Europe's First Farmers

Plants and animals originally domesticated in the Near East arrived in Europe between 7000 and 4000 BC. Was the new technology introduced by migrants, or was it an "inside job"? How were the new species adapted to European conditions? What were the immediate and long-term consequences of the transition from hunting and gathering to farming? These central questions in the prehistory of Europe are discussed here by leading specialists, drawing on the latest scholarship in fields as diverse as genetics and Indo-European linguistics. Detailed studies document the differences between European regions, and fresh generalisations are also proposed and debated.

T. DOUGLAS PRICE is Weinstein Professor of European Archaeology and Director of the Laboratory for Archaeological Chemistry at the University of Wisconsin, Madison. He is the author of more than ten books on the subjects of prehistoric hunter-gatherers, the transition to agriculture and the application of chemistry to the study of the past.

Europe's First Farmers

edited by

T. DOUGLAS PRICE

University of Wisconsin, Madison

CAMBRIDGE
UNIVERSITY PRESS

PUBLISHED BY THE PRESS SYNDICATE OF THE UNIVERSITY OF CAMBRIDGE
The Pitt Building, Trumpington Street, Cambridge, United Kingdom

CAMBRIDGE UNIVERSITY PRESS
The Edinburgh Building, Cambridge CB2 2RU, UK   http://www.cup.cam.ac.uk
40 West 20th Street, New York, NY 10011–4211, USA   http://www.cup.org
10 Stamford Road, Oakleigh, Melbourne 3166, Australia
Ruiz de Alarcón 13, 28014 Madrid, Spain

First published 2000

Printed in the United Kingdom at the University Press, Cambridge

Typeface Swift light   *System* QuarkXPress™   [S E]

A catalogue record for this book is available from the British Library

Library of Congress Cataloguing in Publication data

Europe's first farmers / edited by T. Douglas Price.
    p.   cm.
ISBN 0 521 66203 6.   0 521 66572 8 (pbk)
1. Neolithic period – Europe.   2. Agriculture – Origin.   3. Europe –
Antiquities.   I. Price, T. Douglas (Theron Douglas)
GN776.2.A1E87   2000
306.3'49–dc21   99-15477   CIP

ISBN 0 521 66203 6 hardback
ISBN 0 521 66572 8 paperback

Contents

Illustrations

Tables

Preface

This book is ultimately the product of both enthusiasm and frustration. The enthusiasm comes from the enormous amount of new information about the prehistoric transition to agriculture around the globe and particularly in Europe. There has been a remarkable increase in our knowledge of the Mesolithic and the Neolithic there in the last twenty years and dramatic changes in previous views. The frustration comes from the tenacity of more traditional perspectives among archaeologists who continue to see a continent gradually covered from southeast to northwest by waves of immigrants originating in the Near East. This outdated view continues in vogue; several popular and important theories are firmly based on it. The implications of this concept of continuous colonization for the spread of culture, language, and genes are obvious and strong: newcomers bring new things; change comes from outside. This perspective has significant implications for our perspectives on transformation and interaction. New information that has accumulated in recent years, however, has raised serious questions about how the transition to agriculture took place and, in a larger frame, about the very origins of agriculture and why human society changes at all.

The overture for this publication was a scholarly symposium, held in Minneapolis, Minnesota, in 1995, at the annual meeting of the Society for American Archaeology. This symposium provided an opportunity for the authors of this volume to convene to discuss the ideas and information presented by their colleagues and to collate those facts and views with their own. The participants in the symposium, and the authors of the chapters in this volume, were selected as individuals who were active in field research dealing with the Mesolithic and Neolithic in Europe, and who at the same time were involved in developing revised perspectives for understanding the transition. This combination of hard-won data and new ideas is essential, in my view, for developing a realistic and viable understanding of our human past.

The symposium provided a means for integrating the individual papers in the volume and linking the major themes that we address. The symposium went well, large numbers of people attended, excellent papers were read, voices and tempers were raised in debate, and interest peaked. It also seems that the enthusiasm from the symposium traveled home with the contributors, who then spent a great deal of effort enhancing and elaborating their papers to deal with questions, comments, and concerns that were raised during the symposium. As a result, the chapters are lengthy and deliberate in treating the themes that define the substance of this volume.

Other aspects of the volume should also be noted. We have tried to be consistent throughout in the use of calibrated radiocarbon dates in order to have a coherent discussion of the spread of agriculture in actual calendar years. We have also provided both chronological charts and maps of site locations and the distribution of archaeological cultures as summaries of information and reference for the reader.

The human past is a thoroughly fascinating subject. I am convinced that archaeology has both a great deal to offer, and a great deal to learn, in the development of our understanding of the evolution of ourselves and our society. The transition to agriculture is without question one of the major events in that evolution, shifting human focus from the wild to the tame, from nature to the constructed, from the landscape to the community, from the horizontal to the hierarchical. In addition, as I believe the information in this volume will convince you, our ancestors played a decisive role in bringing about that transition as demands from social, economic, and ideological realms of ourselves and our societies grew.

These have been many pleasures in organizing and putting together this book. One of the primary pleasures has been the assocation with the various contributors whose intellect, alacrity, knowledge, and good nature have made this a relatively easy task. Please accept my sincere thanks and admiration for a job well done. Another pleasure has been the connection and correspondence with other scholars concerned with the transition to agriculture who have generously supplied information, offprints, and other materials to enhance the information presented in the various chapters of this book. A third pleasure has been the association with the publisher, and particularly with the Senior Commissioning Editor for the Social Sciences, Jessica Kuper, who made an effort to put this book in fine form. Thanks also to Frances Brown whose care in copy-editing has made this a cleaner and more accurate book. My appreciation also goes to the two anonymous reviewers who, while perhaps overly opinionated, helped to make this a better book. A final thank you must go to another great pleasure, my colleague, critic, partner, friend, and love, Anne Birgitte Gebauer.

T. DOUGLAS PRICE

Contributors

William K. Barnett, *American Museum of Natural History*

Didier Binder, *CNRS and University of Provence*

Peter Bogucki, *Princeton University*

Michael Jochim, *University of California, Santa Barbara*

Malcolm Lillie, *University of Hull*

T. Douglas Price, *University of Wisconsin*

Ruth Tringham, *University of California, Berkeley*

Peter Woodman, *University College, Cork*

João Zilhão, *Instituto Portugues de Arqueologia*

Marek Zvelebil, *University of Sheffield*

1

Europe's first farmers: an introduction

The transition from hunting and gathering to agriculture is arguably the most important event in human prehistory, representing a shift from foraging to farming, from food collection to food production, from wild to domestic, that sets the stage for most of the significant subsequent developments in human society. For this reason, the beginnings of agriculture have been the subject of scholarly interest since at least the middle of the last century, as evidenced by Charles Darwin's 1868 treatise on *The Variation of Plants and Animals under Domestication,* and subsequent works by various other authors (e.g., de Candolle 1882, Roth 1887).

The search for causality began early as well. Raphael Pumpelly in 1908 first suggested the oasis as the context of domestication in the ancient Near East during the time of desiccation thought to have characterized the end of the Pleistocene, invoking climatic change as a primary cause. The 1920s brought two important concepts to the study of the first farmers (Harris 1996b, Watson 1995). In 1926, the botanist N. I. Vavilov defined "centers of origin" for the domestication of plants and two years later the archaeologist V. Gordon Childe described the origins of agriculture in terms of a "Neolithic Revolution." Employing this new concept of centers, Childe argued that agriculture, along with a number of other innovations, had moved to Europe from its place of origin in the Near East.

Large multidisciplinary projects of archaeological investigation characterized research on agricultural origins after the Second World War (e.g., Braidwood 1960, Byers 1967, Hole *et al.* 1969, Kenyon 1981, MacNeish 1992). The 1960s and early 1970s saw an intensified search for causality (e.g., Binford 1968, Cohen 1977, Flannery 1973). Humans were viewed as forced into agriculture by the uncontrollable circumstances of nature, such as climatic change, environmental degradation, or inherent growth in their own numbers. Consensus views today of the origins and spread of agriculture are generally an outgrowth of these perspectives.

Since the 1970s, many details have been added to the picture and innovative theories have been suggested. The origins and spread of farming have been considered in a variety of new publications (e.g., Anderson 1992, Aurenche and Cauvin 1989, Clark and Brandt 1984, Clutton-Brock 1989, Cowan and Watson 1992, Edmonds and Richards 1998, Gebauer and Price 1992, Harris 1996c, Harris and Hillman 1989, Helmer 1992, Price and Gebauer 1995b, Rindos 1984, Smith 1994, Zohary and Hopf 1993, Zvelebil *et al.* 1998). A synthesis is emerging from the accumulation of information, ideas, and methods that truly provides new insight on the complex process that is the transition to agriculture. More recent perspectives suggest that humans were active players in this process and that changes in the social, economic, and ideological aspects of human society were important forces in bringing about the transition.

With this acknowledged bias toward new evidence and non-traditional perspectives, *Europe's First Farmers* is intended to provide an over-view of the new synthesis, some of the latest information concerning the introduction of farming in prehistoric Europe and the details of that transition in various portions of the continent, as well as the new ideas that have appeared. There is more archaeological information in Europe with which to try and answer these questions than elsewhere in the world in terms of archaeological sites, radiocarbon dates, detailed studies, and published reports. A great deal has been learned about the where, what, and when of the transition to agriculture. Major questions remain concerning who brought the domesticates and why. Fundamental issues in archaeological research are involved in these questions. Colonization vs. indigenous adoption — migration vs. acculturation — is an essential aspect of the study of culture change. Causality — why the transition to agriculture took place — is a relevant concern in every part of the globe where farming replaced foraging. These issues are the major concerns of this volume.

In this initial chapter, I will outline the generally accepted views of the transition to agriculture in Europe, followed by a brief discussion of more recent data and perspectives that document substantive changes in the traditional picture. In the subsequent chapters specialists elaborate the recent evidence, and its interpretation, in detail region by region. These chapters are organized along the lines of the spread of the Neolithic from southern and eastern Europe to the north and west. The concluding chapter provides a summary of these new data and ideas, returning to the major questions of this volume — colonization vs. indigenous adoption and the possible causes of the transition. Several major theories specifically concerned with the introduction of agriculture into Europe are evaluated in the light of the new synthesis.

Traditional views of the transition in Europe

It is important to remember that most of the major innovations in European prehistory — domesticated plants and animals, pottery, writing, and more — came initially from Asia. It is clear that the staple crops and herd animals of the European Neolithic — wheats and barley, pulses, and flax, along with cattle, pigs, sheep, and goats — were originally domesticated in the Near East shortly after 10,000 BC. These plants and animals spread to Europe as agricultural practices moved beyond the boundaries of southwest Asia. The expansion of agriculture across Europe took place relatively quickly, within a period of approximately 3000 years — certainly within less time than it had taken farming first to spread across southwest Asia. Incipient farming communities appeared in the Aegean area and Greece some time around 7000 BC, while the earliest agriculture in northwestern Europe (Britain and Scandinavia) did not arrive until after 4000 BC.

The introduction of agriculture into Europe has, since Childe's original conceptualization in the 1920s, been thought to reflect the spread of foreign colonists bearing ceramic containers and domesticated plants and animals, and bringing permanent villages, new architecture, storage facilities, long-distance trade, and elaborate burial rituals. The indigenous hunter-gatherers of Europe are thought to have been only sparsely present, residentially mobile, socially amorphous, and eventually overwhelmed.

This traditional view of the transition was based on rather limited archaeological data and simple, logical expectations. For the last fifty years or more the textbook map of the introduction of agriculture into Europe has shown a continent riddled by large arrows, the first thrusting from Turkey across the Aegean and into Greece. That initial attack split in two as a pincer movement began, one by land and the other by sea. The inland movement brought farming, pottery, and rectangular mud brick houses to southeastern Europe. The second, maritime arm moved along the Mediterranean shore carrying domesticated sheep and goats, cereals, and pottery. The next step was an explosive expansion across central Europe, with farmers pouring out of Hungary and occupying an area from Holland, Belgium, and France to the Ukraine in the east, and from the Alps to northern Germany and Poland.

At the same time, the arrows began to move from the Mediterranean shore inland as farmers entered the fertile valleys of Italy, France, Switzerland, and the Iberian peninsula. In central Europe the initial spread of farming was followed by a period of "regionalization" as Neolithic groups took on a distinctive, local character and in the west began to erect monumental tombs known as megaliths. By 4500 BC, most of Europe, with the exception of the British Isles and Scandinavia, had been occupied by farmers. Finally around 4000 BC the last arrows made their way to these northwest margins, blanketing most of the continent with the Neolithic.

The apparent regularity of this spread, along with the monotonic decline in radiocarbon dates for the earliest Neolithic across the continent, led Ammerman and Cavalli-Sforza in 1973 — drawing on Clark (1965) — to describe this process as a "Wave of Advance," aptly characterizing the presumed inevitability of colonization by farming communities. This wave model has been the explicit, or implicit, foundation for discussions of the transition to agriculture for twenty-five years. In that same time, however, a proliferation of innovative ideas, new methods, extensive fieldwork, and myriad information has steadily accumulated that does not fit this traditional view.

Toward a new synthesis

The foundation for a new synthesis can be viewed as responses to a series of questions regarding the prehistoric transition to agriculture in Europe that have been revisited and investigated over the last twenty-five years. These questions concern the data used to interpret the onset of the Neolithic, certain methods of analysis, and conceptual frameworks for describing what we know and how we think about it. These questions more specifically involve matters such as the meaning of "Neolithic," the contents of the Neolithic package, the use of radiocarbon dates and other evidence, the nature of farming, who was responsible, the role of the indigenous Mesolithic inhabitants, and why in fact the transition occurred.

The meaning of the term Neolithic itself is highly variable in its use in European prehistory (e.g., Prescott 1996, Thomas 1991b, Whittle 1996, Zvelebil 1986c, 1998) and has changed substantially since first employed. Neolithic has been used as a time period, a cultural phase, an evolutionary step, an economy or mode of production, a population, a social structure, and other variable cultural phenomena. This ambiguity has complicated an understanding of the transition to agriculture. As Dennell (1992: 92) noted, "the concept of the 'Neolithic' as signifying the appearance of agriculture probably has done more to obscure than to illuminate the nature of the processes involved." It is essential to define the meaning of the term in order to know what is being observed and reported in the literature.

Other information has been employed to identify the Neolithic. Radiocarbon dates of a certain age are often the criteria used for designating the Neolithic in Britain, in spite of the fact that there is a great deal of overlap in the dates for the late Mesolithic and early Neolithic (Williams 1989, Woodman, this volume). In Scandinavia and other areas, the presence of distinctive pottery or polished flint is frequently taken as the hallmark of the first farmers. In this context, it is essential to distinguish between characteristics of the Neolithic, such as pottery, settled villages, polished stone, and the like, and the actual evidence for agriculture, the use of domesticated plants or animals. Plant and animal remains of domesticated species are the most reliable indication of cultivation and herding.

One of the reasons that criteria must be clearly stated and consistently applied has to do with the concept of the "Neolithic package." As originally defined, the term was intended to distinguish assemblages of Neolithic artifacts from Palaeolithic ones. Neolithic included pottery and ground stone objects, in addition to the flaked stone technology typical of the Old Stone Age. Since that initial definition, more baggage has been added to the concept, particularly as the notion of colonization as the mechanism for spreading the Neolithic became established. Colonists would have carried a set of knowledge, tools, and concepts with them, in addition to domesticated plants and animals. This package, denoting a Neolithic presence, came to include permanent villages of rectangular houses, religious objects and structures, and domesticated plants and animals, as well as pottery and ground stone tools. These items were expected to appear simultaneously with the arrival of new farming populations. Even though direct evidence of domesticated plants and animals was often missing, they were assumed to have been present as part of the package. In recent years, however, it has become clear that the package did not always arrive intact.

Increasing interest in the indigenous populations of Europe during the transition to agriculture has brought new insights as well. Scholars of the Mesolithic have been particularly active in Europe during the last twenty-five years, elaborating our knowledge and understanding of this period (e.g., Bonsall 1989, Gramsch 1981, Kozlowski and Kozlowski 1973, Vermeersch and Van Peer 1990). Views of the Mesolithic have shifted in that time from a period of quarantine or degradation between the Palaeolithic and Neolithic to a time of dynamic groups of complex foragers. This perspective has emphasized the role of indigenous people in the transition to agriculture.

Several aspects of Mesolithic adaptations are of relevance to the question of the transition to agriculture, including sedentism, population size, and plant foods (Price 1987). These characteristics have traditionally been considered as exclusively Neolithic. The presence of sedentary communities was often used as evidence of the arrival of the Neolithic, but it is now clear that permanent settlements existed in many parts of Europe in the preceding Mesolithic as well, e.g., in the Iron Gates of the Danube (Srejovic 1972), in Scandinavia (Brinch Petersen 1973), and in Ireland (Woodman 1985b).

Discussions regarding Mesolithic population remain fraught with problems in estimating past numbers of people. However, a general pattern is emerging. It now seems clear that Mesolithic foragers were concentrated in marine, riverine, and rich lacustrine environments across Europe. It is less certain how intensive occupation was in less productive river valleys and heavily forested areas of the interior of the continent. A number of authors have suggested that the dense canopy of the mixed oak forest of Atlantic Europe would not have provided substantial biomass for hunters or their prey (Noe-Nygaard 1995, Vencl 1986, Waterbolk 1982). Recent surveys in the interior basins of central Europe have failed to reveal substantial Mesolithic remains (M. Kuna, personal communication). Greece and the southeastern Balkans, with the exception of the Iron Gates, apparently had a very small Mesolithic presence (van Andel and Runnels 1995).

There is mounting evidence for the use of wild plants in the

Mesolithic (Hansen and Renfrew 1978, Price 1989, Zvelebil 1994a). At the Grotto dell'Uzzo in Sicily, the Mesolithic layers, dating before 6000 BC, contained the remains of grass pea, pea, wild strawberry, wild olive, and wild grape (Constantini 1989, Dennell 1992). Holden *et al.* (1995) have identified a number of species in charred plant remains from the Roc del Migdia in Catalonia, including fragments of hazelnut and sloe and several roots and tubers. In northern Europe, there is substantial evidence for the use of nuts (hazelnuts and acorns), water chestnuts, and nettles; fruits such as wild strawberry, apple, and sloe and rowan berries and raspberries have also been found (Price 1989, Regnell *et al.* 1995, Zvelebil 1996). Zvelebil (1994a) has gone so far as to suggest that wild plant food husbandry was practiced in the Mesolithic as a pre-adaptation for the arrival of the Neolithic.

Another issue is the question of domesticated plants and animals in Mesolithic contexts. There have for some years been a number of instances of cereal pollen with early dates from many parts of the continent. In virtually every instance, these have been dismissed on the grounds of weak chronology or questionable identification. Recent evidence, however, suggests that domesticated plants may have been present during the later Mesolithic in some parts of Europe. The best example of this comes from pollen cores from the Zurich region in Switzerland where cereal pollen (*Triticum* sp.) and a seed of flax (*Linum usitatissimum*) have been dated to *c.* 6400 BC cal., almost 1000 years before the accepted start of the Neolithic in this region. Domesticated animals may also appear before the traditionally recognized arrival of the Neolithic. Examples are known from several areas (e.g., Scandinavia, Jennbert 1984; the Mediterranean, Geddes *et al.* 1989, Schvorer *et al.* 1979). Additional examples are needed before these pre-Neolithic contexts are fully accepted, but evidence is certainly accumulating.

Because of an increasing appreciation of the Mesolithic period, significant questions have arisen about the degree and extent of colonization involved in the transition to agriculture. It seems clear that local inhabitants often played an important role in the transition. The simple distinction between demic diffusion (colonization by immigrants) and indigenous adoption obscures a great deal of variability and often is inadequate for explaining observed evidence. This problem has been recognized by a number of authors and various models of diffusion and acculturation have been proposed (van Andel and Runnels 1995, Anthony 1994, Arnaud 1982, Dennell 1985, Gregg 1988, Moore 1985, Renfrew 1987, Whittle 1996, Zilhão 1993). Zvelebil and Lillie in this volume and Zvelebil elsewhere (1995b, 1996) propose several different mechanisms to explain how materials, ideas, and/or people move into new areas. Each of these has implications for the nature and for the kind of evidence that result as new subsistence strategies, technologies, and material culture spread into a given region.

In addition to changing views and methods, there are substantial new data from Europe on the transition to agriculture. Research on this question has resulted in a great deal of fieldwork, analysis, and publication in the last twenty-five years (e.g., van Andel and Runnells 1995, Barker 1985, Biagi 1990, Bogucki 1988, 1996, Bogucki and Grygiel 1983, Chapman 1994b, Coudart 1991, Demoule and Perlès 1993, Dennell 1992, Gregg 1988, Harris 1996c, Hodder 1990, Milles, Williams, and Gardner 1989, Perlès 1992, Price and Gebauer 1992, Price *et al.* 1995, Price 1996b, Renfrew 1989, Rowley-Conwy 1995, Thorpe 1996, Tilley 1996, Whittle 1996, Zvelebil 1986c, Zvelebil and Dolukhanov 1991).

Some of this information is briefly summarized in the paragraphs below to provide a region by region overview of Greece and the Aegean, southeastern Europe, the Mediterranean shore, central Europe, eastern Europe, and northwestern Europe, following the path of the spread of agriculture. It is not my intent to provide a detailed description of all of the new evidence and ideas that have accumulated in the last twenty-five years, but rather to note some of the major developments. The following chapters will provide more of the details for specific areas.

The eastern Mediterranean

The earliest farmers in Europe appeared in the Aegean and Greece by the beginning of the seventh millennium BC (Demoule and Perlès 1993). This has traditionally been seen as a classic case of colonization. There is very little evidence for a human presence on the islands of the eastern Mediterranean until the Neolithic, suggesting a distinct pattern of colonization by sea (Broodbank and Strasser 1991, Cherry 1990, Jarman 1996, Sondaar 1971). These first colonists often quickly diverged from their original character, as Ronen has described for the first Neolithic inhabitants of Cyprus (Ronen 1995).

The early Neolithic sites on the plains of Thessaly in Greece appear to be substantial, long-term communities, largely dependent on domesticated plants and animals (Halstead 1996). These settlements were located on perennially wet floodplains with very fertile soils (van Andel and Runnels 1995). Little is known of the Mesolithic and earliest Neolithic occupation of this area; the low number of sites from this period suggests that a rather empty landscape may have been available for colonization throughout Greece (Runnels 1995). Perlès (1993, 1995) and others have pointed out that the early Neolithic environment of Greece resembled the Near East more than the remainder of Europe. Because the first Neolithic settlements on mainland Greece were villages housing grain-cultivating, cattle-herding agriculturalists, their inhabitants are thought to have arrived as colonists from the Near East (Demoule and Perlès 1993, Papathanassopoulos 1996).

Traditional assumptions regarding the similarities between the Neolithic in the Near East and the Aegean area, however, have been brought into question. Özdogan (1993, 1997) and others, for example, have pointed out that the Neolithic of southwest Asia is not a monolithic entity, that there are substantial regional differences. The Anatolian Neolithic differs significantly from the traditional area of the western Fertile Crescent; in addition to differences in material culture, sedentary communities were dependent on hunting and gathering to a much greater extent than in the Levant (Özdogan 1997). Anatolia may well have been the source of the first Neolithic inhabitants of the Aegean and perhaps the Greek mainland (Özdogan 1989). Direct comparison of the European situation to the Neolithic of the Levant is not warranted.

Other lines of evidence suggest indigenous adoption in mainland Greece, rather than colonization. Very little is known about the earliest Neolithic in this area. There are questions about the completeness of the Neolithic package in this area (Halstead 1996, Tringham, this volume). An enigmatic "preceramic" phase is known at a few sites (e.g., Argissa, Gediki, Sesklo) where pottery is absent but domesticated plants and animals are present. The radiocarbon dates for the Greek Preceramic Neolithic sites all cluster around 6800 BC. The lithic assemblages in these preceramic levels are described as Mesolithic (Tringham, this volume).

To the south, in the more rocky and isolated areas of the Peleponnese, local foragers may have gradually adopted cultigens and herd animals as part of the transition to agriculture. The evidence for this comes largely from the site of Franchthi Cave in the Peleponnese (Jacobsen 1981). A mix of local and foreign traditions can be seen at Franchthi in lithic tradition and faunal remains; moreover, the earliest ceramics are distinct from those elsewhere in Greece (Demoule and Perlès 1993). The use of wild barley and wild lentils is documented in the late Pleistocene and early Holocene and suggests that hunter-gatherers in this area were already consuming substantial amounts of plant foods (Dennell 1985, Hansen 1991, 1992, Hansen and Renfrew 1978). The pieces of the Neolithic package appear to have arrived here sequentially as domesticates were gradually added to the diet over time (Halstead 1996). In this area local adoption of farming and the Neolithic appears to have been the case.

Thus, current views on the transition to agriculture in the Aegean and Greece are mixed. Many authors (van Andel and Runnels 1995, Demoule and Perlès 1993, Lewthwaite 1986b, Perlès 1993, and others) argue for colonization on the basis of the similarity to materials in Anatolia, the fact that the islands of the eastern Mediterranean were inhabited for the first time in the early Neolithic, and the general absence of Mesolithic occupation in the primary areas where the first farmers appear. Others (Budja 1993, Chapman 1994b, Dennell 1983, Theocharis 1973, Tringham, this volume, Whittle 1996), supporting indigenous adoption, point to contrasts with the materials in the Near East, the apparent existence of a preceramic Neolithic with Mesolithic affinities, and the gradual transition indicated at Franchthi Cave. In fact, the varied evidence — and more research and information on both the late Mesolithic and the early Neolithic are badly needed

— suggests a situation in which both colonization and indigenous adoption took place in different areas.

Southeastern Europe

During the seventh millennium BC, farming and pottery followed two main pathways from the Aegean area into the rest of Europe: by land into the southeastern quarter of the continent and by sea along the north shore of the Mediterranean. The Neolithic spread quickly to the Balkan Peninsula (i.e., Bulgaria, Romania, and Hungary, and the present countries of the former Yugoslavia). In the other direction, distinctively impressed Cardial pottery, the bones of domesticated sheep, and cereals are found in caves and rockshelters along the Mediterranean and southern Atlantic coasts of Europe.

Less than 1000 years after the appearance of agriculture in the Aegean, the first farming appears in the interior of southeastern Europe. The radiocarbon dates for the Early Neolithic in the southern Balkan peninsula are 6600–5800 BC and for the northern area around 6500–5200 BC (Chapman and Dolukhanov 1993, Todorova and Vajsov 1993, Tringham, this volume). The traditional view of the Neolithic in the Balkan peninsula involved the expansion of farmers out of the plains of Thessaly and northern Greece, moving up the natural corridors of the major river valleys, into southeastern Europe. Indeed, there are areas such as the Vardar-Morava corridor, the Maritsa basin, and the middle and lower Danube basins which witnessed the simultaneous arrival of early Neolithic material culture and a change in settlement pattern. With a few exceptions, the early Neolithic is known primarily from large tells with deep deposits containing rectangular houses, pottery, and domesticated plants and animals. The similarity of these sites to those known from the Near East gave obvious support to a model of colonization by immigrant farming populations. The subsequent sixth millennium BC witnessed the flowering of Neolithic cultures in southeastern Europe — elaborate religious systems, rich graves, gold and copper mining and metallurgy, and extensive trade networks, again supporting the idea of outside influence.

However, substantive questions have been raised about the colonization of southeastern Europe (Bogucki 1996, Budja 1993, Radovanovic 1996, Whittle 1996). Chapman (1994b) and Whittle (1996) take the position that little evidence exists for incoming farmers in southeast Europe. Deep tell deposits do not easily reveal their lowest levels. Greenfield (1993) reports that variation in faunal assemblages at early Neolithic sites in the Balkans indicates local adoption rather than wholesale insertion of farmers. Van Andel and Runnels (1995) suggest that Neolithic settlement in most of southeastern Europe was quite sparse and irregularly distributed on floodplains and other particularly hospitable areas for agriculture. Willis and Bennett (1994) point to the sparsity of pollen and other evidence for substantial cultivation in southeastern Europe prior to 5000 BC. Such information suggests that initial farming populations in southeastern Europe were relatively small and that networks among foraging populations may have been responsible for the spread of agriculture.

Neither these initial farmers nor the late Mesolithic inhabitants of southeastern Europe are well known or documented, yet one of the most important aspects of the transition to the Neolithic is the relationship between them. The basis for this ambiguity lies in the significance of a series of settlements from the Iron Gates region of the Danube, along the Yugoslavian–Romanian border. Evidence from these settlements, and especially from the site of Lepenski Vir, indicates that Mesolithic hunter-gatherers in southeast Europe already had adopted the complexities of a sedentary way of life (Bonsall *et al.* 1997, Radovanovic 1996,Tringham, this volume).

The stratigraphy and chronology of Lepenski Vir has been debated for some time; the interpretation of the site is critical for understanding the transition to agriculture in the Balkan peninsula. The major question concerns the dating of the Neolithic component at the site. Jovanovic (1975), Tringham (this volume), and others have argued that the radiocarbon determinations from Lepenski Vir place the occupation between 6500 and 5700 BC, making much of the settlement entirely contemporary with early Neolithic sites in the Morava, middle Danube, and Tisza valleys, no more than 100 km distant. Radovanovic (1996) has proposed a detailed chronology for Lepenski Vir with six phases of occupation, dating from approximately 7500–5500 BC. Pottery is present at the site by 6500 BC, indicating connections with Neolithic groups, but domesticated plants and animals are missing in the archaeological remains. Bonsall *et al.* (1997) report a change toward more terrestrial diets at Lepenski Vir also around 6500 BC, correlated, they suggest, with the introduction of domesticated plants and animals, perhaps appearing before the introduction of pottery.

The presence of Neolithic ceramics and other materials at Lepenski Vir is generally seen as evidence for interaction between the Iron Gates foragers and farmers in nearby areas. The archaeological data on subsistence, stability, and use of resources suggest to Tringham that, in a situation of interaction between the two populations, the foragers were the more dynamic partners. Faunal assemblages show pronounced differences between the hunters and farmers: Iron Gates sites were based largely on hunting and fishing; Neolithic sites were dependent on farming and herding. The stone tools of these early Neolithic settlements were made of local pebbles, even though good raw materials were located nearby (Tringham 1988, Voytek and Tringham 1989). The stone artifacts of the late Mesolithic settlements of the Iron Gates (including early Lepenski Vir), however, are made from both local and imported lithic resources. This pattern of limited use of local materials in the early Neolithic is also seen in other areas of Europe in the early Neolithic (e.g., Binder, this volume; Price, this volume). Tringham (this volume) views the interaction between farmers and hunters as the key aspect of the Neolithic transition, "a two-way process of 'Neolithisation', in which the agriculturalists as well as the foragers were radically (and quickly) transformed." Clearly, the long-term survivors of this relationship were the farming populations of southeastern Europe.

The western Mediterranean

The other arm of the early Neolithic, spreading from the eastern to the western Mediterranean in the sixth millennium BC, is characterized by the rapid appearance of stylistically uniform ceramics, domesticated plants and animals, and long-distance exchange of items such as obsidian and ground stone (Lewthwaite 1986a, Tykot 1996). The terms Cardial and Impressed Ware have often been used interchangeably for the pottery; in some areas the terms are distinguished chronologically. The spread of Impressed Wares appears to have taken place in two stages. The first stage carried from the east along the Dalmatian coast to Italy and southern France during the first half of the sixth millennium BC (Binder, this volume, Donahue 1992, Evin 1987, Pluciennik 1998a, Rowley-Conwy 1995). The second stage of this expansion covered the area from southern France around the coast of Spain to the Atlantic coast of Portugal, in the second half of the millennium (Lewthwaite 1986a, Zilhão 1993). In each stage, radiocarbon dates suggest a very rapid expansion (Zilhão, this volume). The coastal location and sporadic distribution of these sites have traditionally been interpreted as the result of colonization by sea.

Until recently, the Cardial culture was generally poorly known because of the limited range of excavated materials, the location of most sites in disturbed caves and rockshelters, and the inundation of the early Neolithic coastline of the Mediterranean (Guilaine 1979, Guilaine *et al.* 1984). Cave and rockshelter sites probably represent only one aspect of Cardial settlement (Chapman and Müller 1990); other facies are not well known. The recent discovery of the underwater lakeshore site of La Draga in Catalonia, Spain, demonstrates that primary Cardial settlements were most probably open-air agricultural villages (Tarrus *et al.* 1994). Excavations revealed the remains of posts and planks, preserved in chalk deposits, from structures estimated to be 3–4 m high, three paved platforms, and more than thirty hearths. The vast majority of the animal bones were from domesticates; large quantities of plant remains (wheat, barley, and legumes) were also recovered. Radiocarbon dates indicate the site was occupied early in the sixth millennium BC.

The appearance of the Cardial culture varies from east to west (Whittle 1996, Zilhão 1993). The earliest dates for the Cardial along the Dalmatian coast are immediately after 6000 BC (Chapman and Müller 1990,

Müller 1993, 1994). In this area a complete "package" of Neolithic materials appeared only in lowland coastal sites, not in the interior. An adjacent area along the Mediterranean coast, the Po basin, experienced a late arrival of agriculture, primarily in the form of ceramics after 5250 BC (Bagolini 1990). This process was marked by the piecemeal adoption of different parts of the Neolithic package. From around 5250 to 4750 BC throughout northern Italy, early Neolithic groups demonstrate a clear link with Mesolithic technology (Bagolini 1990). The Neolithic in this traditional Mesolithic area was accompanied by an impressive amount of exotic, prestige goods, which are generally rare and less diversified in Impressed Ware cultures. These goods included a wide range of raw materials: obsidian from Lipari Island and the Carpathian Mountains, stone axes from the Alps, Veronese flint, and imported pottery. The Early Neolithic in the Po basin, although quite late in time, had an economy based largely on hunting.

In southern Italy, on the other hand, the Cardial culture is marked by the presence of large farming communities in substantial settlements dating early in the sequence, but not before 6000 BC (Donahue 1992, Pluciennik 1998a, Whitehouse 1992, 1994). These sites are marked by ditched enclosures, up to a kilometer in diameter. More than 500 enclosures are reported from the Tavoliere plain, a small area along the east coast above the boot heel (Brown 1991). The largest of these, at Passo di Corvo, is a multi-ringed enclosure of 28 ha containing some ninety small inner compounds of C-shaped ditches (Jones 1987). Little is known of the preceding Mesolithic in this region and colonization is often cited as the mechanism responsible for the arrival of these first farmers. A gap of more than 1000 radiocarbon years between the latest Mesolithic and the earliest Neolithic (with only one or two exceptions, Skeates and Whitehouse 1997, Tinè 1996) supports such a perspective (Pluciennik 1998a)

For northwestern Italy and southeastern France, the Impressed Ware tradition first appears in Liguria around 6000 BC. Excavations at the Pendimoun shelter near the Italian border revealed a complete series of Early Neolithic deposits with two major episodes: Early Cardial in the upper levels with characteristic geometric features and Impressed Ware deposits in the lower layers, with the pottery showing clear affinities with the Adriatic and Balkan regions (Binder *et al.* 1993). The first Impressd Ware economy at the site of Pendimoun was fully Neolithic, with both cultivation and herding present (Binder *et al.* 1993, Binder, this volume).

The Impressed Ware tradition quickly spread along the Tyrrhenian coast between 6000 and 5600 BC. The late Mesolithic has not been identified in eastern Provence or on the Riviera in spite of numerous excavations both along the coast and inland (Biagi *et al.* 1989, Binder 1989). Mesolithic and Neolithic sites in southern France and northern Italy have a mutually exclusive distribution, suggesting the spread of a colonizing Neolithic population along the coast (Binder 1989, 1995, Binder *et al.* 1993, Binder and Courtin 1987). The Impressa and the subsequent Neolithic groups settled only in areas where Mesolithic groups were absent; Mesolithic people were focused on aquatic environments and the Impressed Ware groups were terrestrial. The western Mediterranean Impressed Ware culture in this area has been considered fully Neolithic, producing distinctive ceramics and polished stone and bone artifacts; subsistence was based on food production.

The second stage of expansion dating to *c.* 5400 BC, or perhaps slightly earlier, saw the appearance of Cardial materials in the west Mediterranean region of France and the coasts of Iberia. Evidence from the Aude valley in France documents the local evolution of projectile points and the lithic industry into the early Neolithic (Barbaza *et al.* 1984). In Cantabrian Spain, the transition begins almost 1000 radiocarbon years later and is probably related to the adoption of the new economic system by local populations. Zilhão (1993, this volume) argues that the Cardial arrived in Portugal as a package brought by seafaring colonists from the east. The transition there is signaled by the appearance of new items of material culture (pottery, polished stone axes, bone tools) in association with domesticated plants and animals (cereals and ovicaprids). Enclave colonization is the term used by Zilhão (this volume) to refer to the pattern of small group movement into unoccupied areas. Radiocarbon dates indicate that these agriculturalists were contemporary with Mesolithic foragers less than 100 km away.

There is other evidence, however, contradictory to the larger picture of Cardial as introduced by farmers. One of the important aspects of this controversy has to do with the debate over a number of sites dating to the seventh millennium BC. If accepted, these sites indicate the presence of domesticated animals and pottery in Mesolithic contexts (e.g., Donohue 1992). Barnett (1990a, 1995, this volume) has examined the production and distribution of Cardial ceramics and demonstrates two scales of interaction: long-distance transport of a few, very well-defined ceramic types, and more localized movement of more regionally decorated ceramics. Presumably the smaller scale movements relate to inter-community interaction, perhaps associated with local exchange (Barnett, this volume).

The very rapid expansion of the Cardial culture certainly suggests the prior existence of routes of communication and exchange. The question remains as to who carried domesticates and ceramics along these routes. The evidence presented here and subsequently in this volume indicates that the mechanisms for the spread of the Cardial Neolithic were varied and may have included both colonization of uninhabited regions by small enclaves and local adoption of farming or other aspects of the Neolithic in other parts of the Mediterranean shore.

Central Europe
The next stage in the inland expansion of the Neolithic reached into central and eastern Europe. The first Neolithic communities in central Europe traditionally have been thought to be Bandkeramik groups, based

on a distinctive and remarkably homogeneous pattern of ceramic shape and design. The Bandkeramik originated around 5500 BC in villages along the middle Danube and its tributaries in eastern Hungary.

The expansion of the Bandkeramik, like the Cardial, was very rapid. Within a period of less than two hundred years, around 5500 BC, small farming villages appeared across an area stretching from Belgium and northern France, through central Europe to the Ukraine. Settlement was not continuous but appears to have occurred as scattered clusters of hamlets and farmsteads situated on loess soils in well-watered valleys. These early farming communities produced a suite of crops, including emmer and einkorn wheat, barley, peas, flax, and poppy, and herded cattle and pigs. The uniformity of the architecture, artifacts, burials, subsistence, and set-tlement plan that characterize these communities is striking.

The interpretation of the Bandkeramik has seemed equally clear, as a prime example of colonization by farming groups (Lüning 1988a, Whittle 1987). Bogucki in this volume and elsewhere (1996) summarizes the recent evidence for the Bandkeramik in the northern part of central Europe, between the middle Danube valley and the lower Oder, Vistula, and Elbe rivers to the north and the Paris basin to the west. He examines the ques-tion of colonization vs. adoption in detail and finds no evidence for adop-tion. Keeley (Price *et al.* 1995) also makes an argument for colonization as the mechanism for the spread of LBK. He finds evidence of contact between farmers and foragers on the western and northern fringes of the Bandkeramik distribution in north-central Europe, in the form of imitative ceramics, the fortification of farming settlements, and ultimately the adop-tion of agriculture by foraging communities.

On the other hand, recent studies in central Europe are beginning to ameliorate the dogmatism of LBK interpretations, postulating a greater role for Late Mesolithic inhabitants and at times challenging the entire notion of an agricultural colonization (e.g., Gronenborn 1994, Lüning 1997, Stäuble 1995, Tillmann 1994). These authors point out that the earliest phase of the Bandkeramik in the heartland of central Europe is character-ized by significant heterogeneity among assemblages and patterns of exchange that suggests indigenous change rather than homogenous coloniz-ation. In the southern part of central Europe and the Alpine Foreland, Jochim (this volume) and others (Whittle 1996) report new evidence that has raised questions about the traditional scenario for the Bandkeramik. Whittle (1996), in fact, now views the Bandkeramik as simply another example of foragers becoming farmers.

The most important new evidence comes from a recently identified, earlier archaeological culture, La Hoguette, characterized by the presence of distinctive, bone-tempered pottery and sheep/goat remains (Jeunesse 1995). The earliest remains date to around 5500 BC. The lithic industry asso-ciated with La Hoguette is clearly Mesolithic (Gronenborn 1990b). The La

Hoguette sites show a distribution across the middle Rhône valley, north-ern France, and much of Switzerland and Germany. These materials are thought to be derived from Cardial groups to the south (Lüning *et al.* 1989). La Hoguette materials are often found together with early LBK materials in excavations. The association of LBK and La Hoguette suggests either con-temporary interaction between the two cultures or mixing of diachronic settlement remains. However, relatively pure deposits such as at Stuttgart-Wilhelma (Schütz *et al.* 1992) in the Neckar valley are known.

The earliest known Neolithic settlements in Switzerland and the lake country of the upper Rhine and the Rhône date more than 1000 years later, around 4400 BC, and often contain a mixture of local Mesolithic and early Neolithic elements (Barker 1985, Bogucki 1996, Sakellardis 1979). Mesolithic groups in this area participated in wide-ranging networks of exchange and interaction extending to the southwest and southeast where they encountered early Neolithic communities. Examples of exchange items include the presence of Neolithic polished stone axes in the late Mesolithic of southern Germany and domesticated plants in Switzerland (Erny-Rodmann *et al.* 1997, Jochim 1993, this volume, Nielsen 1997). Very early dates, *c.* 6500–6400 BC cal. – roughly 1000 years before the Early Bandkeramik culture – have recently been obtained for finds of domesti-cated flax seeds and cereal pollen (Erny-Rodmann *et al.* 1997, Haas 1996) in the area around Zurich. Similar situations in the Alpine areas of Italy also suggest that Mesolithic foragers in this area began to use pottery, herd sheep and goats, and cultivate some cereals, but not until after 4000 BC. Technology and settlement were not dramatically changed with the arrival of the Neolithic (Barker 1985, Biagi 1985, 1990).

At the northwestern periphery of the Bandkeramic distribution, distinctive ceramics and settlement remains have been uncovered on areas reclaimed from the sea in the Netherlands. Survey of Mesolithic and Neolithic material in the Meuse valley and elsewhere in the Netherlands documents a gradual intensification in interaction between Bandkeramik farmers and Mesolithic foragers prior to the adoption of agriculture (Verhart and Wansleeben 1997). Early Neolithic sites outside the classic area of the LBK document this pattern. Excavations at Swifterbant, for example, exposed an early Neolithic horizon dating to *c.* 4500 BC (van der Waals and Waterbolk 1976). Neolithic occupations on clay levees contain well-preserved evidence for both animal husbandry (cattle and pigs) and cultiva-tion (barley and emmer wheat), and for ceramics and house construction. The sites were seasonally occupied during the summer months. Wild plants and animals contributed significantly to the diet and fishing was particu-larly important. The pottery is coil-built with thick walls; profiles are gen-erally S-shaped with a pointed base (de Roever 1979). This material most closely resembles early Neolithic ceramics in the Roucador area in France (Roussot-Larroque 1977), dated to *c.* 5000 BC, the contemporary Dummer materials from northwestern Germany (Deichmüller 1969) and the Ertebølle pottery of southern Scandinavia and northern Germany (Andersen 1975). The lithic assemblages contain substantial numbers of trapezes, perhaps indicative of continuity with the local Mesolithic (Deckers 1979).

Eastern Europe

The introduction of agriculture into Europe north and east of the Balkan peninsula is not well understood beyond the basic parameters of characteristic artifacts, chronology, and geographic distribution (Dolukhanov 1979, Potekhina and Telegin 1995, Telegin 1987). The appearance of the Neolithic, at least in its ceramic form, is relatively early. The first agricultural settlements attributed to the Cris-Körös culture in Romania and Moldavia date to the first part of the sixth millennium BC, marked by features which link the culture to the Mesolithic, for example in the technology of stone tools, in house architecture, and in economy (Degarchev 1989, Whittle 1996, Zvelebil and Lillie, this volume).

At about the same time, in the river valleys of the Ukraine, comparatively small sites belonging to the Neolithic Bug-Dniester culture appeared (Lillie 1998). The Bug-Dniester sites show strong continuity with earlier Mesolithic assemblages in lithic industry, settlement pattern, house structures, and economy. Domesticates form less than 20 percent of the faunal assemblage during the early phase; most of the faunal remains are of wild species, notably wild pig, red deer and roe deer, fish, and edible molluscs. Grain impressions in the pottery sherds include a variety of wild and some domesticated cereals (Zvelebil and Dolukhanov 1991).

The contact zone between the Tripolye culture and the Dnieper-Donetz culture in the Dnieper basin is centered on the middle and lower Dnieper valley, with the Tripolye culture to the west, and the Dnieper-Donetz occupying the Dnieper valley itself and the areas to the east (Ellis 1984). There was a period of 800 years or so during which contacts were increasing between the Tripolye farming culture and the essentially hunter-gatherer-fisher Dnieper-Donetz communities, prior to the full transition to farming of the latter.

In the eastern Baltic area, farming was adopted at a very slow rate over a period of some two thousand years (Dennell 1992, Dolukhanov 1979, Zvelebil 1981, 1993, Zvelebil and Dolukhanov 1991). There is little difference to be seen in this region between the artifact assemblages of the late Mesolithic and the early Neolithic. Dennell (1992) describes the earliest Neolithic in the eastern Baltic and western Russia as exhibiting minor changes in basic foraging strategies that were added piecemeal following the introduction of pottery. Cultivation does not appear to have been employed in this area until after 3500 BC; wild resources continued to be heavily used.

Zvelebil and Lillie (this volume) argue for a pattern of gradual, limited adoption of farming by indigenous hunter-gatherers throughout eastern Europe. Within the area of Dnieper-Donetz cultural tradition, as well as in the east Baltic and in the eastern parts of the North European Plain, these interactions appear to follow a similar pattern, marked first by cooperation, then by competition among the forager communities, followed by a shift to farming. This transition was often subsequenly reversed as farming was abandoned in favor of foraging.

Northwestern Europe
The fourth millennium BC witnessed the spread of agriculture to northwestern Europe. This area had been at the margin of the Bandkeramik region during the fifth millennium BC. One of the curious aspects of the Bandkeramik is the fact that its explosive movement stopped before it reached the Atlantic and Baltic coasts. Bandkeramik materials spread from Hungary to southern Holland and northern Germany within a hundred years. Yet further expansion by farmers beyond those borders did not occur for 1500 more years. The reason for this delay must be attributed to the presence of substantial Mesolithic groups along the Atlantic and Baltic coasts of Europe. There is evidence of contact between these late Mesolithic hunters and early Neolithic farmers to the south in the form of early ceramics, distinctive tool types, raw materials, and in a few cases domesticated species (Bogucki 1996, Fischer 1982, Price 1985, 1995, 1996b). Examples are known from northern France, Belgium, the Netherlands, northern Germany, and Scandinavia (e.g., Bogucki 1996, Louwe Kooijmans 1993, Price *et al.* 1995). Intriguingly, however, examples of borrowed Neolithic items are largely unknown in the late Mesolithic of the British Isles.

The archaeology of early farming in Scandinavia and the British Isles is in fact surprisingly different. Both are rather marginal areas on the edge of Europe, separated from the continent by large bodies of water. The transition to agriculture in Scandinavia is extensively documented; the transition to farming in the British Isles is not well known and opinions are more easily discovered than facts (Woodman, this volume). Settlement sites and chronological evidence are often missing or disputed in Britain and Ireland.

Another problem in Britain and Ireland lies in identifying transitional assemblages. Foragers and farmers may both have been present in this area for several hundred years at the end of the fifth millennium BC given the overlap in current radiocarbon dates (Dennell 1983, but see Woodman, this volume). Yet, unquestionable evidence for cereal cultivation is not present in England until after 4000 BC (Helbæk 1952, Thorpe 1996) and only a few Neolithic sites in southern England are older than this date (Woodman, this volume). The contrast between the varied Mesolithic groups of the British Isles and the appearance of a relatively uniform

Neolithic material culture in many areas within a very short period of time around 4000 BC is remarkable. This pattern has suggested to some that colonization was responsible. Yet a similar phenomenon occurred in Scandinavia and in that area there is little evidence for the introduction of agriculture by new peoples. Moreover, the pronounced difficulties in distinguishing between Mesolithic and Neolithic assemblages in the British Isles support an interpretation involving indigenous adoption.

The first evidence for the Neolithic in Scandinavia appears around 4000 BC in the form of Funnel Beaker pottery, large tombs, flint mines, and bog sacrifices (Price, this volume, Price and Gebauer 1992). As in other areas of Europe, farming seems to have spread very quickly into Scandinavia, appearing almost simultaneously across a large area from northern Germany to western Norway and middle Sweden. The demonstrated continuity in settlement location (e.g., Andersen 1991), lithic artifacts (Stafford 1998), aspects of pottery production (Koch 1998), skeletal morphology (Bennike 1995), burial practice, and other criteria, however, indicates that farming was adopted by indigenous peoples in this area.

In sum

Today, archaeologists have reasonable answers for the what, when, and where questions about the transition to agriculture in prehistoric Europe. The important remaining questions concern the who, how, and why of Europe's first farmers. It is with regard to these that the new synthesis has a great deal to contribute; that is what this book is about. The following chapters examine the various regions of Europe with these questions in mind. The major implications of the new synthesis are brought together in the concluding chapter, along with a discussion of their impact on current theories and perspectives.

For the moment, suffice it to say that the spread of agriculture across Europe involved different mechanisms, probably involving new groups of colonizing farmers, exchanges of population between foragers and farmers, and indigenous adoption by foragers. Europe is a large area. There was no single means through which farming and herding became the primary form of human subsistence; rather there were a variety of ways in which agriculture spread, either carried by new people or moving as ideas and materials beyond existing farming groups to local foraging populations. I will return to these questions of who and why in the concluding chapter.

Acknowledgments

This chapter has involved a variety of contributions from a number of individuals but I would particularly like to thank Robin Dennell, Detlef Groenenborn, Martin Kuna, Jens Lüning, Catherine Perlès, Martin Richards, Peter Rasmussen, and Marek Zvelebil for their thoughts and assistance.

2

Southeastern Europe in the transition to agriculture in Europe: bridge, buffer, or mosaic

Southeast Europe as bridge and buffer between the Near East and temperate Europe

The transition to agriculture – the so-called "Neolithization process" – in southeast Europe has been a crucial topic of research at an international scale since the 1960s. In the 1920s, V. Gordon Childe referred to the Balkan peninsula as a "bridge" between Europe and the Near East (Childe 1958). He meant that the area acted as a vital route for the diffusion of plants, animals, techniques, ideas, and people themselves from what was at that time regarded as the heartland of domestication and civilization – the Near East – into temperate Europe, which was barely emerging (in Childe's eyes) from the rigors of the Ice Age. For Gordon Childe, Europe was a continent awaiting transformation into a civilized world that would arrive via this bridge (Fig. 2.1). His idea, based on few empirical data, was taken up by both Balkan archaeologists and international synthesizers in the 1930s and 1940s and was supported by the increasing amount of excavated data that emerged in southeast Europe during those years, documenting the wealth of early agricultural settlements in modern Bulgaria, Romania, Hungary, and former Yugoslavia (e.g., Vinca and Karanovo) (Gaul 1948).

From the mid-1950s onwards, data on the Early Neolithic increased in the east Balkans, as a result of large-scale excavations of impressive tell settlements, funded by the new, centralized, communist-backed regimes (Georgiev 1961). Equally impressive empirical data were being collected at the same time on the process of the domestication of plants and animals in Iraq, Iran, Syria, Israel, Lebanon, and Turkey.

In assigning a bridging role to the Balkan countries, Childe challenged the deep-seated notion in the minds of Europeans that the Balkans or southeast Europe acted as a "buffer zone" between the Islamic empires of the Middle East and the Christian empires of Europe. Such a concept had

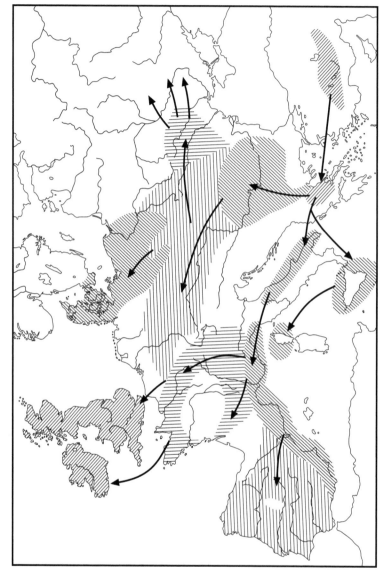

2.1   Europe and the Near East showing the dominant concept of the "agricultural colonization" of Europe from the Near East (after Renfrew 1987).

developed easily during the 500 years' power of the Ottoman Empire and its attempts to make inroads into Europe. Within the metaphor of southeast Europe as buffer, its history was regarded as complicated, chaotic, and meaningless in the bigger picture – an area of fragmentation, disorganization, danger, and unfamiliarity, and settled by wild, uncivilized people (Tringham 1974). It was viewed as an area that civilized Europeans needed to control by setting up military zones and by moving populations around to improve the strategic positions of the great powers (Kaplan 1993).

For most periods of prehistory, that is how southeast Europe has been and is still conceived. The Mesolithic is a good example. The Neolithic of southeast Europe, however, has become the darling of prehistorians world-wide. It has become familiar through the writing of V. Gordon Childe (Childe 1929, 1957, 1958), and more recently of Marija Gimbutas, who has given us a special vision of what the transition to the Neolithic means in southeast Europe (Gimbutas 1991). It has been described in detail by other synthesizers from western Europe and the United States (van Andel and Runnels 1995, Chapman 1981, 1988, 1989b, 1990, Demoule and Perlès 1993, Hodder 1990, Lichardus and Lichardus-Itten 1985, Renfrew 1979, 1989, Runnels and van Andel 1988, Séfériadès 1993, Sherratt 1984, Tringham 1971, 1990, Whittle 1985, 1996). Archaeologists from all over the world excavate its sites. The vertically stratified sites of Neolithic and Eneolithic southeast Europe provide a firm chronological framework almost unequaled in Europe, for a 3000-year period, from 6500 to 3500 BC, that encompasses the so-called Neolithization process.

In spite of the recent political changes, the traditional view of southeast Europe has changed little. The opening of political and commercial opportunities in the previously inaccessible countries of southeast Europe has meant that this is still an area that is controlled by the more intrusive nations of temperate Europe. The petty crime threat against visitors that has followed from these same opportunities in the "newly freed" countries has lent a certain credibility to the traditional vision of this area of Europe as being chaotic. And the horrifying violence and proximity of the civil wars in different parts of the former Yugoslavia (which was the one country that it was easy to visit in the pre-1990 period) have emphasized this impression.

I shall show below that the metaphors of bridge or buffer have led archaeologists into different models and visualizations of the transition to agriculture in southeast Europe. A third metaphor is one which I shall encourage – that is one of a mosaic, altogether a chaotic one, of unexpected and complex variability whose envisaged details can help us, I think, to construct a richer prehistory in this part of Europe.

The transition to the Neolithic in southeast Europe
The area encompassed by my discussion is termed southeast Europe. There is no "official" boundary to it. Its extent is defined by my focus

of interest which at this point is the middle and lower Danube basins, from Vienna (or perhaps Budapest) downstream to the Black Sea. The catchment area of the Danube here includes much of the modern states of Bulgaria, Serbia (former Yugoslavia), Romania, and Hungary. My discussion also includes (in a less intensive way) the catchment area of the rivers that run southwards from here into the Aegean Sea, to include the modern states of Greece and the former Yugoslav Macedonia.

"Southeast Europe" in this definition overlaps with the area defined and discussed by Marek Zvelebil as "eastern Europe." To have the area discussed by two different authors, with such different experiences and backgrounds, should not detract from the value of the discussion but can only enhance it.

What must come through in all the chapters in this volume is the lack of consensus not only in the models for the transition to agriculture in Europe but also in how to define the "Neolithization process." As has been pointed out by both Budja and Séfériadès at a recent conference on the topic, this is not surprising, since the two concepts are intrinsically linked (Budja 1993, Séfériadès 1993). It seems amazing that after all these decades we are still allowing the heuristic device of the Three-Age System to direct our interpretational modeling, but it is a truism that the definition of "Neolithization" depends a great deal on the criteria used to define "the Neolithic."

There is no doubt, however, that although subsistence change, specifically from a subsistence based on foraging to one based on the exploitation of domesticated plants and animals, seems to be a dominant criterion. Since Childe's coining of the term "Agricultural Revolution" there are nevertheless numerous other criteria which define "the Neolithic" and have been seen as significant in the "Neolithization process" in European prehistory. Technological changes of pottery production and polished macrocrystalline stone edge-tools were the original criteria used to define the Neolithic and continued to be used as such in defiance of Childe's dictum (Benac and Brodar 1957, Grbic 1959). Since then many other criteria have been added to the list in different kinds of combinations in the various models of "the Neolithization process": sedentary settlements, architecture, social differentiation, symbolic expression and the humanity of humans (Cauvin 1992), and even their own domestication (Hodder 1990). As will be argued in this chapter, in agreement with both Michel Séfériadès (1993) and Marek Zvelebil in this volume, the Neolithization process – whether transformation of subsistence or technology or settlement – means something different in different parts of the world and in different parts of Europe. What is to be understood in southeast Europe is the complexity of the economic, social, and cultural transformations that took place in this particular historical context.

My main argument in this chapter will be that in the geographical region that we call southeast Europe, many of these complexities have been missed because of the macroscopic scale with which archaeologists have chosen to view the transformations.

The Early Neolithic cultures of southeast Europe have been painted with a uniform brush. They have been called the early farmers of eastern Europe; described as colonists, egalitarian, small-scale, and domus-focused (Hodder 1990, Renfrew 1987, Tringham 1971, Whittle 1985, 1996); called matrifocal and goddess-worshipping participants in the civilization of Old Europe (Gimbutas 1991) . They have been grouped under the rubric of Early Neolithic Painted Pottery cultures or First Temperate Neolithic and contrasted to the Linear Pottery culture(s) of central Europe (Jarman *et al.* 1982, Nandris 1972, Sherratt 1984, Todorova and Vajsov 1993, Tringham 1971), or contrasted with areas in which the process was different, such as that north of the Black Sea or that of the Adriatic and central and west Mediterranean coast (Kozlowski 1989). This same sentiment can be grasped by the organization of this volume (Fig. 2.2).

The Early Neolithic settlements of southeast Europe *do* have much in common. A Neolithic "package" has been identified: pottery, predominantly monochrome, with its surfaces smoothed or roughened; the occurrence of pottery painted before firing; the use of clay in manufacturing figurines, weights, spindle-whorls, etc.; an architecture of rectangular detached houses constructed of wattle-and-daub techniques; polished stone adzes of macrocrystalline rocks; grinding stones; macrolithic flaked stone tools of flint and chert; a subsistence pattern based predominantly on domesticated animals and plants, including sheep, goats, cattle, pigs, wheat, barley, lentils, etc. (Lichardus and Lichardus-Itten 1985, Tringham 1971, Whittle 1985, 1996).

In spite of this seeming homogeneity, there are some important differences among the Early Neolithic settlements of southeast Europe as to how "the Neolithic package" is manifested archaeologically. Regional variation has been constructed by local southeast European archaeologists within this homogenous whole on the basis of variability of ceramics and architecture, and even settlement and subsistence. The Early Neolithic localities have been lumped into named cultures: Karanovo, Kremikovci, Starcevo, Körös, Cris (Tringham 1971, Whittle 1985, 1996) (Fig. 2.2). These groupings do recognize important differences between west, central and east Balkans, and south and north Balkans, but in many cases they seem to be driven by the emotional recognition of modern political territorial boundaries, when Cris refers to the Early Neolithic of all Romania, Körös to the Early Neolithic sites in Hungary, and Starcevo to the Early Neolithic sites in Serbia. In order to describe cultural similarities across modern political boundaries, for example among the sites of the lower Tisza/Tamis area, it is necessary to use hyphenated names such Starcevo-Körös and Starcevo-Cris that do little to capture their distinctive nature (Brukner 1980)!

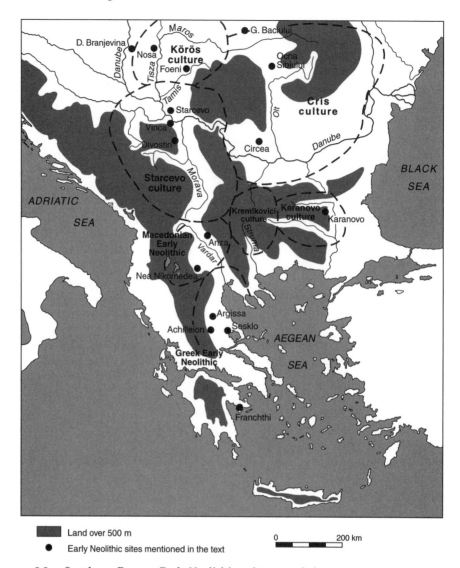

Land over 500 m
● Early Neolithic sites mentioned in the text

0   200 km

2.2   Southeast Europe: Early Neolithic cultures and sites.

An important example of regional variability is that between the
Early Neolithic of the southern Balkan peninsula and those of the catchment area of the middle and lower Danube basin in the northern Balkan
peninsula (Fig. 2.2). In the catchment area of the Danube basin (north of the
Vardar–Morava watershed in Serbia and north of the Sredna Gora mountains in Bulgaria), there is a virtual absence of evidence of long-term occupation (that is of a duration of more than a few years, even if occupation is

year round) in the Early Neolithic settlements. There are few solid surface houses, and there is no spatial differentiation within the settlements; there is little evidence for intensive labor effort put into the modification of the landscape, apart from digging pits (that have frequently been interpreted as dwellings) (Bogdanovic 1988, Brukner 1982, Drasovean 1989, Greenfield and Drasovean 1994). The settlement pattern is one of "tactical," short-term opportunism; a location is occupied according to an immediate need (water availability, a place to cross the river) (Barker 1985, Bogucki 1979, Kaiser and Voytek 1983, Kosse 1968, Nandris 1970). This is in marked contrast to the well-established, long-term settlements at this time south of this region that are characterized by the remains of surface houses, and are at the base of long-lived tell settlements that were consistently located strategically at the spring-line with a view to constant water availability (Demoule and Perlès 1993, Georgiev 1981, Gimbutas 1976, Gimbutas *et al.* 1989, Hiller 1990, Nikolov 1989b, Rodden 1962, Todorova and Vajsov 1993).

The lithic assemblages of the early agriculturalists of the Danube basin catchment area indicate a utilization of secondary (fluvial) sources of minerals for microcrystalline and probably macrocrystalline stone edge-tools (Radovanovic *et al.* 1984, Tringham 1988), compared to the stone tools of the southern Balkans that were from outcrop sources (Demoule and Perlès 1993, Elster 1976, Manolakakis 1987, 1994, Perlès 1990a, 1990b, 1992, Tringham, in press). Moreover, the people were living in an area that was highly suited to large forest mammals (cattle, pigs, deer), yet these figure hardly at all in wild form in their faunal assemblages (Blazic 1992, Bökönyi 1974, 1988, 1989, Clason 1980, Greenfield 1993, Lazic 1988). I have the impression that they were relatively under-utilizing the riches of their local micro- and macro-environments in terms of food and other resources, either through ignorance or through a resistance to venturing far in space or concept into the unknown.

This variability has been predominantly explained as the result of the process of adaptation to changing environment and changing distance from the "source" in the Near East (Gimbutas 1991, Lichardus *et al.* 1985, Todorova and Vajsov 1993). Even if this variability is clearly complicated, archaeologists in the Anglo-American tradition of synthesis have preferred to view it as "noise" that disturbs the overarching concept that the process of the establishment of the Neolithic was a homogeneous one.

Some archaeologists have explored the nature of variability in the southeast European Neolithic in terms that go beyond "ecological-adaptational" or "geo-political" explanation, but their voices have largely been unheard or unheeded (Barker 1985, Brukner 1980, Chapman 1990, Garasanin 1980, Whittle, 1996). For the most part, the Neolithization process itself – the establishment of "the Neolithic package" – is seen as a homogeneous one by foreign and local southeast European archaeologists alike, one which, moreover, was introduced into southeast Europe from the

Near East (Brukner *et al.* 1974, Demoule and Perlès 1993, Dolukhanov 1979, Garasanin 1980, Jovanovic 1972, 1975, Lazarovici 1979, Lichardus and Lichardus-Itten 1985, Nikolov 1989a, Todorova and Vajsov 1993, Vlassa 1976). Although there may seem to be a consensus on the form of the Early Neolithic cultures and the exogenous origin of the domesticates, there are still many points of dissent and debate which continue to be discussed in meetings and publications. Many of the debates may seem to be an endless quibbling over local relative chronologies and claims of chronological priority of local Neolithic settlements. But in fact, as both Budja and Séfériadès have pointed out, these debates have significant implications for our understanding of the bigger picture (Budja 1993, Séfériadès 1993).

When were the domesticates and cultigens introduced in southeast Europe?

In the traditional model of the introduction of "the Neolithic package," it has been assumed that the earliest domesticates were introduced with other technological innovations that appear in the Early Neolithic settlements of southeast Europe: pottery, clay figurines and weights, polished edge-tools of macrocrystalline stone and macrolithic flaked edge-tools of cryptocrystalline stone, grindstones, and wattle-and-daub architecture. This view assumes that the Neolithic of southeast Europe is, from its beginning, a ceramic Neolithic and that there is no earlier preceramic Neolithic.

The dissenting views focus on two aspects of this traditional view. First, the solidity of the "package" itself has been challenged by evidence of certain parts of it without the other – for example, domesticates without pottery, and pottery without domesticates. Second, the process of Neolithization has been argued to be a much longer and more complicated process in southeast Europe than usually assumed.

The challenge to the Neolithic package was first put forward in the 1950s/1960s when aceramic layers were found at the base of Neolithic tells in northern Greece (e.g., Argissa) and Crete (Knossos) (Bloedow 1991, Budja 1993, Demoule and Perlès 1993:365, Milojcic 1960, Theocharis 1973) in which domesticates dominated the faunal and floral remains, yet with a lithic assemblage that included "Mesolithic" geometric microliths. These levels were referred to as "Preceramic" or "Aceramic" Neolithic and created an excited search for similar sites north of Greece (Tringham 1973). The search was for sites which demonstrated the presence of domesticated plants and animals without evidence of pottery, but with evidence of a "Mesolithic" flint industry. It was assumed that this would provide evidence of a very early (pre-pottery) introduction of exogenous domesticates. In other words, the pre-pottery sites challenged the date of the introduction of domesticates and their technological correlates, but not their point of origin.

In the end, the only comparable sites to the preceramic Neolithic levels at Argissa – for example, at Baile Herculane in the southwest Carpathian mountains of Romania (Berciu 1958), or at Murzak Koba in the Crimean peninsula of the Ukraine (Tringham 1971 and see Zvelebil, this volume) – were found in poorly dated contexts and inhospitable areas which had no obvious connection to mainstream ceramic Neolithic settlements (Fig. 2.3). These sites are now explained as the result of a relatively late adoption of domesticated animals by hunter-gatherers (Dennell 1983, Kozlowski 1989, Tringham 1971, 1973, Voytek and Tringham 1989 and Zvelebil, this volume).

The stratified cave of Crvena Stijena in the mountains of Montenegro, former Yugoslavia, in spite of hopes that its Stratum IV would provide evidence of domesticated goat without ceramics, eventually proved to have no domesticated plants or animals in either its Stratum IV or the overlying Stratum III. What makes this site interesting is that, in its Stratum III, it provides an example of a foraging site which has ceramics (Benac and Brodar 1957). The question for Benac and others is whether these ceramics are locally developed or whether they represent interaction between local foragers and Ceramic Neolithic agriculturalists (Benac 1975). This is a situation that occurs several times in the archaeology of southeast Europe, and I will return to it when discussing the role of local foragers in the "Neolithization process."

The calculated duration of the Neolithization process in southeast Europe obviously depends to a certain extent on the dating of its starting point. The radiocarbon dates for the Greek Preceramic Neolithic sites (Argissa, Knossos, Franchthi) all hover at *c.* 8000 BP uncal. (6800 BC). The radiocarbon dates for the Ceramic Early Neolithic in the south Balkan peninsula fall between 7800 and 7000 BP uncal. (6600–5800 BC), and for the Early Neolithic in the north Balkan peninsula are 7500–6400 BP uncal. (6500–5200 BC) (Chapman and Dolukhanov 1993, Demoule and Perlès 1993, Todorova and Vajsov 1993). Within this range, however, and not always with the support of the radiocarbon dates, a complicated series of sequences of ceramic development has been distinguished. The sequences are designed to show that certain areas of southeast Europe have claim to an earlier phase of the "Neolithization" process than others. In most cases the claims fall into two camps, those that suggest that the earliest Neolithic pottery in southeast Europe is painted (Lazarovici 1979, Paul 1995, Vlassa 1972, 1976), and those that suggest that it is monochrome (Dimitrijevic 1974, Garasanin 1973, Todorova and Vajsov 1993:74). As Demoule and Perlès have noted for Greece, such sequences based on ceramic decoration typology are still very much the subject of debate (Demoule and Perlès 1993:377). By now, however, the painted/monochrome debate has resulted in Pre- and Proto-Starcevo (Srejovic 1988), pre-Cris (Paul 1995) and pre-Karanovo (Todorova and Vajsov 1993) phases filling the role of "Early Neolithic" north of Greece,

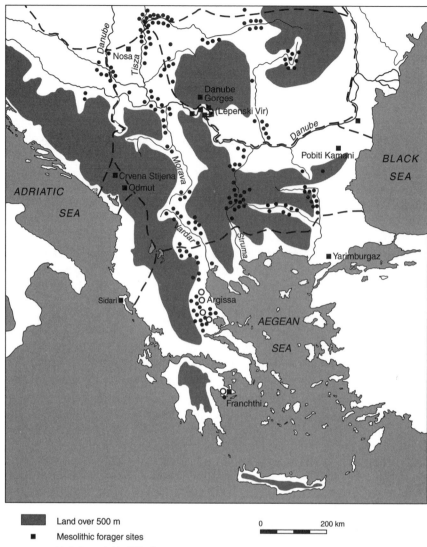

2.3   Southeast Europe: Mesolithic sites and claimed Aceramic Neolithic sites against a background of Early Neolithic sites.

so that the Starcevo, Cris and Karanovo I cultures themselves have been "demoted" to "Middle Neolithic." To readers on the outside of these debates, the designation of this or that phase may not seem crucial to the problem of the bigger picture of Neolithization. On this basis, however, complex scenarios of the Neolithization process have been written, as I shall show in one case in detail below.

Do the domesticates and cultigens in southeast Europe have an exogenous origin?

Most archaeologists writing about and in southeast Europe accept the exogenous origin of the domesticated plants and animals. The candidates for the source of the domesticates are to the southeast of southeast Europe: in the territory of modern Turkey, Iran, and the east Mediterranean coast. Within the consensus that river valleys or sea coasts were involved, the options for which route(s) are many. Western archaeologists in their abstract (but by no means apolitical) view of the geo-political map of Europe have waved magic wands along one or another route. Local southeast European archaeologists, on the other hand, have been motivated by regional politics, territorial boundaries, and national and/or ethnic identities. Opinions have changed also with the increase of archaeological information on Early Neolithic settlements.

The route from Turkey across the Hellespont and up the Maritsa valley has always been dubious because of the lack of Early Neolithic sites in the southeast corner of Bulgaria and the northwest corner of Turkey. The fact that this has long been a military zone may explain the lack of research, but it is only a matter of time before sites are found (Gatsov and Özdogan 1994, Özdogan 1989). The research of Mehmet Özdogan and other Turkish archaeologists underlies a challenge to another set of significant assumptions about the nature of the Neolithization process in "the Near East" that unfortunately I do not have time or space to deal with here (Özdögan 1995, 1997, Séfériadès 1993:147).

Childe himself favored an indirect route from Turkey via Crete and then through the Greek mainland up the Vardar river and down the Morava to the Danube, i.e., through modern Macedonia and Serbia (Childe 1957). Demoule and Perlès suggest an island-hopping route from the east Mediterranean coast to Greece (Demoule and Perlès 1993). Bulgarian archaeologists have tended recently to push for their own Struma/Iskar valley route to the Danube, especially as research on the Early Neolithic in west Bulgaria has accumulated (Lichardus-Itten 1993, Nikolov 1989a, 1990, Todorova and Vajsov 1993) (Fig. 2.1).

The route from the Danube mouth (another military zone) up the lower Danube has always been out of favor. The Black Sea, however, may have been important at some point, particularly for access into the hinterland of the Prut, Siret, and Dniester rivers (Zvelebil, this volume).

The Adriatic coast also has been out of consideration as a route by which domesticates reached the inland valleys of Neolithic distribution. The process of the transition to the Neolithic on the coast is generally considered entirely separate from the Early Neolithic cultures of the central and east Balkans (Budja 1993, Chapman and Müller 1990, Lewthwaite 1986b).

The discussion of routes by which the domesticates reached Europe assumes their exogenous origin. This has always been a strong underlying assumption in the construction of European prehistory, owing to the apparent lack of wild progenitors of the domesticates – sheep and goats and wheat and barley – north of the coastal fringes of the Balkan peninsula. As will be discussed below, another basis for this assumption is the deeply rooted idea that southeast Europe was virtually uninhabited by a post-Pleistocene foraging (Mesolithic) population. A few archaeologists, however, have argued for southeast Europe – especially its southern fringes – being part of the large zone in which domestication had first been achieved and then spread to the rest of Europe. Dennell, for example, has argued that the absence of wild progenitors of especially domesticated wheats and barley, and even sheep and goats, in southeast Europe has been greatly overestimated (Dennell 1983). This idea has recently been resuscitated (Séfériadès 1993:145). Both of these authors have argued that it is quite feasible that all the domesticates seen in the Neolithic of southeast Europe had an indigenous origin. However, the exogenous origin of domesticates and cultigens in Greek Preceramic Neolithic levels in Aegean coastal areas, including the recently excavated cave of Franchthi in southern Greece, is accepted by most archaeologists (Demoule and Perlès 1993, Evans 1964, Perlès and Vaughan 1983, Theocharis 1973, Vitelli 1993).

The conclusions are more ambiguous, however, with regard to domesticates – cattle, pigs, and dogs – whose wild progenitors are clearly present in southeast Europe, especially in the more heavily forested and watered areas inland from the Mediterranean littoral in the northern and central Balkan peninsula. The construction of Mesolithic foragers who were intensively manipulating and exploiting their animal and plant resources for food well along the continuum toward domestication (Harris 1977, 1989) has become a major concept for the study of much of the Mesolithic in northern, western, and eastern Europe (e.g., Higgs and Jarman 1975, Roussot-Larroque 1989, Rowley-Conwy *et al.* 1987). Interpretation of the data in these terms has only recently been applied to the data in the "mainstream" areas of Early Neolithic settlement in central and southeast Europe. The idea of Mesolithic forager quasi-domestic manipulation of "wild" cattle, deer and pigs, and plants such as *chenopoedia*, is still only marginally entertained in these areas, mostly because of the apparent lack of data on the presence of foragers. I believe, as do Zvelebil, Bogucki, and Jochim in this volume, however, that there is a good case to be made for the presence of such foragers in central and southeast Europe that needs to be taken into account in our interpretation of the Neolithization process (Bonsall *et al.* 1997, Budja 1993, Chapman 1993, Dennell 1983, Greenfield 1993, Jarman 1972, Séfériadès 1993, Tringham 1973, Whittle 1996). The archaeologist who has developed the scenario of an indigenous origin of domesticated plants and animals in southeast Europe to its ultimate extent is Dragoslav Srejovic in his reconstruction of the prehistory of the Danube Gorges (Srejovic 1974, 1988).

The dominance of the model that domesticates and cultigens were introduced by a colonizing population has done much to overwhelm the idea that local Mesolithic foragers played a significant part in the history of southeast Europe.

Migration/colonization: the dominant model of the introduction of domesticates and cultigens in southeast Europe

The idea of demic diffusion, i.e., an actual colonization by real people (always without faces, gender, age, etc.) bringing in domestic animals and plants, as well as ceramics, and all of the concomitant knowledge and skills of farming (although perhaps with less knowledge of local resources), has been the most popular means – as far as the southeast European data are concerned – for achieving the transition to the Neolithic. This model was suggested by V. Gordon Childe (1925) and taken up by his synthesizing followers (Ammerman 1989, Ammerman and Cavalli-Sforza 1971, 1984, Barker 1985, Bogucki 1988, Gimbutas 1991, Lichardus and Lichardus-Itten 1985, Milojcic 1960, Renfrew 1989, Tringham 1971, Whittle 1985, 1996) (Fig. 2.1).

Radiocarbon dating of the Early Neolithic sites gave numerical credence to the idea of colonization, since the earlier dates tended to be in the southeast of the Balkans, while later dates were further north and west. The colonization model has been expressed in greatest detail by Albert Ammerman and Luigi Cavalli-Sforza (1984) in their Wave of Advance model, and more recently by Colin Renfrew (1987), who saw the colonization as coinciding with the spread of Indo-European language speakers.

Marek Zvelebil in this volume gives a detailed account of the model's critique. He points out here and elsewhere the flawed assumptions that underlay the model, including the idea that there is a time limit for cultivating land without fertilizers or fallow-field technology, so that the colonists had to keep moving until they reached the Atlantic and North Sea and could move no longer (also see Harris 1977, Zvelebil 1986, 1986b, Zvelebil and Zvelebil 1988). Other supporting data that have been used for this model include the apparently exogenous origins of the domesticated plants and animals that I have discussed above.

The popularity of the colonization model, however, has rested heavily on the impression that southeast Europe – from Greece all the way north into the middle Danube valley – was devoid of a significant indigenous foraging population (e.g., Demoule and Perlès 1993). It seemed as though the colonists were moving into an empty continent.

Participation of Mesolithic foragers in the transition to the Neolithic: a marginal model so far for southeast Europe

Postglacial hunter-gatherers fall into a nebulous gap between the Upper Palaeolithic cave deposits with richly elaborated macrolithic flaked stone tools and the ceramic Neolithic settlements with their decorated ceramics, clay architecture, and figurines. Few systematic, long-term attempts at finding Mesolithic or Epipalaeolithic period sites have been made in southeast Europe (Bonsall 1997, Boroneant 1970, 1981, Dzhambazov 1964, Kozlowski 1989, Kozlowski and Kozlowski 1973, Perlès 1996, Srejovic 1975, Tringham 1973, Voytek and Tringham 1989).

Evidence of Mesolithic hunter-gatherers is found in those places where the "mainstream" Early Neolithic is not found (Séfériadès 1993 and see Zvelebil, this volume): limestone mountains of Montenegro and Serbia, e.g., Odmut (Srejovic 1975) and Crvena Stijena (Benac and Brodar 1957), and Romania; limestone sea cliffs of the Adriatic coast (Budja 1993, Miroslavljevic 1959, Sordinas 1969) and the Aegean coast, e.g., at Franchthi Cave (Jacobsen 1981); sand dunes of the Black Sea littoral, e.g., at the Varna lakes in Bulgaria (Gatsov 1985, Price 1993, Todorova and Vajsov 1993); and in the Dobrogea region of Romania (Bolomey 1978, Paunescu 1987); most recently in Turkish Thrace (Gatsov and Özdogan 1994; Özdogan 1989, 1997); and of course in the Danube Gorges (see citations below) (Fig. 2.3). There exists the very real possibility that evidence for local hunter-gatherer populations in the major valleys lies stratified deeply below the floodplain deposits (Demoule and Perlès 1993 and see Zvelebil, this volume). To date Mesolithic sites have not been found in the Danube and Morava floodplains or terraces, nor have they been looked for.

The rich models of contact, interaction, and exchange between Mesolithic foragers and early Neolithic farmers that are familiar to those working elsewhere in Europe (Bogucki 1988, Gregg 1988, Lewthwaite 1986b, Rowley-Conwy *et al.* 1987, Zvelebil 1986b) have been applied sporadically to the margins of early agricultural settlement in southeast Europe. In this volume, Marek Zvelebil expands his model of moving agricultural frontiers with success to southeast Europe, where contact between foragers and agriculturalists had been hinted at by previous authors, for example, in the Prut, Dniester, and Bug valleys northwest of the Black Sea (Dennell 1983, Dolukhanov 1979, Kozlowski 1989, Tringham 1971, 1973), the Adriatic coastal zone and the Montenegrin mountains (Budja 1993, Chapman and Müller 1990), the marshes of the Tisza–Danube confluence (Nandris 1972, Tringham 1971), and the Danube Gorges (Chapman 1993,

Tringham 1990, Voytek and Tringham 1989), as well as the south Aegean coast.

In these models of interaction, the burden of proof rests on which data can be interpreted as "external" to the foragers' culture or the agriculturalists' culture and therefore can be interpreted as evidence of exchange or some other kind of contact. The problem lies in the fact that the interpretation of, for example, ceramics or domestic animal bones or polished stone edge-tools is ambiguous. For example, the ceramics at Franchthi in some of the "Preceramic" levels have been interpreted as local experimentation and development of ceramics (Theocharis 1973), evidence of colonization by agriculturalists in the early stages of developing ceramic technology (Bloedow 1991), and exchange with a ceramic-producing group outside the Greek mainland (Demoule and Perlès 1993, Vitelli 1993). The ceramics of Crvena Stijena have been interpreted as the independent development of ceramics by foragers (Benac 1975) and as evidence of contact with ceramic-producing agriculturalists (Séfériadès 1993). It is this ambiguity of the data that has opened up the possibilities of interpretations of the data in terms of forager–agriculturalist contact – evidence of Marek Zvelebil's zone of availability – that makes the Neolithization process in southeast Europe suddenly seem much more complex.

Thus Zvelebil's and others' models no longer slip into the debate on colonization or indigenous development. The kind of colonization that is modeled is reduced in speed, distance of movement, and scale; in this demic movement social pressures and the social complexity of fissioning settlements are emphasized (Bogucki 1979, 1988, Chapman 1989, 1990, Renfrew 1989, Séfériadès 1993, Zvelebil 1986).

In the last part of this chapter, I shall explore in detail the potential of these ambiguities of the archaeological data to enrich our models of forager–agriculturalist interaction in the "Neolithization process" in one small area of southeast Europe – the Danube Gorges.

Lepenski Vir and the Danube Gorges sites: a unique or typical history of transition to the Neolithic in southeast Europe?

The exploration of the Danube Gorges in the late 1960s and early 1970s prior to damming of the Danube between Yugoslavia and Romania led to a series of quite unexpected and impressive finds in a terrain that was quite inhospitable for agriculturalists, both prehistoric and modern (Bolomey 1973b, Boric in press, Boroneant 1970, 1981, 1990, Jovanovic 1969, 1972, Letica 1969, Mogosanu 1978, Paunescu 1970, Prinz 1987, Radovanovic 1992, 1996, Srejovic 1966, 1972, Srejovic and Letica 1978) (Fig. 2.4).

The sites of the Danube Gorges present late Pleistocene and early post-Pleistocene forager settlements dating from 10,000 to 4800 BC. Their material is as ambiguous as any that I have discussed so far. It is not surprising, therefore, that various interpretations have been used to construct very

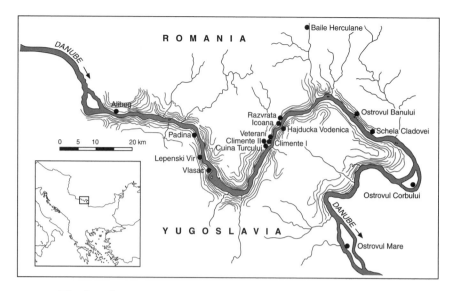

2.4   The Danube Gorges and important archaeological sites (after Voytek and
       Tringham 1988: fig. 1).

different versions of the Neolithization process, not only in this small
regional pocket, but in the whole of southeast Europe. For the sites of the
Danube Gorges – in particular Lepenski Vir – serve as the model for local
forager participation in the Neolithization process in southeast Europe
north of Franchthi cave. From the data of Lepenski Vir, Padina, and Schela
Cladovei are extrapolated scenarios that are assumed to be typical of the
transition to the Neolithic (Gimbutas 1991, Hodder 1990, Price and Feinman
1993).

    Like the excavator of Lepenski Vir – Dragoslav Srejovic – and a few
others (Chapman 1993, Srejovic 1972), however, I think that Lepenski Vir is
unique and that the Danube Gorges sites represent a historically contingent
process.[1] I consider it unjustifiable to assume that the complexities of
hunter-gatherering society and the scenarios of their contact with agriculturalists that have been developed for the Danube Gorges sites also apply
to southeast Europe *outside of* the Danube Gorges. If there is some general
statement that *can* be extrapolated from the Danube Gorges sites, however,
it is that there were hunter-gatherers in southeast Europe who had already
adopted the complexities of a sedentary way of life and that this way of life
could have been severely disrupted, if not destroyed very quickly, by direct
or indirect contact with and proximity to agriculturalists.

    I also agree with Dragoslav Srejovic (and others) in his argument
that the Epipalaeolithic and Mesolithic sites in the Danube Gorges display
an increasing degree of social complexity and sedentism culminating in

phases I–II in the occupation of Lepenski Vir, known as the Lepenski Vir culture. The exploitation of local plants and animals (especially red deer, birds, and fish) was planned and scheduled well along the spectrum toward domestication (Chapman 1993, Dennell 1983, Hodder 1991, Jarman 1972, Jovanovic 1972, Prinz 1987, Radovanovic 1992, 1996, Srejovic 1974, Tringham 1973, Voytek and Tringham 1988). This process had a long, continuous tradition going back to late Pleistocene times (Bolomey 1973, Boroneant 1970) and was fully established by periods I–II in the occupation of Vlasac *c.* 7500–6500 BC (8500–8000 BP uncal.) (Letica 1969, Prinz 1987, Srejovic and Letica 1978).

The Danube Gorges contain a highly concentrated set of microenvironments, because of both the presence of the river and the steep, high sides of the gorges (Misic *et al.* 1969, Radovanovic 1996, Srejovic and Babovic 1981). The area was ideal for the exploitation of a broad spectrum of animal and plant resources from a permanent home base.[2] Such a pattern of subsistence would have needed careful organization and scheduling and might have continued to be practiced indefinitely without modification. But it did not! From 6500 BC (7500 BP uncal.) onward, important socio-economic changes were clearly happening (Lepenski Vir I–II, Padina B1–B2). By 5700 BC (6800 BP uncal.) the foragers' settlements had been abandoned. In a few sites (e.g., Lepenski Vir IIIa–b, Padina B3) the occupation layers of foragers were overlain for a short time by debris of Early Neolithic settlements (5700–4800 BC/6800–6000 BP uncal.). After 4800 BC, the Danube Gorges were largely deserted.

There are a number of scenarios to explain how this may have happened. All involve the transition to a subsistence economy based on domesticated plants and animals and concomitant changes in settlement and social organization. They vary in terms of the timing of the changes and the role played by the indigenous foragers. The scenarios can be divided into two groups depending on which interpretation of the chronological data from the later Danube Gorges sites, particularly those from Lepenski Vir itself, is accepted (Fig. 2.5).

The first interpretation is that proposed by the excavator of Lepenski Vir (Srejovic 1969a, 1974, 1988, Srejovic and Babovic 1981). In this interpretation, Srejovic proposes that there are three main phases of occupation at Lepenski Vir and that the radiocarbon dates from the site (7500–6800 BP uncal.) should be assigned to the final phase of the occupation of Lepenski Vir (phase IIIa–b), even though the samples were originally taken from the deposits (houses) that were assigned to phases I–II. In other words, Srejovic is suggesting that the radiocarbon dates are not reliable. Similarly ceramic sherds that were excavated in many of the phase I–II house remains are viewed by Srejovic as the result of secondary contamination and not part of the original material assemblage of the houses. He suggests that the Lepenski Vir culture (phases I–II of the occupation of Lepenski

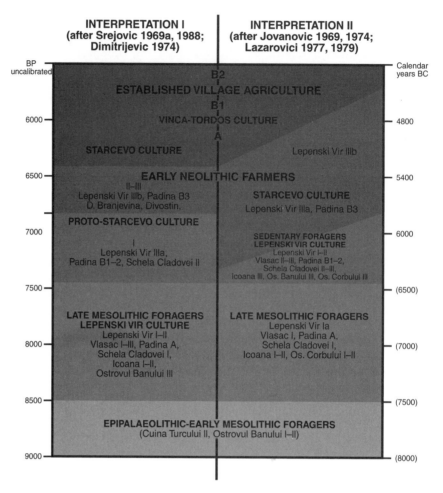

| INTERPRETATION I (after Srejovic 1969a, 1988; Dimitrijevic 1974) | INTERPRETATION II (after Jovanovic 1969, 1974; Lazarovici 1977, 1979) |

2.5   Chronological interpretations of the Danube Gorges sites and the Lepenski Vir stratigraphy.

Vir), with its stone heads, trapezoid houses, and other paraphernalia of material complexity, is *contemporary* with the Mesolithic site of Vlasac. According to this scenario, Lepenski Vir I–II entirely *precedes* the monochrome and painted pottery Neolithic settlements of the Danube basin catchment area (Proto-Starcevo/Pre-Cris and Starcevo/Körös/Cris cultures). In Srejovic's view, the Proto-Starcevo culture is contemporary with phases IIIa–b at Lepenski Vir.

It is worth repeating here that, as mentioned above, Srejovic and others believe that the Starcevo culture, represented, for example, by the type-site Starcevo, does not typify the earliest agriculturalists in the central

Balkan area. Srejovic refers to the painted pottery of the Starcevo culture as "Middle Neolithic" (Srejovic 1988). He feels that the Early Neolithic settlements are defined by monochrome pottery of the Proto-Starcevo culture (that is itself assigned three sub-phases) as seen at Lepenski Vir IIIa–b and a few sites outside the Danube Gorges (Donja Branjevina, Drenovac, Grivac, and Divostin).[3] For Srejovic the origin and inspiration of the Early Neolithic settlements (and ultimately of the Middle Neolithic settlements) lies in the Danube Gorges, with the Lepenski Vir Late Mesolithic culture.

Dragoslav Srejovic used his own discoveries at Lepenski Vir and Vlasac, those of Borislav Jovanovic at Padina, and those of the Romanians at Icoana and Schela Cladovei, to challenge the idea that the Balkans were merely a bridge. He offered his hypothesis of a local, autochthonous origin of agriculture in the Balkans (Srejovic 1972, 1974, 1988). In his opinion, the Balkans are an extension of the Near East, in that experiments in domestication of plants and animals were going on in the Danube Gorges just as they were in other upland regions of the Near East. He conceived of a transition to the Neolithic in the central Balkans that started first in the Danube Gorges. In his scenario, hunter-gatherers in the early Mesolithic period at settlements such as Vlasac (Fig. 2.6b) experimented to domesticate local fauna (especially dogs, cattle, and pigs) and flora (such as wild millet and wild einkorn), and by the late Mesolithic (at places like Lepenski Vir, phases I–II) (Fig. 2.7a) they had developed into a flourishing proto-Neolithic society.

None of the other numerous sites excavated on either the Romanian or Yugoslavian side was comparable to Lepenski Vir in either size or complexity. The settlement during phases I–II at Lepenski Vir, with its extraordinary architectural remains, elaborate stone carvings, and rich material culture in stone and bone, has been described in detail by Srejovic himself, and discussed and interpreted by many archaeologists (Chapman 1993, Gimbutas 1991, Hodder 1991, Price and Feinman 1993, Radovanovic 1996, Voytek and Tringham 1988). For this reason, I shall not describe the site here, but assume that its details are familiar. Srejovic noted that the material elaboration and architecture were not duplicated in the other Danube Gorges sites and interpreted the site in this period (I–II) as having acted as a central settlement or ceremonial place, whose occupants specialized in the accumulation and preservation of the sacred secrets of the knowledge about experiments in domesticating plants and animals and who monopolized the rituals and ceremonies associated with such knowledge.

His scenario continues with the growth of the Late Mesolithic settlements of the Lepenski Vir culture in stability, size, and complexity, along with their need for the more intensive procurement of food and raw materials. This pattern led to removal of the knowledge of domesticated animals and plants out of the secret sacred domain at Lepenski Vir to a wider acceptance as a source of subsistence. In this phase (the Proto-Starcevo

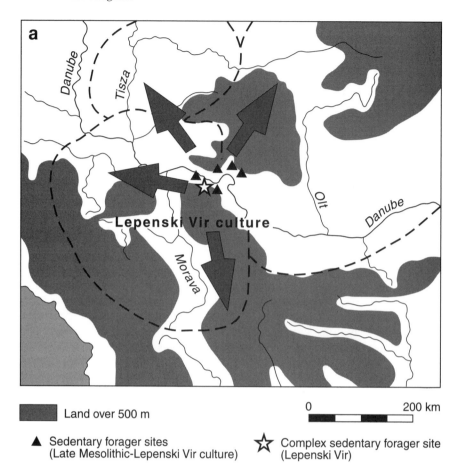

2.6a   Southeast Europe: two models for Mesolithic–Neolithic interaction, 6500–5500 bc (7500–6500 BC).

culture, Lepenski Vir IIIa–b) the Danube Gorges foragers transformed into food-producers (Fig. 2.8a).

Moreover, Srejovic suggests that, with the expansive nature of food-production, the new food-producers were quickly forced to expand beyond the constricting boundaries of the Danube Gorges into the valleys (but not the floodplains) of the Danube tributaries, colonizing the valleys of the Morava, Tisza, and Maros, and beyond. In his eyes, the Starcevo, Körös, and Cris cultures are the ultimate result of this expansion. Meanwhile, the Danube Gorges were occupied less permanently, as seen at the Lepenski Vir IIIa–b settlement (Fig. 2.8a), eventually becoming a marginal backwater to be abandoned. Thus in Srejovic's scenario, the Danube Gorges foragers-turned-food-producers were responsible for the formation of the earliest

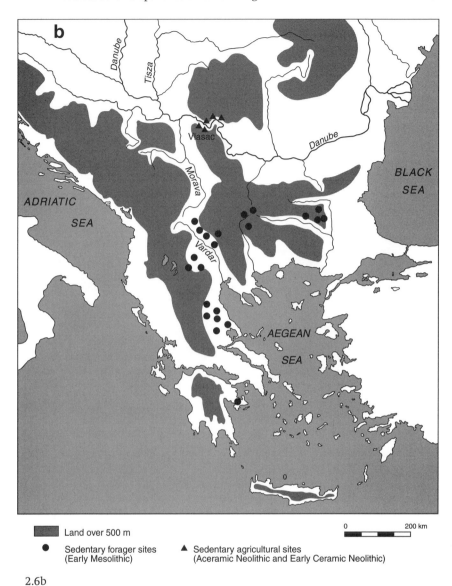

2.6b

Land over 500 m

● Sedentary forager sites (Early Mesolithic)

▲ Sedentary agricultural sites (Aceramic Neolithic and Early Ceramic Neolithic)

0   200 km

agricultural settlements of the Morava and Danube valley closest to the Gorges, and perhaps of those of the whole middle Danube basin catchment area. He would see the Early Neolithic of the south and east Balkans (Kremikovci, Karanovo, Macedonian Neolithic) as a separate phenomenon caused by direct colonization from Anatolia or Greece.

Srejovic's dating of Lepenski Vir I–II is accepted by many archaeologists inside and outside the former Yugoslavia. What is *not* accepted by

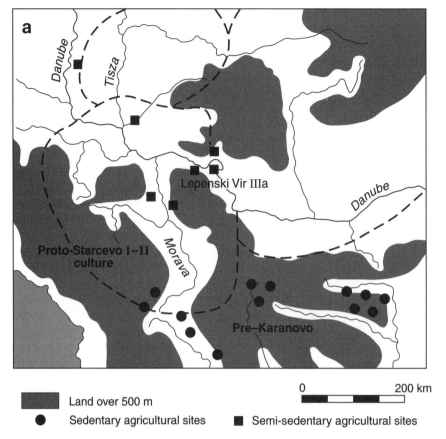

2.7a   The Middle Danube basin: two models for Mesolithic–Neolithic interaction, 5500–4800 bc (6500–5700 BC).

many colleagues, however, is his idea that the Danube Gorges was an
autochthonous center of animal and plant domestication, or his model for
the formation of the Starcevo, Körös and Cris cultures. Foremost among the
objections to his model is the fact that there is no record of the wild progenitors of the domestic animals (sheep and goats) and plants (wheat and
barley) that were the main subsistence source in these latter settlements in
the Danube Gorges, although wild cattle and pigs were found in the
Lepenski Vir I–II faunal assemblage (Bökönyi 1970). Moreover, the only
domesticated species – plant or animal – that has been identified in the
Lepenski Vir I–II contexts is the dog (Bökönyi 1970). Sandor Bökönyi has no
hesitation in calling Lepenski Vir I–II a forager settlement. At Padina,
however, where the faunal assemblage of contemporary "Late Mesolithic"
levels (A–B1–2) contained domesticated animal bones of cattle, pig, and
goat, Clason opted for Jovanovic's chronological interpretation discussed

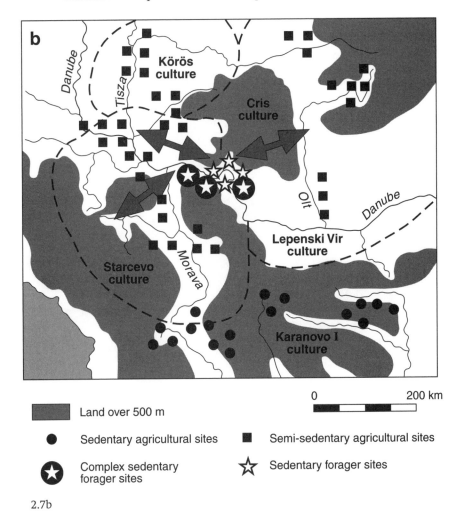

Land over 500 m

● Sedentary agricultural sites

■ Semi-sedentary agricultural sites

⭐ (white) Complex sedentary forager sites

☆ Sedentary forager sites

2.7b

below (Clason 1980). The largest number of bones in all periods of both Lepenski Vir's and Padina's occupation is from red deer.

Other archaeologists have accepted and elaborated on the symbolic and ceremonial aspects of Lepenski Vir material culture. Their scenarios, including Srejovic's own, suggest that a complex system of organization of work, social relations, ceremonial activities, and symbolic expression that developed in the late Mesolithic settlements of the Danube Gorges did so as the result of internal tensions and inspiration, domesticating the wild in humans as well as plants and animals (Handsman 1990, Hodder 1991), allowing the natural riches of the region to inspire the natural riches of humanity to emerge, developing domestication skills, or rich ritual and sacred life associated with the worship of nature and the Goddess

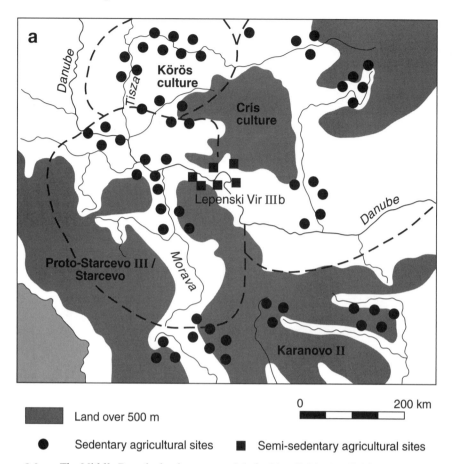

2.8a   The Middle Danube basin: two models for Mesolithic–Neolithic interaction, 4800–4400 bc (5700–5300 BC).

(Gimbutas 1991, Srejovic 1972). In these models (or scenarios) which accept Srejovic's chronological interpretation, the foragers of the Danube Gorges are acting in a blissful vacuum. Neolithic colonists from the east Mediterranean area, for example, played no role in their developments toward social complexity and sedentism, which were all hypothesized to have happened *before* any such people were within reach of the foragers of the Danube Gorges (Fig. 2.6a).

In an alternative chronological interpretation of the Danube Gorges sites, these two populations become chronologically and spatially juxtaposed, which opens up the possibilities for a very different set of interpretations of the transformations in the Danube Gorges. This interpretation was proposed by Borislav Jovanovic on the basis of his excavations at Padina (Chapman 1993:84, Clason 1980, Jovanovic 1969, 1974, 1975, Radovanovic

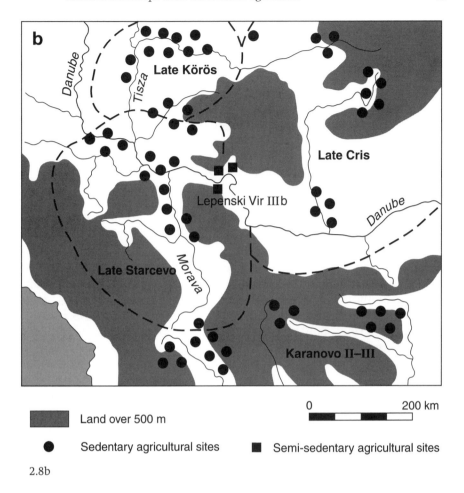

Land over 500 m

0   200 km

● Sedentary agricultural sites   ■ Semi-sedentary agricultural sites

2.8b

1996). Padina is the westernmost of the Danube Gorges forager sites and lies on the Yugoslav side, 27 km from the west end of the Gorges. Two periods of early prehistoric occupation have been recognized at this site: an earlier one (phase A) of foragers possibly contemporary with Vlasac or Lepenski Vir I, and a later one (phase B1–3) that has been dated by several radiocarbon samples at *c.* 5100 BC (Fig. 2.5), that is, contemporary with the infamous dates from Lepenski Vir. In the case of Padina, however, the radiocarbon samples as well as ceramics are unambiguously located in trapezoid houses of the kind that characterize the Lepenski Vir culture and are associated with a context that is very similar to that of Lepenski Vir I–II. On this basis, Jovanovic has proposed that the relative chronological position of these layers based on the ^{14}C dates *is* valid and that the Starcevo (or Proto-Starcevo) culture ceramics and other materials in the deposits are *not* the result of contamination at Lepenski Vir, Padina, or Schela Cladovei, but lie in their original position (Fig. 2.5).

Jovanovic suggests that the occupation of Vlasac I–II precedes entirely that of both Lepenski Vir (with the possible exception of the earliest [Ia] phase) and Padina B, as well as the earliest agricultural settlements of the Danube basin catchment area (Proto-Starcevo, Starcevo-Cris, etc.). He proposes that the radiocarbon dates from Lepenski Vir *do* date the occupation from which the samples were taken. In his interpretation the Lepenski Vir culture (Lepenski Vir I–II) is dated to 6500–5700 BC (7500–6800 BP uncal.) and is entirely *contemporary* with the Early Neolithic settlements of the Morava, middle Danube, and Tisza valleys (Starcevo, Körös, and Cris cultures) (Fig. 2.5).[4]

Both chronological interpretations of the Danube Gorges sites accept the presence of agricultural colonists in the *south* Balkans (northern Greece, Bulgaria, former Yugoslav Macedonia) at the time of the establishment of the late Mesolithic settlement at Vlasac (*c.* 7500 BC/8500 BP uncal.) (Fig. 2.6b). It has been assumed, however, that the distance between the two populations – 400 km – was sufficiently great for it to be highly unlikely that there was either direct contact or any direct effect on the hunting-gathering population of the Danube Gorges by the agricultural people, animals, or plants.

It is not inconceivable, however, that there *was* contact between the two populations in the period before 6500 BC. This has been implied by John Chapman (who accepts Jovanovic's chronological interpretation) in his discussion of the maintenance of exogamous mating networks by exchange of lithic materials and shells in possibly quite distant areas (Chapman 1993:111). It is also possible that already in this period the agriculturalists may have had an indirect effect on the foragers of the Danube Gorges of the kind discussed by Zvelebil in his conclusion in this volume and discussed below. More than serendipity may account for the fact that the earliest presence of agriculturalists in the Balkan peninsula coincides with the earliest occurrence of sedentary foragers in the Balkan peninsula.

According to this interpretation (Fig. 2.5), the complex forager settlements of Lepenski Vir I–II and Padina B (the Lepenski Vir culture) were not contemporary with the early agricultural settlements in the south Balkans and the hunter-gatherer settlement at Vlasac, but occurred later. Moreover Lepenski Vir I–II did not precede but *coincided* with the earliest agricultural settlements of the nearby Morava valley and the Danube basin catchment area. These latter were 100 km from Lepenski Vir but only 50 km distant from settlements at each end of the Danube Gorges – Padina in the west, and Schela Cladovei in the east (Fig. 2.4).

As has probably become clear by now, I, like John Chapman, Marek Zvelebil, and Sandor Bökönyi (see also Lazarovici 1979, Vlassa 1976), am inclined to accept Jovanovic's interpretation of the Danube Gorges chronology. Marek Zvelebil discusses in this volume the possible effect of nearby agriculturalists on the subsequent history of foragers of the Danube Gorges as the agricultural frontier moves into this region. John Chapman has focused on the effect of such contact on the tensions of dominance and power in the settlements of the Gorges as reflected for example in burial location and ritual and symbolic elaboration of architecture and other expressions of material culture. He has interpreted the site of Lepenski Vir not as holding the secrets of domestication, but as holding onto its power (and that of its occupants) as a place of symbolic significance amongst the forager places in the Danube Gorges, contrasting it to Padina and Schela Cladovei which were more exposed and more open to exchanges with agriculturalists outside[5] (Chapman 1993).

In the model or scenario presented below, I view the frontier as more of a two-way process of "Neolithization," in which the *agriculturalists* as well as the foragers were radically (and quickly) transformed by the contact.

As already discussed, the Early Neolithic settlements close to the Danube Gorges in the area of the confluence of the Danube, Morava, and Tisza rivers, and the Danube catchment area, in general display important differences from the Early Neolithic settlements of the south Balkans (Fig. 2.2). They also show some marked contrasts with the hunter-gatherer settlements of the Danube Gorges, especially those of the Lepenski Vir I–II period.

The picture of opportunistic, short-term settlements, instability of food-production, and even ineptitude in the use of resources that has been portrayed earlier in this chapter for the Early Neolithic settlements of the catchment area of the Danube basin is probably exaggerated, and is not entirely applicable to the Körös culture settlements and those of the late phases of the Starcevo and Cris cultures. The picture does, however, apply to the settlements of the earliest agricultural population in the Danube–Morava–Sava–Tisza confluence area and Romanian Banat, in other words to those agriculturalists who came within reach of direct contact with the hunter-gatherers of the Danube Gorges and who may have affected and been affected by them.

The stone tools of these Early Neolithic settlements were made of the most local pebbles even though many of the settlements were located near a more favorable raw material in the form of rich resources of outcrop microcrystalline and macrocrystalline rock (Chapman 1990, Kuijt 1994, Tringham 1978, 1988, Voytek and Tringham 1988). The stone artifacts of the late Mesolithic settlements of the Danube Gorges (including Lepenski Vir I–II), however, show a much greater familiarity with and utilization of local and imported mineral resources (Bonsall 1997, Chapman 1993, Prinz 1987, Radovanovic 1992, 1996, Voytek 1990, Voytek and Tringham 1988).

The built environment of the Early Neolithic settlements in the Danube basin catchment area comprises, as has been mentioned above, virtually no examples of surface structures. Pits which form the main archaeological features at the sites have been claimed to be "pit-dwellings." Such a way of constructing shelter would be in direct contrast not only with impressive later Neolithic architecture in this region and contemporary Early Neolithic architecture in the south Balkans, but also with the carefully prepared structures of the Late Mesolithic settlements of the Danube Gorges. It is possible that surface structures were built in the Early Neolithic of the Danube basin catchment area, but that they were ephemeral and temporary enough not to have survived archaeologically.

The faunal assemblages of the Early and "Middle" Neolithic settlements of the Danube basin catchment area, for example from Divostin, Ludas-Budzak, Starcevo, Donja Branjevina, and Foeni-Salas, comprised over 75 percent of bones of domestic animals – especially ovicaprids and some cattle but very few pigs, even though the forests and valleys of the Danube basin catchment area must have abounded with other rich food resources (Blazic 1992, Bökönyi 1988, 1989, Clason 1980, Greenfield 1993, Greenfield and Drasovean 1994, Lazic 1988).

As was pointed out by Anika Clason and Sandor Bökönyi, this was in direct contrast to the richly varied local fauna exploited by the foragers of the Danube Gorges, that included red deer, wild pig, wild cattle, fish, and birds. It has even been suggested that experimentation in culling, for example, red deer, cattle, or pig was being carried out as a means to intensifying production (Bökönyi 1970, 1978, Bolomey 1973a, Clason 1980, Dennell 1983, Jarman 1972, Prinz 1987). The dog was domesticated for food and – we like to think – for other purposes. Clason has noted that the domestic ovicaprids at Starcevo were smaller than those in Greek Macedonia, for example at Nea Nikomedea (Clason 1980). From this we can imagine that some of the domestic animals, and presumably any domestic plants, had to be carefully nurtured and protected, and, perhaps, did not thrive so well!

Sporadic remains of emmer and einkorn wheat have been found at the Early Neolithic settlements but a lack of required methodology for seed retrieval (e.g., flotation) in the excavations of both Early Neolithic and Late Mesolithic settlements has minimized any empirical support for the hypotheses on the nature of plant exploitation, whether wild or domestic. It is assumed that cultivation of wheat and barley was present at Early Neolithic settlements, since sporadic rich finds of carbonized grains have been made south of the Danube basin catchment area, e.g., at Slatina near Sofia (Todorova and Vajsov 1993:169). John Chapman (Chapman 1990) and Marek Zvelebil (in this volume) have both pointed out that the scale of agriculture may have been quite small at this time, and Willis and Bennett have shown minimal impact on the environment until 6000 BP reflected in local palynological sequences (Willis and Bennett 1994). It is assumed, on the other hand, that the foragers of the Danube Gorges were taking advantage of their local knowledge of the rich variety of plant foods and incorporating them into their diet. This idea is hardly backed up by empirical palaeo-botanical data, but has been suggested by Gloria y'Edynak on the basis of comparative human palaeodental evidence (y'Edynak 1978).

These differences are significant when we examine the implications of the two groups of settlements – forager and agriculturalist – as *contemporary* and no more than 100 km apart at the most at *c.* 6500–5700 BC (7500–6800 BP uncal.) (Fig. 2.7b). At this time in their history, the Early Neolithic settlements of the Danube basin posed no threat to the stability of the hunter-gatherers in the form of competition between their animals, forest clearance, and so on. However, I suggest in my scenario that the agriculturalists did in fact effect important changes on the foragers of the Lepenski Vir culture.

The process through which a complex sedentary settlement like Lepenski Vir I–II with elaborate symbolic expression in the material world and social relations of the kind suggested by Hodder and Srejovic (Hodder 1991, Srejovic 1969a, 1984) grew out of the late Mesolithic settlements such as Vlasac has been modeled by John Chapman and others (see also Bender 1978, Chapman 1993, Harris 1977, 1978, Price and Brown 1985). According to their models, much of the complexity would have grown out of the decreasing degree of mobility or increasing sedentism (Kaiser and Voytek 1983, Tringham 1990, Voytek and Tringham 1988). Factors such as population growth, increasing social inequality, probable competition between households, and the need for the accumulation of goods as concomitants of sedentism must certainly have been important, along with the need for more complex organization of activities to procure the maximum from local resources.

As Zvelebil in this volume has pointed out, however, the presence of the agriculturalists relatively close to the Danube Gorges must certainly have been an important element in this transformation. There is no doubt – if we accept the painted ceramics and ground stone tools in the Lepenski Vir I–II, Padina B, and Schela Cladovei III house assemblages as really belonging there – that there was contact between the two populations. The data described above on subsistence, stability, local knowledge of resources, and motivation suggest that, in such a situation of relations between the two populations, the foragers would have been the more dynamic partners (cf., Peterson 1978). It is even possible that the relatively greater size and material complexity of Lepenski Vir reflects a situation in which they had greater access to exchange relations with the agriculturalists, along with the ceremonial paraphernalia and social complexity that such a status might imply.

Such a situation of stable but dynamic interaction – Zvelebil's and Gregg's "Phase of Co-operation" – between two populations with quite different subsistence strategies may continue for some time, as can be seen from both modern examples (Peterson 1978, Spielmann 1991) and other archaeological examples (Bogucki 1988, Gregg 1988, Zvelebil 1986b, and this volume). In the case of the Danube Gorges, the interaction lasted throughout Lepenski Vir I–II, phase B1–2 at Padina, and phase III at Schela Cladovei. It might have lasted indefinitely in the Danube Gorges, but for certain factors which proved disastrous for the cultural and physical survival of the Danube Gorges foragers. These factors that I have hypothesized have much in common with those discussed by Zvelebil in his conclusion in this volume.

First, the contact and interchange of commodities (including those which might be classed as prestige items, such as ceramics), services, and personnel would eventually have had some important effects on the social relations of the Danube Gorges foragers. If the redistribution of the goods from the agriculturalists among the foragers of the Danube Gorges was channeled through a few places – Padina, Lepenski Vir – it is likely that certain individuals or households would have had greater access than others to the exotic goods, people, and knowledge. The process by which such inequalities in access to such exchanges can lead to inequalities of status and competition and thus act as an incentive for the greater production and accumulation of goods and food has been elegantly traced by a number of researchers (e.g., Bender 1978, 1989, Chapman 1993, Friedman and Rowlands 1978, Testart 1982, Tringham 1990).

Even more spectacular is the potential effect on reproductive behavior which the exchange of personnel may have had. Zvelebil and Chapman have constructed a matrilocal society in which it was suggested that males mated into the Danube Gorges from "outside," meaning, by the time of Lepenski Vir I–II, from agricultural communities (Chapman 1993 and Zvelebil, this volume). As discussed by Zvelebil in this volume (see note 3), it has been suggested that two distinct populations are represented among the burials in the settlements of the Lepenski Vir culture and that through time a physical "Neolithization" is visible in the burials of the Danube Gorges sites (Chapman 1993 and Zvelebil, this volume, y'Edynak 1978, Jovanovic 1972, Menk and Nemeskéri 1989, Mikic 1980, 1988, 1990, Nemeskéri 1969, 1978, Prinz 1987, Roksandic 1999). The smaller, more gracile individuals have been identified as agriculturalists, and the more robust ones as indigenous foragers. Explanations for the differences include both genetic and nutritional factors.

The interpretation of their presence and their blending can include the idea that individuals moved from forager to agricultural villages, and *vice versa*, through exchange for marriage, hostage, or similar purposes. The implications of this interpretation are quite enormous if reproduction was the purpose or at least the result of such exchanges. Two contradictory reproductive strategies are likely to have clashed: the expansive agricultural notion of reproduction in which the aim is to increase the labor force, against the more restrained hunter-gatherer reproductive strategy (Binford

1968, 1978, Harris 1977, Lee 1972). It is feasible that one of the results of such a clash was an upsetting increase (if not explosion) in the birth-rate of the delicately balanced Danube Gorges forager population.

On both counts, therefore, contact with the agriculturalists in the Danube–Morava catchment basins could have led to a perceived need for even more intensive procurement of food by the foragers. And yet it is difficult to conceive of the wild resources being utilized more intensively, with fishing and red deer hunting already being carried out on a large scale. Such a need may have been the incentive for the transformation of their subsistence base to one based more on the production of food from domestic animals and plants. As mentioned above, the intensive exploitation of red deer that is indicated by all the faunal assemblages of the Mesolithic Danube Gorges has been interpreted as experiments in controlling and culling red deer. The same may have been true of wild cattle, pigs, and certain wild plants, such as *Chenopoedia* (Jarman 1972, Tringham 1973, Voytek and Tringham 1988). It is likely that during the period of the Lepenski Vir culture some of the techniques of animal and plant domestication were adopted from the agriculturalists' experience. Whatever the means, by the end of the Lepenski Vir culture (Lepenski Vir IIIa–b), the foragers had become increasingly reliant on domestic sources of food, particularly cattle, although wild animals still made up 60–70 percent of the mammal bones and fish continued to be a very important source of food (Bökönyi 1970, Clason 1980).

An important factor in the destruction of the Lepenski Vir forager culture is the transformation of the agriculturalists themselves. We can imagine (and may see evidence for it in the later Starcevo, Körös, and Cris settlements) that those agriculturalists who had contact with the hunter-gatherers of the Danube Gorges learned a great deal from the latter about local resources, such as wild cattle and pigs, possibly plants, and minerals – their distribution, their behavior, and the techniques with which best to utilize them. It is also likely that the exchanges and interaction with the hunter-gatherers stimulated increased production of food and commodities and other socio-economic changes amongst the agriculturalists, just as they had among the hunter-gatherers.

The conversion of existing techniques of herding and cultivation to local plants and animals, most importantly cattle, that is seen in the late Starcevo and succeeding Neolithic settlements may very likely have been the result of contact and the exchange of information with the hunter-gatherers (Bökönyi 1974, 1989, Clason 1980). The earliest agriculturalists had not been completely unfamiliar with herding cattle (Séfériadès 1993), but until the late Starcevo period, as seen for example in the assemblages from Starcevo (Clason 1980) and Foeni-Salas (Greenfield and Drasovean 1994), cattle did not play a significant role in their subsistence pattern. Sandor Bökönyi and Anika Clason have both noted evidence in the faunal data of local domestication of both cattle and pigs in the Starcevo culture assemblages (Bökönyi 1974, Clason 1980). I imagine, therefore, that a result of contact would have been an intensification of food-production on the part of the agriculturalists to feed a growing population and provide a surplus for exchange.

Such developments in the agricultural settlements of the Danube–Morava catchment basin would have created direct competition between domestic cattle and pigs on the one hand and wild deer, wild cattle, and wild pigs on the other for the same food resources. Such competition would probably have led to more forest clearance and larger garden plots by both populations, resulting in changes of the surrounding micro- and macro-environments, noted in the palynological record at Lepenski Vir and Vlasac (Misic *et al.* 1969).

Another effect of the increasing success of the subsistence strategy and resource utilization of the agriculturalists and growing social inter-change between their settlements was that there would have been less incentive to maintain the exchange relations and alliances with the forag-ers of the Danube Gorges. By the time of Lepenski Vir IIIa such a lack of incentive would have been compounded by the foragers themselves being economically disrupted.

However the foragers of the Danube Gorges acquired the tech-niques of food-production and however the agriculturalists came to rely more heavily on cattle and local resources, the result was increasing com-petition for resources and a pattern of interaction which favored the Morava–Danube valley (Starcevo and Cris cultures) agriculturalists and increasingly marginalized the foragers. The social and economic disloca-tions that would have resulted in the Danube Gorges settlements must have spelled the end very quickly to the hunting-gathering way of life and led to the rapid disappearance of the Lepenski Vir culture – the richest and most successful hunting-gathering culture in southern Europe – and the aban-donment soon after of the Danube Gorges by human occupants.

This stage of the process is represented by Lepenski Vir IIIb which, according to Jovanovic's chronological interpretation of the Danube Gorges settlements, is younger than 5400 BC (6600 BP uncal.) and contemporary with the later phases of the Starcevo culture and possibly (as suggested by Padina phase B3) with its transformation into the Vinca-Tordos culture (Vinca A) (Fig. 2.8b). In Lepenski Vir IIIb and Padina B3, it is possible to see that the Lepenski Vir culture had transformed into a poor copy of the agricultural settlements of the wide Morava–Danube valleys. Gone is the previous complexity of settlement, social organization, and economic pro-duction, as well as the large population. Gone is the elaboration of material culture, including architecture and stone carvings. The only modification of the terraces is by the digging of pits, for garbage or for dwellings.

Food-production may be an expansive strategy, but in the Danube

Gorges it could not satisfy the nutritional and social demands of the enlarged population that existed there during the late stages of the Lepenski Vir culture without some very complex reorganization of the labor force and redistribution and exchange of goods, for which there is no archaeological evidence. Even today, the topographical conditions of the Danube Gorges, which had been so advantageous for the development of sedentary forager communities, restrict the intensification of cultivation and herding there and the expansion of a food-production subsistence base.

The death of the Lepenski Vir culture and the abandonment of the Danube Gorges relatively soon afterwards coincide with two significant phenomena that occurred in the agricultural settlements of the Morava–middle Danube region (Fig. 2.9). One was the establishment of the first clearly sedentary farming villages in this region associated with what might be termed their initial fully productive agricultural system, represented by the formation of the Vinca-Tordos culture (*c.* 5300 BC). Interestingly enough, it is at this point in time that Willis and Bennett have noted an effect of land clearance and, presumably, agriculture on the palynological record (Willis and Bennett 1994; see also Chapman 1990). Second, there was at the same time a rapid expansion, probably as a result of the fissioning of parts of the agricultural communities as mentioned earlier in this chapter, toward the north into areas represented by the Linear Pottery cultures (Bogucki 1979; see also Bogucki, this volume, Bogucki 1988, Tringham 1971).

The Vinca-Tordos settlements form the lowest occupation layers of settlements that are continuously occupied for much of the fifth and even later millennia BC. These settlements are distributed in a pattern which might be called "strategic," that is, with a view to long-term settlement and an understanding of a number of landscape features including resources, soils, and communications (Bogucki 1979, Chapman 1981, 1990, Kaiser 1979, Kaiser and Voytek 1983, Tringham 1990). They represent an irreversible commitment to a sedentary agricultural way of life. The Vinca-Tordos settlements appear in the lower Morava and the area of its confluence with the Danube, that is in those areas in which the early Neolithic (Proto-Starcevo/Pre-Cris, Starcevo, Körös, and Cris cultures) agriculturalists had been in closest proximity to the hunter-gatherers of the Danube Gorges (Brukner *et al.* 1974, Chapman 1981, Jovanovic 1965, 1984, 1990, Lazarovici 1979, Paul 1995, Tasic *et al.* 1979, Tasic *et al.* 1990). From this same area, the Vinca culture (along with a fully sedentary way of life) spread southwards and westwards as the Vinca-Plocnik culture in the late fifth and fourth millennia BC (Chapman 1981, 1990, McPherron and Srejovic 1988, Tringham and Krstic 1990).

In my opinion, this association is more than mere coincidence. In the paragraphs above, I have formulated a model of interaction between agriculturalists and foragers in the middle Danube basin. The ultimate

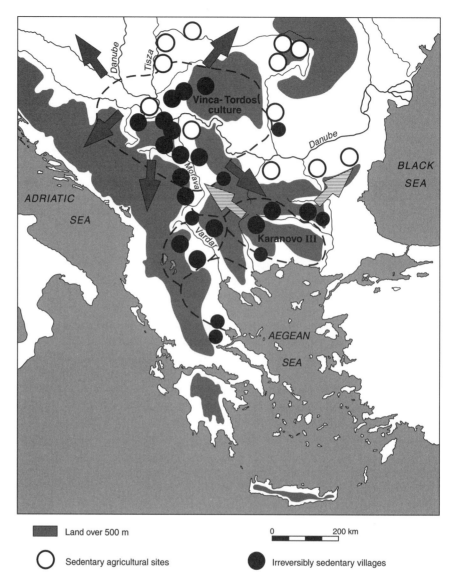

2.9   Southeast Europe: later Neolithic settlements, 4400–4000 BC (5300–
       4800 BC).

historical result of that contact was that the Lepenski Vir culture contributed to the formation of the earliest *successful* long-term agricultural settlements (the Vinca culture) of the Danube basin catchment area, whose
subsistence was based on local animal resources, especially cattle whose
numbers and gene-pool had been stimulated by breeding with local
animals, and probably pigs likewise (Bökönyi 1974, 1988, Chapman 1981,

Greenfield 1991, Lazic 1988, Tringham *et al.* 1992). A broad spectrum of plant resources, including wild plants, is characteristic of Vinca culture plant exploitation (Borojevic 1988, Hopf 1977). Finally the Vinca culture represents a blossoming in the use of a rich variety of materials, minerals for various purposes as well as clays, that were from local sources and from more distant sources by exchange (Chapman 1990, Kaiser and Voytek 1983, Radovanovic *et al.* 1984, Tringham 1990, Voytek 1990).

This is, in fact, not such a dissimilar model to that of Dragoslav Srejovic. Whereas he saw the foragers of the Lepenski Vir culture as involved in the formation of the *first* agricultural settlements (Starcevo, Körös, and Cris cultures) of the Morava–Danube basin, I am suggesting that they contributed to the formation of the first fully established agricultural settlements (the Vinca culture).

Mosaic

I have spent much of this chapter discussing the case of the Danube Gorges Late Mesolithic foragers in order to demonstrate the dialectical poignancy of a situation in which foragers may have initiated contact with inept agriculturalists, thereby providing the stimulus for the latter's development and, at the same time, sowing the seeds of their own destruction.

The situation at Lepenski Vir was not repeated exactly in other contexts, but other contexts of contact between foragers and early agriculturalists certainly shared its speed and completeness of transformation. No single scenario can model the "typical" way in which the transition to the Neolithic took place in southeast Europe, or any other part of Europe. I have found Marek Zvelebil's "Moving Frontier" model to have been useful in provoking a more open-ended visualization of the "Neolithization process." However, I think that he would agree that visualizing the transition becomes much more interesting if the process is not homogenized, but treated as a complex and richly variable set of situations.

Clearly the transition to the Neolithic in southeast Europe took many different forms whose nature is often lost by adherence to local cultural names. But the unique history of each situation is also lost by the generalizing and vast extrapolations that are characteristic of many (not all) western syntheses. As Michel Séfériadès has suggested, "The neolithisation process must be understood in different ways, whether areas develop synchronically or not, because they were paradoxically largely independent, but also in constant interaction" (Séfériadès 1993:139).

It seems that Séfériadès is working toward a metaphor for the Neolithization of southeast Europe that is similar to that proposed by Jean Guilaine for the process in Greece (Guilaine 1987). I find the idea of a mosaic an attractive concept, not just for its expression of environmental diversity, as was meant by Guilaine, but as an expression of diversity in experiencing the Neolithization process. It sits well with the idea of a multiscalar study of the transition to agriculture, in which no one scale in time or space is privileged over another, in which it is as important to write about Lepenski Vir as a site which experienced a unique and poignant history in this process as it is to use it as an example of a more general process.

Some kind of movement of people plus domesticates and cultigens undoubtedly occurred, expressed for example by Zvelebil and others (Zvelebil 1986b: Fig. 10), but we can imagine that this process was experienced in a different way by each family that we assume was housed at Karanovo, or Starcevo, or Vinca. There may have been as many different manifestations of the transition as there were villages and families, each with its own history. This kind of study is very foreign to the research on the transition to the Neolithic as it now stands. Gender and other categories are generalized to whitewash the variability of experience of the individual social actors (matrifocal, victims of the domus, gardeners).

I think it is also clear that some kind of direct contact between foragers and early farmers occurred at Lepenski Vir and other Danube Gorges settlements, as it did in other "Mesolithic" sites, e.g., Crvena Stijena at the margins of the main Early Neolithic agricultural settlement in southeast Europe. The question remains, however, to what extent was there contact and exchange of people, food items, ideas, and minerals between indigenous Mesolithic foragers and Early Neolithic farmers in the "heartland" of agricultural settlement itself, that is, in the valleys of, for example, the Morava, Tisza, Vardar, Struma, Iskar, Tamis, Maros, and Körös rivers? As I have mentioned above, Marek Zvelebil in this volume and many others (Greenfield 1993, Séfériadès 1993) suggest that Mesolithic indigenous forager presence was much greater than its archaeological invisibility in the great valleys of southeast Europe indicates. The problem is that we archaeologists cannot see it, although it may be "standing right in front of us."

If the transformation from forager to agriculturist happened very quickly, as is suggested in the Danube Gorges, but with a more serendipitous interaction between the two populations, the resulting archaeological manifestation of contact may have been more subtle and ephemeral than at Lepenski Vir and the other Danube Gorge sites, and may have escaped the notice of archaeologists. Some vestiges of contact and the agricultural frontier may, however, be visible in the remarkable variability exhibited by the Early Neolithic sites of southeast Europe that is often overlooked, including large proportions of wild animals represented in some faunal assemblages such as Ludas and Golokut (Greenfield 1993). If this variability were examined in the light of Zvelebil's Agricultural Frontier model, much of what passes for "local adaptation by early colonists" might be interpreted, on the contrary, as foragers quickly adopting the innovations of domestication, or foragers in an exchange relationship with farmers in a "zone of availability" (see note 4). The models that are presented in this chapter and elsewhere in this volume that offer alternatives to the Wave of Advance colonization models also encourage examining the evidence of each site and small region, twisting and turning it for different interpretative points of view of the Neolithization process.

James Lewthwaite (Lewthwaite 1986b) argued that complex, sedentary foragers would have been less likely or slower to have adopted the innovations of farmers than less complex foragers. In the scenario that I have set out here, I have suggested that successful complex foragers could indeed have been transformed – if not seduced – very quickly into the "mainstream" Early Neolithic. To have some idea of the rate of change, we should not forget that two thousand years after the first appearance of domestic sheep, cattle, wheat, and barley in the southern edge of southeast Europe, and twelve hundred years after their first appearance in the northern part of the Balkan peninsula, there were no full-time hunter-gatherers left in the Balkan peninsula!

Notes

1 Much of this discussion about Lepenski Vir was originally presented in a paper at the conference that was held alongside the Lepenski Vir exhibit in Cologne, Germany, in 1982. I am grateful for the comments of the other participants in the conference (especially Dr. Dragoslav Srejovic, Dr. Borislav Jovanovic, and Dr. John Chapman) and have tried to incorporate them into my arguments here.

2 There is not a consensus as to the degree of settlement permanence of the Danube Gorges foragers, including those at Lepenski Vir itself. Some such as Whittle (1996) and Boric probably favor greater mobility, whereas I would fall at the other end of the spectrum in suggesting greater permanence of the base settlement.

3 In addition to the radiocarbon dating of the Lepenski Vir levels, the relative chronological position of the Danube Gorges sites hinges to a certain extent on the argument that monochrome pottery holds chronological priority over painted wares in the Starcevo, Körös, Cris, and Karanovo cultures (Dimitrijevic 1974, Garasanin 1973, Todorova and Vajsov 1993). In this case, Lepenski Vir would represent one of the few sites in which it is possible to see a phase of the Starcevo culture with monochrome pottery (Lepenski Vir IIIa) stratified *below* Starcevo culture linear painted ceramics (in Lepenski Vir IIIb) (Srejovic 1971a:12).

Thus in Srejovic's interpretation, Lepenski Vir IIIa would represent one of the earliest sites of the Starcevo culture and one of the earliest agricultural settlements of the Danube basin catchment area; one, moreover, that had a long continuous tradition preceding it in the Mesolithic levels of Lepenski Vir I–II.

If, on the other hand, the monochrome and painted wares occur together right from the start of the Early Neolithic cultures, as has been suggested by research in the Romanian Banat and Transylvania (Lazarovici 1979, 1981, Paul 1995, Vlassa 1972, 1976), then the monochrome ceramics associated with Lepenski Vir IIIa (or II as suggested by Jovanovic) need not necessarily represent an early phase of the Starcevo culture, but could belong to a middle or later phase of its development (Jovanovic 1974:41).

The controversy also hinges on the reported presence of ceramic sherds and ground stone tools in the assemblage excavated in and around the trapezoid houses of Lepenski Vir I–II (Jovanovic 1974, Srejovic 1966:15, 39). Srejovic interprets these artifacts (like the radiocarbon samples) as the result of post-depositional contamination of the I–II levels of Lepenski Vir from the upper (III) levels (Srejovic 1966, 1969a:15). Jovanovic interprets these materials as part of the original debris from the Lepenski Vir I–II and Padina B1–2 houses that represents contact of the hunter-gatherers with the Starcevo culture agriculturalists in the Morava or middle Danube valleys (Jovanovic 1974:39).

4 An example of such variability that can be reinterpreted in this way is provided in the marshlands of the Tisza–Danube interfluve, where Early Neolithic settlements have a high proportion of wild animals (e.g., Ludas). Mesolithic settlements (dated only "postglacial") are nearby (e.g., Nosa), represented by scatters of microlithic stone tools (Brukner 1980, Brukner *et al.* 1974, Greenfield 1993, Nandris 1972, Tringham 1971) (Figs. 2.2 and 2.3). The "Early Neolithic" settlements have traditionally been explained by the adaptation of colonists to an area that is inhospitable to agriculturalists.

5 As reflected for example in the large numbers of ceramic sherds as well as domestic animal bones found at Padina and Schela Cladovei, compared to fewer sherds and no domestic animal bones at Lepenski Vir (Chapman 1993).

MAREK ZVELEBIL

and MALCOLM LILLIE

3

Transition to agriculture in eastern Europe

Introduction

A major issue in the debate surrounding the transition to farming in Europe concerns the manner of its spread. To many, the agricultural transition in Europe represents a spread of people, cultigens and domesticates, and of new technology, from the nuclear zone of the Near East to the peripheral zone of Europe, the latter regarded as a passive recipient, rather than an active element in the process of transition. But, despite many years of investigation of the subject – ever since Gordon Childe's first publication of *The Dawn of European Civilisation* (Childe 1925) – the transition from mainly hunter-gatherer Mesolithic societies to predominantly farming Neolithic ones remains a major unresolved problem in European prehistory, with the reasons for the transition and the manner, the rate, and the mechanism of this transformation all being subjects of debate and controversy (for example, in Britain: Dennell 1983, Ammerman and Cavalli-Sforza 1984, Zvelebil 1986c, Thomas 1988, 1991, Zvelebil and Zvelebil 1988, Ammerman 1989, Zvelebil 1998, etc.; in continental Europe: Lichardus and Lichardus-Itten 1985, Aurenche and Cauvin 1989, Guilaine 1987, Budja 1993, Séfériadès 1993, Zilhão 1993, Cauvin 1994; etc.).

This debate underlines the importance of the issue, which has historical and anthropological, as well as political, implications. Historically, the transition to the Neolithic addresses the origin and constituent elements of the Neolithic and the subsequent cultures in Europe. Anthropologically, it addresses the transformation of material cultures, the processes of diffusion, interaction, and adoption, and their recognition in the archaeological record. Politically, it raises the question of European cultural identity, and of the genetic and linguistic roots of most present-day Europeans (e.g. Renfrew 1987, 1996, Zvelebil and Zvelebil 1988, Sokal *et al.* 1990, 1991, Cavalli-Sforza *et al.* 1994, Cavalli-Sforza 1996, Zvelebil 1995a, b).

Embedded within the problem of the transition to the Neolithic lies the special issue of the mechanism of the spread of farming, which has often been polarized into a debate between the "diffusionists" and "indigenists." This aspect of the debate has particularly strong political con-notations, as it addresses the relationship between the gene-pools, lan-guage, material culture, and ethnicity of present-day Europeans; it is wrong, therefore, to dismiss this debate as sterile, irrelevant, and outdated (Séfériadès 1993, Chapman 1994b). Ever since Childe's seminal publication (1925, 1957), it has become an established view to regard the adoption of farming in Europe as a case of replacement of indigenous hunter-gatherers by farmers migrating from the Near East, and, over generations, colonizing hitherto unfarmed areas in Europe (Piggott 1965, Case 1969b, Lichardus and Lichardus-Itten 1985, Vencl 1986, Aurenche and Cauvin 1989, Cauvin 1994, van Andel and Runnels 1995, etc.). This colonization process is thought to have shaped the genetic map of modern Europe (Ammerman and Cavalli-Sforza 1984, Sokal *et al.* 1991, Cavalli-Sforza *et al.* 1994) and to have been responsible for the introduction of the Indo-European languages to the continent (Renfrew 1987, 1992, 1996).

This view has not gone unchallenged. An increasing number of "indigenists" have been arguing for the local adoption of farming by indig-enous hunter-gatherer communities throughout Europe (Dennell 1983, Barker 1985, Séfériadès 1993, Chapman 1994b), or in most of its regions (Zvelebil 1986b, 1995a; Guilaine 1987; Lüning 1988a, etc.). The two views are not necessarily exclusive. Even though a strong case can be made for the local adoption of farming through contact and exchange by indigenous hunter-gatherers in many parts of Europe, local adoption does not preclude inter-regional migration between hunter-gatherer and farmer communities at several possible scales of transfer of population (see below).

The concept of the agricultural frontier provides the social context within which such genetic and cultural exchanges may be identified. It also serves to reduce the gap in the often polarized discussion about the nature of population transfers at the Mesolithic–Neolithic transition (e.g. Ammerman 1989, Zvelebil 1989) and allows us to contemplate gradual changes in the gene-pool of the first farmers in Europe, as the act of adop-tion of farming moved from the Balkans to northern Europe in the course of some five thousand years.

Neolithization and the transition to farming

The terminology associated with the problem of the Neolithic tran-sition reflects the interpretative confusion that marks the subject at present. Before we can proceed, therefore, it is necessary to elucidate the meaning of a few basic concepts: transition to farming, Neolithization, and agricultural frontier.

First, and in general, the transition to farming is an economic process involving a shift from dependence on biologically wild to biologically domesticated resources. The recognition of such a shift in the archaeological record is not an easy matter. The methodological problems include the adequate sampling of archaeological deposits, the understanding of the formation processes of deposits, the taphonomy of plant and animal remains, the recognition of the domesticated status of plants and animals in question, and the quantitative representation of domesticates within the economy of a settlement and of a regional subsistence pattern of a community.

The recognition of domesticates and cultigens can be especially difficult, if not impossible, if the resources are in a semi-domesticated state – that is, tamed or under some form of management more intensive than hunting and gathering, and yet before such husbandry practices result in a morphological change in the animals and plants by which their domestic status can be identified. This means that resources can be domesticated in a behavioral sense – their freedom of movement may be constrained, for example – yet undomesticated in a biological, morphological sense. It follows, then, that the evidence for behavioral domestication, or husbandry of undomesticated plants and animals, must remain circumstantial. At present there are indications that, during the Mesolithic, predominantly hunter-gatherer communities in many parts of Europe engaged in some form of husbandry of undomesticated pig, cattle, and native plant foods, in particular hazelnut, water chestnut, and small-seeded grasses (Clarke 1976, Dennell 1983, Zvelebil 1994a, 1995c).

From this it follows that the economic transition from the Mesolithic to the Neolithic is not simply a transition to any kind of farming. It must denote a shift from a native system of hunting, gathering, and management of possibly husbanded but biologically undomesticated resources, to a new, agro-pastoral system based on a more productive husbandry of imported domesticates and cultigens, specifically sheep, goat, cereals, and pulses. Despite some doubts (e.g., Dennell 1983, Séfériadès 1993), there is general agreement that Neolithic farming, as a system, was introduced from Anatolia and the Near East, although the subsequent adoption of its components in different parts of Europe was variable. Despite the methodological and conceptual problems outlined above, the shift in the mode of subsistence to agro-pastoral farming remains the only process which is relatively clearly defined, geographically widespread, and archaeologically detectable to act as the key feature of the Neolithic (for an opposing view, see Thomas 1988, 1991b, Séfériadès 1993; for a critique of this position, see Zvelebil 1998).

Second, this process cannot be separated from the cultural, social, and historical contexts in which it occurred. The change in economy may be a cause, or perhaps a consequence, of changes in ideology, material culture, or social organization of participant groups: changes often collectively referred to as "Neolithization." At the same time, it is not clear whether these changes were broadly simultaneous and whether, in Europe as a whole, the shift from undomesticated local resources to agro-pastoral farming can be regarded as a signature for "Neolithization" (e.g. Ammerman and Cavalli-Sforza 1984, Zvelebil 1986c, 1989, 1998, Thomas 1987, 1988, 1991b, Ammerman 1989, Séfériadès 1993, Chapman 1994b, etc.).

Even the parameters of "Neolithization" are not clearly defined. What do we mean by the concept? To some, the key feature of Neolithization is a profound social, ideological, and conceptual change (Thomas 1988, Cauvin 1994), "something different to think with" (Thomas 1991b:181), symbolized by new rituals, ritual objects, and burial architecture; to others, it is technological advances heralded by the appearance of a new lithic technology, ceramics, polished stone, permanent house structures (Ammerman and Cavalli-Sforza 1984, Lichardus and Lichardus-Itten 1985), or a long-term process of social and conceptual domestication, of the taming of the wild, encapsulated in the development of the "domus" (Hodder 1990, Chapman 1994b); to others still, it is "an evolutionary stage of the human societies," marked by "accentuated cultural spread" (Séfériadès 1993:140), and evidenced in the archaeological record by "sedentary lifestyles (real villages), total mastery of chipped stone and bone industries, first polished objects, domestication of selected plants and of selected animals and invention of pottery" (Séfériadès 1993:139).

The problem is that the Neolithization process defined in this way can extend back into the Upper Palaeolithic. Further, it can, depending on the mélange of defining attributes, apply to most regions of the world, or to no more than a single area. Defined in a polythetic way and deprived of a common central characteristic, Neolithization remains a vague and vaporous neologism, any concrete meaning of which is obliterated by the polythetic nature of the phenomenon and the regionally variable composition of its attributes. It is, therefore, deprived of any real meaning. Or, as Pluciennik noted, there is such a great degree of variability evident in the archaeological record of the Neolithic that "there were probably many different neolithics" (Pluciennik 1998b).

Individually, or even coevally, such changes attributed to the Neolithic cannot denote "Neolithization," since they have also occurred in historical conditions and geographical areas far removed from the Neolithic. If the term "Neolithization" is to be retained at all, it must have a common denominator: this common denominator can only be the introduction and the development of agro-pastoral farming. The question of whether this change in the mode of subsistence corresponded to changes in social structure and ideology and to other aspects of Neolithization must be examined within individual regional and historical contexts.

The agricultural frontier
The idea of an agricultural frontier has usually been associated with models of agricultural colonization by farming communities. This is largely because archaeologists have adopted a historical analogue: the

farmer colonization of the colonial period of recent centuries as a model for the prehistoric event. But we have to consider that the situation in prehistoric Europe would have been very different. Neolithic farmers would not have had the same technological superiority over local hunter-gatherers, nor would they have been able to attain the same levels of productivity or population growth as their modern counterparts (Dennell 1983, 1985). Recent research indicates that, in many areas of Europe, Mesolithic hunter-gatherers practiced intensive food-procurement strategies, perhaps even some form of husbandry, while early farmers engaged extensively in hunting (Mithen 1990, Zvelebil 1992a, 1993, 1994a, 1995b). This further reduces the difference in productivity between the complex hunter-gatherers and early farmers at the time of the transition to farming.

Perhaps the most standard depiction of the agricultural frontier is represented by the work of Ammerman and Cavalli-Sforza (1973, 1984). Here, the agricultural frontier is viewed as a Wave of Advance by immigrant farming populations moving from the Near East through the Balkans into central Europe and beyond, to colonize the continent. Assuming high population growth rates among the colonist farmers and no resistance from local hunter-gatherers, the authors proceed to model the spread of farming in Europe and predict the rate of colonization.

The colonization hypothesis, or the demic diffusion version of it as presented by Ammerman and Cavalli-Sforza (1973, 1984), has become a focus for the critical reappraisal of the whole notion of the Neolithic colonization of Europe (Dennell 1983, 1985, Barker 1985, Zvelebil 1986a, 1986b, 1989, 1995b, Zvelebil and Zvelebil 1988, Chapman 1994b; for counterarguments, see Thomas 1988; Ammerman 1989; Cavalli-Sforza *et al.* 1994). There is no need to rehearse these arguments; in summary, the critics of the demic diffusion hypothesis argue that there is no evidence for actual colonization, that the predicted rate of farming dispersal under the hypothesis does not correspond to the observed rate, that there is strong evidence for continuity between the Mesolithic and the Neolithic in most regions of Europe, and that Ammerman and Cavalli-Sforza confuse the meaning of the Neolithic in different regions of Europe and attribute a farming economy to communities that have little or no evidence for farming. Consequently, a good case can be made for the local adoption of farming by the indigenous Mesolithic communities in most (Zvelebil 1986b, 1995b) or all of Europe (Dennell 1983, Séfériadès 1993, Chapman 1994b). The underlying problem with the demic diffusion model is that, in order to subject it to mathematical treatment, Ammerman and Cavalli-Sforza have considerably simplified the complex process of agricultural transition in Europe.

Regardless of these shortcomings, the demic diffusion model has been adopted by Renfrew (1987) as a vehicle for the diffusion of Indo-European languages to Europe, while at the same time research into the genetic patterning of modern European populations has provided further apparent support for these theories (Ammerman and Cavalli-Sforza 1984, Sokal *et al.* 1989, 1991, Cavalli-Sforza 1991, Renfrew 1992, Calafell and Bertranpetit 1993, Sokal and Livshits 1993, Cavalli-Sforza *et al.* 1994). Despite widespread support given to these claims (i.e., Diamond 1992:241; Renfrew 1992:463, Hagelberg 1995:178), the results emerging from both the gross morphological and the genetic evidence have been inconclusive at best[1] (Zvelebil 1995b, Richards *et al.* 1996, Bateman *et al.* 1990).

It must be emphasized that "indigenist" and "colonist" positions regarding the transition to farming in Europe are not as contradictory as may appear at first glance. On the one hand, demic diffusion is only one among several types of population movement which may have contributed to the spread of farming in Europe; on the other, not all indigenists insist on the local adoption of farming throughout Europe. Scenarios combining limited population movement and local adoption are certainly possible (Zvelebil 1986b, 1995a, b, Whittle 1996, Thorpe 1996, Harris 1996a). It is therefore important to clarify different forms of population transfer that may have been implicated in the transition to agriculture throughout Europe.

Demic diffusion as used by Renfrew (1987) and Ammerman and Cavalli-Sforza (1984) denotes a sequential colonization by random migration carried out by family groups. It occurs over many generations and involves slowly expanding farming population, colonizing new areas by the "budding off" of daughter hamlets from the old agricultural settlements.

Folk migration involves a more directional movement of a population, from the old area of settlement to the new, in a more rapid "leapfrogging" or "migration stream" dispersal (Anthony 1986, 1990, Anthony and Brown 1991).

Elite dominance (Renfrew 1987) involves the penetration of an area by a numerical minority who subsequently seize control and impose their culture and (sometimes) language on the indigenous majority. (This does not mean that folk migrations cannot be led by social elites.)

Infiltration (Neustupny 1982) denotes a gradual penetration of an area by small groups or individuals who often assume subordinate positions in a society and perform specialist tasks for the majority.

Leapfrog colonization denotes selective colonization by small, seafaring communities, who establish themselves in selected areas, that perhaps were only marginally exploited by indigenous foragers, creating "enclave" settlements, from which further dispersal of farming proceeds by contact with and the acculturation of the local foragers (Arnaud 1982, Zilhão 1993; see also van Andel and Runnels 1995 for a similar concept of Modified Wave of Advance model).

Individual frontier mobility (Zvelebil 1995a, 1996) through contact and partner exchange involves mostly single individuals or small groups linked

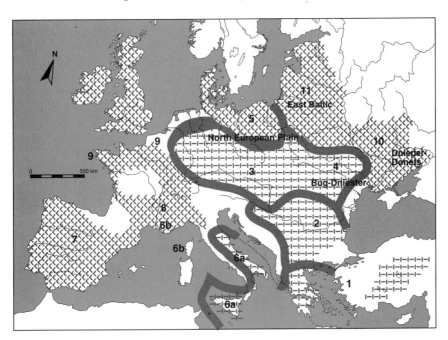

3.1   Major frontier zones, earliest Neolithic cultures, and the spread of farming
       in Europe. Stippled zones indicate major frontiers. Cross hatching indi-
       cates areas where farming was introduced partly by demic diffusion.
       Triangular hatching indicates areas where farming was introduced
       through adoption by local foragers. 1. Early Neolithic of Greece and
       Anatolia. 2. Starcevo-Cris-Körös. 3. Linear pottery and derived cultures. 4.
       Cucuteni-Tripolye culture. 5. Funnel Beaker culture. 6a. Impressed and
       Painted wares of southern Italy. 6b. Impressed wares in the west
       Mediterranean. 7. Iberian Neolithic. 8. Chassey and Cortalloid Neolithic. 9.
       The Neolithic of the British Isles and northwest Atlantic coast. 10. Dnieper-
       Donets and related groups. 11. Corded ware and related groups. (Redrawn
       in part after Renfrew 1987.)

by kinship, who move between hunter-gatherer and farming communities
within the framework of established kinship ties, marriage alliances,
trading/exchange partnerships, or other social ties of reciprocity and obli-
gation. Within this scenario, the direction and the pace of the adoption of
farming would reflect as much the existing Mesolithic social frameworks
and routes of communication, or those established between the Mesolithic
and initial Neolithic communities in the region, as they would reflect the
regional ecological conditions and the demographic parameters of the communities in contact. It is this form of contact, and of socially embedded
mobility, that, in our view, was mostly responsible for the introduction and
spread of farming in the greater part of Europe (Fig. 3.1).

    As an alternative to the colonization hypothesis and the demic diffusion model, an availability model of the agricultural transition was developed to accommodate the role of the local hunter-gatherer communities (Zvelebil and Rowley-Conwy 1984, 1986) and to allow for the effects of the agricultural frontier (Alexander 1978, Dennell 1983, 1985). This model describes the process of agricultural transition in three stages: availability, substitution, and consolidation (Zvelebil and Rowley-Conwy 1984, Zvelebil 1986c, 1995a, 1996). Each is defined by the economic evidence, considered at a regional scale. The model operates within the broader socio-cultural context of an agricultural frontier: a zone of interaction between foragers and farmers, marked by various forms of contact and exchange (Alexander 1978, Leacock and Lee 1982, Schrire 1984, Dennell 1985, Ingold *et al.* 1988, Spielman 1991).

Forager–farmer interactions

Forager–farmer interactions – patterned human behavior – generate structured relationships between individuals, groups, and communities across the frontier, or within the frontier zone. This structure then characterizes different "types" of frontier situations (e.g., Dennell 1983, 1985, Moore 1985). For example, competitive relations in a given historical situation may result in conflict and warfare, and in a "static closed frontier" (see below, Dennell 1985).

The structure of forager–farmer relationships is only a part of the story, however. The historical context and the historical contingency (constraints and opportunities set by earlier developments), ecological conditions, contradictions within the structure of the relationships themselves, ideological considerations, and the broader network of contacts and exchange – the "world system" in modern times – provide the dynamic element which enforces the historically situated process of change. They make up the agency of change and development. In response, the frontier zone is expanded, contracted, and relocated in space and through time, and its characteristics change (i.e., as in the availability, substitution, and consolidation phases [Zvelebil and Rowley-Conwy 1984, 1986]). These activities leave archaeological signatures which then have to be decoded by archaeologists and interpreted in terms of past human behavior.

Conceptually, the agricultural frontier zone can be divided into the mobile and the stationary frontiers (Alexander 1978, Green and Perlman 1985). Mobile or moving frontiers develop during periods of agricultural expansion and are typically associated with models of agricultural colonization by demic diffusion. On the basis of ethno-historical data, farmer communities in such rapidly shifting frontier zones share a number of special features: rapid population growth, extensive land-use patterns, frequent relocation of settlement, low subsistence and high labor costs, preponderance of males and younger people over females and the old.

Drawing on the ethnographic evidence (Sahlins 1974, Leacock and Lee 1982, Woodburn 1982, 1988, Schrire 1984, Moore 1985, Ingold *et al.* 1988, Olsen 1988, Bailey and Annger 1989, Headland and Reid 1989, etc., Spielmann 1991), four types of developments were common within a forager–farmer frontier zone: exchange of technological innovations and imports, exchange of partners and creation of marriage alliances, transmission of diseases, and ecological change. Ethnographic evidence for different types of exchange in subsistence societies shows that social and geographical distance (kin and tribal boundaries) are the two main factors specifying the nature of the exchange. So for example, Malinowski (1922) specified six forms of exchange among the Trobrianders, while Sahlins (1974) used social distance to outline his model of generalized, balanced, and negative reciprocity.

Using this information, we can begin to build a more concrete model of forager–farmer interactions. The role of contact between foragers and farmers across this frontier could have been both supportive (Bogucki 1988, Gregg 1988) and disruptive for the foragers (Moore 1985, Keeley 1992).

In our view, cooperation would prevail in the early phase of forager–farmer contact. At this stage, the effect of the frontier would have been largely supportive: the exchange of foodstuffs across the frontier would reduce stochastic variation in food supply and the risk of failure for both the hunting and farming communities. This would be especially true for farmers who have recently adopted farming, or who have recently moved into a new area. In terms of the local adoption, there may have been kin relations between foragers and farmers, with the result that balanced, rather than negative, reciprocity would occur. In addition to foodstuffs, other forms of exchange, including exchange of information, partners, prestige items, and raw materials, may have played a role equal to or greater than food exchange (Fig. 3.2).

More broadly, movement of livestock may have been of major importance in regional exchange systems (Sherratt 1982:23). Such a system of exchanges would introduce domesticates to hunter-gatherer contexts for social, rather than economic, reasons, and may explain initially low percentages of domesticates on some early so-called Neolithic sites. The early appearance of domesticates in low numbers would also support the general hypothesis by Hayden (1990) and Bender (1978), arguing that farming was initially adopted for social reasons.

With the increasing duration of the agricultural frontier, disruptive effects gained the upper hand (Fig. 3.3). This may have been marked by the following developments.

1 Internal disruption of the social fabric among hunter-gatherers arising from increased circulation of prestige items and increased social competition.

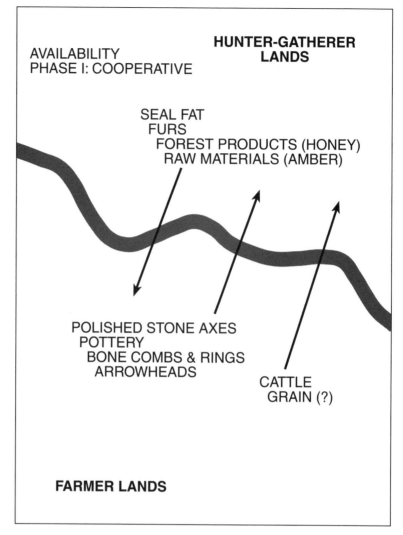

3.2   Forager–farmer exchanges expected during the earlier ("cooperative") part of the availability phase.

2 Opportunistic use of hunter-gatherer lands by farmers, which, as Moore has shown, can cause serious interference in hunter-gatherer foraging strategies and information exchange (Moore 1985) and initiate an ecological change disruptive for foraging strategies.

3 Direct procurement of raw materials and wild foods by farmers establishing their own "hunting lands" in hunter-gatherer territories as part of a secondary agricultural expansion.

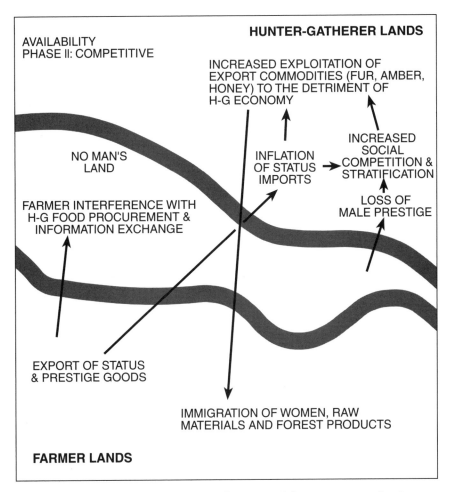

AVAILABILITY
PHASE II: COMPETITIVE

HUNTER-GATHERER LANDS

INCREASED EXPLOITATION OF
EXPORT COMMODITIES (FUR, AMBER,
HONEY) TO THE DETRIMENT OF
H-G ECONOMY

NO MAN'S
LAND

INFLATION
OF STATUS
IMPORTS

INCREASED
SOCIAL
COMPETITION &
STRATIFICATION

FARMER INTERFERENCE WITH
H-G FOOD PROCUREMENT &
INFORMATION EXCHANGE

LOSS OF
MALE PRESTIGE

EXPORT OF STATUS
& PRESTIGE GOODS

IMMIGRATION OF WOMEN, RAW
MATERIALS AND FOREST PRODUCTS

FARMER LANDS

3.3   Competitive relations between foragers and farmers, expected to increase toward the end of the availability phase.

4 Increased exploitation of export commodities by hunter-gatherers to the long-term detriment of the forager economy.

5 Hypergyny: the loss through marriage of forager women to farmers. Hypergyny occurs where foragers are viewed by both parties as culturally and economically inferior to farmers. In such situations the emigration of forager women can amount to 15% of the female population (Bailey and Annger 1989, Speth 1991), causing severe shortage of females among the hunter-gatherer males. Based on case studies in Africa, there seem to be two responses among forager men designed to increase their own standing with the women: an increase in commercial hunting among the men (Speth 1991) or the adoption of farming.

The frontier and Neolithization in eastern Europe: some examples

Southeast Europe

Southeast Europe is, of course, a key area for our understanding of the transition to the Neolithic: it is in this area that we have the earliest evidence for agro-pastoralism and for the appearance of technological, economic, and symbolic traits commonly associated with the Neolithic. It is here, too, that most direct links to the cultural traditions of the Near East and Anatolia have been observed, leading to the generally accepted conclusion that the Neolithic was introduced into the Balkans by colonization of farming groups from Anatolia (Childe 1957, Piggott 1965, Ammerman and Cavalli-Sforza 1984, Lichardus and Lichardus-Litten 1985, Zvelebil 1986c, Renfrew 1987, Aurenche and Cauvin 1989, Cauvin 1994, Demoule and Perlès 1993, Kalicz 1993, van Andel and Runnels 1995, etc.). In the present volume, the southeast Balkans is considered in some detail by Tringham (see chapter 2); here we wish to outline the more general case for the role of the local forager communities in the process of agricultural transition.

The migrationist explanation for the introduction of farming into Greece and the Balkans has been questioned by Theocharis (1973) and Dennell (1983), and challenged by Gimbutas (1988), who believed in the long-term cultural continuity with the Upper Palaeolithic and in the indigenous origin of the Neolithic societies in the area. More recently, these views gained greater currency, with some researchers prepared to consider the local adoption of farming in some regions (e.g., Greece: Lüning 1988a) or in the entire Balkan peninsula (Chapman 1993, Séfériadès 1993), followed by the subsequent dispersal of foragers turned farmers. As a part of this reappraisal, a greater search for forager–farmer contact (e.g. Müller 1988, Chapman and Müller 1990, Chapman 1993) and the reassessment of the palynological evidence (Willis and Bennett 1994) suggested the following.

1 The impact of agriculture, reflected in forest clearance and the development of open agricultural landscape, is not evident until *c.* 6000 BP. This suggests that the introduction of farming by the early Neolithic farmers "was not of sufficient intensity to be detected upon a landscape scale" (Willis and Bennett 1994:327), indicating that population densities at the Neolithic transition were low and that farming techniques had little or no impact on the existing vegetation. Consequently, the hypothesis that the Neolithic transition and subsequent expansion were caused by a surplus and rapidly growing population (Ammerman and Cavalli-Sforza 1984, Childe 1957) is not supported by these results (Willis and Bennett 1994:327–8).

2 Archaeological evidence is in broad agreement with these findings. While there is evidence for a wide-ranging replacement of the material culture of the Mesolithic by that of the Neolithic groups in the fertile lowland plains, major river valleys, and coastal plains, other, less

fertile areas reveal continuity in settlement and material culture between the Mesolithic and the Neolithic (Tringham 1971, Müller 1988, Chapman and Müller 1990, Dergachev *et al.* 1991, Budja 1993, Chapman 1994b, Gatsov and Özdogan 1994), contradicting the notion of a rapid and widespread colonization by farming populations.

Demoule and Perlès (1993) and van Andel and Runnels (1995) present a convincing case for the exogenous origin of the Greek Neolithic. The lack of Mesolithic settlement, the coeval introduction of agro-pastoral economy and of new material culture with links to Anatolia, the absence of hunting and gathering by the Neolithic communities, residential permanence and long-term continuity of the Neolithic settlements in Thessaly and the Argolid, and the spatial discontinuity between the known Mesolithic and the Neolithic settlements are major arguments in favor of the colonization hypothesis (e.g., Demoule and Perlès 1993, van Andel and Runnels 1995).

But, as Chapman argues (1989, 1994), the current distribution of late Mesolithic and early Neolithic sites is biased by the postglacial rise in the sea level and by the post-Neolithic erosion and sedimentation of river basins and valleys. As van Andel and Runnels show (1995), this would have obscured the location of smaller, but not of larger early Neolithic sites. It follows, then, that Mesolithic sites, being earlier and generally smaller, would have been far more affected by erosion and burial than the early Neolithic sites. Yet, while Demoule and Perlès note that "the extensive alluviation may also have hidden Early Neolithic sites in northern Greece, especially if they were short-term occupations" (1993:365), they accept the lack of Mesolithic sites as real (1993:364; see also van Andel and Runnels 1995:481, 494). The conclusion must be that the Mesolithic settlement was far more extensive than arguments biased in favor of the exclusive presence of the Neolithic would lead us to expect.

Even though van Andel and Runnels argue in favor of the demic diffusion model for the spread of farming (1995:494–8), their own calculations fail to substantiate the population growth rates necessary for such a model to operate. They conclude that the Early and Middle Neolithic interval "seems to have been a time of steady but not very rapid growth," so that "even the Larisa basin, region of major growth, required some 1500 years, from about 9000 to 7500 BP, to reach saturation" (1995:497). Even if we allow for the selective, "leapfrog" colonization of optimal farming habitats (van Andel and Runnels 1995:496; see also Zilhão 1993), this is a much slower rate of growth than postulated by Ammerman and Cavalli-Sforza for their demic diffusion model (1984, Cavalli-Sforza *et al.* 1994). The underlying cause for the continuous and widespread colonization by Neolithic farmers – rapid population growth – is therefore called into the question.

3 Correspondingly, the Neolithic package of cultigens, domesticates, ceramics, and new lithic technology – a signature for the colonizing

populations from the Near East – does not appear in the Balkans everywhere. Whilst there are areas such as the Vardar–Morava corridor, the
Maritsa basin, and the middle and lower Danube basins, of coeval introduction of Early Neolithic material culture, cultigens, and domesticates, and
of a change in the settlement pattern, in other areas these features were
not introduced coevally. Rather, we are dealing with a mosaic of different
patterns (Fig. 3.5). Some of these patterns differ from the standard notion
of the Neolithic package, and the areas where they occur are often marked
by at least some continuity in material culture and settlement location
between the Mesolithic and the Neolithic (e.g., coastal Thrace and northwest Turkey: Özdogan 1983, Gatsov and Özdogan 1994, Özdogan and
Gatsov in press; Dinaric Mountains zone of western Yugoslavia: Müller
1988, Chapman and Müller 1990; Slovenia: Chapman and Müller 1988,
Budja 1993; Moldavia: Markevitch 1974, Dergachev *et al.* 1991, etc.; for taphonomic critique, see Chapman and Müller 1990, Kokelj 1993, Biagi *et al.*
1993). In these areas, the case for continuity and local origin of the Balkan
Neolithic seems stronger than for colonization. As Tringham (1971) concluded some time ago, the "Neolithization" process for the Balkan peninsula as a whole included both the demic diffusion and local adoption of
farming by indigenous hunter-gatherer groups, creating conditions for
long-term forager–farmer contacts.

4 Through such reappraisal of the evidence, the existence of the
forager–farmer frontiers within the Balkans is revealed. Fig. 3.4 represents
an early attempt to locate the enduring zones of forager–farmer interaction
in space. While the exchange and contact within the frontier zone along the
Yugoslav Adriatic coast has been assessed by Müller (1988), and the Iron
Gates contact zone has been investigated by several researchers (Srejovic
1969, 1971a, 1971b; Voytek and Tringham 1989, Chapman 1993, 1994b,
Tringham, this volume) other zones of contact have so far received little
attention.

Forager–farmer contact zones undoubtedly existed within the
Aegean area itself (Özdogan 1983, in press; Gatsov and Özdogan 1994,
Özdogan and Gatsov in press). This is suggested, for example, by the contrast
between the ceramic production in the Early Neolithic in Greece,[2] and the
highly developed ceramics of the contemporary, "parental" Anatolian communities. This may be due to "the development by foragers of a local potting
tradition stimulated by the acquisition of ceramic containers within an
exchange network bridging the north Aegean" (Chapman 1994b:138). In the
Early Neolithic, exchange networks are evident throughout Greece in the
long-distance distribution of obsidian, honey flint, and other raw materials
as well as finished artifacts (Perlès 1992). The sudden appearance of these
exotic materials from the Early Neolithic onwards suggests that earlier
Mesolithic exchange systems continued in use – obsidian was already
traded in the Mesolithic – and that indigenous rather than immigrant

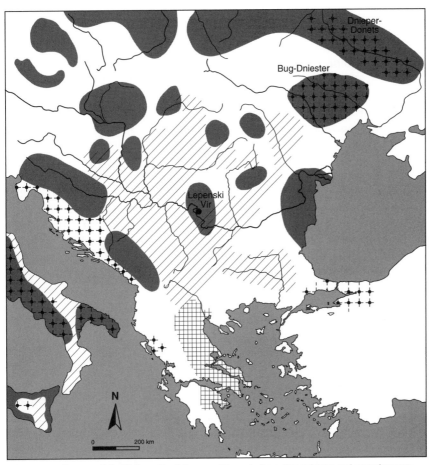

 Starcevo–Cris–Körös or Cardial ware settlement where domesticates and ceramics were introduced coevally

Greek Early Neolithic marked by the limited provision of ceramics and by occasional aceramic layers

+ + + + Areas where pottery was introduced first into forager communities in the "Availability" phase

Areas of concentrated hunter-gatherer settlement

3.4 Frontier zones, concentrations of Mesolithic settlement and the earliest Neolithic cultures in southeastern Europe. (*Sources:* Tringham 1971, Muller 1988, Chapman and Muller 1990, Kozlowski and Kozlowski 1986, Özdogan 1983, Budja 1993, Dergachev *et al.* 1991.)

people were at least partly involved. It is unlikely that such wide-ranging exchange networks could have been established all at once by a population new to the region.

North of the Aegean, we have evidence for Mesolithic hunter-gatherer settlement of relatively high population density and social complexity in several regions of southeast Europe. The Lepenski Vir culture in the Iron Gates of the Danube, and the Bug-Dniester culture in Moldavia provide the most pertinent examples[3] (Srejovic 1969b, 1971, Markevitch 1974, Garasanin 1978, Voytek and Tringham 1989, Dergachev *et al.* 1991, Chapman 1993, 1994b). Prior to the adoption of agro-pastoral farming, these Mesolithic communities engaged in contact and exchange with the Neolithic communities and with those in Greece: Starcevo-Cris-Körös, and Impressed Ware groups who were already practicing agro-pastoral farming (Sordinas 1969, Tringham 1971, Müller 1988, Voytek and Tringham 1989, Chapman and Müller 1990, Budja 1993, Chapman 1993, 1994b, etc.). This confirms that in many parts of southeastern Europe, there were clusters of Mesolithic settlement capable and ready to serve as secondary centers for the adoption of agro-pastoral farming (Lüning 1988a). In the course of this process these communities could be expected to modify the agro-pastoral practices and integrate them with the existing subsistence strategies.

The Bug-Dniester/Cris-Körös frontier

Let us now turn to the Bug-Dniester/Cris-Körös contact zone (Fig. 3.5). The first agricultural settlements attributed to the Cris-Körös culture appeared in Moldavia in the early eighth millennium BP, and correspond to stage 3 of the same culture in Romania. The Cris culture in Romania and Moldavia is marked by features which link it to the Mesolithic, for example in the technology of flint tool manufacture (selective use of local materials, a high proportion of trapezes, slotted bone sickles), in house architecture (semi-subterranean houses), and in the economy (a large amount of wild species in faunal assemblages, wild plant food exploitation), raising the question of whether the Cris-Körös settlement itself was a result of hunter-gatherer "acculturation" (Tringham 1971, Dergachev *et al.* 1991).

At about the same time, in the valleys of the southern Bug, the Dniester, and the Prut, comparatively small sites belonging to the Bug-Dniester culture appeared. The Bug-Dniester sites show strong continuity with the earlier Mesolithic assemblages in lithic industry, settlement pattern, house structures, and economy (Tringham 1969, 1971, Markevitch 1974, Telegin 1987). Although Markevitch (1974) divides the Bug-Dniester culture into five phases, the culture can be more reliably divided only into an aceramic phase (7500–7000 BP) and a ceramic phase (*c.* 7000–6000 BP) (Dolukhanov 1979, Zvelebil and Dolukhanov 1991).

Throughout the period of their existence, the Bug-Dniester communities underwent changes arising from the history of contact with their

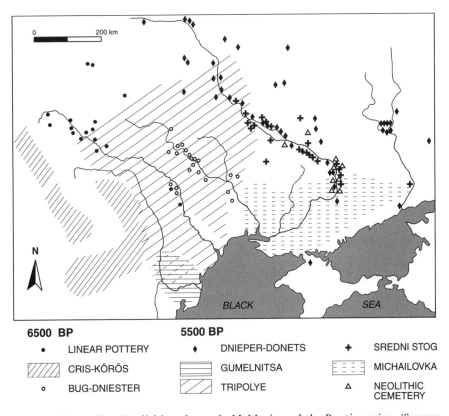

3.5 The earliest Neolithic cultures in Moldavia and the Pontic region. (*Sources: Zvelebil and Dolukhanov 1991, Telegin 1987.*)

farming neighbors: Cris-Körös at first, Linear Pottery culture later. The cultural traditions of the aceramic phase were firmly rooted in the preceding Mesolithic. Between 7000 and 6800 BP ceramic production, showing technological links with the Cris-Körös Ware on one hand (flat-based forms, chaff tempering) and original Bug-Dnietser features on the other (pointed-based forms, undulating incised lines, Unio shell impressions), was introduced through contact with the Cris communities to the west. By the middle of the seventh millennium BP the tool inventory for the first time included polished stone axes and querns. There was an increase in flat-based pottery, and finger-nail impressions – another cultural loan from the Cris culture in Romania – were added to the decorative repertoire. Between 6500 and 6000 BP contacts with the Linear Pottery communities had been established. Semi-subterranean houses, which had been until now the main form of domestic architecture, were beginning to be replaced by above-ground structures, a process completed by 6000 BP. The pottery changed its character: the tempering included for the first time mineral admixtures such as sand, mica, and crushed shell, the majority of vessels were pointed based and some were decorated by comb impressions. This formed a marked contrast with the Linear Pottery Ware, the significance of which has not, so far, been discussed. At about 6000 BP, a shift in settlement pattern to terrace locations and the widespread adoption of above-ground houses and of biconical, flat-based pottery mark the incorporation of the Bug-Dniester communities within the expanding Cucuteni-Tripolye cultural tradition (Markevitch 1974, Dergachev *et al.* 1991).

The economic evidence comes from some eleven sites located in the valleys of the Dniester and the southern Bug. Domesticates form less than 20% of the faunal assemblage during the early phase, which can be accounted for by importation of individual domestic animals (seven pigs and three cattle in all if we use MNI). Most of the faunal remains are of wild species, notably wild pig, red deer and roe deer, fish, and edible molluscs. Grain impressions in the pottery sherds include a variety of wild and some domesticated cereals. Grinders, composite sickles, some with sickle gloss, and antler mattocks supply further evidence for the importance of gathering, possibly cultivation. Even on the later sites, domesticates remain a minority, ranging from 3 to 50% (Markevitch 1974, Zvelebil and Dolukhanov 1991).

Direct contacts between the Bug-Dniester and the Cris-Körös communities are attested by the imports of Cris ceramics and by the similarity between Cris and Bug-Dniester pottery decoration: horizontal rows of shell and fingernail impressions, essentially similar to the barbotine technique. There are also imports of Notenkopf Linear pottery at Soroki 5, Tsikinovka, and Baz'kov ostrov (Tringham 1971, Markevitch 1974, Dolukhanov 1979, Zvelebil and Dolukhanov 1991).

In the opposite direction, Bug-Dniester pots were found at the Linear Pottery site of Novye Rusesty, and at a recently identified cluster of Cris settlements in northern Moldavia between the rivers Reut and Prut. Most of the ceramic sherds on these sites belong to the Cris culture (Dergachev *et al.* 1991). But sites such as Selishte and Sakarovka not only contained pots typical of the Bug-Dniester culture, but also exhibited other features commonly found in hunter-gatherer contexts in eastern Europe, such as semi-subterranean houses, and ornaments of perforated boar tusks and red deer teeth. It is not clear whether these features are a result of exchanges – cultural and genetic – with the Bug-Dniester communities, or whether they are a consequence of the indigenous adoption of farming and ceramic technology by the local hunter-gatherers, who had thus became a part of the Cris-Körös cultural tradition .

Bug-Dniester has been interpreted as an early farming culture based on cultivation of cereals and keeping of domestic pigs. In our view, what we have here is a transitional society, which took some 1500 years to move to agro-pastoral farming. The aceramic phase can be regarded as an availability phase, during which contacts were established with the Körös groups in the Carpathian basin, leading to the adoption of pottery around 7000 BP (Zvelebil and Dolukhanov 1991).

During the seventh millennium BP, these contacts were intensified: this was marked not only by imported farming ceramics, but also probably by imports of grain and domestic animals. We have to remember that on most Bug-Dniester sites, biologically domestic animals remained very few in number: on the lower Bug they never exceed 10% (see Zvelebil and Dolukhanov 1991: Fig. 17). In the course of the seventh millennium, intensified contacts led to the gradual and selective adoption of farming (without caprines) by some Bug-Dniester communities, for example Soroki and Tsikinovka, but not by others, for example the sites on the lower Bug.

By the middle of the seventh millennium BP, some of the sites were in the substitution phase, marked by food procurement from a variety of sources, which included hunting, fishing, gathering, and limited pig and cattle husbandry and cultivation. This process was never completed within the idiom of the Bug-Dniester culture; instead, the Bug-Dniester communities became one of the constituent elements of the Cucuteni-Tripolye culture that replaced it, together with intrusive cultural elements, probably brought by the migration of Linear Pottery and Boian culture groups (Dergachev *et al.* 1991, Zvelebil and Dolukhanov 1991) (Table 3.1).

The middle Dnieper frontier

The contact zone between the Tripolye culture and the Dnieper-Donetz culture in the Dnieper basin is centered on the middle and lower Dnieper valley, with the Tripolye culture to the west, and the Dnieper-Donetz and the related Sredny Stog groups occupying the Dnieper valley itself and the areas to the east (Fig. 3.5). The period in question traditionally dates between 6500 and 5000 BP (i.e. from the middle of the fifth to the third millennium bc; *c.* 5500–3500 BC), and includes the early and middle stages of the Tripolye culture, and the Dnieper-Donetz culture stages 1 and 2. Originally five radiocarbon dates, from the Mariupol-type cemeteries of Yasinovatka, Nikolskoye, and Osipovka, were used in the periodization of the Dnieper-Donetz culture (Telegin 1987). The principal basis upon which the periodization of the Neolithic to ancient Eneolithic is developed consists of ^{14}C dating (the majority of dates, sixty, were obtained from Tripolye culture sites), with stratigraphical sequences, imports from other cultures, and the seriation of the associated ceramic and lithic inventories forming the chronological basis of the Mariupol-type cemetery sequence (Telegin and Titov 1993:464 and 470).

While the agricultural nature of the Tripolye culture has never really been questioned (despite a high proportion of wild animal species on some early sites), the economy and the social organization of the Dnieper-Donetz culture has proved more problematic to define. The material culture

Table 3.1 *Uncalibrated radiocarbon dates, calibrated ranges, context and sample numbers from the Mariupol-type cemeteries of Nikolskoye, Yasinovatka, Derievka I and Osipovka*

	RC date uncal. BP	Calibrated date range 95.4% confidence	Skeleton no.	Context
Nikolskoye				
OxA-5029	6300 ± 80	5430 (1.00) 5050 BC	125	Pit E
Ki-3283	5460 ± 40	4450 (0.01) 4420 BC	125	Pit E
OxA-5052	6145 ± 70	5250 (1.00) 4910 BC	137	Pit 3
Ki-523	5640 ± 400	4950 (1.00) 4000 BC	unknown	Pit 3
Ki-3284	5200 ± 30	4450 (0.01) 4420 BC	115	Pit D
		4370 (0.92) 4220 BC		
Yasinovatka				
OxA-5030	6330 ± 90	5440 (1.00) 5060 BC	64	Pit A4
Ki-2810	5100 ± 40	3980 (1.00) 3790 BC	63 + 64	Pit A4
OxA-5057	6260 ± 180	5550 (1.00) 4750 BC	36	Pit B
Ki-1171	5800 ± 70	4810 (1.00) 4470 BC	36	Pit B
Ki-3033	6240 ± 100	5430 (0.01) 5400 BC	65	Pit A4
		5380 (0.01) 5360 BC		
		5340 (0.98) 4930 BC		
Ki-3032	5900 ± 90	4980 (1.00) 4530 BC	18	Phae B-2
Derievka I				
OxA-5031	6110 ± 120	5300 (1.00) 4750 BC	109	Eastern part
Ki-2177	5190 ± 90	4230 (1.00) 3790 BC	11 (76)	Indeterminate
Ki-3135	4820 ± 40	3700 (0.98) 3510 BC	(31)	Indeterminate
		3400 (0.02) 3380 BC		
Osipovka				
Ki-517	6075 ± 125	5300 (1.00) 4700 BC	53	Collective pit
Ki-519	5940 ± 100	5100 (1.00) 4550 BC	53	Collective pit

Notes:
All Oxford dates are Accelerator dates while Kiev dates are conventional.
Dates calibrated using OxCal program (oxCal v2. 14 cub r:4 sd: 12 prob [chron]), see *Radiocarbon* 35(1), 1993.

has clear roots in the preceding Mesolithic of the area, indicated for example by lithic technology or by the existence of the extended burial rite at both the early Mesolithic site of Vasilyevka 3, and the late Mesolithic Mariupol-type cemeteries of Vasilyevka 2 and Marievka, a rite which continues into the Neolithic period (Lillie 1998). Also, consideration of the anthropological composition of the Mariupol skeletal population supports the conclusion that, whilst not homogenous, these people are genetically linked to the "proto-European" type of the native Mesolithic population (Potekhina unpublished manuscript). With the addition of pottery to the cultural repertoire *c.* 6300–6100 BP (4300–4100 bc; 5450–5250 BC), the hunting-gathering communities have become "Neolithic." However, it must be pointed out that some sites after this date remain aceramic (and therefore essentially Mesolithic), while others have only a few pottery sherds. For example, the cemeteries of Marievka (now shown to be Late Mesolithic in date [Lillie 1998]) and Vasilyevka 5 are aceramic, and Vovnigi 2 and Osipovka have only a few sherds in association (Lillie 1996:136).

The same problem applies to the presence of domesticated plants and animals. While some people have stressed the agricultural nature of the Dnieper-Donetz economy, at least from its second phase (e.g. Shnirelman 1992b, Anthony 1994; also Jacobs 1993), there are good reasons to regard the Dnieper-Donetz communities as predominantly hunter-gatherers at least until the mid-fifth millennium BP. At this point the management of the horse is evidenced by the faunal remains from the settlement of Derievka, situated on a promontory of the river Omelnik (a right-bank tributary of the Dnieper); this, taken together with evidence for domesticated cattle and caprines, indicates a shift in subsistence toward a pastoral-based farming economy.

The reasons for doubting the farming nature of the earlier Dnieper-Donets economy include:

1   Low counts of domesticated animal remains on Dnieper-Donetz sites, suggesting exchange as opposed to economic dependence.
2   Dominance of hunting, fishing, and shell-collecting evidence in faunal remains.
3   Absence of caries and other markers of stress typical of agricultural communities on skeletons belonging to the Dnieper-Donetz culture cemeteries (Mariupol type), prior to the Eneolithic cemetery of Derievka II (Lillie 1996).
4   High delta carbon 13 values obtained from Dnieper-Donetz cemeteries, reflecting a diet which continued to be based on high protein intakes. This observation is reinforced by the high incidence of dental calculus found on the Dnieper-Donetz skeletons, supporting the notion of a predominantly meat-based, non-agricultural diet. The possibility of limited pastoralism in this context is not discounted.

Finally, recent new radiocarbon dating of the Dnieper-Donetz cemeteries (Jacobs 1993, 1994a and b; Jacobs and Price n.d.; Lillie 1996, 1998) has shown that certain of these cemeteries are earlier than previously thought (Fig 3.6; Table 3.1: Vasilyevka 2 now dates to the Mesolithic at 8000–7500 BP, and the Derievka I, Yasinovatka, and Nikolskoye cemeteries are dated to 6300–6100 BP (i.e., Dnieper-Donetz stage 2). Taken together, this information enables us to reinterpret the Dnieper-Donetz/Tripolye interactions and the impact on the Dnieper-Donetz culture as follows.

During Dnieper-Donetz stage 1 (6700–6300 BP), the economy is

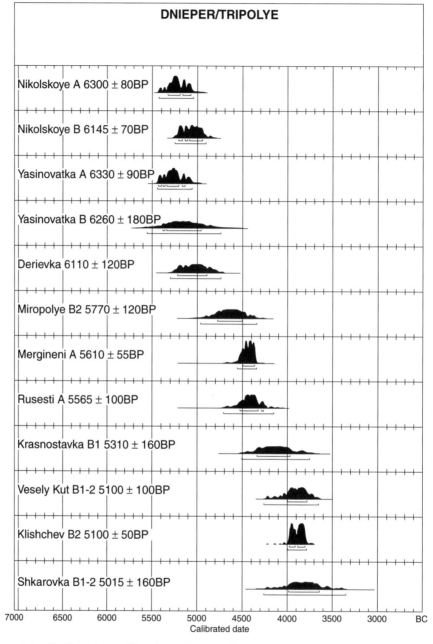

3.6   Radiocarbon calibrations obtained from Nikolskoye, Yasinovatka, Derievka
I and Osipovka. See also Fig. 3.7 and Table 3.1 After Stuiver *et al.* 1993.

almost entirely based on fishing, hunting, and gathering. The few bones of cattle found on sites of this period are indicative of trade/exchange rather than local stock-breeding. This early stage includes imported late Bug-Dniester ceramics at the site of Girli, dated after 6500 BP. Recent stable isotope evidence from the cemeteries of Vasilyevka V, Derievka I, Yasinovatka, and Nikolskoye indicates that a significant part of the diet was composed of aquatic resources; river fish in particular are attested (Lillie 1998). This evidence is supported by the frequent occurrence of fish-tooth pendants, derived from carp and pearl-roach, found in burials of the Mariupol-type cemeteries of the Dnieper Rapids region.

The beginnings of stage 2 of the Dnieper-Donetz culture are now back-dated to *c.* 6300 BP, some 300 years earlier than proposed by Telegin. Despite these early dates, there is evidence for extensive contacts with the Tripolye culture during the middle period of stage 2, as witnessed by the presence of imported Tripolye A2 ceramics at Grini, Strilcha, Piliava, Nikolskoye, and other sites, and imported copper ornaments, gold pendants, and polished maces (Fig. 3.7). It is these extensive contacts that may have contributed to the eventual appearance of a food-producing economy some time after *c.* 5800 BP (cf. Shnirelman 1992b:129–30). Additional contacts with the Balkans can be seen in the development of pottery decoration, the elaboration of boar tusk platelets reminiscent of the north Bulgarian bone figurines, and a shift from point-based to flat-bottomed vessels.

These changes are associated with a decrease in the microlithic element in the flint assemblages, an increase in bifacial tool production and in stone axe production, including polished axes, and an increase in the number and value of grave goods of some individuals. In other words, the volume of exchanged goods and the incidence of status-related objects increases significantly. As Anthony points out, "these changes may be associated with increasing sedentism and perhaps incipient ranking following contact with the more complex Tripolye culture" (1994:51). An alternative hypothesis is that from stage 1 of the Dnieper-Donets culture (the earliest Neolithic) the increasing emphasis upon the exploitation of *r*-selected species such as fish (and probably nuts) is resulting in the development of more complex social relations within these groups. Such a situation has been shown to result in increased residence permanence and the eventual "independent" adoption of domesticates (cf. Hayden 1990).

The significant point is that with the new dates for Nikolskoye, Yasinovatka, and the Derievka I Neolithic cemetery, these changes begin to occur from the very beginning of the Dnieper-Donetz culture, phases 1–2 at between 6500–6100 BP (5550–4750 BC; Figs. 3.6 and 3.7; Table 3.1). These dates are therefore indicative of much earlier interactions than previously suggested by Telegin (1987) between the Dnieper Rapids region and associated pre-Cucuteni-Tripolye culture groups.

STAGE		CEMETERY	1	2	3	4	5	6	7	8	9	10	11	Date cal. BC
Middle fourth millennium bc	C	Vilnyanka												
		Derievka Settlement		-		-		-					-	4460–3350
		Derievka II												4360–3988
		Nikolskoye pit A							—					4450–4220
		Chaply		-									-	
		Sobachy												
	B 2	Mariupol				—	-	—	—	-		-	-	
		Lysaya Gora pits I–V				—		—	—	—	—			
	B 1	Vovnigi 1		-	-		-		-		-		-	
		Vilnyanka pit 6		-	-	-	-							
Early fourth millennium bc	A2	Vovnigi 2		-	-								-	
		Kapulovka		-										
		Nenasytets	-	-	-	-								
		Vilnyanka pit A	-	—	-									
		Vasilyevka 5	-		—				—					
		Maryevka	-		-								-	
		Sobachy pits 1 & 2	-											
		Yasinovatka B-2							-					4980–4460
Mid to late fifth millennium bc	A1	Osipovka	-							-			-	5300–4550
		Derievka I		—		—		—	-	—	-		—	5300–4750
		Nikolskoye pit 3,B,A				-		-	-	—	—	-	—	5250–4910
		Yasinovatka pit B-1		—				—	—		—	-		5550–4750
		Nikolskoye pit E							—	-	-		-	5430–5050
		Yasinovatka pit A	-	—	-								—	5540–4930
End of seventh to early sixth millennium bc		Vasilyevka 2		-									—	8020–7620 Uncal. BP

3.7   Chronological positioning of the radiocarbon-dated cemeteries of Nikolskoye, Yasinovatka, Derievka I and II, and Osipovka, and the settlement site of Derievka in relation to Telegin's 1987 proposed chronological scheme for the Mariupol cemeteries. All other cemeteries remain undated, and as such their positioning in this table reflects Telegin's chrono-typological scheme.

However, consideration of the calibrated dates (Fig. 3.6) shows that some considerable overlap occurs between the earliest phases of the Nikolskoye, Yasinovatka, Derievka, and Osipovka cemeteries. Whilst it is clear from the calibration curves that some discrepancies occur between the dates obtained from the conventional dating facility in Kiev and those obtained from the accelerator facility at Oxford,[4] it is significant that a number of the Kiev dates do indeed support the earlier dating of the genesis of these cemeteries as indicated by the new Oxford dates.

It is therefore evident that the earliest stages in the genesis of the Dnieper-Donets cemeteries begin in the late seventh and early sixth millennia BP at Marievka, continuing into the fifth millennium with the stage 1 cemetery of Vasilyevka V and stage 2 cemeteries of Derievka I and Yasinovatka (6300–5800 BP). At this time contacts may exist with the neighboring pre-Cucuteni-Tripolye culture groups, at a time when the economic and social foundations of the latter, marked by the development of a farming way of life, are barely beginning. During this stage in the Dnieper-Donets culture the skeletal evidence from sites in the vicinity of the Dnieper Rapids does not support a shift toward greater dependence on a farming economy, or the shift to greater sedentism (Lillie in press; Telegin and Potekhina 1987). Indeed, such shifts in economic and residence focus are not evident until later in stage 2, around 5600 BP (3600 bc, 4700 BC), suggesting that culture contacts with neighboring farming groups occur for a period of some 500–800 years prior to the adoption of certain elements of the farming economy by the Dnieper-Donets groups.

The only suggestion of a shift toward greater sedentism in the Dnieper Rapids area is perhaps attested by the first occurrence of porotic hyperostosis on skeletal remains associated with the Derievka I cemetery. However, this site is early in the Neolithic sequence (*c.* 6200–6000 BP) and has no direct settlement evidence associated with it. Consequently, it is not until *c.* 5600 BP that reduced mobility is suggested by the adjacent Derievka settlement complex, suggesting that the cause of the porotic hyperostosis in the Derievka I population may relate to parasitic infestation from fish tapeworms such as has been recorded from Denmark and the Danubian Iron Gates areas (cf. Meiklejohn and Zvelebil 1991:130–1). The three sites of the Dnieper-Donetz culture with high numbers of domestic pigs, cattle, and caprines date to the same period, whilst the single impression of barley in a Dnieper-Donetz pot from Vita Litovskaya could be an example of imported grain. As such, any shift toward sedentism and food production would seem to have occurred at around 5600 BP, and clearly not as early as 6300–6100 BP (5550–4750 BC; Fig. 3.8). This view is also supported by the lack of any changes in the health status of the Dnieper-Donetz populations at around 6300–6100 BP, when compared to that in evidence from the preceding Mesolithic period.

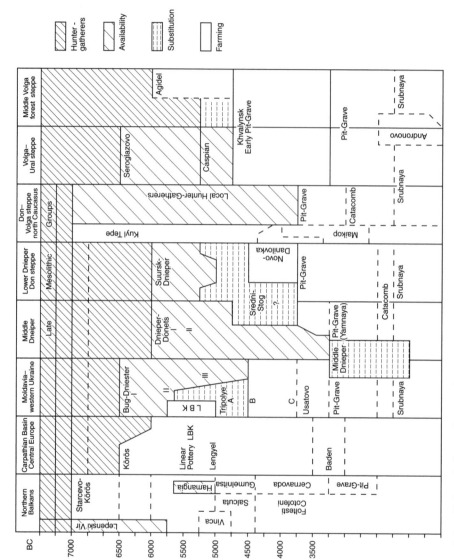

3.8 Cultural chronology and the duration of agricultural transition in different regions of eastern Europe when viewed in terms of the availability model.

In summary, it appears that we have a period of about 800 years or so during which contacts were increasing between the developing Tripolye farming culture and the essentially hunter-gatherer Dnieper-Donetz communities, prior to the integration of a pastoral element into the economic spectrum of the latter. These contacts appear to have resulted in the increased circulation of prestige objects, and increased status differentiation within the Dnieper-Donetz society. They also resulted in imitation of the farming culture's products (boar-tusk plates, flat-bottomed pottery, polished stone axes) and ornamentation.

Finally, it appears that Dnieper-Donetz people had to work harder during this transitional period. Jacobs (1993, 1994b) noted an increase in robusticity of individuals from cemeteries of Igren, Surskoy, Vilnyanka lower level, and Vovnigi, thought to belong to the early Dnieper-Donetz period. As Jacobs notes, "these might have resulted from heavier work loads in the performance of traditional forager chores." Such increases in workloads may reflect more intensive hunting, fishing, and gathering, driven by social competition, which was in turn provoked by contacts with agricultural communities across the frontier, reminding us of the models proposed by Hayden (1990) and Bender (1978) which focus on social competition as a rationale for the adoption of low-intensity farming. Despite this apparent increased social competition, the hunter-gatherer economy remained robust enough to accommodate any intensification in hunting strategies aimed at increasing social status for a period of up to 800 years before the shift toward a food-producing economy became necessary.

North European Plain

Forager–farmer exchange networks, similar to those described for the Bug-Dniester and Dnieper-Donets regions, existed within the agricultural frontier zone which marked the boundary between the farming LBK and daughter communities on one hand, and the hunter-gatherer communities to the north and the northeast. After a rapid spread of farming across the loess soils of central Europe, we see here the establishment of a stationary frontier in the middle of the sixth millennium BP (*c.* 4400 bc; *c.* 5000 BC), a frontier zone which lasted for 500–1200 years (Figs. 3.1 and 3.9). Contacts and exchanges within and beyond this frontier zone have been a subject of many studies (e.g. recently, Madsen 1982, Zvelebil and Rowley-Conwy 1986, Solberg 1989, Larsson 1990, Sherratt 1990, Price and Gebauer 1992, Midgley 1993, Thorpe 1996, Zvelebil 1996, etc.), some contained in this volume (Bogucki, Price).

Two major points are emerging from these studies. First, the exchange networks and transfer of technology from the Neolithic to the Mesolithic contexts were not confined only to the contacts between the Ertebølle culture and the Neolithic communities to the south – the two best-studied groups – but were, in fact, symptomatic for the entire length of the

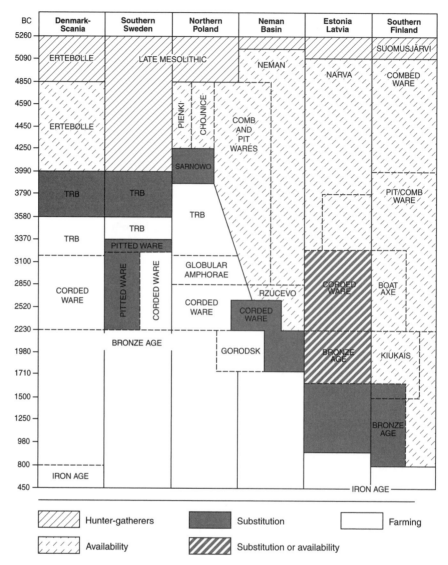

3.9   The transition to farming along the southern rim of the Baltic in terms of the three-stage availability model. In the eastern Baltic, the proportion of domesticates at the Corded Ware and early Bronze Age settlements was very variable, ranging from 0% to 14%; hence this period could be characterised as either availability or substitution, depending on the region. Dates calibrated BC.

frontier zone encompassing the agricultural communities of the Linear Pottery tradition (LBK and derived: for a useful summary east of the Oder, see Thorpe 1996). So for example, the making of pottery was not confined to the Ertebølle groups alone: recent research suggests that this was a widespread practice across the North European Plain, which now can be found in the Boberg group in north Germany, the Chojnice-Pienki group in northwest and central Poland, and the Wistka group in central Poland, while east of the Vistula, pottery made by the hunter-gatherer communities belongs within the broad pit-comb Ware tradition, derived ultimately through contacts with the early Neolithic farmers in Ukraine and central Europe (Dolukhanov 1979, Timofeev 1987, 1990). In a similar way, unperforated LBK shoe-last adzes, or later, perforated forms, are widely distributed within the hunter-gatherer territories north and east of the LBK agricultural frontier, their distribution marking the impact of the agricultural frontier zone (e.g. Fischer 1982, Sherratt 1990, Midgley 1993, Zvelebil 1996: Fig. 6).

A similar exchange system existed within the frontier zone in the east Baltic in the sixth and fifth millennia BP (fifth to third millennia cal. BC), where we have clear evidence for trade in amber (Vankina 1970) and other prestige items (axes, pots) and possibly also agricultural imports (Dolukhanov 1979, 1993) and trade in seal fat (Fig. 3.10), (Zvelebil 1981, 1995c). Local pottery shows the influence of ornamental motifs from the early Neolithic sites in the Dnieper basin (Zvelebil and Dolukhanov 1991) and from the western Baltic (Dolukhanov 1979, Timofeev 1987, 1990), giving rise to hybrid ceramic traditions in northeast Poland and Lithuania (Timofeev 1987). Such contact and exchange networks reached out over a wide area of the Baltic and eastern Europe, creating a pathway for new ideas and cultural innovations, which, in the later stages, may have been manifested archaeologically in the Corded Ware/Boat Axe horizon (Zvelebil 1993).

Second, this early contact phase, marked by exchange and cooperation, appears to have been followed by a later phase of increased competition and conflict. There are several indicators of conflict within the agricultural frontier zone in northern and northeast Europe. These include marks of increased social competition, territoriality, and violence among the late Mesolithic hunter-gatherers around the perimeter of the agricultural frontier on the North European Plain (Keeley 1992) and southern Scandinavia (Persson and Persson 1984, Bennike 1985, Meiklejohn and Zvelebil 1991, Price and Gebauer 1992), the presence of fortified farming villages on the farming side of the frontier, and, in some areas such as in Limburgh and Brabant, the existence of "no man's land" (Keeley 1992). Similar apparently unoccupied areas of 20–40 km in width can be detected between the agricultural Bronze Age and forager Inland Neolithic sites during the first millennium BC in Finland, again suggesting antagonistic relations prior to the transformation of the hunter-gatherer communities there (Zvelebil 1981). Similarly, the presence of Mesolithic armatures for

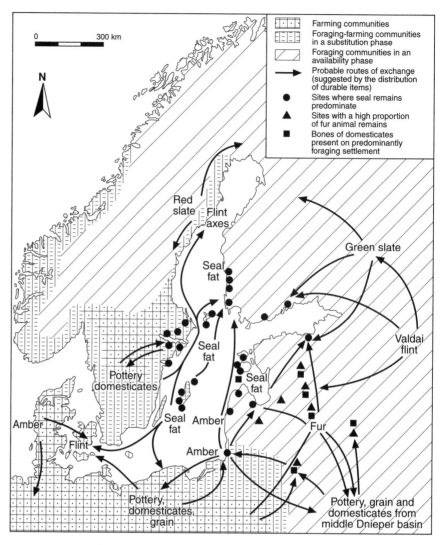

3.10   Forager–farmer interactions in the east Baltic, *c.* 5000–4000 BP; 3000–2000 BC, 4000–2200 cal. BC. (*Sources:* Paaver 1965, Vankina 1970, Zvelebil 1992a, 1993, 1996.)

arrows in Neolithic assemblages in Poland, Germany, and the Low Countries could be explained as a manifestation of conflict between foragers and farmers, while Neolithic artifacts could be seen as loot rather than imports (Tomaszewski 1988, Gronenborn 1990b, Keeley 1992).

The increase in conflict and social competition toward the end of the Ertebølle culture and similar groups across the North European Plain would have reduced the benefits of maintaining complex hunter-gatherer strategies, and shifted the balance in favor of adopting farming. Owing to their relative stability and population numbers, coastal communities were able to acquire farming rapidly and avoid the full destructive impact of competition with farmers. The result was the transformation and evolution of hunter-gatherer social, ideological, and economic strategies, rather than replacement; this is evident in continuities in material culture, economy, settlement location, and burial practices (Jennbert 1985, Madsen 1982, Bogucki 1988, Rowley-Conwy and Zvelebil 1989, Solberg 1989, Sherratt 1990, Price and Gebauer 1992) between the Mesolithic and the first Neolithic TRB culture.

In the western Baltic this process of transformation was accomplished fairly rapidly between *c.* 5200 and 5000 BP (3200 and 3000 bc; 4100–3900 BC); most authorities agree that we are dealing with the acquisition of farming by local groups, with little or no immigration from the more established groups further south (see Madsen 1986, Price this volume for a review; Solberg 1989 for a contrary view). The genesis of the TRB culture in some areas of the North European Plain shows a similar blending of cultural attributes and continuity in settlement, and could be seen in a similar light (Bogucki 1988, Sherratt 1990, Midgley 1993) (Fig. 3.9).

In the eastern Baltic, agro-pastoral farming was adopted at a very slow rate over some two thousand years (Dolukhanov 1979, Zvelebil 1981, 1993, Zvelebil and Dolukhanov 1991, Janik 1998). Despite the presence of low numbers of domesticates on archaeological sites from *c.* 4500 BP (2500 bc; *c.* 3100 BC), and despite a major change in material culture marked by the Corded Ware horizon *c.* 4500–3800 BP (2500–1800 bc; 3100–2200 BC), the decisive shift to an agro-pastoral economy occurred between 3300 and 2600 BP (1300 and 600 bc; 1600–600 BC), attested by the shift in the location of major settlements away from wetland and shoreline locations to areas with lighter, arable soils, by the rise in the presence of domesticates, and by the abandonment of symbolism associated with hunting and gathering in favor of agricultural symbols (Paaver 1965, Zvelebil 1981, 1985, 1992a, 1993).

Between 4500 and 2600 BP (2500 and 600 bc; 3100–600 BC), there was a society based principally on hunting and gathering for subsistence, yet making some occasional use of domesticates and possibly cultigens from about 2500 bc (3100 BC) (Vuorela and Lempiainen 1988, Rimantienè 1992). The presence of domesticates in low numbers has been explained as a result of wide-ranging trading networks, elaborated within the context of the Corded Ware/Boat Axe culture (Dolukhanov 1979, Zvelebil 1993), while their limited use, which continued until the end of the second millennium bc, fits with the notion of their ritual, rather than economic significance (Hayden 1990). In the eastern Baltic, then, the process of agricultural "transition" was arrested in the early stages and became a way of life, and as such remains suspended between our traditional notions of the Mesolithic and the Neolithic (Fig. 3.9).

Conclusions

The concept of the agricultural frontier can be employed as a useful heuristic device in our attempts to understand the process of the transition to the agro-pastoral, farming societies in Europe. While the agricultural frontier, as any other frontier, is primarily a conceptual and a cognitive construct, held both by the prehistoric actors who were engaged in contacts between the two types of communities, and in the minds of anthropologists and prehistorians who study them (not necessarily coeval or conterminous), it should be possible to identify the agricultural frontier zone in the archaeological record as an area in space within which contacts and exchanges occurred, and in which a particular structure of social, economic, and ideological relationships operated. Although the studies explicitly focused on the prehistoric agricultural frontier in Europe are still in early stages, we hope that this chapter has been able to demonstrate the following.

1 Forager–farmer interactions were taking place along the major cultural boundaries – stationary frontiers – which existed at the beginning of the Neolithic in Europe (Fig. 3.1). In eastern Europe, these interactions played a role in the differentiated adoption of farming in the Balkans, in Moldavia and the Ukraine, and in northern and northeastern Europe. It is now clear that forager–farmer interactions were occurring along the entire perimeter of the stationary frontier defined by the limit of the Balkan Neolithic/LBK cultural zone.

2 Within the area of Dnieper-Donets cultural traditions, as well as in the east Baltic and in parts of the North European Plain, these interactions appear to follow a similar pattern, marked first by cooperation, and then by social competition within the forager communities, followed by a shift to farming by the forager communities.

3 Contacts between foragers and farmers, occurring within an agricultural frontier zone, must have had a direct effect on the nature and the rate of the transition. Such contacts may have acted as a delaying mechanism in the process of the transition, as appears to have been the case in the east Baltic, or they may have acted to accelerate the adoption of farming, for example, at the end of the Mesolithic in southern Scandinavia. In particular, by fostering social competition among foragers, and by disrupting their social organization, forager–farmer contacts appear as one of the major causes in the adoption of farming by the indigenous hunter-gatherers. In this way, the adoption of farming can be explained – at least partly – as a result of social and economic developments occurring within the indigenous Mesolithic communities of hunter-gatherers. As Chapman notes, the forager–farmer exchange model "raises serious doubts about the validity of a diffusionist account of the spread of both social and economic domestication from the Near East and Anatolia" (1994b:146).

Acknowledgments

The original version of this chapter was presented at the 60th annual meeting of the Society for American Anthropology in Minneapolis. Marek Zvelebil would like to thank the University of Sheffield for making a financial contribution toward travel to Minneapolis from the Foreign Travel Fund, and Mark Pluciennik, Paul Halstread, and Kostas Kotsakis for advice in the preparation of Fig. 3.4. Malcolm Lillie would like to thank Dmitri Telegin and Inna Pothekina, Ukrainian Academy of Sciences, for hospitality proffered to him during his stay in Kiev, and for access to skeletal collections housed in Kiev; and the University of Sheffield for assistance with travel costs. All errors are our own.

Notes

1 At the phenotypic level, the differences in gross physical morphology between the Mesolithic and Neolithic skeletal remains may reflect a dietary shift to a cereal-based, agricultural diet (y'Edynak 1978, 1989, Meiklejohn and Zvelebil 1991) rather than demic diffusion. From the study of cranial measurements of the relevant skeletal samples, Harding *et al.* have concluded that "there is no evidence from this analysis for Neolithisation of Europe by demic diffusion coupled to the spread of agriculture" (1996:54).

At the genetic level, analyses of genetic patterning of modern European populations have been used to adduce support for the demic diffusion theory (Ammerman and Cavalli-Sforza 1984, Renfrew 1987, Sokal *et al.* 1991, etc.). However, the analysis neither of blood protein polymorphisms (e.g., Ammerman and Cavalli-Sforza 1984), nor of molecular (DNA) or dermatoglyphic traits (Sokal and Livshits 1993), produces clear results, a situation which made Sokal and his co-workers come to different conclusions with each new publication (Sokal *et al.* 1989, 1991, 1992, Sokal and Livshits 1993). In the 1989 study, 59 allele frequencies and 109 cranial measurements were analyzed at 3466 geographical locations in Europe and then compared to different European language families. The results suggested that "for numerous genetic systems, population samples overall differ more among language families than they do within families, and that only Germanic among the language families of Europe exhibits significant homogeneity" (Sokal *et al.* 1989:497), with either gene flow or adaptation capable of accounting for the variation observed in the data (1989:498–500). Although in their 1991 letter to *Nature*, Sokal *et al.* argue that their findings support the demic diffusion hypothesis, only 6 of 26 genetic traits examined showed significant agreement with demic diffusion (1991:144), while "the highly significant negative partial correlation for the ABO system clearly contradicts the demic diffusion hypothesis" (1991:144). The continuing doubts led Sokal to claim a year later that the genetic evidence does not support either Renfrew's or Gimbutas' (the nomadic theory) hypothesis (Roberts 1992). The recent analysis of dermatographic traits from 144 samples in Eurasia (Sokal and Livshits 1993) has again proved inconclusive, showing more convincingly a diffusion from east-central Asia and the Middle East, rather than from the Near East: in the latter case, the epicenter for the diffusion of dermatoglyphic traits was in the southern part of the Arab peninsula, and not in Asia Minor as required by the language–farming hypothesis.

Similarly, the analysis by Calafell and Bertranpetit (1993) of the genetic history of the Iberian peninsula is predicated on the colonization of Iberia from the northeast (i.e. Catalonia) by local populations turned farmers through demic diffusion marked by "short range individual mobility" (1993:739). Even though this simulation is based on such moderate expectations, the goodness of fit between the model and the actual genetic composition in the Iberian peninsula suggests first that the introduction of farming into Iberia must have occurred in more than one place within a short time-span, second, that the inner areas of Iberia as well as the Basque region served as centers of genetic continuity of indigenous populations long after the initial introduction of farming – as the authors themselves admit (1993:741) – and third, that the process of "acculturation," or uptake of the Neolithic culture (i.e. technology and economy), can only be matched with a far more gradual and limited gene replacement than suggested by the model (1993:737, the first principal component, compare Figs. 4 and 5).

The latest recently published study by Richards *et al.* (1996), concerned with the analysis of the mitochondrial DNA of 821 haplotypes from Europe, concludes that the majority of modern Europeans appears to be descended from the local pre-Neolithic population, while the demographic influence of later colonizations from the Middle East is judged to have been small. In Richards *et al.*'s view, "there was selective penetration by fairly small groups of Middle Eastern agriculturists of a Europe numerically dominated by the descendants of the original Palaeolithic settlements. The ensuing conversion of this population from a hunter-gatherer-fishing to an agricultural economy would then have been achieved by technology transfer rather than large scale population replacement" (1996:15). This is in complete agreement with archaeological evidence as presented by Zvelebil (1986b, 1995b, 1996).

2 This is marked by small size of vessels, relative infrequency of pots, and the simplicity of manufacture. The paucity of potsherds in the Early Neolithic in Greece led to the notion of "aceramic Neolithic" (Theocharis 1973; see Lüning 1988a, Budja 1993, Chapman 1994b for recent discussion). Although in some locations such as Franchthi cave, "it is possible that the adoption of domesticates took place piecemeal over a period of several centuries" (Halstead 1996; see also Hansen 1988, Perlès 1990), the presence of cultigens and domesticates in clearly aceramic layers is known from Agrissa, Franchthi, Knossos level X and three small soundings in Thessaly (Demoule and Perlès 1993), and from sites in northwest Turkey (Özdogan 1983, 1997, Özdogan and Gatsov in press).

3 The hunter-gatherer settlements along the Danube in the Iron Gates serve as one of the best examples of sedentary, symbolically and socially complex hunter-fishers, who maintained their way of life coevally with farming

communities in eastern Serbia (Srejovic 1969a, 1971, Tringham 1971, Garasanin 1978, Prinz 1987, Chapman 1989a, 1993, 1994b, Voytek and Tringham 1989). Food procurement strategies of these Mesolithic communities may have included rudimentary forms of plant and animal husbandry, marked by close herding and perhaps selective breeding of local pigs and cattle (Tringham 1971, Bökönyi 1974, Markevitch 1974, Malez 1975, Srejovic 1979, Shnirelman 1992b, Turk 1993) and harvesting, soil preparation, and possibly planting of local small-seeded cereals and possibly root crops (Dennell 1983, Barker 1985, y'Edynak 1989, Budja 1993, Zvelebil 1994a). The settlements at Lepenski Vir and Vlasac, best known for their trapezoidal houses, served as territorial centers for ritual, social, and partner-finding activities (Chapman 1989a, 1993). The evidence for storage, exchange, and delayed-return technologies led Voytek and Tringham to suggest that we are dealing with descent-based, lineage societies where the band organization and egalitarian ideology were in the process of disintegration (Voytek and Tringham 1989). The notion of matrilocal descent-based social organization is additionally supported by the differential patterns of disarticulation of male and female skeletons, by the differences in grave goods between the sexes, and by the sex-specific location of burials (Chapman 1993). In short, females received more formal, elaborate burial, which was clearly linked to the houses.

Between 7500 and 7000 BP (5500 and 5000 BC), Neolithic imports, principally ceramics, stone artifacts and bones of domesticates, occur at Lepenski Vir, Padina, Vlasac, and other sites. The operation of far-flung exchange networks is demonstrated by the presence of obsidian from Hungary, yellow flint from the lower Danube basin and a paligorskite necklace originating either in the Urals or in Anatolia (Srejovic 1969a, Voytek and Tringham 1989, Chapman 1994b). At the same time, human skeletal remains in the burials show a sharp decrease in robusticity which appears to be too sudden to be explained by micro-evolutionary changes. The study of ancient ABO blood groups from Vlasac suggests that females at Vlasac belonged to the resident population, while the males show different, exogenous patterning. These studies suggest the coexistence of two different morphological types and progressive blending of the two populations: the later Starcevo sample is very different from the Mesolithic pattern (Menk and Neméskeri 1989).

One can bring these strands of evidence into a coherent explanation, accounting for the transition to farming in very specific terms. In a matrilineal society the choice of partners by females could have easily included males from farming communities, bearing in mind the economic benefits of an exchange link with a farming society. While pottery, domesticates, and exotic artifacts testify to such trade, yellow flint tools may have been the personal gear of immigrant males, rather than exchange items. It may be the case that males from a farming community, at least initially, were responsible for the production of pottery: ethnographically, ceramic manufacture is not always associated with females; as a specialized activity it is more often associated with males (Hodder 1978, 1982). Finally, this scenario fits the general conditions of an agricultural frontier, which tends to have a surplus of young males and a lack of females, increasing the competition for females and encouraging male migration (Green and Perlman 1985). Recent research by Bonsall *et al.* (1997:82–3) on the dietary patterns and stable isotope markers of the Iron Gates populations lends some support to the hypothesis that males and females came from different communities.

4 Some explanation for the apparent differences between the dates is suggested by date Ki-2810 (Kiev) which is clearly obtained from the grouping of bone samples from pit A4 at Yasinovatka, a factor which could easily result in contamination of the sample. Other dates, such as Ki-3283, apparently obtained from individual 125 at Nikolskoye, appear to be over 500 radiocarbon years younger than the date obtained on the same individual, but which was processed at the Oxford accelerator facility. These younger dates may therefore reflect a tendency of certain conventional dates to age too young, a fact which finds some support with the conventional dates obtained from Osipovka.

The Oxford determinations fit perfectly well with the chronological positioning proposed by Telegin on the basis of the burials and associated artifactual material obtained during excavation, though not in fact with the actual position in terms of calibrated age BC. Telegin (1987:120) places Osipovka at stage B1 of the Mariupol-type cemetery sequence, this being the early to mid-sixth millennium BP/early to mid-fourth millennium BC, despite the fact that the uncalibrated radiocarbon determinations are 6075–5940 BP, i.e. the late fifth to early fourth millennia BC. This cemetery is clearly some 250–300 radiocarbon years earlier in the chronological sequence of the Mariupol cemeteries than its positioning by Telegin would suggest. Whilst certain errors in the radiocarbon dating methods are not fully understood (cf. Neustupny 1969:35–8), it is apparent that further radiocarbon dating of the distinct chronological stages of each of the Dnieper Rapids cemeteries is needed if the resolution of the chronological sequence is to be resolved.

4

Cardial pottery and the agricultural transition in Mediterranean Europe

Introduction

The transition to agriculture in the western Mediterranean is associated with the first appearance of ovicaprids (Geddes 1985) and domesticated wheat and barley (Hopf 1991), species of which originated in the Near East and spread rapidly from Italy to Portugal. This period of prehistory, the Early Neolithic, is primarily identified in the archaeological record by the presence of stylistically uniform wares, such as Cardial or Impressa pottery, domesticated plants and animals, and the use of obsidian and ground stone (Guilaine 1976). Studies of these materials indicate that significant transformations in economy and society began to take shape at this time. Many of these changes do not, however, appear to manifest themselves in terms of dependence on agro-pastoral products or larger village settlements until the Middle Neolithic around a thousand years later (Guilaine 1976). The nature of the agricultural transition in the western Mediterranean has proved, therefore, an interpretative challenge as it represents the rapid appearance but slow assimilation of production-based economies among emergent agricultural societies (cf. Zvelebil 1986c).

By the 1960s, investigations of the first European agricultural societies had shifted in focus from culture historical studies of artifacts to economic and ecological studies based on environmental and subsistence data. Models constructed to interpret these data have been concerned with the relationships between humans and their non-human physical environment, that is to say "nature." This is a logical connection as Neolithic farming represented new subsistence relationships with plants and animals. Sedentary agriculture implied new types of interactions between man and the physical landscape that had not existed in previous foraging societies. To explain the origins of agriculture in these economic and ecological terms, scholars proposed either Neolithic colonization, indigenous invention, or Mesolithic adoption as mechanisms.

The singular importance of full-scale agriculture in the subsistence economies of later complex societies (or the consequences of agricultural development such as population growth) did not, however, necessarily mean that early agricultural societies were similarly dependent. Early agriculture did not present any subsistence advantage to foraging societies that would drive colonization or adoption (Gregg 1988). Equally, early agriculture was not so intrinsically valuable that European foraging societies must have experimented, if not independently adopted, some form of cultivation prior to the arrival of eastern domesticates (Rowley-Conwy 1986, Zvelebil 1994, this volume).

Domesticates did rapidly appear across Mediterranean Europe in the sixth millennium BC (Zilhão 1993, this volume). The relationship of this transformation to the emergence of agriculture by processes of colonization, invention, or adoption is, however, unclear. For the most part, these models conceive of the transition process as monolithic and unidirectional, beginning with foraging and heading along a single, unvarying route toward sedentary agriculture. With few exceptions (e.g., Shnirelman 1992) these models generally have not accounted for a diversity of strategies that may have been employed by transitional societies, for interactions among different groups, and for multiple routes to early agriculture that do not presuppose the subsequent development of full-scale agriculture.

It is possible to question the colonization vs. adoption edifice that has housed current debate on the agricultural transition. In terms of models and measures, colonization and adoption models fail to account for the variety of patterns and processes during the agricultural transition. Attempts to explain what are likely to have been spatially and temporally diverse phenomena through these general models have not been entirely satisfactory, and the data that have been called upon to demonstrate colonization or adoption in the western Mediterranean have proved largely equivocal (Barnett 1995). This chapter attempts to outline those limitations, to explore socio-economic interaction-based regional scale models for understanding the agricultural transition in the western Mediterranean (Zvelebil, this volume), and to examine those models through patterns of Early Neolithic subsistence, settlement, interaction, and technology.

The western Mediterranean Early Neolithic

The archaeology of the western Mediterranean Neolithic is characterized by intriguing patterns on the one hand and significant gaps on the other. Current estimates place the first appearance of Neolithic assemblages, characteristically with impressed pottery, at around 5700 BC in Provence (Evin 1987) and spreading westward to Portugal by at least 5300 BC, if not earlier (Zilhão, this volume; Zilhão and Carvalho 1996). This rapid spread appears to have the characteristic of a single punctuated event (Zilhão, this volume), assuming earlier dates from as yet unexcavated submerged sites in France and Italy are not forthcoming. Domesticated cereals

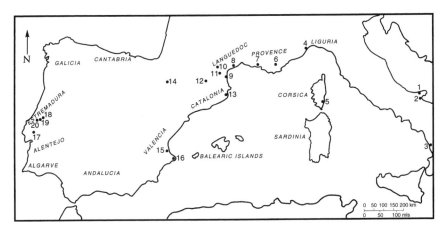

4.1   The western Mediterranean showing sites discussed in the text: 1. Coppa
        Nevigata, 2. Passo di Corvo, 3. Piana di Curinga, 4. Arene Candide,
        5. Curacchiaghiu, 6. Fontbrégoua, 7. Châteauneuf, 8. Peiro Signado,
        9. Leucate-Corrège, 10. Grotte Gazel, 11. Jean-Cros, 12. Balma Margineda,
        13. La Draga, 14. Chaves, 15. Cova de l'Or, 16. Cueva de Cendres, 17. Muge,
        18. Caldeirão, 19. Gruta do Almonda, 20. Cabeço de Porto Marinho.

appear in many Mediterranean Early Neolithic sites (Hopf 1991), and have
recently been documented in Portugal (Sanchez 1996). The appearance of
pottery and domesticates, however, does not necessarily indicate sedentary
agriculture and no Early Neolithic sites can be definitively associated with
full agricultural dependence.

It is doubtful that excavated sites accurately represent Early
Neolithic settlement patterns. Most reliably dated Early Neolithic materials
come from caves or rockshelters such as Arene Candide in Italy;
Curacchiaghiu in Corsica; Châteauneuf, Fontbrégoua, La Grotte Gazel, and
L'Abri Jean-Cros in France; Balma Margineda in Andorra; Cova de l'Or,
Cueva de Cendres and Cueva de Chaves in Spain; and Caldeirão, Gruta do
Almonda, and Cabeço do Porto Marinho in Portugal to name just a few (Fig.
4.1). The ease of identifying cave and rockshelter locations and a traditional
bias for their excavation have undoubtedly slanted investigations toward
these sites.

Only a few open-air sites have been excavated, notably Coppa
Nevigata, Passo di Corvo, and Piana di Curinga in Italy, Leucate-Corrège and
Peiro Signado in France (Fig. 4.1) and, recently, La Draga in Catalonia (Tarrus
et al. 1994). These open-air sites typically represent a single-phase occupation
whose material remains are less complete than contained caves and more
subject to taphonomic effects. Besides the paucity of open-air sites, the role
of coastal sites in the picture of Early Neolithic settlement is unknown. Sea
level rise during the later Holocene has put most coastal sites effectively out

of reach of archaeologists. Submerged and possibly inaccessible coastal sites such as Leucate-Corrège could significantly alter what we know about ceramics, settlement, and economies.

Leucate-Corrège and La Draga are unique, and diverse, examples of open-air Early Neolithic sites. Leucate-Corrège is located at 6 m below sea level in the Etang de Leucate, an embayment on the Mediterranean coast of Languedoc (Guilaine *et al.* 1984). Partially excavated by dredging, it appears to have been a single-phase Early Neolithic coastal settlement with evidence of year-round wide-spectrum occupation. There are domesticated cattle and sheep, but no remains of domesticated cereals were recovered. Excavators recovered 600 decorated sherds representing seven decorative categories (Guilaine *et al.* 1984), exceeding the amount currently known from the rest of the Languedoc. The recent publication of La Draga, an epi-Cardial lakeside site in Catalonia (Tarrus *et al.* 1994), provides a contrasting example. Dating to around 5000 BC, it is a large and apparently permanent single-occupation phase complete with paved areas. The ceramic assemblage is small, but includes a large storage jar filled with wheat. Preliminary examination of the fauna reports 75% domestic animals, with half of those being cow and pig.

Characteristics of the Early Neolithic

Pottery is the most diagnostic feature of this period and has been traditionally seen as the marker of agriculture in Europe even though neither one requires the other (Hoopes and Barnett 1995). The initial pottery horizon in the western Mediterranean shows two different distribution patterns. There are certain decorative and technologically distinct types, such as *Cardial* or *Impressa* wares that span wide areas. Guilaine (1976:37–8) has identified two principal zones: a central *Impressa* pottery zone covering Italy to the Ligurian coast, and a western *Cardial* zone beginning in Provence and extending to Atlantic Portugal. Within these zones Guilaine (1976:21–2) has further identified fourteen more restricted pottery "groups" based on ceramic decoration and vessel form.

The ceramic sequence in the Early Neolithic of this area is traditionally interpreted as an initial horizon of widespread "Cardial" wares followed by a regionalization of decoration during subsequent "epi-Cardial" impressed Ware phases of the Early Neolithic (Fig. 4.2). The widespread patterns appear to overlap (for example, Ligurian Impressa wares appear at Peiro Signado). Critiques of stratigraphies (Zilhão 1993) have bolstered views that these widespread regional ceramic types may have been more contemporaneous than previously thought (Barnett 1990a) and therefore may represent more complex patterns of ceramic production and use. Production and distribution studies show transport of all wares around Languedoc (Barnett 1990b). That they were transported complicates their traditional interpretation as cultural markers since exchange of vessels across political

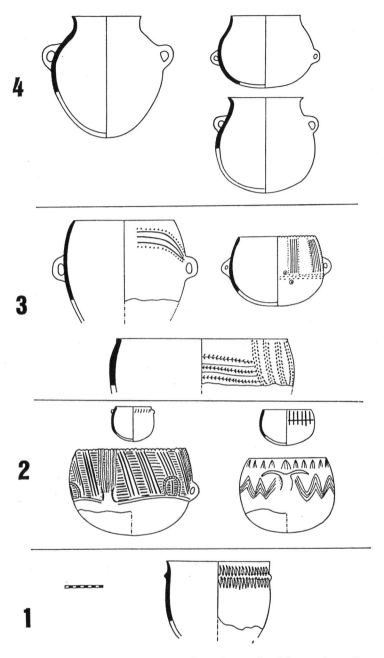

4.2 Early Neolithic ceramic sequence from Grotte Gazel in southern France: Cardial ceramics (Phase 1) to epi-Cardial Impressed wares (Phases 2 and 3) to late undecorated wares (Phase 4) that are transitional to the Middle Neolithic. (From Guilaine 1976:233.)

boundaries implies that their distribution does not necessarily reflect group divisions. Assuming style reflects social group, these patterns may instead reflect socio-political interaction patterns.

Ceramic sample sizes are extremely small for a period that encompasses nearly a thousand years. The relatively small amounts of Early Neolithic pottery at cave and rockshelter sites (typically a dozen or so vessels, rarely more than fifty vessels) in a sequence representing hundreds of years may be due to sporadic production of pottery or the limited habitation of these sites. In contrast to open-air sites, caves and rockshelters were probably inhabited for longer periods of time, as is evidenced by the continuity of habitation at some of these sites from Palaeolithic to modern times. Open-air sites were inhabited for shorter durations, yet may have been significantly larger habitation foci. Leucate-Corrège, a single-occupation open-air site, has produced more, and more diverse, pottery than all other sites in the Aude valley combined.

Flaked stone tools are the most useful artifact class for comparison between Early Neolithic and the preceding Mesolithic assemblages. The shift to Early Neolithic lithics in the western Mediterranean is marked by changes in flaked tool technology and the appearance of different kinds of reduction sequences and formal tools. In southeastern France and Italy, Mesolithic Castelnovian geometric and microburin industries are quite different from Neolithic flake-based industries. Neolithic assemblages also show greater uniformity in raw materials (Binder, this volume, Binder and Courtin 1987).

A gradual progression of geometrics from Epipalaeolithic to Neolithic, however, seems to be more characteristic in eastern Iberia (Fortea Perez *et al.* 1987) although this view is contested by Zilhão (1993, this volume). Ground stone objects, particularly axes, appear in the Early Neolithic and are known to have been widely transported (Ricq-de Bouard and Fedele 1993). Obsidian also begins to be transported in the Early Neolithic, particularly around Italian and Corsican sources (Tykot 1992) but some pieces occur as far west as Peiro Signado in Languedoc (Roudil and Soulier 1983) (Fig. 4.1).

Evidence for the appearance of domesticates themselves is somewhat tenuous. Marnival (1992) reports the presence of *Triticum aestivo-compactum* (bread/compact wheat) and *Hordeum vulgare* var. *nudum* (naked barley) in Spain and southern France in the Early Neolithic. In much of the rest of the Mediterranean basin, early domesticated plant remains have included emmer and einkorn and hulled barley (J. Hansen personal communication). Domesticated plants have recently been recovered from the Early Neolithic in Portugal (Sanchez 1996). Domesticated animals, particularly Near Eastern ovicaprids, are shown to appear at least by the Early Neolithic across the western Mediterranean (Geddes 1985) to Portugal (Rowley-Conwy 1992). Claims for Mesolithic use of domesticated plants

(Vaquer *et al.* 1986) and ovicaprids (Geddes 1985), however, have been largely discounted through the reexamination of site taphonomies (Zilhão 1993).

The picture that emerges is one of tantalizing contradictions, depending on the scale of analysis. On a large scale, the appearance of new technologies and foodstuffs is quite rapid across the western Mediterranean. On a local scale we do not know if the change happened in five years or five generations. New types of technologies and foodstuffs appear in varying quantities almost universally, yet the consolidation of these technologies into a new mode of life may have taken as long as a thousand years (Zvelebil 1986c). On a large scale, the process seems quite similar, particularly when artifact technologies are compared. At the smaller scale, the archaeological record documents more varied strategies and unique settlement patterns that defy general classification. There are numerous sites excavated across the western Mediterranean, yet owing to site selection bias and inundation of coastal areas, it is unclear how representative they are. Likewise there are relatively numerous excavated sites, but the evidence from them relating to the introduction of agriculture is sparse.

Push-me, pull-you: colonization or adoption?

Others in this volume and elsewhere discuss in detail the arguments surrounding models of colonization, invention, and adoption, their theoretical bases (Ammerman and Cavalli-Sforza 1984, Dennell 1992, Zvelebil and Rowley-Conwy 1986), and their fit with the western Mediterranean in particular (Barnett 1995, Binder, this volume, Lewthwaite 1982, Zilhão 1993, this volume). Suggestions of the independent invention of domesticates, such as caprids and cereals, as well as of pottery technology, have been largely discredited (Geddes 1985, Rowley-Conwy 1986, Zilhão 1993) and are not further considered here. In considering colonization and adoption, Zvelebil and Rowley-Conwy (1986) identify three principal positions that have driven explanations of the agricultural transition: agriculture as a superior mode of production, agricultural expansion driven by population–resource imbalance, and social disequilibrium.

Ammerman and Cavalli-Sforza's (1984) demic diffusion hypothesis represents the earliest testable iteration of the traditional "superiority of agriculture" argument. If we assume that early farming was expansive, agriculture resulted in population growth which would have driven population diffusion. This hypothesis linked the expansion of agriculture to the results of subsistence changes such as storable surpluses, population growth, and land consumption through cultivation. Whereas these aspects are certainly characteristic of established sedentary agriculture, there is no evidence that population or resource imbalance drove initial agricultural expansion (Zvelebil 1986) or that early agriculture was sedentary or had any subsistence advantage over foraging (Gregg 1988). Ammerman and Cavalli-Sforza's own analysis of the Wave of Advance model has shown that populations in the western Mediterranean adopted agriculture, or at least pottery, at roughly five times the rate predicted by demic diffusion (Ammerman and Cavalli-Sforza 1984).

It is unlikely, therefore, that early European farming would have supported great demographic growth, provided a real subsistence benefit, or proceeded at the rate that it appears to have in the Mediterranean. Likewise, land consumption through slash-and-burn or other expansive agricultural techniques is not now considered a likely hypothesis for Europe in general (Bogucki 1988:79–82). More recent versions of colonization models across central Europe (Bogucki, this volume) and in the western Mediterranean in particular (Zilhão 1993, this volume) are more realistic in that they describe socio-economic processes, rather than natural ones, as causal agents in population diffusion and avoid many of the inherent difficulties of earlier theories that depend of demographic or environmental stress as causal agents. These models still do not account well for interactions with foraging societies that inhabited areas to be colonized and it is still difficult to evaluate the processes they describe in the western Mediterranean (Barnett 1995).

The assertion that subsistence and environment did not drive the adoption of agriculture has led to the development of social models for the adoption of agriculture (Bender 1978, 1985). These have been based on the interpretation of pre-agricultural foragers adopting agriculture owing to an accumulation ideology (Testart 1982) via prestige exchange through competitive feasting (Hayden 1990, 1995). In order to be successful, adoption models must contend not only with the archaeological evidence, but with how foraging societies suddenly would have become enamored of new foods that did not necessarily provide economic benefit.

One answer may lie in an assumption that human society is essentially competitive and that exchange in a social venue resulted in the adoption of domesticates (Bender 1978, Hayden 1990). Hayden's (1990) prestige model proposes that only certain individuals, or "early adopters," in a society would have needed to experiment with new technologies or foodstuffs as a competitive strategy for its adoption to occur. Such experimentation could set the stage for more pervasive adoption while not committing the entire group to dietary or logistic dependence on domesticates. These models explain how foraging groups could have coped with the qualitative changes in daily or seasonal activities that cultivating plants or breeding herds would have engendered (e.g., Zilhão 1993) without complete adoption of an agricultural way of life.

Adoption has been proposed for the appearance of agriculture in the western Mediterranean (Lewthwaite 1982, 1986). Early models propose the "piecemeal" adoption of the Neolithic beginning in the Mesolithic (Geddes 1985, Vaquer *et al.* 1986). Such selective adoption of individual Neolithic traits (pottery or domesticates or ground stone independently of one another) has been questioned by Rowley-Conwy (1995) and Zilhão (1993) who have argued that the appearance of key features of the Neolithic, particularly domesticated caprids and pottery, was largely contemporaneous. Other arguments for an indigenous role in the spread of Mediterranean agriculture (Barnett 1995, Zvelebil 1986a, 1994a) do not require piecemeal adoption, but rather emphasize that adopted innovations could have operated for some time in a predominantly foraging situation before consolidation into a new subsistence mode.

Building better models

The difficulty in evaluating both colonization and adoption models lies in the unrealistic predictions of these models and in the inability of the available evidence to provide an adequate evaluation. Spatially, population movements among the small-scale societies that existed at the time of the agricultural transition were more complex than monolithic colonization or adoption models predict and these models do not cope well with such complexity. Evidence of sea travel in the Mesolithic (Jacobsen 1976) demonstrates the capacity for widespread, rapid movement. There was probably some amount of population mobility during any period in the past as groups, no matter how small, existed in a social landscape of neighbors with whom interaction of some sort or another was unavoidable. Any innovation would be subject to local or regional expression appropriate to the society in question. Tringham (this volume) has argued that the units of variability can be as small as a household. Testing at this fine scale, however, is tenuous because, as mentioned above, spatial and contextual data are afflicted with excavation biases, remixed stratigraphies, site submergence, and serious gaps in site distributions.

The principal technique for providing temporal resolution is radiocarbon dating, whose precision for mid-Holocene dates is typically a first standard deviation of around 100 years, as can be noted in any publication of collected dates for mid-Holocene prehistory (also cf. Zilhão 1993 for the western Mediterranean). Radiocarbon dating has produced, on a large scale, evidence for the rapid overall spread of pottery and domesticates across the Mediterranean. These gross patterns are, however, of little relevance for the time scale which is necessary for identifying colonization or adoption events. A single standard deviation can represent up to five generations (assuming twenty years per generation), which precludes its usage for identifying local punctuated events such as migration or adoption. The "sudden" appearance of domesticates or pottery in a stratigraphic layer only demonstrates that changes occurred roughly between two sets of estimated dates, each with a 64% chance of being internally consistent within 100 years. Multiple dates cannot significantly narrow this inherent error.

We can build models that are more satisfying in terms of their expectations and testable in terms of the data in the ground. Socio-economic models of interactions or frontiers among foragers and small-scale agriculturalists are anthropologically viable in terms of their expectations and provide a fertile ground for evaluating this transformation (Zvelebil 1986a). These models provide an explanatory framework for processes that occurred during the Neolithic transformation in the historical and environmental context of the western Mediterranean. They are conceived at scales necessary to provide additional insights into the agricultural transition in the western Mediterranean.

Several models of interaction among foraging and early agricultural societies already exist (e.g., Moore 1985, Zilhão 1993, this volume, Zvelebil, this volume). Each of these models plays out effectively in terms of rate of transition and testability of evidence on a regional basis. Certain specific models may predict different rates of the transition in a frontier situation. The power of these models is that they can be constructed at a regional scale that more appropriately reflects the diversity of early agricultural manifestations (see Jochim, Tringham, Zvelebil, all this volume).

These may be related to ecological diversity or seasonality where products are transported across zones as part of transhumant movements or exchanges. They may be related to the extent of social networks, the degree of exogamy, or the relative degree of conflict within or among communities. Interaction patterns may be governed by territoriality and social restrictions regarding who may participate in extra-community interactions. They may be related to inter-group predatory (i.e., theft) or violent interactions. These models can then be compared to data on subsistence, settlement, interaction, and technology. They do not depend solely on dates and the presence of "type fossils" such as domesticates or pottery. As they operate at a regional scale, they consider material evidence through landscape approaches that have the potential to identify smaller-scale dynamics.

Zvelebil (this volume) describes six interactive relationships in a mobile frontier situation that can characterize the transition at the Mesolithic/Early Neolithic boundary in the western Mediterranean: Demic Diffusion, Folk Migration, Elite Dominance, Infiltration, Leapfrog (Enclave) Colonization, and Individual Frontier Mobility. Each of these has implications for the nature of the agricultural transition that are clearly more complex than a simple colonization versus adoption dichotomy. They can operate at a regional, or even single-village (Tringham, this volume) spatial scale; they have implications for the rate of spread and the degree to which subsistence strategies, settlement, technologies, and material culture change with the appearance of domesticates.

Colonization, adoption, or what?

As discussed above, the rapid overall rate of the initial spread of the earliest Neolithic in the western Mediterranean appears as punctuated, mobile frontier events involving populations of roughly equal scale. Thus Demic Diffusion, Folk Migration, or Elite Dominance can probably be excluded from consideration in this case. Such processes would have occurred in a later consolidation phase when subsistence strategies shift to year-round dependence on agricultural products (Zvelebil 1986). Such a consolidation appears to have occurred at the Early to Middle Neolithic transition when Chasséen agricultural villages begin to appear (Mills 1983).

Current formulations of Enclave (Leapfrog) Colonization models describe socio-economic processes as causal agents in population diffusion both in the western Mediterranean (Zilhão 1993, this volume) and in central Europe (Bogucki 1995a). For the western Mediterranean, Enclave Colonization involves resettlement by small seafaring groups of agriculturalists across the western Mediterranean (Zilhão 1993, this volume). Enclave Colonization is described as the budding off of small groups to found new agricultural colonies (Zilhão, this volume). Colonization events may have been driven by offspring required to homestead enclaves as part of entry into adulthood or inheritance or as part of planned navigational enterprises. Upon arrival, they would have assimilated or displaced local foragers, despite their smaller numbers, owing to the inherent superiority of an agricultural economy. According to Zilhão, these groups would have had to be small enough so that their replacement of foragers would have resulted in the negligible effects on modern human genetic patterning as modeled by Calafell and Bertranpetit (1993) for the Iberian peninsula. Colonizing groups could then have reconnoitered new, distant areas, utilizing interaction frameworks established by the foragers with whom they interacted (Zilhão, this volume).

Enclave Colonization requires the identification of a discontinuity between Mesolithic and Neolithic settlement, either spatially or temporally, and a rapid establishment of fully agricultural enclave sites in locations uninhabited by or adjacent to Mesolithic groups. It also requires a population discontinuity as foragers are replaced by farmers. It implies local production of new material goods such as pottery according to a uniform technology and style that has a utilitarian component, particularly for storage. It is difficult to test through evidence from physical anthropology, as the colonizers would have represented a small proportion of the population in colonized areas; thus colonizers would have had a small effect on genetic patterning. Subsequent leaps would have further thinned the colonists' "genetic" ranks.

In this, Enclave Colonization resembles a rapid Infiltration (Zvelebil, this volume), where small groups of individuals penetrate the territory of, and participate in, the socio-economic activities of indigenous groups. As Zvelebil (this volume) points out, in the Infiltration model, the infiltrators are required to participate in interactions based on the rules of the resident population and are usually in a subordinate or specialist role. Were this the case, it is germane to ask who might have been assimilating whom and therefore engaging (or not) in subsequent leaps in a real Enclave situation. If settlers are establishing their own rules in an Enclave Colonization, an increase in violence may be expected as foragers are displaced or assimilated; otherwise such colonization may not be distinguishable.

Adoption models have largely been recast as Individual Frontier Mobility (Zvelebil, this volume) where existing socio-economic relationships form the framework for the arrival of new foods and technologies through competitive intra-group exchange (Hayden 1990), or through the maintenance of inter-group alliances (Barnett 1990a, 1995), possibly utilizing social storage (Halstead and O'Shea 1989) to accumulate obligations. In this view, there was an active set of intra- and inter-group relationships amongst Mesolithic foraging groups that may have included exchange of goods, marriage partners, or labor obligations. It is also possible that only certain individuals participated in inter-group exchange and so would have had access to innovations.

It would be difficult to distinguish the temporary mobility of Individual Frontier Mobility from the permanent mobility of Infiltration, accomplished by individual pioneers bearing innovations being assimilated in a foraging group, possibly through exogamy. There would be only slight initial modification of settlement as individual innovators adopted new modes of subsistence or technologies, followed by significant resettlement in a few generations as agriculture took hold. New material culture would arrive as a technology transfer, maintaining a technological and decorative style. Decorative style would be most variable with initial widespread wares replaced by locally produced wares that continue to exhibit smaller-scale interaction.

Radiocarbon dating is ineffective in distinguishing the Enclave Migration, Individual Mobility, and Infiltration models under consideration here. Infiltrations, mobile interactions, or colonization events simply took places at a much finer temporal scale. Artifact and contextual data patterns, however, can provide more insight into the initial transformation process. It is helpful to view these models through the lenses of subsistence, settlement, interaction, and technology in order to gain a better view of the socio-dynamics of the agricultural transition in the western Mediterranean. Ceramic analysis in particular is a rich information source that provides some relevant documents.

Subsistence

Enclave Colonization requires the complete suite of interrelated domesticated plants and animals in a developed agricultural economy to appear as a package at colonial settlements, then spreading to indigenous populations. Individual Mobility can support the arrival of items independently or in a linked fashion amongst early adopters who would have experimented with new items or technologies at each settlement. Infiltration may imply more "piecemeal" importation of individual food items by socially peripheral or prestigious individuals. Each innovation could creep in over a period of a few generations or be linked, such as ceramic vessels and grains. In either of the latter models, new foods could have been introduced to the wider populations through feasting events (Hayden 1995) that involved the exchange of social obligations. Individual Mobility and Infiltration imply the proportional increase in domesticates in the diets of transitional populations; however, subsets of these populations may have switched over sooner.

The direct evidence for subsistence across the agricultural transition is currently too thin to provide an adequate evaluation of these models. In most areas only general presence or absence information on domesticated plants and/or animals is available, only enough to provide an overall rate of spread, not a regional identification of process. For the most part, these patterns show the appearance of domesticated cereals and ovicaprids in the Early Neolithic across the western Mediterranean. The single exception may be La Draga (Tarrus *et al.* 1994), where cattle and pig have been claimed in an epi-Cardial context along with a ceramic storage vessel containing wheat. The incidence of caries in Portuguese Mesolithic populations appears to indicate the use of carbohydrates and starchy foods and significant use of plants (Zvelebil 1994). The relation to Neolithic subsistence in this area is still unclear.

Taphonomic considerations have put claims for Mesolithic intense seed use, that is to say production, at Abeuradour (Languedoc) and Fontbrégoua in doubt (Binder, this volume), although in general there should be an expectation that plant foods composed a significant proportion of Mesolithic diet (Zvelebil 1994). Additional lines of research may provide better insight into the subsistence strategies practiced by transitional groups. Physical anthropology studies (e.g., Meiklejohn and Zvelebil 1991, Zvelebil 1995) and bone chemical analyses (e.g., Lubell *et al.* 1989) provide important complements to studies of plant and animal remains recovered from sites, yet their results have not yet provided definitive answers.

Settlement
The implications for settlement of the three models are fairly distinct. Enclave Colonization predicts that Neolithic enclaves were founded either in a separate location from forager settlements, or in a region where there was no significant Mesolithic settlement. The ideal loci for these enclaves may have been coastal zones that were proximal to their presumed maritime arrival routes and in areas not settled by foragers. In cases where there was a significant and resistant Mesolithic community, the enclaves may have been forced to settle peripherally, possibly leading to inter-group conflict. Individual Mobility and Infiltration are equally clear: innovations would occur in the context of extant Mesolithic settlements. Although one

would not necessarily expect the same exact locations to have been always inhabited, there should have been a consistent logic to settlement strategies in the Earliest Neolithic that might have then become modified as foraging activities were replaced by agricultural ones during the course of the Early Neolithic.

Settlement data must be considered with the caveats of incomplete survey, site inundation, and excavation bias. In some areas, such as Languedoc, caves and rockshelters generally have both Mesolithic and Early Neolithic habitation (Guilaine 1976), as predicted by Individual Mobility and Infiltration models. These sites, however, would have been easily located independently by foragers, pastoralists, or farmers, so long-term occupation of these sites confers no continuity of habitation. Binder and Zilhão (this volume) have proposed northern Italy and Cantabrian Spain as areas of possible adoption. Provence, Languedoc (Binder, this volume), Valencia, and the Portuguese Estremadura (Zilhão, this volume) have been proposed as regions of enclave settlement. It is, however, difficult to distinguish Neolithic resettlement by migrating colonists from that of adoption through mobility or infiltration.

Portugal is an example of the difficulties of using settlement data. The Estremadura region in central Portugal witnessed Palaeolithic settlement, but a relative lack of Mesolithic sites with habitation focused in estuarine sites such as Muge in the northern Alentejo (Zilhão 1993). Resettlement in the Estremadura during the Early Neolithic borders or overlaps dates for the latest Mesolithic levels at Muge (Zilhão 1993). Zilhão (1993) has argued that this pattern represents the appearance of enclaves in the Estremadura. The Estremaduran coast, however, has never been surveyed as has the interior, and there are rare Mesolithic sites in the interior. It is as likely that there was a significant coastal population in the Estremaduran Mesolithic or that Estremaduran Early Neolithic sites represent expansions of Mesolithic populations centered just to the south as it is that Neolithic colonists bypassed the rich estuaries of the Tagus and Sado and settled the Estremadura. The current settlement data cannot distinguish the various scenarios.

Interaction

Enclave Settlement predicts an independent settlement of agriculturalists. As such, initial interaction with local populations would have been low, particularly if Mesolithic populations were sparse. During the course of a few years (instantaneous in archaeological terms), it is likely that enclaves would have begun to interact and exchange goods with surrounding populations. There would, however, be items such as grain storage vessels, that would have application only to enclave economies and so would not have been exchanged until foragers adopted domesticates. There could also have been some interaction between an enclave and its parent settlement.

Table 4.1 *Numbers and types of transported ceramic vessels at Aude valley early Neolithic sites in southern France*

Archaeological site	Cardial vessels	Number transported	Other imported vessels	Number transported
Grotte Gazel	3	2	17	1
L'Abri Jean-Cros	–	–	7	7
Peiro Signado*	4	0	7	0
Camprafaud	2	2	16	7
Balma Margineda	1	1	10	0
Leucate-Corrège*	3	2	6	0

Note:
* Counts represent decorative groups, not individual vessels.

Individual Mobility models predict a high degree of local interaction and hence artifact movement as innovations traveled through an extant socio-economic network. As novel artifacts, technologies, and domesticated foods moved among existing territories through established relationships, transmission of innovations could have been quite rapid. Adopted items would have been only those that would fit the evolving strategies of the indigenous populations. One would also expect widespread movement of objects to have been accomplished through local mechanisms such as down-the-line exchange (Renfrew 1977). Infiltration would probably have operated only at a regional level, without mechanisms for the regular long-distance movement of objects.

Studies of ceramic production and distribution have been few in number, but have shown a high degree of transport of Early Neolithic pottery in southern France (Barnett 1989) and the existence of ceramic transport in Portugal (Barnett 1992). Not surprisingly, the classic distinctive wares such as Cardial pottery are most frequently exchanged. In southern France, distribution studies revolved around petrographic analyses of assemblages from six Early Neolithic sites in and around the Aude valley in Languedoc (Barnett 1989). The numbers of vessels transported to these sites varies, but classic Cardial decorated vessels are frequently found as imports, whereas "epi-Cardial" wares are much less likely to have been imported (Table 4.1). Single Cardial vessels from Balma Margineda (Barnett 1989) and Caldeirão in Portugal (Barnett 1992) had pastes totally different from locally produced vessels and from local clays and sedimentary lithologies.

The classic widely distributed wares such as Cardial and Impressa types show the widest distributions, possibly as far as 100 km. On the other hand, epi-Cardial vessels with more regional design motifs show small-scale movement. Epi-Cardial vessels show movement across the Aude valley or between upland and coastal areas. Fig. 4.3 shows patterns of Early Neolithic

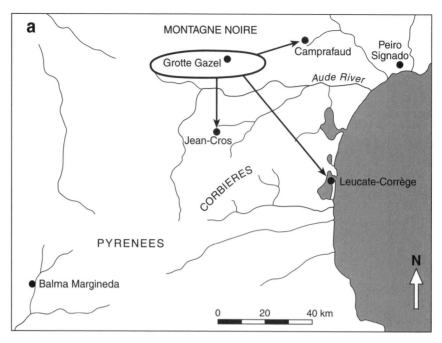

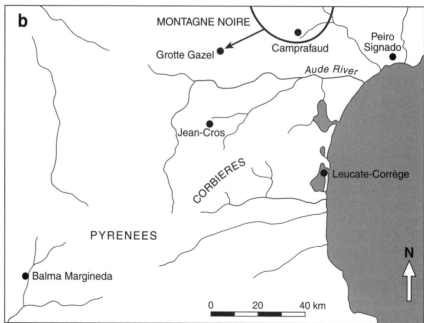

4.3   Maps of the Aude valley showing the transport vectors for Early Neolithic pottery originating from (a) the southern flank of the Montagne Noir, (b) the eastern flank of the Montagne Noir, (c) the Têt valley and (d) the Hérault valley.

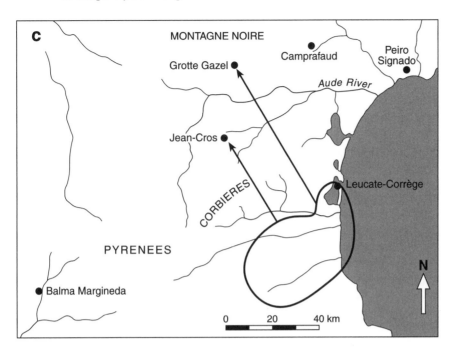

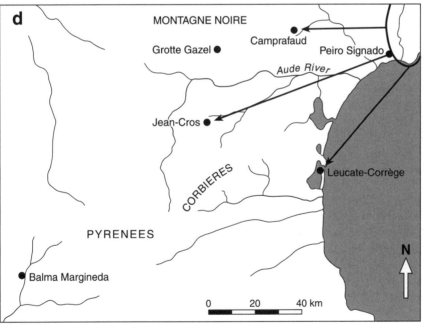

ceramic movement within the Aude valley from four source regions identified by petrographic analysis of vessels and clays: the southern flank of the Montagne Noir, the eastern flank of the Montagne Noir, the Têt valley, and the Hérault valley. The vectors of ceramic transport are along the coast, among inland areas, and between drainages, as well as highland–lowland transport predicted by seasonal transhumance. Peiro Signado is an interesting contrast in this regard; its assemblage appears to be all locally made but is either derived Cardial (cardium decoration, but not the distinct Cardial ware) or highly diagnostic Impressa wares that typically occur much farther to the east, notably at Arene Candide in Liguria. Whether Impressa was exchanged or a widely copied style is still an open question, but it has been established that the Peiro Signado Impressa was locally produced.

These patterns appear to demonstrate two scales of interaction: broader-scale transport of a few very well-defined ceramic types, and more localized transport of more regional and varied decoration ceramics (Barnett 1990b). Presumably the larger-scale movements relate to long-distance exchange of the particular wares (possibly as aggregates of shorter transport events) and the smaller-scale movements relate to inter-community interaction possibly associated with local exchange across territorial boundaries or as part of a settlement system.

The transport of ceramic containers begs the question of what, if anything, may have been transported in them. Cardial and other distinct and widely exchanged wares may have had value that transcended any contents; however, epi-Cardial wares may have been used to carry, store, and prepare foods such as animal products or the domesticated grains that begin to appear across the western Mediterranean at this time. There are, however, only rare examples (such as at La Draga, noted above) of storage containers in the Early Neolithic. Vessel types in the earliest Neolithic appear to be designed for food preparation or serving. Ceramics would also have easily improved the ability of populations to transport and process non-domesticated plants such as seeds or nuts, enhancing their role as surplus or exchanged good.

Exotic polished stone tools (Ricq-de Bouard and Fedele 1993) and obsidian (Tykot 1992) began to appear in the Early Neolithic and their incidence increased in later periods. Some antecedents exist in the form of Mesolithic shell exchange in Provence (Rähle 1980) that has clear links to central Europe (Jochim, this volume) and this pattern continues into the Neolithic (Gallay *et al.* 1987). Presumably, domesticated plants and animals that began to appear at this time could easily have been included, though their exchange cannot be documented archaeologically, as part of the interactions surrounding the movement of pottery, stone, and other items.

These documented interactions amongst Early Neolithic societies are most consonant with Individual Mobility in that the first phase of ceramic production appears to be associated with distinct, highly decorated wares that are exchanged over long distances. Exchange prior to the Neolithic, a proposition of Individual Mobility (or at least prestige exchange adoption models), is supported by evidence of Mesolithic shell exchange in Provence. Long-distance and local interaction could also be logically expected in Enclave Colonization, although it is not explicitly required. The wide exchange of ceramics, such as Cardial wares, ground stone, and obsidian, indicates that they could have carried symbols and been valued objects utilized in Individual Mobility situations such as prestige exchange and that such exchange may have been pervasive, if occasional, across the western Mediterranean. The evidence of long-distance exchange indicates that Infiltration, a regional phenomenon, may not have a predominant role in the spread of agriculture in the western Mediterranean although it may have accounted for local dynamics.

Technology

One implication of Enclave Colonization is that an enclave artifact assemblage was a more or less standard agricultural tool kit whose technology was transported to the enclaves as part and parcel of their economy. Ceramics in this situation would have had important roles as food storage, transport, processing, and serving vessels (Arnold 1985) in support of these expansive economies. Some vessels could have been decorated for ceremonies or for exchange with local foragers. Lithic assemblages would have had reduced percentages of formal tools intended for hunting and more tools related to food, particularly plant, processing. The Individual Mobility model would predict the initial use of pottery, a novel technology, in the socio-political realm. Early ceramics associated with novel foods could have been exchanged and heavily decorated to convey identity (e.g., Weissner 1984). Increasing experimentation and investments in domesticated plants and animals acquired through trade would have resulted in increasing sedentism and a reduction in portable lithic tool kits (Parry and Kelly 1987). In Infiltration situations, limited innovations arrived in a new area and the manufacture and use of these items were probably modified to meet existing socio-economic needs and strategies.

Examination of Early Neolithic ceramic production and distribution has already contributed a great deal to the understanding of technologies of production and use and patterns of interaction. Certain wares, such as *le Vrai Cardial* pottery (Guilaine 1976) and Impressa pottery, have distinctive technologies of manufacture. In the case of Cardial pottery, grog tempering met technological and aesthetic requirements. Tempering was necessary so the clay body would have sufficient strength to form walls. The use of grog for tempering gave the appearance of an untempered, smooth surface that was enhanced by burnishing. This technology is noted for Cardial pottery in both southern France (Barnett 1989) and Portugal (Barnett 1992, Masucci 1994), demonstrating a uniformity in the manufacturing technology of these specific wares over a surprisingly large area. Other impressed wares in southern France show a wide variety of clay and temper processing and mixing that are more site specific and include the addition of sand, crushed rock, and organics (Barnett 1989). Although early, these wares were neither simply nor hastily constructed, and tempering appears to have been a central feature of a generic technology "recipe" (Barnett, in press).

Vitelli (1995) reports ceramic vessel construction in Early Neolithic wares in Greece, specifically slightly uneven surfaces (Fig. 4.4) even in highly burnished wares, that she attributes to occasional and individual pottery manufacture as opposed to production as part of regular or specialized manufacture. These patterns are also noted in western Mediterranean Early Neolithic wares (Barnett 1989). As noted above, Early Neolithic ceramics were not produced in great quantity and may not have played a regular utilitarian role. The extensive use of techniques such as burnishing are quite labor intensive (Vitelli 1995), and demonstrate a great deal of investment in each vessel.

Decorations are quite specific and complex and there is evidence of particular design motifs being copied, for example Cardial-like decoration by other means presumably in the absence of cardium shells for a tool. In some cases, holes were drilled through decorated pots (Fig. 4.5), compromising their utility for storage or holding liquids but possibly not as ritual items (Barnett 1989, in press). As later perforated ceramics were used to process milk products, it is possible that these early perforated vessels performed a similar function at a smaller scale. Decorative and technological studies suggest that ceramic production was occasional, possibly event based, involving individual manufacture of vessels whose decoration played a significant role, possibly in symbolic terms.

It is not clear whether the changes in lithics that occur in the Early Neolithic are due to changes in populations, subsistence activities, or spheres of interaction. Changes in lithic reduction sequences and formal tools that occur with the Early Neolithic have been interpreted as resulting from new populations (Zilhão, Binder, both this volume). The assertion that changes in these *chaînes opératoires* are necessarily related to new populations may be premature. Such changes are noted during the Mesolithic from the Sauveterrian to the Castelnovian in the Mediterranean (Binder, this volume) and elsewhere in Europe (Rowley-Conwy 1986:22) without suggestions of colonization. Explicit comparisons of Epipalaeolithic to Mesolithic and Mesolithic to Neolithic flaked stone technologies, particularly in the style of formal tools, are not yet available to the degree that might identify population changes.

Changes in lithic technology can, in any particular instance, be due to changes in available lithic resources, shifts in food procurement or processing strategies, or changes in mobility. Shifts in quality and type of flint

4.4   An Early Neolithic vessel from Furninha, central Portugal, showing slightly
uneven form and surface.

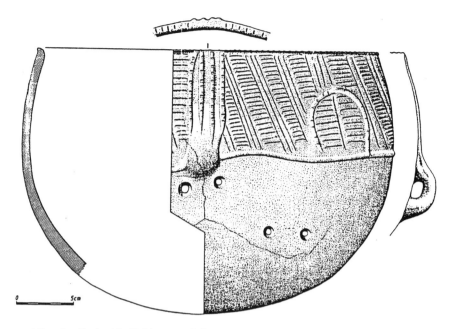

4.5   An Early Neolithic vessel from Grotte Gazel showing post-production drilled holes (drawing by J. Coularou).

are noted from Mesolithic to Neolithic at the sites of Oullins and Fontbrégoua (Binder, this volume). The Early Neolithic saw the introduction not only of domesticated animals and plants but also of tools, specifically pottery (see Arnold 1985) and ground stone (Ricq-de Bouard and Fedele 1993), that would have necessarily altered food procurement and processing strategies regardless of how they arrived. These, no doubt, would have had an impact on the manufacture and use of lithics. In addition, reduced mobility can of itself result in changes in reduction sequences. Mobile populations would have preferred more portable, prismatic, tool kits whereas sedentism in general tends to result in more varied tasks, more varied tool kits, and the use of amorphous cores and more expedient reduction sequences (Parry and Kelly 1987). This is precisely the pattern we see in the replacement of Castelnovian prismatic *chaînes opératoires* with "Impressed culture" flake-based technologies (Binder, this volume). Certainly flake-based technologies existed from the Lower Palaeolithic to the age of metals, and both blade- and flake-based technologies would not have been difficult to master by Holocene foragers, farmers, or pastoralists as the need arose.

In sum, Early Neolithic ceramic production in the western Mediterranean shows the occasional production of labor-intensive, highly stylized wares, extensive paste modification, and broad similarities in technology and decoration of distinct wares such as Cardial pottery. These types of technological patterns are more diagnostic of an Individual Mobility situation, where ceramic vessels and ceramic technology filter into a frontier of existing relationships, than of the importation of a production oriented tool kit through enclave settlements. Lithic technology patterns reinforce our understanding of the Early Neolithic as a period of increasing sedentism. Future examination of stylistic attributes of formal tools may provide some insight into the behavior of the populations that utilized them.

Conclusions

Is there any way to move forward past the blockade of untestable assertions of monolithic colonization versus adoption toward a better understanding of the transition to agriculture in the western Mediterranean? Evaluating the evidence through a series of regional frontier models has provided a better handle on the range of interactions that may have taken place during this transition. As noted above, radiocarbon dating of the earliest Neolithic sites has shown an apparently rapid spread of pottery and ovicaprids from Italy to Portugal. Unfortunately, at a local scale, dating alone cannot provide the resolution to distinguish any sort of punctuated process that may have occurred at this critical juncture.

Subsistence data so far are too meager to provide any sufficient information on the agricultural transition in any region of the western Mediterranean. Dietary evidence from osteological remains may prove the only way to evaluate subsistence changes among transitional populations but sample sizes, with notable exceptions such as the Muge middens, may be too small for any detailed assessment. Likewise, settlement data, owing to historical excavation biases and Holocene coastal inundation, present limits to interpretation. We can acknowledge the gaps in our information on settlement patterns, but we cannot yet fill those gaps. Better survey or the investigation of submerged sites may help resolve some settlement issues.

The realms of interaction and technology currently offer the greatest opportunity to identify processes that may have operated across the agricultural transition. In a dynamic frontier situation, each model discussed above has implications for patterns of artifact technology and interaction that are unique and that would have left material evidence. Changes in lithics and lithic technology may relate to mobility, resource utilization, and food processing yet do contain stylistic elements. Studies of lithic typologies need to isolate aspects that relate to mobility and technological requirements of hunting, foraging, and food processing from stylistic components that describe social group. The study of stylistic aspects of formal tools, such as surface flaking patterns on projectile points, may in the future provide more insight on changes in the social aspects of hunting across the agricultural transition. Changes in the stylistic investment of formal tools, such as projectile points for example, may indicate changes in the social organization of those activities that would have implications for the nature of the Neolithic transition.

Ceramics, as a constructed technology, are complex and contain a great deal of technological and decorative information. Current evidence of the production and distribution of Early Neolithic ceramics shows patterns of high investment in manufacturing and decoration, significant exchange, a production schedule that appears to have been occasional and event based rather than predominantly part of a production based economy, and a generic technological style. This evidence, despite an absence of temporal resolution and complete settlement data, seems currently best to support models of Individual Mobility among existing populations rather than the establishment of far-flung agricultural enclaves or small-scale infiltration as the principal mechanism for the spread of agriculture. The Mediterranean was quite diverse during the agricultural transition and there were probably many processes at work that involved the movement of people and items that are beyond our ability to grasp. Future research should expand on the examination of interaction among transitional agricultural groups using a variety of lines of evidence and attempt to investigate more fully the dietary changes associated with the arrival of the earliest Neolithic.

Acknowledgments

This chapter was greatly improved by insightful comments from Douglas Price, John Shea, João Zilhão, and Marek Zvelebil. All errors, omissions, or misinterpretations are my own doing.

5

Mesolithic and Neolithic interaction in southern France and northern Italy: new data and current hypotheses

Since the 1980s, the theories related to the emergence of agropastoral economies in Europe have witnessed a significant evolution. During the 1970s, researchers pursued a hypothesis of independent processes of Neolithization that might explain the variability seen in the European Neolithic. In other terms, this allowed them to consider the introduction of production processes as a natural phenomenon, induced by "global change" at the end of the Pleistocene. For many reasons developed below, this framework of investigation is now obsolete, and partisans of a polygenic model have become rarer (Olaria 1988). We must effectively agree with the idea that there is no explicit tendency through the Holocene hunting economies in western Europe to move toward more and more production. If we consider the entire Mediterranean area, we must note that true Neolithization processes are largely confined to the Near East.

In consequence, this chapter will focus on the different processes of interaction between Mesolithic and Neolithic groups in southern France and northern Italy (Fig. 5.1). These phenomena are the consequence of the spread of the Near Eastern Neolithic. Theoretically speaking, this spread goes through significant transformation along the way and these modifications are not at all clear. Several important themes come out in this examination.

1 Mesolithic and Neolithic entities considered here show a clear geographical and ecological disjunction, reflecting the settlement of a colonizing Neolithic population along the coast. It is still difficult to give a precise and credible picture of the radiocarbon data. This is due, first, to the variable accuracy of measurement of samples submitted for radiocarbon analysis, and second, to the limits of intercomparison of the results provided by different methods and laboratories (Baxter 1990).[1] It is also necessary to keep in mind the fact that major ecological changes have taken place in this area

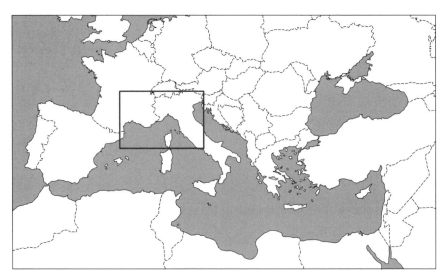

5.1   The location of the study area in the Mediterranean basin (M. Clatot, CNRS-
CRA).

over the last ten millennia. These changes in the Mediterranean shoreline are particularly significant. There is no doubt that, because of the coastal focus of the first Neolithic spread, many data related to the very first immigrants are today submerged and missing. Thus, primary interaction processes escape us.

2 Information on the transition from Mesolithic to Neolithic is generally nowhere to be found. Only a few cases exist, often prone to a fierce criticism of primary data. When the information survives this criticism, these transitional phenomena generally turn out to be late, partial, and/or peripheral. This fact is seen clearly through the study of the material culture, and notably in the lithic technology, that constitutes, when all is said and done, the only common products available for study from both periods.

3 Consequently, one may today see that interaction between the Mesolithic and the Neolithic was not linear and did not constitute a major mainspring for the spread of Neolithic practices in Mediterranean Europe. Therefore, this spread is probably the consequence of economic and social trends that were inherent in Neolithic ideology.

Preamble: the Sauveterrian complex, 9000–6500 BC
Cultural aspects

During twenty-five centuries, which coincide with the whole Near Eastern pre-pottery Neolithic, southern France and northern Italy were inhabited by the Sauveterrian cultural complex. In this area, the distribution is continuous from the Pyrenees to the Alps and beyond. Kozlowski (1976) has shown the significant role of this complex in western Europe. The characteristic lithic industry is made up of narrow bladelets and microliths (and often hypermicroliths). Segments and triangles are shaped by abrupt direct retouch. This industry is clearly linked to the Upper Palaeolithic and Early Epipalaeolithic traditions, and, most particularly in the eastern region, to the Final Italian Epigravettian. Evolutionary tendencies may be seen in projectile point morphology (progressive elongation, loss of truncation symmetry, decline of the microburin technique). An early stage with isosceles triangles or segments can be distinguished from a later one, called "Montclusian," marked by an abundance of elongated scalene triangles with three retouched sides. These patterns have been particularly well discussed in the recent work of N. Valdeyron (Barbaza *et al.* 1991). The homogeneity of the Sauveterrian complex in southern France and northern Italy is most pronounced during the development of the Montclusian facies, some time between 7000 and 6500 BC.[2]

The variability of these lithic assemblages is rather limited, although specific techniques are seen in different regions, particularly during the early stage. This technology is not dependent on raw material availabilty. The microlithic nature of the industries, based on a shaping retouch, and not on the predetermination of artifact morphology, allows it to adapt to any situation, including a great scarcity of lithic resources. Such adaptability in the Sauveterrian technical system may partly explain the fact that the entire territory was occupied.

This cultural homogeneity at some point reaches stagnation. The slow replacement of projectile types emphasizes the integration and the stability of these groups. The variability of the equipment, particularly the ratios of "common" tools to projectiles, seems first a functional one, in connection with the relative importance of hunting activities and the processing of secondary animal products. Technical, and probably functional, differences can be seen in the different lithic equipment that belongs to a base camp or to a more specialized site (Philibert, in Barbaza *et al.* 1991).

In the middle Rhône valley,[3] symmetrical trapezes with an abrupt retouch appear in a Sauveterrian context, with a basic blade technology produced by direct percussion. These trapezes are sometimes twisted and are not produced by the microburin technique. This phenomenon seems to extend further to the west as well.[4] It is also known that different trapeze types, whether symmetrical or not, are sometimes present in an earlier context.[5] Thus, the presence of trapezes may be considered as a latent phenomenon, present in the entire Sauveterrian complex (and, in any case, from the end of the Palaeolithic). On the other hand, the development of a new and more complex prismatic blade technology within the Mesolithic technical system should be considered as a most important change.

Economic aspects
The Sauveterrian economy was a highly diversified and predacious one, with both specialized and generalized hunting of large game in the

lowlands,[6] as well as hunting and collecting in the forests,[7] small ruminant hunting in the mountains,[8] and predation in aquatic environments as well.[9] This was a broad-spectrum economy, probably based in a series of complementary settlements. It will be important, indeed, to clarify the details of the eighth- and ninth-millennium BC economies compared to the latest Paleolithic.

The pronounced variation in faunal assemblages contrasts with the relative homogeneity of the tool kits; in the early Holocene, however, it is difficult to distinguish patterns related to human decisions in exploitation from environmental and climatic changes. Such natural changes do exist, and their effects are perceptible in such situations where constraints are more strongly expressed. For example, the intense exploitation of the Dolomite highlands may be explained by the progressive expansion of the forest, pushing the ibex toward the higher-elevation meadows. Subsequently, during the climatic optimum, the decline in resources from the mountains may be linked to the shrinkage of the alpine pastures in relation to the forest (Bagolini *et al.* 1983).

Numerous seed samples, composed of many pod plants from this period and this cultural complex, are well known from Fontbrégoua cave in central Provence (Courtin 1975) and Abeurador cave in western Languedoc (Vaquer *et al.* 1986, Marnival 1988). These finds have led investigators to suggest that intensive gathering was practiced, and in some cases to argue for a kind of protoagriculture. Such a pattern would have supported to some extent Zvelebil's (1986a, 1994a) concept of availability. In a previous paper (Binder 1989), however, I have suggested that humans were not responsible for these accumulations; the seeds, associated with numerous bird bones, were a result of animal activity. These seeds were actually from toxic (as *Lathyrus*) or inedible plants. But more importantly, at both Fontbrégoua and Abeurador, they were always associated with pigeons, granivorous birds whose resistance to lathyrism is an acknowledged fact.[10]

J. Wattez (1992) has clearly demonstrated this pattern in a micromorphological study of both deposits.[11] The anthropogenic remains associated with Mesolithic settlements alternated with deposits produced by the activity of birds, containing no cultural remains. The avian accumulations were characterized by plant litter and lenticular deposits high in phosphate whose micromorphological structure has shown evidence for the feces of granivorous birds.

Thus, the Sauveterrian protoagricultural pattern, inferred from an underestimation of taphonomical problems, appears to be incorrect.[12] The possibilities for substitution, in Zvelebil's concept, are unlikely in terms of plants, as there was a lack of available species. Moreover, one cannot observe any subsequent amplification of such phenomena in the later Mesolithic. This means that the Sauveterrian people are better described as hunters, rather than hunter-gatherers, because gathering is not seriously evidenced.

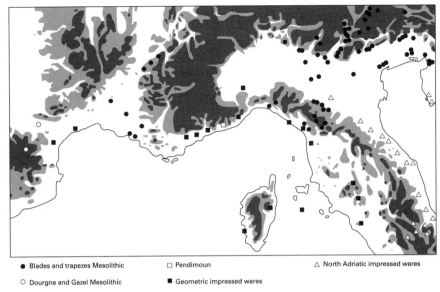

● Blades and trapezes Mesolithic   □ Pendimoun   △ North Adriatic impressed wares

○ Dourgne and Gazel Mesolithic   ■ Geometric impressed wares

5.2   Location of Blade and Trapeze late Mesolithic sites and earliest Neolithic sites, showing their distinct distributions (M. Clatot, CNRS-CRA).

The definitive rejection of the use of wild sheep in a Sauveterrian context must be included with these observations:[13] in fact, the remains found were not sheep, but ibex (Poplin *et al.* 1986). Increasingly, the Sauveterrian seems to be clearly excluded from the processes that led finally to food production.

Cultural interaction in the western Mediterranean, 6500–5250 BC

Current evidence therefore suggests that the Sauveterrian complex is not involved in the transition to agriculture. There are two clearly distinctive traditions related to the spread of the Neolithic: the Castelnovian Blade and Trapeze Mesolithic and the Mediterranean Impressed Ware Neolithic (Fig. 5.2). Relationships between these two groups are quite different depending on the area under consideration.

The Impressed Ware tradition first appears around 6000 BC in Liguria, through a facies marked with Adriatico-Balkanic influence. It quickly becomes widespread along the Tyrrhenian coasts between 6000 and 5600 BC, with two geometric facies. One of them is probably the origin of the classical Cardial culture that expands between 5750 and 5500 BC in Provence, Languedoc, and the Rhône valley. In the Cardial fringe, outlier groups, with more or less evidence for a food-production economy, exhibit a lithic tradition closely linked to Neolithic patterns. An important question is whether these were Mesolithic groups in transition under a Neolithic influence, or if they were functional facies directly linked to Neolithic areas.

In eastern Provence and along the Riviera, the Castelnovian has never been identified, in spite of numerous excavations in caves and rockshelters and at open-air sites, on the coast as well as in the hills (Biagi *et al.* 1989, Binder 1989). The absence of this Mesolithic has to be considered an archaeological reality and not in the slightest as a research deficiency. In this area, there was probably no interaction, for there was probably only one actor.

The Castelnovian tradition began *c.* 7000–6500 BC in a Late Sauveterrian context, with the appearance of a standardized blade technology and trapezes made from prismatic bladelets. This culture is well established between 6250 and 5500 BC in the Rhône basin, and between 6000 and 5500 BC in the Po basin. The links between the Castelnovian and the other Blade and Trapeze industries that occupy the continental regions of France are not well understood.

To the east, this tradition does not seem to exhibit any marked evolution; one may suggest a strong cultural inertia. The Padan region was to be the scene of a late Neolithization, expressed above all through a "ceramization," particularly after 5250 BC, under many influences (Bagolini 1990). This process was marked by the rise of a patchwork of local groups, showing different interaction processes with one another, and incorporating specific elements within the Neolithic system without simultaneously adopting all of its characteristics.

Further to the west, Castelnovian dynamics appear stronger. It becomes possible to define different stages on the basis of material culture. This evolution stopped around 5500 BC with the spread of the Cardial culture. Tardocastelnovian facies continued in some refuges. The Castelnovian tradition perhaps continued to the west with the rise of the Roucadourian Neolithic.

The Blade and Trapeze Castelnovian tradition

The origin of the Blade and Trapeze complex, and particularly prismatic blade technology, poses a problem whose history is important from the perspective of this volume. It is indeed possible that these *chaînes opératoires* had been intrusive within Sauveterrian technology. Perhaps, then, we are able to speak reliably of adoption and acculturation processes in this special case,[14] since specific Sauveterrian techniques continued in Castelnovian assemblages.

In any case, it would be premature to isolate the origin of this Blade and Trapeze phenomenon in space, and very rash to link it with the Neolithic spread.[15] As I do not perceive any instant intellectual benefit from invoking the Upper Capsian from the Maghreb or the Initial Neolithic from

Greece, I would merely like to point out that, at that time, such a phenomenon is highly developed in the central and western Mediterranean.

The development of the new blade and trapeze techniques began probably before 6500 BC. The two regional groups identified at that time — Rhodano-Provençal and Padan — subsequently follow very different cultural trajectories. In this sense, the appearance of the new blade technology is in sharp contrast to the homogeneous distribution of Epipalaeolithic and Sauveterrian settlements. Asymmetric trapezes associated with a prismatic blade technology are found in the highlands (Trentino, Vercors) as well as in the alluvial plains (Rhône, Po).

Lithics may also be involved in decisions regarding settlement location for Mesolithic people. It is quite clear that the Castelnovian shows a preference for zones where flint is more abundant and suitable for complex blade technology: the Tuscan Apennine, the Verona region, the Marseilles littoral, the Vaucluse, the Vercors, etc. The qualitative increase observed in the technology involved in blade production is a common characteristic among the diverse elements of this complex and probably is responsible for the location of Castelnovian settlements close to the major sources of raw material.

After the appearance of these new techniques, the eastern group in the Po basin shows a strong conservatism between 7000 and 5500 BC.[16] This conservatism, linked to the appropriateness of the technical system for natural resource management, probably retarded the spread of the Neolithic in northern Italy. Clear adoption processes there occur very late under several cultural influences.

On the other hand, the western group in the Rhône basin shows evolutionary dynamics in great typological diversity, reflecting *a priori* a kind of adaptability. Nevertheless, one must note that this adaptability does not readily lead to the adoption of the Neolithic, neither material equipment nor domesticated plants and animals. Alternatively, if one argues that such an adoption might have occurred, it is also necessary to explain that it did not leave the least trace of the preceding Mesolithic system. And this seems opposite to what we know from any duly recorded situation of acculturation. The simplest hypothesis is therefore that there was generally no acculturation of the Mesolithic people by the Neolithic ones. This situation is very similar to that recorded in the Iberian peninsula.[17]

The Rhodanian Castelnovian

The Rhodanian group was identified in the 1950s by M. Escalon de Fonton (Escalon 1956) at La Font-des-Pigeons shelter at Châteauneuf-les-Martigues (Fig. 5.3). It was first regarded as a coastal facies of the Tardenoisian. Recent research, however, has shown that this culture occupied both the low and middle Rhône valley[18] and the highlands of the Alps (Bintz *et al.* 1995).[19] In western Languedoc, a group including the sites of

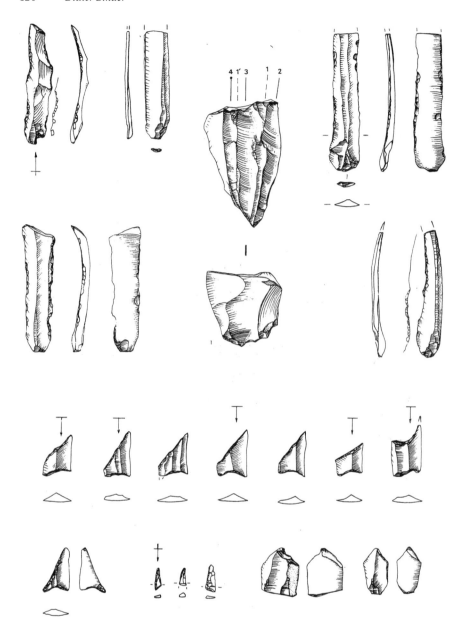

5.3   Castelnovian blades, core, geometric microliths, and microburins from
La Font-des-Pigeons rockshelter, Châteauneuf-les-Martigues, Bouches-du-
Rhône, France. (After Binder 1987.)

Dourgne and Gazel (Guilaine *et al.* 1993) may reasonably be considered a facies belonging to the same cultural complex. Moreover, a direct relationship may exist between the Castelnovian and the Blade and Trapeze Mesolithic observed in the Massif Central.[20]

The Early Castelnovian is dated between 6250 and 5850 BC in the lower Rhône valley (Châteauneuf) and between 6600 and 6000 BC in the middle Rhône valley (Mourre-du-Sève). In the Vercors, earlier dates have been obtained for the Pas-de-la-Charmatte shelter (7030–6490 BC); these dates are comparable with the determinations for the Early Castelnovian in the Trentin (Romagnano III, layers AB1–2, 6990–6470 BC), but the style of the trapezes in the Vercors is closer to the Late Castelnovian.

The Middle and Late phases may be dated between 5950 and 5500 BC. At this stage, the complex may have been practically contemporaneous with the first phases of the Ligurian Neolithic (Impressa) and even with the later phases (classical Cardial with banded decoration). The dates are such that interaction between the Rhodanian Castelnovian and the Early Neolithic was certainly possible.

Since the Early phase, the Rhodanian Castelnovian included different types of triangular or trapezoidal projectiles made from regular prismatic blades[21] truncated with the microburin technique. The lithic industry also includes burins and, when the *chaînes opératoires* are complete, some denticulates shaped with successive Clactonian notches. Small endscrapers with a flat retouch on the dorsal face are also present. Many blades were utilized without any shaping retouch. The technical characteristics of the projectile points are diagnostic (Binder 1987).

1 The vertical crossed retouch of the major truncation is easily produced by pressure. This retouch was observed on one-third of the Castelnovian projectiles from Châteauneuf and Montclus, but, toward the end of the sequence (i.e., Montclus layers 8–10), it is generally associated with a flat direct retouch superimposed on this vertical crossed retouch. In any case, this flat-over-crossed retouch is present during the Early phase; this thinning technique was used at places such as Dourgne or Gazel, where the poor quality of the raw material did not permit standardized knapping; the thinning retouch makes up for this flaw.

2 The inverse flat retouch, obtained by pressure from the minor truncation, is also distinctive. It appears on one-third of the geometric projectiles, and it increases in frequency from the Early phase. Quite obviously, the frequency of this retouch increases as the minor base of the microliths decreases in size, and of course it exhibits a high incidence in the Late phase with the abundance of triangles. The technical characteristics indicate that most of these trapezoidal or triangular microliths were notched points for piercing arrowheads. This hypothesis is confirmed by the observation of impact marks found equally along both the long truncation and the long base.

3 The remnants of the *piquant-triédre* facet on the major truncation may be unique to the Early Castelnovian at Châteauneuf (layer C8) and Montclus (layers 13–14); this trait brings the Early Rhodanian Castelnovian closer to the Padan Castelnovian, and they may have a common origin.

Recent work on this subject in Provence has revealed a phenomenon already known in northern Italy; I refer to the existence of a Sauveterrian component within Early Castelnovian industries. Hypermicroliths are well represented within these tool kits, but at a much lower frequency than in the previous Sauveterrian. The hypermicroliths in the Sauveterrian are more irregular in size and shape as well. Current knowledge about the Late Castelnovian (i.e., Montclus layers 8–10, or Molières) is not sufficient to assert that the Sauveterrian narrow bladelets and microliths had completely disappeared by this stage. Crenate shells of *Mytilus* or *Unio* are among the most peculiar elements of the material culture. The Rhodanian Castelnovian also contains striking artistic work. A pebble with engraved geometric decoration driven into the ground at La Font-des-Pigeons in Châteauneuf must be related to the pebbles driven into a circle at Montclus (layer 13d). The uses of red ochre are well developed.

Dourgne style

The Pyrenean Piedmont contains some Mesolithic settlements (e.g., Dourgne, Gazel, Buholoup) that belong to a parallel Castelnovian facies. The recent publication of Dourgne (Guilaine *et al.* 1993) shows that layers 7–9 were characterized by an industry including blades, asymmetric trapezes made from prismatic blades, and numerous triangular projectiles with a flat direct or bifacial retouch, stemming from an abrupt crossed truncation.

Trapezes at Dourgne decrease from 50 to 17%, and triangles or triangular points increase, along with a strong increase in the flat inverse retouch and in the flat-over-crossed truncation (the latter rising from 20 to 30%). The remaining tools include some small flat end-scrapers and prismatic bladelets with irregular, wear-induced retouch. The bone industry includes a few antler tools.

The proportions of different projectile points allow us to compare the Dourgne style with the latest stages of the Rhodanian Castelnovian,[22] where trapezes reach no more than 25%, and where the crossed retouch attains between 10 and 20%. One or two flat, bifacially retouched items at Dourgne (layer 7) may constitute a specific Neolithic element. This facies, that dates *c.* 5960–5550 BC at Dourgne (layer 7),[23] is found at Montclus around 5950–5530 BC.

A similar situation is known in the Grande Rivoire shelter (Vercors) (Bintz *et al.* 1995). Layer B2 contains asymmetric trapezes associated with a triangle with flat direct-over-crossed retouch. This layer is well defined in the stratigraphy between a Sauveterrian layer with symmetric trapezes (B3) and a post-Cardial or peri-Cardial layer full of Mediterranean cutting arrowheads (B1). Layer B2 provided a very late radiocarbon age, around 5000–4700 BC, hardly credible even if we accept that the "Tardocastelnovian" continues for a long time.

Castelnovian cultural remains in the western Mediterranean Neolithic

The distinctive Castelnovian lithics are not found in the Impressed Ware culture west of the Alps (Binder 1987). Isolated Neolithic assemblages that show characteristics which may be inherited from the Castelnovian are found in some special facies corresponding to one of the Roucadourian forms (Roussot-Larroque 1977). In the Aveyron, a region quite distant from the Impressed Ware distribution, good examples are provided by the industry at Combe Grèze (Costantini and Maury 1986) and at Les Usclades (Maury 1997), probably associated with original ceramics, showing a clear cultural mixing. However, the nature of such evidence has to be more precisely evaluated. Many recent excavations in southwestern France have shown in fact that deposits containing such mixed assemblages had been disturbed by significant post-depositional processes, so that the associated industries may not be reliably employed (Kervazo and Mazière 1989).

In the same vein, the debates about La Hoguette also come to mind (Jeunesse *et al.* 1991), where a similar phenomenon may be present. Even in that case, we need more evidence to establish a clear association between La Hoguette pottery and the Mesolithic blade and trapeze assemblages.[24]

The Padan Castelnovian

The eastern Castelnovian group is well known both from stratigraphic excavations with associated radiocarbon dates and from numerous surface finds. It is distributed through the Triestin Karst and along the Venetian coast,[25] and throughout the Trentin and the Eastern Alps,[26] the Lombardian Prealps,[27] and the Tuscan[28] as well as the Emilian[29] Apennines. Looking at this assemblage, and particularly at the stratified sites, it is quite clear that the industry is basically a Sauveterrian one, with the addition of a variable number of typical trapezes with a right-handed major base and, most of the time, an unretouched *piquant-triédre* facet. But the primary difference here too is the introduction of numerous bladelets produced either by careful indirect percussion or by pressure. No significant trend has ever been detected in the evolution of the eastern Castelnovian until around 5500 BC, except for a possible increase in trapezes, which show a greatly reduced technical diversity. The eastern Castelnovian also includes a bone industry, especially barbed harpoons, and striking art work as well. The use of ochre is well known.

The Padan Castelnovian may be distinguished from the Rhodanian primarily by a strong cultural inertia reflected in the stagnation of tool kits after 6500 BC (even 7000 BC) to 5500 BC. During the emergence of Impressed

Ware in Liguria and later in the Rhône valley, between 6000 and 5500 BC, this Mesolithic is largely represented in Trentino and Emilia.

Ceramics and the Padan Castelnovian

The primary elements of the Neolithization in the eastern Castelnovian are limited to a few sherds in the Romagnano 3 shelter (layer AA, 5470–5290 BC). However, these sherds cannot be ascribed to any identified culture and may be local intrusions from the upper layers.[30] On the other hand, from around 5250 to 4750 BC, throughout northern Italy, diverse Neolithic groups demonstrate very clear genetic links with eastern Castelnovian technology, as seen at Gaban, Fiorano, Vho, and Fagnigola.[31] Among these groups, Gaban is the one that presents the clearest affinities with the Impressed Ware culture,[32] while Fiorano seems to exhibit the most pronounced changes, particularly with the widespread diffusion of ceramics among the other north Italian groups. Such a "ceramization" process in the Mesolithic (Bagolini 1990), however, seems to occur under many influences, including, according to Bagolini, the Late Northern Adriatic Impressed Ware, as well as the Linearbandkeramik[33] (but see Bogucki, this volume) or the Latest Starcevo.[34] Many typological items suggest that some relationship existed between the Padan groups and the Ligurian Middle Neolithic, also dated between 5250 and 4750 BC.[35]

The appearance of the Neolithic leads everywhere to the final disappearance of the hypermicrolithic Sauveterrian tools,[36] an increase in long rhomboids, and the appearance of a peculiar lateral burin, probably borrowed from the north Adriatic Impressed Ware, to be used in plant processing.[37] For the most part, however, the style of the industry does not change. The Po basin is a particularly good example of the nature of a late cultural integration, with clear technological transfers and minimal modifications of existing economic structures (Biagi 1990).

The Neolithic came last to the Padan region, where the Blade and Trapeze Mesolithic shows the greatest inertia and primary settlement, at least 750 years after it appeared in Liguria, where the Middle Neolithic cultures followed the primary Impressed Ware Neolithic at the same time. This implies essentially that the presence of a significant and consistent Mesolithic population acted as a brake on the spread of the Neolithic; obviously, this acknowledgment is antagonistic to the view that the Late Western European Mesolithic is a Proto-Neolithic phenomenon. The presence of a resistant Mesolithic group in the Pô basin shows in the same way the discontinuity of the areas occupied by the Impressed Ware, respectively in the north of Dalmatia and on the northwestern coasts of the Adriatic.

The subsequent appearance of the Neolithic in this traditional Mesolithic area was accompanied by an impressive amount of prestige goods, which are generally rarer and less diversified in Impressed Ware cultures. In Sammardenchia (Ferrari and Pessina 1996), as well in the Frioul, the spectrum of raw materials is quite extraordinary: obsidian from Lipari Island and the Carpathians, alpine stone axes, Veronese flint, Fiorano imported pottery. We may thus suggest that Mesolithic people had succumbed more readily to symbolic pressure and changes in status differentiation than to the benefits and facilities of food production.

Hunting economies and the Castelnovian tradition

No actual remains indicate that the Castelnovian had anything to do with gathering, with the exception of some pistachio nuts at Châteauneuf (Marnival 1988). In any case, the Castelnovian economy shares many aspects with the Sauveterrian. In Italy, precise data come from Romagnano and Pradestel in the Trentin and from Azzura cave in the Triestin Karst. At Azzura (layers t1–t3), the economy seems to be based on forest hunting, primarily for red and roe deer, secondarily for wild pig and carnivores. Sea fishing is well attested, as is shellfish and/or tortoise collecting. However, tortoises are less common here than in the lower Sauveterrian layers, where freshwater fish are also abundant. Birds are present also in both layers (Cremonesi *et al.* 1984).

In the Aurine Alps and the High Adige, mountain sites were used by Castelnovian hunters for seasonal hunting of caprids, such as ibex, and secondarily for cervids (Biagi 1990). In this region, there was no comprehensive acquisition of the Neolithic but rather the irregular adoption of one or another techniques. Agriculture was less developed here. The Early Padan Neolithic, although quite late in time, remained largely a hunting economy, retaining the pattern of Castelnovian conservatism. Hunting activities were also significant later in this area during the fifth millennium BC, as seen in the faunal assemblages of the Square Mouthed Pottery.

In France, data concerning the Castelnovian economy come mainly from Châteauneuf and from the Mourre-du-Sève shelter. At Châteauneuf, freshwater fishing and shellfish and egg collecting were important activities. Hunting involved rabbits for the most part, along with the usual species such as aurochs, wild boar, and red deer. Bird species from open environments were also quite common (Courtin *et al.* 1985, Desse 1987).

At Mourre-du-Sève, the latest excavations have shown that, throughout the Mesolithic, hunting was focused on aquatic environments, as seen in the large quantities of fish and turtles. At this site, terrestrial species are low in number (Helmer, pers. comm.). At Montclus, river fishing has also been recorded. In the Vercors and Chartreuse, as in Italy, high elevation settlements are probably linked to seasonal hunting activities. In Dourgne, with the exception of *Ovis/Capra* discussed below, hunting mainly involved a kind of ibex, wild boars, and carnivores, and, to a small degree, cervids and chamois (Guilaine *et al.* 1993).

According to current research, in northern Italy as in southern France the Castelnovian economy seems to be based upon a logistic complementarity between coastal or open plain settlements on the one hand and mountain pastures on the other. But the outstanding fact obviously in the lowlands is the importance of aquatic habitats over terrestrial ones. This is a specific feature common to the principal cultures of the Mesolithic Blade and Trapeze complex in northern Italy as well as in southern France and the Iberian peninsula.[38]

Sheep, cattle, and the Mesolithic economy

The presence of sheep in Late Mesolithic assemblages may be evidence for interesting patterns of interaction, if one accepts that sheep and goat belonged to the cultural package of the Neolithic and came without question originally from the Near East (Poplin *et al.* 1986, Helmer 1992). This question, however, remains difficult to resolve since uncertainties always arise in the taphonomic and/or archaeozoological data.

Three faunal assemblages, Azzura cave, Châteauneuf, and Dourgne, are of relevance to this question. At Azzura cave, Wilkens (1992) has identified 8 bones of *Ovis* in layers t1–t3, to which we must add 4 bones of *Ovis/Capra* in layer t1, in a total of 103 faunal remains. Ducos (1958) counted 66 *Ovis* bones in Castelnovian layers at Châteauneuf in a total of 189 determinable bones (excluding rabbits). At Dourgne, Geddes counted 6 *Ovis/Capra* bones (and 18 caprins) in layer 7 and 22 *Ovis/Capra* bones (and 110 caprins) in layer 8, in respective totals of 196 and 504 identifiable bones. One of the suggestions made for the site of Dourgne was acquisition of sheep by way of exchange or theft from the surrounding Neolithic communities.

At Azzura cave, Wilkens ascribes the presence of sheep to intrusions from the overlying ceramic layers. At Châteauneuf, the excavations of Courtin in 1979 in the Castelnovian levels did not produce evidence of Mesolithic sheep (Helmer 1984). On the other hand, a precise faunal inventory of each layer is not available from the earlier excavations at the site, which would have allowed us to deal with the question of Neolithic intrusions as has been previously suggested (Binder and Courtin 1987); there was, however, no question about Ducos' identifications at the site.

The stratigraphical situation is certainly the clearest at Dourgne. On the other hand, the distribution of different sheep bones, compared to those of ibex and chamois, is most surprising. If one considers the richest layer (designated as 7), *Capra pyrenaica* and *Ovis/Capra* are represented so unevenly that a clear complementarity may be emphasized in this situation. Thus, the absence of sheep phalanges is difficult to explain in view of the abundance of ibex phalanges. In the same way, the absence of ibex cranial remains is not clear, considering that cranial remains constitute half of *Ovis/Capra* bones. Under such circumstances, it is not easy to claim that there was no analytical bias,[39] unless we envision some different methods of procuring the two species of animals.

With the notable exception of Châteauneuf, the low rates reported for medium and large mammals[40] would seem completely to invalidate the possibility of cattle herding.

Another kind of phenomenon is recorded in the mountains of the Vercors. In layer B2 from the Grande Rivoire shelter, Chaix observed the bones of a domestic ox in a very late Castelnovian context (5000–4700 BC), without any sherds or other specifically Neolithic features (Bintz *et al.* 1995). This situation may be compared to the generally late diffusion of the Neolithic through the eastern Castelnovian as rare evidence of the adoption of Neolithic traits in the western Alps.

The Impressed Ware tradition in the western Mediterranean (Fig. 5.4)

The western Mediterranean Impressed Ware culture has to be considered fully Neolithic, possessing the skills necessary for ceramic manufacture and stone or bone polishing, and basing its subsistence on food production. For the chipped stone industries also, this complex is distinctive in both style and the techniques involved in manufacturing. The main questions today concern the architectural practices.

Basically, this tradition bears the marks of both differentiated and centralized mechanisms for territorial management. Through specific economic and social mechanisms – such as long-distance exchange and specialization – this system permits the reduction of discontinuities in natural resources. This pattern also permits the development of a larger scale of territorial appropriation and resource control. Such a pattern does not seem to have an equivalent in previous periods. In this sense, the so-called Neolithization seems to be of a different order than a "simple" modification of subsistence base or technological customs that have sometimes been perceived as diagnostic. This phenomenon of the spread of the Neolithic then appears much more connected with the ideological sphere, and thus more closely related to the symbolic revolution that might have brought about, or at least initiated (Cauvin 1994), the origins of the Neolithic in the Near East. The question of interaction between Mesolithic and Neolithic, as far as I am concerned, may also be examined in this light.

One of the important current questions concerning the Neolithic spread from east to west regards remodeling phenomena (Guilaine 1987). Starting from the idea that the Impressed Ware facies existed within the Early Neolithic of the Syro-Palestinian and Cilician coastal settlements (e.g., around 6500 BC at Ras Shamra), it must be asked if genetic links do exist between this culture and western Mediterranean Impressed Ware culture and, if so, what was the route of the spread, and the role of the Balkans, of Apulia, and of the islands in remodelling this Neolithic. Given the biological

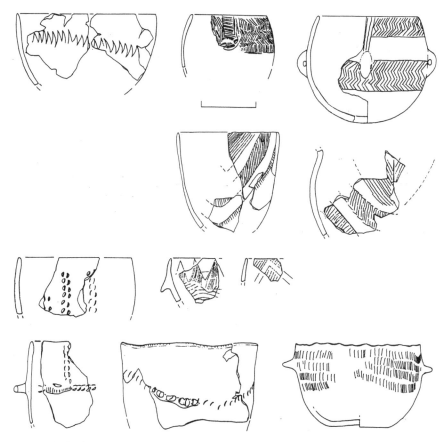

5.4   Principal pottery styles from the Early Impressed Ware Neolithic in south-ern France. From bottom to top: Impressa from Pendimoun rockshelter (Castellar, Alpes-Maritimes), Geometric Impressa from Peiro Signado (Portiragnes, Hérault), Geometric Cardial from Pendimoun; Classical Cardial from Fontbrégoua cave (Salernes, Var) and from Lombard cave (Saint-Vallier de Thiey, Alpes-Maritimes). (After Binder 1995.)

links that relate western and eastern sheep, goats, wheat, and barley, it is probable that the two cultural entities are also related.

Even quite recently, the features of the western Cardial, taken as a homogeneous entity, were such that one could accept the idea of an insular remodelling (Lewthwaithe 1986b). The recent identification in a strati-graphic context of an earlier Ligurian stage, closer to some Adriatic facies than to most of the Tyrrhenian ones (Binder *et al.* 1993), means that one must question a linear diffusion from east to west as in the oversimplifica-tion of Ammermann and Cavalli-Sforza (1984). For this purpose, let us keep in mind the uncertain evolution of sailing in the Mediterranean[41] as well as its antiquity.[42] The westward spread of the Neolithic along the Mediterranean shore occurred through very different mechanisms than those that governed the spread of Danubian Linearbandkeramik through continental Europe (Bogucki, this volume). Thus, the identification of Neolithic remodeling centers in the central and western Mediterranean remains elusive.

Recently, I tried to reclassify the different Impressed Ware styles in southern France and Liguria. New stratigraphic data made it possible to separate more precisely an early entity (Impressa) from a later one (Cardial). This stylistic classification was then used as a template for the Gulfs of Genoa and Lions (Binder *et al.* 1993, Binder 1995). In my opinion, a consequence of this study is that the Impressa and the subsequent geometric groups only occupied territories absent of any Castelnovian settlement. Mesolithic people were focused on acquatic environments, and this pattern is unknown in the Impressed Ware period. These observations support the idea of a complete disjunction in the distribution of the two complexes.

Impressed Ware in Liguria

The Ligurian area exhibits very strong cultural dynamics marked by rapid cultural change from the end of the seventh and the beginning of the sixth millennia BC. This situation makes Liguria a nuclear zone for Neolithic deployment toward the northwestern Mediterranean.

Early Impressa

New data have been obtained from excavations at the Pendimoun shelter (Binder *et al.* 1993). This rockshelter, near the Franco-Italian border, contained thick deposits including an entire series of Early Neolithic layers with two major episodes: (1) in the upper layers, Early Cardial deposits with characteristic geometric Tyrrhenian features (Basi, Filiestru, and Pienza style) and (2) in the lower layers, Impressa deposits with pottery showing affinities with the Adriatic and Balkan regions. The interface between these episodes is marked by several individual burials equipped with grave markers.

The data collected to date suggest that the Tyrrhenian cultures, with geometric pottery decoration, were the starting point for the spread of the Neolithic toward the west, whether from the Guadone stage (Tinè and Bernabo Bréa 1980), or through an insular filter (Lewthwaite 1986b, Vaquer 1989). The evidence from the site of Pendimoun shows that an earlier diffusion took place. Perhaps this phenomenon is closer in age to Rendina 1 (6220–5660 BC) and at least contemporaneous with Trasano 1, according to new AMS measurements at Coppa Nevigata and Trasano (5950–5660 BC) (Guillaine *et al.* 1991) and according to a new AMS date for the Early Cardial levels at Pendimoun itself (5960–5600 BC).

Pendimoun Impressa pottery includes many burnished pots as well as pots decorated with discontinuous impressions made with a small tool (small shell, fingernail, etc.) and arranged in bands or panels. Handles generally have a vertical perforation. Shapes are diverse and open, often with quite regular decoration of the lip and the flat bottoms as well.

The rare lithic assemblage is composed of some blades (unretouched, used as sickles, truncated, and transformed into points with an abrupt retouch). Cutting projectiles are triangular with a flat retouch, sometimes equally covering both sides or more classically on the dorsal side over an inverse, abrupt retouch, according to the feature that was to become standard in the Rhodano-Provençal Cardial industries. At the moment, this Pendimoun Impressa style is unique in the area.

Geometric facies

The geometric facies following the Pendimoun Impressa Neolithic are composed of two different styles, with rare borrowing. Radiocarbon dates place both these styles between 5980 and 5600 BC.[43] Their distributions slightly overlap, and it is easier to work with the hypothesis of competition between two distinctive groups than chronological succession. Geometric Impressa is characterized by stab-and-drag decoration, with a few features inherited from the Pendimoun phase, such as burnished wares, pinched decoration, and flat bases. It is quite common in Liguria,[44] and present in the Maritime Alps and the Central Var,[45] and also in the Hérault.[46] To the south, this style is well represented near Elba,[47] and is present in Latium, although in an uncertain context.[48] The marked geographic distribution of the pottery is emphasized by the presence of Liparian obsidian at Portiragnes (Guilaine and Vaquer 1994), Liparian and Sardinian obsidian at La Pollera, and Sardinian obsidian at Arene Candide (Thorpe *et al.* 1979).

The Geometric Cardial, decorated with cardium shell, is present in Tuscany, in Corsica and in Sardinia.[49] Some cultural features are attested in various contexts near Elba, in Latium and in Sicily.[50]

The lithic industry is similar in both the Impressa and Cardial geometric: symmetric trapezoidal projectiles with a flat direct retouch over inverse truncations, or with a direct abrupt retouch, long borers or points on blades, blade truncations (e.g., Arene Candide), microdenticulated sickles (e.g., Pendimoun). Green stone adzes are present, albeit rare, at Pendimoun (perhaps made of imported eclogite, yet to be confirmed) and at Caucade (perhaps made of local stone), but they are numerous at Arene Candide, closer to some of the major raw material sources (Ricq-de Bouard *et al.* 1990).

The Impressa and Geometric style economy

A major question concerns the relative importance of hunting, herding, and farming in Early Impressed Ware contexts. Few data are currently available for these phases. The Pendimoun Impressa economy appears to have been fully Neolithic, based on the fact that both cultivation and herding are present (Binder *et al.* 1993). The cereals present are *Triticum dicoccuum* and *Hordeum* var. *nudum*. Herding involved domestic caprids of an as yet unidentified species. The deposits also contain evidence for a geo-archaeological facies indicating the penning of small ruminants. Shellfish collecting is also recorded.

Our information on food production is no more precise for the next stage. Wherever it has been studied, that is to say at Pendimoun and at Arene Candide (Rowley-Conwy 1991, Tinè 1986), the fauna shows the predominance of domestic cattle. At Pendimoun, sheep are more numerous than goats; this fact connects this facies to the Apulian ones (Vigne and Helmer 1994). Traces of penning exist at Arene Candide as well as at Pendimoun, according to geo-archaeological analyses (Binder *et al.* 1993, Courty *et al.* 1992). Contextual studies of Geometric Impressa deposits revealed discreet penning episodes and the incorporation of the cave in a complex agro-pastoral system. Hunting is very rare at Pendimoun, and much more common at Arene Candide, with some cervids present. In both places, shellfish collected along rocky coasts have a significant place (C. Cade, pers. comm.); sand shark fishing is a speciality at Arene Candide (Tinè 1986). At Pendimoun, during this period, cultigens included *Hordeum*, *Triticum dicoccum*, and also *T. aestivum-compactum*.

Development of the Neolithic in the Rhodanian and Provençal regions

Zoned Cardial Ware

This facies contains round-bottomed pots with a zoned decoration of cardium impressions, arranged into horizontal bands and delimited by linear impressions. Most of the time, the small rounded handles have a horizontal perforation. It seems that this style evolved by the progressive loss of geometric attributes such as the descenders, that suggest stylistic links between the Early Zoned Cardial Ware and the Geometric Cardial Ware. From the early stage (Châteauneuf, Baratin, Fontbrégoua), the Zoned Cardial Ware was composed of bulky pots with relief modeled features. It is clear that the only stylistic links are with Geometric Cardial and not at all with the earlier Impressa.

The lithic industries are better known than in previous phases (Binder 1987, Binder *et al.* 1993). They are based upon a blade technology using indirect punch percussion on smooth platforms. The first stages of the *chaîne opératoire* produced thick flakes, made into end-scrapers and denticulates. Prismatic blades were used as knives and sickles, or retouched as end-scrapers, truncations, points, and cutting arrowheads. Projectile points were often triangular in the early stage, trapezoidal in the later one, generally made with a flat, direct retouch over an inverse abrupt preparation. Polished green stone adzes and a rich bone industry are present everywhere.

This industry is unrelated to the Castelnovian at Châteauneuf and at Montclus, particularly in terms of blade technology and arrowheads. At Châteauneuf, transition layers between the Mesolithic and Neolithic are difficult to define. The sequence does allow us to suggest important geological changes in the initial Neolithic. Therefore, the presence of a very few intrusive elements between later Mesolithic and younger Neolithic layers cannot be opposed to the fact that reliable Cardial tool kits exhibit no obvious link with the Castelnovian. This Cardial facies may be dated with high probability around 5750–5500 BC.

Peri-Cardial

Recent studies at Dourgne (Guilaine *et al.* 1994) show that the Mesolithic (layers 9 to 7) lies beneath an assemblage (layer 6) with Neolithic affinities in the lithic artifacts (cutting arrowheads with flat, direct-over-abrupt inverse retouch) and associated with undecorated pottery. According to radiocarbon measurements, this facies may be dated around 5560–5240 BC, while the subsequent post-Cardial occupation lies around 5490–5325 BC. This facies from Dourgne 6, peri-Cardial according to Guilaine (Guilaine *et al.* 1994), is contemporaneous with Montclus 5–7 and identical with regard to the lithics. One may relate them to Jean-Cros shelter in the Aude valley, as well as to Couffin 1–F and Balme Rousse in the Vercors. The latter is dated between 5260 and 4540 BC. All the sites apparently are peripheral to the primary zone of Impressed Ware diffusion. All these lithic assemblages are exclusively composed of Cardial projectile points, without any Castelnovian examples. All of them apparently spread over the time and are peripheral to the primary zone of Impressed Ware diffusion. These assemblages show varying degrees of Neolithic affiliation: ceramics and cattle at Dourgne 6 as at Jean-Cros, only cattle at Couffin and Balme Rousse, and probably nothing more than Neolithic projectiles at Montclus. But it must be noted today that only the late dates allow us to relate these manifestations to the Cardial Ware, rather than Impressa.

It is necessary to ask whether these sites represent groups in transition to the Neolithic or whether they are different functional aspects of the Neolithic, expressing the complexity of agro-pastoral logistics (Beeching 1995, Binder 1991). It is not unreasonable to favor the second hypothesis, in view of the total absence of evidence for interaction between Mesolithic and Neolithic complexes.

Economic and social structures of the Cardial and the Neolithic in the western Mediterranean

Current information on economic and social structures comes almost exclusively from the classical and late phases of the Early Neolithic, and particularly the Zoned Cardial Ware period. A pattern has been suggested by data from Courthézon-Le Baratin, Salernes-Fontbrégoua, Le Garn-Baume d'Oullins, and Saint-Vallier-Lombard cave.

This hypothesis suggests a hierarchical organization in three zones: (1) in the center, social concentration around stable open-air settlements oriented toward agriculture and pastoralism, (2) in the surrounding circle, seasonal settlements oriented toward herding and hunting, and (3) in a second circle, most specifically hunting and probably the location of pioneer settlements.

The importance of hunting in the faunal assemblages is a measure of economic and social distance, rather than cultural distance, to major centers. At Courthézon-Le Baratin (Fig. 5.5), preliminary studies by Courtin and Poulain have indicated that domestic animals comprised close to 80% of the fauna. Grinding stones here might have been related to domesticated plants, and several sickles have been found. Arrowheads are less than 27% of the retouched tools. At Fontbrégoua, geo-archaeological, taphonomical, and archaeozoological studies (Brochier 1990, Courtin 1975, Helmer 1984) show that the cave has been used since the Cardial as much for a sheep pen as for a place for processing hunted animals. Taphonomic studies clearly show that the site had been used to prepare meat for storage and not for immediate consumption. Agriculture is attested by a series of cereal grains, but sickles are not in use, as they were recycled for other activities. Wild animals comprised between 40 and 60% of the fauna in the different Cardial layers. Projectile points reached 39% among the retouched tools. At the Lombard cave, wild animal remains are close to 90%. In this situation, domestic animal remains might be considered provisions brought in prior to hunting activities. Hunting seems to have had the same purpose as at Fontbrégoua: to obtain supplies of meat. This was hunting by food producers, very different from the previous Sauveterrian pattern. There are no traces of agricultural activities. Geometric projectiles reach 50% among retouched tools.

Among these different settlements, cultural unity is evidenced by the similarity of lithics, bone tools, and shell, tooth and stone ornaments, as well as the pottery. This cultural unity is further demonstrated by the fact that all these settlements belong to the same exchange networks. At Fontbrégoua as at Lombard, Echallier has distinguished both local pottery production and imports (Binder *et al.* 1993, Echallier and Courtin 1994). At both sites, almost identical pottery has been made both with local sandy clays with carbonate and with non-local materials derived from the alteration of crystalline rock. Such diversity has also been observed in the Pendimoun Impressa and the Caucade Geometric Impressa.

One of the strongest features that link these different economic states as a whole is certainly the special pattern of raw material distribution and the long distances implied by the exchange. Several examples show

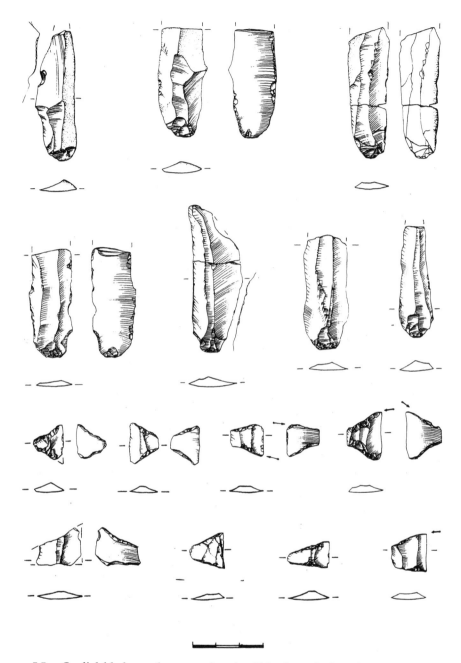

5.5   Cardial blades and geometric microliths from Le Baratin, Courthézon, Vaucluse, France. (After Binder 1987.)

long-distance diffusion of stone axes, adzes, or rings of green alpine stone: eclogites from the Italian Alps at the Lombard cave, Gemenos-La Grande Baume, Fontbrégoua, and Courthézon; jadite at Fontbrégoua, Châteauneuf, and Escanin; glaucophane metabasite from the Durance basin at Leucate-Corrège (Ricq-de Bouard 1987). Above all, Cretaceous honey flint from Vaucluse used in chipped industries is present in different forms depending on the distance from the source. Near the core area, the site of Courthézon-Le Baratin shows complete *chaînes opératoires* wasteful of honey flint, and subsequently a low proportion of blades. Raw material had been collected at the source. This situation is obviously different from the neighboring Castelnovian site at Mourre-du-Sève, where the knappers used only whole local resources, including tertiary flints and diverse flint pebbles.

In the second circle, various situations are observed, depending on the availability of local resources. (1) Oullins is located very close to a source of tertiary tabular flint. The latter had been exploited by the Castelnovian people at Montclus. In the Oullins Cardial layers, one can observe, on the one hand, a knapping of local material producing a lot of thick flakes and some very irregular blades and, on the other hand, many regular prismatic blades made of Cretaceous honey flint from the best examples of indirect percussion. Here particularly, it is clear that the import of finished honey flint products was not a technical necessity; rather, the reasons for its spread belong in the social arena and to cultural identity. (2) At Fontbrégoua, far from any suitable flint sources, finished honey flint products were also found, including prismatic blades and tools largely made from blades. (3) In the third circle, some data are provided by the site of Lombard, where blade removals had been made using a different *chaîne opératoire*. Imported flint is the most abundant here, especially Cretaceous honey flint, more than 150 km from its sources. In this situation, honey flint probably circulated as preformed cores. This honey flint exchange also reached western Languedoc (Gazel cave) at the end of the Early Neolithic (Vaquer 1989).

Such a pattern of distribution also points to disruptions in the organization of technical processes, in time as well as in space. It suggests indirect procurement and redistribution via central places. Down-the-line exchange, perhaps the mechanism for the distribution of individual prestige goods,[51] does not operate easily for flint, a complete and utilitarian material to be used expediently.

Skill is another internal difference that must be considered among Cardial assemblages. At Oullins, for example, it is clear that the quality of blades made from local flint is lower than the quality from honey flint punch technology. This difference raises the question of incipient craft specialization from the beginning of the western Mediterranean Neolithic in terms of raw material procurement and control. This situation was to be significantly amplified during the Middle Neolithic, particularly during the Chassean complex (Binder and Perlès 1990).

All these patterns emphasize the impression that mobility among Early Neolithic groups was a structural phenomenon, corresponding to a specific means of appropriating territory (Binder *et al.* 1993). This mode, involving a gradient of interaction from the center to the periphery of the Neolithic territory, favors the implementation of exchange processes at the margin between hunters and farmers, specifically through the distribution of prestige goods (ornaments, polished stones, or even projectiles).

The evidence from northern Italy suggests that this mode of interaction may have been strong enough to establish cultural complexes intermediate between the Cardial and Danubian areas (cf. above and note 24). This differentiated management of geography and resources that emerges more from ideology than from functionality allows us to distinguish between the western Mediterranean Neolithic spread and the expanding front of Danubian farmers (Jeunesse 1990). It is well known that the Linearbandkeramik economy invested very little in hunting activities (around 5% of the faunal remains are of wild species). Hunting was probably more important for acquiring raw materials as skins and antlers, rather than meat (Arbogast and Jeunesse 1990). Such differences may also explain the stronger influence of the Mediterranean farmers on hunter groups living in central and northern France.

Some current questions

The complexity of the Cardial economy, in terms of hunting vs. food production, could be interpreted as a result of a complete acculturation between Neolithic (i.e., Impressa) and Mesolithic hunters, abandoning all the distinguishing marks of their material cultures. There are probably two good reasons to reject this hypothesis. First, Impressa (e.g., at Arene Candide) has no link with Mesolithic, and a diversified and complementary economy with farming, herding, and hunting. Second, Castelnovian predation focused on fish and other aquatic resources; these activities were not so important in the Cardial economy.

What are the origins of this mixed system?

In central and southern Italy, the situation is still not clear. Recently studied villages show a great predominance of herding relative to hunting, in the same proportion as in the Linearbandkeramik (Vigne and Helmer 1994, Wilkens 1992). That observation led several authors to suggest that the Apulian Neolithic was quite similar to eastern Mediterranean prototypes, notably Thessalian examples. However, the discovery of Impressa cave settlements with a pronounced hunting emphasis in southern Italy (Latronico, Continenza) may document a similar pattern of economic diversity (subject to a clear affirmation of their Neolithic affiliation). Moreover, one must keep in mind that the Mesolithic in central and southern Italy is not well known; it is not currently possible to identify a

Mesolithic tradition which can be compared with the Rhodanian or Padan Castelnovian in scale.

In Dalmatia, the evidence from the sites of Zelena Pecina or Crvena Stijena (Benac 1957b) may correspond closely to economic processes in the Provence Cardial, rather than to the acculturation process of Mesolithic groups.[52] Further to the east, it is difficult to evaluate the role of hunting in the Neolithic economy. In Thessaly, the optimal pattern of territorial exploitation probably remained an exclusively agropastoral one, based on the low physiographic contrasts present (Perlès 1989). But it is likely that the Thessalian pattern does not match that of the Peloponnese or Franchthi Cave. In this area a pattern similar to the Mediterranean Neolithic, adapted to the management of varied environments, might be suggested.

In the nuclear zone of the Near East itself, economic differentiation appeared before the end of the Pre-Pottery Neolithic B, with, on the one hand, sedentary villages where ceramics were developed and, on the other hand, a pastoral nomadism on the desert margins (Stordeur 1993). It is not yet clear whether both these patterns were functional facies of the same culture, or whether they marked the beginnings of a major cultural, economic, and social dichotomy.

Given the fact that the mechanisms that led to the spread of the Neolithic from the nuclear zone are poorly understood, one must admit that many questions remain unanswered. New fieldwork will particularly focus on the characterization of settlement sites and the architectural transitions. Nevertheless, we have a great deal more information today, compared to twenty years ago, in southern France and northern Italy.

Acknowledgments

I would like to thank G. B. Rogers, J. Gaudey, and O. Gazenbeeck for their cooperation and help in translating this chapter, and T. D. Price for his critical comments.

Notes

1 The radiocarbon dates cited here are expressed in calendar years (BC cal.) with an interval of two standard deviations.
2 Fontfaurès superieur, Montclus, Pey de Durance, Fontbrégoua, Lombard, Pradestel F, Vatte di Zambana.
3 At Montclus, layers 15–16, dating around 6620–6010 BC and earlier in the Mourre du Sève (layer Cinf around 7540–7300 BC; the latter date has not been confirmed.)
4 Rouffignac, layer 5a (Rozoy 1978).
5 The Early Sauveterrian at Fontfaurès layer 6 (Barbaza *et al.* 1991), the Sauveterrian at Gramari, or the Late Magdalenian at La Gare de Couze (Rozoy 1978)
6 Aurochs at Sénas-La Montagne; aurochs and horse at Gramari.
7 Hunting for cervids and collection of *Cepaea nemoralis* at the Lombard cave.

8 Alpine meadows in the Adige.

9 Fish, water tortoise, and freshwater shells at Montclus, Fontbrégoua, Romagnano, Pradestel, and Azzura.

10 Poisoning caused by *Lathyrus* consumption.

11 Fontbrégoua, layers 54 and 63; Abeurador, layer C4FA.

12 The question of a cultivated lentil in the Mesolithic layers at Franchthi Cave has been rejected by J. Hansen (in Anderson 1992).

13 Previously suggested from the investigations at Gramari.

14 That this is a rare case should be underlined here.

15 In spite of the previous reservations concerning the absence of data from coastal settlements during the Mediterranean Holocene.

16 Thus, the disappearance of Sauveterrian projectiles is attested only by the appearance of pottery.

17 Cf. Zilhão (1993 and this volume), Juan-Cabaniles (1990) and Bernabeu (1996).

18 Châteauneuf in the Bouches-du-Rhône; Montclus in the Gard; Chinchon, Le Mourre du Sève and Les Molières in the Vaucluse.

19 Bouvante, Machiret, Lachau, Jaboui, Pas de la Charmatte in the Drôme; La Grande Rivoire in the Isère.

20 Particularly Longetraye in the Haute-Loire (Rozoy 1978).

21 These are bladelets with a generally faceted butt for which I have suggested a pressure technique (Binder 1987).

22 Montclus, layers 10 to 8.

23 Measurement obtained from Cepaeae shells.

24 Association suggested by the excavations at La Cure shelter in Baulmes (Switzerland) and to the north at Bavans (Doubs).

25 Grotta Azzura, grotta Benussi, and grotta della Tartaruga.

26 Mainly Romagnano III, Pradestel, Gaban; secondarily Stufles in the Aurine Alps, and Frea III and IV in the Dolomites.

27 Fienile Rossino, Iseo.

28 Isola Santa 4ab.

29 Passo della Comunella.

30 Layer T4 attributed to the Gaban Group.

31 Particularly Sammardenchia in the Frioul.

32 Notably, the links with the north Adriatic Impressed Ware whose presence is observed in the Romagna.

33 The contested Notenköpfe decoration on Gaban and Fiorano ceramics, Meissel at Sammardenchia.

34 Incised and scratched pottery, as well as a bicephalic figurine in the Vho group.

35 Ligurian scratched Ware at the Arene Candide (layer 13) and at La Pollera (ensemble II).

36 This phenomenon is quite clear at Sasso di Manerba, on the banks of Lake Garda.

37 The use of Ripabianca burin is not directly linked to agricultural activities (D'Errico 1988).

38 Cf. Zilhão in the same volume.

39 We must recall here the reservations expressed by Helmer (1992) in regard

to the supposed presence of sheep in the Spanish site of Cova Fosca (Olaria 1988) and concerning the risks of confusing sheep and chamois.

40 8% at Azzura; 3–4% at Dourgne; 30% at Châteauneuf.

41 Remember Ulysses' journey!

42 The peopling of Corsica by sea took place more than a millennium before the spread of the Neolithic in the Tyrrhenian Islands.

43 La Pollera layers 21–24, 5970–5630 BC; Arene Candide layer 14 around 5980–5630 BC; Pendimoun Geometric Cardial layers around 5960–5600 BC.

44 Arene Candide, Arma dell'Acqua, and secondarily La Pollera.

45 Caucade at Nice, Grasse-Sans Peur, Sainte-Catherine at Figanière.

46 Peiro Signado at Portiragnes; Grotte des Fées at Leucate.

47 Giglio is a not well-defined context.

48 La Marmotta (Fugazzola Delpino *et al.* 1993)

49 Pienza, Basi, and Filiestru.

50 Giglio, La Marmotta, and L'Uzzo respectively.

51 Polished alpine stone axes and adzes, and shell ornaments.

52 It is very difficult to identify specific Neolithic features at Zelena Pecina or at Crvena Stijena.

6

From the Mesolithic to the Neolithic in the Iberian peninsula

Introduction

As exemplified by the open air art and habitation sites of the Douro basin, particularly those recently found in the Côa valley (Zilhão *et al.* 1997), the interior of Iberia knew an important settlement throughout the Upper Palaeolithic. However, after the end of the Ice Age, *c.* 11,400 calendar years ago, it shows no sign of human occupation (with the exception of some areas in the upper Ebro basin) until 5000–4500 BC, when the protagonists of such occupation are already clearly defined agro-pastoral societies. This pattern seems to be a genuine reflection of regional settlement history. Many systematic survey projects in both Portugal and Spain (Iglesias *et al.* 1996, Arias 1997) have consistently identified large numbers of late early Neolithic (epi-Cardial or Impressed Ware) sites all over this vast area, as well as, particularly in Portugal, fair numbers of Upper Palaeolithic sites. None, however, is of Mesolithic age, and there is not a single typical Cardial sherd.

The abandonment of the Iberian interior in the early Holocene may be related to the particular geographic and climatic characteristics of the peninsula. Unlike European areas north of the Pyrenees where Mesolithic occupation of the hinterland is well documented, the Meseta lacks important lakes, and the rivers, even the largest (such as the Douro, the Tagus, and the Guadiana), are susceptible to drying out in the summer. Therefore, aquatic resources, which were critical in known Mesolithic instances of successful settlement of mainland Europe (as along the Danube), may have been subject to periodic failure in interior Iberia. In contrast, last glacial settlement had been possible because, at the time, the main rivers were permanent (melting of the winter snow and of the ice accumulated in the glaciers of surrounding mountain chains kept them running throughout the dry season) and the open steppe landscapes provided year-round pasture for large herds of grazing animals. Once forests covered the land and the herbivore biomass was drastically reduced, fish and other aquatic foods may not have been there in the amount and with the reliability necessary to compensate for such a decrease.

An alternative explanation would be that the absence of Mesolithic sites in the Meseta results from the operation of as yet unidentified biases in preservation or research. It must be noted, however, that the absence of human settlement from vast regions with a very dense tree cover is known in other parts of the world and that, in this regard, the Iberian pattern is not unique and does not necessarily require special qualifications. In fact, a similar situation has been observed in southwest Tasmania, where, after many thousands of years of occupation throughout the last glacial period, its inland valleys were abandoned by humans at the beginning of the Holocene, when they were colonized by a very dense temperate forest, and remained that way until the time of contact (Porch and Allen 1995).

In any case, the implication is that the problems of the transition from early Holocene hunter-gatherer adaptations to food-production economies in the peninsula can only be approached from a perspective based on the archaeology of coastal areas. This chapter will begin with a brief overview of the empirical evidence and conclude with some observations regarding its relevance for the interpretation of the process of agricultural expansion in southern Europe. The location of the primary sites mentioned in the text can be found in Fig. 6.1 and more detailed maps of the cultural geography of Portugal during the transition from the Mesolithic to the Neolithic are given in Fig. 6.3.

North of the Cantabrian mountains

The Mesolithic–Neolithic transition in northern Spain has been recently reviewed by Arias (1991, 1992, 1994a, 1997) and González Morales (1992, 1996). Both agree that the areas defined by the present-day national-administrative boundaries of Asturias, Cantabria, and Euzkadi, which extend southwards into the Douro and the Ebro drainages, are not appropriate units of analysis, and that the process should be considered from the perspective of natural geography. Their analytical framework, therefore, is restricted to the ecologically differentiated, narrow coastal strip and the adjacent northern slopes of the Cantabrian mountains, which isolate the study area from the rest of Iberia.

Pottery is present in this region from *c.* 4900 BC, as demonstrated by an AMS radiocarbon date on charcoal collected in the fabric of a sherd from the cave site of Los Canes (Arias 1992) – 5865 ± 70 BP (AA-5788). From this, Arias argues the presence from that time on of the rest of the Neolithic package as well. He bases this inference on two main arguments: that elsewhere in Iberia pottery and domesticates appear simultaneously; and that

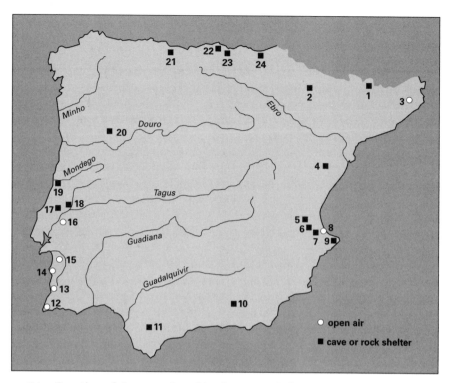

6.1   Location of sites mentioned in the text: 1. Balma Margineda, 2. Chaves, 3. La Draga, 4. Fosca, 5. Cocina, 6. Sarsa, 7. Or, 8. El Collado, 9. Cendres, 10. Cariguela, 11. La Dehesilla, 12. Cabranosa, 13. Fiais, 14. Vale Pincel, 15. Sado shell-middens, 16. Tagus shell-middens, 17. Almonda, 18. Caldeirão, 19. Buraca Grande, 20. Buraco da Pala, 21. Los Canes, 22. Pico Ramos, 23. Arenaza, 24. Marizulo.

pottery and ovicaprids do appear at the same time in the relevant stratigraphic sequences of the region, particularly those excavated at Marizulo and Arenaza.

González Morales (1996), however, has argued that, except for dogs (which are well documented in the local Mesolithic), no evidence for domesticates exists in the area before *c.* 4100 BC, at about the same time construction of megalithic monuments begins. Such concrete evidence is supplied by the burial found in the cave of Marizulo, where a human skeleton was accompanied by sheep and dog bones. Radiocarbon has provided a date for this context of 5285 ± 65 BP (GrN-5992) (Arias 1994a), that is, *c.* 4130 BC. As for Arenaza cave, fair numbers of ovicaprids have indeed been found in level IC2, where domesticates amount to 79% of the faunal remains and are associated with decorated pottery. It is such an association that leads Arias to compare this occupation with the epi-Cardial contexts dated to before 4500 BC elsewhere in Iberia. So far, however, no absolute chronology has been obtained for that level, so all that can be said with certainty is that it should be older than the overlying level IC1, which dates to 4965 ± 195 BP (I-8630), that is, *c.* 3800 BC. More recently, Arias (1997:375) has also remarked that the decorative styles of the pottery from IC2 are reminiscent of those found in the late Neolithic of the Meseta, which would set them apart from the epi-Cardial tradition and indicate that this level probably is not much older than the overlying level IC1 and, therefore, that its age may be similar to that of Marizulo.

It seems fair to conclude, thus, that no signs of food production in the pottery-bearing contexts of the region can be securely dated to a time period before *c.* 4100 BC. Results from recent work point in the same direction. At Cueva de la Trecha, a sequence of four coherent radiocarbon dates established the accumulation of the shell-midden excavated there, which contained neither pottery nor domesticates, as having taken place between 6300 and 4300 BC (González Morales 1996). Further evidence for the continuation of traditional subsistence patterns until after 4900 BC is reported by Zapata (1994) from the shell-midden in level 4 of Pico Ramos cave, radiocarbon dated to 5860 ± 65 BP (Ua-3051), that is, *c.* 4700 BC: it contained no domestic animals and flotation failed to provide any evidence for domestic plants. In this context, González Morales argues that even if one accepts that the evidence from Los Canes and Arenaza is indeed a genuine reflection of the relatively early introduction in the region of pottery and of other technological aspects of the Neolithic package, the best models for the Mesolithic–Neolithic transition would still be those supplied by other regions of Atlantic Europe with a similar ecology. That is, the archaeological situation in the Cantabrian strip between 4900 and 4100 BC would be best described as an Ertebølle-type pottery Mesolithic, not as an Iberian-type epi-Cardial Neolithic.

In their discussion of the transition in Great Britain and Denmark, Zvelebil and Rowley-Conwy (1986) have shown that the appearance of megalithic monuments post-dates by a few centuries (four, in the Danish case) the first establishment of agro-pastoral economies (although monumental earthen barrows are present from the very beginning of the Neolithic – Price *et al.* 1995). The interpretation of the Cantabrian data in this light would carry the implication that the replacement of hunting by food production as the main subsistence activity would have taken place some time before the accepted dates for the earliest megaliths in the region, that is, some time before 4100 BC, as Arias has claimed on the basis of artifactual evidence. Other regions of Atlantic Europe, however, may resemble Cantabria in that the existence of a pre-megalithic Neolithic is problematic, or altogether unaccepted. Such is the case, for instance, in Galicia and northern Portugal, where no peasant-shepherd groups have been documented before the time of the first megalith builders, whose material culture is, on the other hand, in total discontinuity with that of local Mesolithic hunter-gatherers (Vázquez Varela 1994).

Progress in this debate seems to be possible in two ways only: a reliable direct dating by AMS of the ovicaprids found in level IC2 of Arenaza; and the collection of additional palaeonutritional data by stable isotope analyses of human remains from the critical time period (such as those from the Marizulo burial). However, in spite of the disagreements over chronology, there seems to be a consensus among researchers that, in Cantabria, we are observing an essentially indigenous process. In the view of González Morales (1992), continuity is implicit in the explanation of the introduction of ovicaprid husbandry as possibly caused by a situation of extreme stress brought about by the very high sea levels recorded *c.* 4300 BC, resulting in a mixed forager-herding way of life, with agriculture presumably becoming important only in the later Neolithic and Chalcolithic. In the view of Arias (1992), continuity is explicit in his interpretation of pottery-bearing shell-middens as part of a subsistence system where the novel agro-pastoral resources complemented the exploitation of forest game and of sea foods; the regional early Neolithic would simply represent, therefore, a further broadening of the traditional "broad spectrum" hunter-gatherer economy.

Along the shores of the Mediterranean

As in Mediterranean France (Guilaine 1976; Binder, this volume), the earliest Neolithic of Catalonia, the Ebro basin, Valencia, and Andalucía is defined by the presence of Cardial pottery (Navarrete 1976, Baldellou and Castán 1983, Fortea and Martí 1984–5, Baldellou and Utrilla 1985, Martí *et al.* 1987, Navarrete and Molina 1987, Bernabeu 1989, Martín 1992). In all known deeply stratified cave sequences (such as Chaves, Or, Cendres, or Cariguela), such contexts date to between *c.* 5900 and *c.* 5400 BC and represent the simultaneous first appearance of a series of technological and subsistence innovations in the archaeological record of these regions.

In the realm of subsistence, those innovations include ovicaprids (which make up most of the fauna from the base of the Or sequence) and domestic plants. Wheat and barley, very abundant at Or, have also been recovered in all other cave sites of the Cardial "culture" in Valencia and were present in the Cardial levels of Balma Margineda, in Andorra, as well. In the realm of technology, such innovations include, in addition to pottery, polished stone items and, at least in the case of Valencia, a wide variety of new types of bone tools and a new lithic production system (Fortea *et al.* 1987, Juan-Cabanilles 1992). All microliths are geometrics (almost exclusively trapeze) but use of the microburin technique is not documented; blade debitage probably resulted from pressure flaking and there is evidence of heat pretreatment of the flint; laminary products were systematically short-ened through flexure breaking techniques to be used as parts of composite tools, for the most part, as indicated by the numerous specimens bearing the characteristic use wear, as sickle blades; and borers with thick, long points make their first appearance in the regional sequences. This lithic production system is in total discontinuity with the autochthonous Geometric Mesolithic, where triangles and crescents were clearly domi-nant, produced by the microburin technique, and extensively retouched with *doble bisel*, which is extremely rare in the Cardial sites. The presence of some Cardial pottery sherds in the uppermost levels of the long strati-graphic sequences where the evolution of this Geometric Mesolithic can be followed (such as La Cocina) is interpreted as evidence of interaction between the local hunter-gatherers and the contemporaneous groups of allochthonous farmers established elsewhere at such sites as Sarsa and Or (Juan-Cabanilles 1992).

Traditional research biases explain why most of these contexts have been recovered in caves. That an important open-air late Mesolithic settle-ment focused on estuarine or lacustrine areas must have characterized the coasts of Mediterranean Spain has been recently demonstrated by the dis-covery of the El Collado shell-midden which, like its Atlantic counterparts in Portugal and Scandinavia, also contained a cemetery (Aparicio 1988). Unfortunately, the site remains essentially unpublished, although Arias (1994b) refers to the excavation of fourteen burials and two radiocarbon dates on human bone around 6300 BC, at the beginning of the climatic optimum. The nature of the relations that may have existed between this coastal settlement and the cave and rockshelter habitats known in the adja-cent limestone mountains (exemplified by La Cocina) remains, however, to be investigated.

That Cardial settlement must also have been largely open air and organized in aggregates of wood huts that can only be described as peasant villages has been recently demonstrated beyond any reasonable doubt by the lakeside site of La Draga (Banyoles, Catalonia). Tarrus *et al.* (1994) describe the finding of posts and planks stuck in the chalk bedrock beneath the archaeological horizon and they report the excavation of three stone paved platforms and thirty-two associated hearths. From the depth attained by the posts they reconstruct wood structures at least 3–4 m high, some of which may have been granaries. Of the animal bone fragments, 93% belong to domesticates (sheep, goats, pigs, and cattle) and enormous amounts of plant remains (mostly wheat, but also barley and some legumes) were recov-ered in hearths, dumping areas, and large ceramic vessels. Pottery is often decorated with cardial shell impressions and, besides traditional lithic types (blades, borers, trapezes, polished adzes), material culture also included a cylindrical, finely polished marble vessel, a kind of object that, so far, was known only in early Neolithic contexts in eastern Mediterranean areas and in southern Italy. Eight radiocarbon dates on charcoal, cereal grain, animal bone, and wood from oak posts suggest the site was occupied between *c.* 5900 and *c.* 4900 BC.

Based on the marked discontinuity observed at all levels with the material culture of local Mesolithic traditions and on the affinities with the earliest Neolithic to the east, most researchers working in Mediterranean Spain consider this Cardial complex to represent a cultural and demic intrusion, not an essentially local development, as is widely accepted for the areas north of the Cantabrian mountains. Some, however, have taken the opposite view. Acosta and Pellicer (1990), on the basis of data from the Andalucian cave site of La Dehesilla, believe that Neolithization was an ongoing process already by 6900 BC (well before Mediterranean France and Italy), when domestic sheep and rabbits would already be present in the region. Olaria (1988) suggests a similar process in northern Valencia and Catalonia, based on data from Cova Fosca, where goats would have been domesticated from autochthonous ibex populations.

As exhaustively discussed elsewhere (Zilhão 1993), these interpretations are based on seriously disturbed and poorly excavated sites, with highly questionable associations between the radiocarbon dates and the archaeological evidence relating to the Neolithic. At Cova Fosca, for instance, the dates came from samples made up of charcoal collected in badger burrows mistakenly identified as "storage pits." Furthermore, such models are flawed at a very basic level: as demonstrated by genetics and palaeontology, Neolithic sheep and goats are undoubtedly of Near Eastern origin and it was not until very recent times that rabbits were domesticated (Vigne 1989).

The western façade

Tables 6.1 and 6.2 list all radiometric dates available in Portugal for the period between 6000 and 4500 BC. The ranges of occupation for each site derived from the one sigma calibrated radiocarbon ages are given in Fig. 6.2 and their geographical distribution is represented in Fig. 6.3 for three different moments separated by 500 years each: 6000–5750, 5500–5250 and 5000–4750 BC. Only Mesolithic sites are known until 5750 BC and well-defined Cardial Neolithic assemblages are present from *c.* 5500 BC onwards in Estremadura and the Algarve. Remarkable similarities in pottery decoration between the early "baroque" Cardial wares of Cova de l'Or and those from several undated sites in Estremadura, such as Almonda and Eira Pedrinha (Fig. 6.4), suggest contemporaneity. On the Atlantic shores of Iberia, therefore, the Neolithic may be as old as in Mediterranean Spain, that is, its first appearance in Portugal may date precisely to the period between 5750 and 5500 BC not represented in the maps of Fig. 6.3.

Table 6.1 *Chronology of the late Mesolithic in Portugal*[1]

Site	Provenience	Sample[2]	Lab number	Date BP	cal BC 1	cal BC 2
Buraca Grande	Layer 8a	Ch	Gif-9940	7000 ± 60	5944–5753	5964–5702
	Layer 7c	Ch	Sac-1461	6850 ± 210	5943–5525	6112–5336
	Layer 7c	Es	Sac-1459	6940 ± 140	5583–5332	5680–5243
Bocas	Layer 2	Es	ICEN-899	7490 ± 110	6017–5836	6170–5709
Forno da Telha	Layer 2	Es	ICEN-417	7360 ± 90	5947–5710	5981–5632
Cabeço da Arruda	Skeleton III	Hbc	TO-360	6990 ± 110	5980–5730	6090–5640
	Skeleton A	Hbc	TO-354	6970 ± 60	5960–5740	5980–5650
	Skeleton 42	Hbc	TO-359a	6960 ± 60	5960–5734	5980–5640
	Skeleton D	Hbc	TO-355	6780 ± 80	5732–5573	5810–5490
	Skeleton N	Hbc	TO-356	6360 ± 80	5380–5235	5480–5210
Moita do Sebastião	Skeleton 22	Hbc	TO-131	7240 ± 70	6129–5993	6219–5970
	Skeleton 29	Hbc	TO-133	7200 ± 70	6108–5886	6180–5886
	Skeleton 24	Hbc	TO-132	7180 ± 70	6097–5974	6170–5848
	Skeleton 41	Hbc	TO-134	7160 ± 80	6091–5966	6170–5830
	Skeleton CT	Hbc	TO-135	6810 ± 70	5739–5629	5830–5540
Arapouco	Middle level	Es	Q-2492	7420 ± 65	5959–5779	5992–5715
Cabeço do Rebolador		Es	ICEN-277	7140 ± 70	5680–5529	5733–5481
		Es	ICEN-278	7100 ± 60	5627–5526	5693–5448
Várzea da Mó		Es	ICEN-273	7110 ± 50	5628–5528	5687–5488
Poças de São Bento	Lower level	Es	Q-2493	7040 ± 70	5595–5448	5668–5435
	Middle level	Ch	Q-2494	6780 ± 65	5726–5584	5770–5530
	Middle level	Es	Q-2495	6850 ± 70	5443–5313	5566–5259
Cabeço do Pez	Middle level	Es	Q-2497	6730 ± 75	5373–5229	5437–5081
	Middle level	Es	Q-2496	6430 ± 65	5064–4908	5214–4805
Amoreira	Level 2b	Es	Q-(AM85B2b)	6370 ± 70	4946–4787	5064–4715
	Level 2a	Ch	Q-(AM85B2a)	5990 ± 75	4944–4789	5060–4718

Table 6.1 (cont.)

Site	Provenience	Sample[2]	Lab number	Date BP	cal BC 1	cal BC 2
Vale de Romeiras	Layer 2	Abc	ICEN-144	7130±110	6043–5854	6175–5723
	Layer 2	Es	ICEN-150	7390±80	5956–5732	5997–5672
	Layer 2	Es	ICEN-146	7350±60	5936–5716	5960–5672
Vale Pincel (hearths)	Levels 2/3	Ch	ICEN-724	6700±60	5601–5525	5668–5448
	Levels 2/3	Ch	ICEN-723	6540±60	5520–5389	5573–5331
Samouqueira I	Level 3	Es	ICEN-729	7520±60	6011–5889	6117–5833
	Level 2	Hbc	TO-130	6370±70	5382–5238	5480–5220
Vidigal	Level 3	Abc	Ly-4695	6640±90	5593–5443	5668–5348
	Level 2	Abc	GX-14557	6030±180	5220–4770	5330–4510
Medo Tojeiro	Level 4?	Es	BM-2275R	6820±140	5448–5256	5590–5067
Fiais	Level 30–35	Es	ICEN-103	7310±80	5924–5679	5960–5597
	Level 30–35	Abc	ICEN-110	6870±220	5953–5526	6156–5336
	Level 20–30	Abc	ICEN-141	6180±110	5252–4946	5321–4836
		Ch	TO-806	7010±70	5973–5750	6075–5668
		Ch	TO-705	6840±70	5725–5609	5807–5582
		Abc	TO-706	6260±80	5270–5076	5333–4990
Montes de Baixo	Layer 4	Es	ICEN-720	7910±60	6419–6230	6461–6183
	Layer 2	Es	ICEN-718	7590±60	6116–5971	6176–5888

Notes:

[1] *References:* Buraca Grande – Aubry et al. (1997); Bocas – Bicho (1993); Forno da Telha – Araújo (1993); Moita do Sebastião and Cabeço da Arruda – Lubell et al. (1994); Amoreira, Arapouco, Cabeço do Pez, Cabeço do Rebolador, Poças de São Bento, Vale de Romeiras – Arnaud (1989, 1997), Soares (1989); Vidigal – Straus and Vierra (1989); Samouqueira and Medo Tojeiro – Lubell and Jackes (1985, 1988), Bowman et al. (1990), Soares (1995); Fiais – Lubell and Jackes (1988), González Morales and Arnaud (1990), Soares (1989); Montes de Baixo – Soares (1997).

[2] Es – estuarine shells; Hbc – human bone collagen; Ch – charcoal; Abc – animal bone collagen; the dates on estuarine shells were calibrated with the curve for continental samples after subtraction of 380±30 years, apparent age of this material in archaeological sites from this time range (Soares 1993).Page numbers in bold denote illustrations.

Table 6.2 *Chronology of the early Neolithic in Portugal*[1]

Site	Provenience	Sample[2]	Lab number	Date BP	cal BC 1	cal BC 2
Buraco da Pala	Level IV, base	Ch	ICEN-935	5860±140	4905–4540	5060–4369
	Level IV, base	Ch	GrN-19104	5860±30	4780–4714	4798–4627
Senhora das Lapas	Layer C	Hbc	ICEN-805	6100±70	5206–4908	5230–4847
Caldeirão	Layer Eb	Ch	ICEN-296	6870±210	5970–5570	6120–5370
	Horizon NA2	Abc	OxA-1035	6330±80	5348–5231	5480–5079
	Horizon NA2	Abc	OxA-1034	6230±80	5302–5072	5340–4940
	Horizon NA2	Hbc	OxA-1033	6130±90	5226–4941	5296–4843
	Horizon NA1	Abc	OxA-1037	5970±120	5048–4770	5220–4583
	Horizon NA1	Abc	OxA-1036	5870±80	4894–4685	4941–4540
	Horizon NA1	Hbc	TO-350	5810±70	4782–4588	4895–4510
Pena d'Água	Layer Eb (base)	Ch	ICEN-1146	6390±150	5441–5149	5579–4962
Picoto	Surface	Hbc	ICEN-736	6000±150	5063–4723	5256–4528
Casa da Moura	Level 1a	Hbc	TO-953	5990±60	4944–4800	5192–4780
CPM IIIS[3]	Neolithic hearth	Ch	SMU-2477	5710±155	4780–4366	4938–4245
Pedreira de Salemas	Neolithic hearth	Hbc	ICEN-351	6020±120	5059–4783	5226–4616
São Pedro de Canaferrim	UE-4, 69–73 cm	Ch	ICEN-1151	6020±60	4951–4836	5060–4781
	UE-4, 46–63 cm	Ch	ICEN-1152	6070±60	5055–4908	5202–4830
Cabeço do Pez	Upper level	Abc	Q-2499	5535±130	4510–4247	4720–4043
Cabranosa	Neolithic hearth	Es	Sac-1321	6930±60	5563–5389	5579–5325
Padrão	Neolithic hearth	Es	ICEN-873	6920±60	5521–5386	5577–5318
	Neolithic hearth	Es	ICEN-645	6800±50	5432–5278	5442–5255

Notes:

[1] *References:* Buraco da Pala – Sanches *et al.* (1993); Senhora das Lapas – Oosterbeek (1997); Caldeirão, Pena d'Água, and Picoto – Zilhão (1992, 1993), Zilhão and Carvalho (1996); Casa da Moura – Straus (1988); CPM IIIS – Marks *et al.* (1994); São Pedro de Canaferrim – Simões (1996); Pedreira de Salemas and Cabranosa – Cardoso *et al.* (1996); Cabeço do Pez – Arnaud (1989); Padrão – Gomes (1994, n.d.). The dates for the caves of Salemas and Correio-Mor published as early Neolithic (cf. Cardoso *et al.* 1996) were not considered given that there is no secure association between the dated samples and the artifact assemblages.

[2] Es – estuarine shells; Hbc – human bone collagen; Ch – charcoal; Abc – animal bone collagen. The dates on shell were calibrated with the curve for continental samples after subtraction of 380±30 years, apparent age of this material in the archaeological sites from this time range (Soares 1993).

[3] CPM = Cabeço de Porto Marinho.

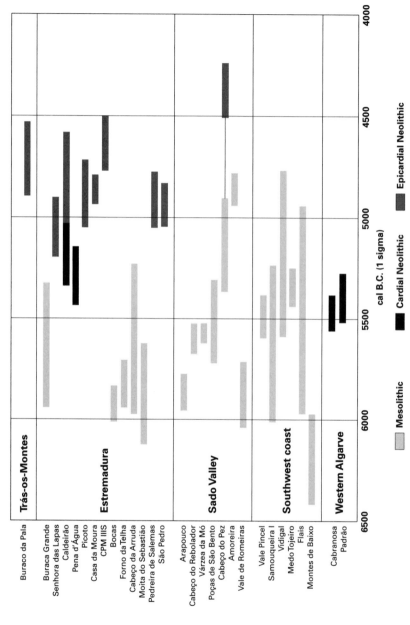

6.2   Calibrated radiocarbon chronology of early Neolithic and late Mesolithic sites known along the western façade of Atlantic Iberia. The bars represent occupation ranges defined with the earliest and the latest limits of all one sigma calibrated intervals derived from the dates obtained for each site or level (cf. Tables 6.1, 6.2).

By comparison with similar western Mediterranean pottery styles, the ceramics found in the Neolithic sites dated to the period between 5500 and 5250 BC can be described as "late Cardial" (Fig. 6.5), in good agreement with their radiometric ages (Zilhão *et al.* 1991, Zilhão 1992, Moura and Aubry 1995, Zilhão and Carvalho 1996, Aubry *et al.* 1997). Accelerator radiocarbon dating of sheep bones from Gruta do Caldeirão has demonstrated that these "late Cardial" contexts are associated with animal domesticates and must be defined as Neolithic not only from the perspective of material culture but also from that of economics (Rowley-Conwy 1992; Zilhão 1992, 1993). Slightly before 5000 BC, impressed or epi-Cardial wares replace Cardial pottery and Neolithic groups begin their expansion toward the interior. The transition is completed by 4750 BC, when Neolithic people reach eastern Trás-os-Montes (Sanches 1996; Sanches *et al.* 1993) and the last Mesolithic hunter-gatherer systems surviving in the Sado valley and the Alentejo coast disappear. Mesolithic–Neolithic cultural interaction in this time range is documented by the *in situ* occurrence of a few decorated sherds in the very late shell-midden of Amoreira, in the Sado valley (Arnaud 1990).

Cardial Neolithic cave sites from Estremadura are located in the interior limestone massifs of the region, which contain many Upper Palaeolithic and some early Mesolithic sites, but where no evidence of a late Mesolithic settlement has so far been recovered (Fig. 6.3). In the several sedimentary sequences bridging the Pleistocene/Holocene boundary that are known in the area, the late Mesolithic is always represented by a hiatus in both sedimentation (no deposits) and occupation (no diagnostic artifacts intrusive in underlying Palaeolithic levels or displaced in overlying Neolithic ones). However, a few late Mesolithic sites radiocarbon dated to between *c.* 6000 and *c.* 5750 BC are known in the periphery of these massifs, at the head of tributaries of the larger rivers of the region: the Mondego, in the case of Buraca Grande (Aubry *et al.* 1997), and the Tagus, in the cases of Forno da Telha (Araújo 1993) and Bocas (Heleno 1956, Zilhão 1992, 1995, Bicho 1993). At these three sites, the late Mesolithic levels could be defined as shell-middens or, at least, as containing large amounts of shells. This suggests that they functioned as logistical outposts of settlement-subsistence systems centered on the exploitation of the very extensive estuaries created in the major rivers of Portugal by the Flandrian transgression.

Thus, on present evidence, it would seem that the onset of the Atlantic period corresponded to a major reorganization of the human settlement of Estremadura (Zilhão 1993): as the limestone massif forests grew denser and less productive, they were gradually abandoned and people concentrated along the margins of estuaries, basing their subsistence strategies on the exploitation of aquatic resources. A similar process seems to have developed in southern Scandinavian, whose interior regions also became largely devoid of human occupation at the time of the mid-Holocene climatic optimum, when "the vast majority of Mesolithic settlement took place along the coasts and at the mouths of river systems . . . as the inland

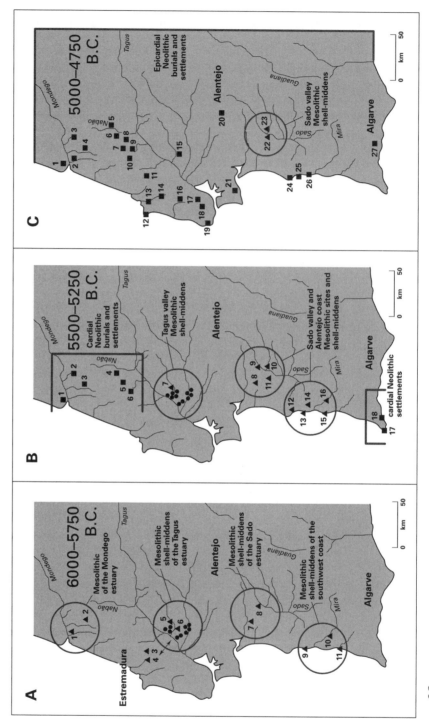

A

6000–5750 B.C.

Mondego

Nabão

Tagus

Estremadura

Mesolithic of the Mondego estuary

1 ▲ 2

4 ▲ 3

Mesolithic shell-middens of the Tagus estuary

5 ● 6

Alentejo

Sado

Mesolithic shell-middens of the Sado estuary

7 ▲ 8 ▲

Guadiana

Mira

Mesolithic shell-middens of the southwest coast

9 ▲

10 ▲

11 ▲

Algarve

0   km   50

B

5500–5250 B.C.

Mondego

Nabão

Tagus

Cardial Neolithic burials and settlements

1 ■ 2 ■

3 ■

4 ■

5 ■

6 ■

Tagus valley Mesolithic shell-middens

7 ▲

Alentejo

8 ▲ 9 ■

11 ▲ 10 ▲

Sado

Sado valley and Alentejo coast Mesolithic sites and shell-middens

12 ■ 14 ▲

13 ▲ 16 ▲

15 ▲

Guadiana

Mira

18 ■

17 ■

Algarve

cardial Neolithic settlements

0   km   50

C

5000–4750 B.C.

Mondego

Nabão

Tagus

Epicardial Neolithic burials and settlements

1 ■

2 ■

3 ■

4 ■

5 ■

6 ■

7 ■

8 ■

9 ■

10 ■

11 ■

12 ■

13 ■

14 ■

15 ■

16 ■

17 ■

18 ■

19 ■

Alentejo

20 ■

Sado

22 ■ 23 ▲

Sado valley Mesolithic shell-middens

Guadiana

Mira

21 ■

24 ■ 25 ■

26 ■

27 ■

Algarve

0   km   50

6.3

Caption to Fig. 6.3

A Geographic and cultural distribution of archaeological sites in southern Portugal c. 6000–5750 BC. 1. Forno da Cal, 2. Buraca Grande, 3. Forno da Telha, 4. Bocas, 5. Cabeço da Arruda, 6. Moita do Sebastião, 7. Arapouco, 8. Vale de Romeiras, 9. Samouqueira I, 10. Fiais, 11. Montes de Baixo. Buraca Grande is a cave and Bocas a rockshelter. All the other are open air. The small dots represent numerous undated shell-middens, some already destroyed, known around the Muge and Magos streams, left-bank tributaries of the Tagus; their accumulation may have begun in this time range or slightly earlier, as at Moita do Sebastião.

B Geographic and cultural distribution of archaeological sites in southern Portugal c. 5500–5250 BC. Only the Cardial contexts defined by pottery assemblages, radiocarbon dating, or stratigraphic position that can be confidently placed in this age range were considered (neither isolated finds, such as the Santarém vessel, nor the odd sites where a few Cardial sherds have been found but most likely belong to later epi-Cardial contexts, were included). 1. Várzea do Lírio and Junqueira, 2. Eira Pedrinha, 3. Buraca Grande, 4. Caldeirão, 5. Pena d'Água, 6. Almonda, 7. Cabeço da Arruda, 8. Cabeço do Rebolador, 9. Várzea da Mó, 10. Cabeço do Pez, 11. Poças de São Bento, 12. Vale Pincel, 13. Samouqueira I, 14. Vidigal, 15. Medo Tojeiro, 16. Fiais, 17. Cabranosa, 18. Padrão. Sites 2–6 are caves or rockshelters; all the others are open air. The small dots represent the undated Tagus middens, some which may have been contemporary with Cabeço da Arruda. The mutually exclusive distribution of late Mesolithic and Cardial sites and the absence of known late Mesolithic settlement in the areas with the earliest Neolithic suggest that the latter is intrusive.

C Geographic and cultural distribution of archaeological sites in southern Portugal c. 5000–4750 BC. 1. Várzea do Lírio and Junqueira, 2. Forno da Cal, 3. Eira Pedrinha, 4. Buraca Grande, 5. Nossa Senhora das Lapas, 6. Caldeirão, 7. Pena d'Água, 8. Picoto, 9. Almonda, 10. Laranjal de Cabeço das Pias and Forno do Terreirinho, 11. Cabeço de Porto Marinho and Bocas, 12. Furninha, 13. Casa da Moura, 14. Lapa do Suão and Gruta das Pulgas, 15. Moita do Sebastião, 16. Cova da Moura, 17. Pedreira de Salemas, 18. Correio-Mor, 19. São Pedro de Canaferrim, 20. Escoural, 21. Lapa do Fumo, 22. Amoreira, 23. Cabeço do Pez, 24. Vale Pincel I, 25. Samouqueira II, 26. Vale Vistoso, 27. Caramujeira. Sites 3–9, 12–14, 16, 18, 20 and 21 are caves, Bocas and Pena d'Água are rockshelters, and all the other are open air. The persistence of Mesolithic groups on the coast of the Alentejo into this time range suggested by radiocarbon (Fig. 6.2) may be an artifact of the large standard deviations of the ICEN-141 and GX-14557 dates for Fiais and Vidigal (Table 6.1). The epi-Cardial ceramics recovered in the Sines area sites suggest that the transition to the Neolithic in this region took place around 5000 BC. The last Mesolithic people in Portugal seem to have been those who persisted in the inner estuary of the Sado until c. 4750 BC.

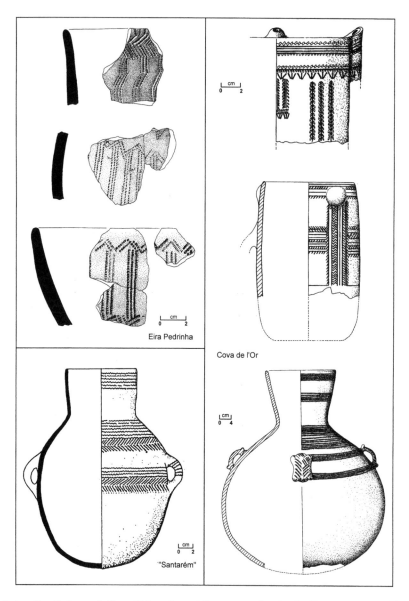

6.4   Cardial vessels from Valencia and from cave sites in the limestone massifs of Portuguese Estremadura with stylistically similar decorative patterns. *Top left*: Sherds from Eira Pedrinha (after Vilaça 1988); identical specimens have been recovered in the 1988–9 excavations at Almonda (Zilhão *et al.* 1991). *Bottom left*: The Santarém vessel (after Guilaine and Ferreira 1970), a ceramic vessel recovered in the nineteenth century from a now unknown location in that district (probably a cave site in the limestone plateau of Santo António, whose southeastern boundary runs only a few kilometers north of that city). *Right*: Ceramic vessels from Cova de l'Or (after Bernabeu 1989).

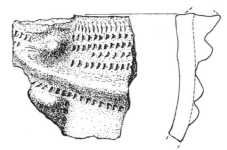

Buraca Grande

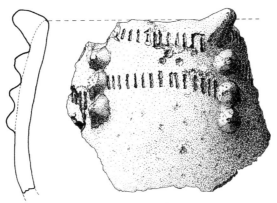

Gruta do Almonda

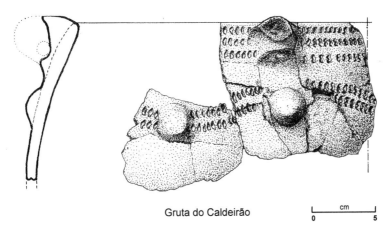

Gruta do Caldeirão

6.5 "Late Cardial" ceramic vessels from Buraca Grande, Caldeirão, and Almonda. These vessels belong to archaeological contexts radiocarbon dated to *c.* 5300 BC at Pena d'Água and Caldeirão. Although as yet undated, the Cardial vessel recovered at Buraca Grande was found directly atop the latest Mesolithic level.

forests increased in density and decreased in biomass and human population" (Price *et al.* 1995:115). In Portugal, this reorganization coincides in
time with a major technological transformation, although no simple relation between the two is easily discernible: flake/bladelet lithic production
systems, often based on the debitage of carinated "scrapers" and featuring
marginally retouched hypermicroliths ("Areeiro bladelets"), were replaced
by blade/bladelet technologies oriented toward the production of geometric armatures, especially trapezes. Technological observation of the Forno
da Telha lithics indicates that indirect percussion was used to extract the
blade/bladelet blanks found in these later assemblages.

The late Mesolithic settlement-subsistence strategy is well documented by the numerous sites known in the inner parts of the estuaries of
the Tagus (particularly the famous shell-middens of Muge, whose excavation began in the mid-nineteenth century), Sado, and Mira rivers (Arnaud
1989, González Morales and Arnaud 1990). Examination of the lithic assemblages recovered in the open-air sites excavated near Figueira da Foz at the
turn of the century, traditionally considered to be exclusively early
Neolithic, has led to the identification of a late Mesolithic component
(Aubry *et al.* 1997). One of these sites, Forno da Cal, was described by the excavator, A. Santos Rocha, as containing a large shell-midden, spreading for
more than 40 m and containing abundant remains of estuarine molluscs
(Vilaça 1988). In Portugal, however, such extensive accumulations of shells
are unknown in both cave and open-air Neolithic sites. It is quite likely, thus,
that Forno da Cal actually featured a stratigraphic sequence identical to
that found in some of the better-known similar sites of the Tagus and Sado
estuaries: an important late Mesolithic shell-midden, overlain by deposits
containing scattered remains of the use of the area in late Early Neolithic
times. The decoration of the small ceramic assemblage recovered (eight
vessels), which is of an epi-Cardial style (Jorge 1979), is compatible with such
a model. If confirmed by future research, this would indicate, as was to be
expected, that the estuary of the Mondego also witnessed the development
of the same kinds of late Mesolithic adaptations that are well known further
to the south. Accordingly, Forno da Cal was included in Fig. 6.3 as representing the estuary-focused adaptations of the lower Mondego basin with which
the late Mesolithic use of the Buraca Grande cave must have been related.

In the Sado and Mira estuaries, these adaptations persisted until
c. 5000 BC and were, therefore, fully contemporaneous for at least 500 years
with the early Neolithic of the limestone massifs of Estremadura and the
Algarve. In the Muge area, the most recent accelerator age obtained for the
skeletons dated by Lubell and Jackes (1988) was 6360 ± 80 BP (from skeleton
N at Cabeço da Arruda), that is *c.* 5200 BC. However, a charcoal date obtained
for the upper part of Cabeço da Amoreira – 6050 ± 300 BP (Sa-194) (Roche
1977) – could be interpreted, despite the large standard deviation, as suggesting a similar late persistence of the Mesolithic. Photographs from the

original excavations show that even the burials located higher up in the stratigraphy were still overlain by at least 1 m of midden fill, suggesting that the accumulation of shells continued well after the most recent skeleton dates. On the other hand, given the stable isotope data for the human bone (Lubell *et al.* 1994), such dates are probably somewhat affected by the reservoir effect, that is, the skeletons are probably at least 100 years younger than indicated by the radiocarbon results (Schwarcz, personal communication). This suggests that the overlap between Cabeço da Arruda, Caldeirão and Pena d'Água shown in Fig. 6.2 is genuine and that the Mesolithic settlement of the estuary of the Tagus did persist for as long as that of the Sado and the Mira.

Stable isotope data (Lubell *et al.* 1994) also show that, although contemporaneous, Cardial pottery sites in the limestone massifs of Estremadura and shell-midden sites in the river estuaries represent separate adaptive systems, not different functional or seasonal poses of a single, highly diversified, system (Zilhão 1992, 1993). The cave site of Caldeirão, located in the valley of the river Nabão, a subtributary of the Tagus, was mainly used, in early Neolithic times, as a cemetery. Accelerator radiocarbon dating of human bone has demonstrated the contemporaneity of the burials with the sheep bones from the same levels (Table 6.2). Stable isotope analysis of those human bones indicated that the people buried at Caldeirão had a terrestrial diet (Fig. 6.6). In contrast, the people buried in the contemporaneous clusters of Mesolithic shell-midden sites located in the Tagus estuary had a diet where the aquatic component amounted to about 50%, as is also indicated by the analysis of faunal remains (Arnaud 1987). Burial practices were also different. The Tagus and Sado Mesolithic shell-middens feature individual burials with very few associated items (mostly shell beads), while Caldeirão represents the beginning of a long tradition of Neolithic collective interment in caves, with ceramic vessels and polished stone tools accompanying the bodies of the deceased.

Although direct evidence of domestic plants remains to be obtained, the fact that the sheep-owning people buried at Caldeirão were able to survive without the aquatic resources upon which their hunter-gatherer contemporaries were so strongly dependent suggests that cereal agriculture must have been the critical element in their successful colonization of the interior limestone massifs. Data from Buraco da Pala, a rock-shelter in Trás-os-Montes, northeastern Portugal, confirm this view. Wheat and barley were recovered from the base of level IV, in association with impressed wares, polished stone tools, and stone mills (Sanches *et al.* 1993; Sanches 1996). In good accord with its archaeological content, the base of the level has yielded two radiocarbon dates placing it in epi-Cardial times (Table 6.2). Buraco da Pala thus physically demonstrates that cereal agriculture existed in the most interior region of Portugal at the end of the early Neolithic. In this context, it seems entirely reasonable that cereal agricul-

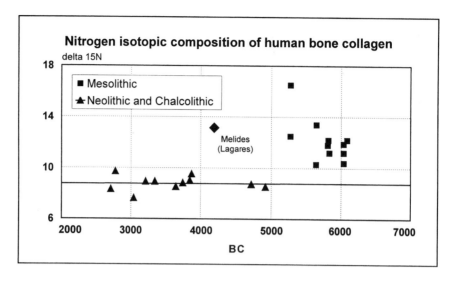

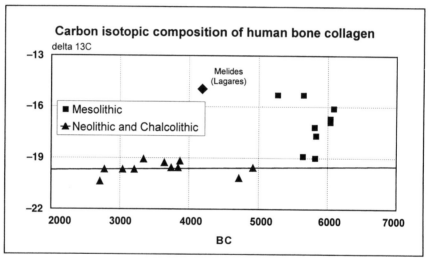

6.6   Isotopic composition of human bone collagen from Portuguese Mesolithic, Neolithic and Copper Age sites (after Lubell *et al.* 1994:Table 1). The retrodiction of Neolithic values into Mesolithic times highlights the marked discontinuity in diet at the Mesolithic–Neolithic boundary.

ture was associated with the few centuries earlier Cardial settlement of the coastal regions, as happens in west Mediterranean areas wherever the relevant artifact suites are present.

The contemporaneity, the mutually exclusive geographical distribution, the economic differentiation, the discontinuity in material culture, and the distinctive burial practices that characterize the late

Mesolithic and the earliest Neolithic of Portugal indicate that the latter is intrusive. The only alternative hypothesis admitted by available evidence is that of a precocious adoption of the Neolithic package by hunter-gatherers living in the limestone massifs of Estremadura, while those living along the river estuaries would still have retained the traditional way of life for several hundred years. This hypothesis faces, however, two major problems, one empirical, the other theoretical: first, that no signs of the putative late Mesolithic adopters have been found so far in the limestone massifs before the putative adoption (an absence that persists even after the intensive archaeological surveys carried out over the last fifteen years); second, that an explanation would have to be provided for the reasons why adaptations in the two areas followed such different strategies after the Neolithic "package" became available through the long-distance exchange networks in which all human groups living in coastal Portugal presumably participated.

Alternatively, it could be argued that the Cardial Neolithic of the massifs of Estremadura exemplified by Caldeirão and Pena d'Água originated in Mesolithic people living in the estuary of the Tagus who decided to move on to unsettled land whose exploitation was made possible once new resources (ovicaprids and cereals) were made available through such exchange networks. The cultural and economic differences with the groups that continued to live in the margins of the estuary as fisher-hunter-gatherers, exemplified by Cabeço da Arruda, would have developed very rapidly once those that had left to settle the interior limestone areas successfully adapted to a new environment and a new way of life. This explanation would require, however, that the arrival of ceramics and ovicaprids to the estuarine areas, whence those settlers presumably originated, pre-dated their first occurrence at Caldeirão and Pena d'Água. The opposite is true – no ceramics and no domestic animals have been found in the Muge Mesolithic shell-middens, except for a few sherds in disturbed, surficial deposits from Moita do Sebastião (Ferreira 1974). The latter are of epi-Cardial style, documenting the use of the area by agriculturalists at a time when the middens had ceased to accumulate and the local hunter-gatherer Mesolithic adaptive systems had already gone extinct. Furthermore, there is no evidence, at the critical moment in time (5750–5500 BC), that the late Mesolithic adaptations of the estuarine regions of Portugal were undergoing processes of population pressure or resource depletion that might have originated such a drive toward the settlement of the interior.

The Alentejo coast in close-up view

The dates for the Cardial sites of Cabranosa and Padrão (Gomes 1994, n.d., Cardoso *et al.* 1996) (Table 6.2), in the Algarve, confirm their contemporaneity with those from Estremadura and, therefore, the isolation of the hunter-gatherer adaptive systems that persisted for several hundred years in the coast and estuaries of the geographically intermediate region of Alentejo. Although this further strengthens the mosaic frontier pattern previously described for Portugal and the maritime pioneer colonization model derived from it (Zilhão 1992, 1993), the opposite view has recently been taken by Soares (1992, 1995, 1997). She states that the large majority of the Alentejo sites should be described as Neolithic and that, given the radiocarbon dates obtained for Vale Pincel (Table 6.2), they represent an early, gradual, local transition from fisher-hunter-gatherer to food-production economies. A detailed analysis of the arguments shows, however, that her position is in direct contradiction with the empirical data.

In the time period of relevance, the Alentejo coast features three kinds of sites: (a) large shell-middens with no indisputably Neolithic artifacts (pottery and polished stone tools) and a mammal fauna featuring exclusively wild species, such as Fiais or Samouqueira I; (b) small shell-middens with no domesticates but with a few Neolithic artifacts of questionable association with the midden deposit, such as Medo Tojeiro; (c) large non-midden sites with pottery (and in some instances with hearths and other features as well) but yielding no direct evidence on subsistence (owing to the acidity of the sandy soils, which has precluded the preservation of bone), such as Vale Pincel.

Soares argues that the first kind of site represents Mesolithic base camps but that the other two would belong to a single, logistically organized, Neolithic settlement-subsistence system developed through indigenous integration in the traditional way of life of domesticates and related new kinds of artifacts: the small sites, featuring low artifact densities, where only hunting and gathering activities are represented, would be temporary camps; the large sites, with high artifact densities, would represent the more permanent village settlements related to agricultural activities. At the same time, she argues that this Neolithic settlement of coastal Alentejo was contemporary with the Mesolithic occupation of the inner estuary of the Sado, explaining the presence in shell-middens such as Cabeço do Pez of ceramics and other Neolithic items (stone mills), acquired through contacts with the coastal forager-farmers.

However, with the already mentioned single exception of the very late midden of Amoreira, in the Mesolithic sites of the inner estuary of the Sado ceramics and other Neolithic artifacts, when at all present, only appear in the upper sections of the sequences, above the midden deposits, not inside them (Arnaud 1982, 1987, 1989, 1990); that is, the deposition of such items post-dates the Mesolithic occupations represented by the shell-middens. Similarly, the Medo Tojeiro midden contained no Neolithic artifacts; as the excavators state, "the only artifacts . . . considered to be indisputably Neolithic were found on the deflated surface of the midden, overlain by dune sand" (Lubell, *in litteris*, 9 June 1991). Furthermore, the small-sized assemblage of decorated ceramics recovered at Vale Pincel is of an epi-Cardial style elsewhere dated in Portugal to the period after *c.*5100

BC; it is also strikingly similar to the pottery recovered in the deposits that overlie the Mesolithic middens of the Sado. Thus, both style and stratigraphy indicate that such pottery cannot be older than *c.* 5100 BC and, consequently, that the hearths dated at Vale Pincel cannot possibly be associated with the Neolithic occupation documented by the epi-Cardial ceramics recovered at that site.

Soares's argument is also internally contradictory since radiocarbon indicates that her "Mesolithic base camp" of Samouqueira I would be a few hundred years later than her supposed locally evolved "Neolithic village settlement" of Vale Pincel (Table 6.1, Fig. 6.2). She tries to avoid this contradiction through defining the site of Samouqueira I as "Mesolithic" and the human skeleton from which the date was derived as "Neolithic" (Soares 1997). The implicit assumption is that the site is earlier than that date and the burial intrusive, but the excavators (Lubell and Jackes 1985) mention no archaeological evidence of intrusion and no Neolithic artifacts were associated with the skeleton (in actual fact, none was recovered at the site). Finally, isotopic evidence shows that the individual in question had a marine diet identical to that of the people buried in the Mesolithic shellmiddens of Muge (Lubell *et al.* 1994).

The functional differentiation argument is also inconsistent. Medo Tojeiro, the prototype of the "Neolithic temporary camps," had a lithic artifact density of $8/m^3$. Although this is exceedingly low indeed, Vale Pincel, the prototype of the "Neolithic village settlements," is no different – from the data supplied by Silva and Soares (1981), the corresponding value can be calculated to be of $8.5/m^3$ and, in the 40 m² excavated at Vale Pincel in 1975, there were only 1.4 lithic artifacts per square meter in levels 2d/3 (the base of the occupation, where the dated hearths and other features described as "hut-floors" were found). Such extremely low lithic artifact densities are incompatible with the definition of Vale Pincel as a permanent village settlement. For comparative purposes, it may be worth noting that the corresponding values obtained at geologically *in situ* sites in this time range were of approximately $520/m^3$ in the epi-Cardial open-air settlement of Laranjal de Cabeço das Pias, Estremadura (Carvalho and Zilhão 1994), and of some $470/m^3$ in the Sado valley Mesolithic shell-midden of Poças de São Bento (modern Arnaud/Larsson excavations) (Araújo 1998); at Mesolithic Samouqueira I, Soares (1997) herself gives values of *c.* $400/m^3$.

In this context, it would seem that the hearths dated at Vale Pincel belong to the Mesolithic occupation previously inferred from stratigraphic and material culture data alone (Zilhão 1993:33–6). In fact, Vale Pincel is a seriously disturbed site, as indicated by the low density of finds, the slope of the sandy deposits containing the Neolithic material, and the presence of obvious erosional features at the interface between levels 2 and 3 – the most striking are the extensive, irregularly shaped pockets and channels excavated in level 3 and filled with darker material wrongly interpreted as "hut-floors" by the excavators (Silva and Soares 1981). Since these hearths (*cuvettes* of hardened, reddish sands containing charcoal and burnt cobbles) are encrusted in level 3 and since their topographical relation with the overlying Neolithic level 2 indicates that they too were affected by the erosional processes ante-dating the accumulation of the latter (the upper part of the *cuvettes* is convex and protuberant, outcropping from the surface of level 3 extant during excavation), their radiocarbon dating to the Mesolithic should come as no surprise. The scant data available on vertical distributions also suggest the presence of a Mesolithic component among the lithics recovered in levels 2d/3.

Similar taphonomic patterns are known from sites in identical geological contexts excavated in Estremadura and in the Algarve. At Ponta da Vigia (Zilhão *et al.* 1987), in coastal Estremadura, several early Mesolithic hearths were identified encrusted on an eroded, deflated surface of hard sands, and the lithics presumably related with this occupation were scattered around at very low densities, as is the case at Vale Pincel. In the 80 m² excavated at Padrão, in the Algarve, the surface with the dated hearth and associated Cardial Neolithic material was cut by Roman burials and the negative of the basis of a fallen menhir. It was the discovery of the latter that prompted the excavation and its close proximity to the hearth initially led the excavator to believe that its erection actually dated back to the earliest Neolithic (Gomes 1994). A sequence in unconsolidated sands presenting exactly the same characteristics as those suggested for Vale Pincel (two occupations in direct stratigraphic contact, with material from the later occupation found in discontinuous pockets excavated by erosion in the underlying deposits containing the earlier occupation), but featuring upper Solutrean and final Magdalenian instead of late Mesolithic and early Neolithic, has also been described at Olival da Carneira, in Estremadura (Zilhão 1995).

There is nothing solid in the Alentejo data, therefore, that can be taken to indicate a slow, piecemeal adoption by local hunter-gatherers of the several elements of the Neolithic package starting as early as 5750 BC. Whether the epi-Cardial Neolithic that appears throughout the region around 5000 BC represents an expansion of the farmer groups that previously settled the neighboring regions of Algarve and Estremadura or the adoption by local hunter-gatherers of the new subsistence system remains, however, to be clarified.

Traditional explanatory frameworks and their limitations

Genetic data indicate that two very different population clusters can be distinguished in Iberia, with the Basque group well isolated from the rest (Calafell and Bertranpetit 1993). These authors interpret such a differentiation in terms of population history. The Basque would represent a pre-Neolithic population that survived in cultural isolation. The pattern of homogeneity revealed by the gene frequencies everywhere else in Iberia would in turn be the result of the Neolithic expansion of farming populations originating in Catalonia and spreading southwestwards. This process would have led to the assimilation of the autochthonous hunter-gatherers, whose genetic contribution to subsequent populations, given their small numbers, would have been extremely diluted.

These conclusions find some support in the results of a simulation study also carried out by Calafell and Bertranpetit (1993), which was based on the "Wave of Advance" model of Ammerman and Cavalli-Sforza (1984). Mapping of the first principal component of the simulated data (interpreted as pre-Neolithic) shows good accord with the real gene frequencies (Fig. 6.7). The isolation of the Basque shown by this map is also in good accord with linguistic and ethnohistorical data and is compatible with the archaeological evidence. As mentioned above, both Arias (1991, 1992, 1994a) and González Morales (1992, 1996) consider that the Neolithization of the Cantabrian coastal strip is best interpreted as the local acquisition of novel resources by local hunter-gatherers. Mapping of the second principal component (interpreted as indicating the consequences of the Neolithic expansion), however, does not show a similar degree of accordance with the real gene frequencies. Instead of the regular east–west gradient predicted by the simulation, we have a pattern where the highest recorded frequencies outside the presumed area of origin of the expanding populations are to be found in central Portugal, not along the adjacent coasts of Valencia and Andalucía, as it should be expected, given the assumptions of the model (Fig. 6.7).

Other exceptions to the east–west gradient predicted by gradualist demic Wave of Advance models of the expansion of agriculture are given by Jackes *et al.* (1997a, 1997b), who find that the Portuguese cluster with the French instead of with neighboring Spaniards in the analysis of some genes. They quote similar findings when blood groups, red cell enzymes, and serum protein polymorphisms are used. It is possible that these contradictions between genetics and geography result from the impact of recent historic processes such as the medieval Berber invasions or the western Crusades. Since the information on conditions at the time of the Neolithic transition contained in modern samples is necessarily confused by the passage of time and the impact of documented large-scale population movements of the recent past, the only conclusion that can be safely derived from these analyses is that the palaeodemography of the Mesolithic–Neolithic transition should be addressed by looking at the extinct populations themselves. This is all the more so since the interpretation of prehistoric patterns through modern ones is dependent on the conditions at start, when the process of hypothesized Neolithic expansion began.

The shortcomings of the Wave of Advance have the implication that the appearance of agro-pastoral economies in Spain and Portugal cannot be simplistically self-explained as the result of the spread of the populations

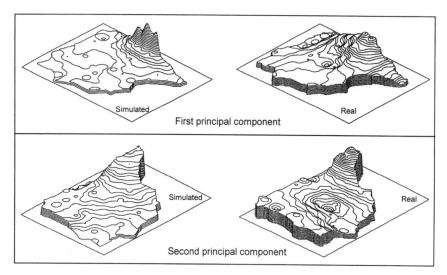

6.7   The genetic history of the Iberian peninsula after Calafell and Bertranpetit (1993:Figs. 4–7, modified). The first principal component is interpreted by these authors as representing the pre-Neolithic population background and the second principal component is interpreted as reflecting the consequences of Neolithic demic diffusion. Simulations were based on the assumptions of Ammerman and Cavalli-Sforza's Wave of Advance model for the spread of agro-pastoral economies across Europe. If the historical significance of the second principal component was correctly interpreted, the disagreement between simulated and real gene frequencies constitutes a refutation of the idea that such a spread was a gradual, southwestwards "oil-spill" process.

that practiced them. Alternative explanatory frameworks available in the literature can be grouped in two categories: (a) independent invention and (b) acculturation models. Independent invention in Iberia was favored, among others, by Acosta and Pellicer (1990) and Olaria (1988). As mentioned above, the empirical foundation of their models is seriously faulty and forces us to eliminate them from further consideration. Acculturation models have been put forward by Guilaine (1976) and Lewthwaite (1986a, 1986b) for the western Mediterranean area and, more recently, by Whittle (1996) for Europe as a whole. According to these models, the local hunter-gatherer populations would have been driven to the adoption of agro-pastoral economies by a number of different causes. They would have gradually acquired the different items of the Neolithic package as needed, doing so by means of long-distance exchange routes that were already operative in the Mesolithic. The classic example of such a scenario is southern France. There, according to data from several sites, mainly located in the Languedoc, the process would have begun with the introduction of sheep in traditional economies. A few hundred years later, pottery would have made its first appearance, to be followed, in the centuries to come, by the other domesticates, such as pigs and cattle. Sedentary villages, however, would not become a feature of the landscape until the Chasséen Middle Neolithic, when cereal agriculture would have become dominant and the region entered the "consolidation phase" of Zvelebil and Rowley-Conwy (1986).

As previously argued, this scenario needs to be submitted to a taphonomic critique (Zilhão 1993). Examination of the published evidence raises serious doubts about the concept of "Mesolithic sheep" put forward by Geddes (1983) (see also Binder, this volume, and Rowley-Conwy 1995). In some cases, such bones are probably intrusive, as was recently demonstrated in the case of Châteauneuf-les-Martigues (Courtin *et al.* 1985). The Languedoc sites (such as Dourgne and Gazel), on the other hand, have high-altitude catchments, which suggests that in many cases we may be dealing with bones of ibex or chamois, particularly since the remains in question tend to be mainly composed of immature animals. In his recent revision of the faunal material from the Mesolithic levels of the Dourgne rockshelter, Geddes (1993) has acknowledged this possibility. As a result, definite ovicaprids dropped to 4% in level 7 and to 3% in level 8 of the total number of identifiable specimens recovered, instead of 29% and 38%, as before. Faced with this evidence, Guilaine (1993) has accepted that the supposedly Mesolithic ovicaprid remains in level 8 are probably intrusive and tentatively reinterpreted the overlying level 7 as a palimpsest of two different occupations, one Mesolithic and one Neolithic, attributing the latter to the first explorations of the Corbières by shepherds coming into the area from coastal villages.

The idea of an early adoption of sheep by the Mesolithic hunter-gatherers of southeastern France is also contradicted by the evidence from Mediterranean Spain reviewed above, which demonstrates that Neolithic innovations appear (for instance at Cova de l'Or) as a "complete package" some time before 5500 BC. Therefore, as suggested by Binder and Courtin (1986) and Binder (this volume), the absence or rarity of cereal remains and of evidence of sedentary agricultural settlement in the Cardial "culture" of southern France may be simply a consequence of differential preservation (or preferential excavation) of site types (caves and rockshelters) that, in the Neolithic, would have been used in a logistic way, for special purposes (herding or hunting). In this perspective, the now submerged, open-air site of Leucate (Guilaine *et al.* 1984) would be the French equivalent of La Draga, that is, an example of the vastly under-represented agricultural villages that would have constituted the sedentary focus of the Cardial Neolithic settlement systems.

The mechanisms suggested for the piecemeal introduction of Neolithic domesticates and items of material culture in the hunter-gatherer economy of west Mediterranean Europe are not exempt from criticism either. Arguments based on sheep (Lewthwaite 1986a, 1986b) or pottery

(Barnett 1990b) as prestige items accumulated in a socially competitive environment have to face the objections that: (1) pottery is not recorded in pure hunter-gatherer contexts such as the Muge shell-middens, in Portugal; (2) pigs do not seem to have been domesticated until the later part of the early Neolithic and sheep are likely to have been an unbearable burden in the framework of a mobile economy based on the resources of the temperate forest (Rowley-Conwy 1986, Helmer 1993); (3) there is no indication in the archaeological record of the existence in the Mesolithic of long-distance exchange networks through which domesticates might have arrived to the shores of Mediterranean France (such as those that were responsible for the presence of Sardinian obsidian at Arene Candide – Ammerman and Polglase 1997, Tykot n.d.); (4) wherever exchange networks across a Mesolithic–Neolithic frontier are documented, as happens in Scandinavia (Price 1991, this volume), it is artifacts, not domesticates, that initially circulated; (5) although Zvelebil (1994b) thinks that burial practices in the Mesolithic of north temperate Europe show "some degree of social hierarchy," Knutsson (1995:204) considers that there are no real clues in the archaeological record of the area, when interpreted in the light of ethnographic evidence, of social inequality and ranking, "with the exception of the somewhat doubtful circumstances at Olenij Ostrov," and Price *et al.* (1995:122) note that "no evidence of elite burial treatment is found in the Ertebølle" (see also Larsson 1990); and (6) even if Zvelebil's interpretation is accepted for the circum-Baltic area, nothing even remotely resembling ranking can be inferred from the interment practices of western Mediterranean Mesolithic hunter-gatherers as exemplified in the hundreds of burials contained in the shell-midden sites of the estuaries of the Tagus and the Sado (Arnaud 1987).

An alternative model: maritime pioneer colonization

The complete absence of serious evidence of independent invention and the problems encountered by models of indigenous adoption when confronted with the empirical data indicate that some form of demic diffusion is still the most powerful explanation for the appearance of Neolithic economies in western Mediterranean Europe and, in particular, in Iberia. However, the above-mentioned contradiction between Calafell and Bertranpetit's simulation and the real genetic data indicates that gradualist "Wave of Advance" models cannot be accepted either. This is also brought forward by the fact that such models predicted that, at the rate of spread calculated by Ammerman and Cavalli-Sforza (1984), agro-pastoral economies would have reached the Pyrenees some time between 4900 and 3800 BC. However, such economies are present in Portugal from at least 5500–5250 BC, as is shown by the accelerator radiocarbon dating of sheep bones from Caldeirão, and probably as early as 5750–5500 BC, as suggested by the typology of some Cardial vessels recovered at other cave sites located in the limestone massifs of Portuguese Estremadura.

Therefore, the spread of the Neolithic package from the Gulf of Lions to the estuary of the Mondego seems to have been, in historical perspective, a punctuated event, rather than a gradual process. Given the littoral orientation of the Neolithic settlement, and the existence of well-documented navigational capabilities in the Mediterranean since at least the early Holocene (recently confirmed by the discovery of ceramic toy boats in the early Neolithic underwater lake site of La Marmotta, near Rome – Fugazzola Delpino and Pessina 1994), it is likely that we are dealing here with leapfrogging colonization by small seafaring groups of agriculturalists, as previously suggested (Zilhão 1993) and as is becoming to be increasingly accepted in the literature (Budja 1996, Harris 1996b, Renfrew 1996).

In the present state of our knowledge, such seems to be the only kind of process capable of explaining both the enclave situation of the earliest Neolithic sites of Portugal and the punctuated, irregular nature of the spread of agro-pastoral economies along the northern shores of the west Mediterranean. Neither of these features can be accounted for in the framework of Wave of Advance or "adoption through prestige exchange in a socially competitive environment" models, since both carry the implication that the spread of food-production economies should proceed at a regular and continuous pace and leaving no "gaps" behind. If early cereal agriculture was economically superior and expanded through the gradual assimilation of neighboring people and neighboring resources into the new system as the latter required more and more land, as assumed by Wave of Advance models, how did it get to Estremadura first, further away from the nearest possible source than the Alentejo, and why did the hunter-gatherer groups of the Alentejo maintain their traditional way of life for at least another 500 years after agriculture was introduced only 150 km to the north? If Mesolithic society was competitive and ranked, and pottery and sheep entered Estremadura in the framework of the accumulation strategies of prestige-seeking leaders or would-be leaders, why did the the latter's Alentejo peers not compete in the same way for the accumulation of the same prestigious items? And, if it is from mortuary data that incipient social ranking is inferred, why are there no signs of those (or any other) prestigious items to be found in the burials of the estuarine food consumers of the Tagus and Sado shell-middens while, in contrast, they are always associated with the human remains of their contemporaneous terrestrial food consumers buried in the cave sites of the limestone massifs of Estremadura?

In a pioneer colonization model, these patterns of the process are easily explained. Early cereal agriculture was not economically superior to European Mesolithic adaptations in terms of work load and long-term stability (Zvelebil and Rowley-Conwy 1986, Gregg 1988), especially when productive and reliable aquatic resources were available, as was the case in coastal Portugal. There would be, therefore, no economic incentive for adoption, and no adoption did in fact occur, even when the new economic system was immediately available as a result of the establishment of farming settlements nearby. Relatively peaceful coexistence between the two systems was made possible by the fact that, at first, farmers only occupied the interstitial areas of the local hunter-gatherer settlement. Peasant economies, however, are more productive, in terms of the amount of people they can feed per area unit of territory. Their specific demographic dynamic would lead, therefore, to a greater population growth among the pioneer groups, resulting in the gradual assimilation, through intermarriage, of neighboring hunter-gatherers, and in the correlative expansion of the new system to all the surrounding areas where it was ecologically viable and socially feasible. Given the discontinuous nature of the distribution of good agricultural land in the broken limestone terrain of the northern shores of the west Mediterranean where the Cardial "culture" developed, this process would require, at a certain point in time, that pioneers would leave to settle in distant areas that might have been previously reconnoitered through the communication and travel routes used by the assimilated local hunter-gatherers. That areas such as the coasts of the Alentejo were "skipped" over may have to do with their different geography, as is indicated by the fact that the expansion of the Cardial "culture" stopped at the mouth of the Mondego, north of which Mediterranean limestone ecosystems no longer exist. In Mediterranean Iberia, the subsequent expansion from the initial enclaves led to the integration of these "skipped" areas, which seems to have been accomplished between 5000 and 4750 BC, at a time when farming had also begun to expand to the interior Meseta, making it possible for pottery to be introduced into the Mesolithic of the Cantabrian strip.

Economic pressure, however, is not necessarily the only reason for the budding off of pioneer groups, as is shown by the archaeological and ethnohistorical data concerning the mechanisms and the motives for the colonization of the Pacific islands, which was initiated by primitive agriculturalists whose technology probably was not more sophisticated than that available to the peoples living around the shores of the Mediterranean in early Holocene times. Such colonization was the result of purposeful and planned navigational enterprises and, often, the movement from one island or archipelago to the next would take place long before any pressure on resources is documented in the archaeological record (Kirch 1984, Irwin 1992). As in the Pacific, social reasons or the prevalence of a "pioneer ethic" enforced by tradition and rooted in the previous history of farming groups may actually account better, therefore, for the apparent swiftness that seems to characterize the spread of the Neolithic package along the shores of west Mediterranean Europe.

Özdogan (1997:16–17) has recently suggested that the initial westwards spread of agriculture out of central Anatolia coincided with the collapse of the Pre-Pottery Neolithic B, for which there are strong indications of a stratified society and a strong impact of cult practices. In contrast, the succeeding Neolithic societies of western Anatolia and southeastern Europe lack any archaeological evidence of specially built temples and of social ranking in settlement or in burial. Özdogan's hypothesis is that these egalitarian rural societies were originated by the migration of groups carrying to the west "all aspects of their culture except central authority." It may not be too bold to extend this hypothesis a little further and to suggest that the driving force behind the expansion of the Neolithic across the west Mediterranean may have been a social imperative rooted in a tradition going back to the events leading to the collapse of the Pre-Pottery Neolithic B: the imperative to fission before groups get too large and conditions arise for the development of social inequality. In sum, agriculture may have been brought to Europe by pioneers escaping from dominance in ranked societies and striving to maintain egalitarianism through the application of strict controls to group size. Along the shores of the north Mediterranean, this tendency to fission and move on would have been further reinforced because opportunities for settlement and expansion around initial enclaves were limited by physical geography and the presence of local hunter-gatherer groups.

Continuity and discontinuity in physical anthropological data

The comparison of the spread of agriculturalists in the west Mediterranean with the colonization of the Pacific islands must not overlook the major difference that exists between the two: the shores of the Mediterranean were not uninhabited at the time of the postulated farmer maritime dispersals and, therefore, the action of the local Mesolithic populations needs to be considered in the process. If people moved along with domestic resources, it should be possible, using Iberian fossil samples – those farthest away from the presumed origin of European agriculturalists – to establish mtDNA or Y-chromosome lineages extending to the earliest Neolithic of the Fertile Crescent, where wheat, barley, sheep, and goats were first domesticated and from where they spread into the continent. If Iberian early Neolithic people were shown to belong to such lineages and Iberian Mesolithic people were shown to be different in this regard, population movement would be proved, regardless of the extent to which the input of incoming agriculturalists affected the gene pool of succeeding populations.

If the input of external farmer groups was important, as might have been the case if local hunter-gatherers were rapidly absorbed by incoming agriculturalists with higher fertility, one would have considerable changes; for all practical purposes, the end-result would be population replacement, even if local Mesolithic groups participated in the process; the extent, nature, and regional variation of such a participation, in turn, would affect the degree of heterogeneity of succeeding Neolithic populations. If, on the contrary, it had been local hunter-gatherers who rapidly absorbed the newcomers and changed their way of life to become farmers and shepherds, one might have very few changes except as regards those brought about by the new nutritional patterns or by adaptation to different kinds of work patterns and new types of terrain; the end-result would be Neolithic homogeneity or Neolithic heterogeneity depending on which was the situation in the Mesolithic, and the external input, although perhaps visible in fossil samples, might have since vanished, or become of little significance, in modern populations.

Since no fossil DNA data are available at present for this time period, the extent to which local Mesolithic people contributed to the later gene-pool of Iberian populations and, conversely, the impact of agricultural colonists on the demographic patterns extant once the transition to food production was completed, can only be evaluated from physical anthropological evidence. Unfortunately, not enough data are available for late Mesolithic skeletal morphology outside Portugal and the scant data on the osteology of the earliest Neolithic people of the west Mediterranean do not allow, in most cases, significant comparisons. Arguments based on skeletal morphology also have to face the complicating possibility that external farmer groups may not have been significantly different from local Mesolithic people and that, therefore, their impact on the osteological record may be undetectable. In the extreme case, that is, if west Mediterranean Mesolithic groups were morphologically homogeneous and if the northwestwards spread of agriculture from southern Italy was initiated by local Mesolithic people who had become Neolithic through indigenous adoption of novel resources with insignificant external population inputs from areas further to the east, total population replacement could have occurred in spite of apparent continuity in osteology.

Over the past fifteen years, Lubell and Jackes (1985, 1988), Jackes and Lubell (1992, n.d.), Lubell *et al.* (1994) and Jackes *et al.* (1997a, 1997b) have tried to address the issue of population continuity or population replacement in the Mesolithic–Neolithic transition through the analysis of the rich skeletal material available in Portugal. In the non-metrical dental traits dendrogram reproduced in Fig. 6.8, Jackes *et al.* (1997a) show that there is less difference between samples from the late Mesolithic and the late Neolithic of Portugal than there is between southern Ontario proto-historic and historic Iroquois groups belonging to the Huron and Neutral nations. Given that the latter are considered to correspond to populations that are known to have been culturally and biologically homogeneous, these results would indicate genetic continuity across the Mesolithic–Neolithic boundary in Portugal. From the previous discussion it necessarily follows, however, that the biological homogeneity inferred from this dendrogram may exist even if the introduction of agriculture was indeed associated with pioneer colonization, given the demographic features of the model: the small size of the colonist groups and the nature of the process through which local Mesolithic people were assimilated (intermarriage, leading to

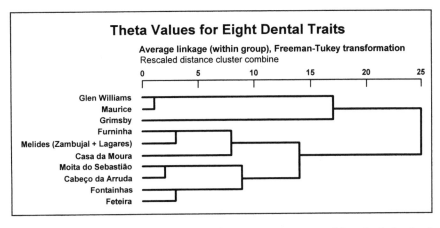

6.8 Results of the cluster analysis of seven Portuguese prehistoric skeletal collections using eight non-metrical traits from dentition and controlling for
sample size through the application of the Freeman-Tukey transformation
(after Jackes *et al.* 1997a). Moita do Sebastião and Cabeço da Arruda are
close-by Mesolithic sites belonging to the Muge cluster of shell-middens.
Melides, Furninha, Casa da Moura, Feteira and Fontainhas were used as
burial caves mostly in the Late Neolithic and Copper Age periods, between
c. 4000 and *c.* 5000 BP (the collections from Casa da Moura and Furninha
also contain an epi-Cardial human bone component, probably small). The
North American samples date to late proto-historic or historic times:
Maurice is Iroquois Huron, Glen Williams, 150 km to the south, is Iroquois
Neutral, as is Grimsby, located another 50 km further south of Glen
Williams, across Lake Ontario.

appropriation by the agriculturalists of the reproductive potential of the
local populations and of their genetic heritage – Moore 1985).

   Furthermore, as exhaustively argued elsewhere (Zilhão 1998), the
interpretation of the American Indian data provided by Jackes *et al.* (1997a)
is questionable. In fact, the collections they analyzed group according to
geography and ethnicity, which can be taken as an indication that the
Huron and the Neutral may have been biologically more distinct than
assumed by the authors. Thus, the comparison would highlight simply that
the degree of biological difference between Portuguese Mesolithic and
Neolithic people may not have been greater than that between neighboring
populations documented ethnohistorically. This is entirely compatible with
the maritime pioneer colonization model, which places the presumed
origin for the earliest Neolithic Portuguese in the nearby Spanish regions
of Andalucía and Valencia, as indicated by the close stylistical similarities
between ceramic assemblages from the two regions.

   Jackes *et al.* (1997b:884), however, argue against demic mechanisms
on the basis that they would require "a massive advantage for the incoming

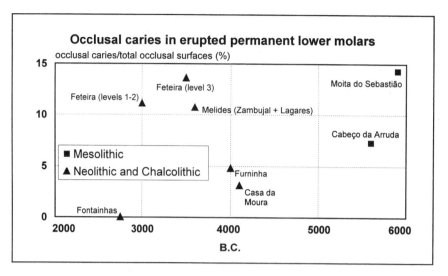

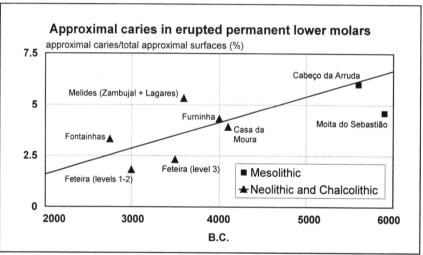

6.9   Dental evidence for the Mesolithic–Neolithic transition in Portugal (after Lubell *et al.* 1994 and Jackes *et al.* 1997a). Late Neolithic–Copper Age values were retrodicted into Mesolithic times but, given the small sample sizes, the trend line was computed without consideration of the early Neolithic material. Caries rates do not show variation through time. The retrodiction of the average bucco-lingual breadth of lower second molars gives results lower than those actually observed and the values for the earliest Neolithic molars are already in the range of those from later periods. The late Neolithic–Copper Age tooth size pattern cannot be considered as the outcome of a gradual trend beginning in the Mesolithic. Instead, it seems to have become established rather abruptly at the Mesolithic–Neolithic boundary.

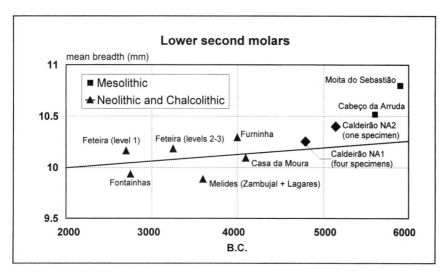

6.9 (*cont.*)

Neolithic population, one that would permit the newcomers an extremely high fertilty rate." The assumption that population replacement can occur only in situations of extreme imbalance is unwarranted. Zubrow (1989), for instance, has demonstrated, in the case of Neanderthal/early modern human interaction, that a difference of no more than 2% in mortality would suffice to bring about the total extinction of the autochthonous European population in thirty generations. Since peasant economies are more productive (the simplification of the ecosystems enables them to feed more people in less space), in situations of initial pioneer settlement they can grow much faster than local hunter-gatherers. As shown by Zubrow's models, this different dynamics would easily result, even if the demographic advantage of pioneer colonists was minor, in the rapid assimilation of neighboring hunter-gatherers, particularly if both groups intermarried. It is interesting to note, in this regard, that elsewhere Jackes *et al.* (1997a:652) state that fertility did increase significantly, by something like 50%, in the Portuguese Neolithic. In fact, on the basis of data from Mesolithic Cabeço da Arruda and late Neolithic Casa da Moura, they estimate that "while Mesolithic women had four children on average, Neolithic women had about six."

Their other results also suggest that, in Portugal, there is a lot more biological discontinuity at the Mesolithic–Neolithic boundary than they are willing to admit (Figs. 6.6, 6.9 and 6.10). Jackes *et al.* (1997b:844) conclude that "the Mesolithic–Neolithic transition period shows a shift in diet and related patterns of dental pathology, but it is neither sudden nor at the boundary . . . instead, it is gradual and continuous across the boundary." In

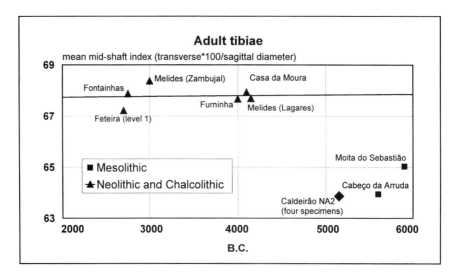

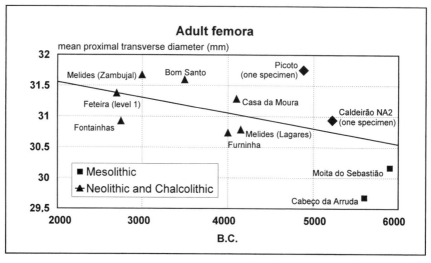

6.10   Lower limb morphological evidence for the Mesolithic–Neolithic transition in Portugal (after Jackes and Lubell n.d. and Jackes *et al.* 1997a). Late Neolithic–Copper Age values were retrodicted into Mesolithic times but, given the small sample sizes, the trend line was computed without consideration of the early Neolithic material. Mesolithic adult tibiae are saber-shinned, while those from the late Neolithic–Copper Age are much rounder in mid-shaft. It is impossible to retrodict the later Neolithic trend and obtain Mesolithic values. The mean proximal transverse diameter of adult femora is consistently larger in the late Neolithic–Copper Age than in the Mesolithic and the odd early Neolithic specimens available for analysis already display the later condition. In late Neolithic collections from the Alentejo, the antero-posterior diameter is also larger and, as a result,

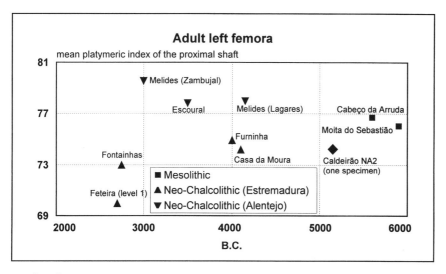

Adult left femora

mean platymeric index of the proximal shaft

6.10 (*cont.*)

values for the proximal platymeric index of adult left femora are closer to those found in the Mesolithic. If femoral shape is genetically controlled, this might indicate that the contribution of local Mesolithic people to the gene-pool of subsequent populations was more important than in Estremadura.

good accord with the pattern revealed by our Fig. 6.6, however, Lubell *et al.* (1994:213), using the same data, have stated exactly the opposite: "there is stable isotopic evidence for a marked difference in diet between Mesolithic and Neolithic Portuguese human remains. The Mesolithic diet can be characterized as a mixture of terrestrial and marine foods, while the Neolithic population appears to have consumed only terrestrial foods (herbivore flesh and plant foods)." Since this difference is already apparent in early Neolithic samples, the conclusion seems inescapable that the shift was indeed sudden and at the boundary.

Data on molar size and caries (Fig. 6.9) are more ambiguous. Teeth from Cabeço da Arruda fit a trend of gradual decrease from the Mesolithic to the Neolithic in the incidence of approximal caries, but those from Moita do Sebastião do not, and no trend can be established for occlusal caries. Thus, dental pathology does not seem to change across the transition. Tooth size, however, undergoes a marked change at the boundary: retrodicting the values obtained for late Neolithic/Copper Age molar breadth into Mesolithic times would give results lower than those actually observed, and the values for the earliest Neolithic molars are already in the range of those from later periods. As is the case with palaeoisotopic data, the late Neolithic/Copper Age tooth size pattern is not the outcome of a gradual trend beginning in the Mesolithic.

Fig. 6.10 charts the information on limb bone morphology in Table 2 of Jackes and Lubell (n.d.) and in Figs. 5–6 of Jackes *et al.* (1997b). Mesolithic adult tibiae are saber-shinned, while those from the late Neolithic and the Copper Age are much rounder in mid-shaft. It is impossible to retrodict the later Neolithic trend and obtain Mesolithic values although it is not yet clear which was the condition prevalent in the early Neolithic, since the average for Caldeirão has a very large standard deviation (there is no statistically meaningful difference between Caldeirão and Lagares). The mean proximal transverse diameter of adult femora is consistently larger in the late Neolithic/Copper Age than in the Mesolithic and the odd early Neolithic specimens available for analysis already display the later condition: Mesolithic values fall way below the retrodictions of the trend. However, in some Neolithic collections, the antero-posterior diameter is also larger and, as a result, values for the proximal platymeric index of adult left femora are not very different from those found in the Mesolithic.

If these differences in the size of teeth and in the morphology of leg bones are related to changes in nutritional patterns, they are in good accord with the occurrence of the abrupt dietary shift indicated by the palaeoisotopic evidence. The same is true if, as sustained by Jackes *et al.* (1997a), the differences are related to activities, since they would then correlate well with the replacement of the hunter-fisher-gatherer way of life of the local Mesolithic by farming and ovicaprid herding. In fact, such simultaneous shifts in diet and in activities would coincide with the appearance of pottery and sheep in the archaeological record of Portugal *c.* 5500 BC.

American Indian archaeological, historic, and forensic data have led Gilbert and Gill (1990) to suggest that proximal femoral shape is under genetic control rather than environmentally regulated. If so, the patterns in Fig. 6.10 may be interpreted as indicating that the marked discontinuities in material culture, settlement patterns, burial practices, diets, and teeth size are indeed associated with pioneer colonization. In this context, the regional differentiation in late Neolithic/Copper Age proximal femoral platymeria may also indicate that, in the Alentejo, the contribution of local Mesolithic people to the later gene-pool may have been larger than in Estremadura, as previously hypothesized on the basis of archaeological and chronometric data alone (Zilhão 1992, 1993).

Concluding remarks

Inter-regional comparisons, such as those upon which both the Wave of Advance and the maritime pioneer colonization model are based, have to rely heavily on radiocarbon dating. However, even if it is fairly easy to compensate for systematic inter-laboratory differences and even if the use of the appropriate taphonomic filters enables us to eliminate those dates and contexts that are mixed or not related to the Neolithic at all, the impact of other factors in the patterns revealed by the available dates also needs to be evaluated. For instance, differences between bone and charcoal samples suggest that an old-wood effect may be hindering a better understanding of the LBK expansion across the Danubian basin (Whittle 1990a). To what extent this may affect the west Mediterranean patterns is currently unknown, but the fact that, at La Draga, the dates on the oak pillars are some four hundred years earlier than those obtained from seeds or from charcoal collected in the hearths (Tarrus *et al.* 1994) may be an indication that a similar problem does exist in southern Europe and suggests that the issue should be explicitly addressed in the future. To overcome these kinds of problems, a collaborative inter-regional program for the accelerator dating of short-lived samples of materials that can in themselves be taken as proof that domesticates are indeed present at a certain point in time is an obvious necessity and should deserve priority efforts by all researchers concerned.

Such a program should also include stable isotope determinations, aimed at establishing palaeonutrition data for the human populations across the Mesolithic–Neolithic boundary, in order to evaluate the real impact on subsistence of those domesticates that are actually shown to be present. The issue of colonization might also be further clarified by more in-depth comparative studies of anatomical data on bone morphology and of ancient DNA obtained from the different late Mesolithic and early Neolithic regional populations of Mediterranean Europe. In fact, given the shortcomings of historical reconstructions of population movements based on modern genetic information and in light of the limitations of the skeletal material to address issues of colonization involving human groups that, originally, may have been biologically identical and morphologically similar, it would seem that a definitive test of competing explanations for the physical anthropological patterns can only come from direct comparison of genetic material extracted from the prehistoric human remains themselves.

Finally, as Barnett (this volume) points out, radiocarbon dating only allows us to work with time units that, at best, encompass at least as much as five human generations. Thus, although useful in terms of testing processual models, radiocarbon dating does not enable us to address real-time historical events. When we state, for instance, that the Neolithic may have appeared simultaneously in Valencia and in Estremadura, we are actually talking about processes best described as penecontemporaneous and resulting in patterns that subsume a few hundred years of human activity. Even at such a low resolution, however, it would seem that, in Iberia, "indigenous adoption" only operates in the Cantabrian strip, and that the expectations derived from Wave of Advance models that are testable against the archaeological record are not met in Mediterranean Spain and Atlantic Portugal. "Maritime pioneer colonization" seems to fare better in this regard, but still needs to be more thoroughly tested, particularly through simulation studies such as that performed by Gregg (1988) for southern Germany. With the help of biological, ethnographical, and historical data, such studies might provide sophisticated models for the contact and interaction between pioneer colonist farmers and indigenous hunter-gatherers that operate in real human time and with adequate consideration of the reconstructed geographical characteristics and economic potential of the spatial scenario in which the process takes place.

Acknowledgments

This paper was originally presented at the Symposium on "The Transition to Agriculture in Prehistoric Europe," held at the 60th Annual Meeting of the Society for American Archaeology (Minneapolis, May 1995). My participation in this event was made possible thanks to the financial support granted by the *Fundação Luso-Americana para o Desenvolvimento*. I also wish to thank Cidália Duarte and José Arnaud for making available results from their unpublished work on the Neolithic collective burial site of Algar do Bom Santo. Pablo Arias, William K. Barnett, Cidália Duarte, Antonio Gilman, Mary Jackes, David Lubell, T. Douglas Price and an anonymous Cambridge University Press reviewer provided useful comments on previous versions and were valuable sources of diverse information. Any errors or omissions are my own.

7

The origins of agriculture in south-central Europe

Introduction

The heartland of Europe, encompassing southern Germany together with adjacent parts of Austria and Switzerland, has long possessed what seemed to be a clear chronology of the Mesolithic–Neolithic transition (Fig. 7.1). The Late Mesolithic, clearly distinguishable from the Early Mesolithic by the presence of trapezoidal microliths, regular blade technology, and extensive antler-working, is known from caves and rockshelters and a few open-air sites dating to the period beginning around 7800 BP. The best-known sites are situated in the limestone formation of the Jura/Swabian Alb that extends from eastern France through Switzerland and across southern Germany. Most notable among these sites are Birsmatten-Basisgrotte in Switzerland (Bandi 1963) and Jägerhaushöhle, Falkensteinhöhle, Felsdach Inzigkofen and Felsdach Lautereck in Germany (Taute 1973; Fig. 7.2). This Late Mesolithic has an economy based solely on wild foods, emphasizing red and roe deer and wild boar among the larger game, together with fish, small mammals, and birds.

One recently excavated site of this period is Henauhof NW 2 (Jochim 1992). This site was discovered by test trenches placed along the old shoreline of the Federsee lake and a total of 72 m² was excavated in 1991. Artifacts were found in several layers, but the majority lay in a sandy peat and date to the Late Mesolithic. A hearth was found in this sandy peat layer, composed of a roughly oval ash and charcoal lens on a thin layer of yellow clay and measuring 75 by 140 cm. On one side of the hearth was a small concentration of stone artifacts and on the other side a concentration of bone and antler fragments. Several burned stones and bone fragments lay within the hearth itself. Two radiocarbon dates were determined on charcoal from this level: 7260 ± 180 and 6940 ± 60 BP (BETA 46907, 46909). Among the total of 142 stone artifacts were two microliths, including a trapeze, two borers, two burins and three scrapers, two cores, a number of well-made, regular blades,

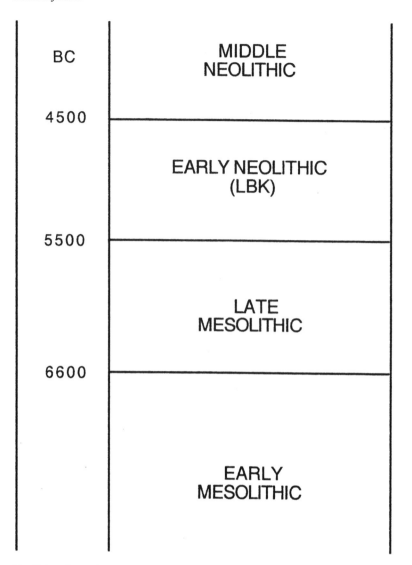

7.1   Traditional south German chronology.

and numerous flakes. The raw materials are mostly local, with a few pieces deriving from approximately 200 km away in Bavaria.

Organic materials were well preserved, but very fragmentary, and include remains of red deer, roe deer, aurochs, boar, beaver, birds, and fish. Red deer remains were most abundant and consist primarily of cranial elements and extremities. One deer metapodial was worked as a hide-scraper. Also among the finds were 142 pieces of antler, comprised of 130 of red deer

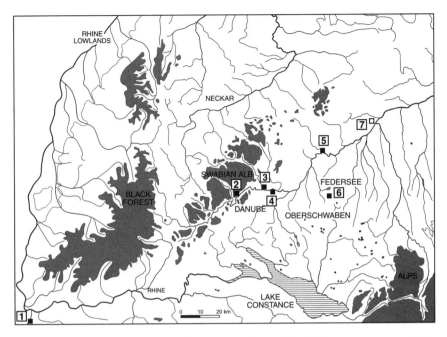

7.2   Distribution of sites. Filled squares: Late Mesolithic; open square: Early Neolithic. 1. Birsmatten-Basisgrotte, 2. Jägerhaushöhle, 3. Falkenstein-höhle, 4. Inzigkofen, 5. Lautereck, 6. Henauhof NW and Henauhof NW 2, 7. Ulm-Eggingen.

and 12 of roe deer. A few of the red deer antler fragments showed cut marks. One unshed roe deer antler suggests a death between April and September. This site appears to represent a very short-term, generalized activity camp, forming part of a seasonal settlement system.

The Neolithic begins in this area around 6700–6500 BP with the appearance of Bandkeramik or LBK villages such as Hienheim (Modderman 1977) and Ulm-Eggingen (Kind 1989) in the Danube drainage and a large number of other sites in the Neckar, Main and Rhine valleys (Sielmann 1971). The economy of these villages is focused largely on agriculture and domestic animals, with varying contributions by wild foods.

One recently excavated example of an important LBK site in this area is Ulm-Eggingen, which lies on a flat hilltop facing southeast over a small tributary valley of the Danube. Although a good portion of the site appears to have been destroyed by modern activities, a total of 16,100 m^2 was excavated from 1982 to 1985. The posthole remains of thirty-four house out-lines were uncovered, including twelve longhouses divided into three parts, twelve smaller houses with only two sections, seven small, single-room houses, and three partial structures. Two of the longhouses had adjoining fenced areas interpreted as gardens. All the houses were accompanied by long ditches that contained most of the recovered artifacts. These included over 100,000 ceramic sherds representing both a coarse and a fine ware, 3220 chipped stone artifacts, and a number of polished stone axes, grinding stones, and hammerstones. The stone raw materials were all locally available. Among the botanical remains were forty-four species of plants, including wheat, barley, linseed, poppy, peas, and a variety of weeds. The few preserved bones could be attributed to domestic cattle and pig. Based on ceramic seriation and analysis of house overlaps, eight different phases of occupation could be distinguished. Radiocarbon dates from the site fall primarily in the period of 6500–5500 BP.

The huge differences between the sites of these two periods suggest a dramatic change in lifeways. The interpretation of this change has traditionally emphasized an agricultural colonization: the LBK was seen to represent an immigration by farming groups originating in western Hungary. Their migration followed the Danube and other river corridors and targeted loess soils in the warmer and drier portions of the area. In its earliest phase, this expansion rapidly reached the Rhine and Neckar valleys, pausing before a secondary expansion in later phases (Fig. 7.3). The fate of the local Late Mesolithic inhabitants of the area was unknown, but seemed inconsequential to cultural developments, given the small number of sites dating to the critical period of transition.

This interpretation is still widely held, so that this area persists as one of the few in Europe where agricultural colonization remains the dominant explanation of this critical economic transformation. Nevertheless, a variety of new excavations and analyses have raised questions about this simple scenario, suggesting that developments were more complex than previously thought, postulating a greater role in later developments by Late Mesolithic inhabitants, and at times challenging the entire notion of an agricultural colonization. My purpose here is to summarize briefly some of this new work, organized around four topics: (1) evidence for agricultural colonization, (2) contrasting expectations for models of local acculturation and borrowing, (3) new studies suggesting local Mesolithic involvement, and (4) issues of contemporaneity between hunter-gatherer and agricultural groups.

Agricultural colonization

The traditional interpretation of an agricultural migration with displacement or absorption of local hunter-gatherers rests on a number of lines of evidence. These include the following.

1 *Non-local origins of foods.* The earliest LBK agricultural crops included einkorn and emmer wheat, barley, millet, peas, lentil, and linseed (Kreuz 1990). Because the wild ancestors of these plants are not native to central Europe, their domesticated forms must have been brought in from elsewhere. Along with them came at least twelve different non-native weed

7.3   Distribution of earliest Linearbandkeramik (LBK) in central Europe.

species that have been identified in the earliest LBK sites. Furthermore, domesticated animals at these sites include sheep, goats, cattle, and pigs, only the latter two of which have wild ancestors native to central Europe. This impressive array of non-native foods suggests to many that they were brought in as part of the functioning economy of immigrants, rather than as items of exchange.

    2 *The rapidity of change.* The appearance of a Neolithic economy and technology is abrupt and instantaneous in archaeological time, with no evidence of incipient stages in this region. Late Mesolithic sites show no signs of incipient cultivation or a long period of experimentation. Rather, agricultural economies appear full-blown with the appearance of LBK sites in the period of approximately 6700–6500 BP.

    3 *The number of different changes.* Most aspects of the archaeological

record show change. The transformation in the economy includes the appearance and immediate dominance of agriculture and animal domestication. Both ceramic and ground stone technology appear as new components of material culture. Settlements are much larger and more permanent, with sturdy houses, large pits and other features, forming a dramatic contrast to the temporary Late Mesolithic camps with no structural remains. Site locations change as well, concentrating on loess soils and river terrace placement rather than the valley caves and lakeside situations that characterize the Late Mesolithic.

4 *The simultaneity of all changes.* These new developments do not appear piecemeal, but rather occur together as a "package" at the new village sites, presumably carried in by a new group of people. This situation contrasts with that in north Europe, for example, where certain items of new technology, such as polished stone axes, appear long before agriculture.

5 *The uniformity across the entire area of change.* The LBK culture area is notable for the uniformity of material culture across its range, although slight differences in the relative importance of certain features are evident (Modderman 1988). The general similarities include specific crops, tools such as polished stone axes, patterns of house layout and construction, site location, and ceramic manufacture and decoration. On the other hand, projectile points appear to be more frequent along the western fringes of the overall LBK distribution (Milisauskas 1978) and the roles of animal husbandry and hunting show considerable variability among sites (Pucher 1987).

6 *The spatial coherence of the area showing change.* A culture zone of earliest LBK is often mapped as one contiguous zone (e.g. Sherratt 1980), easily interpretable as a population continuously expanding along a front, following major river valleys and initially selectively targeting the warmer and drier portions of this region.

7 *The low density of Late Mesolithic sites.* In comparison to the Early Mesolithic, the Late Mesolithic is known from relatively few sites in this region (Jochim 1990). The scarcity of sites has been interpreted as indicating a low population density, which, if true, would have facilitated unhindered LBK expansion and minimized any role for local hunter-gatherers in later developments.

Contrasting explanations and their implications

Because of the non-local origins of important Neolithic crops and domestic animals, completely independent local development of agricultural economies has never been a serious alternative explanation for Neolithic origins in this area. Rather, challenges to the migration hypothesis, best articulated by Whittle (1996), have suggested local adoption of non-local resources and technologies, facilitated through contacts and interaction extending outside of central Europe. In order to discuss the new research that challenges the simple migration model, therefore, a framework of expectations that are consistent with models of local acculturation and borrowing, and that contrast with the types of evidence for migration mentioned above, will first be presented.

1 *Evidence of prior contact between local hunter-gatherers and agricultural groups elsewhere in Europe.* If the Late Mesolithic groups in fact acquired non-local resources and technologies, there should exist some evidence for their interaction beyond the region of central Europe.

2 *Slow, gradual change.* Borrowing and acculturation are likely to be less abrupt than population replacement, and should show some incipient stages of development.

3 *Smaller range of changes.* It is less likely that every aspect of life would be transformed through borrowing than through migration and replacement; borrowing should be more selective, at least initially, so that some continuity should exist in other aspects of the archaeological record across the transition.

4 *Different rates of change in different aspects of the record.* A process of acculturation might show a pattern of piecemeal changes, as different items are adopted at different times and rates.

5 *Differentiation within the area of adoption.* Different local groups, responding to their own contexts and needs, should show differing patterns of borrowing and acculturation, in terms of both what is borrowed and the rate at which it is incorporated into local economies.

6 *Patchy spatial appearance of changes.* Rather than forming a continuous distribution, borrowing might be spatially patchy, depending on the reasons for borrowing. For example, domestication of plants and animals might appear first only in areas of greatest resource stress among Late Mesolithic groups, resulting in a mosaic of contemporary "Neolithic" and "Mesolithic" sites.

7 *Higher local hunter-gatherer populations.* If local groups were responsible for the successful development of the local Neolithic through borrowing and acculturation, these people should be readily apparent in the archaeological record before these changes as well.

Challenges to the colonization model

Challenges to the prevailing migration hypothesis rest upon a number of types of evidence, all related to the various points mentioned above.

1 It is now clear that Late Mesolithic groups in this area participated in wide-ranging networks of exchange and interaction. These linked them indirectly to regions in the southwest and southeast where Early Neolithic developments occurred (Fig. 7.4). Rähle (1978) has documented at Late Mesolithic sites along the upper Danube the presence of shells that derive ultimately from the western Mediterranean, for which he infers a

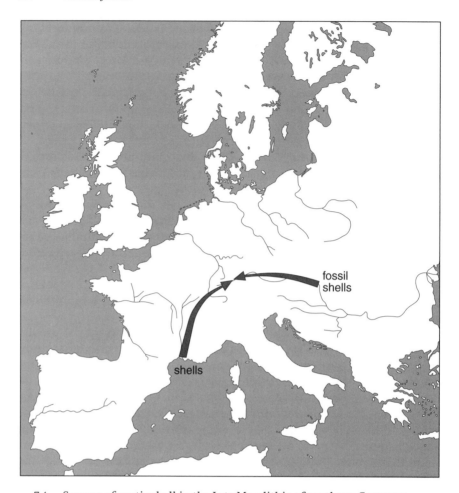

7.4   Sources of exotic shell in the Late Mesolithic of southern Germany.

route of exchange up the Rhône and into Switzerland and southern
Germany. Similarly, fossil shells in these same sites have been traced to
deposits far down the Danube to the east into Hungary. Furthermore, Clark
(1980) suggests that the appearance of regular blade technology and trapezes, which characterize the Late Mesolithic, derive ultimately from southeastern Europe and indicate easy communication across the continent.
Through such networks, Late Mesolithic groups could have gained knowledge of new technologies and resources, and even the resources themselves,
well before 6500 BP.

2 Although the transformation of Mesolithic economies in this area
still appears to be rapid, recent work provides hints that this impression
derives in part from our level of chronological resolution. Gronenborn

(1990b, 1997), for example, points out that recently excavated sites of the earliest LBK show relatively fewer sickle blades than do later LBK sites, suggesting that initially agriculture may not have had the economic importance it later achieved. At the same time, projectile points appear to be somewhat more abundant in the earliest LBK, perhaps indicating a more important initial role for hunting. Whittle (1996) has also suggested that the evidence of small, dispersed settlements of the earliest LBK is compatible with an interpretation of some mobility, implying that full sedentism was slower to develop than previously thought. Another development of relevance here is the more precise dating of this earliest phase of the LBK, suggesting that it may have lasted up to 400 years, much longer than previously thought, beginning perhaps as early as 6700 BP (Kind 1992). If so, then the potential exists for differences within this phase and a more gradual appearance of Neolithic traits.

3 A hypothesis of borrowing and acculturation implies that there may be some evidence of continuity in the archaeological record between the Late Mesolithic and earliest LBK. Despite earlier work that emphasized clear discontinuities in the lithic assemblages of these two periods (Kozlowski 1973, Tringham 1968), it is precisely in this aspect of the material record that some continuities are now being suggested. Kozlowski (1973), in fact, recognizes some continuity in projectile point forms, including trapezes, in the upper Danube region. Gronenborn (1990b, 1997) points out the strong similarities between Late Mesolithic and earliest LBK in the high degree of blade regularity, a similarity that diminishes in later LBK phases. Both Gronenborn (1990b, 1997) and Tillmann (1994) emphasize the dominance of primary faceting as a technique of core preparation in both the Late Mesolithic and earliest LBK in this area.

Finally, Gronenborn (1990b, 1997) argues for the presence of asymmetric, triangular microliths with bifacially retouched bases in both Late Mesolithic assemblages of France and the Low Countries and the westernmost earliest LBK near the Rhine. Such points also occur in the Late Mesolithic of northwest Switzerland and apparently the Swiss morainic lowlands as well, a region where no early Neolithic is known (Nielsen 1992). On the basis of such continuities in lithic technology and typology, all of the authors mentioned argue for a greater local Mesolithic role in LBK developments.

4 Evidence is also accumulating that suggests that all aspects of a Neolithic way of life did not appear in this area simultaneously. Pollen data indicating forest clearance have been reported for several regions in southern Germany and Switzerland well before 6500 BP (Liese-Kleiber 1990). Although some of this evidence has recently been redated and attributed to later periods, a portion still remains to fuel speculation about Late Mesolithic agricultural activities prior to the appearance of other Neolithic elements (Erny-Rodmann *et al.* 1997, Haas 1996, Nielsen 1997).

7.5   Distribution of La Hoguette ceramics. Black squares: sites with La Hoguette ceramics; shaded area: distribution of earliest LBK.

More secure is the evidence for the independent appearance of ceramics and domesticated sheep/goats in parts of this area at the same time or prior to the appearance of the LBK. This evidence takes the form of the La Hoguette phenomenon. La Hoguette refers to a type of ceramics, quite different in tempering, treatment, form, and decoration from those of the LBK, with clear links in these traits to ceramics from southern France (Lüning *et al.* 1989). Although named after a site in northwestern France, the major distribution of these ceramics occurs in the Rhine and Neckar valleys, and extends across southwest Germany into Bavaria (Fig. 7.5). They occur primarily in sites associated with LBK ceramics, and to the east of the Rhine, particularly with those of the earliest LBK phase. Nevertheless, some "pure"

La Hoguette deposits are also known, for example Stuttgart-Wilhelma in the Neckar valley (Schütz *et al.* 1992). At several sites, such as Bavans in north-eastern France, the ceramics may be associated with a Late Mesolithic lithic industry. Another notable association of these ceramics is with domestic sheep/goats at several sites. There seems to be growing acceptance of this phenomenon as a "culture" of Late Mesolithic people who adopted ceramics and domestic sheep from Cardial Neolithic populations in southern France and gradually expanded into the Rhineland and farther east. The co-occurrence of La Hoguette and LBK pottery has been variously interpreted as exchange between groups or mixing of once separate occupation debris (Cziesla 1993, Tillmann 1994).

5 New evidence is also suggesting greater regional differentiation within the LBK area, consistent with differing local contributions to its development. According to Gronenborn (1990b), the triangular points mentioned earlier occur only in the western portions of the earliest LBK, whereas trapezes predominate farther east. In addition, Tillmann (1994) suggests that the earliest LBK of Hessen, on the northern periphery of LBK distribution, differs from that of southern Germany in the dominant core preparation techniques. In Hessen these are characterized by plain and pecked platforms rather than the primary faceting common farther south. He points out that this distinction parallels one existing in the Late Mesolithic of the two areas as well.

6 Although the distributions of earliest LBK and Late Mesolithic sites still appear largely as discrete and segregated, it is now apparent that, at least in a number of areas, LBK sites were patchily distributed in settlement "cells." This, of course, leaves open the possibility that contemporary hunter-gatherer groups persisted in higher elevations and intervening spaces (Cziesla 1993). No evidence presently confirms this, however, although little systematic, regional survey has been done in the area. It should be pointed out here that a number of non-traditional LBK sites, such as caves and rockshelters, have been found to contain LBK ceramics. One of these, Level D of the rockshelter of Lautereck on the Danube, has been interpreted as a temporary fishing camp of the Neolithic farmers (Taute 1967). Such sites often occur outside of the normally mapped areas of LBK distribution and suggest a greater complexity of both site function and site distribution than traditionally described, and amplify the possibilities for interaction (and competition) with local hunter-gatherer groups.

7 A number of recent excavations have uncovered Mesolithic sites dating to the period 7000–6000 BP, and thus extending the Late Mesolithic well into a period of contemporaneity with the LBK (Fig. 7.6). These include Henauhof NW, level 3 (6720 ± 70 BP), Henauhof Nord II (5940 ± 65, 6560 ± 65 BP) and Lautereck Level E (6440 ± 45 BP) in south Germany, Abri Gripons, Mésolithique récent (5964 ± 80, 6510 ± 110 BP) and Bavans 5 (6410 ± 95, 6500 ± 100 BP) in eastern France, and Liesbergmühle VI, Komplex I

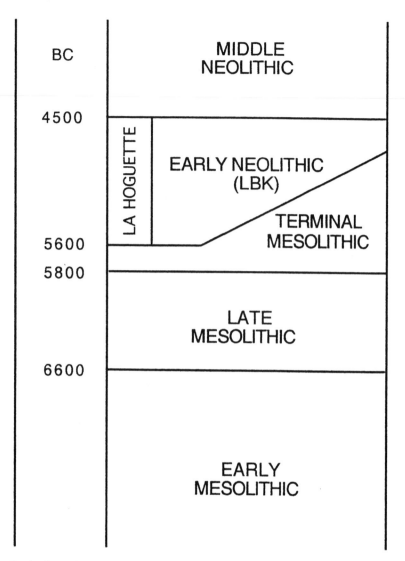

7.6   Revised south German chronology.

(6220±340 BP) in northwest Switzerland (Jochim 1993, Kind 1992, Taute 1967). Nevertheless, Late Mesolithic sites in general, and particularly of this later phase (called here the Terminal Mesolithic), are still scarce in relation to earlier Mesolithic sites (Jochim 1990). Different interpretations for this decrease in site numbers have been offered, including population decline (Taute 1973), differential site destruction by natural processes (Hahn 1983), and reorganization of settlement patterns to emphasize areas that happen to have lesser visibility (Jochim 1990, Tillman 1994). The fact that several of the Terminal Mesolithic sites recently discovered lay buried in the peat of lake edges and alluvial clays of valley bottoms, with no surface indications, suggests that we may indeed be overlooking many buried sites, and that the apparent decline in site numbers may tell us little about population density (Jochim 1993, Kind 1992). The possibility has also been raised that in certain areas such as the Palatinate near the middle Rhine, the Late Mesolithic may lack many diagnostics such as trapezes, leading archaeologists to fail to recognize Late Mesolithic materials in surface scatters (Cziesla 1993).

Contemporaneity and interaction between foragers and farmers

Although both scenarios for Neolithic origins in this area – colonization and borrowing – allow for contemporaneity between hunting and gathering and agricultural ways of life, little evidence of such contemporaneity has been available until recently. Not only are there now greater numbers of sites dating to the Terminal Mesolithic after 7000 BP, but several Late and Terminal Mesolithic sites have clear evidence of Neolithic artifacts associated with them. These include polished stone axes in the Late Mesolithic of Jägerhaushöhle and Falkensteinhöhle and grinding stones in the Terminal Mesolithic of Henauhof Nordwest (Jochim 1993, Taute 1978).

This issue of contemporaneity deserves consideration because the processes leading to the Neolithic should have influenced the nature of interactions between the two, and should be visible in the archaeological record of the period. A few expectations for each scenario may be suggested.

One stimulus to local borrowing of a Neolithic economy, for example, might have been a situation of increasing subsistence difficulty over the course of the Mesolithic, perhaps because of the increasing forest density of the Atlantic period, leading ultimately to the adoption of new food-producing techniques. One way this stress might be visible is through evidence of increasing diet breadth and butchering intensity during the Mesolithic. In fact, the local Mesolithic does show some such evidence, with potentially costly resources (because of processing requirements) such as hazelnuts and shellfish added to late Early Mesolithic diets and the diversity of small mammal prey increasing through time at the site of Henauhof Nordwest (Jochim 1993). In addition, this same site shows a dramatic decrease through time in the average size of large mammal bone fragments, independent of preservational conditions and suggestive of increasing butchering intensity (Jochim 1993).

The colonization hypothesis has a number of different possible implications. If incoming agricultural groups encountered local foraging populations, three simple types of reaction by the hunter-gatherers can be envisioned: hostility, avoidance, and peaceful exchange. Hostility has been suggested to have characterized relations in Belgium, on the northwestern periphery of the LBK distribution, based on the apparent fortification of LBK villages and the occurrence of Late Mesolithic projectile points in these sites (Keeley and Cahen 1989).

Each of these reactions would have had different economic effects on the foraging groups. Hostility, by interfering with normal subsistence movements, may have led to greater subsistence stress during the Terminal Mesolithic in comparison to the Late Mesolithic. Avoidance may have had little effect (except, perhaps, a shift in settlement areas). Peaceful exchange may actually have improved subsistence, allowing for the inclusion of grain and milk into the economy, coupled perhaps with an intensification of hunting to provide surplus meat and hides for exchange.

A detailed comparison of Late and Terminal Mesolithic economic evidence would be required to pursue these ideas further. At this point, however, it is worth noting that the Late Mesolithic assemblage of Henauhof Nordwest 2 shows much greater bone fragmentation than the Terminal Mesolithic assemblage of the nearby site of Henauhof Nordwest (Jochim 1992, 1993). As both sites occur in similar peat deposits, this difference is not likely to be due to preservational factors, although aspects of site function and depositional processes may play a role. If the differences, however, reflect differential butchering intensity and general subsistence difficulties, then they are consistent with an improvement of Terminal Mesolithic economies due to food exchange. The presence of grinding stones in the Terminal Mesolithic of Henauhof Nordwest, dating to 6720 ± 70 BP and perhaps representing exchange items from agricultural groups, lends support to the idea of food exchange in this period as well. The implications of such exchange have been explored in detail through computer simulations by Gregg (1988).

Conclusions

Few conclusions are possible, for the story of the origins of the Neolithic in this region is a work in progress. Certain topics clearly deserve research priority in order to clarify the nature of this crucial economic transition. Further research, including subsurface survey, must be done to determine the density and distribution of Late and Terminal Mesolithic sites, for which we may have only a very partial and biased sample. Additional excavations and detailed comparisons of Late and Terminal Mesolithic economies and settlement patterns are required in order to investigate the processes underlying this economic transformation. The distribution and meaning of La Hoguette materials need further clarification. Continuation of research into the earliest LBK will help illuminate chronological and spatial patterns within this period.

Since the late 1980s considerable amounts of new data have become available from excavations and analyses that are relevant to this transition. At the very least, these data suggest that the cultural landscape of this period was much more complex than previously thought.

8

How agriculture came to north-central Europe

Introduction

Agriculture came to north-central Europe somewhat over 7000 years ago. In the last century of archaeological research, we have been able to establish the archaeological record of these communities in some detail and have adequate, but not perfect, control over their chronology. The "how" and "why" of the establishment of these agricultural communities have been much more elusive. Since 1980, concerted research in many different parts of north-central Europe has been focused on the earliest farming communities (Bogucki and Grygiel 1993). The first goal of this chapter will be to review the current status of this research and establish a baseline for knowledge as the new millennium begins.

A central issue, as it is in all the chapters in this volume, is whether agricultural communities in north-central Europe spread through colonization by populations which had originated elsewhere or through the adoption of Neolithic economy and technology by indigenous foraging peoples. For reasons which will be explained more fully below, the current evidence strongly favors colonization as the mechanism of agricultural dispersal in this region. The second goal of this chapter will be to argue this point against competing hypotheses.

The final goal of this chapter is much more ambitious. Explanations for the dispersal of the first farming communities in north-central Europe, and especially for its rapidity, have all been unsatisfactory and often not supportable with empirical evidence. An attempt will be made here to introduce a framework for considering this dispersal as a member of a category of phenomena called "complex adaptive systems" which exhibit a number of common properties (Waldrop 1992). While this may not be an explanatory model in the 1970s sense, it may obviate the need for the single-factor, "prime mover" explanations sought in the past.

197

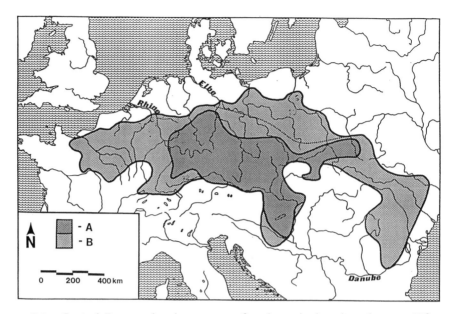

8.1   Central Europe showing extent of early agricultural settlement. (After Lüning 1988b.) *Key:* A — earliest Linear Pottery settlement; B — subsequent expansion of Linear Pottery settlement; the dotted line indicates the approximate northern limit of loess in central Europe.

Geography and chronology

Before going further, let us locate this process in space and time. Geographically, we are concerned with an area which reaches from the middle Danube valley where Hungary, Austria, and Slovakia come together, north to the lower Vistula and Oder rivers, and west to the Paris basin, an area of approximately 750,000 km² (Fig. 8.1). The period that concerns us here lies between 5500 and 4000 BC in calibrated radiocarbon years. Of particular interest is the period between 5500 and 5000 BC, which saw the establishment of farming-based communities throughout this area by several phases of the Linear Pottery culture. The next millennium saw the consolidation of agricultural settlement by post-Linear Pottery cultures such as the Stroke-Ornamented Pottery, the Rössen, and the Lengyel. These later groups continue many of the characteristics of the Linear Pottery culture and can be said to be part of a single tradition (Fig. 8.2).

In the millennia that preceded agriculture in this region, postglacial climatic conditions and vegetation had been established. By the sixth millennium BC, north-central Europe enjoyed somewhat warmer conditions than today, by about 2°C or even slightly more (Huntley and Prentice 1988). Humidity levels, however, exhibit regional variation. Although

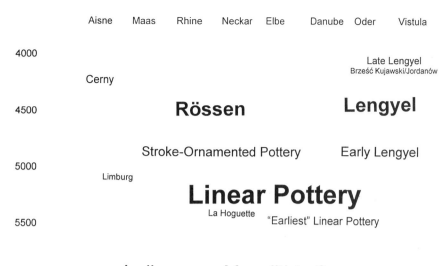

Aisne	Maas	Rhine	Neckar	Elbe	Danube	Oder	Vistula

8.2 Chronological chart showing major cultural units involved in the establishment of agricultural communities in north-central Europe and their distribution in major drainage systems. Dates are given in calibrated years BC.

Scandinavia and northwestern Europe appear to have experienced wetter conditions during this period, recent research indicates that central Europe and much of eastern Europe were relatively dry (Starkel 1995). This observation may have relevance for the spread of agriculture in this area, in that central Europe during the sixth millennium BC was perhaps more similar in temperature and humidity to southeast Europe and Anatolia than at any time either previously or since. The forested terrain sheltered modern forest fauna along with bands of postglacial foragers.

In order to understand how agriculture came to north-central Europe, it is important to know something of the geography of this region. I prefer to simplify the very complicated patchwork of hills, mountains, plains, and streams into two major landscape zones which have relevance for the study of early farmers of north-central Europe. These are the upland basins drained by the major river systems of north-central Europe and the flat lowlands of the North European Plain. I am putting aside the mountain chains like the Carpathians, Sudetens, and Harz, and the glacial outwash plains of central Poland and Niedersachsen, for these became of interest to farming peoples only later. The upland basins of interior central Europe had served as traps during the last glaciation for wind-blown dust, which became fertile loess soils. The North European Plain is covered with thinner soils which had been moved around quite a bit by glacial action. In the upland basins, streams formed a dendritic pattern separated by dry watersheds. On the North European Plain, the drainage pattern was the result of glacial action; the bogs and brooks that formed in meltwater valleys and kettle lakes connected with meandering small streams and the broad floodplains of major rivers like the Oder and Vistula.

Within the upland basins, the habitats of greatest interest to the early farming populations were the valleys of the smaller streams which drained patches of the loess. Loess is fertile but dry; these stream valleys were oases of moistness from runoff from the adjacent watersheds and from upstream. Early farming populations settled in these habitats along the smaller rivers and creeks. In the lowlands of the North European Plain, there was also one very important habitat type, among the chains and clusters of lakes left in meltwater valleys and dead-ice features that interrupt patches of ground moraine in several parts of the plain. In some respect, these features are analogues of the upland creeks, in that they are moist habitats in the midst of drier areas of fertile soil.

The archaeological record

The sites of the earliest farming communities in north-central Europe are almost exclusively open settlements with little vertically stratified accumulation of debris. Thousands have been identified, and several hundred have been systematically investigated. It is important to stress that the archaeological record of the earliest farming communities in central Europe is among the best in the world in terms of the size of the sample and the meticulousness of the excavations. Only in a few key aspects, such as faunal samples, can regional deficiencies be identified owing to preservation conditions in the loess soil.

Ceramics

There is an initial uniformity of ceramic styles in the earliest phases of Linear Pottery, followed by regionalization and differentiation in later Linear Pottery, Rössen, and particularly Lengyel. Linear Pottery fine ware, as its name implies, is decorated with progressively more complex patterns of incised lines (Fig. 8.3). Over time, these lines came to be accented with incised dots (the so-called "music note" motif), and the spaces between the lines were often filled with rows of tiny punctates or strokes. Remarkably, however, most Linear Pottery fine ware vessels are in a single form, the ¾–spherical bowl, or *Kumpf*, in sizes ranging from miniatures to 60 cm in diameter. There was also a coarse ware in a variety of forms, commonly decorated with rows of fingernail impressions.

Linear Pottery is succeeded by the so-called Stroke-Ornamented Pottery culture (expressed more elegantly in German as *Stichbandkeramik*), which in turn is followed by Rössen in the west and Lengyel in the east. In

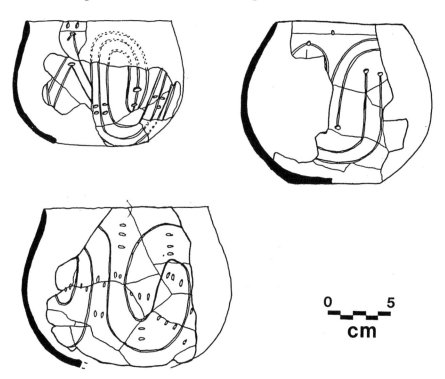

8.3 Examples of Linear Pottery fine-ware ceramics with typical decoration. (After Bogucki 1995b.)

the Rössen culture, baroque patterns of decorations cover the vessels, with "hanging chevrons" a common motif. At the same time, however, Lengyel Ware is hardly decorated, except for painting in some areas, although there is proliferation of vessel forms.

Two anomalous ceramic types, called "Limburg Ware" and "La Hoguette Ware," which appeared in the western part of central Europe during the earliest Linear Pottery phases (Lüning *et al.* 1989), are discussed further below.

Chipped stone industry

Early Neolithic sites in north-central Europe typically yield large assemblages of chipped stone tools and flaking debris. Blade production is the key step in the manufacturing sequence, leading to a variety of tools including knives, scrapers, borers, and (rarely) projectile points. An elaborate reduction sequence for Dutch Linear Pottery sites has been documented by de Grooth (1987), and both she and Keeley (Keeley and Cahen

1989) have argued for domestic specialization in tool manufacture. Examination of the tools both macroscopically and using microwear analysis has revealed their use as sickles and in hide-working. Recently, Silva and Keeley (1994) have used microwear analysis of polish at the edges of thick Early Neolithic flake-blades to suggest a technique for dressing hides using a plant-based compound.

The earliest European farmers placed great importance on the procurement of high-quality flint. In Poland, for instance, the Jurassic flint from north of Kraków and the "chocolate" flint from the Holy Cross mountains of south-central Poland were widely distributed. At the western edge of Linear Pottery distribution, the Rijckholt flint from the Netherlands was used at sites in the Rhineland to the east and in Belgium to the west (de Grooth 1987). At sites distant from high-quality flint sources, however, the inhabitants contented themselves with the local raw material, whatever its quality (e.g., Heussner 1989).

Ground stone tools

With the earliest farmers, ground stone tools appear for the first time in central Europe. They take various forms, but the "classic" adze type is the so-called "shoe-last celt," an elongated chisel-like tool with a roughly square cross-section at its midpoint. Flat adzes are also common in Linear Pottery contexts, while later, during the Lengyel and Rössen cultures, shaft-hole tools make their appearance. Other ground stone implements include querns and grooved polishing stones. The latter have been interpreted as having been used for smoothing wooden arrow shafts (Gaffrey 1994).

Raw material selection was also important in the manufacture of ground stone tools, and considerable effort has been expended in trying to identify sources. Early European farmers were very selective in their choice of raw material for adzes. Green schist from Silesia was used at sites in southern Poland and Bohemia about 150 km away (Modderman 1988:105). The sources of the amphibolite used in adzes in the Rhineland and the Netherlands are difficult to pinpoint, although the material apparently did not come from as far away as Silesia as was once believed (Schietzel 1965). Claims have been advanced that amphibolite used in central Germany came from sources on the Bohemian massif (Schwarz-Mackensen and Schneider 1983), although the evidence for this is equivocal. Nonetheless, it seems clear that in many cases stone from sources up to 200 km distant was used for adzes. Even raw material for grinding stones was carefully selected. For example, the phtanite used for querns at Darion in Belgium came from a source 65 km to the west (Keeley and Cahen 1989).

Longhouses

Probably the most distinctive characteristic of the early farming cultures in north-central Europe after their pottery was the tradition of longhouse architecture, which is found in the earliest Linear Pottery communities and continues through Rössen and Lengyel. These remarkable timber structures were the largest free-standing buildings in the world at the time (Bogucki 1995a). Up to 40 m long (typically closer to 30) and about 5 m wide, the longhouses of the early farmers in north-central Europe are known exclusively from the traces in the soil from their posts and from burnt daub with impressions of structural members and wattle. The earliest houses are known from the investigations of Jens Lüning and his collaborators at sites such as Schwanfeld in central Germany (Lüning 1986, 1988b).

Linear Pottery houses were rectangular structures, normally with five rows of posts: two which formed the outside walls, and three running down the interior. These structures have been the topic of exhaustive analysis (Soudsky 1969, Modderman 1970, 1988, Startin 1978, Milisauskas 1986, von Brandt 1988, Hampel 1989), and only a few summary details need be recapitulated here. The dimensions of the larger houses were relatively constant from Slovakia to the Netherlands, but construction details vary. For example, in Linear Pottery houses in the Netherlands and the Rhineland, Modderman identified a tripartite modular construction which recurs from house to house. Some smaller houses may consist of only one or two of the modules, while the classic longhouses all have three. Further east, in central Germany, Poland, and Bohemia, this modular construction is not observed.

The early farming settlements of north-central Europe were once characterized as "villages," which implies a concentration of population and small physical and social distances among residential groups. More recently, however, they have come to be seen more as collections of farmsteads in which the longhouses standing at any one time were separated by some distance (Lüning 1988a). Over time, rebuilding and incremental relocation of habitation sites led to a palimpsest of house plans to give an impression of greater density of settlement than may actually have been the case (Fig. 8.4). A particularly noteworthy characteristic of the longhouse settlements is that all houses are oriented in roughly the same direction. In the east, they are oriented largely N–S, or NW–SE, while in the west, their orientation shifts to roughly E–W. The explanation for this is unclear but may have some connection to as yet poorly understood climatic factors.

The rectangular Linear Pottery house construction is succeeded by trapezoidal forms in the Rössen and Lengyel cultures (Hampel 1989). In these houses, one end is wider than the other, for some unknown reason. Another change is seen in the use of continuous bedding trenches rather than single postholes to anchor the upright timbers. The tradition of longhouse architecture persisted over a 1500-year period and was a distinctive feature of the earliest farming communities of north-central Europe.

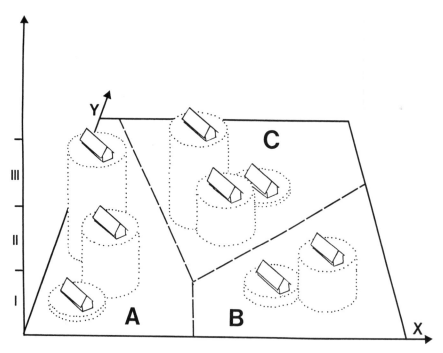

8.4   Schematic representation of a Linear Pottery settlement showing the progressive occupation and rebuilding of three house locations. Note that all
locations are occupied in Phases I and II, while in Phase III only A and C are
occupied. (After Lüning 1988a.)

Subsistence

The earliest farming communities in north-central Europe grew a
suite of crops, including emmer and einkorn wheat, barley, peas, flax, and
poppy (Milisauskas and Kruk 1989). Barley appears to have been more
common in the eastern part of the Linear Pottery realm than in the west.
Poppyseed has an interesting distribution, occurring almost exclusively in
the western reaches of Linear Pottery. Since it is not indigenous to central
Europe, it appears to have entered the area through contact with the
Mediterranean zone in southeast France (Bakels 1982). A recurring set of
weeds of cultivation occurs among the carbonized seed samples, but otherwise no wild plants figure prominently in the subsistence of the early
farmers.

Although animal bones are often poorly preserved on the loess,
several dozen Linear Pottery faunal assemblages have been studied (discussed most recently in Döhle 1993.) They are composed predominantly of
the bones of domestic animals, among which domestic cattle are most
numerous. There are markedly fewer sheep and goat, and pigs are relatively
scarce, which is surprising given the suitability of that species for the

forested habitats preferred by the early farmers. The large proportion of domestic cattle makes economic sense only if they were used for all possible products: males for their meat, and females for their milk and eventually their meat. Ceramic sieves found on Linear Pottery sites are evidence of cheese-making (Bogucki 1984). A scarcity of bones from wild animals indicates that hunting was not a major activity, although large samples of small fish bones from Singen am Hohentwiel near Lake Constance (Aufdermauer *et al.* 1986) and Place Saint-Lambert in Belgium (Desse 1984) indicate that this resource was not overlooked.

In the subsequent Rössen and Lengyel cultures, the record of animal exploitation is considerably more varied. Overall, it is clear that pigs increased in importance, as did sheep and goats, although cattle continued in the dominant role. Some sites also indicate an increase of hunting, possibly as the landscape became more open and fields were defended against crop-robbing species like deer (Uerpmann 1977). Fishing continued to be important in some regions, such as at Lengyel sites in the Polish lowlands.

Settlement Patterns

The settlement patterns of the earliest farmers of north-central Europe are remarkably consistent. In the loess basins, settlements are generally found on the margins of the floodplains of smaller streams (although the location of Hienheim on the Danube indicates that the valleys of major rivers were not ignored). In general, they are not located directly on the banks of the streams, but rather are set back at the junction between the floodplain and the watershed. Such habitats can be called "energy-subsidized" (Odum 1983) in that the nutrient content of the nearby soils is continually recharged through flooding and through groundwater movement in the adjacent slopes.

On the North European Plain, along the lower Oder and Vistula rivers, there is no loess, but the early farmers in these areas sought similar energy-subsidized habitats. Here, the depressions which resulted from glacial sub-ice meltwater channels were the foci of early farming settlement. In the flat lowland terrain, these meltwater channels contained streams or chains of lakes whose shorelines had the ideal combination of high soil moisture and fertile soil for grain agriculture, as well as meadows for pasture.

Burials

Linear Pottery burials are generally found in a contracted position and frequently are grouped in cemeteries of several dozen or more graves. The cemetery at Wandersleben in Germany has over 200 scattered burials, while the recently discovered cemetery at Schwetzingen in southern Germany (Behrends 1990) may also contain several hundred. Other well-known cemeteries include those at Nitra (Slovakia), Rixheim (France), Aiterhofen-Ödmühle (Bavaria), Flomborn (central Germany), Elsloo

(Netherlands), Niedermerz (Rhineland), and Sondershausen (central Germany). In some cemeteries, such as Elsloo and Niedermerz, the acidic loess has destroyed the bones, leaving stains in the soil and grave goods to indicate the location of a grave. Cremations are known from Schwetzingen, Elsloo, and Niedermerz, indicating an alternative burial rite of unknown significance.

Grave goods frequently accompany Linear Pottery burials (e.g., van de Velde 1993). In addition to pots and flint tools, stone adzes and shell ornaments are frequently found. Of particular note are the ornaments made from *Spondylus* shell, which served as armrings and belt decoration (Nieszery and Breinl 1993). The source of this marine shell has been traced to southeastern Europe, probably to the Aegean, and its distribution from Slovakia to France reflects a network of contacts among Linear Pottery communities. Although attempts have been made to associate specific types of grave goods with each sex, such as adzes with males, contradictory examples can often be found.

The discovery of a Linear Pottery mass burial at Talheim in Baden-Württemburg indicates that not all early farmers met a peaceful end (Wahl and König 1987). The skeletons of about thirty-five men, women, and children were found piled together, not buried in the typical orderly Linear Pottery style. Many of the crania bore traces of the impact of stone adzes, including the characteristic square sections of "shoe-last celts," indicating that the violence that befell them was probably at the hands of other Linear Pottery farmers.

In the subsequent Lengyel and Rössen cultures, burial practice becomes diversified. Rössen graves continue to occur in cemeteries, although the burials were now in an extended position. Some cemeteries, such as the one at Wittmar in Lower Saxony, continued in use from Linear Pottery times, a further indication of continuity between these periods. Elsewhere, such as at the Lengyel settlements of northern Poland in the late fifth millennium BC, burials are found interspersed among the houses.

Fortifications

Earthworks are found at a number of early farming settlements in north-central Europe. They take the form of ditch systems, which were presumably backed by a berm of excavated soil. Breaks in the ditches indicate the location of gates or at least passages into the interior of the settlements. There are also indications at some sites, such as Eitzum in central Germany, of the combination of a ditch with a palisade. Most of the Linear Pottery earthworks have been found at the northern and northwestern edge of the distribution of this culture (Lüning 1988b, and see Fig. 8.1); of particular note are those in the Geer valley in Belgium, at sites like Darion (Keeley and Cahen 1989). Recently, a noteworthy fortified Linear Pottery site has been excavated at Vaihingen/Enz in Baden-Württemberg (Krause 1995, 1997). The tradition of fortified sites continued into the late fifth millennium BC, as indicated by a Lengyel ditch system discovered by Ryszard Grygiel and the author at the site of Osłonki in northern Poland (Grygiel and Bogucki 1997).

Most earthworks built by the early farmers of north-central Europe clearly were of a defensive character. They either enclosed settlements or took advantage of natural defensive features of the terrain such as lakes or streams to complete the fortification. Some, however, such as the small triple-ditch enclosure at Langweiler in the Rhineland, have a more ambiguous character, since they neither enclose settlement remains nor are located in defensible places.

Key recent developments

The three most important developments in the investigation of the earliest farmers of north-central Europe since 1980 have been: (1) a much improved understanding of the very earliest Linear Pottery settlements, developed through the work of Jens Lüning and his colleagues in central Germany; (2) the northward extension of the known range of settlements of the Linear Pottery tradition, along the lower Oder and Vistula; and (3) the recognition of Limburg and La Hoguette wares and the definition of their geographical extent. Each of these developments has contributed a significant new dimension to our understanding of the earliest farmers in this region.

Although the chronological position of the earliest Linear Pottery ceramics (*älteste LBK*) was established over four decades ago by Quitta (1960), the settlements associated with this pottery were poorly known. For a long time, the only one investigated to any extent was Eitzum, near Wölfenbüttel in Lower Saxony (Schwarz-Mackensen 1983). There was a particular absence of houses, leading the present author to propose that this was a pioneer phase of ephemeral short-term occupations (Bogucki 1982). In the early 1980s, however, a series of settlements with Quitta's earliest Linear Pottery were excavated in central Germany. The most notable among these are Schwanfeld near Schweinfurt in Franconia (Lüning 1986, 1988b) and Bruchenbrücken in Hessen (Gronenborn 1990b, 1994). Of particular importance are the houses, which are more complicated in their construction than the "classic" Linear Pottery houses although similar in their dimensions (Lüning and Stehli 1989). Additional houses from the earliest Linear Pottery phase have been found recently near Tübingen in southern Germany (Reim 1995).

Although Linear Pottery sites have long been known from the lower drainages of the Oder and Vistula in northern Poland and Germany (Kostrzewski 1929, Kunkel 1934), they were thought to be aberrant outliers of the main current of early farming settlement. Since 1980, however, survey and excavation in these areas has revealed a remarkable abundance of early farming sites. For example, in the area north of Toruń in northern

Poland, about ten Linear Pottery sites were known prior to 1980. In the last two decades, however, intensive survey has revealed over 200 Linear Pottery sites and over 160 Lengyel sites in this area (Kirkowski 1994). Along the lower Oder, sites such as Zollchow (Heussner 1989) indicate that this area was also a center of early farming settlement. The sites along the lower Vistula are within 100 km of its mouth, while those in the lower Oder drainage are less than 90 km from the Baltic coast. It now seems highly probable that at some moment 7000 years ago, a Linear Pottery farmer looked out at the Baltic from the coastline in northern Germany or Poland.

Finally, the identification of the anomalous Limburg and La Hoguette wares and the definition of their geographical extent has been a significant addition to our knowledge of early farming communities in north-central Europe. These types differ in their technique of manufacture, their vessel forms, and their style of decoration from coeval Linear Pottery Ware. Limburg vessels, usually bowls, are characterized by their light brown or tan color and herringbone decoration which frequently covers the entire surface. La Hoguette vessels are generally deep conical pots (one might say, "¾–egg shaped") with bands of stroked decoration. Both Limburg and La Hoguette wares are characterized by their use of ground-up bone fragments as temper.

Limburg Ware was first identified by Modderman (1974) at sites in the southern Netherlands, although reexamination of old collections has indicated that such anomalous sherds had long been found on Linear Pottery sites. By the early 1980s, it was possible to trace the distribution of Limburg Ware throughout eastern France and parts of Belgium (Constantin 1985). In many respects, the term "Limburg Ware" is a misnomer, in that its distribution centers more to the south and west.

La Hoguette Ware has a more curious distribution. First identified at the outlying site of La Hoguette on the Normandy coast, its geographical distribution centers on the Rhine and Neckar valleys in Germany. It is closely associated with the earliest Linear Pottery, and in the last decade, several settlements have been excavated at which the two wares occur together (e.g., Lüning *et al.* 1989, Langenbrink and Kneipp 1990). Recently, a site which appears to have been settled exclusively by the makers of La Hoguette Ware has been found at Stuttgart-Bad Cannstatt in Baden-Württemberg (Schütz *et al.* 1992). The significance of the La Hoguette and Limburg Wares is still equivocal, but a likely possibility is that it represents the adoption of ceramic technology by local foraging groups on the fringes of Linear Pottery settlement (Keeley 1992, Price *et al.* 1995).

Colonization versus local adoption

The major issue to be considered in this volume is that of colonization by farming populations versus the adoption of domesticated plants and animals by indigenous foragers. In the late 1990s, the colonization versus indigenous development debate has reemerged, despite the apparent consensus a decade earlier that colonization was clearly the main process of agricultural dispersal in central Europe (Bogucki 1988). The most recent presentation of the indigenist argument is that of Whittle (1996:151), who focuses on the rapidity of the spread of Linear Pottery settlements across central Europe. In his view, the speed with which Linear Pottery communities were established from Slovakia to eastern France is inconsistent with the demic diffusion model of a low-density colonization and suggests instead an *in situ* transformation of indigenous foraging society. Others, including Bogucki (1995b) and Keeley (1992), have stubbornly held to the colonization model.

In this regard, it is helpful to consider the criteria laid down by Rouse (1958) when evaluating whether population movement is a better explanation for change in the archaeological record than *in situ* development.

1   Identify the migrating people as an intrusive unit in the region they have penetrated.
2   Trace this unit back to its homeland.
3   Determine that all occurrences of this unit are contemporaneous.
4   Establish the existence of favorable conditions for migration.
5   Demonstrate that some other hypothesis, such as independent invention or diffusion of traits, does not better fit the facts.

Sanger (1975:73) added a sixth rule.

6   Establish that all cultural subsystems are involved and not just an isolated one (such as burial practice).

In the case of the earliest farmers of north-central Europe, it is extremely clear that the establishment of sedentary communities with an economy based on cultivation and the keeping of livestock was *not* the product of the localized adoption of these characteristics by indigenous foraging peoples. There are a number of factors that argue in favor of this position.

1   There is no *in situ* development of pottery in north-central Europe. Pottery manufacture appears fully developed within this area, with clear antecedents outside the region in Hungary. The anomalous Limburg and La Hoguette wares appear *contemporaneous* with Linear Pottery and do not pre-date it.
2   The house forms and settlement patterns of the first farmers of this region are completely different from any preceding ones in the region (as poorly known as the latter are).
3   The chipped stone tool types of the first farmers are also markedly different from preceding microlithic forms.
4   The key domestic plant species and two of the major livestock species – sheep and goats – have no native, wild, conspecific forms

in central Europe and were introduced from southeast Europe and ultimately from southwest Asia.

5   The pottery, house forms, and settlement locations are extraordinarily uniform in their general appearance, although with minor local variations over time, from Slovakia to eastern France; local *in situ* development and adoption of sedentary food production would be expected to produce numerous local variations from the very beginning (see Greenfield 1993 and the chapter by Ruth Tringham in this volume).

The evidence, then, conforms to Rouse's criteria: the Linear Pottery culture is intrusive, it has a clear source outside the region, its appearance across central Europe occurs in a very short span of time, and favorable conditions existed for migration. The clincher, however, lies in its conformity with Sanger's additional qualifier. All Linear Pottery cultural subsystems – technology, subsistence, settlement, mortuary practice – are involved.

In opposition to this evidence, relatively few contradictory data can be adduced. The lack of evidence for forager activity in the zone of Linear Pottery colonization following the establishment of agricultural communities suggests the immediate engagement of indigenous peoples with the farmers and the rapid fusion of the two populations or the relegation of foragers to refugia such as the outwash plains of central Poland. Flint assemblages provide some evidence of interaction between these populations. On the basis of his analysis of several early Linear Pottery flint assemblages, Gronenborn (1994) argues that the Linear Pottery culture dispersed across central Europe and assimilated indigenous traditions, particularly La Hoguette. He attributes the subsequent regionalization of Linear Pottery styles to the residual effects of this assimilation. The colonization model does *not* necessarily exclude indigenous foragers from participation in the establishment of agricultural communities in Europe. Rather, it assigns a primary causal role to the dispersal of farming populations across the region rather than to the widespread, simultaneous transformation of local foragers.

The question is how to characterize the alternative to *in situ* development more accurately. Terms such as "colonization" and "migration" have already been applied here, but these are actually imprecise. "Colonization" is acceptable (Bogucki 1995b), but it implies a certain degree of intentionality and directedness, with a clear core area from which the colonizing population originated and identifiable colonies which they founded some distance away. "Migration" is coming back into favor as a valid archaeological explanation (Anthony 1990, Snow 1995), but it implies large-scale and sustained movement of a unified population, which is difficult to envision or document for the Linear Pottery culture.

Ammerman and Cavalli-Sforza (1984:61) have described this

process as *demic diffusion*: "demic" because it involves people and "diffusion" in the proper meaning of dispersal, rather than the archaic anthropological usage as a hypothesized means of transmitting a cultural trait. Indeed, one might speak of a "Neolithic diaspora," in which farming communities dispersed across central Europe between 6000 and 5000 BC. In the demic diffusion model, the *cumulative* effect of small-scale Neolithic population movements brought agriculture from the middle Danube valley almost to the North Sea and the Baltic within only a few centuries. There was no clear intentionality behind this movement: Neolithic Hungarian farmers did not decide to move *en masse* to the lower Rhine valley. Instead, the small incremental movements of Neolithic farmers resulted in the occupation of the desirable riverine habitats across central Europe.

Yet can such a model account for the rapid, almost explosive, appearance of early farming communities throughout the 750,000 km^2 of north-central Europe? A diffusion model is predicated on a normal distribution of distances of movement, resulting from local random walks, leading to a steady, but relatively slow dispersal at a very low density. Those who argue for *in situ* development of agricultural communities would propose that the rapid spread of Linear Pottery, covering 1500 km in about 250 years, does not conform to such a model, thus vitiating the colonization hypothesis.

An effective rejoinder to this position has been provided by advances in dispersal theory in plant ecology (Kot *et al.* 1996, Pitelka *et al.* 1997, Clark *et al.* 1998). Many biological invasions are characterized by great leaps forward and rare (and difficult to observe) long strides. These are undertaken by a small minority of the population, while the majority takes small steps and determines the *average* dispersal distance. So while average dispersal distances may be small, the range of variation in relocation distances may include some very long strides. Episodic, long-distance colonization events violate a diffusion model (Clark *et al.* 1998). Under such conditions, the dispersal of an organism will not be a smooth and steady diffusion wave but rather a rapid – even accelerating – spread whose rate may vary considerably from one area to another. This body of theory reconciles the rapid establishment of Linear Pottery communities across central Europe with a dispersal of intrusive agricultural peoples and provides a promising point of departure for future attempts to model this process.

It is very important to differentiate among the various elements of the dispersal process and to avoid the tendency to conflate exploratory activity with the actual establishment of sedentary agricultural communities. Clearly, there must have been forays into the central and northern European forests in advance of the eventual establishment of long-term farming settlements. Nonetheless, exploration of primeval forests does not equate with the transition to agriculture, although it is certainly an element of the process.

A number of years ago, I suggested that Linear Pottery cattle herders may have moved ahead of the actual farming frontier in search of pasturage and forest grazing (Bogucki 1982), practicing a form of transhumance, and in this way identified optimal habitats for subsequent agricultural settlement. To say that this proposition did not meet with widespread support is an understatement. The subsequent discovery of long-term settlements associated with the earliest Linear Pottery and of so many new Linear Pottery sites in the lowlands of the lower Oder and Vistula drainages, including evidence of longhouses (Czerniak 1994), has effectively vitiated this argument.

Nonetheless, I find it difficult to abandon the idea that at least some members of early Linear Pottery communities penetrated the lands beyond the farming frontier and in that way identified the optimal habitats described above. A recent reminder that otherwise sedentary societies may have a mobile component is Philip Smith's 1995 description of non-pastoral transhumance practiced by early settlers in Atlantic Canada. The incorporation of the sparse indigenous foraging populations into Linear Pottery and later communities also would have contributed to the process of environmental mapping, which was a precondition for the rapid establishment of farming communities.

As already noted, the most remarkable aspect of the Neolithic diaspora in central Europe is its speed (Bogucki 1988, Price *et al.* 1995). Even the low resolution afforded by conventional radiocarbon dating indicates that virtually all 750,000 km^2 of this region had been penetrated by farming peoples prior to 5000 BC, perhaps much earlier. The rapidity of this spread is reflected in a marked homogeneity in material culture during the early Linear Pottery phases. The present author has argued (Bogucki 1995b) that the ability of Linear Pottery farmers to rely on a basic repertoire of artifact types and to build houses which used a consistent, modular form facilitated (but does not explain) the rapid dispersal of farming communites throughout central Europe.

After this dramatic rapid dispersal, however, the spread of farming communities in central Europe halted. The "stop line," as currently known, runs across northern Poland and Germany and loops through eastern France to the upper Rhine. For nearly a millennium, until nearly 4000 BC, a frontier existed with farmers to the south and east and foragers to the north and west. This frontier was not impenetrable. For example, there is evidence that ground stone tools from central Europe were traded to the foragers of southern Scandinavia (Fischer 1982). Eventually crops and livestock also made their way through the frontier to the hunter-gatherers to the north and west.

"Engines" of agricultural dispersal

Archaeologists who deal with the process of agricultural dispersal in north-central Europe have long sought to identify an *engine* which propelled it forward (or a "prime mover," to use a 1970s processual term). The Neolithic diaspora across this region constituted such a dramatic change in the archaeological record that it seemed to demand a concrete explanation. The Neolithic of north-central Europe became perhaps the first instance in the history of archaeology in which ecology, subsistence, and demography were woven together in a series of explanatory models for the spread of agriculture, beginning in the first quarter of the twentieth century.

V. Gordon Childe (1925, 1929) and his contemporaries saw the earliest European farmers as people who frequently relocated their settlements owing to exhaustion of soil fertility. In their view, these "classically Neolithic" farmers were "primitive agriculturalists," and modern analogues of such farmers practiced shifting agriculture. Hence, the first farmers of central Europe were presumed to have done likewise, with soil depletion causing them to shift not only their fields but also their settlements at frequent intervals. This shifting would have driven the agricultural frontier forward across central Europe. Overlooked in this model, of course, was the fact that shifting agriculture today is practiced almost exclusively on thin, tropical soils. Such a model is not sustained by work done since the 1970s (Modderman 1971, Lüning 1980, Rowley-Conwy 1981), which indicates not only that early farming settlements were occupied for long durations, but also that the rich soils of the central European floodplains can sustain crop yields almost indefinitely.

Woven together with the Childean soil-depletion hypothesis was often a demographic thread, again in advance of the wider popularity of demographic explanations in archaeology. This idea (e.g., Clark 1952:97) held that early agriculture resulted in such explosive population growth that the surplus population so generated was pushed out across central Europe. Obviously, population growth did occur during this period in north-central Europe, but it is not evident, at least to this author, that it was so precipitous that it caused great pressure on available land and resources. There was no "population machine" on the Hungarian plains pumping out Neolithic farmers to go and colonize the riverine habitats of north-central Europe. Moreover, the gradual infilling of prime floodplain habitats, demonstated in studies such as those of Kruk (1973), indicates that there was still ample fertile land available after the initial dispersal of farming throughout the area.

Recently, the hypothesis has been advanced that a major marine transgression of the Black Sea continental shelf approximately 7500 years ago was a factor in the dispersal of agriculture in many parts of Europe (Ryan *et al.* 1997). Under this hypothesis, the postglacial Black Sea was a freshwater lake whose level was over 100 m below the Bosporus sill. According to marine geologists William Ryan, Walter Pitman III, and their colleagues, the Mediterranean breached this sill about 7500 years ago and caused the Black Sea to inundate over 100,000 km^2 of its continental shelf.

They hypothesize that this triggered population displacements which may have accelerated the dispersal of farmers into the interior of Europe. Although this is an intriguing theory, there are nonetheless nearly 1000 km between the northwest coast of the Black Sea to absorb groups that might have been so displaced and the arc of the Carpathians to deflect them from interior central Europe.

If soil depletion and population pressure are ruled out as "prime movers" in the dispersal of agriculture in north-central Europe, what did cause this process? I have suggested elsewhere (Bogucki 1988) that we should consider the causes to lie in the goals and aspirations of individual households as they mature through their developmental cycle. As offspring establish their own households, for example, some may find relocation from the immediate environs of their birth household to be an attractive social option. Proving that such social factors lay behind the Neolithic settlement of north-central Europe is very challenging, but with the dismissal of traditional explanations such as soil depletion and population growth we need to examine the feasibility of such suggestions.

How, one might ask, could such small, local factors have resulted in such a rapid spread of agricultural settlements? I would like to propose that the Neolithic settlement of north-central Europe belongs to a category of phenomena called "complex adaptive systems" which are only in the 1990s being subjected to systematic study in the physical sciences, life sciences, and social sciences (Waldrop 1992). In such systems, individual elements spontaneously organize themselves into a pattern and acquire collective properties. The result is not merely complicated, but also dynamic, sometimes disorderly, and almost with a life of its own. Note that this usage of "complex" differs from its usage in evolutionary anthropology. It expresses the fact that the overall properties of its system are not measurable by a single system attribute. Similarly, the term "adaptive" differs from its traditional ecological use in that it connotes the ability of the system to learn and change, not necessarily to return to equilibrium.

Complex adaptive systems have several important characteristics. A fundamental trait is that they are composed of many *agents*. Each such system is a network of many agents working in parallel and making separate decisions, and these agents make mistakes and learn. Moreover, the results of individual decisions are not averaged away and forgotten but may be magnified in impact as a result of other decisions and may decide the direction the system takes. This may cause the system at times to rush forward, at times to stand still, and at times to retreat.

The mutual interdependence of the many agents in such a system results in a characteristic which has been termed *self-organization*: an economy develops without anyone overseeing it or planning it; geese flying south organize themselves into a V-formation. Waldrop (1992:11) expresses this phenomenon in general terms: "groups of agents seeking mutual accommodation and self-consistency somehow manage to transcend themselves, acquiring collective properties ... that they might never have possessed individually." In addition, such systems are *adaptive* in that these new collective properties respond to new conditions in order to seek new advantages and to exploit opportunities.

Many complex adaptive systems are characterized by what economists would call "increasing returns." While conventional economic theory is based on an assumption of diminishing returns, since the 1980s some economists have embraced the existence of situations of positive feedback resulting in increasing returns and multiple equilibria (Arthur 1990). In such increasing returns systems, it is often the case that small chance events and decisions early in the history of the system can determine its course. Moreover, these initial decisions are based on limited experience and may cause a potentially inefficient or sub-optimal technology or product to be chosen and to persist as the system evolves. The economist W. Brian Arthur (1989) refers to this as *lock-in by historical events*: "increasing returns can cause the economy gradually to lock itself in to an outcome not necessarily superior to alternatives, not easily altered, and not entirely predictable in advance."

It is important to realize that, by itself, the idea of complex adaptive systems has little explanatory strength if one is seeking a sequential model with causality proceeding in a single direction. Some archaeologists find this unsatisfactory. Yet Flannery (1986) suggests that there are different sorts of causality and that the interpretative frameworks used in the life sciences, which focus on multivariate concepts, are more appropriate paradigms for archaeology than the deterministic models used in the physical sciences. The notion of a complex adaptive system is one such multivariate concept which might be profitably used to approach archaeological problems such as the spread of agriculture in Europe.

This sketch does not do justice to the richness of recent scholarship on complex adaptive systems, but with it as background, I would like in the remaining available space to consider the Neolithic settlement of north-central Europe as a complex adaptive system with increasing returns but locked in to a subsistence and settlement system which, while successful, did not turn out to be the best way to exploit the central European environment.

The Neolithic settlement of north-central Europe as a complex adaptive system

How can we model the introduction of agriculture to north-central Europe as the outcome of a dynamic web of individual and small-group interests rather than the product of a stable system in equilibrium? Let us first try to identify the agents, the network among them, and the conditions which permitted increasing returns for the earliest farmers of this region.

It is relatively straightforward, I believe, to view the kin-based co-residential units of the Neolithic longhouses, characterized as "house-holds," as the effective decision-making units of Neolithic society (Bogucki 1988). The case for Neolithic households has also been made persuasively recently by Ruth Tringham (Tringham and Krstić 1990) and Ryszard Grygiel (Grygiel 1994), although it has not met with universal acceptance. Nonetheless, in virtually every small-scale agrarian, agro-pastoral, and pastoral society extant in the world today, the household is the fundamental locus of economic and social decision-making. This perspective has been widely adopted in the archaeological study of such societies (e.g., Lightfoot 1994).

Hundreds of longhouses have been found in the sixty-five years since they were first noted by Buttler and Haberey (1936) at Köln-Lindenthal in Germany and Jażdżewski (1938) at Brześćae Kujawski in Poland, and countless more have been eradicated by erosion, development, and more than seven millennia of cultivation. These longhouses are of very similar dimensions from one end of central Europe to another, suggesting domestic units of constant size. These residential units – let us call them "house-holds" – can be considered the *agents*, who were the individual adaptive units of this complex system. They were its grains of sand, its snowflakes, its flying geese.

Of course, although households may have been the primary unit of decision-making for the early farming cultures of north-central Europe, they were not completely independent. I believe that they would have been linked by a network of kinship bonds (Bogucki 1988). In light of the geographical dimensions of the demic diffusion of farmers across north-central Europe, such bonds would have extended beyond the immediate environs of the settlement to link settlement cells in a web of relationships of various strengths. Perhaps an analogy may be drawn with a pond in which water lilies are floating. On the surface, the lily pads appear as discrete plants, but beneath the surface there is a tangled network of stems and branches. Similarly, the Neolithic longhouse households appear on site plans and regional maps as very independent units, but drain the metaphorical pond of Neolithic central Europe and the interconnections among the households emerge.

I would argue that this web of individual decision-making entities was a fundamental characteristic of the Neolithic adaptive system in central Europe. Although the system did require certain inputs, it did not require a powerful engine to drive its development. There is no evidence of soil depletion, nor is there good reason to assume that the pressure of surplus population caused the explosive dispersal of agricultural communities across Europe. Instead, the developmental cycle of the individual house-holds would have provided the system with a certain "metabolism" which, I would maintain, was sufficient to propel it forward. Spontaneously self-organizing systems often suddenly rush forward as the small incremental behavior of individual agents tips them at a critical point (Waldrop 1992:36–7). The effects of such decisions are often then magnified. Thus individual local decisions about household relocation echoed throughout this web of self-interested agents to result in the agricultural settlement of almost all of north-central Europe within a matter of centuries.

Let us now make a connection to the economic model of increasing returns. Conventional economists would argue that agricultural systems are subject to diminishing returns caused by limited amounts of fertile land. On the other hand, Arthur (1990) points out that knowledge-based aspects of the economy, such as high technology, are those sectors that are largely subject to increasing returns. The initial large investment is rewarded by progressively cheaper unit costs and rapidly accumulated experience and knowledge in making the process function more efficiently. I would argue that in light of the condition of effectively unlimited fertile land at the beginning of the Neolithic in north-central Europe, the introduction of agriculture to this area was very much a knowledge-based process. After a demanding initial investment, accumulated experience, with adapting the cultigens and livestock to central European habitats led to progressively greater understanding of soils, climate, landforms, plants, and animals which enabled the Neolithic farmers to disperse rapidly across the continent. "Costs" in mistakes, labor, and start-up effort would have fallen sharply as knowledge increased. Use of a standard settlement format would have helped to keep the learning curve flat. Moreover, there would have been an incentive to share information, which would have further magnified the effects of individual decisions and chance events.

A cost in such situations, however, is the potential for inefficiency as conservative but generalized technologies and methods are "locked-in" by initial choices. The Early Neolithic settlement system of concentrations of household settlements within particular microregions may have been a good choice for frontier agriculturalists, but in the central European environment it may not have been the most sustainable system over time. Changes in temperature and humidity around 4000 BC (Starkel 1995) may also have had an impact on the adaptive system. After about 4000 BC, there is considerable dispersal of settlement in many parts of this area, and nucleation of settlement is not seen again for several millennia. Moreover, it appears that the complex of domesticated plants and animals used at the earliest farming sites did not yet represent an optimized and integrated "mixed farming" system that characterizes later European prehistory. In particular, it is characterized by imbalances such as the very heavy concentration on domestic cattle and a low reliance on domestic pigs which later prehistoric communities in this area avoided. Yet, for about 1500 years, it was the system of choice in north-central Europe, and it worked.

Conclusion

I have presented a general sketch of the introduction of agriculture to north-central Europe and outlined what I believe is a promising way to think about it. Early agriculture in north-central Europe was the result of the rapid dispersal of agricultural peoples from the southeast to the north and northwest about 7500 years ago, resulting in the establishment of very similar communities across this region within the brief span of several centuries. Foragers who were present in the core area of early farming settlement in north-central Europe were either quickly absorbed into agricultural communities or displaced into refugia like the glacial outwash of central Poland. Subsequent regional differentiation in the archaeological record does not obscure the persistence of very similar subsistence and settlement patterns throughout this area until about 6000 years ago.

Earlier attempts to search for "prime movers" or "engines" behind this diaspora have been unsatisfactory. Neither soil depletion necessitating settlement relocation nor explosive demographic growth appear to be supported by current evidence, although it is possible that localized short-term population imbalances may have occurred. I have argued instead that viewing this process as an example of a complex adaptive system is a profitable avenue for research. In such a system, small decisions by individual households, increasing returns, and the "metabolism" of the household developmental cycle resulted in sudden and dramatic dispersal of agricultural communities across north-central Europe. This chapter represents only an initial attempt to connect the concept of a complex adaptive system with the Neolithic dispersal in north-central Europe, but perhaps subsequent work will reveal whether this approach will provide a useful analytical framework.

Acknowledgments

Timothy Kohler and Douglas Price made helpful comments on earlier drafts of this essay, although responsibility for content and interpretations rests solely with the author.

9

Getting back to basics: transitions to farming in Ireland and Britain

Introduction

In the case of Britain and Ireland changes from a hunter-gatherer to a farming lifestyle have been written about with a prolific frequency. Any objective assessment of the problems must emphasize the fact that opinions are much more easily discovered than information based on the observation of actual archaeological data. While this is not something peculiar to this topic or region, given that so much of our later prehistory is based on the presumed impact of agriculture, it places this particular topic in a special position.

Problems associated with the lack of information have obviously been compounded by the realization since the 1970s that the use of simple chronological phases, based on observed changes in material culture, may have masked a more complex process of change. However this realization has resulted in the collapse of one framework of investigation and a substitution of a much more relative approach which has often lacked its own critical framework of analysis. There is often a substitution of the implicit assumptions of traditional archaeology with an over-reliance on a few economic indicators, which are also used to express an equally simple view. The archaeological record, particularly radiocarbon dating and pollen analysis, is raided for information which supports a particular perspective.

Britain and Ireland should provide a fascinating case study of a group of islands where the processes of change from hunter-gatherer to farmer can be studied, a point emphasized in an Irish context by Zvelebil and Rowley-Conwy (1986:75). Yet the British Isles is a region where, for a variety of reasons, there is a limited range of information which can contribute meaningfully to these discussions. Much of Ireland and northern Britain is covered with acidic soils which do not allow for good preservation of organic materials while the earliest known Neolithic of southern Britain is documented through the investigations of monument types which almost certainly post-date any initial phase of the Neolithic.

Our information on the transition is truly limited. In the case of Ireland, a distinctive later Mesolithic technology would appear to form a portion, if not all, of the lithic assemblages. In Britain there is no satisfactory and coherent account of the lithic typology, particularly for the final millennium of the English Mesolithic (see Darvill 1987; it is further noticeable that the late sites chosen by Smith in his 1992 survey of late glacial and Mesolithic sites lie in Scotland). Distinctive assemblages of bone and antler tools are absent from Ireland; in Britain they are usually found in coastal middens in the north of Scotland. The fact that the northern Scottish late Mesolithic middens in the fully developed Obanian period produce such a rich faunal and bone/antler artifact assemblage and that the early Neolithic is still best documented in the south of England, does not help any informed analysis of the transition to farming in Britain. Thus, within the Mesolithic it can, in some cases, be quite difficult to identify the type-fossils which would clearly indicate a final Mesolithic presence in an area or on a site.

Therefore, it is not surprising that the beginnings of the Neolithic/farming are discussed in the context of several theoretical perspectives which have virtually been elevated into self-evident truths. These perspectives are themselves a product of the growing dissatisfaction with the ideas of Childe (1940) in *Prehistoric Communities of the British Isles* and Piggott (1954) in *Neolithic Cultures of the British Isles*. Thus the second half of the century started with a certainty that the Neolithic had begun through the immigration of agriculturalists while the possibility that there was an indigenous contribution was never mentioned. "The material culture of the immigrant agriculturalists which can on various grounds be assigned to an early phase of settlement seems invariably to represent the introduction of completely novel equipment, and there are no signs that an immediate fusion took place with any Mesolithic traditions" (Piggott 1954:15). In spite of Piggott's assumption that farmers migrated to the British Isles there is never any clear idea as to where they came from. All the elements of the British Neolithic could be found elsewhere in western Europe, i.e., carinated pottery, piercing leaf-shaped arrowheads and megalithic tombs, but as these did not conveniently occur in one place, Piggott (1954) coyly describes them as follows: "Initially it is a record of the arrival at various points of the long coastline of the British Isles of smaller or larger groups of colonists from various regions of the Atlantic and channel coasts of Western Europe" (Piggott 1954:15). Usually the mechanisms for this immigration were not discussed but this problem was addressed by Case (1969b) in "Neolithic explanations." However, while he accepted the immigration model and focused on the problems associated with the transfer of people, seed corn, and livestock to new areas across the sea, his paper had exceptional influence in introducing the concept of an initial pioneering phase of farming within a now generally recognized much longer Neolithic. This phase could have been preceded by several exploratory phases and all would have had a minimal presence in the archaeological record. Many later authors were to develop this concept of a pioneering phase which implied either an unknowable early Neolithic or a phase at the beginning of the Neolithic which would be difficult to identify in the archaeological record.

During the 1970s and 1980s there was a realization that the Mesolithic had been treated as a passive phenomenon and that some consideration should be given to either an indigenous contribution to the establishment of farming in the British Isles or a Neolithic which was created through Mesolithic adaptations.

Mercer (1986), in examining the Neolithic of Cornwall, developed Case's model by suggesting that much of the indigenous early Neolithic could be initiated through contacts across the English Channel but these contacts were developed by Mesolithic communities rather than Case's Neolithic pioneers. Bradley (1984:11) felt that the social potential of British Mesolithic communities had been underrated. He noted (quoting Jacobi 1979) the suggestion that social territories existed in the later Mesolithic of Britain and that their social organization would allow them to make at least a substantial contribution to the initiation of farming in Britain. Thus Bradley's famous statement: "successful farmers have social relations with one another, while hunter-gatherers have ecological relationships with hazelnuts." Whittle (1985:125–8) again emphasized the potential Mesolithic contribution within Britain. Many authors relied heavily on the observations of palynologists that there is evidence for extensive forest clearance before the Neolithic (Simmons 1979). In that context Irish evidence, in the form of early ^{14}C dates from sites such as the passage tombs at Carrowmore, Co. Sligo, and early occurrences of cereal-type pollen at Cashelkeelty, Co. Kerry, was seen as supporting the concept of early farming already in existence in Ireland well before 5,500 bp (see below for discussion of these points). Similar evidence was expected to exist in Britain.

Thus by the late 1980s there was a general consensus that in southern Britain the pioneering phase of initial farming would have contained a substantial Mesolithic component and that initial farming settlements were in coastal regions where near-sedentary Mesolithic communities had already developed.

In recent years discussions have centered on the factors which caused a change to farming. Thus, Zvelebil and Rowley-Conwy (1984:86) suggested that the appearance of farming was due to a series of economic or ecological factors while Thomas (1988) emphasized the role of social factors in bringing about these changes. In a further debate with Mithen (1991) Thomas has argued, like so many before, that "some of the social changes which took place in the Neolithic of Britain might have had their origins in processes and tensions already present in the Mesolithic" (Thomas 1991a:19). Thomas' view has been further developed with the suggestion that the accepted 'Image of a Neolithic Economy' based on a mature sedentary mixed farming economy needed to be challenged. His *Rethinking the Neolithic* begins by pointing to the limited nature of the evidence for farming in the southern English Neolithic.

The way of life imagined during the earlier Neolithic is a mobile one with at least part of the population following herds of cattle seasonally between upland and lowland. The whole community, gathering roots and berries as they went or part (most) of each group might have stayed in one place year round tending gardens, crops of cereals and pulses. Indeed these two extremes might mark the poles between which actual variables existed. (Thomas 1991a)

To an extent this represents a continuation of the debate about the representative nature of the southern English chalklands. This debate, initiated by Barker and Webley (1978), drew an immediate response from J. Evans which the editor of the *Proceedings of the Prehistoric Society* took the unusual step of including at the end of Barker and Webley's paper.

Therefore by the 1990s it had become axiomatic that the latest Mesolithic communities of southern Britain were following a "sophisticated" and near-sedentary way of life which would, for a number of reasons, allow a shift from a hunter-gatherer to a farming economy. These changes were not thought to have been necessarily coeval with the traditional shift from a Mesolithic (microlithic) to a Neolithic (piercing arrowhead, pottery) material culture.

Case, however, had specifically discussed the problems of the beginnings of the Irish Neolithic in a second paper in 1969, and discussed these problems within a framework in which the primacy of the northern Irish Neolithic was accepted (Case 1969a). This view had been reinforced by De Valera's contention that the Irish court tombs were part of an initial Neolithic package (De Valera 1960) and, therefore, as these monuments were found in the northern third of Ireland, there was a continued justification for the traditional belief that the Irish Neolithic first became established in the north. Case suggested that, owing to similarities in material culture, "the earliest Neolithic settlers are more likely to have come from or through the wolds than from elsewhere in the British Isles or the Continent" (Case 1969a:11). Case also argued strongly for an acculturation of indigenous Irish Mesolithic communities, an idea which was reinforced by Woodman (1976:78) when the apparent presence of Neolithic elements and domesticates on late Mesolithic sites was contrasted with an absence of diagnostic Mesolithic elements on early Neolithic sites (Case felt that these Mesolithic elements could be identified in the later Neolithic, an idea which had also been championed by Piggott in 1954 when, admittedly, it had been assumed that the Neolithic of the British Isles had lasted a few centuries rather than more than a millennium).

The debate in Ireland had been rather limited, as most authors (Waddell 1978, Woodman 1985a, Cooney and Grogan 1994) continued to emphasize the role of outside stimuli, if not actual immigration, in the beginning of farming. With early ^{14}C dates from the Neolithic site of Ballynagilly and the apparent presence of domesticates on Mesolithic sites there was also an acceptance of a chronological overlap between Mesolithic and Neolithic economies. Even many authors from Britain (Whittle 1985, Zvelebil and Rowley-Conwy 1986, as well as Williams 1989) emphasized the fact that farming may have begun in Ireland through a different set of circumstances. Only Burenhult (1984) felt that the major contributors to the Irish Neolithic were the indigenous Mesolithic communities. This was embedded in his argument that the Carrowmore megalithic tombs pre-dated traditional dates for the beginning of the Neolithic and the associated economic indicators suggested that a full farming economy was not established until the Iron Age.[1]

Several general trends can be seen in the discussions on the transition to farming in the British Isles. Perhaps the most obvious is the general lack of attention being paid to the nature of the geographical unit. Authors are often unclear as to whether Britain and Ireland should be considered together or separately. In fact there has also been little discussion as to whether Britain should be considered as one or several regions. In the latter case then it is possible that even within Britain transitions to farming may have taken place in a number of different ways.

In the rush to identify the Mesolithic contribution to the indigenous development of farming one caveat should be noted. Many authors working primarily on Mesolithic material either have not supported the concept of an indigenous contribution (e.g. Woodman 1978, 1985a) or have been very circumspect about the Mesolithic contribution (see Smith 1992, Epilogue, or Wickham-Jones 1994, chapter entitled "End of an Era")!

Very little specific consideration has been given to chronological issues *per se*. Williams (1989), on a limited selection of ^{14}C dates, reinforced what had been already established, i.e., that there was an overlap between ^{14}C dates from Mesolithic and Neolithic sites both in Britain and Ireland. She did, however, correctly identify that some of the ^{14}C dates which had been used in the past were dubious because of pre-treatment, old-wood factor, etc. Baillie (1992), in contrast, noted that between 5000 and 5200 BP there was a sudden increase in ^{14}C dates from Neolithic sites and therefore some major factor, such as climate change, might have forced a rapid shift to farming throughout the British Isles. Pennington (1975) had, of course, suggested that the elm decline took place during a phase of high rainfall at a similar point in time.

These debates have been noted for one remarkable characteristic.

Like most good stories, the discussions rarely let factual information get in the way! They have been based on the relative merits of the different theoretical perspectives rather than on archaeological criteria which might be used to calibrate when or how farming spread to the British Isles. Gaps or overlaps were dealt with by using a number of convenient ^{14}C dates to push Neolithic assemblages back or pull Mesolithic ones forward in time. The context of ^{14}C samples was rarely discussed or the consequences for related material culture considered. Similarly, suggested indications from palynology of the presence of early cereal-type pollen grains were rarely related to the rest of the archaeological record. Instead, invisible pioneering farmers, with an unspecific economy and unknown material culture, were called upon to fill the gaps.

This virtual absence of evidence can almost be raised to a virtue. Simmons in his recent survey (1996), observing the paucity of evidence in parts of Britain, notes: "This makes inferences at once easier since there are fewer 'hard' points of reference that have to be built into models, and more difficult in the sense that a very little extra information has the potential to require a great deal of revision." In this lacuna anything is possible, including recent suggestions that the discovery of Neolithic material and activity in a wetland context at Carrigdirty, Co. Clare, on the Shannon Estuary, is an indication of a Mesolithic–Neolithic transition simply because it is found outside the "Domesticated Landscape" (O'Sullivan 1997). There is a danger that too much can be made of hunters who gather plants or farmers who fish. Each is a valid activity in its own economy without indicating precognition of a change in lifestyle or reaffirming ancestral traditions!

Some of the problems which will be discussed in this paper have already been alluded to by Rowley-Conwy (1995). In the context of Fritz's discussion of the dates for the beginning of agriculture in the Americas (Fritz 1994), he has correctly observed that there may be certain biases in our approach to the same topic in western Europe and this bias has led to a too ready acceptance of early dates for the appearance of agriculture.

This chapter, therefore, proposes to take the Irish archaeological record and examine the problems associated with using ^{14}C dates and other attributes to establish evidence for early farming or transitional assemblages and economies. In that context working from generally accepted later Mesolithic and Neolithic criteria the evidence for very early or pioneering farming in Ireland will be examined. Finally issues such as the alternative mechanisms for the spread of farming to Ireland will be considered along with the questions as to whether it was part of a unitary phenomenon within the whole of the British Isles.

One must simply note Whittle's observations at the end of his 1990 survey of the Mesolithic–Neolithic transition in Britain and Ireland.

He concludes with four alternatives: early or late colonization by farmers and early or late process of indigenous acculturation. It is not surprising that his last paragraph begins with the sentence: "Much further research is needed, and the outlook is unfortunately gloomy" (Whittle 1990b).

The use of radiocarbon dating and other approaches to identify the transition

It seems likely that problems in identifying transitions have been greatly compounded by the manner in which ^{14}C dating has been used. In certain areas of Europe, such as south Scandinavia, stratigraphic evidence can be employed to back up interpretations based on typology, environmental archaeology, and ^{14}C dating (e.g. at the site of Bjørnsholm, Andersen 1993). However, in Britain and Ireland, other than radiocarbon determinations, it is rare to find alternative objective criteria which can provide independent dating of an assemblage. Yet, if we must move away from a traditional approach where typological and economic change are seen as one and the same, then a rigorous approach to the establishment of an independent framework for documenting change should be a prerequisite. Usually this would be a framework based on ^{14}C dating, yet our use of radiocarbon often falls well below any minimum standard. A spurious scientific objectivity is thus created by the uncritical use of ^{14}C dates.

The problems of ^{14}C dating

This is not a chapter on ^{14}C dating and only a few references will be made to the types of problem encountered.

1   Baillie (1991), for example, has pointed out the degree of variation in dates obtained from wood of known age from the Sweet Track (covering a range of several hundred years); yet archaeologists tend to ignore the problem of statistical variation and accept the earliest or latest date, i.e., the dates which are least probable.

2   It is often conveniently and erroneously assumed that a single radiocarbon date provides an adequate estimate of age of all the archaeological material within a single layer (see below for discussion on Dalkey Island).

3   Frequently the question of the integrity of the sample is ignored, i.e., was charcoal, in particular, created by one event or did it accumulate from several?

4   As Warner (1990) has pointed out, many buildings have had structural timbers dated and an allowance of at least 200 years should be made for ^{14}C dates deriving from such contexts.

Pilcher (1993:28), in discussing the reliability of radiocarbon dating in palynology, summarizes the problem: "The routine radiocarbon dates

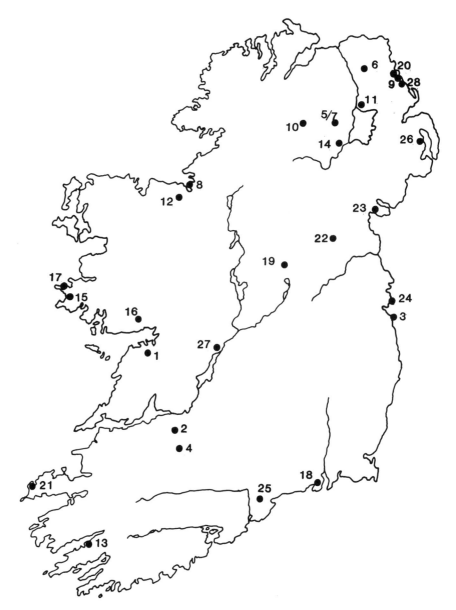

9.1   Location of sites referred to in text: 1. Poulnabrone, Co. Clare, 2. Lough Gur, Co. Limerick, 3. Dalkey Island, Co. Dublin, 4. Tankardstown, Co. Limerick, 5. Ballynagilly, Co. Tyrone, 6. Ballymacaldrack, Co. Antrim, 7. Ballybriest, Co. Tyrone, 8. Carrowmore, Co. Sligo, 9. Mad Mans Window, Co. Antrim, 10. Altanagh, Co. Tyrone, 11. Newferry, Co. Antrim, 12. Croaghan, Co. Sligo, 13. Cashelkeelty, Co. Kerry, 14. Weirs Lough, Co. Tyrone, 15. Connemara National Park, Co. Galway, 16. Lough Namackenbeg, Co. Galway, 17. Lough available from most laboratories have been shown to have inaccuracies that only allow the calendrical date to be specified to the nearest half millennium. Attempts to interpret time differences or real ages closer than 500 years by conventional dates are simply not valid." See also Lanting and van der Plicht (1993–94) for a general discussion on the problems of ^{14}C dating in archaeology.

Some examples of the problematic use of ^{14}C dates from an Irish context may provide an insight into the potential pitfalls.[2] A list of all the uncalibrated ^{14}C dates referred to in this chapter is provided in the appendix, pp. 257–58.

The tendency to focus on one date from a series, often the earliest, is best illustrated at Poulnabrone portal tomb, Co. Clare (Lynch 1988) (Fig. 9.1). Reference is usually made to the date of 5100 BP (Woodman 1992b, Twohig 1990). However, while the later use of the tomb is recognized, little significance is placed on the fact that there are a number of individuals dated to between 5000 and 4800 BP in the tomb (Hedges, Housley, Bronk and Van Klinken 1990). This could represent reuse of the tomb, but the date range may simply be considered as a typical product of the ^{14}C dating technique, and therefore the earliest and/or latest date should be treated with caution.

In fact, taking the nature of ^{14}C dates into account, an overlap between series of so-called late Mesolithic and early Neolithic dates should be expected (see Baillie 1992 for discussion on this point).

Probably the least reliable situations are those in which general, non-specific charcoal collections have been made – particularly on sites which have been used episodically. Similarly, the collection of charcoal from pits, where the function of the pit is unclear and the origin of the charcoal uncertain, is fraught with danger. In the case of Mt Sandel (Woodman 1985a), a number of relatively recent tree falls contained charcoal which had been derived from the Mesolithic settlement. A very clear example of the dangers of dating charcoal of uncertain origin can be seen in two dates obtained from the same burial at Churchtown near Lough Gur, Co. Limerick (Cleary, pers. comm.).

| GrN19477 | 5990 ± 60 BP | charcoal |
| OxA5821 | 2935 ± 60 BP | bone |

Caption for fig. 9.1 (*cont.*)

> Sheeauns, Co. Galway, 18. Ballylough Project, Co. Waterford, 19. Lough Derravaragh, Co. Westmeath, 20. Bay Farm, Carnlough, Co. Antrim, 21. Ferriter's Cove, Co. Kerry, 22. Moynagh Lough, Co. Meath, 23. Rockmarshall, Co. Louth, 24. Sutton, Co. Dublin, 25. Kilgreaney Cave, Co. Waterford, 26. Ringneil Quay, Co. Down, 27. Stoney Island, Co. Galway, 28. Ballygalley, Co. Antrim.

At Dalkey Island, Co. Dublin (Liversage 1968), Woodman (1976:78) argued for contemporaneity between the domesticates and later Mesolithic artifacts based on the assumption that one ^{14}C date could be used to date everything in two small shell-middens. AMS ^{14}C dates on bone from the Quaternary Faunas Project (Woodman *et al.* 1997) provide a rather different picture. Even allowing for the marine effect, it would appear that there is a very significant variation in age within the two small shell-middens. The dates range from 7250 ± 100 BP (a seal rib) to 3050 ± 70 BP (a cattle bone). This date range shows an accumulation and addition to the middens over a 4000-year period. The original charcoal ^{14}C date of 5290 ± 170 BP (Liversage 1968) provided a spurious precision, possibly based on the accumulation of separate pieces of charcoal over a significant time span. There is a certain irony in the fact that if 400 years are subtracted from the seal dates to allow for a marine effect, and we allow for dates taken from two middens, then the arithmetic mean of 5450 lies quite close to the original ^{14}C date![3]

The lesson from the many instances of the inclusion of residual charcoal from forest fires and old wood are almost too numerous to document. In an Irish context large pieces of charcoal from one small area at Newferry Site 3, Zone 7, were ^{14}C dated to 8895 ± 125 BP. However other dates from this zone ranged from 7485 ± 115 BP to 6915 ± 60 BP. In this case the oldest date was also a stratigraphic impossibility as the underlying peat layer, Zone 8, produced a date of 7630 ± 195 BP (Woodman 1977).

An obvious problem with the use of structural timbers is reflected in the dating of the Neolithic house at Tankardstown, Co. Limerick (Gowen and Tarbett 1988). Here a burned house has both charcoal and wheat grain dates, the latter from the Oxford accelerator lab. The wheat grain dates are significantly younger, over 200 years, than the structural timber dates. The tendency for dates of structural timbers to be older than dates derived from other types of plant remains, such as wheat, can also be seen at Balbridie in Scotland (Hedges, Housley, Bronk and Van Klinken 1990a) and Buxton in Derbyshire (Hedges *et al.* 1991; see also below). Therefore in situations where Neolithic house or tomb structural timbers have been dated and compared to dates from Mesolithic sites where twigs or hazelnuts have often been dated, there is an obvious danger of a false contemporaneity being created.

Within mainland Europe the debate on the impact of AMS ^{14}C dates in an area where structural timbers and residual charcoal have been used is best illustrated by the proposed revisions of the duration of the LBK culture (see Lanting and van der Plicht 1993–4, appendix 1, and Whittle 1990a).

The ^{14}C date obtained from a hearth beneath the bank of the Cleavden Dyke (Tayside), Scotland, shows that the problems of old wood are not confined to structural timbers (Barclay *et al.* 1995). In this instance careful examination of the charcoal submitted for ^{14}C dating showed that "the wood had already been rotten prior to becoming charred." It was suggested that the wood had been dead up to 200 years before it had been placed in the fire!

Identifying transitional sites on the basis of ¹⁴C dates can be difficult when the nature of the sample and statistical uncertainty are taken into consideration, but when samples of uncertain context and integrity are used then the possibility of creating spurious chronological frameworks increases exponentially.

Problems associated with the use of ¹⁴C dates are not confined to the beginnings of the Neolithic; where a specific time horizon is being identified through the use of ¹⁴C dates the nature of the samples can have an immeasurable impact on the problem. Anderson (1991), in reviewing the radiocarbon evidence for the human colonization of New Zealand, noted the lack of reliability of certain materials which have been used for ¹⁴C dating. He noted: "Dates on charcoal of minimum inbuilt age should be closest to the actual calendrical period . . . unidentified charcoal is the most problematic sample type."

Radiocarbon chronologies have been essential in documenting the transition to agriculture but in the case of both Ireland and Britain the study of this crucial period has often relied on a range of poorly contexted ¹⁴C dates carried out on material of uncertain origins. The very nature of the surviving archaeological record of this phase has, unfortunately, forced a reliance on such dates. In summary, it should be remembered that in most cases ¹⁴C dating rarely provides dates of the events which archaeologists seek to study (obviously AMS dates obtained from worked organic materials can be an exception). Instead it provides dates based on materials which it is hoped are chronologically associated with these events.

Other problems in identifying a transition to farming in Ireland

Another problem in the study of the transition is difficulty in identifying actual transitional assemblages. Those that exist may be a product of post-depositional processes or an artifact of our research strategies. At Newferry Site 3, Co. Antrim (Woodman 1977) Neolithic pottery and occasional Neolithic artifacts were found in a river channel along with a range of Mesolithic implements (Zone 2). However, this late channel cut through a series of rich Mesolithic horizons mixing two potentially chronologically distinct assemblages together; the occasional occurrence of sherds of Neolithic pottery just below this channel is likely to have been caused by intrusive contamination. The Dalkey Island case, referred to earlier, is another classic instance of contamination. Another case was the apparent occurrence of cattle with Mesolithic artifacts at Moynagh Lough (Bradley 1991; see also below). Here, as a result of an AMS ¹⁴C date, it was shown that the cattle bone had penetrated down into Mesolithic levels through 50 cm of later deposits.

The Ballylough Project (Zvelebil *et al.* 1987) has enhanced our knowledge of the prehistory of southeast Ireland through its identification of numerous scatters of artifacts. However, the observation that Mesolithic and Neolithic artifacts occur in the same location and are, therefore, transitional assemblages is based on surface collection.

The discovery of Mesolithic and Neolithic artifacts in the same field does not imply contemporaneity or the existence of transitional assemblages. The argument that Mesolithic and Neolithic materials come from the same coastal environment and therefore represent a transition in which both "Mesolithic" and "Neolithic" communities exploited the same environment ignores two facts: (a) the availability of flint in beaches means that all stone-using communities, even into the Bronze Age, use coastal areas and leave a very visible presence in the form of industrial waste, and (b) even in the Ballylough Project, few diagnostic artifacts of Mesolithic type were found away from the coast.

Identifying the transition in Ireland
The Irish Neolithic at 5000 BP

Obviously the implication of the introduction of this chapter is that while propositions for the transition to agriculture abound, the use of the available limited information has been selective. Archaeology only develops on the basis of what previous generations have made available to us; we cannot wipe the slate clean but rather must reevaluate the reliability of our database. It is perhaps simpler to begin by defining both the known early Neolithic of Ireland and the latest Mesolithic, and then consider the evidence for changes through time, overlaps, or discontinuities.

Based on his excavations at Ballynagilly, Co. Tyrone, ApSimon (1976) suggested a division of the Irish Neolithic. The period after 5000 BP would be described as the Middle Neolithic, while the period before 5500 BP was described as the Earliest Neolithic. This was to distinguish it from the period between 5500 and 5000 BP which he described as the Early Neolithic. As will be shown below, there is no difficulty identifying the fully developed (Middle) Neolithic. The problem is identifying the extent and nature of the Early Neolithic and whether ApSimon's Earliest Neolithic really exists.

At 5000 BP the ceramic material culture consists of plain bag-shaped, shouldered bowls (Western Neolithic Pottery *pace* Case 1961) and is associated with a simple flint industry of surface retouched and pointed projectile heads, end scrapers, and possibly elongated plano-convex knives (Woodman 1994) (Fig. 9.2). The blade technology would appear to vary significantly between localities (Woodman 1992b). Williams (1989) mistook the restricted range of artifacts typical of the early Neolithic as an indication of a transitional assemblage. Woodman (1994) has shown that the range of flint artifacts from sites such as Ballynagilly compares with that from other Neolithic sites of comparable age in Britain. The remarkable

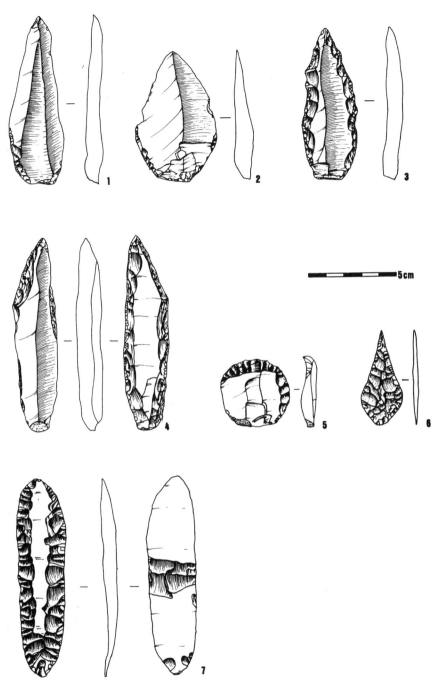

9.2 Irish later Mesolithic and early Neolithic artifacts: 1. tanged flake, 2. Bann flake, 3. blade point, 4. bar form, 5. scraper, 6. leaf-shaped arrowhead, 7. plano-convex knife.

aspect of this 5000 BP assemblage, i.e., the similarity of both much of its pottery to the Grimston style pottery and the early Neolithic lithic assemblages in many parts of England, is often ignored.

Faunal assemblages are relatively rare, but in the case of Tankardstown (Gowen and Tarbett 1988) the limited number of fragments of bone suggested a reliance largely on cattle and sheep (McCarthy, pers. comm.). In addition to the emmer wheat remains, some burnt apple fragments were also recovered (Monk, pers. comm.). Few megalithic tombs have faunal remains which can be convincingly described as primary, but a survey carried out by McCormick (1985–6) showed the presence of domesticated cattle and sheep. The middle Neolithic, at least, is characterized by the occurrence of large timber-framed houses, e.g., Tankardstown, Ballynagilly, etc. (see Simpson 1995). In the case of the Ballynagilly house (ApSimon 1976) the dates of 5100 BP are also based on samples of structural timber and, therefore, likely to be older than the actual house (see below). The Tankardstown AMS dates on wheat may be more accurate, i.e., 4900 BP.

The contents of the court tombs, which are particularly common in the northern part of Ireland, have often been regarded as typical of the Early Neolithic (Herity and Eogan 1976). However, it would appear more likely that the dates of the tombs identified by archaeologists represent successive stages of use, which may have occurred some considerable time after they were erected. Based on the few charcoal ^{14}C dates available from within the court tombs, there is no real evidence of their use before 5000 BP (Woodman 1994).

The earliest dates from a court tomb come from beneath the cairn at Ballymacaldrack, Co. Antrim. These appear to belong to a pre-cairn structure similar to those found in the British unchambered long barrows. It is also probable that the dated charcoal was derived from structural timbers (Collins 1976). One of the other early dates which is frequently quoted comes from *below* Ballybriest court tomb, Co. Derry (ApSimon 1976).

The accepted chronological sequence of Irish tombs is also beginning to break down. Many authors, e.g., ApSimon (1976), have argued that portal tombs are earlier than court tombs. Ronayne (1994) also has made a case that in some areas, such as south Armagh, they may pre-date court tombs. The range of dates from Poulnabrone (Lynch 1988) starts with OxA1906, 5100 ± 80 BP, which could suggest this general trend, but there is a group of four dates between 4940 and 4720 BP (Hedges, Housley, Bronk and Van Klinken 1990). This could suggest that OxA1906 is part of Baillie's statistical tail. The bulk of the dates after 5000 BP should not be ignored. If Thomas (1991b) is correct and material could also be moved from older monuments, then even Poulnabrone may not pre-date 5000 BP.

Berg's (1995) balanced review of the passage tomb dates, particularly those from Co. Sligo, suggests that the two earliest dates, Carrowmore 3 (formerly 4) and Carrowmore 7, are not reliable (see below). In general the trend is for some of the passage tombs to be as early as the other monuments, but they are unlikely to be earlier. The Linkardstown-style megalithic cists, which produce single or limited numbers of articulated inhumations, were often thought of as late, and are probably contemporary with other forms of tomb-building, as the skeletal remains have been ^{14}C dated as far back as 4800 BP (Brindley and Lanting 1989–90). Most dates from other tomb types are based on charcoal, often from below the monument, thus creating a spurious antiquity. Instead of a presumption of chronological primacy for one monument type (Herity and Eogan 1976, ApSimon 1986), there is growing evidence of extensive megalithic tomb-building in certain parts of Ireland beginning at, or more likely after, 5000 BP. As strict chronological order no longer seems a necessary criterion, there are now numerous other explanations for the development of and differences among these tombs (Woodman 1992b, Cooney and Grogan 1994).

It is therefore the middle Neolithic, or the period immediately after 5000 BP, that sees the existence of tombs, perhaps of several varieties, substantial houses, and a farming economy. The problem is, of course, to identify the earlier Neolithic and to assess its relationship with the latest phases of the Mesolithic.

An early/earlier/earliest(?) Irish Neolithic

One site in particular has influenced our expectations for the earliest Neolithic in Ireland and even Britain. This site is Ballynagilly. By the late 1960s it was apparent, based on ^{14}C dates, that an argument might be made for a Neolithic phase of occupation at Ballynagilly well before 5500 BP. For the last two decades this purported early phase for an Irish Neolithic has colored the judgments of many searching for early evidence of Neolithic occupation well before 5000, if not 5500 BP (see Whittle 1985:196). Although caution was recommended by many (Woodman 1985a, Kinnes 1985), the site created the expectation that other early Neolithic sites would soon be found. However, as pointed out by Baillie (1992), early Neolithic Irish and British dates cluster at around 5200 BP and the ones earlier than that date may represent a normal statistical tail which would be expected in a large batch of dates.

ApSimon (pers. comm.) has recently indicated his unease with the early dates from Ballynagilly. His concern is that the material culture associated with the early dates and that associated with the later house are identical. It is also difficult to find a suitable earlier progenitor for such a clearly common set of equipment in Britain and Ireland. Baillie (1992) has noted that while some skepticism was correctly expressed over the dates based on the structural timbers from the house (Williams 1989), not enough attention had been given to the fact that the so-called early phase dates were based on samples of what was potentially residual charcoal of uncertain origin. What is also remarkable is that twenty years after the publication of Ballynagilly no other early assemblage of material like Ballynagilly with a consistent series of ^{14}C dates from reliable contexts has yet been found.

One of the few possible examples of a pre-5000 BP date is that from a small hearth placed on a large stone slab and associated with a simple carinated bowl at Mad Mans Window, Co. Antrim, dated to 5100 ± 150 BP (Woodman 1992a); even this date has a large standard deviation. Other dates obtained include those from Altanagh, Co. Tyrone (Williams 1986), where an enigmatic megalithic tomb had been badly disturbed. These are two dates from closely related pits.

| F137 | GrN10557 | 4590 ± 80 BP | charcoal |
| F136 | UB2560 | 5685 ± 70 BP | charcoal |

F137 is a burial pit which was stratigraphically later than F136. F136 was a large irregular hollow nearly 3 m across which contained lenses of soil and charcoal. The excavator had reservations about the date for F136 as the material culture was identical to F137 and the pit was so clearly associated with F136. This is clearly another case of the use of relict charcoal as in the Lough Gur burial.

Examples such as these are not uncommon, but bigger problems occur when charcoal which is only a few hundred years older than the settlement is used for ^{14}C dating. One possible example in this category is the extensive Neolithic settlement excavated by Simpson at Ballygalley, Co. Antrim (Simpson 1995). Here seven ^{14}C dates were associated with pits and foundation trenches (appendix, p. 257). A difference of 600 years between ^{14}C dates is present (UB3491, 4830 ± 117 BP to UB3362, 5469 ± 69 BP). It is therefore questionable as to whether ^{14}C dating has contributed much to the dating of the Neolithic occupation of this site. Instead it can only be stated that a series of charcoal samples of diverse origins have been ^{14}C dated. It would be difficult to state with any certainty that this site was in existence before 5000 BP. The excavator has stated a preference for UB3491, 4830 ± 117 BP.

Burenhult (1984) has claimed an early origin for the Sligo passage tombs. However, as Berg (1995) has pointed out, the date from Carrowmore Tomb 7 of 5240 ± 80 BP (Lu1441) must be regarded as suspect as the charcoal was taken from four separate contexts. Other early dates also come from the Co. Sligo passage tombs. In two cases, Carrowmore 3 and Croaghan, there must be serious reservations about the stratigraphic context and range of dates. In the case of Carrowmore 3, Berg (1995:104) and others have commented on the fact that there is a 1500 year difference between two dates which are both associated with an early phase of the monument.

| Lu1840 | 5750 ± 85 BP | charcoal around base of orthostats |
| Lu1750 | 4320 ± 75 BP | charcoal, inner stone packing |

At Croaghan two dates from the chamber were obtained. Both dates came from the cremation deposit and, in fact, the later date is from a disturbed deposit.

Ua713   6680 ± 100 BP   charcoal
St10453   5685 ± 85 BP   charcoal

The manner in which passage tombs are open to disturbance and contamination is perhaps best exemplified in that not only *late* Neolithic and early Bronze Age ^{14}C dates occurred at Croaghan but also modern charcoal was obtained from below the cairn. In three cases, Carrowmore Tomb 3, Croaghan, and Altanagh, an apparently early date has been matched by a ^{14}C date which is at least 1000 years different in age and yet comes from a context which may be associated. Ultimately it is difficult to date passage tombs in use in Ireland even to 5000 BP, and an earlier date seems even more improbable.

The investigations at Ballynagilly also encouraged palynologists to find traces of early farming well before 5000 BP. Early traces of large grasses and possible cereals were documented at numerous sites, first at Ballynagilly (Pilcher and Smith 1979), and then at Cashelkeelty (Lynch 1981) and Weirs Lough (Edwards and Hirons 1984). In recent years, after enthusiastic support for the early farming evidence, caution has been expressed by many of the same authors (Edwards 1989) although Edwards has also noted that there is a tendency for most cereal-type pollen to occur in the period shortly before the Elm Decline (Edwards 1989). Confidence in these early data received a further setback when O'Connell (1987) identified what appeared to be cereal pollen at Connemara National Park, Co. Galway, and Lough Namackenbeg, Co. Galway. This cereal-type pollen grain is associated with a ^{14}C date of (GrN13145) 6915 ± 40 BP. At Lough Namackenbeg a ^{14}C related date is inferred from its position in the pollen profile. O'Connell suggests a date of 7570 BP.

In some instances, through the identification of numerous indicators in the pollen diagram, e.g., Lough Sheeauns, Co. Galway (Molloy and O'Connell 1988), there is no question regarding the presence of Neolithic farming activity. However the rather more limited indicators which occur well before 5000 BP do present a greater problem. Objectively, there is no easy way to distinguish between early human clearances and natural variations in pollen density, contamination, and genetic spores, e.g. polyploidy. The tendency amongst archaeologists seems to be to believe in clearances which occur within an archaeologically acceptable chronological framework. Dates after 6000 BP appear to be considered as acceptable indicators of farming, but not those before!

The expectation of Neolithic activity extending back to, or before, 5500 BP is typified by Monk (1993: Fig. 5.5, while in Britain the idea of a very early Neolithic is also becoming enshrined in chronological charts (Darvill 1996: Fig. 6.1)). Assumptions of a farming presence can be met by accepting so-called cereal-type pollen when it occurs at or after 5600 BP and combining that information with ¹⁴C dates from charcoal which are used to suggest an early presence of cattle on non-specified sites. As noted earlier with the use of AMS dates, some of the domesticates can be shown to date rather later in time. The reality of the archaeological record is that expectations of a significantly earlier Neolithic are not being met.

In summary, much of the evidence for either very early farming activity or a Neolithic material culture was previously acceptable because of the early dates from Ballynagilly. However, this type of evidence alone is much more difficult to sustain. The evidence from palynology cannot be used with confidence and the ¹⁴C dates from most archaeological contexts must also be treated as suspect.

While a case can be made for an early Neolithic before 5000 BP there is no clear evidence of a fully developed or mature Neolithic, similar to the middle Neolithic, at a significantly earlier date. Obviously the case can be made for a transitional phase or substitution phase. Thus the whole question of a possible chronological overlap between the Irish Mesolithic and Neolithic needs to be re-examined.

The chronological position of the latest phases of the Irish Mesolithic

The definition of the Irish later Mesolithic has often seemed simple. At 6000 BP a hard hammer percussion technique was producing, in various raw materials, a series of robust and often quite stubby, thick blades averaging between 6 and 9 cm in length. The most distinctive of these artifacts are the so-called Bann Flakes and backed blades and flakes (Fig. 9.2), but there is also a series of roughly notched flakes, triangular picks, and numerous polished stone axes. Large concentrations of these pieces are found at key fishing locations on islands, lakeshores, and river fords, possibly in the last instance associated with the building of fish weirs.

While many of the known later Mesolithic range of tools give the impression of being task specific for wood-working, in particular the large numbers of polished stone axes, the range of implements is found in different environments. Dalkey Island, off the east coast of Ireland, in contrast to river ford/valley locations such as Newferry, would probably have been used in a different manner. There is only a small scatter of Mesolithic artifacts away from the rivers and even when they occur at 300 m above sea level they are still the same artifact types.

There is a question as to whether the material from these sites represents the entire later Mesolithic. Woodman and Anderson (1990) have suggested that emphasis on blade production, where raw materials were freely available, and their subsequent transportation to key locations, may have led to the creation of sites where few, if any, artifacts were left behind. At the other extreme, Peterson (1990), working with surface-collected material in the Ballylough Project, has suggested that because the percussion technique is simple it could be considered as expedient, arguing then that other even less controlled techniques using small pebbles were also Mesolithic – a point questioned by many of those working in Ireland (Anderson 1995; see also below).

It has always been accepted that many large land mammals, e.g., elk and aurochs, never lived in early Holocene Ireland. Recently, through the work of the Quaternary Faunas Project, it has become obvious that no single verifiable red deer bone (*Cervus elaphus*) exists on any Mesolithic site in Ireland (Woodman *et al.* 1997). Therefore, aside from pigs (*Sus scrofa ferus*), Mesolithic communities in Ireland must have relied on gathering, fishing in lakes and rivers, and the exploitation of a range of marine species and shellfish.

The significance of the identification of the Irish later Mesolithic as a robust blade industry associated with a distinct range of artifacts which are largely concentrated on sites in a narrow range of coastal, river-ine, and lacustrine environments is not to be underestimated. In the absence of any known alternative technologies in secure later Mesolithic contexts, and given the exceptional scarcity of later Mesolithic artifacts from other environments, the appearance of the known material is, even in preferred environs such as Strangford Lough, of limited numbers of shoreline campsites often with a particular procurement purpose. There are no groups of artifacts or locational indicators which would suggest a heavy reliance on either plant food collection and processing or extensive mammal hunting.

As noted in the introduction, many authors have pointed to chron-ological overlaps between the later Mesolithic and early Neolithic in Ireland. Williams (1989) interpreted a rather restricted selection of dates as an indication that a process of change from hunter-gatherer to farmer life-style was taking place. This view relied extensively on the evidence from Ballynagilly although, as Baillie noted, the structural timber dates were excluded and emphasis was placed on the non-specific charcoal date.

There is a series of ^{14}C dates from Mesolithic sites which could suggest a continued Mesolithic occupation of Ireland at or after 5500 BP (see appendix for details). These sites include (1) Lough Derravaragh, Co. Westmeath (Mitchell 1972b), with a date derived from charcoal probably associated with a chipping floor;[4] (2) Bay Farm, Carnlough, Co. Antrim (Woodman and Johnson 1996), with discrete charcoal patches dumped within flint working debris; and (3) Newferry [Site 3] Zone 3, where the con-tribution of relict charcoal in waterlain contexts might have caused the dates to be slightly too old. These would be confirmed by the dates obtained from the coastal site of Ferriter's Cove, Co. Kerry, where charcoal and hazel-nuts from a hearth and hazelnuts from beside two small activity areas suggest later Mesolithic occupation at 5600–5700 BP (Woodman *et al.* 1999).

As will be seen from the appendix, there are other ^{14}C dates from the Ferriter's Cove excavation, including indicators of a later presence on the site.

Context 488	Q2641 5241	5245 ± 55 BP	charcoal
	Q2634 5634	5680 ± 70 BP	shell
Context 302	OxA3869	5510 ± 70 BP	bone

C488 was a pit cut through the silt in which most of the material was embedded; cattle bones which have been ^{14}C dated (C302) also appeared to have been embedded in the same silt. These dates confirm the stratigraphic observation of later activity at Ferriter's Cove, but they do not of themselves necessarily confirm a continuity of a Mesolithic presence on the site. However, fragments of a human femur and tooth have also been ^{14}C dated:

Context 213	OxA4918	5545 ± 65 BP	bone
	OxA5770	5590 ± 60 BP	tooth

The δ^{13}C level of $-14‰$ and 4.1‰ suggests a marine diet; given that there may be an associated old carbon effect the mean point of the date might be 200 years later. The femur, stratified at a higher level than the main phase of occupation, is still associated with a hunter-gatherer economy. Thus the presence of occasional cattle bones does not necessarily indicate a major shift in diet.

Some of the Mesolithic sites which have produced the most recent ^{14}C dates are less secure. There is a date from a layer beneath an early medieval crannog at Moynagh Lough. Bradley (1991) quotes this as 5270 ± 60 BP (charcoal). This layer contained Mesolithic artifacts but was also subject to some contamination, i.e., an early medieval cattle bone was found within the layer (see above).

As noted earlier, the information from Dalkey Island shows how spurious contemporaneity can be created. It is of interest that in this case the domesticates, i.e., cattle and sheep, date to 5000 BP and later – at best more than 500 years younger than the dates which might be associated with the Mesolithic use of the same location. As can be seen in the Appendix there is a suggestion that the Mesolithic occupation which created the shell-middens was dated to 5600 BP or earlier.

Similarly at the Sutton shell-midden (Mitchell 1956, 1971, 1972a), the charcoal date, 5250 ± 100 BP (I5067), would appear to be over 1000 years younger than the AMS bone dates. Therefore the large bone which was originally thought to be cattle is more likely to be bear (Woodman *et al.* 1997).

At Rockmarshall III, Mitchell (1949, 1971) obtained one charcoal ^{14}C date.

I5323	5470 ± 110 BP	charcoal

The age of the Mesolithic middens was cross-checked by obtaining a date for a human bone from Site III.

OxA4604   5705 ± 75 BP   bone

Again this suggests occupation around or before 5500 BP.

In general, these sites indicate that the Later Mesolithic may have continued until quite late, possibly until after 5500 BP but it is not clear how much later a Mesolithic presence can be documented. Therefore the question of a chronological overlap and the existence of a Neolithic or farming component in the latest phases of the Mesolithic needs careful examination.

Identification of an overlap/transition

One possible indicator of contact between the Mesolithic and Neolithic is the presence of early cattle or sheep bones. As noted, one group of cattle bones found at Ferriter's Cove (C302) occurs in what may be a Mesolithic context. Only one clearly diagnostic Neolithic artifact was recovered from all the excavations and this was out of context on a cliff edge. Unlike Dalkey Island or the Dundrum sand dune sites, where coastal Neolithic settlement is known, there are no concentrations of Neolithic artifacts such as arrowheads, scrapers, or pottery from Ferriter's Cove. The cattle bones thus may be contemporaneous with a human bone with a high marine diet; they are probably associated with Mesolithic activity.

A second occurrence of a cattle bone dating to before 5000 BP, [OxA4269] 5190 ± 80 BP, is less satisfactory. This comes from investigations at Kilgreany Cave (Layer E), Co. Waterford. Unfortunately this site was disturbed stratigraphically (Movius 1935) and, while there are a number of Neolithic burials and some sherds of early plain western Neolithic pottery, there is no clear indication that this cattle bone and the Neolithic material are associated. There is also evidence of modern fauna working their way into the same layer; early Holocene and even late glacial faunal remains also occur at the same level.

The least satisfactory is Ringneill Quay, Co. Down (Stephens and Collins 1961; Jope 1965). Here cattle and sheep bones were recovered from a series of beach and marine deposits along with an undiagnostic lithic assemblage. However, the often quoted ^{14}C date came from another excavation carried out nearby (see Woodman 1978 for discussion).

Q770   5380 ± 120 BP   charcoal

Obviously, as noted earlier, the Dalkey Island and Sutton charcoal dates do not, as suggested by Woodman (1976), indicate early presence of cattle and sheep. It is interesting, however, that the sheep bone which was dated by the Oxford Accelerator Lab is still quite early (see Appendix).

One occurrence of human remains which epitomizes the intangible nature of the evidence is the Stoney Island, Co. Galway, burial. This bog body was noted in a possible early context (Shea 1931; O Floinn 1995), but was only dated recently, with average age for three dates (OxA2941–3) of 5210 ± 50 BP (Brindley and Lanting 1995). No artifacts have been associated with this burial, which has been assumed to be Neolithic. Certainly the $\delta^{13}C$–21‰ would suggest a land-based diet which is more likely to indicate a farming economy.

It is quite difficult to find a transitional assemblage within which faunal remains and other indicators can be placed. In the Irish case, no reliable examples exist. The possible abruptness of the change is best illustrated by the juxtaposition of sites in southwest Ireland.

At Ferriter's Cove, Co. Kerry, ^{13}C values suggest a continuation of a marine-based diet down to 5200 BP. However, at Poulnabrone portal tomb, Co. Clare (Lynch 1988), many of the human bones may have been from individuals who died at or just after 5000 BP. This is a site within 10 km of the coast yet three $\delta^{13}C$ determinations from the human remains center on 21.0‰ which indicate the likelihood of a land-based diet. Even the Stoney Island burial should have had a "marine" component if salmon had played a major role in its diet.

In contrast is the inland Neolithic settlement at Tankardstown where substantial farmhouses existed at 4900 BP. There is an associated Neolithic assemblage along with cereal grain (Monk pers. comm.) and a fauna dominated by domesticates (McCarthy pers. comm.). This evidence, although based on only two sites, would appear to suggest that there is an abrupt shift at the end of the Mesolithic from a gathering-fishing-hunting economy to a farming economy (Woodman forthcoming).

As can be seen from the previous discussion, the period before 5000 BP is poorly understood. It lacks the houses and artifact traps such as the tombs of the middle Neolithic and is, therefore, slightly better known from its later Mesolithic assemblages and sites. An examination of the chart of ^{14}C dates (Fig. 9.3) also shows, however, that there is a problem in that the latest ^{14}C dates from Mesolithic sites are the least trustworthy, i.e., those after 5400 BP; the original Dalkey Island and Sutton charcoal dates are examples while again in the case of Moynagh Lough there is always the possibility of later charcoal intruding. It is also difficult to identify Neolithic assemblages with trustworthy ^{14}C dates which date to before 5100 BP.

This could, of course, be due to ^{14}C variation in the atmosphere at that time which has created a perceived gap in the record. When calibrated the ^{14}C dates for this time span range between 3900 and 4200 cal. BC. According to the Pearson *et al.* (1986) calibration curve, the period between 4000 and 4200 BC seems to have been one where there had been considerable fluctuation in ^{14}C levels in the atmosphere (Fig. 9.4). There are, there-

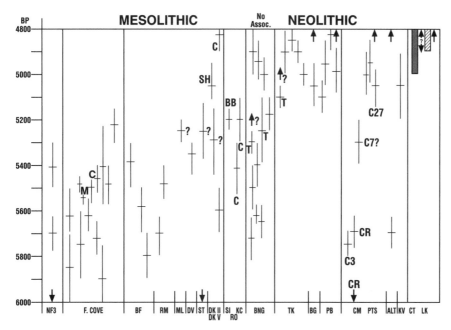

9.3   Range of ¹⁴C dates from the latest phases of the Mesolithic and the early
      Neolithic in Ireland: 1–4 Later Mesolithic; 5–7 Neolithic. An arrow indi-
      cates either possible allowance for old-wood factor or the existence of dates
      outside the chronological range of the chart. *Key:* NF3 = Newferry Site 3, Co.
      Antrim; F. Cove = Ferriter's Cove, Co. Antrim; BF = Bay Farm, Carnlough,
      Co. Antrim; RM = Rockmarshall, Co. Louth; ML = Moynagh Lough, Co.
      Meath; DV = Lough Derravaragh, Co. Westmeath; DKII/V = Dalkey Island,
      Co. Dublin; SI = Stoney Island, Co. Galway; RQ = Ringneil Quay, Co. Down;
      KC = Kilgreaney Cave, Co. Waterford; BNG = Ballynagilly, Co. Tyrone;
      TK = Tankardstown, Co. Limerick; BG = Ballygalley, Co. Antrim; PB =
      Poulnabrone, Co. Clare; CM = Carrowmore tombs, Co. Sligo; PTS = Passage
      tombs; CR = Croaghan, Co. Sligo; ALT = Altanagh; KV = Knockiveagh, Co.
      Down; CT = Court tombs; LK = Linkardstown cists; C = Cattle bone;
      SH = Sheep; T = Structural timbers; BB = bog body; M = midden.

fore, a number of points within that time span when less than usual reliability can be placed on dates. However, there is no reason to believe that
dates are either clumping or being scattered arbitrarily over certain time
periods to the same extent as has happened in the period 2000–2500 cal. BC.
Aside from this problem and the lack of credibility of some of the latest
dates from Mesolithic sites, none post-dates this 4200–4000 BC phase, while
it is noticeable that if a 200-year allowance is made for the use of structural
timbers and their impact on the ¹⁴C chronology then there is a very notice-

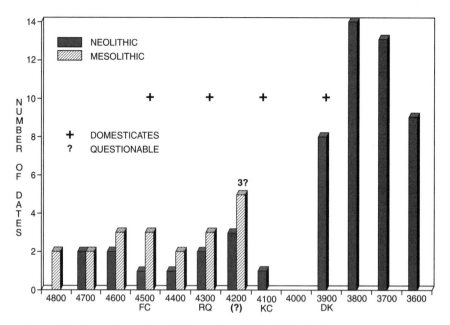

9.4   Number of later Mesolithic and early Neolithic ^{14}C dates per century after calibration and, where appropriate, adjusted for a 200–year-old wood factor. (For key, see Fig. 9.3.)

able increase in ^{14}C dated Neolithic assemblages at around 3800 BC (Fig. 9.4). Most of those which are earlier fall into the category of non-specific charcoal samples. Whether raw ^{14}C dates or calibrated dates are used, apparent overlaps between the Mesolithic and Neolithic are more a product of our research strategies than of past activities.

In summary, the difficulties in finding reliably dated later Mesolithic sites after 5500 BP and early Neolithic sites before 5000 BP are compounded by a scarcity of securely dated assemblages from the intervening period. Many of both the Mesolithic and the Neolithic assemblages from this period have been dated using non-specific (probably relict in some instances) charcoal out of uncertain contexts. Instead, the few firm indicators of a change in economy and lifestyle are based on the occurrence of cattle bones in ephemeral or stray contexts. There is neither a clear continuity of classic Mesolithic assemblages close to 5000 BP nor, taking securely dated Neolithic assemblages, significant evidence in Ireland to indicate the occurrence of classic middle Neolithic assemblages before 5000 BP. Making allowances for timelags in the dating of structural timbers, there is little reason to believe that any of the Irish timber houses of the Neolithic date before 5000 BP. Similarly if the few bone dates from tombs are reliable, with the exception of one date from Poulnabrone, there appears to have been a floruit of tomb use after 5000 BP. Even if the uncertain indicators of palynology point towards an earlier Neolithic, it may have differed significantly from the well-known Middle Neolithic of 5000 BP and later.

It is with this paucity of evidence at a key point in time that questions are asked about the means by which farming was established in Ireland.

By what means did the transition from hunter-gatherer to farmer take place in Ireland?

In the absence of any objective chronological framework, it is not surprising that personal preferences color interpretation to such a great extent, but certain underlying trends can be recognized.

Thomas (1991b) correctly noted that "the Neolithic" need not necessarily be a single phenomenon, thus the earliest phases need not resemble the middle Neolithic. Therefore, what form of earlier Neolithic or transitional assemblage might exist before 5000 BP? However in Ireland no substantive occurrence of a full Neolithic exists well before 5000 BP. It is unfortunate, for example, that there is no clear association between the pottery and the early cattle bones from Kilgreaney cave (see above).

As a background to the beginnings of the Neolithic, it is useful at this stage to compare and contrast the latest phase of the Mesolithic in Ireland and Britain. As noted earlier, the Irish later Mesolithic is characterized by a distinct series of implements, namely large blade tools, a series of simple retouched artifacts, and core tools such as picks, borers, and the like. In effect there appears to be a narrow range of artifacts in a narrow range of environments. It has been noted by Woodman and Anderson (1990) that there are few sites from this period which could be described as substantial base camps. Many of the sites have a very limited purpose, i.e., a valley floor fishing site at Newferry, flint-working at Bay Farm, shellfish collection on many of the Strangford Lough sites and at Rockmarshall. In general, later Mesolithic artifacts are found in riverine, lacustrine, and coastal locations (see mid Antrim, Fig. 9.5). Even the apparently ideally located coastal site at Ferriter's Cove has produced evidence only of several relatively ephemeral uses of this area. This has led Woodman and Anderson (1990) to suggest either that there are substantial camp-sites from Ireland's later Mesolithic which have yet to be discovered or that, in spite of the fashionable trend to assume a degree of sedentism and complexity amongst Holocene hunter-gatherers, e.g. Rowley-Conwy (1983), there is a possibility that the latest phases of the Irish Mesolithic were characterized by low density, more mobile patterns of settlement.

Obviously this raises questions as to the representativeness of the

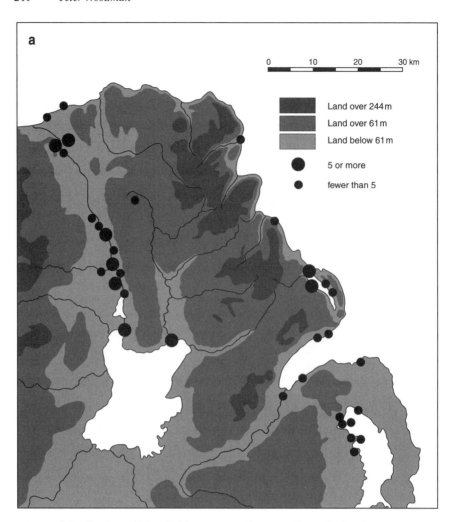

9.5a   Distribution of Mesolithic core axes from northeast Ireland.

known Later Mesolithic. The Ballylough Survey team (Peterson 1990) have argued for greater technological variation within the Irish later Mesolithic. Cooney and Grogan (1994) have expressed concern about the apparent difference of the Irish Mesolithic from that of Britain and would argue that the Irish Mesolithic should be fitted into models based on the received wisdom of other regions. While it is correct to ask why the Irish later Mesolithic differs from the perceived norms of other parts of western Europe, the ecological distinctiveness of Ireland must also be considered. The isolation of Ireland and its reduced fauna and flora have always been recognized (Sleeman *et al.* 1984), but recent work by the Quaternary Faunas Project has

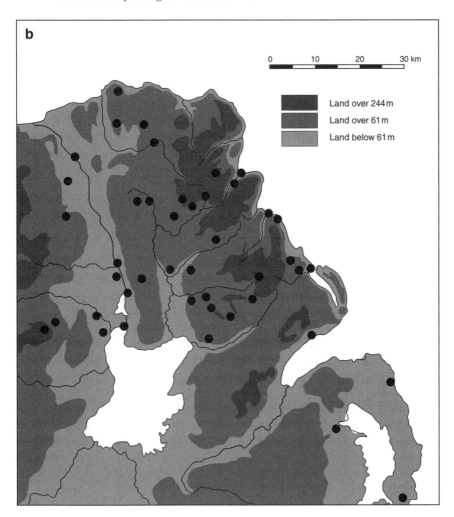

9.5b   Distribution of Neolithic polished flint axes from northeast Ireland.

suggested that the differences are even greater than thought. While the absence of elk, aurochs, and roe deer has long been recognized (van Wijngaarden-Bakker 1989), the ¹⁴C dating of a range of red deer has suggested that it may have had a minimal presence in Ireland until after 5000 BP (Woodman *et al.* 1997). Therefore, the absence of scrapers and burins in Mesolithic contexts in particular makes sense, i.e., no antler and no antler equipment from Irish Mesolithic sites. The only large mammal to occur consistently on Irish Mesolithic sites is the wild pig. An economy of fishing, sea mammal hunting, and shellfish collecting in coastal areas and intensive use of fish traps on rivers therefore makes sense. This was not the totality of the

Irish Mesolithic economy, but it is difficult to identify other major alternatives. The distribution of artifacts along the rivers and coasts suggests that plant gathering or even Zvelebil's (1994a) "Proto Horticulture" did not play an important role. Therefore, in spite of MacLean's (1993) suggestion that plant foods would have played a significant role in the Mesolithic of Ireland, it should be noted that there is no evidence of the extensive use of plant processing equipment on sites from the Irish later Mesolithic. Therefore while there is a natural tendency to underestimate the importance of plant foods on Mesolithic sites, it is more likely that they played an important but not dominant role in Irish Mesolithic economies.

This returns us to the question of the potential danger of an overnarrow interpretation of the typology of the Irish later Mesolithic. In particular in the Ballylough Survey (as noted earlier), Peterson (1990) has assumed that if a few potentially diagnostic implements of later Mesolithic character are found in ploughed field contexts, along with very simple lithic technologies including scalar cores, then, as the later Mesolithic technology is also simple, any artifacts made with a simple technology found in the same vicinity can be considered as later Mesolithic or part of a continuum into the Neolithic. However in all reliable later Mesolithic assemblages, even where small beach flint pebbles were used, the overall trend in Ireland is for the use of a platform and hard hammer technology. Any claim that uncontexted assemblages using scalar cores or similar techniques should also be regarded as later Mesolithic should be treated with extreme caution.

In summary, there is, so far, little evidence for "transitional" assemblages or economies in the period before 5000 BP. Objectively, it is difficult at this stage to find evidence of the type of Mesolithic economy or society in Ireland which could evolve into a "mature" Neolithic form simply as a result of minimal contact with other parts of Europe. Thus it is important to place this process of change or substitution in the context of events taking place before 5000 BP in the whole of these islands.

Transitions to farming in Britain

In contrast to much of Europe and Ireland, the later Mesolithic of southern Britain is associated with the continued use of microliths. In contrast to Ireland, English Mesolithic assemblages frequently contain numerous scrapers and burins. In common with many parts of Europe, the submergence of the Mesolithic coastline in Britain represents not only the loss of a potential area of exploitation but also the loss of an environment which would have been more likely to preserve organic remains. In the absence of late Mesolithic sites with faunal remains, an expectation of an economy based on the exploitation of red deer has arisen. Significant changes in mid-Holocene vegetation in regions such as the North York Moors (Simmons 1979, 1996) and Dartmoor (Casseldine and Hatton 1993) have often been explained as a product of human activity. This in turn has led others such as Mellars (1976) to argue for fire manipulation to attract large herbivores, in particular red deer. However, the limited faunal remains from Westward Ho! (Balam *et al.* 1987) and Cherhill (Evans and Smith 1983) would suggest that the role of red deer may have been over-rated. Other species such as aurochs or pig could have been of equal importance. While Simmons (1979) has documented over 100 instances of apparent Mesolithic interference with vegetation, a cautionary comment is worth repeating: "What remains puzzling in view of all the evidence for Mesolithic impact is the relative lack of similar evidence from elsewhere in North West Europe" (Bell and Walker 1992). There is also no doubt that the later Mesolithic of southern Britain relies heavily on attitudes created by the study of the mammalian fauna from the early Mesolithic site of Star Carr (Legge and Rowley-Conwy 1988). While some reservations can be expressed in the red deer economy model for the English Mesolithic, the location of Mesolithic settlement across the Pennines (Jacobi *et al.* 1976) and in parts of southern England (Mellars and Rheinhardt 1978, Jacobi 1979) (Fig. 9.6) suggests a substantial mammal hunting component in many parts of England. Indications of a coastal component can be seen in the Portland area (Palmer 1968) and at Eskmeals in Cumbria (Bonsall *et al.* 1989) but the loss of the mid-Holocene coastal areas of southern England presents a problem as it is impossible to gauge the importance of marine resources to the later Mesolithic communities of that region. It has recently been suggested that the rising relative sea level may have flooded an important series of ecological niches in areas such as the lower Thames valley (M. Bates and T. Barham lecture to the Palaeo/Meso Day meeting, London, March 1996).

Further north the so-called Obanian sites (Mellars 1987) as well as the site of Morton (Coles 1971) show that coastal resources were exploited. (However, see Coles [1983] for a reevaluation of the Morton evidence which suggests that coastal resources were balanced by a substantial land-based component in the late Mesolithic economy practiced in the Morton area.) Investigations in the southern uplands of Scotland suggest a significant riverine and lakeshore element in the late Mesolithic use of the landscape, e.g., in the Tweed valley or the Loch Doon area (Edwards *et al.* 1983, Affleck 1986). It would, however, be a mistake to assume that the economic strategies of late Mesolithic communities in southern England and parts of Scotland were the same. In that context the comparative scarcity of burins and scrapers on many Scottish Mesolithic sites may reflect a significant difference between the Mesolithic of England and Scotland.

In essence, while the usually accepted models for the economic strategies of late Mesolithic communities in the British Isles are to some extent a matter of convenience rather than substance, there can be no doubt that there are significant typological and economic differences between the two islands and perhaps even within mainland Britain.

One of the most overlooked aspects of this phase of prehistory is the contrast between the diverse Mesolithic occupation of the British Isles and the emergence by 5000 BP of a relatively uniform Neolithic material culture

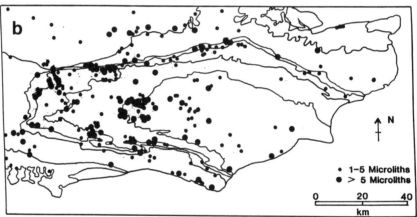

9.6   Distribution of microliths in (a) southwest England (after Jacobi 1979) and
       (b) southeast England (after Mellars and Rheinhardt 1978).

in many regions of these islands. Apparently by or just after 5000 BP communities had appeared which were using a similar range of lithic artifacts,
i.e., leaf-shaped, surface-retouched piercing arrowheads and end scrapers
in particular, and a range of pottery styles whose common traits easily
outweigh some decorative differences. Within the suite of ritual monuments there is a remarkable degree of continuity throughout the British

Isles. The range of unchambered barrows (long and round) and the various types of megalithic tombs may show regional clustering but, on the basis of portal tombs in western Britain and in parts of Ireland, as well as a number of instances of wooden structures pre-dating megalithic tombs, e.g., Wayland Smithy in England (Whittle 1991), Lochill in southwestern Scotland (Masters 1973) and Dooey's Cairn, Ballymacaldrack (Collins 1976), there are some striking similarities throughout the British Isles. As has been suggested for the Irish sites, Kinnes (1992) finds little clear evidence that the unchambered long barrows were begun before 5000 BP. Similarly, although they are as yet rare in Ireland, Donegore (Mallory and Hartwell 1984) has provided an indication that causewayed camps existed at the same time as in England.

This virtual homogeneity can be contrasted with a series of changes which may have happened within the following 500 RCYBP. Distinctive regional styles of pottery emerged from Sandhills in Ireland, through Unstan in parts of Scotland, to Peterborough wares in parts of England, as did local forms of flint tools including polished javelin heads in Ireland and daggers in Britain.

Given the appearance of an almost uniform middle Neolithic by 5000 BP, it is not surprising that there has been an almost unwritten assumption that the beginning of the Neolithic in Britain and Ireland was a phenomenon which began throughout the whole region within a very short period of time. The early dates from Ballynagilly in Ireland may have contributed to this view, while Baillie's suggestion that there was a cluster of dates from the 'British Isles' beginning at 5200 BP again implied a Neolithic beginning with a single event, albeit at a later date.

A closer examination of the British evidence could indicate a phased arrival of a Neolithic economy. Kinnes (1985) argued for an abrupt change to a Neolithic economy in Scotland, possibly around 5200 BP. However this is to some extent based on dates from Dalladies (Piggott 1972) and Balbridie (Ralston 1982). In the case of Dalladies, a substantial timber beam was dated to 5190 ± 110 BP, again probably an old wood sample which should be taken into consideration. In the case of Balbridie, dates before 5100 BP are often quoted, but these have again been based on the use of structural timbers. However ^{14}C dates from plant remains at the site suggest a structure in use around 5000 BP or slightly later (Hedges *et al.* 1990a). There is little good evidence for a fully developed middle Neolithic in Scotland well before 5000 BP.

In the case of southern England, identifying early phases of a Neolithic presents its own problems. Although the chalklands have a potential for organic preservation, the fact that there has been a significant loss from the surfaces which existed in the Neolithic has led to a reliance on information from more substantial monuments. Yet as Thomas (1991b) has noted, much of the information has come from ritual monuments and therefore one must be cautious about economic inferences. Similarly

Kinnes (1992) has expressed a very pessimistic view as to the validity of using information derived from the non-megalithic long barrows to search for origins. To him it is "in a sense non permissible, since it cannot be resolved archaeologically. Chronological precedence, the standard technique is derived from a variable almost random pattern of excavated sites . . . Since it would seem that the formation process was brief, the statistical probabilities of the radio-carbon technique are incompatible with quasi-historical chronology" (Kinnes 1992:139).

On the other hand, even in 1986 Zvelebil listed a number of early dates for the early Neolithic from the southern half of England. Many are dates in which individually no great confidence can be placed, e.g., the dates from Hembury (5280 ± 150 to 5100 ± 150 BP) have been obtained from charcoal, possibly from timbers. The Church Hill mine date (5340 ± 150 BP), although obtained from antler, still has a large standard deviation. In total they could suggest occupation well before 5000 BP. It is unfortunate that the Broom Heath charcoal date of 5424 ± 117 BP comes from an old ground surface below a bank and so is not clearly associated with much of the Neolithic settlement. On the other hand, the lesser-known Neolithic material from Peacock's Farm is stratified between two ^{14}C dates based on peat at 5465 ± 120 and 5295 ± 120 BP.

There are of course other sites which should receive some consideration. Kinnes and Thorpe (1986) cast doubts on the early dates of 5500 BP from Briar Hill (Northants) (Walker and Otlet 1985). However some consideration should be given to the fact that while there may be a certain old-wood effect from charcoal dates derived from palisade timbers, there are a number of these early dates and even allowing for an age lapse of 200–300 years it would appear that a causewayed camp may have been constructed in central England well before 5000 BP. In contrast some of the early individual dates from unchambered long barrows such as that from Raisthorpe in Yorkshire, 5505 ± 145 BP (Manby 1988), could fall into the category of the risky non-specific charcoal category identified earlier.

Although many of these dates come from a period of ^{14}C dating when the technique was not refined and large standard deviations were common, they would suggest a robust trend indicating a relatively early Neolithic settlement in parts of England. They also have the advantage over the Irish data in that the chronological agenda is not being set by one or two sites nor is there over-reliance on non-specific charcoal dates.

The recently published ^{14}C dates from Whitewell long cairn in Derbyshire could indicate the presence of well-established Neolithic communities at an early date (Hedges *et al.* 1994).

OxA4176	5380 ± 90 BP	bone
OxA4177	5190 ± 100 BP	bone
OxA4325	5115 ± 70 BP	bone

In this case the 4176 and 4325 dates reflect the stratigraphic sequence of bones in a bone accumulation. In this context the dates from antler at sites such as Horslip and Fussells Lodge make sense.

Fussells Lodge	BM134	5180 ± 150 BP
Horslip	BM180	5190 ± 150 BP

Perhaps, therefore, a full Neolithic was established in southern and parts of eastern Britain by 5200 BP if not earlier. If indications of the Buxton Neolithic house (Garton 1987) are taken into consideration, these were communities which not only kept domesticated animals but also grew cereals; there have of course been suggestions that the Neolithic economy of southern England was not based on arable farming (e.g., Thomas 1991b), but the evidence from Buxton along with Balbridie in Scotland and Tankardstown in Ireland shows some use of cereals by about 5000 BP throughout the British Isles.

The major problem in southern Britain is to assess how the change took place. As can be seen from the introduction, various explanations have been put forward: near-sedentary hunter-gatherers who manipulated their environment and lived in a manner which allowed them to develop through to farmers (Darvill 1987), or sedentary hunter-gatherers exploiting the now drowned estuarine landscapes of southern England, again shifting over to farming. There is at the moment no great confidence in the chronology of the final stages of the Mesolithic. There is a definite lack of easily identifiable type fossils for the final phase of the Mesolithic. Again as has been demonstrated at Eskmeals, Cumbria (Bonsall *et al.* 1989), it can be remarkably difficult to separate Mesolithic from later phases of occupation at sites such as Williamsons Moss. However the possibility of an earlier Neolithic of unknown origin occurring in southern and eastern Britain still remains.

If fully fledged farming communities had emerged in the southern part of Britain by 5200 BP and had been in a process of development before that date then it is possible that Ireland and northern Britain may have existed in an interaction zone in which certain ideas and technologies would have spread independent of major economic changes. There are numerous examples in Scandinavia where technological elements associated with the Neolithic have turned up in Mesolithic contexts. In particular pottery is found in the latest phases of the Ertebølle, while the T-shaped antler axes found in Jutland are also derived from the German Neolithic (Price and Gebauer 1992; Price, this volume). Even in Finnmark in Arctic Norway there have been discoveries of south Baltic polished flint axes (Johansen 1979), while some of the Younger Stone Age sites in Varanger Fjord, e.g., Nordic, again in Finnmark, have produced the distinctive early Finnish pit-comb wares (Helskog 1984). In some cases, as in the Ertebølle, new elements become incorporated into the material culture. In the case of the Arctic Younger Stone Age they coexist as occasional intrusive elements in the local Younger Stone Age, which also remains as a hunter-gatherer economy.

It is possible therefore that the presence of individual items such as axes or pottery may not of themselves herald the beginnings of a Neolithic as they may be little more than items which have been exchanged into areas where the normal economy continues to be that of the hunter-gatherer. Thus the jadeite axe found at the Sweet Track is not necessarily an indication in itself that the Sweet Track was constructed by farmers.

There is of course the form of gift which was highlighted by Jennbert (1985), writing on the productive gift. The presence of cattle bones at an early date in Ireland has already been noted. In particular those at Ferriter's Cove suggest the presence of domesticated cattle well before 5200 BP. One explanation would be to assume that this simply indicates the establishment of a Neolithic economy in Ireland at an early date but, as shown above, there is so far little substantial evidence that this existed. The alternative is to consider the possible introduction of cattle as part of this interaction zone, perhaps as a productive gift.

In an Irish context the relative absence of large mammals in the mid-Holocene might have created a situation where the addition of a new large species, namely cattle, would have created a new source of food. This interaction zone could also be interpreted as an "availability" (*pace* Zvelebil and Rowley-Conwy 1984) phase, but an availability phase should also contain the possibility that new elements or ideas were not always taken up. It must be remembered that the limited $\delta^{13}C$ indicators as well as the distribution of so much archaeological material on lakes and rivers suggests that marine resources and fish played an important role in the Irish Mesolithic. While an additional large mammal would provide some advantages in terms of an extra resource, it is also possible that a new element within the economy would not necessarily fit in, for either social or economic reasons – in other words, its advantages would have to outweigh the disadvantageous consequences. Again like Jembert's concept of the productive gift, the addition of something such as cattle could have long-term consequences in the manner in which hunter-gatherers in Ireland organized their society and economy, particularly if they had been following an intensive fish exploitation strategy. It is possible therefore that the limited addition of some elements such as cattle caused changes in the nature of the final Mesolithic. This could also explain some of the suggested 'pre-Elm-Decline" disturbances which have been noted in the pollen record, i.e., clearances for cattle rather than the, so far, invisible red deer!

It may of course seem probable that the occurrence of elements such as cattle in late Mesolithic communities suggests a transition to agriculture as a process of acculturation, but it should be remembered that these changes are not part of a preordained series of irrevocable character.

It is possible that they would create changes which were self-sufficient in themselves and that the emergence of a full Neolithic in the west and north of the British Isles could to some extent still be a product of a limited population infiltration by groups of farmers bringing an established economic and social package to regions such as Scotland and Ireland. In fact immigrant groups of farmers could have settled in areas where preexisting exchange systems had already established connections and perhaps a knowledge of new landscapes.

A summary of scenarios
   It was noted at the beginning of this chapter that ideas and opinions about the nature of the transition to agriculture are numerous, but recent research perhaps indicates that certain proposed scenarios are less likely and that a more conservative chronology is probable (Fig. 9.7).

a   The Burenhult concept of a megalith-building, near-sedentary hunter-gatherer community slowly evolving through a process of pastoralism to a full agrarian economy by as late as the Iron Age is based on a small local study and more on the absence of evidence than anything else. A particular problem with this model would be the claim advanced by Goransson (1984) that Mesolithic communities were creating clearings in the forest. The consistent failure to find red deer bones which pre-date 5000 BP makes it difficult to establish a reason why clearances were being created.

b   The evidence of a fully developed Neolithic economy associated with tombs and a material culture similar to the middle Neolithic at or earlier than 5500 BP is very weak and relies on a limited number of questionable ^{14}C dates.

c   If the shift to agriculture happens in different regions at different times, the Baillie model in which climatic change is a prime mover is also less likely. In an Irish context, it is difficult to see how a climatic change would cause the primarily fishing communities to change to farming.

d   The Irish evidence for "proto garden horticulture" is also very weak.

There are indications that elements of a Neolithic economy and lifestyle were present in Ireland before 5000 BP and their presence could be explained by two scenarios.

(a)   As a result of outside stimulus, the indigenous Mesolithic communities may have shifted over to a Neolithic economy. The problems here are in identifying why in an Irish context such a radical change should take place and why the remarkable similarity in Neolithic economy, material culture, and ritual exists in two islands whose Mesolithic was so different.

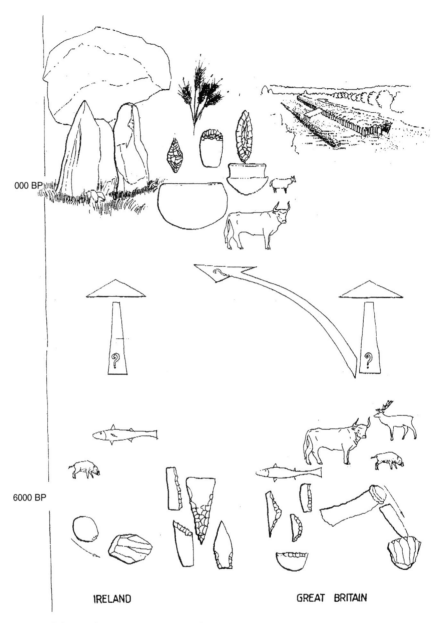

000 BP

6000 BP

IRELAND   GREAT BRITAIN

9.7   Schematic representation of resources and artifacts used in the later
Mesolithic and early Neolithic of Ireland and Britain.

(b) Mesolithic communities may have obtained elements of a Neo-
     lithic economy and technology through contact with adjacent
     islands, but the adoption of elements of a "Neolithic" did not of
     itself cause an immediate development of an agrarian society.
     Perhaps if the concept of an interaction zone, which allows certain
     elements of the so-called Neolithic into Ireland in the period
     5500–5000 BP, is explored then certain other matters must be
     taken into consideration.

As noted earlier the existing evidence for the Irish later Mesolithic
suggests communities which relied heavily on fishing, probably sea
mammal hunting, and gathering. The known sites suggest transitory occupation, and while there is always a possibility that more sedentary settlement sites remain to be discovered, there is no evidence of a type of
land-based Mesolithic economy such as that suggested for Britain. Therefore
some consideration should be given to the impact of new elements on an
existing Irish later Mesolithic.

In themselves new elements in the latest phase of the Irish later
Mesolithic do not necessarily represent evidence of an evolutionary stage
from hunter-gatherer to farmer. The presence of domesticates such as cattle
could represent a logical acquisition by hunter-gatherers taking advantage
of new elements. They may of course have created a situation where their
introduction causes other changes which make a shift to agriculture inevi-
table. Even if indigenous changes had taken place in the latest phases of the
later Mesolithic it does not preclude the shift to a full agricultural economy
through the infiltration of a small number of farmers bringing in a tested
economy to an area where some contact had already been established. In
returning to some of the ideas proposed by Case in 1969b and Mercer in
1986, perhaps we should envisage an "Interaction Zone" covering large
parts of Britain and Ireland. Ideas, both social and economic, as well as gifts,
could spread throughout this zone, with each region accepting some elements and developing in their own distinctive manner.

One other aspect of the transition to farming should receive serious
reconsideration. There is still a tendency to look to the northern part of
Ireland to assess how early the full Neolithic was established. Yet aside from
the "early" phase at Ballynagilly there is no earlier evidence in the north
than in the south of Ireland. This zone of interaction could focus attention
on the southern third of Ireland where the earliest cattle bones are turning
up and where the earliest full Neolithic may be entirely different from that
which has been traditionally sought. For too long the "Neolithic" has been
presumed to have "trickled" down from the megalith-rich areas of the north
of Ireland. A Neolithic without megaliths had to be explained as a deviation
from an expected norm, but in the case of parts of southern Ireland the
Neolithic may have developed in an entirely different manner.

Summary

In one sense this returns the debate to the question of how farming spread throughout the British Isles and, in an Irish context, challenges the primacy of "the North" which has dominated Neolithic research in Ireland through much of this century. However, at another and more general level, it addresses the problem of the role of a series of necessary social constructs as prerequisites for the change to a full farming economy. We could be doubly mistaken both in searching for the origins of the Neolithic through the study of ritual monuments, such as megalithic tombs, and in assuming that public display, in the form of megalithic tombs, unchambered long barrows, etc., was an essential component in any farming society. For the same reasons this chapter has not explored the questions associated with the identification of an area or areas in mainland Europe which might have been the source for ideas or elements of a farming economy. The comparison of mature Neolithic cultures in a search for origins is more likely to reinforce a belief in Bradley's (1984) "Lethe"-like effects of the stretches of water round these islands than it is to contribute to an appreciation as to how the ideas of farming spread.

Research on this topic can only be advanced by careful use of ^{14}C dates from sites in the period 5500–5000 BP. This may require more than the careful reevaluation of excavations. The growing tendency to use AMS dates is placing a strain on the traditional use of ^{14}C dates. There is a trend towards the use of dates based on material that is often more closely associated with the events or artifacts studied. Therefore there will soon by an imperative that only secure, well-dated samples of reliable material are dated and as a consequence these can only be considered in the context of a calibrated chronology.

In the interim one can only recognize the lacuna in a chronology of the period associated with the transition to farming. The recognition of an initial Neolithic, which would be difficult to identify and perhaps rather heterogeneous, was in itself a major step forward in Denmark (e.g., Madsen 1987). In that context one must simply observe the limited evidence available and ask the following question. Could it be that the economy and material culture of this period is something very different from the classic Mesolithic or Neolithic packages and we are therefore unsure of what we should be looking for?

Appendix: ^{14}C dates

Altanagh, Co. Tyrone			
F136	UB2560	5685 ± 70 BP	charcoal
F137	GrN10557	4590 ± 80 BP	charcoal
Ballygalley, Co. Antrim			
Site 1	UB3471	5219 ± 104 BP	charcoal (sieved) foundation slot
	UB3491	4830 ± 117 BP	charcoal foundation slot
	UB3362	5046 ± 101 BP	charcoal pit
	UB3363	5469 ± 69 BP	charcoal pit
	UB3374	5002 ± 92 BP	charcoal pit
Site 2	UB3368	4821 ± 67 BP	charcoal pit
Ballynagilly			
F174	UB306	4880 ± 110 BP	charcoal hearth
F134	UB301	4910 ± 90 BP	charcoal pit
F162	UB625	4945 ± 55 BP	charcoal pit
	UB199	5230 ± 125 BP	charcoal house timbers
	UB201	5165 ± 50 BP	charcoal house timbers
F67	UB551	5290 ± 50 BP	charcoal pit
F211	UB304	5370 ± 85 BP	charcoal pit
F135	UB559	5500 ± 85 BP	charcoal pit
F135	UB197	5625 ± 50 BP	charcoal pit
F46	UB307	5640 ± 90 BP	charcoal pit
F16	UB305	5745 ± 90 BP	charcoal pit
Bay Farm, Carnlough			
IID	UB2603	5810 ± 100 BP	charcoal
II	UB2604	5470 ± 95 BP	charcoal
II	UB2606	5595 ± 100 BP	charcoal
Carrowmore			
Tomb 3	Lu1840	5750 ± 85 BP	charcoal
	Lu1750	4320 ± 75 BP	charcoal
Tomb 7	Lu1441	5240 ± 80 BP	charcoal
Tomb 27	Lu1698	5040 ± 60 BP	charcoal
	Lu1808	5000 ± 65 BP	charcoal
	Lu1818	4940 ± 85 BP	charcoal
Croaghan	Ua713	6680 ± 100 BP	charcoal
	St10453	5685 ± 85 BP	charcoal
Dalkey Island			
Site II	OxA4566	5050 ± 90 BP	sheep bone
	OxA4567	3050 ± 70 BP	cattle bone
	OxA4568	6870 ± 90 BP	pig bone
Site V	OxA4569	7250 ± 100 BP	seal/sheep bone
	OxA4570	5600 ± 80 BP	wild pig bone

		OxA4571	4820 ± 75 BP	cattle bone
		OxA4572	6410 ± 110 BP	seal bone
Ferriter's Cove				
Trench 1		Q2641	5245 ± 55 BP	charcoal
		Q2634	5680 ± 70 BP	shell
		BM2227R	5400 ± 220 BP	charcoal
		BM2227AR	5420 ± 150 BP	charcoal
Trench 2		BM2228R	5750 ± 140 BP	charcoal
		BM2228AR	5850 ± 140 BP	charcoal
		GrN18769	5900 ± 110 BP	charcoal
		GrN18770	5620 ± 130 BP	hazelnut shell
		GrN18771	5620 ± 80 BP	hazelnut shell
		GrN18772	6300 ± 140 BP	charcoal
		UB3598	5727 ± 81 BP	charcoal
		UB3599	5503 ± 45 BP	charcoal
		UB3597	5479 ± 56 BP	charcoal
		OxA3869	5510 ± 70 BP	bone
Trench 3		BM2229R	5490 ± 160 BP	charcoal
		BM2229AR	5500 ± 130 BP	charcoal
Kilgreaney Cave		OxA4269	5190 ± 80 BP	bone
Lough Derravaragh		I4234	5360 ± 110 BP	charcoal
Moynagh Lough			5270 ± 60 BP	charcoal
Newferry Site 3				
Zone 3		UB489	5415 ± 90 BP	charcoal
		UB630	5705 ± 90 BP	charcoal
Zone 4		UB490	6215 ± 100 BP	charcoal
Poulnabrone, Co. Clare[5]		OxA1906	5100 ± 80 BP	bone
		OxA1910	4940 ± 80 BP	bone
		OxA1905	4930 ± 80 BP	bone
		OxA1912	4810 ± 80 BP	bone
Ringneil Quay		Q770	5380 ± 120 BP	charcoal
Rockmarshall Site III		I5323	5470 ± 110 BP	charcoal
		OxA4604	5705 ± 75 BP	bone
Sutton, Co. Dublin		I5067	5250 ± 100 BP	charcoal
		OxA3691	6660 ± 80 BP	bone
		OxA3960	6560 ± 75 BP	bone
		OxA4449	7140 ± 100 BP	bone (contaminated?)
Tankardstown		GrN	5105 ± 45 BP	charcoal
		GrN15386	5005 ± 25 BP	charcoal
		GrN15387	4880 ± 110 BP	charcoal
		OxA	4880 ± 45 BP	Triticum
		OxA	4840 ± 70 BP	Triticum

Acknowledgments

This chapter would not have been possible without the constructive help of the late Liz Anderson, MA, whose advice and pertinent observations turned it from a conference presentation into a text. Drawings were provided by Ms. E. Anderson, Mr. D. Anderson and Ms. R. Cleary.

While the ideas expressed are ultimately those of the author, it has to be admitted that over a decade of "Palaeoecology Lunch Clubs" has left a healthy skepticism of ^{14}C dates and an ever greater concern about the manner in which archaeologists use them.[6]

Notes

1 It is not entirely clear whether his statements refer only to the Knocknarea area of Co. Sligo or are more regional statements.

2 Because so much of this chapter will be devoted to a critical analysis of individual ^{14}C dates and their context, the dates used in this paper will usually be left uncalibrated in the text.

3 A more exhaustive list of ^{14}C dates from key sites is provided in the appendix.

4 As this material was recovered from contexts exposed through drainage ditch activity there is a presumed relationship between the charcoal and the artifacts. However, as the material occurs within a bog context it is unlikely that there is any contamination from relict charcoal.

5 These are the four earliest dates from a series of ten. One was a late insertion (1904) while the others ranged in age down to OxA1913, 4390 ± 90 BP.

6 Since the completion of this chapter one extra date has become available from Ferriter's Cove. This date has been obtained from a cattle bone and is OxA 8775, 5825 ± 50 bp. It is three hundred years older than the Ferriter's Cove date referred to in the text, and taken together the two are strongly suggestive of the need to reconsider the traditional range of paradigms used in discussing the transition to farming in Ireland, if not Britain. In particular they emphasize the need to consider the transition as a process rather than an event, although whether it should be seen as a passive "availability phase" rather than a more positive interaction phase will be the subject of much further discussion.

10

The introduction of farming in northern Europe

Introduction

The Mesolithic period in northern Europe ended around 4000 BC as ideas, practices, and artifacts of the first farming communities heralded the onset of the Neolithic. Within a period of little more than two thousand years, from approximately 5400 to 3300 BC, it is possible to examine one of the major transitions in human prehistory in some detail in this area.

Several factors make this possible. The excellent preservation afforded by the many bogs and marine deposits of southern Scandinavia has made the organic part of that past accessible. Because of a long history of archaeological research in Scandinavia, the time and space parameters of early hunting and farming cultures are well known. The transition to agriculture has been a subject of interest and debate in Scandinavia for nearly 150 years, essentially since the distinction between the Older (Palaeolithic and Mesolithic) and the Younger (Neolithic) Stone Age was made. This debate continues. There are several books and articles on the subject in addition to the materials cited in the following pages. There is an important volume, *Introduksjonen av jordbruk i Norden* [The Introduction of Agriculture into Scandinavia], edited by Thorleif Sjøvold in 1982, with a series of studies from northern Europe. Several books on the Early Neolithic Funnel Beaker culture in this area have appeared recently (Hoika 1994, Jankowska 1990, Midgley 1993). There is a series of debate articles concerning the transition that have appeared in both the *Journal of Danish Archaeology* (vols. 4 and 5) and the *Norwegian Archaeological Review* (esp. vol. 18, 1–2). There are a number of useful summary publications available on both the Mesolithic (e.g., Brinch Petersen 1973, Larsson 1992, Nygaard 1989, Price 1991) and the Neolithic (e.g., Åkerlund 1996, Ahlfont *et al.* 1995, Bostwick Bjerck 1988, Bratt 1996, Ebbesen 1975, Jennbert 1987, Larsson 1985, 1988, Mikkelsen 1989, Nærøy 1993, Nygaard 1988, Østmo 1990, Persson 1987, Price 1996b, Solberg 1989, Zvelebil 1996).

In this chapter, I begin with a brief discussion of landscape and geography, followed by a general overview of the Late Mesolithic and the Early Neolithic in northern Europe. I then outline current views on the origin of the earliest Neolithic. I subsequently discuss the basic details of the earliest Neolithic in three important areas of northern Europe and describe several sites that provide important new evidence on the transition. I then consider the mechanisms and the causes – the how and the why – of the transition to agriculture in northern Europe. I conclude with an overview of our current understanding of this transition.

Geography

Northern Europe is defined for this essay as the classic area of Scandinavia – the countries of Denmark, Sweden, and Norway. This is an enormous region, extending from deep inside the Arctic Circle more than 2000 km to the border of Germany. It is further from the northern tip of Norway to Copenhagen than it is from Copenhagen to the bootheel of Italy. Scandinavia is surrounded by several bodies of water – the Norwegian Sea, the North Sea, the Baltic Sea, and the Gulf of Bothnia. The landscape varies from the mountainous highlands of Norway to the rolling forest and rivers of central and northern Sweden to the flat morainic landscape of Denmark and southern Sweden.

For purposes of this discussion I will focus on that part of Scandinavia in which the Neolithic is found, basically the area within the limits of cultivation, defined largely by a line drawn from approximately 100 km north of Stockholm to the Oslo area and then along the south and west Norwegian coast to north of Bergen (Fig. 10.1). These areas of cultivation approximate the distribution of the limits of oak (Berglund 1985). The northern two-thirds of Scandinavia is largely unsuitable for agriculture, essentially above the sixty-eighth parallel. Neolithic pottery is rare to absent north of this line in Sweden and uncommon in Norway as well. Previous reports of finds of domesticated plants and animals (e.g., Baudou 1982, Engelmark 1982) in the Early Neolithic of northern Scandinavia have largely been discounted (Ahlfont *et al.* 1995, Engelstad 1985, Prescott 1995, 1996). The area of Scandinavia where agriculture was practiced in the Neolithic is approximately 800 by 600 km in size, of which approximately 200,000 km^2 is dry land.

The southern third of Scandinavia differs greatly from the highlands and wilderness of the north. Extending from the sandy stretches of the North European Plain, the peninsula of Jutland lies as an entry point from the continent into Scandinavia. Denmark and southern Sweden were leveled by the action of glacial ice leaving a flat and hummocky topography with small, short rivers and numerous bogs and lakes inland. River valleys draining this area flow slowly into the Baltic and Skagerak; rivers in western Norway are steep, with frequent falls into the deep fjords that are the hallmarks of the coasts of Norway. The glaciers left southern Scandinavia

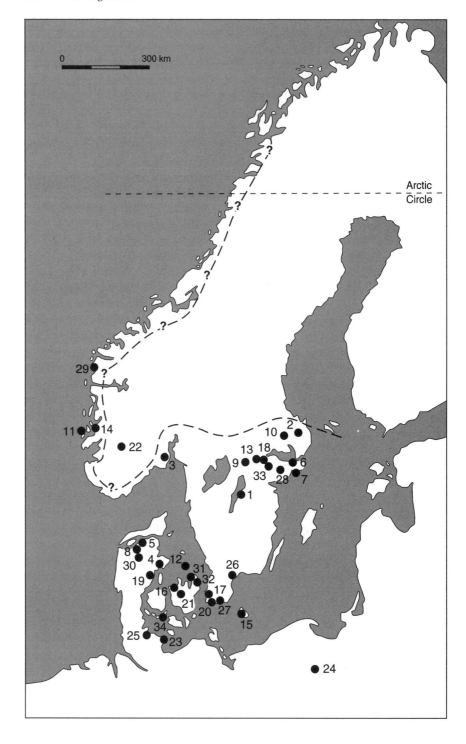

without mountains, but rich in a maritime environment. No spot in Denmark is more than 75 km from the coast; deep inlets, long peninsulas, and islands characterize the Danish coast; more than 400 islands make up the eastern part of the Danish state. The west coast of Sweden and the south coast of Norway are a boater's paradise with hundreds of rocky islands and inlets.

Climate and environment

Scandinavia lies far to the north; Stockholm and Oslo sit at 60°N, above Juneau, Alaska. Yet the present-day climate surprises the uninitiated. The effect of the North Atlantic Current, originating in the Gulf Stream, cannot be overstated; these warm waters keep western Scandinavia more temperate than might be expected given the northern latitude. Bergen on the west coast of Norway has an average temperature of 35°F in January and 61°F in July. Snow is unusual in southern Scandinavia today; temperatures rarely fall much below freezing in the winter. Even in Finnmark, at the northern end of Norway, the sea does not freeze in the winter. Only at elevation to the interior and in the far north are winters severe; less than 50 km east of Bergen herds of reindeer roam the high inland tundra of the Norwegian highlands.

Climatic and environmental change in the last 15,000 years played an important role in shaping the landscape of the Mesolithic and Neolithic. The end of the Pleistocene was marked by the retreat of the Fennoscandian ice sheet, gradually exposing the landmass of Scandinavia. Rising seas in the early Holocene submerged the coastlines of that landscape until they reached and slightly exceeded modern levels around 4000 BC. This period, around the time of the transition to agriculture, was marked by a series of transgressions and regressions as the sea gradually adjusted to modern levels (Christensen 1993). At the same time, the isostatic rebound of the

Caption for Fig. 10.1 opposite
>   Location of sites and research areas mentioned in the text. Limits of agriculture in the early Neolithic are shown with a dashed line (after Berglund 1985, Berglund *et al.* 1994, and Spång *et al.* 1976); west of the Oslofjord area the evidence for early agriculture is uncertain. Key: 1. Alvastras, 2. Anneberg, 3. Auve, 4. Barkær, 5. Bjørnsholm, 6. Bjørktorp, 7. Brunn, 8. Ertebølle, 9. Frotorp, 10. Fågelbacken, 11. Hespriholmen, 12. Heselø, 12. Hjulbjerg, 6. Häggstra III, 14. Kotedalen, 15. Limensgård, 16. Lindebjerg, 17. Löddesborg, 18. Mogetorp, 19. Mosegården, 20. Mossby, 21. Muldbjerg, 22. Normanslågen, 6. Parlangsberget, 21. Præstelyngen, 23. Rosenhof, 16. Saltbæk Vig, 24. Sarnowo, 25. Siggeneben-Süd, 26. Siretorp, 27. Skateholm, 10. Skogsmossen, 6. Smällen II, 28. Soderbytorp, 29. Stakaneset, 34. Stengåde, 30. Storgård, 31. Sølager, 32. Vedbæk, 20. Ystad, 21. Åmose, 21. Øgårde, 33. Østra Vrä.

glacially depressed land surface continued, slowly raising most areas of Scandinavia. The east coast of Sweden along the Gulf of Bothnia, for example, continues today to rise at a rate of several millimeters per year. Mesolithic rock carvings made along coast of the Oslo fjord some 6000 years ago are today more than 25 m above sea level.

The two climatic episodes of particular interest for the transition to agriculture are the Atlantic (7200–3900 BC) and Subboreal (3900–1000 BC). The early Atlantic period (7200–6000 BC) was dominated by rising sea level; current estimates suggest a rise of 5 m per 100 years at the beginning of the Atlantic (Christiansen 1993). After 6500 BC the present coastline of Scandinavia took shape as a series of minor transgressions and regressions of the sea occurred during the late Atlantic and Subboreal. Gradually rising temperatures and sea level culminated in the late Atlantic with slightly higher temperatures and precipitation than today. Winters were milder and the growing period was longer (Berglund 1991:65). Annual July temperatures in southern Scandinavia in the Atlantic episode averaged 18°C and gradually declined to about 17°C in the Subboreal period, compared to the modern average of 16°C. A period of decreasing humidity began in the Atlantic and culminated in the early Subboreal, between roughly 5600 and 3150 BC (Berglund 1991, Noe-Nygaard 1995). More continental conditions prevailed in the Subboreal, with somewhat colder winters and warmer summers.

Forest composition during the Atlantic and Subboreal climatic episodes was generally similar, with some differences introduced by human activity. Southern Scandinavia during these periods was covered by a forest dominated by lime on drier, fertile soils. Oak and hazel were more common in poorer soils and lower areas where the forest was more open (Aaby 1993). Alder was common in wet areas with rich soils. Beginning primarily in the Subboreal this forest was substantially modified by human activity. Cutting of large trees, coppicing of trees for fodder, and grazing of domestic animals resulted in a decline of the forest and the creation of larger and larger openings for fields and pasture.

Cultures and chronology

The chronology for the period of the transition to agriculture is known in some detail, based on typological changes in the artifacts, chronometric dating (e.g., Tauber 1972), pollen data, and sea level changes (Fig. 10.2). In the last twenty years, hundreds of radiocarbon dates have been obtained from the Mesolithic and Neolithic period in Scandinavia, providing much higher resolution and reliability for these chronologies (e.g., Persson and Sjögren 1996). Recent AMS assays of short-lived specimens have greatly enhanced the reliability of dates and reduced the effects of problems such as older wood samples (e.g., Nielsen 1993).

In this discussion, I will focus on the Late Mesolithic (5400–3900 BC)

	Years BC	Denmark Scania	Sweden		Norway	
			West	East	East	West
Subboreal	3000—		PITTED WARE	PITTED WARE	PITTED WARE	
		FUNNEL BEAKER	FUNNEL BEAKER	FUNNEL BEAKER	FUNNEL BEAKER	FUNNEL BEAKER
Atlantic	4000—					
		ERTE-BØLLE	LIHULT	QUARTZ AND FLINT GROUPS	NØSTVET	NØSTVET
	5000—					

10.2   The chronology of the Late Mesolithic and Early Neolithic in Scandinavia.

and the Early Neolithic (3900–3300 BC) in the southern third of Scandinavia; in addition, I will concentrate on the Early Neolithic, known in most areas as the early Funnel Beaker culture (or TRB). The early TRB is found throughout Denmark and southern Sweden and into eastern Norway. The Early Neolithic in western Norway is related to TRB. The first part of TRB in much of southern Scandinavia is referred to as Early Neolithic (EN) and divided into EN I and EN II; EN I is slightly longer in duration than EN II, which begins *c.* 3500 BC. The TRB is replaced by the the Pitted Ware culture or the Single Grave/Corded Ware/Battle Axe culture in various areas of Scandinavia.

The Mesolithic

The later Mesolithic of Scandinavia is characterized by several related, but distinctive, regional groups. In the discussion below, I focus on four areas: southern Norway, western Sweden, eastern Sweden, and the southernmost part of Scandinavia incorporating Denmark and Scania. The presence or absence of high-quality flint raw material for the production of stone tools plays a large role in how Mesolithic assemblages in these areas are manifest. Sources for flint are found as natural deposits in chalk across northern Denmark and southwestern Sweden, redeposited in the ground moraine of Denmark and Scania, or as beach deposits along the coasts of western Sweden and Norway.

The Mesolithic of Norway differs significantly between the north and the south of the country (Nygaard 1989, Price 1991, Woodman 1992c). Inland sites are known in both areas, but human occupation was focused on the coast. Coast/inland patterns of interaction were established early in the Mesolithic and continued into later periods (Bang-Andersen 1996). In southern Norway the later Mesolithic is known as Nøstvet. Subsistence was based on fish, seals, and whales, supplemented by some terrestrial species. Around 5000 BC, the successful and long-lived Nøstvet Mesolithic disappears in the southernmost part of eastern Norway and is replaced, apparently rapidly, by assemblages dominated by transverse points and blade and flake technology. This transition was time transgressive; further north in the Oslofjord it is dated to between 4700 and 4200 BC. However, in the interior there was no replacement; Nøstvet elements (like microblades) and transverse points are found together from about 4400 BC until the beginning of the Neolithic. After 4000–3800 BC, at coastal sites in southern Norway the density of occupation increases significantly and the contents of these sites become more varied. These changes have been interpreted as the beginnings of sedentary occupation during the Mesolithic (Nygaard 1989), but new discoveries suggest that this shift may coincide with the arrival of the Neolithic (Olsen 1995). The issue of the meaning of Neolithic in Norway emerges again below.

The later Mesolithic of western Sweden is known as the Lihult culture, characterized by flaked and ground stone and flint axes, handle cores for microblades, and an absence of microliths (Larsson 1990). The Lihult axe is flaked to a rough form and ground with one arched side and one rounded side. The vast majority of the sites are known from coastal areas. Little is known of the final Mesolithic in this area.

The Mesolithic of interior middle and eastern Sweden is also not well known and only a small number of sites are reported (Larsson 1990). Sites in this area are generally described as small scatters of quartzite artifacts with little organic preservation. Fig. 10.3 shows the boundaries between the flint and quartzite areas of Mesolithic occupation (Åkerlund 1996). The typical Late Mesolithic site in eastern Sweden is located along the Baltic coast, contains pecked stone axes, and artifacts of quartz and quartzite, but lacks flint and ceramics. Some Lihult axes indicate exchange networks to the west. Dates from the latest Mesolithic sites are virtually contemporary with the earliest Neolithic, e.g., Parlangsberget, 4100–3900 BC (Hallgren et al. 1995); Soderbytorp, 4200–3800 BC (Runeson 1994). The Mesolithic on the Swedish island of Gotland contains almost no diagnostic stone materials, although organic materials are well preserved. A number of bone tools show connections across the eastern Baltic (Larsson 1990).

The Late Mesolithic Ertebølle (also known as the Ellerbek in northern Germany, e.g., Hartz 1991) is found across the coastal areas of northern Germany, in Denmark, and in the provinces of Scania and Hålland in Sweden. The Ertebølle dates from approximately 5400–3900 BC and reflects

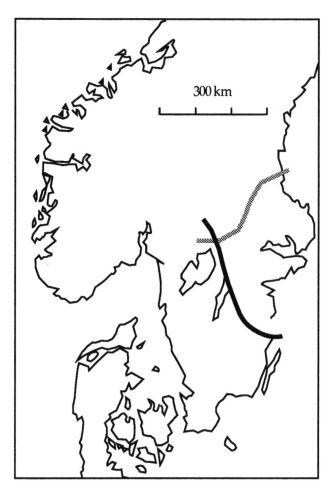

10.3   The distribution of flint and quartzite groups in the Mesolithic of Sweden
(after Åkerlund 1996). Flint groups are found in southern, western, and
northern Sweden; quartzite groups in eastern middle Sweden.

the culmination of several trends in the Mesolithic (Blankholm 1987, Price
1985, 1991). More artifact types and facilities, and more complex facilities,
occurred; previous forms become more functionally specific. This equipment is both diverse in form and specialized in function. The Late
Mesolithic is characterized by both flaked and ground stone technologies.
An elaborate blade technology, projectile points, and flake and core axes,
are hallmarks of the Ertebølle. Ground stone artifacts appear as axes, celts,
and other tools. Projectile weapons were armed with an array of specialized
tips made of bone, wood, antler, and stone. A wide range of fishing gear,
including nets, weirs, leisters, hooks, and harpoons, is known from this

period. Pottery appeared during the Ertebølle period after 4600 BC and takes two major forms: pointed-base cooking vessels and small oval bowls that probably served as oil lamps (Andersen 1989, Gebauer 1995).

The primary focus in the Mesolithic of Scandinavia was on coastal, lacustrine, or riverine environments; inland sites are known largely from small summer camps. Carbon isotope ratios in human bone point to the predominance of marine foods in the diet (Tauber 1981). These groups used boats and paddles, erected large fishing weirs, and successfully exploited the rich resources of both the sea and the land. Fish species from a wide range of both marine and freshwater habitats (e.g., Enghoff 1993) were taken during this period, with a variety of elaborate equipment; eels seem to have been especially important (Pedersen 1997). Shellfish were incorporated into Mesolithic diets, as indicated by the distribution of shell-middens along some coasts. Fish, fowl, molluscs, crustaceans, and sea mammals were all prey for coastal dwelling hunter-gatherers.

Terrestrial resources were varied and apparently abundant in the Late Mesolithic. The Late Mesolithic coastal settlement at Skateholm in southern Sweden, for example, contained the remains of some eighty-six different kinds of animals, including marine and terrestrial species. Red deer, wild pig, and roe deer were the primary terrestrial animals of economic importance. Other animals were also hunted and trapped, including a variety of small fur-bearing species: marten, otter, wolf, and squirrel. The domestic dog was common at most Mesolithic settlements and a number of intentional dog burials, some with grave gifts, are known from cemeteries at Skateholm (Larsson 1984) and elsewhere. Large quantities of hazelnut shells are known at many Mesolithic sites, along with the remains of acorns, water chestnut, and nettles; fruits such as wild strawberry, apple, and sloe and rowan berries and raspberries have also been found (Price 1989, Regnell *et al.* 1995, Zvelebil 1996). Evidence for the use of thatch (*Cladium mariscus*) has recently been reported from the inland Swedish settlement of Bokkeberg III (Regnell *et al.* 1995).

Evidence is present at many sites for summer, autumn, and winter residence, making year-round occupation likely, particularly in Denmark and Scania. The general picture is often one of large settlements ranging up to 200–300 m along the coastlines (Andersen 1991). House structures are rare (cf., Sørensen 1995). Cemeteries are another important hallmark of the later Mesolithic (e.g., Albrethsen and Brinch Petersen 1977, L. Larsson 1984, 1988a). Examples of trauma and violent death in all the Mesolithic cemeteries suggest a pattern of conflict, perhaps as a result of inter-group raiding.

Significant regional variation in artifact types and styles is documented from the later part of the Ertebølle; differences between eastern and western Denmark, and among smaller areas within Zealand, have been reported (Andersen 1981, Vang Petersen 1984). Some form of territoriality can be inferred from the limited, local distributions of certain artifact types

(Vang Petersen 1984). Areas exhibiting such distinctive patterns range in size from approximately 200 km to 20 km in diameter (Price 1981).

The general picture of the Late Mesolithic in Scandinavia then is one of rather substantial, autonomous, and self-sufficient local groups, intensively exploiting the natural environment. These peoples were adept foragers, using an elaborate technology to exploit the resources of the land and the sea. Fish, shellfish, and marine mammals seem to have contributed a substantial part of the diet. Groups lived in substantial and sedentary communities at least in the southern part of Scandinavia. The dead often were buried in cemeteries. There was contact with Neolithic groups on the European continent to the south. Social relationships appear to have been largely egalitarian; there is no evidence for status differentiation or inequality in the later part of the Mesolithic. Outside of the coastal areas, the intensity of Mesolithic occupation declines. The intensity of occupation also decreases from Denmark and Scania into middle Sweden and southern Norway, both in number of sites and in the amount of material present. It seems likely that foraging populations in these areas were somewhat less sedentary and lived in smaller groups. It is also the case, however, that material culture is less well preserved in these areas; sites are less visible and our impression more ephemeral.

The Early Neolithic

This section on the Early Neolithic and the Funnel Beaker culture is intended to provide some overview of the general characteristics of TRB as well as some of the local variation that is present in Scandinavia. I will first outline the origins and spread of TRB, followed by an overview of its introduction into Scandinavia. This section also contains a discussion of several recently excavated sites from Denmark, Sweden, and Norway that have had a significant impact on our understanding of the Early Neolithic.

The origins and spread of TRB

The earliest manifestation of TRB is not well understood and its origins are still debated. Several recently excavated sites containing stratified layers of Mesolithic and Early Neolithic materials may provide more information on this transition, including Friesack in eastern Germany (Gramsch 1981), Tanowo at the mouth of the Oder (Galinski 1992) and Dabki in central Poland (Ilkiewica 1989).

One good candidate for the place of origin is found in central Poland as the Sarnowo group (Gabalówna 1968, Midgley 1992). In the region known as Kujavia, both distinctly TRB pottery and earthen long barrows appear around 4400 BC (Midgley 1993, Sherratt 1990). Until recently the Funnel Beaker culture was thought to have originated as a fusion of late Linear Pottery culture farmers and Mesolithic hunter-gatherer groups in north-central Europe (e.g., Balcer 1980, 1983, Hulthén 1977, Kowalczyk

1970, Wislanski 1973). However, evidence of interaction between Late Mesolithic and Danubian farmers is very limited in the area of origin in Poland. Kruk (1980) on the other hand argued for connections between late Linear Pottery Lengyel culture and the earliest TRB. Kruk focused on the shift from Lengyel horticulture on loess soils to TRB swidden cultivation of drier, lighter soils. Sherratt (1981) argued that TRB adaptations resulted from the introduction of oxen as draft animals and the plow. Domanska's (1995) study of lithic assemblages from Mesolithic, LBK and its descendants, and TRB assemblages in Kujavia sheds a great deal of light on the origins of TRB. Domanska demonstrates that the closest parallels to early TRB lithics in this area are to be found in later Danubian cultures of the Lengyel tradition. The appearance of shell beads in Lengyel style at Sarnowo supports this contention (Midgley 1993).

The first TRB ceramics include funnel neck beakers, handled amphorae, flasks, bowls, and flat clay disks. Decoration is rare in the earliest phases and more common through time. The long barrows of the earliest TRB have been argued to represent copies of timber houses from the latest Lengyel phases (Midgley 1985). Sherratt (1990) similarly sees the long barrows on the outwash sands of the North European Plain as a means of maintaining a link to the ancestral Lengyel culture on the loess lands to the south.

The TRB probably spreads from Poland west across the North European Plain. A second early center is located in Holstein in northern Germany, known as the Rosenhof group (Hoika 1994, Schütrumpf 1972, Schwabedissen 1979). In direct contrast to the evidence from Kujavia, the flint industry of TRB in northern Germany is clearly related to the local Mesolithic (Hartz 1995, Weber 1981, Wechler 1993); blade production techniques, transverse projectile points, flake axes, and convexly truncated blade knives are heirlooms of the Late Mesolithic Ertebølle-Ellerbek. The site of Rosenhof in Holstein contains a stratified sequence with a Late Mesolithic occupation under a sterile layer of *gyttja*, waterlain organic mud. A recent radiocarbon date of *c.* 4850 BC on the bone of a domesticated cow in this layer probably confirms an association between domesticated animals and the Late Mesolithic (Hedges *et al.* 1993). Above the Mesolithic layer is found the earliest TRB in northern Germany, dating from 4260 to 4100 BC (Hoika 1994, Schütrumpf 1972). Vessels of the Rosenhof phase are largely undecorated and occur in four forms: amphorae, oval shaped bowls, small spherical bowls, and funnel beakers (Hoika 1994). The pottery is similar to Sarnowo, but clay disks, collared flasks, and lugged beakers do not appear until the succeeding Satrup phase of the Early Neolithic in Holstein. In addition to the distinctive TRB pottery, this layer contains examples of the ceramic bowl lamps belonging to the late Ertebølle-Ellerbek Mesolithic in this area (van Diest 1981). In the subsequent Siggeneben phase, dating from 4000 to 3700 BC, clay disks appear along with collared flasks and lugged beakers with occasional decoration. This assemblage also includes oval lamps known from the Ertebølle and the classic thin-butted polished flint axes of the Early Neolithic (Hoika 1994, Meurers-Balke 1983).

The TRB thus probably began in Poland around 4400 BC and moved from there through Holstein in Germany shortly before 4200 BC. TRB pottery, usually accompanied by domesticated plants and animals and earthen long barrows, then began to appear across much of southern Scandinavia. The transition from hunting to farming societies in northern Europe took place in a very short time between 4000 and 3800 BC. It is essential to note that the spread of TRB from the Danish/German border across virtually the entire southern third of Scandinavia to the limits of cultivation thus takes place within a period of less than 200 years. Radiocarbon dates from some of the earliest sites with TRB pottery document this very rapid spread (Fig. 10.1): from the peninsula of Jutland (e.g. Barkær, north of Aarhus, 4000 BC; Bjørnsholm, in northern Jutland, 3960 BC), the Danish islands (e.g., Lindebjerg, in western Zealand, 3800 BC), the Swedish peninsula (e.g., Mossby, east of Malmö, 4150 BC; Frotorp in central Sweden, 3800 BC; Smällan II, near Stockholm, 3960 BC), and along the south and west coast of Norway (e.g. Auve, near Oslo, 3725 BC; Kotedalen, north of Bergen, 3850 BC).

The dates for the earliest Neolithic are virtually indistinguishable throughout Scandinavia, given the resolution of radiocarbon dating. Radiocarbon dates from some of the earliest Neolithic sites in Scandinavia are summarized in Figure 10.4 to emphasize the synchronicity of the spread of the Funnel Beaker culture. The distance from the Danish/German border to Bergen or Stockholm at the edge of Early Neolithic distribution is approximately 800 km as the crow flies, and certainly much further along the very irregular coasts of Scandinavia that would have been the principal routes of movement. The rapidity of this spread of the Early Neolithic across such a large area is remarkable, and comparable to the often discussed explosive expansion of Linearbandkeramik in central Europe in the middle of the sixth millennium BC.

The spread of agriculture can also be seen as a slow process, however, depending on the criteria chosen. The first appearance of domesticated cattle and wheat, along with polished flint axes and earthen long barrows for elite burial, is almost simultaneous across much of the lower one-third of Scandinavia, from southern Norway, southern Sweden, and Denmark. The earliest dates for these distinctly Neolithic items are consistently around 4000–3900 BC. This is a large area, almost 500,000 km^2, and the sudden appearance of these goods and practices suggests that the transition was rapid indeed.

The magnitude and abruptness of this transition, the sudden appearance of domesticates, can hardly be questioned. Even so, the very long period of contact between hunters and farmers prior to the use of cul-

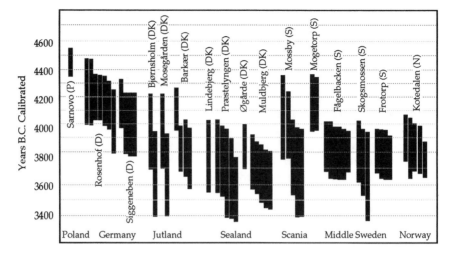

10.4   Radiocarbon dates by region for a select group of the earliest TRB sites in Scandinavia. With the exception of a few very early dates (one from Bjørnsholm, one from Mosegården, one from Barkær, two from Mossby, and two from Mogetorp), there is a very clear pattern in which the earliest dates for TRB in Scandinavia fall very close to 4000 BC. The basic diagram is adopted from Hallgren (1996) with additions. One aberrant date from Rosenhof was deleted; the dates from Kotedalen are from Layer 12, designated as Neolithic (Olsen 1992), with oldest and youngest date deleted.

tigens and the very slow development toward full reliance on agriculture remains a puzzle. Farmers were present only 200 km to the south in northern Germany and Poland before 5000 BC. Certain ideas or actual objects such as pottery, stone and antler axes, and bone combs were obtained from these farmers (Fischer 1982, Jennbert 1984), yet it takes more than 1000 years before domesticates appear in Scandinavia. It is also the case that the evidence for farming during the earliest part of the Neolithic is not abundant. Settlements are rare and there is no evidence for substantial forest clearance or extensive cultivation until 3300 BC. From this perspective, the transition to agriculture takes more than 2000 years.

The general characteristics of TRB

The introduction of farming into northern Europe was accompanied by a number of technological innovations: thin-walled pottery and new pot shapes, large polished flint axes for forest clearing and timber work, along with a related flint mining industry, weapons like ground stone battle axes and mace heads, grinding stones for processing cereals, copper axes as well as flint daggers, and personal ornaments made of amber and copper. Not all of the pieces of the Neolithic package arrived simultaneously across Scandinavia, or in the same form. Cereal cultivation and animal husbandry were probably introduced along with pottery and polished flint axes in most areas, but organic evidence is not well preserved at most Early Neolithic sites. In the discussion below I provide a generic description of the early TRB, but it is essential to keep in mind that there is a great deal of local variation across Scandinavia. I will consider some of these local variations in a discussion of three zones in the spread of the Early Neolithic – Denmark/Scania, middle Sweden, and Norway.

TRB pottery is the primary diagnostic for Early Neolithic in much of the area (Gebauer 1995, Koch 1994, 1998), although there is very little present on the earliest Neolithic sites in Norway. Pottery is found in several contexts in the Early Neolithic, at settlements, from votive offerings in bogs, and at places of burial. TRB pottery exhibits a variety of vessel shapes used for a wide range of domestic and ritual purposes. The early TRB inventory contained seven types of pots, compared to the two types in the preceding Mesolithic. The major forms of TRB pottery are bowls, beakers/jars, and flasks. These definitions are based on the ratio of vessel height to the diameter of the orifice (Koch 1994, 1998, E. K. Nielsen 1987). Beakers are by far the most common form and can be divided into three size classes of small, medium, and large. Medium and large vessels appear to have been used for cooking and storage; the smaller vessels were probably drinking cups. Medium and large vessels are common at settlement sites while medium-size beakers are dominant in ritual deposits in bogs. Small drinking cups and flasks and bowls are found primarily in burial contexts.

Polished flint axes are another important diagnostic for the Neolithic (Nielsen 1985, Nordqvist 1991, Stafford 1998). In Norway, where Early Neolithic pottery is very rare, such axes are used as the primary evidence for the arrival of the Neolithic (Østmo 1986, 1990). Polished flint axes are usually made from large tabular cores, available largely from deposits of fresh flint. Mines and quarries dating to the earliest Neolithic are known from the chalk belts that cross northern Denmark and southwestern Sweden and a number of manufacturing sites have been identified (Becker 1980, 1993, Madsen 1993, Rudebeck 1987). Outside of the chalk zone, large flint nodules are known primarily from beach deposits. The axes are manufactured through a process involving the flaking of a preform and polishing (Madsen 1993, Stafford 1998). The labor for the production of a finished axe is estimated to require several hours for flaking and up to thirty hours for polishing, depending on the size of the axe (Madsen 1993). One type of early polished flint axe is known as the pointed-butt type and appears closely related to the core axes of the latest Mesolithic (Nielsen 1979, Stafford 1998). Thin-butted axes are most common in the Early Neolithic and are known throughout the distribution of early TRB. These axes are polished on all four sides and are made in a range of sizes, up to 50 cm in length. The extent of the polish and the remarkable size of some of these axes, along with their discovery in hordes and offerings, suggests that at least some of the axes were important in terms of status and display.

The exact nature and extent of Neolithic cultivation and herding has been debated for many years. Iversen (1941) used the term *landnam* to describe a pattern of extensive swidden agriculture that he thought characterized the Neolithic and was responsible for the dramatic decline in elm trees that took place almost simultaneously with the transition to agriculture at the beginning of the Subboreal period. Göransson (1982) has viewed the elm decline as a natural event that made the pollen of cultigens visible. Berglund (1985) has described the time period as one of unstable forest ecosystems with indications of cultivation and pasture. During the first part of the Early Neolithic (EN I), pollen analyses provide a picture of a population practicing swidden cultivation. New pollen studies of samples from beneath Early Neolithic barrows show very local conditions and indicate two primary modes of agriculture in Denmark, (1) clearance of lime forest for pasture, and (2) swidden cultivation of cereals in burned-over birch woodlands (Andersen 1992, Andersen *et al.* 1991). Cleared areas were small in size; a mosaic of small fields, fallow, and pasture, in the larger context of the Subboreal forest seems characteristic. Microwear analysis of Early Neolithic sickles, however, reveals little evidence of grain harvesting; these implements were used primarily for reeds and rushes (Jensen 1994).

The majority of Early Neolithic settlements are found in inland locations, at some distance from coastal areas, placed at lakes or streams where fresh water was easily obtainable and conditions for grazing were favorable. This shift from a coastal focus is also seen in stable carbon isotope ratios in Neolithic skeletons, which indicate a greater dependence on terrestrial resources at this time (Tauber 1981). Remarkably, carbon isotope values from two of the earliest dated Neolithic human skeletons from bog sacrifices on the north coast of Zealand (Ferle Enge and Tagmosegård) reflect largely terrestrial diets, indicating this shift may have happened quickly (Koch 1998). On the other hand, the carbon isotope evidence may be somewhat misleading. Recent experimental studies (Ambrose and Norr 1994) have demonstrated that the carbon isotope ratios in collagen are largely a product of the protein intake of the individual. Carbonate in bone apatite is a better measure of both carbohydrate and protein consumption. This information suggests that minor changes in the amount of marine foods in the diet might appear as large shifts in subsistence patterns in collagen ratios. In addition, Lanting and van der Plicht (1996) have demonstrated that freshwater fish contain reduced levels of ^{14}C isotopes, resulting in radiocarbon dates for consumers that may be as much as 400 years too old. Thus the age of the skeletons used in the stable carbon isotope studies will have to be reevaluated. New studies of bone isotopes will be needed in southern Scandinavia.

As in the Mesolithic period, very few actual residential structures

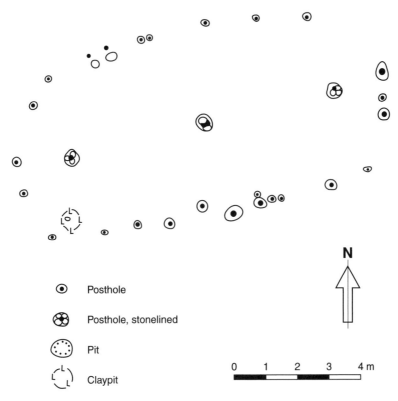

N

Posthole

Posthole, stonelined

Pit

Claypit

0   1   2   3   4 m

10.5   The Early Neolithic house at Mossby (Larsson 1992), marked by postholes and a scatter of burned daub. The house is approximately 12 m long. (Courtesy of Mats Larsson.)

are known from the Early Neolithic (Eriksen 1992). Based on a handful of examples, the general pattern appears to be an oval structure with a central row of support posts (Fig. 10.5). The size of these structures varies from 5 to 15 m in length and 4.5 to 7 m in width (Eriksen 1992: 15). Madsen (1982) and Larsson (1992) argue that Early Neolithic residences were regularly relocated a short distance and rebuilt. Residential sites are small in size with a thin cultural layer compared to Late Mesolithic settlements, suggesting that co-resident groups in the Neolithic were smaller and perhaps more mobile (e.g., Andersen 1993). The significance of this shift is not clear. This change may represent a reduction in population or perhaps changes in settlement associated with cattle pastoralism. In truth, because of the sparsity of evidence, we know very little about settlement patterns in the Early Neolithic.

The timing of the arrival of domesticated plants and animals is debated and contradictory evidence exists. Some researchers have argued for food production in the Late Mesolithic, citing evidence such as the presence of *Cerealia* in pollen cores from the late Atlantic period (Göransson 1988, Kampffmeyer 1983, Kolstrup 1988, Schütrumpf 1972). In general, however, virtually all of the claims for early cereal pollen have been questioned (e.g., Rowley-Conwy 1995); this pollen is difficult to distinguish from other grasses and stratigraphic context is often uncertain (e.g., Edwards 1989). However, cereal impressions have been found in late Ertebølle pottery at one or two sites in southwestern Sweden, such as Löddesborg (Jennbert 1984, 1987). Clearly there was some domesticated wheat present in the latest Ertebølle, whether imported or locally cultivated is unknown.

Löddesborg is dated between 4200 and 4050 BC, very early and transitional in age. The question is whether this site is actually a combination of EBK and EN or if it is a mixed deposit. Ertebølle and TRB ceramics are found together in the same layers, along with cattle bones; the proportion of TRB pottery increases through time. The remains of domestic animals have also been reported at late Ertebølle/Ellerbek sites in Germany but there are questions regarding stratigraphy (Meurers-Balke 1983, Schwabedissen 1979, 1981). The majority of evidence suggests that cereals and domesticated animals arrived primarily with TRB pottery and that cultivation and animal herding were only minor components of subsistence during the early part of the Funnel Beaker period. Cereals, and perhaps domesticated animals, arrived slightly later in Norway than in the rest of southern Scandinavia.

The Funnel Beaker period then started with an extended, 600–year-long period that saw the gradual adoption of farming. The basic pattern of subsistence involved terrestrial hunting, seal hunting, fishing, cereal cultivation, cattle breeding, and pig herding. Domesticated plants and animals may have been somewhat more important in Denmark and Scania during the later part of the Early Neolithic, but in the rest of Sweden and Norway seal hunting and fishing seem to have been primary pursuits. Faunal assemblages in southwest Sweden are dominated by cattle in the Early Neolithic, along with a number of wild species. A number of hunting sites are known from the Early Neolithic and contain either a mixture of wild and domesticate fauna, or purely wild species. Activities included hunting for red deer, wild boar, baby seals, ducks, and swans, and collecting of shellfish, berries and nuts, and fishing. At the site of Siretorp in southern Sweden only 7% of the bones are of domestic species and the remainder are seals (86%) and deer (7%). At Muldbjerg, a summer lakeside camp in Denmark, for example, traces were found of a hut measuring 7×3 m together with evidence of domestic cattle and sheep, red deer, wild boar, and beaver, and strawberries, raspberries, and hazelnuts (Troels-Smith 1953). Early Neolithic sites along the coasts of southern Scandinavia are probably associated with very large fishing facilities (Pedersen 1997). Fishing appears to have been very important in the Early Neolithic in Sweden and Norway as well and sites are often situated in prime fishing locations.

Domesticated plants in the Early Neolithic include emmer and einkorn wheat, and naked and hulled barley. These species are known from grain impressions in pottery and from carbonized remains (Andersen 1992). The oldest reliably dated cereal grains in Scandinavia have been found at Limensgård on the Danish island of Bornholm from 3775 BC and at Mossby near Ystad, Sweden, from 3700 BC or perhaps even earlier (Sjögren 1994). In addition to the wheats and barleys, certain weeds with oil-rich seeds were also collected, along with apples, berries, and nuts (Sjögren 1994). Impressions of grape pips have also been discovered in potsherds from the Early Neolithic, indicating that vines were cultivated in Scandinavia in this period. Radiocarbon dates from grape pips at the sites of Mogetorp and Østra Vrä in eastern Sweden are very early, probably too early, between 4350 and 4160 BC (Rausing 1990).

The oldest accepted radiocarbon date for a domestic animal other than the dog comes from a cow bone at the site of Øgårde on Zealand, *c.* 3850 BC (Sjögren 1994). Cattle, pig, sheep/goat, and dog are present at most sites. Cattle were the most important livestock and increased in number through the Funnel Beaker period, representing more than 80% of the domestic animals at some later sites. Lidén (1995b) has documented the importance of cattle in the diet in a bone chemistry study of Swedish Neolithic populations. The primary importance of cattle was for meat; milk production and their use for transportation or as draft animals seem less important. Pigs were the second most common domestic species, clearly more significant at inland sites where they roamed the forest. Sheep and goats were also present but it is unclear whether textiles were produced from wool in the TRB period (Higham 1969, Rowley-Conwy 1987). Numerous cord impressions are seen on pottery, but only a few spindle whorls have been found. Fur and leather may have been preferred for garments in the Early Neolithic.

Denmark and Scania

The earliest radiocarbon dates for the Neolithic in Denmark and Scania come from small settlements, large earthen long barrows with timber burial chambers, flint mines, and bog offerings, not from domesticated animals or pots filled with grain. Early Neolithic long barrows with wooden structures were first recognized in Denmark in the early 1970s (Madsen 1979). Almost forty non-megalithic barrows are known today, predominantly in western Denmark. These long barrows are almost always found in conjunction with settlement remains from the earliest Neolithic (Liversage 1992, Madsen 1979). In eastern Denmark, simple inhumations without mounds were more common. Only one or two earthen long barrows are known from southern Sweden. The barrows show much variation in both construction and size. Normally the barrows are low (about 1–2 m high) and vary in the length from 20 m to more than 100 m. Certain

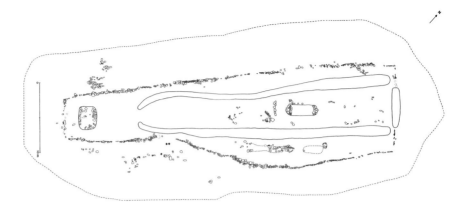

10.6   The ground plan of the Early Neolithic earthen long barrow at Storgård IV
(Kristensen 1991). This example shows a trapezoidal earlier barrow with
one grave and a post trench for a timber façade on three sides, and a later
long barrow surrounded by a palisade with a large grave at one end. The
long, straight side of the later palisade is 50 m in length. (Courtesy of Inge
Kjær Kristensen.)

distinctive features are normally incorporated in their construction: rectangular or trapezoidal palisade enclosures surround the mound, the interior of the barrow is transversely partitioned by rows of stakes, and massive timber façades are usually placed at the east end of the mound, associated with deposits of pottery (Fig. 10.6). Only one, or a very few, graves have been found in each of these mounds, providing substantial evidence for emerging social differentiation in Early Neolithic society.

Flint mines are another category of the earliest Neolithic sites (Becker 1980, 1993, Rudebeck 1987). One of the most archaeologically visible remains of the Neolithic are the tens of thousands of polished flint axes scattered across the landscape of southern Scandinavia. Much of the tabular flint for the manufacture of these axes came from mines and quarries in the chalk belts across northern Denmark and southwestern Sweden. These flint mines and finished polished stone axes are the evidence remaining from extensive networks that involved trade of amber and other materials.

Bog offerings, the third category of earliest Neolithic sites, are generally small sets of pottery vessels and other material deposited in lakes, springs, and bogs. Hundreds of such votive deposits are known. Animal and human sacrifices were also occasionally placed in the bogs (Bennike and Ebbesen 1987, Koch 1994, 1998). Detailed investigation of the ceramics in bog offerings from Zealand, Denmark (Koch 1998), has documented an early Funnel Beaker with a pointed base (Type O), intermediate in form between Ertebølle and TRB vessels (Fig. 10.7). No differences can be seen in Type O

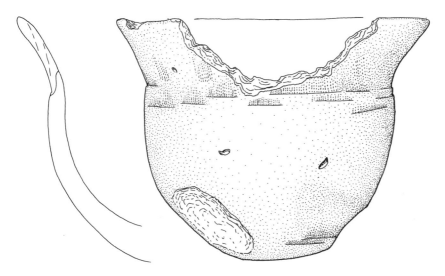

10.7 A small, complete type O Funnel Beaker, unornamented, with several seed impressions, at least one of cereal. The vessel is 8.2 cm high; thickness is 0.52 cm. (Courtesy of Eva Koch.)

vessels between coastal and inland areas, indicating similar and simultaneous changes in both zones. This intermediate phase appears to last for only 100–200 years at the very beginning of the Early Neolithic.

The earliest Neolithic settlements in Denmark and Scania are known from two contexts: either as continuations of Late Mesolithic settlements in coastal locations or as new inland sites, scatters of residential debris, usually discovered beneath early long barrow excavations. This pattern of coincidental barrow and settlement is repeated at a number of early TRB settlements in Denmark such as Lindebjerg (Liversage 1981), Stengade (Skaarup 1975), and Mosegården (Madsen and Petersen 1984). The association between barrows and settlement may represent legitimization of claims to land and place through ancestry. In the discussion below the sites of Bjørnsholm and Barkær are discussed as examples of Early Neolithic settlements with long barrows; Mossby is a very early coastal occupation, on the south coast of Scania. These descriptions are intended to provide some information on recent finds and interpretations regarding the transition to agriculture.

Bjørnsholm is a well-known shell-midden in the central Limfjord area of northern Jutland, dating from the Late Mesolithic and Early Neolithic (Andersen 1991, Andersen and Johansen 1992). The site is of particular importance because of the presence of midden and settlement remains from both periods, along with evidence for an earthen long barrow. Excavations here in recent years have provided a number of important observations. The Ertebølle layers at Bjørnsholm date from 5050–4050 BC and the Early Neolithic from 3960–3530 BC. The location of residence clearly did not change from the Mesolithic to the Neolithic; in fact, residence continued in virtually the same spot following a ninety-year gap in the occupation record. The latest Mesolithic occupations are enormous, extending more than 300 m along the coastline of the fjord and 10–50 m in width. The earliest Neolithic midden is smaller and a meter or so lower on the coastline, in response to lowering sea levels. There was a shift from oysters to cockles in the shell-midden around the time of the transition, suggesting that changes in the environment may have been taking place. However, the earliest Neolithic pottery was present in the sequence before this shift in the midden occurred (Andersen and Johansen 1992).

The evidence for Early Neolithic settlement at Bjørnsholm comes from two small scatters of artifacts, in close association with an earthen long barrow (Fig. 10.8). Neolithic subsistence remains were very similar to those from the Mesolithic, with the addition of small amounts of wheats, barley, sheep, cattle, and pig (Bratlund 1993). Fishing was a very important component of the subsistence base and a variety of both freshwater and saltwater species appear in the middens (Enghoff 1993). Eels were particularly abundant among the remains. The long barrow held a massive timber chamber with a single burial furnished with a large thin-butt polished flint axe and a diabase copy of a central European copper axe. The diabase axe lacks a cutting edge, which clearly marks its symbolic significance (Andersen and Johansen 1992).

The site of Barkær is located on a low hill along the former coast of Djursland, northeast of Aarhus, western Jutland, Denmark (Fig. 10.1). Barkær was excavated in the 1930s and 1940s by P. V. Glob. David Liversage conducted limited test excavations at the site in the late 1980s and published all the excavations in 1992. Madsen (1979) and Liversage (1992) describe the site as a scatter of settlement artifacts overlain by two non-megalithic long barrows, each almost 80 m long, with two wooden tombs in each barrow. The grave finds included a substantial amount of pottery, more than 100 beads and other pieces of amber, and two fragments of copper artifacts. Assay of the copper suggests it may have come from a source in Saxo-Thuringia in central Germany (Liversage 1992).

Originally these mounds were interpreted as residential structures, but the discovery of earthen long barrows in Denmark in the 1970s has helped clarify their function. The settlement remains under the barrows are probably mixed and include early TRB pottery, numerous polished flint axes and other flaked stone tools, and scatters of shell, black earth, and burnt clay. The axes at the site are early pointed-butt forms; several of the TRB pottery styles resemble those known from Germany and Poland. Other pottery designs at Barkær are more local in derivation. Four radiocarbon dates on the shell scatters at Barkær provide an age for the settlement

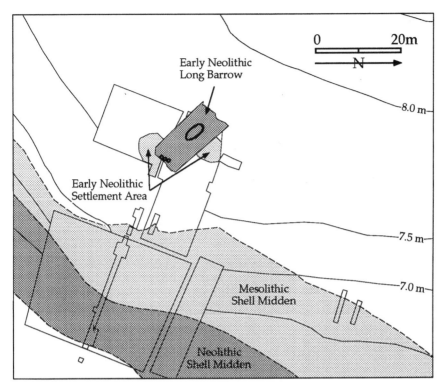

Early Neolithic
Long Barrow

0   20m

N

-8.0 m-

Early Neolithic
Settlement Area

-7.5 m-

-7.0 m-

Mesolithic
Shell Midden

Neolithic
Shell Midden

10.8   Ground plan of the site of Bjørnsholm, showing the relationship between the Mesolithic and Neolithic middens, the Early Neolithic settlements, and the earthen long barrow. (After Andersen and Johansen 1992.)

between 3786 and 4213 BC, and, if reliable, include one of the earliest dates for the Neolithic in Scandinavia.

The site of Mossby in the Ystad area of southwestern Scania, Sweden, is one of the earliest Neolithic settlement in Scandinavia and very close in age to the end of the classic Lengyel period in Poland (Larsson 1992). Radiocarbon dates from food residues on pottery date the site between 4233 and 3900 BC. The two earliest radiocarbon dates for the site, prior to 4000 BC (Fig. 10.4), in all likelihood pre-date the Neolithic occupation. Features at the site included postholes, pits, and hearths, along with a brown-black sandy midden layer 15–30 cm thick. The site contains a house construction about 12×6 m in size, marked by burned daub with wattle impressions, and three central posts, 40–50 cm in diameter (Fig. 10.5). Similar house types are known from the early TRB in Poland. House constructions are rare in both Mesolithic and Early Neolithic Scandinavia (Sørensen 1995). The pottery from Mossby is cord-marked in a fashion similar to the eastern Danish Early Neolithic, but only about 5% of the ceramics are decorated.

Other materials at the site included flaked flint artifacts, polished pointed-butt axes, grinding stones, and carbonized grains and seeds. The total site area was 300–400 m², similar in size to other small Early Neolithic settlements across Denmark and southwestern Sweden, and in strong contrast to the larger earliest Neolithic settlements in middle Sweden.

The transition from EN I to EN II in Denmark and Scania, around 3500 BC, is marked by major changes in settlement, subsistence, and tomb construction. The beginnings of continuous settlement within specific ecological zones, increased cattle herding, the introduction of the ard, and the initial settlement of clay soils are some of the hallmarks of this period. The number of known sites increases at this time and occupation evidence becomes more substantial. Settlement size varies from the small hunting sites of 100 m² to residential sites up to 8000 m². In some western areas, a pattern of permanently inhabited sites at 2 km intervals is observable, each with one or more large tombs and offering sites (Madsen 1982, Madsen and Jansen 1986) (Fig. 10.9). Finds of prestige items including copper axes and jewellery, long thin-butted axes, and amber also increase.

There is evidence of settlement over much of southern Scandinavia in EN II. Regional forest clearance is seen in the pollen diagrams. Domesticates were more common and plow marks have been preserved below mounds (Thrane 1991). However, cereal growing still appears to be limited; specialized hunting and fishing sites are still in use. Exchange of local and exotic materials appears to have intensified. An enormous amount of energy was invested in ancestor cult and other rituals. Large-scale offerings, including human sacrifices (Bennike and Ebbesen 1987), took place at bogs and lakes.

Late in the Early Neolithic period, around 3400 BC, the simple inhumation graves of eastern Denmark and Scania were replaced by dolmens – large stone cists, covered with a round or rectangular mound, circumscribed by a row of huge stones. There are more than 3000 dolmens on the island of Zealand alone. Passage and gallery graves are two other, larger forms of megalithic tombs from this period. A recent study by Persson and Sjögren (1996) summarizes the radiocarbon evidence from these tombs and suggests that dolmens, passage graves, and gallery graves in Scandinavia were roughly contemporary and show no chronological sequence in construction. Many of the 30,000 or more megalithic tombs known from Scandinavia were built during a brief span of perhaps 200 years during the Early Neolithic II phase. The erection of these monuments ended everywhere around 3000 BC. Like the simple inhumation graves, the megaliths were apparently originally intended for a single funeral (Skaarup 1988). The dead were placed in a similar position and given the same equipment as in the inhumation graves. Only later in the Neolithic were these graves reused as collective tombs for tens or hundreds of individuals. More elaborate offerings, involving tens of pottery vessels, were made at the entrance of the

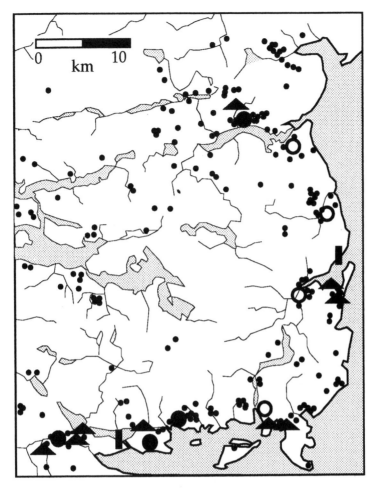

● Causewayed camp   ▮ Procurement site   • Grave
○ Possible causewayed camp   ▲ Settlement

10.9   The distribution of Early Neolithic sites in east-central Jutland, showing the
location of megalithic tombs, settlements, exploitation sites, and causewayed camps. (After Madsen 1982.)

tombs. Similar offerings of a few pots were made at the long barrows at the
beginning of the Neolithic.

Another type of site dating to EN II is the causewayed camp, a type
of fortified, regional ceremonial center (N. H. Andersen 1990, 1993). These
sites are represented by large open areas enclosed by natural or built
defenses such as palisades and ditches that enclose natural promontories or
heights (N. H. Andersen 1993). It appears that all of the more than twenty

causewayed sites now known were built between 3500 and 3100 BC. Ritual deposits at the bottom of the ditches in these enclosures contain whole pots, heaps of tools and bones, human skulls and bones, and dark greasy layers of organic materials. Celebrations at the causewayed enclosures may have involved several hundred people, based on the size of these structures and the area enclosed (N. H. Andersen 1993).

It is not until the beginning of the Middle Neolithic around 3300 BC – at least 600 years after the first appearance of the Funnel Beaker culture – that significant agricultural activities are seen in the landscape of southern Scandinavia. Vast areas of forest were cleared, and there is substantial evidence of cattle herding and the use of pasture as well as cereal cultivation, predominantly of wheat. Settlements increased dramatically in size and number. More substantial houses were constructed. Territorial divisions appeared to have been fixed; each territory was marked by a cluster of megalithic tombs, and a group of hamlets shared a common regional ceremonial center at a causewayed enclosure. Trade and exchange of flint axes, copper, and amber items was intensive at this time. After 3300 BC there is an influx of amber from western to eastern Denmark, suggesting an intensification of inter-regional trade relations. The heavier reliance on food production apparently was associated with a need for more rituals and for status symbols to support rival demands for power and control of people and resources (Kristiansen 1987, Skaarup 1988).

Middle Sweden

Until recently, the Neolithic of middle Sweden was known largely from megalithic tombs along the west coast and the presence of a small number of inland settlements (e.g., Hjulbjerg: Hulthén and Welinder 1981). The primary source on this area before 1990 was Sten Florin's 1958 volume *Vråkulturen*. In the 1980s, however, renewed investigations of the Neolithic in eastern middle Sweden were undertaken as part of a rescue program (Åkerlund 1996). Several of the newly discovered sites show continuous occupation from the Late Mesolithic into the Early Neolithic.

A number of large, well-dated sites from middle Sweden – Anneberg, 3950 BC (Segerberg 1986), Smällen II, 3960 BC, (Olssen and Kihlstedt, per. comm.), Frotorp, 3900 BC (Eriksson *et al.* 1994), Fågelbacken, 3925 BC (Apel *et al.* 1995, Lekberg 1996) – demonstrate that the TRB culture is at least as old in this area as it is in Denmark and Scania (Kihlstedt 1996). It also appears that some settlements of hunter-gatherers containing quartzite artifacts and lacking pottery continued in use in this area during the Early Neolithic (Hallgren 1993, Hallgren *et al.* 1995). Interestingly, western middle Sweden, where megalithic tombs are concentrated, contains relatively little other evidence of the Early Neolithic (Sjögren 1986, 1994). The majority of sites are small, seasonal, coastal procurement sites.

The Early Neolithic of middle Sweden varies greatly between the east and west. The west is characterized by a large number of megalithic tombs and few settlements. The east contains a number of large settlements and other sites, but no megalithic tombs. Coastal sites document the continued importance of marine resources in this area. Domesticates are lacking at coastal sites and domesticated animals are known from only two Early Neolithic sites in eastern Sweden. Agriculture was clearly only a minor part of the first TRB occupation in middle Sweden. The site of Anneberg, located on the former Baltic coast near Uppsala, is one of the earliest in middle Sweden, dated to 3950–3700 BC. The excavations revealed sealed deposits with rich organic remains. The organic material contains almost no evidence for domesticated plants; about 10% of the faunal remains are pig and cattle. Fågelbacken (Apel *et al.* 1995, Lekberg 1996, Welinder 1987), another large coastal site, is located at the edge of the city of Västerås in middle Sweden. Materials from TRB, Pitted Ware, and Battle Axe cultures have been found at this location. There is no evidence of domesticates, a situation typical of the coastal Neolithic in middle Sweden. The TRB portion of the site has been dated from food residues on pottery from approximately 3900 BC to 3600 BC. The TRB pottery is heavily decorated and may be associated with a number of graves at the site. Fågelbacken is interpreted by the excavators as an agglomeration camp used by inland farming groups on a seasonal basis and focused on marine resources.

There are also a number of inland TRB sites in central and eastern middle Sweden. New excavations at Östra Vrä have uncovered the remains of both domesticated plants (wheat and barley) and animals (sheep/goat, pig, and cattle). More than eighty saddle-shaped grinding stones were found at this site as the stone packing in two graves of children (Olsson and Kihlstedt, pers. comm., Kihlstedt 1996). The site of Frotorp near the city of Örebro contains finds of carbonized domesticated cereals (Eriksson *et al.* 1994). Radiocarbon dates range from 3900 to 3550 BC. TRB pottery at this site, in contrast to Fågelbacken, is decorated only with simple lines of dots under the rim, associated with an early phase of the Early Neolithic. The early TRB inland site of Skogsmossen, excavated by Arkeologikonsult in 1995, contained both a farmstead area with a house construction and bog deposits (Hallgren, pers. comm.). The bog deposits adjacent to the farmstead include more than 100 kg of TRB pottery, including funnel beakers, collared flasks, clay disks, and bowls. The rich decoration on several of the vessels includes cord and twisted cord and various types of impressions and belongs to the middle Swedish Early Neolithic Vrä group (Florin 1958). Also in the bog, probably also as votive offerings, were various stone axes including a battle axe, thin-butt polished axes of flint and porphyrite, and pecked stone axes of porphyrite and diabase. Many of the axes were intentionally broken. Radiocarbon dates on food crusts from the pottery in the bog date the site to approximately 3720 BC.

The Pitted Ware culture (GRK) appears very soon after TRB in middle

Sweden as an alternative subsistence strategy focused more on marine resources and hunting than farming and herding. The earliest dates for Pitted Ware culture in eastern Sweden range from 3700 BC (at Häggsta III), to 3500 BC (at the site of Brunn, Welinder 1978) and 3350 BC (at Björktorp) (Olsson and Kihlstedt, pers. comm.). Browall (1991) points out that TRB in southern Scandinavia is always older than Pitted Ware culture wherever the two occur in the same area and that the first appearance of GRK marks the end of TRB. Browall suggests a relationship between the retreat of the megalithic culture of TRB and the advance of GRK between *c.* 3200 and 2700 BC from central Sweden to northern Denmark. Evidence for this argument comes from the site of Alvastra in western Östergötland, Sweden (Browall 1986), where Neolithic ceremonial platforms on pilings are located in a bog next to megalithic graves (Malmer 1984). The bog deposits contain both TRB and GRK pottery, as well as artifacts common to both groups. The transition to GRK follows the disappearance of TRB pottery and the abandonment of the megalithic grave.

Norway

Polished flint axes and pollen evidence for cultivation and pasture have been used as the primary evidence for the beginning of the Neolithic in Norway. The earliest Neolithic generally lacks both TRB pottery and domesticated plants and animals. There are important questions as to what the transition from Mesolithic to Neolithic in Norway actually represents and whether agriculture was present in Norway outside of the Oslofjord area during the Early Neolithic (Bostwick Bjerck 1988, Mikkelsen and Høeg 1979, Nygaard 1988, Prescott 1996). This issue is addressed below.

In both coastal and interior areas of southeastern Norway, tanged points and polished flint axes appear around 4000 BC (Boaz 1994, Hinsch 1955, Mikkelsen 1984). Thin-butt axes appear at both Late Mesolithic and Neolithic sites in eastern Norway (Hinsch 1955). Østmo (1986) noted that the distribution of early pointed-butted axes in Norway was almost exclusively around the Oslofjord area and corresponded very closely with the location of arable land. This pattern is supported by pollen evidence for *Cerealia, Plantago lanceolata,* and *P. major* which is found in this area during or immediately after the elm decline (Østmo 1986, 1990), dated to *c.* 3900 BC (Griffin *et al.* 1990). The presence of a few megalithic tombs and TRB pottery in the Oslofjord area also suggests that this area may have been closely related to the west coast of Sweden during the Early Neolithic (Østmo 1988, 1990). Norwegian archaeologists generally regard this introduction of TRB as evidence of immigration, as Late Mesolithic materials are markedly different from TRB (Hinsch 1955, Mikkelsen 1982, Østmo 1986).

The site of Auve, located in the Sandefjord of southeastern Norway, produced flint and ceramic artifacts, along with slate, pumice, and other stone, and more than seventy pieces of amber (Østmo 1993, Østmo *et al.* 1996). The archaeological layer lies in a sand dune that was active during the occupation. Pottery is decorated primarily with whipped cord marking, characteristic of the later Early Neolithic (also known as Middle Neolithic in Norway), but includes cord-marked TRB-related vessels. These materials are similar to contemporary west Swedish sites. Two of the earliest AMS radiocarbon dates at the site were made from food crusts on pots decorated with pits, *c.* 3750 and 3725 BC, and may be associated with the earliest Neolithic in this area. On this basis, Østmo argues that pottery in the Early–Middle Neolithic of Norway does not belong to the Pitted Ware culture *per se*, as described in earlier publications, but rather is a local manifestation of TRB. Østmo (pers. comm.) would prefer a new cultural designation for the Early Neolithic in Norway to distinguish it from the complex of TRB that characterizes this period further to the south.

The Hardangarvida, the largest mountain plateau in Europe, was a zone of contact between eastern and western Norway in the southern part of the country. Survey and excavations in this area (Indrelid 1994, Indrelid and Moe 1983) have recorded both distinctive stone and ceramic artifacts, documenting the use of this region in the Early Neolithic. Polished flint axe fragments were found at Normanslågen dated to 3950 BC and TRB pottery is also found in this area dating from 3650 BC. Direct evidence of domesticated plants or animals is absent.

Significant new information comes from western Norway where excavations at the site of Kotedalen have forced a reconsideration of the Mesolithic–Neolithic transition. Kotedalen, on the shore of Fosnstraumen some 60 km north of Bergen (Fig. 10.1), contains sixteen phases of occupation from the Late Mesolithic to the Early and Middle Neolithic (Olsen 1992, 1995). Radiocarbon dates place the occupation of the site from 6000 to 2500 BC. A number of important changes take place at the site around 4000 BC, including an increase in site size, an increased thickness of the cultural horizon suggestive of longer occupation duration, and new technologies (cylindrical cores) and materials (flint, slate) in stone artifacts. Evidence for permanent occupation is seen in the faunal assemblage at the site, along with an increase in both the number of species and the number of bones present. Imported vessels of Funnel Beaker ceramics also appear in the Early Neolithic levels, dating to *c.* 3650 BC. These early dates for the Norwegian Neolithic are surprising in that they are almost simultaneous with the earliest TRB in Denmark and Sweden. Given the great distances involved, this synchronicity is nothing short of remarkable. The pollen of cultigens such as barley, of weed species associated with cultivation, and of pasture plants, however, does not appear until 3400 BC. At the same time the landscape changed from forested to more open, as seen in the pollen record. A local pottery tradition also emerged at this time.

Thus it appears that agriculture did not arrive, if in fact it was present, until some several hundred years after the evidence for TRB pottery at Kotedalen. The most characteristic finds from "Neolithic" settlements are artifacts associated with hunting and fishing. No domestic animal bones were found in the faunal remains and no cereal impressions were found in the pottery from the Neolithic levels. Prescott (1996) questions the presence of agriculture at this site and elsewhere in Norway outside of the Oslofjord region and argues that food production does not arrive until the Late Neolithic. Others argue that some form of animal husbandry was practiced in western Norway in the Early Neolithic (Bakka and Kaland 1971, Bostwick Bjerck 1988, Næroy 1993), In this sense, the Early Neolithic of Norway may resemble the Late Mesolithic in Denmark and Scania, reflecting sedentary hunter-gatherers in contact with farming groups to the south, exchanging a variety of materials and ideas (Prescott 1996).

The excavator of Kotedalen, Asle Bruen Olsen (1995), suggests that successful hunter-fisher societies in this region were only minimally influenced by eastern Norwegian TRB groups in the Oslo area. Olsen argues that the first farmers of Norway occupied the coastal landscape, one of the richest biotopes for marine exploitation anywhere. In this context, farming and herding were probably minor concerns in a larger strategy of hunting, gathering, and fishing employed by sedentary groups. The Early Neolithic in Norway is distinct from the rest of southern Scandinavia and in this sense just barely Neolithic. A number of innovations in the Early Neolithic probably reflect both the dynamics of such complex hunter-gatherers and long-distance exchange among many different groups. Items such as cylindrical core technology and the use of slate in lithic production may be innovations that subsequently travel to southern Scandinavia.

The distribution of the finished products from two source-specific quarries on the west coast of Norway is also very informative with regard to the nature of the Early Neolithic in this area (Olsen and Alsaker 1984). A greenstone quarry at Hespriholmen and a diabase quarry at Stakaneset were used throughout the Mesolithic and Early Neolithic for the production of stone axes and adzes. Radiocarbon dating, typology, and shoreline displacement provide good chronological information on the use of these raw materials. During the Mesolithic, these materials were used to produce ground and pecked core adzes. There is a clear shift to small, rectangular, polished adzes at the beginning of the Neolithic, shortly after 4000 BC. What is remarkable is the fact that the distribution of these axes does not change with the introduction of the Neolithic in this area. Greenstone artifacts are found in the southern part of western Norway and diabase artifacts in the northern portion. Each type of material is found up to 650 km from the source but 95% of the materials occur within 200 km. Each type of material covers an area of roughly 25,000 km^2 but there is very little overlap in their distribution (Fig. 10.10).

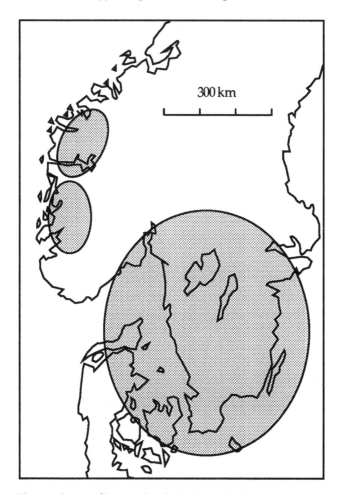

10.10   Three spheres of interaction in Early Neolithic Scandinavia (after Bostwick
        Bjerck 1988). Two networks can be identified in the movement of green-
        stone and diabase ground and pecked axes in western Norway (Olsen and
        Alsaker 1984) and a third is identified by the distribution of diabase axes,
        Funnel Beaker ceramics, and Danish flint and polished axes, and Swedish
        battle axes.

Mesolithic and Early Neolithic artifacts are found in the same favorable locations for hunting and fishing activities at the shore along the outer
coast and in the fjords. Clearly the initial introduction of domesticates and
some new technologies did not significantly disrupt the basic pattern of
stone axe manufacture and exchange. It is not until the beginning of the
Late Neolithic in Norway, *c.* 2200 BC, that this pattern changes in the wake
of major farming expansion and the large-scale import of flint axes from
Jutland (Clark 1965, Bakka and Kaland 1971).

Mechanisms and causes

Information from northern Europe, because of both its abundance and its quality, is particularly well suited to addressing questions regarding the transition to agriculture: how and why did the introduction of agriculture take place? In the discussion below I consider these questions, specifically the mechanism for the spread of farming, whether through colonization by foreign peoples or local adoption by indigenous groups. I also consider several of the major theories regarding the cause of this transition, including resource stress, population growth, and social change.

Colonization vs. indigenous adoption

The question of how agriculture was introduced in southern Scandinavia is a difficult one. There are three major hypotheses: (1) the Early Neolithic was intrusive, brought by colonists (Becker 1948, 1955, Lichardus 1976, Solberg 1989); (2) the Early Neolithic developed from the local Mesolithic, under the influence of various Danubian cultures to the south (Ahlfont *et al.* 1995, Fischer 1982, Jennbert 1984, 1985, Larsson 1987, Madsen and Petersen 1984, Nielsen 1985, Price 1991, Price *et al.* 1995, Schwabedissen 1979); or some combination of the two, such as (3) small groups of immigrants brought the basic Neolithic package into Scandinavia where it was adopted by local inhabitants (Larsson 1987, Madsen 1987, 1991).

Clearly there was contact between late Danubian farming groups in central Europe and Mesolithic groups in southern Scandinavia, considering the evidence of a number of imports in the Ertebølle culture. Certain ideas or actual objects were obtained in trade from farmers to the south during this period, but agricultural foodstuffs were among the last items to be brought into the Late Mesolithic. In addition to pottery, bone combs, "t-shaped" antler axes, and "shoe-last" adzes of amphibolite appear in an Ertebølle context in Denmark (Andersen 1973, Fischer 1982, Jennbert 1984). These materials are present in southern Scandinavia at least 500 years before the beginning of the Early Neolithic. The only reasonable explanation for the delay is the presence in northern Europe of successful fishing-hunting peoples who had little immediate use for other aspects of the Neolithic. The question then is not one of interaction, which is clear, but rather of colonization vs. indigenous adoption.

The evidence for and against colonization comes largely from material culture. Arguments in favor of colonization cite the simultaneous introduction of a variety of new materials such as TRB pottery and polished flint axes and new practices involving domestic plants and animals and monumental tombs (e.g., Solberg 1989). However, a number of similar lines of evidence – lithic and ceramic technology, settlement location, and burial practice – support an argument for indigenous adoption. Nielsen (1985) has described the similarities and differences in lithic assemblages between Late Mesolithic and the Early Neolithic in Zealand and south Scania. Flint

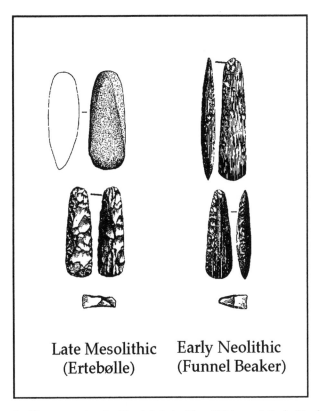

Late Mesolithic   **Early Neolithic**
(Ertebølle)   **(Funnel Beaker)**

10.11   Artifact types in the Danish Late Mesolithic and Early Neolithic (Stafford
1995). *Top*: Groundstone Limhamn axe from the Late Mesolithic and Early
Neolithic thin-butted axe. *Middle*: Late Mesolithic specialized core axe and
Early Neolithic polished pointed-butt axe. *Bottom*: Transverse projectile
points.

technology appears to be derived from the Ertebølle. Certainly polished
flint axes are new and there is a distinct decrease in the use of blade technology in the Early Neolithic. Quantitative study of Late Mesolithic and
Early Neolithic assemblages from sites in the Åmose area of Denmark show
almost no change in the technology of stone tool production (Stafford 1998).
Throughout much of Scandinavia the only way to distinguish Early
Neolithic surface sites lacking pottery is the presence of polished axe fragments. All of the technology for the production of polished flint axes is
present in the Mesolithic (Nordqvist 1991, Stafford 1998). Pecked and polished greenstone axes are known from much of southern Scandinavia
during the later Mesolithic. The earliest polished flint axes, the pointed-butt
forms, closely resemble Late Mesolithic core axes (Fig. 10.11). Some of these
specialized core axes from the last part of the Ertebølle period have polished
edges. Many of the characteristic flaked stone artifacts from the Early

Neolithic, such as flake axes, flake scrapers, and backed knives, were made on the flakes from axe production (Madsen 1991).

The pottery tradition of the Funnel Beaker culture, and perhaps the technology of food preparation, are relatively new. The funerary pottery of TRB reflects clear innovation in shape and decoration. However, only minor differences exist between the Ertebølle ceramics and the utilitarian wares of the early TRB; the two groups of pottery can be seen as developmental stages within the same tradition of pottery production (Gebauer 1995, E. K. Nielsen 1987, P. O. Nielsen 1985). Decorative technique and motifs and new forms allow distinctions to be made between the two stages but some rim designs show common features such as rows of punctates or nail and finger impressions (Jennbert 1984, P. O. Nielsen 1987, Skaarup 1983). As noted earlier, Koch (1998) has distinguished a beaker form intermediate between Ertebølle and TRB.

There are also similarities to be seen in the continuation of regional differences. Andersen (1973) and Vang Petersen (1984) have reported on a number of regionally distinct stylistic and artifact distributions in the Mesolithic, such as decorative motifs on Ertebølle ceramics, bone combs, T-shaped antler axes, greenstone axes, and the like. These distributions show a marked distinction between western Denmark and Zealand and Scania. In a pattern reminiscent of these divisions during the Late Mesolithic, three major groups of TRB pottery can be identified in Denmark and southern Sweden. The Volling style ceramics of western Denmark were influenced by the Rössen-inspired Dümmer pottery from northwest Germany (Gebauer 1988, 1995); the Oxie style TRB vessels of eastern Denmark and and the Mossby style in southern Sweden more resemble the earliest TRB from Sarnowo in Poland (Madsen and Petersen 1984, Nielsen 1985). As Jennbert (1987) has noted, southern Scandinavia was not a homogeneous region in either period, but rather contained different regional groups. The presence of these distinct groups at the very beginning of the Early Neolithic is a strong argument for the indigenous adoption of agriculture.

The earliest sites with TRB pottery are often found at the same location as latest Mesolithic sites, emphasizing continuity in settlement (Koch 1994). Settlement evidence from Bjørnsholm (Andersen 1991) and elsewhere also indicates the continuity of Early Neolithic at the places of Ertebølle residence. In addition to residential sites, hunting and fishing stations continue in use from the Late Mesolithic well into the Early Neolithic, e.g., in the Åmose area of eastern Denmark (Fischer 1991), on Hesselø, an island in the Kattegat, and at the site of Sølager on the north coast of Sealand (Skaarup 1973). Clearly the initial appearance of TRB settlement follows the pattern of the latest Mesolithic.

Compared to the previous Ertebølle period, the monumental appearance of the earthen long barrow burials of the Funnel Beaker is certainly a new phenomenon. These graves were covered by a mound and framed by a timber palisade. However, the fully extended position of the body in the central tomb resembled Ertebølle practices. The grave goods consisted of similar kinds of artifacts, translated into different materials: amber beads instead of tooth beads, flint axes or a stone battle axes instead of antler axes, pots instead of bark containers. Part of the burial ritual thus seems to be a continuation of the Ertebølle tradition. The simple, flat graves of the Early Neolithic in eastern Denmark are largely indistinguishable from the Late Mesolithic.

Radiocarbon dates have been used in recent years to assign chronological periods to a number of previously undated skeletons (Bennike and Ebbesen 1987). Today there are several hundred Mesolithic skeletons and more than fifty Early Neolithic individuals. The anatomical characteristics of the Neolithic remains differ only slightly from their Mesolithic predecessors. Several minor changes are seen in the Early Neolithic skeleton; bones and skulls are less robust and the teeth are smaller (Bennike 1993). There are also minor changes in stature; Mesolithic males and females are 1 cm taller than their Early Neolithic counterparts (Bennike 1993). The overall impression is one of continuity rather than replacement.

In sum, while there is a rapid influx of new kinds of pottery and decoration, new burial rites, house forms, and domesticated plants and animals, a number of very basic aspects of life did not change during the transition to agriculture. Today, it is generally agreed that the last hunters of southern Scandinavia became the first farmers. It is important to remember the very explosive spread of the TRB into Scandinavia is directly comparable to the classic spread of the Linearbandkeramik in terms of speed and distances involved. There is no substantive evidence to suggest the colonization of southern Scandinavia by agriculturalists from the south. The possibility that small groups of immigrants came into the area and introduced local inhabitants to the "Neolithic" is very difficult to resolve; at the same time the question remains as to why it took more than 500 years after contact between farmers and foragers for this introduction to take place.

Causes of the transition

The question of *why* hunters became farmers is not easily answered. The reasons for the transition are not well understood and are subject to significant debate and interpretation. Three major factors are considered below: population growth, resource stress, and social and economic change.

Population

One of the major hypotheses attempting to explain the transition to agriculture suggests that human population growth resulted in too many people and too little food (e.g., Binford 1968, Cohen 1977). Agriculture then was a means of increasing food yields per unit of land to feed growing numbers of people. In southern Scandinavia, changes in the environment increased population density even if population numbers were stable. Rising sea levels and forest climax operated during the Mesolithic to reduce the amount of land available for the population (Noe-Nygaard 1995). Marine transgression was the hallmark of the early Holocene, while at the same time the vegetation was changing from open birch and pine woodlands to more dense, closed deciduous forest with greatly reduced biomass. This may be one of the reasons that the sea becomes such an important source of food. Gaillard and Göransson (1991), on the other hand, suggest that the presence of light-demanding species and high pollen values of *Corylus* (hazel) in southwest Sweden indicate that Late Atlantic forests were not as dense as generally assumed.

Archaeologically the question of population pressure is difficult to answer; population levels are a notoriously slippery variable to measure. One approach is to examine the number and size of sites by time period. Two published systematic survey projects provide some information from regional studies: the Ystad project and the Saltbæk Vig project.

The Ystad project, in southernmost Sweden (Fig. 10.1), was carried out in the 1980s as a study of changes in the cultural landscape from 4000 BC to the present (Berglund 1991, Larsson *et al.* 1992). The Ystad project focused on four study areas in both coastal and inland contexts in the parish of Ystad. This huge undertaking involved palaeoecologists, geologists, archaeologists, and others in the analysis and reconstruction of the cultural landscape in this area over the last 6000 years. Settlement patterns in the Ystad area are revealing with regard to changing land use. Mesolithic settlement focused on lagoons and rivers along the coast. Little evidence of settlement was found inland. Fewer than ten settlements from the Mesolithic were reported from the four study areas; Late Mesolithic sites were poorly represented. During EN I, settlements were smaller and more widely distributed on sandy soils. These sites are found in two zones, along the coastal strip and in a hummocky, inland landscape. The small size of the settlement suggests family units as the primary co-residential unit. There are more EN I settlements than during the Mesolithic but the number is no more than ten. A significant change in settlement occurs in EN II. Site size increases slightly; settlements are located along the coast and adjacent lands in areas of wetlands, river mouths, lagoons, and archipelagos. Inland sites are few in number. Sites are concentrated around megalithic tombs, constructed in this period. There are more than thirty settlements recorded from this period by the Ystad project.

The Saltbæk Vig project is an ongoing investigation of the transition to agriculture in eastern Zealand, Denmark (Price and Gebauer 1992). Systematic survey was conducted along the coastline and immediate adjacent areas of the Saltbæk Vig, a small inlet near the town of Kalundborg, Denmark (Fig. 10.1). More than 18 km^2 was intensively surveyed and more than 350 localities were collected and mapped. There is no noticeable change in the number of settlements between the Late Mesolithic and the Early Neolithic. A dramatic threefold increase in site frequency is seen in the later Early Neolithic and Middle Neolithic.

The results from the Ystad and Saltbæk Vig projects are generally comparable and provide an approximation of population changes in southern Scandinavia during the transition to agriculture. The number of sites from the Mesolithic is never particularly large and it is difficult to imagine that population pressure on resources was a factor at this time. No increase in the total number of settlements is seen in the earliest Neolithic. In fact, sites from the earliest Neolithic were smaller in size than in the preceding Mesolithic. In the larger view, current information suggests that population was not a primary cause of the transition to agriculture in northern Europe.

Resource availability

Climatic or environmental change is often invoked as a cause for changes in subsistence and settlement. One early model for the introduction of agriculture into Scandinavia was closely tied to the decline of the elm forest that Iversen (1941) identified at the end of the Atlantic climatic episode. A shift toward cooler, more moist conditions was argued to have caused the marked decrease in elm and created conditions favoring the introduction of agriculture. Troels-Smith (1953, 1960, 1982), on the other hand, suggested that the elm decline was related to activities of early farmers, pruning elm for leaf fodder. More recent investigations of the elm decline have convincingly connected this event with the spread of disease, not climatic change (Groenman-van Wateringe 1983, Peglar 1993, Rasmussen 1990).

Other lines of evidence do, however, suggest climatic disruption at the time of the transition. In Ireland, for example, tree ring evidence has suggested a major interruption in oak growth at 4000 BC (Baillie 1992). Some evidence of environmental disruption is also seen in Scandinavia. This is the time of the transition between the Atlantic and Subboreal climatic episodes, the decline in elm, and a series of marine transgressions and regressions. The tree line dropped in the Scandes Mountains in central Sweden around 4000 BC (Kullman 1988) and glaciers in northern Scandinavia advanced in the period 4000–3500 BC (Karlén 1988). In southern Sweden, there is some evidence to suggest that the Subboreal period began with drastic ecological change that brought about the opening of the landscape with the recession of the broad-leafed trees and a succession of hazel, birch, and alder. The incidence of forest fires increased and some erosion took place (Berglund *et al.* 1991).

Some crisis in resource availability in southern Scandinavia at the time of the transition is implied in a number of papers (Andersen 1973, 1981, Larsson 1987, Paludan-Müller 1978, Rowley-Conwy 1983, 1984, 1985, Zvelebil and Rowley-Conwy 1984). Rowley-Conwy (1984) has argued that changes in water levels and salinity reduced the availability of shellfish, causing a food shortage. However, Late Mesolithic shell-middens are found only in limited areas of southern Scandinavia; shellfish were not important in the diet in most regions. Strand Petersen (1992) has documented a decrease in the tidal range and water salinity. A change in water levels in the Kattegat and Baltic would reduce the availability of fish and sea mammals in the long fjords and straits of southern Scandinavia. There is an observed shift from oysters to mussels or cockles from the Mesolithic to the Neolithic layers in shell-middens in Jutland (Andersen 1991). Others (Larsson 1992, Larsson and Larsson 1991) have argued that stable sea level and marine erosion resulted in the closure of marine estuaries and a decrease in the amount of biomass at the end of the Atlantic climatic episode. Madsen (1987, 1991) has argued that resource-poor inland groups sought a productive source of food to compete with their coastal neighbors.

Clearly, some changes in the environment do take place at the end of the Atlantic episode. Yet there is no substantial evidence to indicate that these had a profound impact on human population. Other evidence exists to suggest that environmental change and food stress were not significant factors in the transition to agriculture. Several climatic indicators, includ-ing a species of mistletoe and a tortoise today found only in central and southern Europe, were present in Denmark during the Subboreal period, indicating that conditions remained warmer than today (Troels-Smith 1960). Food stress is not seen in skeletal material from the Late Mesolithic; individuals were large and robust, with few indications of nutritional defi-ciency (Meiklejohn and Zvelebil 1991). It is also notable that the TRB expanded, one could say exploded, across the southern one-third of Scandinavia into a variety of different environments. In Norway, moreover, it seems to be the case that certain accouterments of the TRB such as axes and pottery were more important than cultivation and herding. Such evi-dence strongly argues against climatic or environmental factors in the expansion of the Neolithic and supports an argument for changes in social and economic organization as important factors in the transition.

Social and economic change

Other scholars have suggested that the transition was caused not by forces external to society such as population growth or resource strain, but rather by factors involving changes in social structure and the emergence of inequality (e.g., Bender 1978, 1990, Hayden 1990). For southern Scandinavia, Fischer (1982) and Jennbert (1984, 1985) have argued that these successful foragers did not require additional sources of food, that the only obvious reason for farming was to generate surplus. They point to the close connec-tions between the farmers of north-central Europe and the foragers of Denmark, and the variety of "borrowed" artifacts and ideas. Jennbert argues that a few leaders were probably responsible for encouraging cultivation and herding for the accumulation of wealth. Sjögren (1986, 1994) similarly argues that Early Neolithic societies in western Sweden were not ephemeral swidden agriculturalists, but rather depended on relatively intensive agriculture in permanent fields. He suggests that cultivation gave increased value to the land and supported the rise of a hierarchical society. Competition between higher-status individuals for prestige then might explain why successful foragers adopted farming.

The appearance of barrows at the onset of the Neolithic indicates that substantial changes in social organization took place at the time of the transition. Nothing like these elite, mound-covered interments is known from the Mesolithic period. Obviously, a limited segment of the Neolithic population was entitled to monumental burial. Clear communal involvement and participation in the construction, maintenance, and enlargement of these monuments suggests that the barrows represent more than just places for the disposal of the dead. The earthen long barrows probably formed local ceremonial foci, some of which were maintained for several centuries. This pattern continued during the construction of the megalithic monuments after 3500 BC. These tombs appear to have been built originally for only a few inhabitants (Skaarup 1988) and only later became communal burial places.

Ceremonial sites in the bogs with sacrificial deposits of flint axes, amber beads, and copper ornaments and axes are further evidence of wealth accumulation and exchange at this time. Bog sacrifices also represent communal involvement and were part of a ceremonial landscape. Even the Early Neolithic tradition of sacrifice appears to have its roots in the Mesolithic (Johansen 1989, Karsten 1994). Consumption of labor is evident in the withdrawal of luxury items from circulation with the deposition of fine flint axes, amber beads, and copper items in votive hoards from the Early Neolithic. This expenditure of labor and materials in the Early Neolithic represents a considerable increase in surplus production invested in activities beyond basic subsistence.

Changes in economic organization in the Early Neolithic may also be informative with regard to social differentiation. Differences in the amounts of raw materials and exotic goods in Mesolithic and Neolithic contexts probably reflect shifts in the organization of both productivity and exchange. Specialization of production at the settlement level may well be a characteristic of the Early Neolithic. Evidence for such specialization is seen in several realms, including large-scale fishing, variation in site activities, and access to raw materials. The large size and number of Early Neolithic fishing weirs and other equipment in Denmark would easily have harvested more fish and eels than could have been consumed at the settlement level (Pedersen 1997). The obvious conclusion is that fishing resulted in surplus production for exchange. Such evidence also argues against environmental change as a major factor in the transition.

There are clear differences in technology, in the composition of artifact assemblages, and in the raw materials present at Early Neolithic sites in Denmark, a distinct change from the preceding Mesolithic (Price *et al.* 1995). Neolithic stone tools are without question less well made than their Mesolithic counterparts; with only a few exceptions, craftsmanship declined precipitously across the transition. The long and slender blades that were the hallmark of the Mesolithic almost disappear as a flake tradition comes to dominate in the Early Neolithic. In the Mesolithic, lithic technology is generally wasteful, utilizing quantities of large nodules of high-quality Danish flint for the production of a relatively small number of tools. In the Neolithic, the flint raw material is generally lower in quality and smaller in size.

Information from the Saltbæk Vig project in northwest Zealand provides some information on this issue (Price *et al.* 1995). Early Neolithic sites differed substantially in assemblage composition; various sites contained extraordinary numbers of scrapers, axe production flakes, types of flint, or specialized tools. At the same time access to raw materials was clearly changing. In the Mesolithic period in this small area in northwest Zealand, there was abundant flint for the production of a wide range of artifact types. Waste material was common at sites and less than 5% of the total artifacts were retouched tools. This picture changed dramatically in the Early Neolithic. Large nodules of high-quality flint are no longer available to all settlements; there appears to be more recycling of materials. Flint cores are much smaller in size, with more cortex, and appear to come from very local sources in the ground moraine rather than the coasts where high-quality flint was readily available. Retouched artifacts comprise a larger proportion of the artifact assemblage, more than 10%. Flint artifacts generally are noticeably smaller and more irregular. The general picture from this area suggests that local, community-level specialization in production has emerged, with certain co-residential groups controlling available raw materials and surplus production for exchange.

Long-distance exchange systems also characterize the Early Neolithic; these networks expand dramatically in extent and in the amounts and types of materials moving. Trade in flint, ground and polished axes, amber and other materials was part of an apparently extensive network of exchange (L. Larsson 1988a). Flint axes of Danish or southern Swedish origin are known from the Neolithic in the Netherlands and Germany (Rech 1979) and also from middle and northern Sweden and Norway (Clark 1948, Simonsen 1988, 1996, Welinder 1988). Several generalized networks for the exchange of axes can be suggested for the Early Neolithic (Bostwick Bjerck 1988); greenstone and diabase axe distributions mark two zones in western Norway (Olsen and Alsaker 1984); another network exists between Denmark, Sweden, and eastern Norway involving the movement of flint and stone axes and TRB pottery (Fig. 10.10). Exotic imports include copper ornaments, jewellery, and axe blades, including a model for the Scandinavian polygonal battle axes in the Early Neolithic (Randsborg 1975, 1979). Metallurgical analyses indicate that these copper artifacts have a very low arsenic content similar to copper from southern Europe, perhaps from sources in central Germany or western Austria (Madsen and Petersen 1984). The materials traded from Scandinavia in return are unknown. Organic products such as fur, feathers, lamp oil from seals, and honey were probably included among the exports.

Community specialization and long-distance exchange in prestige items were important aspects in the introduction of agriculture in Scandinavia (Simonsen 1975). The simultaneous appearance of status differentiation, community specialization in production, and trade and exchange of both local and exotic materials reflect a largely new pattern of social and economic organization that may be more important hallmarks of the "Neolithic Revolution" than the domestication of plants and animals and new subsistence strategies.

In summary

There are several conclusions to be drawn from the current evidence for the transition to agriculture in southern Scandinavia, specifically concerning colonization versus local adoption, rates of change, and causality – the who, the how, and the why questions raised at the beginning of this chapter.

The transition to agriculture in southern Scandinavia probably represents a case of local hunters adopting the materials, practices, and ideology of farming from agricultural groups to the south. This introduction was accompanied by a number of innovations and changes in economic and social organization. Trade in flint, polished axes, and amber and probably many other materials was part of an apparently extensive network of exchange. It is clearly the case that these changes in social, economic, and religious spheres in the earliest Neolithic are more pronounced than are changes in subsistence. Local inhabitants were the actors responsible for the transition in Scandinavia. In spite of the influx of new materials and techniques, there is a remarkable continuity in the basic aspects of lithic and ceramic technology, settlement, and burial rite.

The rate of change is very informative with regard to how the transition occurred. There are two answers to questions about the rate of change – it is both fast and slow. On the one hand, the period from first contact with farmers until the full adoption of agriculture extends over more than 1000 years, from around 4600 until 3500 BC. Sedentary foragers in the Late Mesolithic began to import items of Neolithic manufacture from the south after 4600 BC. The appearance of TRB pottery, domesticates, and long barrows marks the recognized beginning of the Neolithic around 3900 BC, but a fully Neolithic economy is not in place until after 3500 BC.

On the other hand, the almost simultaneous appearance of the evidence for domesticated plants and animals, TRB pottery, and earthen long barrows across Denmark, southern and middle Sweden, and the eastern part of Norway within roughly a 100-year period around 3900 BC is remarkable and reflects a very different phenomenon, the very rapid spread of new technologies, subsistence practices, economic and social organization, and ideology. The view from the north thus suggests that colonization was not a necessary factor in the almost instantaneous spread of agriculture over large areas. The spread of the Funnel Beaker culture across northern Europe is comparable in time and distance to the explosive movement of the Linearbandkeramik culture in the preceding millennium.

Current evidence suggests that the search for causality should focus in the realm of internal decisions within Mesolithic society, rather than external changes in climate, environment, or population. Human groups at the onset of the Neolithic participated in a larger sphere of trade and formalized the higher status of certain individuals through burial and other practices. It seems most reasonable to suggest a scenario in which interaction through exchange networks among foragers and farmers involving both ideas and materials fostered the rise of an elite component in Late Mesolithic societies. The Neolithic ushered in surplus production available through domestication and the establishment of extensive, long-distance trade.

Acknowledgments

I would like to extend my sincere appreciation to Agneta Åkerlund, Søren Andersen, Jan Apel, Sveinung Bang-Andersen, Pia Bennike, Björn Berglund, Joel Boaz, Lucyna Domanska, Anders Fischer, Fredrik Hallgren, Sönke Hartz, Svein Indrelid, Dobochna Jankowska, Kristina Jennbert, Britta Kihlstedt, Kjel Knuston, Eva Koch, Inge Kjær Kristensen, Kristian Kristiansen, Lars Larsson, Mads Larsson, Kerstin Lidén, Torsten Madsen, Bengt Nordqvist, Asle Bruen Olsen, Eva Olsson, Einar Østmo, Per Persson, Kristian Petersen, Peter Rasmussen, Anne Segerberg, Povl Simonsen, Karl-Gøran Sjögren, Michael Stafford, Peter Vang Petersen, K.-P. Wechler, and Stig Welinder. These individiuals provided assistance above and beyond the call to long-distance requests for information. I am indebted to the kindness and openness of my north European colleagues and thank the stars for email and fax machines. Obviously, errors in the manuscript will be mine. As usual, this work would not have been possible without the extraordinary care and attention of Anne Birgitte Gebauer.

11

Lessons in the transition to agriculture

Two concerns were emphasized at the beginning of this volume, colonization vs. indigenous adoption and causality. These questions of how and why agriculture spread to Europe are important ones, both in regard to the specific situation on the continent, and for understanding the global process that was the transition to agriculture. A number of insights into these questions have come from the study of the transition to agriculture in prehistoric Europe summarized in this volume. These insights demand fundamental changes in our explanations of how and why that transition took place. The paragraphs below summarize new perspectives on these questions.

Colonization vs. indigenous adoption

It is clear from recent studies that the introduction of farming in Europe involved both colonization by migrant farmers and the adoption of agriculture by indigenous inhabitants. Monolithic or even dichotomous patterns cannot define the processes that resulted in the introduction of agriculture. There was, as Tringham noted in this volume, a mosaic of mechanisms that brought farming into Europe; a range of migration (such as demic diffusion, leapfrog colonization, elite dominance, infiltration, folk migration) and varieties of local adoption (exchange of materials and information, exchange of mates, individual frontier mobility, or independent local adoption) must be considered. These patterns have been discussed in detail in the chapter by Zvelebil and Lillie in this volume.

Was a single process dominant in the spread of agriculture? Beyond the example of the first farmers in the Aegean islands, it is difficult to make an uncontested case for colonization. Certainly the evidence is incomplete and more information is needed in a number of regions. The aceramic Neolithic in mainland Greece remains to be fully described as a possible local precursor for a fully developed Neolithic; the evidence from Franchthi Cave in the south of mainland Greece suggests local adoption (Halstead

1996, Tringham, this volume). There are unanswered questions about the nature of the transition both in the Balkans and along the Mediterranean shore. We know very little of the Mesolithic in southeastern Europe with only one or two exceptions. It does seem there was interaction between foragers and farmers in the Iron Gates of the Danube and, perhaps, elsewhere in southeastern Europe. More work remains to be done to clarify the relationship between the Late Mesolithic and the Early Neolithic in the Cardial zone (Barnett, this volume). The sporadic coastal distribution of the Cardial culture along the Mediterranean shore has been seen as the result of colonization by many (e.g., Zilhão, Binder, this volume). Information from the study of human skeletal remains from both the Mesolithic and the early Cardial culture in Portugal indicates that there is little change in the morphology or stature, supporting the concept of indigenous adoption (Jackes *et al.* 1997a), but this evidence is contentious (Zilhão, this volume). In fact, we know little of the Cardial; what we do know is biased by a limited range of archaeological deposits (Barnett, this volume). It is almost certain that the primary settlements of the Cardial lie under the waters of the Mediterranean and Atlantic.

Outside southern and southeastern Europe, the role of local Mesolithic groups in the transition seems more prominent. Zvelebil and Lillie in this volume make a strong argument for the occasional and piecemeal adoption of agriculture by local groups throughout much of eastern Europe. In central Europe, evidence is accumulating for the La Hoguette culture as a predecessor of the fully Neolithic Cortailloid and Bandkeramik. La Hoguette is a mixture of Early Neolithic elements such as pottery and domesticated sheep and goat, found in Late Mesolithic contexts from the middle Rhône valley to Switzerland and north to Belgium and the middle Rhine (Lüning *et al.* 1989, Jochim, this volume). This new information suggests that the Bandkeramik, previously thought to represent colonists in central Europe, was not the earliest manifestation of the Neolithic. Moreover, detailed investigations of the Bandkeramik (Gronenborn 1994, Jochim, this volume, Tillmann 1994) indicate that the earliest phase of this culture was heterogeneous and shared several elements with the Late Mesolithic. In light of this new evidence, the well-known homogeneity of the Bandkeramik may be a development subsequent to the first arrival of the Neolithic.

The evidence against colonization in northern Europe is substantial and points to indigenous adoption of agriculture by local groups. Continuity is seen in lithic and ceramic artifacts as well as aspects of burial in Scandinavia. New settlement locations, diets, and monumental burials are among the notable changes that occur with the arrival of the Neolithic. Views of the transition in the British Isles have shifted back and forth from colonization to indigenous adoption. As Woodman has noted in this volume, the absence of evidence in the British Isles makes resolution of the question of colonization vs. adoption difficult. There is a chronological gap between the last Mesolithic and the earliest Neolithic before 4000 BC in Ireland. The absence of archaeological materials and an uncertainty about how this evidence might appear emphasizes the need for detailed studies of this period.

Biological information on the relationship between Mesolithic and Early Neolithic populations in Europe is limited. Reports by European anthropologists on physical differences among skeletal remains from the Mesolithic and Neolithic in the 1970s indicated relatively few differences (Schwidetsky 1973). Since that time many more Mesolithic graves have been found and more recent comparisons with Neolithic skeletal materials corroborate the previous result of relatively few differences between the two groups (Formicola 1986, Jackes *et al.* 1997a, Jacobs 1994b, Lillie 1996, Meiklejohn *et al.* 1984, y'Edynak and Fleisch 1988).

Most of the observed differences in skeletal morphology between Mesolithic and Neolithic individuals are the result of longer-term trends and do not reflect significant physical differences between the two populations (Meiklejohn and Zvelebil 1991). There is a general decrease in stature from the Upper Palaeolithic to the Neolithic, changing to increase in the later Neolithic (Meiklejohn 1985). There are general trends that continue in the Mesolithic and Neolithic such as a general reduction in tooth size (Frayer 1984, Meiklejohn *et al.* 1988). The incidence of dental caries increases dramatically in the Neolithic, resulting from a change to a diet with more carbohydrates (Meiklejohn and Zvelebil 1991).

There are very few studies that involve the direct comparison of Mesolithic and Neolithic populations in the same local area with regard to the question of replacement. One such investigation in central and southern Portugal provides intriguing results. Comparison of craniometric features between two Mesolithic populations and one Neolithic group almost 3000 years younger and located in a different ecological zone showed no differences (Jackes *et al.* 1997a, 1997b). Stature was similar; the incidence of caries displayed a distinct decrease in the Neolithic population. Jackes *et al.* (1997a) further suggest that their data indicate the Mesolithic population of Iberia was demographically stable and only modest growth took place in the Neolithic. This evidence appears to show clear continuity between the Mesolithic and Neolithic and to negate the likelihood of population replacement at the time of the transition.

Human genetics may provide another avenue for the assessment of the relationship between Mesolithic and Neolithic populations. Cavalli-Sforza and colleagues have examined the geographic patterning of modern human genetic traits in Europe (Ammerman and Cavalli-Sforza 1984, Bertranpetit and Cavalli-Sforza 1991, Cavalli-Sforza 1991, 1996). Some ninety-five different gene frequencies were used in their latest study (Cavalli-Sforza *et al.* 1994) to generate principal components; the first principal component explains approximately 26% of the variability among the gene frequencies. A map of the first principal component scores shows a clinal distribution of frequencies that closely resembles another map of the dates for the spread of the Neolithic in Europe (Ammerman and Cavalli-Sforza 1973). Cavalli-Sforza argues that these gradients are the result of population expansion, "the spread of agricultural settlers . . . into regions inhabited sparsely by hunter-gatherers, who initially had a different genetic background" (Cavalli-Sforza 1996:53). At the same time, he suggests that both demic diffusion and indigenous adoption operated in the spread of agriculture across Europe, otherwise "the observed genetic gradient would not form" (Cavalli-Sforza 1996:53).

There are significant concerns regarding the correlation of maps of genetic traits (or their principal components) and the spread of agriculture. There is in fact no evidence to link the two phenomenon other than speculation. Pluciennik (1996) has noted the absence of correspondence between modern genetic patterns and prehistoric groups of people because of the distance in time and changing identities among ethnic groups. The distribution of these genetic groups could have resulted as easily from the initial colonization of Europe, the expansion of fully modern *Homo sapiens*, the Roman empire, or later population displacements in Europe (Sokal, Oden, *et al.* 1996). Renfrew (1996:85), points out that modern gene frequencies, which represent more recent dispersals of human population, cannot be the same as those in Europe at the time of the Neolithic.

There are also questions regarding the mechanisms invoked to produce these genetic gradients. For example, if colonization were responsible for the spread of agriculture, why would genetic frequencies change so dramatically; colonists would presumably have carried the same genetic frequencies across the continent. Cavalli-Sforza suggests that the observed gradient pattern is the result of a mixing or dilution of genes between farmers and hunter-gatherers. This argument assumes that there would have been a genetically homogenous population of hunter-gatherers distributed evenly across the continent. Such an explanation is difficult to comprehend in light of what we know about the Mesolithic of Europe.

Questions have also been raised regarding the distribution of other genetic characteristics (see also Zvelebil and Lillie, this volume). It appears that while some genetic frequencies follow the gradients observed by Cavalli-Sforza, others do not. Sokal *et al.* (Sokal *et al.* 1991, Sokal, Jantz, *et al.* 1996, Sokal, Oden, and Thompson 1992) and Barbujani *et al.* (1995) have attempted to confirm the relationship between maps of Early Neolithic radiocarbon dates and gene frequency, but were unable to find conclusive evidence (Sokal, Oden, *et al.* 1996). Fix (1996) has argued that modern gene frequency clines in Europe are the result of natural selection, rather than demic diffusion. Examination of the distribution of modern cranial measurements revealed no correlation with Neolithic patterning (Harding 1990, Harding *et al.* 1996).

Recent studies of modern mitochondrial DNA (mtDNA) in

European samples indicate a very different pattern from that proposed by Cavalli-Sforza (Richards *et al.* 1996, Wilkinson-Herbots *et al.* 1996). Analysis of mtDNA in modern populations suggests that more than 85% of European genes probably date to the Upper Palaeolithic, rather than the Neolithic (Richards *et al.* 1996). The most recent publications on this issue in fact bring some concordance. Cavalli-Sforza and Minch (1997:248) indicate that the 26% of variability explained by their first component is probably "not far from" the actual proportion contributed by farming populations to the European gene-pool. Richards *et al.* (1996, 1997) suggest this value is less than 15%, not far from the value of Cavalli-Sforza and Minch. Other aspects of the mitochondrial DNA study are also of interest. It is important to note that the mtDNA evidence does indicate some small-scale colonization (10–15% of total mtDNA lineages) of Europe from southwest Asia during the Neolithic. The pattern of this colonization as indicated by the geographic distribution of mtDNA lineages indicates a "rapid penetration from the southeast, both westward and northwestward, followed by a much more gradual intermixing with the numerically dominant indigenous Mesolithic inhabitants" (Richards *et al.* 1997:253). While these results are preliminary, they do fit current views of the transition to farming in Europe as outlined in this volume.

There are several models of the expansion of human populations, languages, and gene groups, closely related to questions concerning colonization and the spread of farming in Europe. These models are strongly impacted by the new synthesis of the transition to agriculture. If the process of agricultural introduction involved a variety of mechanisms, and if the process was one of explosive leaps and often involved local Mesolithic groups rather than migrant farmers, as has been argued in this volume, previous models and theories must be reviewed in this new light. Focus will be on the Wave of Advance model, the spread of Indo-European languages, and the "availability" model.

The Wave of Advance

Albert Ammerman, an archaeologist, and Luca Cavalli-Sforza, a human geneticist, proposed a Wave of Advance model to describe the spread of agriculture across Europe (Ammerman 1989, Ammerman and Cavalli-Sforza 1973, 1984), a phenomenon noted earlier by Clark (1965). Ammerman and Cavalli-Sforza documented the regularity of radiocarbon dates showing the gradual spread of the Neolithic across Europe and argued that this was a reflection of human colonization. They suggested that this pattern, showing the expansion of the Neolithic at about 1 km/year, was best explained by rates of population growth and individual migration that resembled a wave of expansion or advance. This model has had enormous impact on concepts about the past and thinking about the spread of human population.

The Wave of Advance model is essentially a *description* of how farmers spread across Europe, based on the process of colonization. Farming is assumed to have been advantageous and its spread explained by high rates of population growth among the farmers. This model also has been heavily critiqued over the years, with questions raised about the criteria for "Neolithic," the specific contexts of the dates themselves, and assumed rates of growth and migration (e.g., Dennell 1985, Meiklejohn 1985, Thomas 1996a, Whittle 1996, Zvelebil 1989, Zvelebil and Lillie, this volume, among others). As has also been noted (Barnett, this volume, Keeley in Price *et al.* 1995), the Wave of Advance model does not fit the two generally accepted cases of agricultural colonization in Europe. The spread of both the Bandkeramik and the Cardial cultures took place at a rate at least five times faster than the 1 km/year predicted by the Wave of Advance model.

The rate of the spread of farming in fact is informative with regard to the question of how this process took place. For many years, the introduction of agriculture was understood as a gradual, inexorable process operating at a constant and continuous rate, rather like water slowly running downhill. Today, however, it is clear that the spread of agriculture, where evidence for the rate of change exists, is marked by a series of very rapid expansions followed by long periods of statis in a stop and go fashion, of leaps and stands, of punctuated equilibrium (Gould and Eldridge 1977, Kozlowski 1988). This explosive spread is seen most clearly in the Bandkeramik, Cardial, and Funnel Beaker areas. Following phases of rapid expansion in these areas, there were apparently hundreds of years without any further expansion (e.g., Dennell 1985, Price, this volume, Zvelebil 1989). A simple model such as the wave of advance cannot adequately describe this process. The rate of spread of agriculture into Europe can in fact best be described in terms of a step model (or punctuated equilibrium, Gould and Eldridge 1977), rather than the ramp model of Ammerman and Cavalli-Sforza. Recent evidence discounts any Wave of Advance of Neolithic colonists.

Language and the Neolithic

Colin Renfrew and others (de Laubenfels 1981, Krantz 1988) have raised the argument that the distinctive Indo-European languages spread originally with the first agriculture into Europe (Renfrew 1987, 1989). Initially Renfrew suggested that colonization was the only mechanism through which this process took place (1987). He offered the reasonable argument that the spread of population into an uninhabited or sparsely occupied area would result in the establishment of the language of the colonists. The explicit assumption of this model was that Europe was colonized by farmers who carried the proto-Indo-European language as part of the Neolithic package. This view, sometimes known as the Language Steamroller model, has been disseminated widely and is often referenced in discussions of the introduction of agriculture into Europe. More recently, Renfrew (1994, 1996) has suggested as a global generalization that the distribution of language families and the spread of agriculture in the past are closely related.

Renfrew's views have been soundly critiqued (e.g., Hines 1997, Mallory 1989, Otte 1995, Sherratt and Sherratt 1988, Zvelebil 1995b, Zvelebil and Zvelebil 1988). One of the primary criticisms of Renfrew's formulation has been that there is no demonstrated, or perhaps demonstrable, association between the distribution of Indo-European language and the Early Neolithic (e.g., Gimbutas 1988, Mallory 1989). More recent discussions have added new dimensions to this argument. Renfrew (1994, 1996) has consented, in the face of mounting evidence, that the spread of agriculture, and hence of a language family, can take place through either colonization or the indigenous adoption of agriculture.

In favorable cases the language or languages of the nuclear area are transmitted along with plant and animal domesticates, either through demic diffusion of the farming population (the Wave of Advance model), or through adoption by local hunter-gatherer groups of the new language along with the agricultural economy (acculturation: the "availability" model). The genetic effects of the two mechanisms are significantly different. (Renfrew 1996:77)

When Renfrew accepts both colonization and adoption as mechanisms for the spread, it becomes more difficult to evaluate the argument. If migration is not essential to the spread of language, then the spread of the Neolithic need have little to do with this issue. Language could have spread at any time before or after the introduction of farming.

To support the Renfrew argument, it is essential to explain how languages are adopted when agriculture spreads through indigenous adoption; the mechanism for language transmission in such situations is nowhere made clear. Language transmission and replacement is a fascinating subject and has been the focus of debate for more than a century without resolution. Recent revival of the controversy (e.g., Bateman *et al.* 1990, Bellwood 1996, Moore and Romney 1992, Welsch *et al.* 1992, Welsch and Terrell 1994) points out how vexing a question the replacement of language is. As Bellwood (1996:881), Greenburg (1995), and others have noted, human languages, cultures, and gene-pools do not always co-vary in unison. Bellwood distinguishes between phylogeny (descent or historical relations) in language and cultural relationships, and reticulation (interaction between contemporary groups such as assimilation, intermarriage, borrowing, or diffusion). The essential question here is whether language families have developed through linguistic diffusion alone (convergence), or have spread through language shift in populations speaking previously unrelated languages or through dispersal of the actual speakers of the language. It is clear that our understanding of the process is limited and that there is no direct correlation between the spread of artifacts, people, and language.

Availability and the Neolithic

As we have seen, it is the case that although the actual introduction of domesticates took place very rapidly in a series of steps, there were often lengthy periods of contact between adjacent foragers and farmers prior to the actual spread of the Neolithic. Evidence for this interaction is seen in several areas, including the Mediterranean shore, the Alpine Foreland, central and eastern Europe, and Scandinavia as described in this volume. Agriculture became the primary subsistence regime in these areas only following a period of exchange, experimentation, and changes in technology and settlement. This is the context of "availability," as described by Zvelebil and Rowley-Conwy (1984, 1986) and Zvelebil (1986a).

The availability model distinguished three phases in the transition to the Neolithic: availability, substitution, and consolidation, beginning with contact between foragers and farmers and ending with agriculture as the principal source of food. The availability model argued that hunter-gatherers were familiar with the products and practices of the Neolithic for some period before adoption. The very rapid spread of the Neolithic reflects the fact that pathways for exchange and interaction, for the movement of goods, ideas, and perhaps people, were operating in the Late Mesolithic. The existence of such connections is confirmed by the variety of materials that were moving in the later European Mesolithic (e.g., Larsson 1988, Newell *et al.* 1990, Runnels and van Andel 1988). Tykot (1996), for example, has documented the movement of obsidian and other stone across much of the eastern Mediterranean in the period prior to the introduction of farming. Shoe-last celts made of amphibolite from eastern Europe are found in Late Mesolithic sites in Scandinavia (Fischer 1982). A number of other Neolithic items (e.g., bone combs, t-shaped antler axes) also make their way to Scandinavia from farming groups to the south (Andersen 1970, 1981, Vang Petersen 1984). Certainly the presence of domesticated plants or animals in reliable Mesolithic contexts, discussed previously, further exemplifies interaction between farmers and foragers.

The availability model emphasizes the role of indigenous hunter-gatherers in the transition to farming, as an alternative to colonization, but "availability" is applicable in either context. The availability model is not intended as an explanation of why agriculture spread, rather as a means for describing the conditions under which it did.

Causality and the Neolithic

Causes of the transition are unresolved and the subject of substantial debate. A variety of theories have been put forth in recent years that are related to the spread of agriculture across Europe. For the discussion here, three groups of explanations are considered: external factors, arguments for social change, and ideological approaches to the Neolithic. These perspectives reflect a wide range of conceptual and analytical frameworks for examining the causes of the transition to agriculture across the European continent.

External factors

External forces such as climatic change, resource degradation, or population growth have often been invoked to explain the origins of agriculture as well as its spread. These explanations generally involve large-scale factors in nature that are beyond the control of human society – changes in climate or the environment, inherently high rates of population growth. These factors are usually understood as forcing human populations to change, creating stress or problems that push society to seek new solutions (e.g., Binford 1968, Cohen 1977). These factors have often been explicitly invoked in discussions of the origins of agriculture in the Near East (Bar-Yosef and Belfer-Cohen 1992, Binford 1968, Childe 1928, McCorriston and Hole 1991, Wright 1977).

In their most basic form, explanations involving climatic change as a cause for the transition to agriculture generally rely on shifts in temperature or precipitation. The original version of this was probably Pumpelly's explanation of the origins of agriculture in the Near East (1908), arguing that desiccation at the end of the Pleistocene resulted in the formation of oases. Plants, animals, and humans living in these limiting conditions were forced to find a mutually beneficial relationship – cultivation and herding.

In Europe, changes in climate or environment have been cited, or implicitly invoked, for many years as causes of the spread of agriculture (e.g., Jarman *et al.* 1982) as archaeologists have attempted to correlate climatic events and the arrival of the Neolithic. The elm decline in northern Europe is a classic example – a sharp reduction in elm pollen was cited as an indication of climatic change that coincided with the introduction of agriculture. In another example, Rowley-Conwy (1984) has argued that changes in salinity in the North Sea reduced marine resources, specifically oysters, and caused Ertebølle foragers to turn to farming.

Most of these explanations involving climate or environmental change can be questioned or refuted. The elm decline is now understood to be a result of disease, rather than climate, and in some instances took place after the appearance of agriculture (Peglar and Birks 1993). While it is true that oysters disappeared from Mesolithic shell-middens, the Neolithic levels of these same middens contain mussels and cockles. Moreover, it is clear that fishing continued at a large scale in the Early Neolithic (Pedersen 1997). Shell-middens are present at only a small number of Mesolithic settlements and were not ubiquitous during the Mesolithic. Thus the loss of a dietary supplement such as oysters is unlikely to have created resource stress throughout the area of the Ertebølle culture.

Arguments based on changes in climate or environmental conditions or on population growth are very difficult to evaluate. We know little about the relationship between changes in climate or the environment and how human populations reacted. The relationship between environmental and cultural change may well be coincidental. Climate is now recognized as much more variable than previously thought and is in essence always changing (Lamb 1995, O'Brien *et al.* 1995). It is often possible to find a change in climate that corresponds with cultural change; it is very difficult to demonstrate that the two are correlated.

Also relevant in this context are the parameters of the spread of the Neolithic in Europe. This process takes place over a span of 3000 years, across a variety of environmental regimes, from the islands of the Aegean to the forested plains of central Europe, to the islands and peninsulas of Scandinavia, essentially to the limits of cultivation. Such a widespread, long-term process seems *prima facie* evidence that climate change and environmental conditions had little to do with forcing people to become farmers. A sequential and serendipitous set of changes in climate and/or environment would have to be invoked to explain the multiple events in the spread of agriculture across Europe. The fact that domesticated plants and animals spread so far, over such long distances and diverse environments, in the relatively brief period of 3000 years argues against external causality.

Population is notoriously difficult to measure archaeologically, but present information suggests that human numbers in both the Late Mesolithic and the Early Neolithic were not large. Population appears to have been small to absent in much of the interior of the continent where Mesolithic groups were few and far between (Price 1987, Waterbolk 1982). The difficulty of locating sites from this period in much of Europe is probably an indication of relatively low population numbers. Archaeological surveys in the interior of Europe have revealed very little Mesolithic presence away from major lakes and waterways. In the resource-rich coastal areas of Atlantic Europe, it is difficult to imagine that even substantial population numbers could have put pressure on the abundant resources of the land and sea. Most of the papers in this volume report relatively low levels of Mesolithic population across Europe. The evidence of the Early Neolithic also leaves an impression of low levels of population. Pollen evidence from southeastern Europe records the sparsity of agricultural fields (Willis and Bennett 1994). Evidence from the Bandkeramik indicates that fields were small and shaded by surrounding forest (Keeley 1992). In Scandinavia, pollen evidence also documents the small size and short-term use of agricultural fields (Andersen 1992).

Present information and perspectives suggest that external forces such as climate, environment, and population growth were not primary causes of the transition to agriculture. Several important points emerge in this context: (1) in many areas of Mesolithic habitation, particularly coastal and riverine zones, food resources were relatively abundant and productive; (2) environmental changes did not significantly reduce the amount of food available to Mesolithic groups; and (3) populations numbers do not appear to be substantial in either the Late Mesolithic or the Early Neolithic. Causality should be sought elsewhere.

Social change and the Neolithic

The origin and spread of agriculture has been reconsidered in recent years. In contrast to earlier views, which argued for the beginnings of farming among populations in marginal areas under resource stress, more recent evidence suggests that agriculture appeared in areas with stable and abundant resources (e.g., Bar-Yosef and Meadows 1995, Hayden 1990, Price and Gebauer 1992). Emphasis has shifted from external forces, such as food crisis or population pressure, to factors internal in human society and individuals. A number of scholars have suggested that the transition to agriculture involved changes in social organization and the emergence of inequality (e.g., Bender 1978, 1985, 1990, Hayden 1990, 1992, Jennbert 1984, 1985, Price 1996a, Price and Gebauer 1992, Tilley 1996).

Bender in her 1978 examination of the beginnings of farming argued that "the enquiry into agricultural origins is not, therefore, about intensification per se, not about increased productivity, but about increased production and about why increased demands are made on the economy" (p. 206). Bender pointed out that food production was a question of commitment and social relations, about alliance structures and the individuals operating within such structures, not about technology or demography. Bender was among the first to point out that leadership, alliance, and exchange gave rise to a need for surplus production. Hypotheses invoking social causes for the transition suggest that leaders or higher-status individuals may have encouraged relatives and neighbors to adopt agriculture as a means for producing food surpluses in order to increase wealth and exchange. Exchange in exotic materials is another aspect of the accumulation of wealth.

Hayden (1990, 1992, and elsewhere) has elaborated this concept. Hayden argued that domestication first appeared among hunter-gatherer societies with highly developed technologies, living in areas of abundant resources and usually characterized by relatively dense population, semi-sedentism, socio-economic inequalities, status display, and regional exchange of exotics. He suggested that food production may have developed specifically in the context of feasting and other competitive mechanisms among ambitious individuals. Competition among individuals can be closely related to social hierarchy in evolutionary ecological theory (Boone 1992).

How does the emergence of status differentiation relate to the spread of agriculture? Brunton (1975), in a consideration of why the Trobriand Islanders have chiefs, noted that participation in a closed system of exchange limited the range of people who could compete for leadership.

This situation resulted in the emergence of a few Big Men who encouraged the production of surplus. Elmendorf (1971) and Rubel and Rosman (1983) have reported a similar situation from the Northwest Coast of North America where status relations were dependent on a network of inter-village relations that involved kinship, economic exchange, and ceremonial activities. Cross (1993) views changes in production as important in creating interpersonal ties and redefining differences in status and power in non-stratified societies. Clark and Blake (1994) have noted that political competition privileges those members of the group who can control external interaction. Clark and Parry (1991) and Costin (1991) have documented the correlation between production, in the form of craft specialization, and cultural complexity.

Certainly the relationship between specialization and exchange is very close in more complex societies (Brumfiel and Earle 1987). The production and exchange of valuable, labor-intensive goods is important in societies where marking and maintaining prestige is critical. Feinman (1995) and Spencer (1993a, 1993b) have focused attention on different modes of leadership in transegalitarian societies. Feinman distinguishes corporate vs. network modes of leadership; Spencer (1993a) points to the internal and external relations of leadership and argues (1993b:45) that the shift to status differentiation and ascribed roles of authority requires the establishment of links between both internal and external leadership functions. Aldenderfer (1992) argues that such linkages, leading to the institutionalization of inequality, often take place in the context of ritual activities.

Long-distance exchange of labor-intensive or rare prestige items, community specialization in production, and the intensification of ritual activity can best be understood in terms of emerging social inequality in the Neolithic. It can be argued that most of the important changes in the Early Neolithic in Europe lie in the realms of economy, social organization, and ideology, rather than subsistence (Chapman 1994a, Coudart 1991, Price 1996a, Runnels 1988, Sherratt 1982). These changes are closely intertwined and suggest that a new set of practices, organization, and beliefs accompanied the spread of domesticated plants and animals. Social and economic changes are considered in this section; ideological approaches are discussed in the next.

The evidence for dramatic social and economic changes is not yet conclusive; only bits and pieces are seen in different areas of Neolithic Europe. The chronology of the appearance of inequality, trade in exotic items, and specialized community production in the Neolithic is not well resolved. This evidence varies from place to place. Nevertheless the accumulating picture is suggestive of a larger pattern that may well emerge given future research.

Substantial increases in the exchange of exotic materials occur in a number of areas of the continent with the introduction of farming. This evidence indicates that the transition to the Neolithic involved participation in long-distance networks of exchange for highly valued materials and information. Evidence for economic changes is seen in dramatic increases in production of items for exchange and the widespread distribution of exotic materials. A variety of items were involved in trade and exchange in the Greek Neolithic, including both raw materials and finished products such as stone, shell, figurines, and seals (e.g., Halstead 1996, Miller 1996, Perlès 1992, Runnels and van Andel 1988). Greenfield (1991) has invoked a model of exchange, alliance, and status in the Neolithic of southeastern Europe to explain developments in the Neolithic of that region, pointing to the wide range of valued materials involved in production and exchange. Tykot (1996) has documented the widespread distribution of source-specific obsidian and other stone raw materials along the Mediterranean coast. Copper produced in the Balkans spread far across Europe in the Neolithic (e.g., Ottaway 1973, Randsborg 1979), appearing in very early Neolithic contexts in northern Europe (Andersen and Johansen 1992). Polished flint axes were a major export from flint-rich regions in central and northwestern Europe (Bradley and Edmonds 1993, Nielsen 1979, Sherratt 1982, 1987). Flint mines in southern Sweden, northern Denmark, southern Netherlands, Belgium, France, and Britain date from the Early Neolithic and document the importance of specialized production for exchange (Becker 1980, Bosch 1979, Sieveking 1972).

Indications of social inequality in the Early Neolithic come from several lines of evidence, including differences in house sizes (e.g., Rodden 1962) and the differential distribution of exotic materials (e.g., Chapman 1991, Gimbutas 1977, Price 1996a). Dramatic changes in social organization also can be suggested on the basis of the appearance of megalithic graves throughout western Europe. These megaliths have generally been understood as communal tombs for large numbers of individuals. However, evidence from northern Europe indicates that such tombs may have initially been built for a limited number of individuals. The earliest monumental tombs in the Funnel Beaker area are earthen long barrows containing one or a few graves. The construction and content of these tombs suggest clearly that these are burials of higher-status individuals (e.g., Andersen and Johansen 1992). Earthen long barrows evolve into long barrows with dolmens, and eventually into other megalithic tombs. The earliest levels in these later megalithic tombs, in the rare instances where they are preserved, indicate that the structures were also originally intended for a limited number of individuals or a single person (e.g., Madsen 1991). This pattern may well be widespread throughout the megalithic tradition of western Europe (e.g., Kinnes 1982, Lidén 1995b, Sherratt 1990).

In addition there are suggestions of a shift from production for use to production for exchange in the Neolithic, seen in specialized community production of various items in a number of areas. An early and clear pattern of community production and exchange in several items of stone and pottery is seen in Neolithic Greece (Perlès 1992). In spite of the remarkably

homogeneous appearance of the later Bandkeramik, community production of items such as ceramics, grinding stones, and flint blades is clearly in
evidence (Keeley and Cahen 1989). In Scandinavia, specialized production of
polished flint axes, pottery, and other materials, as well as important foodstuffs such as fish, is likely (Price *et al.* 1995). Specialized community production of domestic items suggests that local exchange networks may have
been part of a larger economic system. Such specialized production impli-
cates the household as the primary locus of both social and economic
decison-making (Bogucki 1988, this volume, Lightfoot 1994, Tringham and
Krstic 1990). A focus on households in Early Neolithic communities is likely
to result in new information critical for understanding the operation of production and exchange.

Social perspectives are intriguing because they are able to explain
some of the phenomena we see with the appearance of the Neolithic, such
as trade in exotic materials, rich graves, and specialized production.
However, the pattern of social change is not the same everywhere in Europe.
Status differentiation cannot be seen in all areas. The impact or amount of
trade in exotic items varies between regions. Not much is known about local
production for exchange.

The term evidence has been used throughout this discussion and it
is appropriate. The evidence is suggestive, an indictment is possible, but the
jury is not yet in. The implications of a causal role for social changes in the
transition to agriculture are strong, but a verdict is not yet possible. Future
investigations in this realm are likely to prove fruitful. A final, thorny
problem, however, lurks behind such social explanations: if the rise of
social and economic changes is the driving force behind the transition to
agriculture, we must answer the question of what brought about the rise of
status differentiation in the first place?

Ideological change and the Neolithic

Another direction in recent years, associated with the post-
processual school of archaeology, has emphasized the symbolic and structural aspects of the human past. As Bradley (1996) has noted, Neolithic
archaeologists tend to fall into two camps. Those who work in areas where
settlements are the primary evidence tend to focus on subsistence and adaptation to resources, while those who work where mounds and earthworks
dominate tend to focus on ritual and ideology. What is more important
from this latter perspective is the movement, not of people or products such
as domesticates or pottery, but of ideas, symbols, and perceptions. As Olsen
(1988: 431) has noted, "farming is not only an 'economy' or a 'mode of production', but also a cultural and symbolic construct."

One of the leading proponents of an ideological perspective is
Hodder (1990). Hodder relies on structural opposition and interplay, at the
conceptual level, between culture and nature, tame and wild, *domus* and

agrios, to make a case for the social domestication of communities, prior to the economic domestication of plants and animals. He emphasizes the change in perspective and worldview that must accompany a transformation as substantive as the introduction of agriculture, an acceptance of the restraints of settled and structured life, and the values of continuity and nurturing. As Whittle (1996:8) has noted: "For Hodder the house was the location of the concept of *domus*. The *domus:agrios* model utilizes a set of concepts based around the idea and practice of the house, the *domus*, which was both a metaphor and a mechanism for the domestication and socialization of people."

In a far-reaching review of the European Neolithic, Whittle (1996) takes a specifically indigenous view of the transition, arguing that in every region local foragers became farmers. Whittle emphasizes values, ideals, and social sanctions rather than social structures in his approach. He envisions the transition as "patterns of slow change, of convergence, of continuity of indigenous population" (p. 9). He calls upon a "sense of community and the values which underpinned it . . . linked to a sense of time and descent and to a sense of the sacred" (p. 9) as dominant principles in the transformation of the Neolithic.

Tilley, in a recent survey of the introduction of agriculture to southern Scandinavia (1996), employs what he terms a post-positivist interpretive archaeology "to think difference" (p. 2). Tilley asserts that the great strength of archaeology is its focus on the relationship between people and material culture, and how material culture is a medium used by society or individuals "to construct, manipulate and transform their world" (p. 3). He summarizes the evidence for the Late Mesolithic and Early Neolithic in southern Scandinavia in a surprisingly straightforward, traditional fashion, involving both data and analogy. Interpretive archaeology, or speculation, comprises only a small portion of the study. For Tilley, the Late Mesolithic was a state of primitive communism in a kind of Garden of Eden. The transformation of the Neolithic was, according to Tilley, a new ideology which "restructured notions of time and space, death and the body, prestige and social competition" (p. 73) and was adopted by Mesolithic groups as they gradually were integrated into the Neolithic system. Social inequality was one of the consequences of this change that emerged in the course of the Neolithic.

Thomas (1988, 1991b), initially rethinking the Neolithic in 1988, viewed the transformation as an integrated ideological package with material expressions (funerary monuments, ceramic vessels, house forms, polished axes, and domesticates) that was adopted intact by Mesolithic groups across Europe. In a recent reanalysis (1996a), however, he repudiated that view: "all that was shared by groups of people in different parts of Europe was a 'material vocabulary', a range of legitimate artefactual forms which were combined and rendered meaningful in day-to-day practice"

(1996a:135). In the 1996 volume, Thomas embarked on an explicitly hermeneutical approach to the archaeological record, considering time, culture, and identity with a focus on the Neolithic of northwestern Europe. He considered the "descent" of the Neolithic: "a concatenation of numberless events by which a particular set of material resources came to crystallise and to be widely adopted in a particular place at a particular time" (p. 98). Special emphasis is on historical relations between different groups in the Mesolithic and Neolithic. While providing an alternative view to the interpretation of the content of the Neolithic and its possible meaning to the prehistoric inhabitants of northwestern Europe, there is again an absence of focus on causality, on the reasons for the transition to agriculture. The question remains: why did Mesolithic hunter-gatherers give up autonomy and a long-term, successful adaptation to become members of a larger Neolithic community?

Proponents of ideological approaches generally argue that "the Neolithic was primarily not an economic phenomenon, nor a new set of social relations, nor the manifestation of an immigrant group, but the material manifestation of a new set of ideas restructuring Late Mesolithic societies and changing their social and economic conditions of existence" (Tilley 1996:72). This is undoubtedly true. These ideological views certainly raise our awareness of the context and content of the Neolithic transformation and provide additional scenarios for the transition. Yet two substantial problems remain. Such interpretative archaeologies are very difficult to evaluate from the archaeological record and they fail to deal with the question of why new ideas and perspectives were spreading.

In sum

Much attention has been given to the *origins* of agriculture as perhaps the most important event in human history. It is, however, not so much the origins, but the *spread* of farming that has had the major impact on human society. It seems more useful to consider the origins of agriculture, or domestication, as a biological phenomenon. Genetic and phenotypic changes in plants and animals mark the impact of domestication, but it is the commitment to an agricultural way of life that is the hallmark of the transition (Bender 1978, Price and Gebauer 1995).

The initial domestication of wheats and barley in the ancient Near East may have been accidental, simply the result of planting the seeds of these species in new zones in an attempt to reproduce wild stands which grew abundantly. Zohary has argued that each of the seven founder species of the earliest crops was domesticated in a separate locale in the Near East (Ladinsky 1989, Zohary and Hopf 1993). The same is probably true for the various species of animals that were domesticated. The "package" of domesticated flora and fauna in the Early Neolithic was in fact the result of the exchange and spread of these species among the communities of the ancient Near East. This distribution was the result of human activity and decision. From this perspective, then, questions regarding agricultural transitions have more to do with the spread of farming than with its invention.

Farming quickly became an important part of subsistence across Europe. The Neolithic combination of domesticates, artifacts, beliefs, and practices must have been an effective new mode for human societies: rare new materials, new havens for the dead, organizational restructuring, extended alliances and relationships, and exotic plants and animals. Farming was apparently not an option; it replaced foraging everywhere within the limits of cultivation. This transformation took place in the brief period in archaeological time of 3000 years. Clearly the Neolithic represented a successful new arrangement that changed human society forever.

The new synthesis of the introduction of the Neolithic in Europe, and the important implications of these data, has dramatic consequences for our understanding of the more general and global phenomena of agricultural transitions. A pattern emerges from European prehistory in which local adoption is the primary mechanism operating to bring farming to the continent. Colonization appears to operate in areas where there are few or no local inhabitants. There are only one or two possible situations of colonization (demic diffusion) in the introduction of agriculture in Europe, especially in the Aegean Islands. At the same time, there are a variety of mechanisms between these two extremes. Modern genetic data, discussed earlier, suggest that small numbers of immigrants may well have been involved in the spread of farming. Small-scale infiltration and mate exchange between farmers and foragers may well account for such a pattern.

The questions who and how regarding the spread of agriculture to Europe now have been largely answered; only the details in specific places remain to be filled in. The question of why agriculture spread across Europe remains unresolved. Several models have emerged since the 1970s and have received wide attention because of their larger anthropological and archaeological implications. These models have generally depended heavily on the assumption that colonization was the single, or preeminent, mechanism that brought new language and new genes to Europe, along with the Neolithic. In the light of the new synthesis for the introduction of farming into Europe, however, serious reservations must be raised about the Wave of Advance model. The relationship between the spread of the Neolithic in Europe and the distribution of both gene frequencies and the Indo-European language family cannot be demonstrated. Given the overwhelming evidence against population replacement in the spread the Neolithic, it is difficult to imagine how these models can now be useful or appropriate.

At the same time, it is clear from the chapters in this volume and other recent literature that no consensus has been reached on why the transition to agriculture took place. Social and ideological approaches have dominated much of the discussion of the transition in recent years. Social models emphasize organizational and economic changes that rely on emerging social inequality to drive accumulators in society to encourage surplus production. Ideological models vary but generally emphasize cognitive aspects of the Neolithic; changes in concepts and perspectives are considered preeminent in the changes that mark early farming societies.

It is essential to note, however, that the overall congruity between social and ideological approaches is pronounced. In spite of an emphasis on different schools, on processual vs. post-modern perspectives, the two sets of models have significant overlap. The extension of the abstract is accompanied by rather dramatic and important correlative activities in social and economic realms (Price 1995). Language, knowledge, concepts, ideas do not travel out of context (Ehret 1988). It may be useful to consider the means through which concepts, symbols, and perceptions are mobile. That context must involve material things – people, materials, or facilities – and therefore will be social, economic, or technological in nature. The social, economic, and ideological realms of human behavior are intimately related, more so in non-western societies. To isolate these branches of the tree is to obscure the importance of their integral relationships. An approach which considers the totality of these aspects of human society, which disregards the political and philosophical loadings of a particular interpretive position, combining concept and material, information and artifact, belief and burial, may allow us to move beyond the present explanatory stalemate and begin to understand why the Neolithic happened.

For the present, it is useful to view the Neolithic as a set of social, economic, and ideological information and material, borrowed or occasionally carried, that spread in fits and starts across the European continent. In light of the new synthesis of the transition to agriculture in Europe, it seems more appropriate that we understand the larger global phenomenon of the origins and spread of agriculture in terms of factors internal to human society. The European evidence suggests that we need to admit that climate, environment, and population growth played a minor role, if any, in comparison to the changes that human groups chose with regard to their livelihood and way of life. In this context, the Neolithic revolution probably had less to do with subsistence and technology and more to do with social and economic organization and ideology. The answer to the question of causality will be found in these arenas in the coming years.

Bibliography

Aaby, B., 1993. Flora. In S. Hvass and B. Storgaard (eds.), *Digging into the Past,* pp. 24–7. Aarhus: Aarhus Universitetsforlag.

Acosta, P., and M. Pellicer, 1990. *La cueva de la Dehesilla (Jerez de la Fontera).* Jerez, Consejo Superior de Investigaciones Científicas.

Affleck, T. L., 1986. Excavations at Starr, Loch Doon 1985. *Glasgow Archaeological Society Bulletin* 21: 14–21.

Ahlfont, K., M. Guinard, E. Gustafsson, C. Olson, and S. Welinder, 1995. Patterns of Neolithic farming in Sweden. *Tor* 27: 133–84.

Åkerlund, A., 1996. *Human Responses to Shoreline Displacement: Living by the Sea in Eastern Middle Sweden during the Stone Age.* Stockholm: Riksantikvarieåmbetet.

Albrethsen, S. E., and E. Brinch Petersen, 1977. Excavation of a Mesolithic cemetery at Vedbæk, Denmark. *Acta Archaeologica* 47: 1–28.

Aldenderfer, M., 1992. Ritual, hierarchy, and change in foraging societies. *Journal of Anthropological Archaeology* 12: 1–40.

Alexander, J., 1978. Frontier studies and the earliest farmers in Europe. In D. Green, C. Haselgrove, and M. Spriggs (eds.), *Social Organisation and Settlement,* pp. 13–29. Oxford: British Archaeological Reports International Series 4.

Ambrose, S. H., and L. Norr, 1994. Experimental evidence for the relationship of the carbon isotope ratios of whole diet and dietary protein to those of bone collagen and carbonate. In J. Lambert and G. Grupe (eds.), *Prehistoric Human Bone: Archaeology at the Molecular Level,* pp. 143–67. Berlin: Springer Verlag.

Ammerman, A. J., 1989. On the Neolithic transition in Europe: a comment on Zvelebil and Zvelebil (1988). *Antiquity* 63: 162–5.

Ammerman, A. J., and L. L. Cavalli-Sforza, 1973. A population model for the diffusion of early farming in Europe. In C. Renfrew (ed.), *The Explanation of Culture Change,* pp. 343–57. London: Duckworth.

1984. *The Neolithic Transition and the Genetics of Population in Europe.* Princeton: Princeton University Press.

Ammerman, A., and C. R. Polglase, 1997. Analyses and descriptions of the obsidian collections from Arene Candide. In R. Maggi (ed.), *Arene Candide: A Functional and Environmental Assessment of the Holocene Sequence (Excavations Bernabo' Brea-Cardini 1940–50),* pp. 573–92. Rome: Istituto Italiano di Paleontologia Umana.

Andersen, N. H., 1990. Sarup. Two Neolithic enclosures in south-west Funen. *Journal of Danish Archaeology* 7: 11–34.

1993. Causewayed camps of the Funnel Beaker culture. In S. Hvass and B. Storgaard (eds.), *Digging Into the Past*, pp. 100–3. Aarhus: Aarhus Universitetsforlag.

Andersen, S. H., 1970. Brovst, en kystboplads fra ældre stenalder. *Kuml* 1969: 67–90.

1973. Overgangen fra ældre til yngre stenalder i Sydskandinavien set fra en mesolitisk synsvinkel. In P. Simonsen and G. Stamsø Munch (eds.), *Bonde – Veidemann: Bofast – ikke bofast i nordisk forhistorie*, pp. 26–44. Tromsø: Universitetsforlaget.

1975. An inland Ertebølle settlement in Jutland. *Kuml* 1974: 94–108.

1981. Ertebøllekunst. Nye fund af mønstrede Ertrebølleoldsager. *Kuml* 1980: 3–41.

1989. *Fra jæger til bonde: den ældste bondekultur i Danmark*. Acta Jutlandica 65, 3. Naturvidenskabelig Serie 8. Aarhus Universitetsforlag.

1991. Norsminde. A Køkkenmødding with Late Mesolithic and Early Neolithic occupation. *Journal of Danish Archaeology* 8: 13–40.

1993. Bjørnsholm, a stratified køkkenmødding on the Central Limfjord, North Jutland. *Journal of Danish Archaeology* 10: 59–96.

Andersen, S. H., and E. Johansen, 1992. An Early Neolithic Grave at Bjørnsholm, North Jutland. *Journal of Danish Archaeology* 9: 38–59.

Andersen, S. T., 1992. Early and Middle Neolithic agriculture in Denmark: pollen spectra from soils in burial mounds of the Funnel Beaker culture. *Journal of European Archaeology* 1: 153–80

Andersen, S. T., B. Odgaard, and P. Rasmussen, 1991. *Pollenanalytiske undersøgelser 1988–89–90 in gravhøje, Hassing Huse Mose, Skånsø, Gudme Sø, Kragsø og Kobbelhøje Mose*. Copenhagen: Dansk Geologisk Undersøgelse.

Andersen, S. T., and P. Rasmussen, 1993. *Geobotaniske undersøgelse af Kulturlandskabet Histories*. Copenhagen: DGU, Miljø ministeret.

Anderson, A., 1991. The chronology of New Zealand colonisation. *Antiquity* 65: 767–95.

Anderson, E., 1995. Flint technology in the Irish Later Mesolithic. MA thesis, University College Cork.

Anderson, P. (ed.), 1992. *Préhistoire de l'agriculture: nouvelles approches expérimentales et ethnographiques*. Paris: Editions du CNRS.

Anthony, D. W., 1986. The Kurgan culture, Indo-European origins, and the domestication of the horse: a reconsideration. *Current Anthropology* 27: 291–313.

1990. Migration in archaeology: the baby and the bathwater. *American Anthropologist* 92: 895–914.

1994. On subsistence change at the Mesolithic–Neolithic transition. *Current Anthropology* 35: 49–59.

Anthony, D. W., and D. Brown, 1991. The origins of horseback riding. *Antiquity* 65: 22–38.

Aparicio, J., 1988. *Les arrels del poble valencià y de la seua cultura*. Valencia: Academia de Cultura Valenciana.

Apel, J.-E., Y. Bäckström, F. Hallgren, K. Knutsson, P. Lekberg, E. Olsson, M. Steineke, and L. Sundström, 1995. Fågelbacken och trattbagarsamhallet. Samhallsorganisation och rituella samlingsplatser vid overgangen till en bofast tillvaro östra Mellansverige. *Tor* 27: 47–132.

ApSimon, A., 1976. Ballynagilly and the beginning and end of the Irish Neolithic. In S. J. de Laet (ed.), *Acculturation and Continuity*, Proceedings IVth Atlantic Colloquium, pp. 15–30. Bruges.

    1986. A chronological context for Irish megalithic tombs. *Journal of Irish Archaeology* 3: 5–15.

Araújo, A. C., 1993. A estação mesolítica do Forno da Telha. *Trabalhos de Antropologia e Etnologia* 33: 15–45.

    1998. A indústria lítica do concheiro de Poças de São Bento (vale do Sado) no seu contexto regional. *Revista Portuguesa de Arqueologia* 1(1).

Arbogast, R., and C. Jeunesse, 1990. Ensisheim 'Ratfeld'. Quelques données sur la chasse et l'élevage au Néolithique rubané en Alsace. In D. Cahen and M. Otte (eds.), *Rubané et Cardial*, pp. 287–98. Etudes et recherches archéologiques de l'université de Liège 39. Liège: Université de Liège.

Arias, P., 1991. *De cazadores a campesinos: la transición al neolítico en la región cantábrica*. Santander: Universidad de Cantabria, Asamblea Regional de Cantabria.

    1992. Estrategias económicas de las poblaciones del Epipaleolítico avanzado y el Neolítico en la región cantábrica. In A. Moure (ed.), *Elefantes, ciervos y ovicaprinos: economía y aprovechamiento del medio en la prehistoria de España y Portugal*, pp. 163–84. Santander: Universidad de Cantabria.

    1994a. El Neolitico de la región cantábrica. Nuevas perspectivas. *Trabalhos de Antropologia e Etnologia* 34: 93–118.

    1994b. Iberian hunter-gatherers and death. A review of Palaeolithic and Mesolithic funerary remains in the Peninsula. Paper presented at the International Conference on the Mesolithic of the Atlantic Façade, Santander (Spain), 1994.

    1997. Nacimiento o consolidación? El papel del fenómeno megalítico en los procesos de neolitización de la región cantábrica. In A. A. Rodríguez Casal (ed.), *O Neolítico atlántico e as orixes do megalitismo*, pp. 371–89. Santiago de Compostela: Universidade de Santiago de Compostela.

Arnaud, J. M., 1982. Néolithique ancien et processus de néolithisation dans le sud du Portugal. *Archéologie en Languedoc*, no. spécial (Actes du Colloque International de Préhistoire), pp. 29–48.

    1987. Os concheiros mesolíticos dos vales do Tagus e do Sado: semelhanças e diferenças. *Arqueologia* 15: 53–64.

    1989. The Mesolithic communities of the Sado Valley, Portugal in their ecological setting. In C. Bonsall (ed.), *The Mesolithic in Europe*, pp. 614–31. Edinburgh: John Donald.

    1990. Le substrat mésolithique et le processus de néolithisation dans le sud du Portugal. In D. Cahen and M. Otte (eds.), *Rubané et Cardial*, pp. 433–46. Etudes et recherches archéologiques de l'université de Liège 39. Liège: Université de Liège.

    1997. Mesolithic land-use in the Portuguese territory. Paper presented at the Annual Meeting of the European Association of Archaeologists. Ravenna, September 1997.

Arnold, D., 1985. *Ceramic Theory and Cultural Process*. Cambridge: Cambridge University Press.

Arthur, W. B., 1989. Competing technologies, increasing returns, and lock-in by historical events. *The Economic Journal* 99: 116–31.

1990. Positive feedbacks in the economy. *Scientific American* 262(2): 92–9.

Aubry, T., M. Fontugne, and M. H. Moura, 1997. Les occupations de la grotte de Buraca Grande depuis le Paléolithique supérieur et les apports de la séquence holocène à l'étude de la transition Mésolithique/Néolithique au Portugal. *Bulletin de la Société Préhistorique Française* 94: 182–90.

Aufdermauer, J., B. Dieckmann, and B. Fritsch, 1986. Die Untersuchungen in einer bandkeramischen Siedlung bei Singen am Hohentwiel, Kreis Konstanz. In D. Planck (ed.), *Archäologische Ausgrabungen in Baden-Württemberg 1985* pp. 51–4. Stuttgart: Konrad Theiss.

Aurenche, O., and J. Cauvin (eds.), 1989. *Néolithisations: Proche et Moyen Orient, Méditerranée orientale, Nord de l'Afrique, Europe méridionale, Chine, Amérique du sud.* Oxford: British Archaeological Reports International Series 516.

Bagolini, B., 1990. Contacts entre les courants danubiens et méditerranéens en Italie du nord. In D. Cahen and M. Otte (eds.), *Rubané et Cardial*, pp. 73–81. Etudes et recherches archéologiques de l'université de Liège 39. Liège: Université de Liège.

Bagolini, B., A. Broglio, and R. Lunz, 1983. Le Mésolithique des Dolomites. *Preistoria Alpina* 19: 15–36.

Bailey, R. C., and J. R. R. Annger, 1989. Net hunters vs. archers: variation in women's subsistence strategies in the Ituri forest. *Human Ecology* 17: 273–97.

Baillie, M. G. L., 1991. Suck in and smear: two related chronological problems for the 1990s. *Journal of Theoretical Archaeology* 2: 12–16.

1992. Dendrochronology and past environmental change. *Proceedings of the British Academy* 77: 5–23.

1995. *A Slice through Time.* London: Batsford.

Bakels, C. C., 1982. Der Mohn, die Linearbandkeramik und das westliche Mittelmeergebiet. *Archäologisches Korrespondenzblatt* 12: 11–13.

Bakka, E., and P. E. Kaland, 1971. Early farming in Hordaland, western Norway. *Norwegian Archaeological Review* 37: 41–60.

Balam, N. D., M. G. Bell, A. E. U. David, B. Levitan, R. Macphail, M. Robinson, and G. Scaifer, 1987. Prehistoric and Romano-British sites at Westward Ho! Devon archaeological and palaeoenvironmental surveys 1983–84. In N. D. Balam, B. Levitan, and V. Straker (eds.), *Studies in Palaeoeconomy and Environment in South West England*, pp. 163–264. Oxford: British Archaeological Reports British Series 181.

Balcer, B., 1980. A study of the socio-economic aspects of Neolithic flint working on the example of the Funnel Beaker culture (FBC). In R. Schild (ed.), *Unconventional Archaeology: New Approaches and Goals in Polish Archaeology.* Warsaw: Institute of Archaeology and Ethnology, Polish Academy of Sciences.

1983. *Wytwó rczosc Narzedzi Krzemiennych w Neolicie Ziem Polskich.* Wrocław: Polska Akademia Nauk.

Baldellou, V., and A. Castán, 1983. Excavaciones en la Cueva de Chaves de Bastaras (Casbas – Huesca). *Bolskan* 1: 9–37.

Baldellou, V., and P. Utrilla, 1985. Nuevas dataciones de radiocarbono de la prehistoria oscense. *Trabajos de Prehistoria* 42: 83–95.

Bandi, H., 1963. *Birsmatten-Basisgrotte: Eine mittelsteinzeitliche Fundstelle im unteren Birstal.* Bern: Acta Bernensia 1.

Bang-Andersen, S., 1996. Coast/inland relations in the Mesolithic of southern Norway. *World Archaeology* 27: 427–43.

Bar-Yosef, O., and A. Belfer-Cohen, 1992. From foraging to farming in the Mediterranean Levant. In A. B. Gebauer and T. D. Price (eds.),*Transitions to Agriculture in Prehistory*, pp. 21–48. Madison, WI: Prehistory Press.

Bar-Yosef, O., and R. Meadows, 1995. The origins of agriculture in the Near East. In T. D. Price and A. B. Gebauer (eds.), *Last Hunters – First Farmers: New Perspectives on the Prehistoric Transition to Agriculture*, pp. 39–94. Santa Fe: School for American Research Press.

Barbaza, M., J. Guilaine, and J. Vaquer, 1984. Fondaments chrono-culturels du Mésolithique en Languedoc occidental. *L'Anthropologie* 88: 345–65.

Barbaza, M., N. Valdeyron, J. André, F. Briois, H. Martin, S. Philibert, D. Allios, and E. Lignon, 1991. *Fontfaurés en Quercy*. Archives d'écologie préhistorique 11. Toulouse: Centre d'anthropologie des sociétés rurales.

Barbujani, G., R. R. Sokal, and N. L. Oden, 1995. Indo-European origins: a computer simulation test of five hypotheses. *American Journal of Physical Anthropology* 96: 109–32.

Barclay, G. J., I. A. Maxwell, G. S. Simpson, and D. A. Davidson, 1995. The Cleaven Dyke: a Neolithic cursus monument/bank barrow in Scotland. *Antiquity* 69: 317–26.

Barker, G., 1985. *Prehistoric Farming in Europe*. Cambridge: Cambridge University Press.

Barker, G. and D. Webley, 1978. Causewayed camps and Early Neolithic economies in central southern England. *Proceedings of the Prehistoric Society* 44: 161–86.

Barnett, W. K., 1989. The production and distribution of Early Neolithic pottery in the Aude valley, France. Ann Arbor, MI: University Microfilms International.

    1990a. Production and distribution of early pottery in the west Mediterranean. In W. D. Kingery (ed.), *The Changing Roles of Ceramics in Society: 26,000 BP to the present*, pp. 137–57. Ceramics and Civilization 5. Westerville: The American Ceramic Society.

    1990b. Small-scale transport of Early Neolithic pottery in the west Mediterranean. *Antiquity* 64: 859–65.

    1992. The physical analyses of Early Neolithic Impressed pottery from Gruta do Caldeirão. In João Zilhão (ed.), *Gruta do Caldeirão: O Neolítico Antigo*, pp. 297–312. Trabalhos de Arqueologia 6. Lisbon: Instituto Português do Património Arquitectónico e Arqueológico.

    1995. Putting the pot before the horse: earliest ceramics and the Neolithic transition in the western Mediterranean. In W. K. Barnett and J. W. Hoopes (eds.), *The Emergence of Pottery: Technology and Innovation in Ancient Societies*, pp. 79–88. Washington, DC: Smithsonian Institution Press.

    in press. Forming and fashion: manufacturing technologies and the spread of early pottery. In R. Harrison and M. Gillespie (eds.), *Eureka! The Archaeology of Innovation and Science*. Calgary: Proceedings of the 29th Annual Chacmool Conference, University of Calgary, Alberta.

Bateman, R. L., I. Goddard, R. O'Grady, V. A. Funk, R. Mooi, W. J. Kress, and P. Cannell, 1990. Speaking of forked tongues: the feasibility of reconciling human phylogeny and the history of language. *Current Anthropology* 31: 1–24.

Baudou, E., 1982. Det förhistoriska jordbruket i Norrland: bakgrunden i det arkeologiska fyndmaterialet. In T. Sjøvold (ed.), *Introduksjonen av Jordbruk i Norden*, pp. 163–72. Oslo: Universitetsforlag.

Baxter, M. S., 1990. Report of the international workshop of intercomparison of radiocarbon laboratories: a summary of the meeting. *Radiocarbon* 32: 389–91.

Becker, C. J., 1948. Mosefundne lerkar fra Yngre Stenalder. Studier over yngre stenalder i Danmark. *Aarbøger for Nordisk Oldkyndighed og Historie* 1947: 1–318.

1955. Stenalder bebyggelsen ved Store Valby i Vestsjælland. Problemer omkring tragtbægerkulturens ældste og yngste fase. *Aarbøger for Nordisk Oldkyndighed og Historie* 1954: 127–97.

1980. Katalog der Feuerstein/Hornstein-Bergwerke, Dänemark. In G. Weisberger (ed.), *5000 Jahre Feuersteinbergbau*, pp. 456–74. Bochum: Deutschen Bergbbau-Museum.

1993. Flintminer og flintdistribution ved Limfjorden. In J. Lund and J. Ringsted (eds.), *Kort- og Råstofstudier omkring Limfjorden*. Aalborg: Limfjordsprojektet.

Beeching, A., 1995. Nouveau regard sur le Néolithique ancien et moyen du bassin rhodanien. *Société préhistorique rhodanienne* 20: 93–111.

Behrends, R.-H., 1990. Ein Gräberfeld der Bandkeramik von Schwetzingen, Rhein-Neckar-Kreis. In D. Planck (ed.), *Archäologische Ausgrabungen in Baden-Württemberg 1989*, pp. 45–8. Stuttgart: Konrad Theiss.

Bell, M., and Walker, M. J., 1992. *Late Quaternary Environmental Change*. London: Longmans.

Bellwood, P., 1996. Phylogeny vs. reticulation in prehistory. *Antiquity* 70: 881–90.

Benac, A., 1957a. Crvena Stijena. *Bulletin du Musée de la République Populaire de Bosnie et Herzégovine (Sarajevo)* 12: 19–50.

1957b. Zelena Pecina. *Bulletin du Musée de la République Populaire de Bosnie et Herzégovine (Sarajevo)* 12: 61–92.

Benac, A. (ed.), 1975. *Crvena Stijena: Zbornik Radova*. Niksic.

Benac, A., and A. Brodar, 1957. *Crvena Stijena*. Sarajevo: Godisnjak.

Bender, B., 1978. Gatherer-hunter to farmer: a social perspective. *World Archaeology* 10: 204–20.

1985. Prehistoric developments in the American midcontinent and in Brittany, northwest France. In T. D. Price and J. A. Brown (eds.), *Prehistoric Hunter-Gatherers: The Emergence of Cultural Complexity*, pp. 21–57. New York: Academic Press.

1989. The roots of inequality. In D. Miller, M. Rowlands, and C. Tilley (eds.), *Dominance and Resistance*, pp. 83–95. London: Unwin, Hyman.

1990. The dynamics of nonhierarchical societies. In S. Upham (ed.), *The Evolution of Political Systems*, pp. 62–86. Cambridge: Cambridge University Press.

Bennike, P., 1985. *Palaeopathology of Danish Skeletons: A Comparative Study of Demography, Disease and Injury.* Copenhagen: Akademisk Forlag.

1993. The people. In S. Hvass and B. Storgaard (eds.), *Digging into the Past: 25 Years of Danish Archaeology*, pp. 34–9. Aarhus: Universitetsforlag.

1995. Danmarks første bønder. *Humaniora* 4: 6–10.

Bennike, P., and K. Ebbesen. 1987. The bog find from Sigersdal. Human sacrifice in the Early Neolithic. *Journal of Danish Archaeology* 5: 83–115.

Berciu, D., 1958. Neolithic preceramic in Balcani. *Studii si Cercetari de Istorie Veche* 9: 1–100.

Berg, S., 1995. *Landscape of the Monuments*. Stockholm: Arkeologiska Undersökningar Skrifter Nr 6.

Berglund, B. E., 1985. Early agriculture in Scandinavia: research problems related to pollen-analytical studies. *Norwegian Archaeological Review* 18: 24–70.

Berglund, B. E. (ed.), 1991. *The Cultural Landscape during 6000 years in Southern Sweden – the Ystad Project*. Ecological Bulletin 41. Lund.

Berglund, B. E., S. Helmfrid, and Å. Hyenstrand, 1994. Landscape and settlements: ten thousand years in Sweden. In S. Helmfrid (ed.), *National Atlas of Sweden*, p. 17. Copenhagen: Munksgaard.

Berglund, B. E., L. Larsson, N. Lewan, E. Gunilla, A. Olsson, and S. Stankjö, 1991. Ecological and social factors behind the landscape changes. In B. E. Bjerglund (ed.), *The Cultural Landscape during 6000 Years in Southern Sweden – the Ystad Project*, pp. 425–45. Ecological Bulletin 41. Lund.

Bernabeu, J., 1989. *La tradición cultural de las cerámicas impresas en la zona oriental de la Península Ibérica*. Valencia, Servicio de Investigación Prehistórica, Serie de Trabajos Varios, 86.

1996. Indigenismo y migracionismo. Aspectos de la Neolitizacion en la fachada oriental de la Peninsula Ibérica. *Trabajos de Prehistoria* 53: 37–54.

Bertranpetit, J., and L. L. Cavalli-Sforza, 1991. A genetic reconstruction of the history of the population of the Iberian peninsula. *Annals of Human Genetics* 55: 51–67.

Biagi, P., 1985. Neue Aspekte zur Neolithisierung Norditaliens. *Zeitschrift für Archäologie* 19: 11–22.

Biagi, P. (ed.), 1990. *The Neolithization of the Alpine Region*. Monografie di Natura Bresciana 13. Brescia: Museo civico di Scienze naturali.

Biagi, P., L. Castelletti, M. Cremaschi, B. Sala, and C. Tozzi, 1989. Popolazione e territorio nell'Appennino tosco-emiliano e nel tratto centrale del Bacino del Po, tra il IX ed il V millenio. *Emilia Preromana* 8: 13–36.

Biagi, P., E. Starnini, and B. Voytek, 1993. The Late Mesolithic and Early Neolithic settlement of northern Italy: recent considerations. *Porocilo* 21: 45–69.

Bicho, N. F., 1993. Late glacial prehistory of central and southern Portugal. *Antiquity* 67: 761–75.

Binder, D., 1987. *Le Néolithique ancien provençal: typologie et technologie des outillages lithiques*. Supplément, Gallia Préhistoire 24. Paris: CNRS.

1989. Aspects de la néolithisation dans les aires padane, provençale et ligure. In O. Aurenche and J. Cauvin (eds.), *Néolithisations*, pp. 199–226. Oxford: British Archaeological Reports International Series 516.

1995. Eléments pour la chronologie du Néolithique ancien à céramique imprimée dans le Midi. In *Chronologies néolithiques: de 6000 à 2000 avant notre ére dans le Bassin rhodanien*. Documents du Département d'Anthropologie de l'Université de Genéve 20.

Binder, D. (ed.), 1991. *Une économie de chasse au Néolithique ancien: la grotte Lombard à Saint-Vallier de Thiey*. Monographies du CRA 5. Paris: CNRS.

Binder D., J. E. Brochier, H. Duday, D. Helmer, P. Marinval, S. Thiébault, and J. Wattez, 1993. L'abri Pendimoun à Castellar (Alpes-Maritimes): nouvelles données sur le complexe culturel de la céramique imprimée méditerranéenne dans son contexte stratigraphique. *Gallia Préhistoire* 35: 177–251.

Binder, D., and J. Courtin, 1986. Les styles céramiques du Néolithique ancien provençal. In J.-P. Demoule and J. Guilaine (eds.), *Le Néolithique de la France*, pp. 83–93. Paris: Picard.

1987. Nouvelles vues sur les processus de la néolithisation dans le sud-est de la France. In J. Guilaine, J. Courtin, J.-L. Roudil, and J.-L. Vernet (eds.), *Premières communautés paysannes en Méditerranée occidentale*, pp. 491–9. Paris: CNRS.

Binder, D., and C. Perlès, 1990. Stratégies de gestion des outillages lithiques au Néolithique. *Paléo* 2: 257–83.

Binford, L. R., 1968. Post-Pleistocene adaptations. In S. R. Binford and L. R. Binford (eds.), *New Perspectives in Archaeology*, pp. 313–41. Chicago: Aldine.

1978. *Nunamiut Ethnoarchaeology*. New York: Academic Press.

1983. *In Pursuit of the Past*. London: Thames and Hudson.

Bintz, P., J. Evin, and R. Picave, 1995. Evolutions culturelles du Mésolithique au Néolithique moyen en Vercors et dans les Alpes du Nord. In *Chronologies néolithiques: de 6000 à 2000 avant notre ére dans le Bassin rhodanien*. Documents du Département d'Anthropologie de l'Université de Genéve 20.

Blankholm, H. P., 1987. Late Mesolithic hunter-gatherers and the transition to farming in southern Scandinavia. In P. Rowley-Conwy, M. Zvelebil, and H. P. Blankholm (eds.), *Mesolithic Northwest Europe: Recent Trends*, pp. 155–62. Sheffield: University of Sheffield Department of Archaeology and Prehistory.

Blazic, S., 1992. Fauna Donja Branjevina: preliminary report. In D. Srejovic (ed.), *Arheologija i Prirodne Nauke*, pp. 65–7. Belgrade: Serbian Academy of Sciences and Arts.

Bloedow, E. F., 1991. The "Aceramic" Neolithic phase in Greece reconsidered. *Journal of Mediterranean Archaeology* 4:1–43.

Boaz, J., 1994. Site utilization in the Dokkfløy, eastern Norway, 8000–2500 B.P. PhD thesis, Department of Anthropology, University of Wisconsin-Madison.

Bogdanovic, M., 1988. Architecture and structural features at Divostin. In A. McPherron and D. Srejovic (eds.), *Divostin and the Neolithic of Central Serbia*, pp. 35–142. Ethnology Monographs 10. Pittsburgh: University of Pittsburgh.

Bogucki, P., 1979. Tactical and strategic settlements in the early Neolithic of lowland Poland. *Journal of Anthropological Research* 35(2):238–46.

1982. *Early Neolithic Subsistence and Settlement in the Polish Lowlands*. Oxford: British Archaeological Reports International Series 150.

1984. Ceramic sieves of the Linear Pottery culture and their economic implications. *Oxford Journal of Archaeology* 3(1): 1530.

1988. *Forest Farmers and Stockherders: Early Agriculture and Its Consequences in North-Central Europe*. Cambridge: Cambridge University Press.

1995a. The largest buildings in the world 7,000 years ago. *Archaeology* 48(6): 57–9.

1995b. The Linear Pottery culture of Central Europe: conservative colonists? In W. K. Barnett and J. W. Hoopes (eds.), *The Emergence of Pottery: Technology and Innovation in Ancient Societies*, pp. 89–97. Washington: Smithsonian Institution Press.

1996. The spread of early farming in Europe. *American Scientist* 84: 242–53.

Bogucki, P., and R. Grygiel, 1983. Early farmers of the North European Plain. *Scientific American* 248(4): 104–12.

1993 The first farmers of northcentral Europe. *Journal of Field Archaeology* 20(3): 399–426.

Bökönyi, S., 1970. Animal remains from Lepenski Vir. *Science* 167:1702–4.

1974. *History of Domestic Mammals in Central and Eastern Europe.* Budapest: Akademiai Kiadó.

1978. The vertebrate fauna from Vlasac. In D. Srejovic and Z. Letica (eds.), *Vlasac*, pp. 35–68. Belgrade: Serbian Academy of Sciences and Arts.

1988. The Neolithic fauna from Divostin. In A. McPherron and D. Srejovic (eds.), *Divostin and the Neolithic of Central Serbia*, pp. 419–46. Ethnology Monographs 10. Pittsburgh: University of Pittsburgh.

1989. Animal husbandry of the Koros-Starcevo Complex: its origin and development. In *Neolithic of Southeastern Europe and its Near Eastern Connections* 2, pp. 13–16. Budapest: Varia Archaeologica Hungarica.

Bolomey, A., 1973. An outline of the late Epipalaeolithic economy at the "Iron Gates": the evidence on bones. *Dacia* 17:41–52.

1978. Why no Early Neolithic in Dobrogea? *Dacia* 22: 5–16.

Bonsall, C. (ed.), 1989. *The Mesolithic in Europe: Proceedings of the IIIrd International Symposium on the Mesolithic.* Edinburgh: John Donald.

Bonsall, C., R. Lennon, K. McSweeney, C. Stewart, D. Harkness, V. Boroneant, L. Bartosiewica, R. Payton, and J. Chapman, 1997. Mesolithic and Early Neolithic in the Iron Gates: a paleodietary perspective. *Journal of European Archaeology* 5: 51–92.

Bonsall, C., D. Sutherland, R. Tipping, and J. Cherry, 1989. The Eskmeals Project: Late Mesolithic settlement and environment in north west England. In C. Bonsall (ed.), *The Mesolithic in Europe*, pp. 175–205. Edinburgh: John Donald.

Boone, J. L., 1992. Competition, conflict, and development of social hierarchies. In E. A. Smith and B. A. Winterhalder (eds.), *Evolutionary Ecology and Human Behavior*, pp. 301–38. New York: Aldine de Gruyter.

Borojevic, K., 1988. Differences in plant macro remains from the neolithic level at Gomalava and the Neolithic site of Opovo. In N. Tasic and J. Petrovic (eds.), *Gomalava: hronologija i stratigrafija u praistoriji i antici podunavlja i jugoistocne Evrope*, pp. 109–16. Novi Sad: Vojvodanski Muzej and Balkanoloski Institut SAN.

Boroneant, V., 1970. La période Epipaléolithique sur la rive roumaine des Portes de Fer du Danube. *Praehistorische Zeitschrift* 45(1): 1–25.

1981. Betrachtungen über das Epipalaeolithikum (Mesolithikum) in Rumänien. In B. Gramsch (ed.), *Mesolithikum in Europa* 2, pp. 289–94. Berlin: Deutscher Verlag der Wissenschaften.

1990. Le site de Schela Cladovei: problèmes posés par la transition de la culture Cris Starcevo à la culture Vinca. In D. Srejovic and N. Tasic (eds.), *Vinca and its World*, pp. 143–7. Belgrade: Serbian Academy of Sciences and Arts.

Bosch, P. W., 1979. A Neolithic flint mine. *Scientific American* 240: 126–32.

Bostwick Bjerck, L. G., 1988. Remodelling the Neolithic in southern Norway: another attack on a traditional problem. *Norwegian Archaeological Review* 21: 21–52.

Bowman, S. G. E., J. C. Ambers, and M. N. Leese, 1990. Re-evaluation of British Museum radiocarbon dates issued between 1980 and 1984. *Radiocarbon* 32: 59–79.

Bradley, J., 1991. Excavations at Moynagh Lough, County Meath. *Journal of the Royal Society of Antiquaries of Ireland* 121: 5–26.

Bradley, R., 1984. *The Social Foundations of Prehistoric Britain*. London: Longman.

1996. Long houses, long mounds and Neolithic enclosures. *Journal of Material culture* 1: 239–56.

Bradley, R., and M. Edmonds, 1993. *Interpreting the Axe Trade*. Cambridge: Cambridge University Press.

Braidwood, R. J., 1960. The agricultural revolution. *Scientific American* 203: 130–42.

Brandt, D. von, 1988. Häuser. In U. Boelicke, D. von Brandt, J. Lüning, P. Stehli, and A. Zimmermann, *Der bandkeramische Siedlungsplatz Langweiler 8, Gemeinde Aldenhoven, Kreis Düren*, pp. 36–289. Rheinische Ausgrabung 28. Cologne: Rheinland-Verlag.

Bratlund, B., 1993. The bone remains of mammals and birds from the Bjørnsholm shell-mound. A preliminary report. *Journal of Danish Archaeology* 10: 97–104.

Bratt, B., 1996. *Stenalder i Stokholms Lan: Tva Seminarier vid Stockholms Lans Museum*. Stockholm: Lans Museum.

Brinch Petersen, E., 1973. A survey of the Late Palaeolithic and the Mesolithic of Denmark. In S. K. Kozlowski (ed.), *The Mesolithic in Europe*, pp. 77–127. Warsaw: Warsaw University Press.

Brindley, A., and J. N. Lanting, 1989–90. Radiocarbon dates for Neolithic single burials. *Journal of Irish Archaeology* 5: 1–7.

1995. Irish bog bodies. The radiocarbon dates. In R. C. Turner and R. G. Scaife (eds.), *Bog Bodies: New Discoveries and New Perspectives*, pp. 133–6. London: British Museum Press.

Brochier, J. E., 1990. Des techniques géoarchéologiques au service de l'étude des paysages et de leur exploitation. Archéologie et espaces. *Rencontres Internationales d'archéologie et d'Histoire d'Antibes* 4: 453–72.

Broodbank, C., and T. F. Strasser, 1991. Migrant farmers and the Neolithic colonization of Crete. *Antiquity* 65: 233–45.

Browall, H., 1986. *Alvastra på lbyggnad: social och ekonomisk bas*. Theses and Papers in North European Archaeology 15. Stockholm: Institute of Archaeology.

1991. Om förhållandet mellan trattbägarkultur och gropkeramisk kultur. In H. Browall, P. Persson, and K. G. Sjögren (eds.), *Västsvenska stenålderstudier*, pp. 111–42. GOTARC Serie C, Arkeologiska skrifter 8. Göteborg: Institute of Archaeology.

Brown, K. A., 1991. Settlement and social organization in the Neolithic of the Tavoliere, Apulia. In E. Herring, R. Whitehouse, and J. Wilkins (eds.), *Papers of the Fourth Conference of Italian Archaeology, 1: The Archaeology of Power*, pp. 9–25. London: Accordia Research Centre.

Brukner, B., 1980. A contribution to the investigation of similarities and differences between the Starcevo and Körös group. In J. Kozlowski and J. Machnik (eds.), *Problémes de la Neolithisation dans certaines regions de l'Europe*, pp. 49–55. Kraków: Ossolineum.

Brukner, B., 1982. Ein Beitrag zur Formierung der neolithischen und äneolithischen Siedlungen im jugoslawischen Donaugebiet. In D. Papenfuss and V. M. Strocka (eds.), *Palast und Hütte: Beiträge zum Bauen und Wohnen im Altertum von Archäologen, Vor- und Frühgeschichtlern*, pp. 141–51. Mainz am Rhein: Verlag Philipp von Zabern.

Brukner, B., B. Jovanovi, and N. Tasi, 1974. *Praistorija Vojvodine*. Novi Sad: Institut za Izuçavanje Istorije Vojvodin.

Brumfiel, E. M., and T. K. Earle (eds.), 1987. *Specialization, Exchange, and Complex Societies*. Cambridge: Cambridge University Press.

Brunton, R., 1975. Why do the Trobriands have chiefs? *Man* 10: 544–58.

Budja, M., 1993. Neolitizacija Evrope: Slovenska Perspectiva. The neolithization of Europe. *Slovenian Aspect. Porocilo o rziskovanju paleolitika, neolitika in eneolitika v Slovejini* 21: 163–93.

1996. Neolithization in the Caput Adriae region: between Herodotus and Cavalli-Sforza. *Porocilo o rziskovanju paleolitika, neolitika in eneolitika v Slovejini* 23: 6976.

Burenhult, G., 1984. *The Archaeology of Carrowmore, Co. Sligo*. Theses and Papers in North European Archaeology 14. Stockholm: Institute of Archaeology.

Buttler, W., and W. Haberey, 1936. *Die bandkeramische Ansiedlung bei KölnLindenthal*. Berlin: Walter de Gruyter.

Byers, D. S., 1967. *The Prehistory of the Tehuacan Valley*. Austin: University of Texas Press.

Calafell, F., and J. Bertranpetit, 1993. The genetic history of the Iberian peninsula: a simulation. *Current Anthropology* 34: 735–45.

Cardoso, J. L., J. R. Carreira, and O. V. Ferreira, 1996. Novos elementos para o estudo do Neolítico antigo da região de Lisboa. *Estudos Arqueológicos de Oeiras* 6: 9–26.

Carvalho, A. F., and J. Zilhão, 1994. O povoado neolítico do Laranjal de Cabeço das Pias (Torres Novas). In *Actas das V Jornadas Arqueológicas (Lisboa, 1993) 2*, pp. 53–67. Lisbon: Associação dos Arqueólogos Portugueses.

Case, H., 1961. Irish Neolithic pottery: distribution and sequence. *Proceedings of the Prehistoric Society* 27: 174–233.

1969a. Settlement patterns in the north Irish Neolithic. *Ulster Journal of Archaeology* 32: 3–27.

1969b. Neolithic explanations. *Antiquity* 43: 176–86.

Casseldine, C., and J. Hatton, 1993. The development of High Moor on Dartmoor, fire and the influence of Mesolithic activity on vegetation change. In F. M. Chambers (ed.), *Climate Change and Human Impact on the Landscape*, pp. 119–31. London: Chapman and Hall.

Cauvin, J., 1989. La néolithisation au Levant et sa première diffusion. In O. Aurenche and J. Cauvin (eds.), *Néolithisations*. Oxford: British Archaeological Reports International Series 516.

1992. Problèmes et méthodes pour les débuts de l'agriculture: point de vue de l'archéologue. In P. C. Anderson (ed.), *Préhistoire de l'agriculture*, pp. 265–8. Monographie du CNRS. Paris: CNRS.

1994. *Naissance des divinités. Naissance de l'agriculture. La Révolution des symboles au Néolithique*. Paris: CNRS.

Cavalli-Sforza, L. L., 1991. Genes, peoples and languages. *Scientific American* 265(5): 72–8.

1996. The spread of agriculture and nomadic pastoralism: insights from genetics, linguistics and archaeology. In D. Harris (ed.), *The Origins and Spread of Agriculture and Pastoralism in Eurasia*, pp. 51–70. London: UCL Press.

Cavalli-Sforza, L., and E. Minch, 1997. Paleolithic and Neolithic lineages in the European mitochrondrial gene pool. *American Journal of Human Genetics* 61: 247–51.

Cavalli-Sforza, L. L., A. Piazza, and P. Menozzi, 1994. *The History and Geography of Human Genes*. Princeton, NJ: Princeton University Press.

Chapman, J., 1981. *The Vinca Culture*. Oxford: British Archaeological Reports International Series 117.

1988. From "space" to "place": a model of dispersed settlement and Neolithic society. In C. Burgess (ed.), *Enclosures and Defences in the Neolithic of Western Europe*, pp. 25–46. Oxford: British Archaeological Reports International Series 403.

1989a. Demographic trends in neothermal south-east Europe. In C. Bonsall (ed.), *The Mesolithic in Europe*, pp. 500–15. Edinburgh: John Donald.

1989b. The early Balkan village. In S. Bökönyi (ed.), *Neolithic of Southeastern Europe and its Near Eastern Connections*, pp. 33–55. Budapest: Varia Archaeologica Hungarica.

1990. Regional study of the North Sumadija region. In R. Tringham and D. Krstic (eds.), *Selevac: A Neolithic Village in Yugoslavia*, pp. 13–44. Monumenta Archaeologica 15. Los Angeles: UCLA Institute of Archaeology Press.

1991. Social inequality on Bulgarian tells and the Varna problem. In R. Samson (ed.), *The Social Archaeology of Houses*, pp. 31–44. Glasgow: Cruithne Press.

1993. Social power in the Iron Gates Mesolithic. In J. Chapman and P. Dolukhanov (eds.), *Cultural Transformations and Interactions in Eastern Europe*, pp. 71–122. Aldershot: Avebury Press.

1994a. Social power in the early farming communities of eastern Hungary – perspectives from the Upper Tisza region. *Josa Andras Muzeum Evkönyve* 36: 79–99.

1994b. The origins of farming in southeast Europe. *Préhistoire Européenne* 6: 133–56.

Chapman, J., and P. Dolukhanov, 1993. Cultural transformations and interactions in eastern europe: theory and terminology. In J. Chapman and P. Dolukhanov (eds.), *Cultural Transformations and Interactions in Eastern Europe*, pp. 1–36. Aldershot: Avebury Press.

Chapman, J., and J. Müller, 1990. Early farmers in the Mediterranean basin: the Dalmatian evidence. *Antiquity* 64: 127–34.

Cherry, J. F., 1990. The first colonization of the Mediterranean islands: a review of recent research. *Journal of Mediterranean Archaeology* 3: 145–221.

Childe, V. G., 1925. *The Dawn of European Civilisation*. London: Kegan Paul.

1928. *The Most Ancient East: The Oriental Prelude to European Prehistory*. London: Kegan, Paul, Trench and Trubner.

1929. *The Danube in Prehistory*. Oxford: Oxford University Press.

1940. *Prehistoric Communities of the British Isles*. London: Chambers.

1957. *The Dawn of European Civilisation*, 6th edn. London: Kegan Paul.

1958. *The Prehistory of European Society*. London: Penguin Books.

Christensen, C., 1993. Land and sea. In S. Hvass and B. Storgaard (eds.), *Digging into the Past*, pp. 20–3. Aarhus: Aarhus Universitetsforlag.

Clark, J. D., and S. A. Brandt, 1984. *From Hunters to Farmers: The Causes and Consequences of Food Production in Africa*. Berkeley: University of California Press.

Clark, J. E., and M. Blake, 1994. The power of prestige: competitive generosity and the emergence of rank societies in lowland Mesoamerica. In E. M. Brumfiel and

J. W. Fox (eds.), *Factional Competition and Political Development in the New World*, pp. 17–30. Cambridge: Cambridge University Press.

Clark, J. E., and W. J. Parry, 1991. Craft specialization and cultural complexity. *Research in Economic Anthropology* 12: 289–346.

Clark, J. G. D., 1948. Objects of south Scandinavian flint in the northernmost provinces of Norway, Sweden and Finland. *Proceedings of the Prehistoric Society* 9: 219–32.

1952. *Prehistoric Europe: The Economic Basis*. London: Methuen.

1965. Radiocarbon dating and the expansion of farming culture from the Near East over Europe. *Proceedings of the Prehistoric Society* 31: 57–73.

1980. *Mesolithic Prelude*. Edinburgh: Edinburgh University Press.

Clark, J. S., C. Fastie, G. Hurtt, S. T. Jackson, C. Johnson, G. King, M. Lewis, J. Lynch, S. Pacala, C. Prentice, E. W. Schupp, T. Webb III, and P. Wyckoff, 1998. Reid's paradox of rapid plant migration – dispersal theory and interpretation of paleoecological records. *BioScience* 48: 13–24.

Clarke, D. L., 1976. Mesolithic Europe: the economic basis. In I. Sieveking, I. J. Longworth, and K. E. Wilson (eds.), *Problems in Economic and Social Archaeology*, pp. 449–81. London: Duckworth.

Clason, A. T., 1980. Padina and Starcevo: game, fish, and cattle. *Palaeohistoria* 22:142–73.

Clutton-Brock, J. (ed.), 1989. *The Walking Larder: Patterns of Domestication, Pastoralism, and Predation*. London: Heinemann and The British Museum.

Cohen, M. N., 1977. *The Food Crisis in Prehistory*. New Haven, CN: Yale University Press.

Coles, J., 1971. The early settlement of Scotland: excavations at Morton, Fife. *Proceedings of the Prehistoric Society* 38: 284–366.

1983. Morton revisited. In A. O'Connor and D. V. Clarke (eds.), *From the Stone Age to the Forty Five*, pp. 9–18. Edinburgh: Edinburgh University Press.

Collins, A. E. P., 1976. Dooeys Cairn, Ballymacaldrack, Co. Antrim. *Ulster Journal of Archaeology* 39: 1–7.

Constandse-Westermann, T. S., and R. R. Newell, 1989. Limb laterisation and social stratification in western Mesolithic societies. In I. Herskovitz (ed.), *People and Culture in Change*, pp. 405–34. Oxford: British Archaeological Reports International Series 508.

Constantin, C., 1985. *Fin du Rubané: céramique du Limbourg et postRubané*. Oxford: British Archaeological Reports International Series 273.

Constantini, L., 1989. Plant exploitation at Grotta dell'Uzzo Sicily: new evidence for the transition from Mesolithic to Neolithic subsistence in southern Europe. In D. H. Harris and G. C. Hillman (eds.), *Foraging to Farming: The Evolution of Plant Domestication*, pp. 197–206. London: Unwin Hyman.

Cooney, G., and E. Grogan, 1994. *Irish Prehistory: A Social Perspective*. Dublin: Wordwell.

Costantini, G., and J. Maury, 1986. Le néolithique ancien de l'abri de la Combe-Grèze, commune de la Cresse (Aveyron). *Bulletin de la Société Préhistorique Française* 83: 436–51.

Costin, C. L., 1991. Craft specialization: issues in defining, documenting, and explaining the organization of production. *Archaeological Method and Theory* 3: 1–56.

Coudart, A., 1991. Social structure and relationships in prehistoric small-scale societies: the Bandkeramik groups in Neolithic Europe. In S. Gregg (ed.), *Between Bands and States*, pp. 295–320. Carbondale, IL: Southern Illinois University Press.

Courtin, J., 1975. Le Mésolithique de la Baume Fontbrégoua à Salernes (Var). *Cahiers Ligures de Préhistoire et d'Archéologie* 24: 227–43.

Courtin, J., J. Evin, and Y. Thommeret, 1985. Révision de la stratigraphie et de la chronologie absolue de Châteauneuf-les-Martigues (Bouches-du-Rhône). *L'Anthropologie* 89: 543–56.

Courty, M. A., R. I. McPhail, and J. Wattez, 1992. Soil micromorphological indicators of pastoralism, with special reference to Arene Candide, Finale Ligure, Italy. *Istituto Internazionale di Studi Liguri*: 127–50.

Cowan, C. W., and P. J. Watson (eds.), 1992. *The Origins of Agriculture: An International Perspective*. Washington, DC: Smithsonian Institution Press.

Cremonesi, G., C. Meluzzi, C. Pitti, and B. Wilkens, 1984. Grotta Azzurra, scavi 1982. *Societa per la Protohistoria della Regione Friuli-Venezia Giulia* 5: 21–64.

Cross, J. R., 1993. Craft specialization in nonstratified societies. *Research in Economic Anthropology* 14: 16–84.

Czerniak, L., 1994. *Wczesny i ´Srodkowej Okres Neolitu na Kujawach, 5400–3650 p.n.e.* Poznan: Polish Academy of Science, Institute of Archaeology and Ethnology.

Cziesla, E., 1993. The 6. millennium BC in southwestern Germany: regional Late-Mesolithic, La Hoguette and Bandkeramik. Unpublished manuscript.

Darvill, T., 1987. *Prehistoric Britain*. London: Batsford.

1996. Prehistoric buildings in England, Wales and the Isle of Man. In T. Darvill and J. Thomas (eds.), *Neolithic Houses in Northwest Europe and Beyond*, pp. 77–112. Oxbow Monographs 57. Oxford: Oxbow Books.

Darwin, C., 1868. *The Variation of Plants and Animals under Domestication*. London: J. Murray and Sons.

de Candolle, A., 1882. *Origine des plantes cultivées*. Paris: Germer Baillière.

de Laubenfels, D. J., 1981. Ethnic geography of the Neolithic. *Mankind Quarterly* 22: 119–43.

de Roever, P., 1979. The pottery from Swifterbant – Dutch Ertebølle? *Helinium* 19:13–27.

De Valera, R., 1960. The court cairns of Ireland. *Proceedings of the Royal Irish Academy* 60: 9–140.

Deckers, P. H., 1979. The flint material from Swifterbant, earlier Neolithic of the northern Netherlands. I. Sites S-2, S-4, and S-51. *Palaeohistoria* 21:143–80.

Degarchev, V., 1989. Neolithic and Bronze Age cultural communities of the steppe zone of the USSR. *Antiquity* 63:793–802.

Deichmüller, J., 1969. Die Neolithische Moorsiedlung Hüde 1 am Dümmer, Kreis Grafschaft Diepholz. *Neue Ausgrabungen und Forshungen in Niedersachsen* 1: 28–36.

Demoule, J.-P., and C. Perlès, 1993. The Greek Neolithic: a new review. *Journal of World Prehistory* 7: 355–416.

Dennell, R. W., 1983. *European Economic Prehistory: A New Approach*. London: Academic Press.

1985. The hunter-gatherer:agricultural frontier in prehistoric temperate Europe.

In S. Green and S. Perlman (eds.), *The Archaeology of Frontiers and Boundaries*, pp. 113–39. London: Academic Press.

1992. The origins of crop agriculture in Europe. In C. W. Cowan and P. J. Watson (eds.), *The Origins of Agriculture: An International Perspective*, pp. 71–100. Washington, DC: Smithsonian Institution Press.

Dergachev, V., A. Sherratt, and O. Larina, 1991. Recent results of Neolithic research in Moldavia. *Oxford Journal of Archaeology* 10: 1–16.

D'Errico, F., 1988. Le burin néolithique sur encoche latérale ou "bulino di Ripabianca": approche fonctionnelle. In S. Beyries (ed.), *Industries lithiques: tracéologie et technologie*, pp. 127–64. Oxford: British Archaeological Reports International Series 411.

Desse, J., 1984. Les restes des poissons dans les fosse omaliennes. In M. Otte (ed.), *Les fouilles de la Place St-Lambert á Liège*, pp. 239–40. Etudes et recherches archéologiques de l'Université Liège. Liège: Université de Liège.

1987. La pêche: son rôle dans l'économie des premières sociétés néolithiques en Méditerranée occidentale. In J. Guilaine, J. Courtin, J.-L. Roudil, and J.-L. Vernet (eds.), *Premières communautés paysannes en Méditerranée occidentale*, pp. 281–6. Paris: CNRS.

Diamond, J., 1992. *The Rise and Fall of the Third Chimpanzee*. London: Vintage.

Dimitrijevic, S., 1974. Problem stupnjevanja starcevacke kulture s posebnim obziram na doprinos juznopanonskih nalazista resavanju ovih problema. *Materijali Srpskog Arheoloskog Drustva* 10: 59–122.

Döhle, H.-J., 1993. Haustierhaltung und Jagd in der Linienbandkeramik? Ein Überblick. *Zeitschrift für Archäologie* 27: 105–24.

Dolukhanov, P. M., 1979. *Ecology and Economy in Neolithic Eastern Europe*. London: Duckworth.

1986. The late Mesolithic and the transition to food production in eastern Europe. In M. Zvelebil (ed.), *Hunters in Transition*, pp. 109–20. Cambridge: Cambridge University Press.

1993. Foraging and farming groups in north-eastern and north-western Europe: identity and interaction. In J. Chapman and P. Dolukhanov (eds.), *Cultural Transformations and Interactions in Eastern Europe*, pp. 122–45. Aldershot: Avebury.

Domanska, L., 1995. *Geneza Krzemienizrstwa Kultury Pucharó w Lejkowatych na Kujawach*. Lódz: University Press.

Donahue, R., 1992. Desperately seeking ceres: a critical examination of current models for the transition to agriculture in Mediterranean Europe. In A. B. Gebauer and T. D. Price (eds.), *Transitions to Agriculture in Prehistory*, pp. 73–80. Madison, WI: Prehistory Press.

Drasovean F., 1989. Observatii per marginea unor materiale inedite privind raporturile dintre culturile Starcevo-Cris, Vinca A si lumea liniara in nordul Banatului. *Apulum* 24:9–48.

Ducos, P., 1958. Le gisement de Châteauneuf-les-Martigues (B.-du R.). Les mammifères et les problèmes de la domestication. *Bulletin du Musée d'Anthropologie Préhistorique de Monaco* 5: 118–33.

Dzhambazov, N., 1964. Prouchvania na Paleolitnata i Mezolitnata Kultura v Balgaria. *Arheologiya* 6: 67–76.

Ebbesen, K., 1975. *Die jüngere Trichterbecherkultur auf den dänischen Inseln*. Arkæologiske Studier 2. Copenhagen: Akademisk Forlag.

Echallier, J. C., and J. Courtin, 1994. Approche minéralogique de la poterie du Néolithique ancien de la baume Fontbrégoua à Salernes (Var). *Gallia Préhistoire* 36: 267–97.

Edmonds, M., and C. Richards (eds.), 1998. *Understanding the Neolithic of North-Western Europe*. Glasgow: Cruithne Press.

Edwards, K., 1989. The cereal pollen record and early agriculture. In A. Milles, D. Williams, and N. Gardner (eds.), *The Beginnings of Agriculture*, pp. 113–47. Oxford: British Archaeological Reports. International Series 496.

Edwards, K., M. Ansell, and B. Carter, 1983. New Mesolithic sites in S.W. Scotland and their importance as indicators of inland penetration. *Transactions of the Dumfriesshire and Galloway Natural History and Antiquarian Society* 58: 9–14.

Edwards, K. J., and K. R. Hirons, 1984. Cereal pollen grains in pre-elm decline deposits: implications for the earliest agriculture in Britain and Ireland. *Journal of Archaeological Science* 11: 71–80.

Ehret, C., 1988. Language change and the material correlates of language and ethnic shift. *Antiquity* 62: 564–73.

Ellis, L., 1984. *The Cucuteni-Tripolye culture: A Study in Technology and the Origins of Complex Society*. Oxford: British Archaeological Reports. International Series 217.

Elmendorf, W. W., 1971. Coast Salish status ranking and intergroup ties. *Southwestern Journal of Anthropology* 27: 353–80.

Elster, E., 1976. The chipped stone industry of Anzabegovo. In M. Gimbutas (ed.), *Neolithic Macedonia*, pp. 257–78. Monumenta Archaeologica I. Los Angeles: UCLA Institute of Archaeology Press.

Enghoff, I. B., 1993. Mesolithic eel-fishing at Bjørnsholm, Denmark, spiced with exotic species. *Journal of Danish Archaeology* 10: 105–18.

Engelmark, R., 1982. Ekologiska synpunkter på jordbrukets spridning och etablering i Norrland. In T. Sjøvold (ed.), *Introduksjonen av Jordbruk i Norden*, pp. 153–62. Oslo: Universitetsforlag.

Engelstad, E., 1985. The Late Stone Age of Arctic Norway. *Arctic Anthropology* 22: 79–96.

Eriksen, L. B., 1992. Ornehus pa Stevns – en tidligneolitisk hustomt. *Aarbøger* 1991: 7–19.

Eriksson, T., D. Fagerlund, and B. Rosborg, 1994. Sten- och jarnaldersbonder i Frotorp. *Fran Bergslag och Bondebygd* 1994: 29–50.

Erny-Rodmann, C., E. Gross-Klee, J. Haas, S. Jacomet, and H. Zoller, 1997. Früher human impact und Ackerbau im Übergangsbereich Spätmesolithikum-Frühneolithikum im schweizerischen Mittelland. *Jahrbuch des Schweizerischen Gesellschaft für Ur- und Frühgeschichte* 80: 27–56.

Escalon de Fonton, M., 1956. *Préhistoire de la Basse-Provence*. Paris: Presses universitaires de France.

Evans, J. D., 1964. Excavations in the neolithic settlement of Knossos, 1957–60, Part I. *Annual Report of the British School of Archaeology at Athens* 59:132–240.

Evans, J. G., and I. F. Smith, 1983. Excavations at Cherhill, North Wiltshire 1967. *Proceedings of the Prehistoric Society* 49: 43–118.

Evin, J., 1987. Révision de la chronologie absolue des débuts du néolithique en Provence et Languedoc. In J. C. Guilaine, J.-L. Roudil, and L. L. Vernet (eds.),

Premières communautés paysannes en Méditerranée occidentale, pp. 27–36. Paris: CNRS.

Feinman, G. M., 1995. The emergence of inequality: a focus on strategies and processes. In T. D. Price and G. M. Feinman (eds.), *Foundations of Social Inequality*, pp. 255–79. New York: Plenum Press.

Ferrari, A., and A. Pessina (eds.), 1996. *Sammardenchia e i primi agricoltori del Friuli*. Banca di credito cooperativo di Basiliano.

Ferreira, O. V., 1974. Acerca das cerâmicas neolíticas encontradas na parte superior dos concheiros da região de Muge. *Comunicações dos Serviços Geológicos de Portugal* 57: 191–7.

Fischer, A., 1982. Trade in Danubian shaft-hole axes and the introduction of Neolithic economy in Denmark. *Journal of Danish Archaeology* 1: 7–12.

1991. *Store Åmose: Danmarks hidtil største kulturhistorisk begrundede fredninssag*. Hørsholm: Skov- og Naturstyrelsen.

Fix, A. G., 1996. Gene frequency clines in Europe: demic diffusion or natural selection. *Journal of the Royal Anthropological Institute* 2: 625–43.

Flannery, K. V., 1973. The origins of agriculture. *Annual Review of Anthropology* 271–310.

1986. A visit to the Master. In K. V. Flannery (ed.), *Guila Naquitz: Archaic Foraging and Early Agriculture in Oaxaca, Mexico*, pp. 511–19. Orlando: Academic Press.

Florin, S., 1958. *Vråkulturen: Stenåldersboplatserna vid Mogetorp, Östra Vråoch Brokvarn*. Stockholm: KVHAA.

Formicola, V., 1986. Postcranial variations in late Epigravettian and Neolithic human remains from Arene Candide cave (Liguria, Italy). *Human Evolution* 6: 557–63.

Fortea, J., and B. Martí, 1984–5. Consideraciones sobre los inicios del Neolítico en el Mediterráneo español. *Zephyrus* 37–8: 167–99.

Fortea, J., B. Martí, and J. Juan, 1987. La industria lítica tallada del Neolítico antiguo en la vertiente mediterránea de la Península Ibérica. *Lucentum* 6: 7–22.

Fortea Perez, J., B. Martí Oliver, M. Fumanal Garcia, M. Dupré Ollivier, and M. Perez Ripoll, 1987. Epipaleolítico y Neolítizacion en la Zona Oriental de la Peninsula Iberica. In J. Guilaine *et al.* (eds.), *Premières communautés paysannes en Méditerranée occidentale*, pp. 581–91. Paris: CNRS.

Frayer, D. W., 1984. Biological and cultural change in the European late Pleistocene and early Holocene. In F. Smith and F. Spencer (eds.), *The Origin of Modern Humans: A World Survey of the Fossil Evidence*, pp. 211–50. New York: Alan R. Riss Co.

Friedman, J., and M. Rowlands, 1978. Notes towards an epigenetic model of the evolution of civilization. In J. Friedland and M. Rowlands (eds.), *The Evolution of Social Systems*, pp. 201–78. London: Duckworth.

Fritz, G. J., 1994. Are the first American farmers getting younger? *Current Anthropology* 35: 305–9.

Fugazzola Delpino, M. A., G. D'Eugenio, and A. Pessina, 1993. La Marmotta (Anguillara Sabazia, RM). Scavi 1989. Un abitato perilacustre di età neolitica. *Bullettino di Paletnologia Italiana* 1993: 181–342.

Fugazzola Delpino, M. A., and A. Pessina, 1994. Le Néolithique ancien et moyen de l'Italie centro-occidentale. Paper presented to the XXIVème Congrès Préhistorique de France, Carcassonne.

Gabalówna, L., 1968. Report on the 1967 excavations of sites 1 and 1A at Sarnowo, distr. Wloctawek (summary). *Pracei Materialy Muzeum Archeologicznego i etnograficznego w Lodzi. Seria archeologiczna* 15: 145–7.

Gaffrey, J., 1994. Die Steininventare der bandkeramischen Siedlungsplätze Laurenzberg 7, Langweiler 16 und Laurenzberg 8. In J. Lüning and P. Stehli (eds.), *Die Bandkeramik im Merzbachtal auf der Aldenhovener Platte*, pp. 395–531. Bonn: Rheinland-Verlag.

Gaillard, M.-J., and H. Göransson, 1991. Vegetation and landscape through time. In B. E. Bjerglund (ed.), *The Cultural Landscape during 6000 Years in Southern Sweden – the Ystad Project*, pp. 167–74. Ecological Bulletin 41.

Galinski, T., 1992. Obozowisko mezolitycne i protoneolitycne na stanowisku w Tanowie badane w latach 1989–1991. *Materialy Zachodniopomorskie* 38: 121–2.

Gallay, A., R. Carazzetti, and C. Brunier, 1987. Le Néolithique ancien des Alpes Centrales (fin Vème millénaire) et ses relations avec la Méditerranée. In J. Guilaine *et al.* (eds.), *Premières communautés paysannes en Méditerranée occidentale*, pp. 479–85. Paris: CNRS.

Garasanin, D., 1980. Origine et relations des groupes du complexe Balkano-Pannonien du Nèolithique ancien. In J. Kozlowski and J. Machnik (eds.), *Problèmes de la Neolithisation dans certaines régions de l'Europe*, pp. 73–7. Krakow: Ossolineum.

Garasanin, M., 1973. *Praistorija na tlu SR Srbije*. Belgrade: Srpska Knjizhevna Zadruga.
   1980. Les origines du Néolithique dans le bassin de la Mediterranée et dans le sud-est de l'Europe. In J. Kozlowski and J. Machnik (eds.), *Problèmes de la Néolithisation dans certaines régions de l'Europe*, pp. 57–72. Krakow: Ossolineum.

Garasanin, M. (ed.), 1978. *Vlasac: A Mesolithic Settlement in the Iron Gates*. Belgrade: Serbian Academy of Sciences and Arts Monograph 62.

Garton, D., 1987. Buxton. *Current Archaeology* 103: 250–3.

Gatsov, I., 1985. Early Holocene flint assemblage from the Bulgarian Black Sea coast. In C. Bonsall (ed.), *The Mesolithic in Europe*, pp. 471–5. Edinburgh: John Donald.

Gatsov, I., and M. Özdogan, 1994. Some epi-palaeolithic sites from NW Turkey. *Anatolica* 20: 97–120.

Gaul, J. H., 1948. *The Neolithic Period in Bulgaria*. Bulletin of the American School of Prehistoric Research 16. Cambridge, MA: Peabody Museum, Harvard University.

Gebauer, A. B., 1988. Stylistic variation in the pottery of the Funnel Beaker culture. In T. Madsen (ed.), *Multivariate Archaeology: Numerical Approaches in Scandinavian Archaeology*, pp. 91–117. Aarhus: Jutland Archaeological Society Publications.
   1995. Pottery production and the introduction of agriculture in southern Scandinavia. In W. K. Barnett and J. W. Hoopes (eds.), *The Emergence of Pottery*, pp. 99–112. Washington, DC: Smithsonian Institution Press.

Gebauer, A. B., and T. D. Price (eds.), 1992. *Transitions to Agriculture in Prehistory*. Madison, WI: Prehistory Press.

Geddes, D. S., 1983. Neolithic transhumance in the Mediterranean Pyrenees. *World Archaeology* 15: 51–66.

1985. Mesolithic domestic sheep in west Mediterranean Europe. *Journal of Archaeological Science* 12: 25–48.

1993. *La faune de l'abri de Dourgne: paléontologie et paléoéconomie.* In J. Guilaine, M. Barbaza, J. Gasco, D. Geddès, J. Coularou, J. Vaquer, J. E. Brochier, F. Briois, J. André, G. Jalut, and J. L. Vernet, *Dourgne: derniers chasseurs-collecteurs et premiers éleveurs de la Haute-Vallée de l'Aude,* pp. 365–97. Toulouse and Carcassonne, Centre d'Anthropologie des Sociétés Rurales/Archéologie en Terre d'Aude.

Geddes, D., J. Guilaine, J. Coularou, O. Le Gall, and M. Martzluff, 1989. Postglacial environments, settlement and subsistence in the Pyrennes: the Balma Margineda, Andorra. In C. Bonsall (ed.), *The Mesolithic in Europe,* pp. 561–71. Edinburgh: John Donald.

Georgiev, G., 1961. Kulturgruppen der Jungstein- und der Kupferzeit in der Ebene von Thrazien. *L'Europe à la fin de l'âge de Pierre.* Prague.

1981. Die Neolithische Siedlung bei Chavdar. *Izvestia na Arkheologicheski Institut* 36: 63–109.

Gilbert, R., and G. W. Gill, 1990. A metric technique for identifying American Indian femora. In G. W. Gill and S. Rhine (eds.), *Skeletal Attribution of Race,* pp. 97–9. Albuquerque: Maxwell Museum of Anthroplogy.

Gimbutas, M., 1977. Varna: a sensationally rich cemetery of the Karanovo civilization, about 4500 BC. *Expedition* 19(4): 3–47.

1988. Book review: Archaeology and Language. The Puzzle of Indo-European Origins, by Colin Renfrew. *Current Anthropology* 29(3): 453–6.

1991. *Civilization of the Goddess.* San Francisco: Harper and Row.

Gimbutas, M. (ed.), 1976. *Neolithic Macedonia as reflected by excavation at Anza, southeast Yugoslavia.* Los Angeles: UCLA Institute of Archaeology Press.

Gimbutas, M., S. Winn, and D. Shimabuku, 1989. *Achilleion: A Neolithic Settlement in Thessaly, Greece, 6400–5600 B.C.* Monumenia Archaeologica 14. Los Angeles: UCLA Institute of Archaeology Press.

Gomes, M. V., 1994. *Menires e cromeleques no complexo cultural megalítico português – trabalhos recentes e estado da questão.* In *O Megalitismo no Centro de Portugal. Actas do Seminário (Mangualde, Novembro de 1992),* pp. 317–42. Viseu.

n.d. Escavações arqueológicas em Padrão 1 – Vila do Bispo. Relatório da campanha de 1994. Unpublished manuscript.

González Morales, M., 1992. Mesolíticos y Megalíticos: la evidencia arqueologica de los cambios en las formas productivas en el paso al megalistismo en la Costa Cantábrica. In A. Moure (ed.), *Elefantes, ciervos y ovicaprinos: economía y aprovechamiento del medio en la prehistoria de España y Portugal,* pp. 185–202. Santander: Universidad de Cantabria.

1996. La transición al Neolítico en la Costa Cantábrica: la evidencia arqueológica. *Actes I Congrés del Neolític a la Península Ibérica, Gavà, Museu de Gavà* 2: 879–85.

González Morales, M., and J. Arnaud, 1990. Recent research on the Mesolithic of the Iberian Peninsula. In P. M. Vermeersch and P. Van Peer (eds.), *Contributions to the Mesolithic in Europe,* pp. 451–61. Leuven: Leuven University Press.

Göransson, H., 1982. The utilization of the forest in north-west Europe during the Early and Middle Neolithic. *PACT* 7:207–21.

1984. Pollen analytical investigations in the Sligo area. In G. Burenhult (ed.), *The Archaeology of Carrowmore*, pp. 154–93. Thesis and Papers in North European Archaeology 14. Stockholm: Institute of Archaeology.

1988. *Neolithic Man and the Forest Environment around Alvastra Pile Dwelling.* Theses and Papers in North European Archaeology. Stockholm: Institute of Archaeology.

Gould, S. J., and N. Eldridge, 1977. Punctuated equilibrium: the tempo and mode of evolution reconsidered. *Paleobiology* 3: 115–51.

Gowen, M., and C. Tarbett, 1988. A third season at Tankardstown. *Archaeology Ireland* 2(4): 156.

Gramsch, B. (ed.), 1981. *Mesolithikum in Europa.* Veröffentlichungen des Museums für Ur- und Frühgeschicht Potsdam 14/15.

Grayson, D. K., 1979. On the quantification of vertebrate archaeofaunas. *Advances in Archaeological Method and Theory* 2: 199–237.

Grbic, M., 1959. Starcevo kao najraniji neolitske ekonomike na Balkanu. *Starinar* 9–10: 11–16.

Green, S., and S. Perlman, 1985. *The Archaeology of Frontiers and Boundaries.* New York: Academic Press.

Greenburg, J. H., 1995. Genes, languages, and other things. *Review of Archaeology* 16(2): 24–8.

Greenfield, H., 1991a. Fauna from the Late Neolithic of the central Balkans: issues in subsistence and land use. *Journal of Field Archaeology* 18: 161–86.

1991b. Kula ring in prehistoric Europe? A consideration of local and interregional exchange during the Late Neolithic of the central Balkans. In S. Gregg (ed.), *Between Bands and States,* pp. 287–308. Carbondale, IL: Southern Illinois University Press.

1993. Zooarchaeology, taphonomy, and the origin of food production in the central Balkans. In R. W. Jamieson, S. Abonyi, and N. A. Mirau (eds.), *Culture and Environment: A Fragile Coexistence,* pp. 111–17. Calgary: University of Calgary Archaeological Association.

Greenfield, H., and F. Drasovean, 1994. An Early Neolithic Starcevo-Cris settlement in the Romanian Banat: preliminary report on the 1992 excavations at Foeni-Salas Annale Banatului. *Journal of the Museum of the Banal* 3:5–50.

Gregg, S., 1988. *Foragers and Farmers.* Chicago: University of Chicago Press.

Griffin, K., H. Høeg, and E. Østmo, 1990. Postglacial vegetation changes and early agriculture in southeast Norway. *5th International Palynological Conference. Abstracts.* Cambridge.

Groenman-van Wateringe, W., 1983. The early agricultural utilization of the Irish landscape: the last word on the elm decline. In T. Reeves-Smyth and F. Hammond (eds.), *Landscape Archaeology in Ireland,* pp. 217–232. Oxford: British Archaeological Reports British Series 116.

Gronenborn, D., 1990a. Eine Pfeilspitze vom ältesband-keramisachen Fundplatz Friedberg-B Bruchenbrocken in der Wetterau. *Germania* 68: 223–31.

1990b. Mesolithic–Neolithic interactions/The lithic industry of the Earliest Bandkeramik culture site at Friedberg-Bruchenbrücken. In P. Vermeersch and P. van Peer (eds.), *Contributions to the Mesolithic in Europe,* pp. 173–82. Leuven: Leuven University Press.

1994. Überlegungen zur Ausbreitung der bäuerlichen Wirtschaft in Mitteleuropa

– Versuch einer kulturhistorischen Interpretation ältestbandkeramischer Silexinventare. *Praehistorische Zeitschrift* 69(2): 135–51.

1997. *Silexartifakte der ältestbandkeramischen Kultur, mit einem Beitrag von Jean-Paul Kaspar.* Universitätsforschungen zur prähistorischen Archäologie 37. Bonn: Verlag Dr Rudolf Habelt.

Grooth, Marjorie E. T. de, 1987. The organisation of flint tool manufacture in the Dutch Bandkeramik. *Analecta Praehistorica Leidensia* 20: 27–52.

Grygiel, R., 1994. Untersuchungen zur Gesellschaftsorganisation des Früh- und Mittelneolithikums in Mitteleuropa. In P. Koötuøík (ed.), *Internationales Symposium über die Lengyel-Kultur 1888–1988*, pp. 43–77. Brno and Lódź: Masaryk University-Museum of Archaeology and Ethnography.

Grygiel, R., and P. Bogucki, 1997. Early farmers in north-central Europe: 1989–1994 excavations at Oslonki, Poland. *Journal of Field Archaeology* 24(2): 161–78.

Guilaine, J., 1976. *Premiers bergers et paysans de l'occident méditerranéen.* Paris: Mouton.

1979. The earliest Neolithic in the west Mediterranean: a new appraisal. *Antiquity* 53: 22–30.

1987. Les néolithiques européens: colons et/ou créateurs. *L'Anthropologie* 91: 343–50.

1993. Questions ouvertes sur la néolithisation de la haute vallée de l'Aude. In J. Guilaine, M. Barbaza, J. Gasco, D. Geddès, J. Coularou, J. Vaquer, J. E. Brochier, F. Briois, J. André, G. Jalut, and J. L. Vernet, *Dourgne: derniers chasseurs-collecteurs et premiers éleveurs de la Haute-Vallée de l'Aude*, pp. 443–76. Toulouse and Carcassonne: Centre d'Anthropologie des Sociétés Rurales/Archéologie en Terre d'Aude

Guilaine, J., M. Barbaza, J. Gasco, D. Geddès, J. Coularou, J. Vaquer, J. E. Brochier, F. Briois, J. André, G. Jalut, and J. L. Vernet, 1993. *Dourgne: derniers chasseurs-collecteurs et premiers éleveurs de la Haute-Vallée de l'Aude.* Toulouse and Carcassonne: Centre d'Anthropologie des Sociétés Ruralés Archéologie en Terre d'Aude.

Guilaine J., G. Cremonesi, G. Radi, and J. Coularou, 1991. Trasano et la céramique gravée matérane. In J. Guilaine and X. Gutherz (eds.), *Premières communautés paysannes*, pp. 123–37. Montpellier: Autour de Jean Arnal.

Guilaine, J., and O. Ferreira, 1970. Le Néolithique ancien au Portugal. *Bulletin de la Société Préhistorique Française* 67: 304–22.

Guilaine, J., A. Freises, and R. Montjardin, 1984. *Leucate-Corrège: habitat noyé du Néolithique cardial.* Toulouse: Centre d'Anthropologie des Sociétés Rurales.

Guilaine, J., and J. Vaquer, 1994. Les obsidiennes à l'ouest du Rhône. *Gallia Préhistoire* 36: 323–7.

Haas, J., 1996. *Pollen and Plant Macrofossil Evidence of Vegetation at Wallisellen-Langachermoos (Switzerland) during the Mesolithic–Neolithic Transition 8500 to 6500 Years Ago.* Dissertationes Botanicae 267. Berlin and Stuttgart: J. Cramer.

Hagelberg, E., 1995. Digging into our genes. A book review *of The History and Geography of Human Genes* by L. L. Cavalli-Sforza, P. Menozzi, and A. Piazza. *Antiquity* 69: 177–9.

Hagen, A., 1987. Behov og vekst. Ekspansjon og arealbruk i Øst-Norge i neolittisk tid og bronsealder. *Viking* 50: 37–64.

Hahn, J., 1983. Die Frühe Mittelsteinzeit. In H. Müller-Beck (ed.), *Urgeschichte in Baden-Württemberg*, pp. 363–92. Stuttgart: Konrad Theiss Verlag.

Hallgren, F., 1993. Bosättningsmönster i gränsland. Gästriklands stenålder. MA thesis, Uppsala University.

    1996. Sociala territorier och exogamirelationer i senmesolitisk tid, en diskussion utifrån boplatsen Pärlängsberget, Södermanland. *Tor* 28: 3–27.

Hallgren, F., A. Bergstrom, and A. Larsson, 1995. *Pärlängsberget, en kustboplats från övergången mellan senmesolitikum och tidigneolitikum.* Tryckta rapporter fran Arkeologikonsult AB, 13.

Halstead, P., 1996. The development of agriculture and pastoralism in Greece: when, how, who and what? In D. H. Harris (ed.), *The Origins and Spread of Agriculture and Pastoralism in Eurasia*, pp. 296–309. London: University of London Press.

Halstead, P., and J. O'Shea, 1989. *Bad Year Economics.* Cambridge: Cambridge University Press.

Hampel, A., 1989. *Die Hausentwicklung im Mittelneolithikum Zentraleuropas.* Bonn: Habelt.

Handsman, R., 1990. Whose art was found at Lepenski Vir? Gender relations and power in archaeology. In J. Gero and M. Conkey (eds.), *Engendering Archaeology*, pp. 329–65. Oxford: Basil Blackwell.

Hansen, J., 1988. Agriculture in prehistoric Aegean: data versus speculation. *American Journal of Archaeology* 92: 39–52.

    1991. *Excavations at Franchthi Cave, Greece. Fascicle 7: The Paleoethnobotany of Franchthi Cave.* Bloomington: Indiana University Press.

    1992. Franchthi Cave and the beginnings of agriculture in Greece and the Aegean. In P. Andersen (ed.), *Préhistoire de l'agriculture: nouvelles approches experimentales et ethnographiques*, pp. 231–47. Paris: CNRS.

Hansen, J., and J. M. Renfrew, 1978. Palaeolithic–Neolithic seed remains at Franchthi Cave, Greece. *Nature* 271: 349–52.

Harding, R. M., 1990. Modern European cranial variables and blood polymorphisms show comparable spatial patterns. *Human Biology* 62: 737–45.

Harding, R. M., F. W. Rösing, and R. R. Sokal, 1996. Cranial measurements do not support neolithization of Europe. *Homo* 40: 45–58.

Harris, D. H., 1996a. The origins and spread of agriculture and pastoralism in Eurasia: an overview. In D. H. Harris (ed.), *The Origins and Spread of Agriculture and Pastoralism in Eurasia*, pp. 552–73. London: Routledge.

    1996b. Themes and concepts in the study of early agriculture. In D. H. Harris (ed.), *The Origins and Spread of Agriculture and Pastoralism in Eurasia*, pp. 1–9. London: University of London Press.

Harris, D.H. (ed.), 1996c. *The Origins and Spread of Agriculture and Pastoralism in Eurasia.* London: University of London Press.

Harris, D. H., and G. C. Hillman, 1989. *Foraging and Farming: The Evolution of Plant Exploitation.* London: Unwin Hyman.

Harris, D. R., 1977. Alternative pathways toward agriculture. In C. A. Reed (ed.), *Origins of Agriculture*, pp. 179–244. The Hague: Mouton Publishers.

    1978. Settling down: an evolutionary model for the transformation of mobile bands into sedentary communities. In J. Friedman and M. Rowlands (eds.), *Evolution of Social Systems*, pp. 401–18. London: Duckworth.

    1989. An evolutionary continuum of people–plant interaction. In D. R. Harris and G. C. Hillman (eds.), *Foraging and Farming: The Evolution of Plant Exploitation*, pp. 11–26. London: Unwin Hyman.

Hartz, S. 1991. Hochatlantische Besiedlung in Schleswig-Holstein. Ein Beispiel. *Offa* 48: 115–32.

1995. Die Steinartefakte des endmesolithischen Fundplatzes Grupe – Rosenhof LA 58 (Ostholstein). PhD thesis, Christian-Albrechts-Universität, Kiel.

Hastdorf, C. A., and V. S. Popper (eds.), 1988. *Current Palaeoethnobotany*. Chicago: University of Chicago Press.

Hayden, B., 1990. Nimrods, piscators, pluckers and planters: the emergence of food production. *Journal of Anthropological Archaeology* 9: 31–69.

1992. Contrasting expectations in theories of domestication. In A. B. Gebauer and T. Douglas Price (eds.), *Transitions to Agriculture in Prehistory*, pp. 11–20. Madison, WI: Prehistory Press.

1995. The emergence of prestige technologies and pottery. In W. K. Barnett and J. W. Hoopes (eds.), *The Emergence of Pottery: Technology and Innovation in Ancient Societies*, pp. 257–65. Washington, DC: Smithsonian Institution Press.

Headland, T., and L. Reid, 1989. Hunter-gatherers and their neighbours from prehistory to the present. *Current Anthropology* 30: 43–66.

Hedges, R. E., H.-J. Bandelt, and B. Sykes, 1996. Palaeolithic and Neolithic lineages in the European mitochondrial gene pool. *American Journal of Human Genetics* 59: 185–203.

Hedges, R. E. M., R. A. Housley, C. R. Bronk, and G. J. Van Klinken, 1990. Radiocarbon dates from the Oxford AMS system: archaeometry datelist 11. *Archaeometry* 32: 211–37.

1991. Radiocarbon dates from the Oxford AMS system: archaeometry datelist 13. *Archaeometry* 33: 279–96.

1993. Radiocarbon dates from the Oxford AMS system: archaeometry datelist 17. *Archaeometry* 35: 305–26.

1994. Radiocarbon dates from the Oxford AMS system: archaeometry datelist 18. *Archaeometry* 36: 337–74.

Hedges, R. E. M., R. A. Housley, I. A. Law, and C. R. Bronk, 1990. Radiocarbon dates from the Oxford AMS system: archaeometry datelist 10. *Archaeometry* 32: 101–7.

Helbaek, H., 1952. Early crops in southern England. *Proceedings of the Prehistoric Society* 12: 194–223.

Heleno, M., 1956. Um quarto de século de investigação arqueológica. *O Arqueólogo Português* 3: 221–37.

Helmer, D., 1984. Le parcage des moutons et des chèvres au Néolithique ancien et moyen dans le sud-est de la France. In J. Clutton-Brock and C. Grigson (eds.), *Animals and Archaeology, 3: Early Herders and their Flocks*, pp. 39–45. Oxford: British Archaeological Reports International Series 202.

1992. *La domestication des animaux par les hommes préhistoriques*. Paris: Masson.

1993. Les suidés du Cardial: sangliers ou cochons? In J. Guilaine, J. Roudil, and J. L. Vernet (eds.), *Premières communautés paysannes en Méditerranée occidentale*, pp. 215–20. Paris: Centre National de la Recherche Scientifique.

Helskog, K., 1984. The Younger Stone Age settlement in Varanger, north Norway. *Acta Borealia* 1(1): 39–69.

Herity, M. J., and G. Eogan, 1976. *Ireland in Prehistory*. London: Routledge and Kegan Paul.

Heussner, K.-U., 1989. Bandkeramische Funde aus Zollchow, Kreis Prenzlau. *Bodendenkmalpflege in Mecklenburg* 1988: 7–23.

Higgs, E., and M. Jarman (eds.), 1975. *Palaeoeconomy*. Cambridge: Cambridge University Press.

Higham, C. F. W., 1969. The economic basis of the Danish Funnel-Necked Beaker (TRB) culture. *Acta Archaeologica* 40: 200–9.

Hiller, S., 1990. Tell Karanovo. In *Die ersten Bauern* 2, pp. 77–89. Zurich: Schweizerisches Landesmuseum.

Hiller, S. (ed.), 1989. *Tell Karanovo und das Balkan-Neolithikum*. Salzburg: Institut für Klassische Archäologie der Universität Salzburg.

Hines, J., 1997. Language and culture in an archaeological perspective. *Archaeological Pol.* 34: 183–97.

Hinsch, E., 1955. *Traktbegerkultur – megalitkultur. En studie av Øst-Norges eldste, neolitiske gruppe*. Universitetets oldsaksamling Årbok 1951–53. Oslo.

Hodder, I., 1982. *Symbols in Action*. Cambridge: Cambridge University Press.

1990. *The Domestication of Europe*. Oxford: Basil Blackwell.

Hodder, I. (ed.), 1978. *The Spatial Organisation of culture*. London: Duckworth.

Hoika, J., 1994. Zur Gliederung der frühneolithischen Trichterbecherkultur in Holstein. In J. Hoika and J. Meyers Balke (eds.), *Beiträge zur Frühneolithischen Trichterbecherkultur im westlichen Ostseegebiet*, pp. 85–131. Neumünster: Wachholz Verlag.

Hoika, J., and J. Meyers Balke (eds.), 1994. *Beiträge zur Frühneolithischen Trichterbecherkultur im westlichen Ostseegebiet*. Neumünster: Wachholz Verlag.

Holden, T. G., J. G. Hather, and J. P. N. Watson, 1995. Mesolithic plant exploitation at the Roc del Migdia. *Journal of Archaeological Science* 22: 769–78.

Hole, F., K. V. Flannery, and J. A. Neely, 1969. *Prehistory and Human Ecology of the Deh Luran Plain*. Ann Arbor: University of Michigan Museum of Anthropology.

Hoopes, J. W., and W. K. Barnett, 1995. The shape of early pottery studies. In W. K. Barnett and J. W. Hoopes (eds.), *The Emergence of Pottery: Technology and Innovation in Ancient Societies*, pp. 1–7. Washington, DC: Smithsonian Institution Press.

Hopf, M., 1977. Pflanzenreste aus Siedlungen der Vinča-Kultur in Jugoslawien. *Jahrbuch des Römisch-Germanischen Zentralmuseums, Mainz* 21, 1974:1–13.

1991. South and southwest Europe. In W. van Zeist, K. Wasylikowa, and K.-E. Behre (eds.), *Progress in Old World Paleoethnobotany*, pp. 241–77. Rotterdam: A. A. Balkema.

Hulthén, B. 1977. *On Ceramic Technology during the Scanian Neolithic and Bronze Age*. Theses and Papers in North-European Archaeology. Stockholm: Institute of Archaeology.

Hulthén, B., and S. Welinder, 1981. *A Stone Age Economy*. Theses and Papers in North-European Archaeology. Stockholm: Institute of Archaeology.

Huntley, B., and I. C. Prentice, 1988. July temperatures in Europe from pollen data, 6000 years Before Present. *Nature* 241: 687–90.

Iglesias, J. C., M. A. Rojo, and V. Alvarez, 1996. Estado de la cuestión sobre el Neolítico en la Submeseta Norte. *Actes. I Congrés del Neolític a la Península Ibérica*, 2, pp. 721–34. Gavà: Museu de Gavà.

Ilkiewica, J., 1989. From studies on cultures of the 4th millennium BC in the central part of the Polish coastal area. *Przeglad Archeologicny* 36: 17–55. Warsaw.

Indrelid, S., 1994. *Fangstfolk og bønder i fjellet*. Oslo: Universitets Oldsaksamlings Skrifter.

Indrelid, S., and D. Moe, 1983. Februk på Hardangervidda i yngre steinalder. *Viking* 46: 36–71.

Ingold, T., 1988. Notes on the foraging mode of production. In T. Ingold, D. Riches, and V. Woodburn (eds.), *Hunters and Gatherers, 1: History, Evolution and Social Change*, pp. 269–85. Oxford: Berg.

Ingold, T., D. Riches, and J. Woodburn (eds.), 1988. *Hunters and Gatherers*, 2 vols. Oxford: Berg.

Irwin, G., 1992. *The Prehistoric Exploration and Colonisation of the Pacific*. Cambridge: Cambridge University Press.

Iversen, J., 1941. *Landnam i Danmarks Stenalder: en pollenanalytisk Undersøgelse over det første Lantbrugs Indvirkning paa Vegetationsudviklingen*. Copenhagen: Danmarks Geologiske Undersøgelse 66.

Jażdżewski, Konrad, 1938. Cmentarzyska kultury ceramiki wstęgowej i związane z nimi ślady osadnictwa w Brześciu Kujawskim. *Wiadomości Archeologiczne* 15: 1105.

Jackes, M., and D. Lubell, 1992. The Early Neolithic human remains from Gruta do Caldeirão. In J. Zilhão (ed.), *Gruta do Caldeirão: O Neolítico Antigo*, pp. 259–95. Lisbon: Instituto Português do Património Arquitectónico e Arqueológico.

n.d. Human skeletal biology and the Mesolithic–Neolithic in Portugal. In P. Bintz (ed.), *Epipaléolithique et Mésolithique en Europe: peuplements, systèmes culturels et paléoenvironnements*. Grenoble: CNES (in press).

Jackes, M., D. Lubell, and C. Meiklejohn, 1997a. On physical anthropological aspects of the Mesolithic–Neolithic transition in the Iberian peninsula. *Current Anthropology* 38: 839–46.

1997b. Healthy but mortal: human biology and the first farmers of western Europe. *Antiquity* 71(273): 639–58.

Jacobi, R., 1979. Early Flandrian hunters in the South West. *Proceedings of the Devon Archaeological Society* 37: 48–93.

Jacobi, R. M., J. H. Tallis, and P. A. Mellars, 1976. The Southern Pennine Mesolithic and the archaeological record. *Journal of Archaeological Science* 3: 307–20.

Jacobs, K., 1993. Human postcranial variation in the Ukrainian Mesolithic–Neolithic. *Current Anthropology* 34: 311–24.

1994a. On subsistence change at the Mesolithic–Neolithic transition. *Current Anthropology* 35: 52–9

1994b. Human dento-gnathic metric variation in Mesolithic/Neolithic Ukraine: possible evidence of demic diffusion in the Dnieper Rapids region. *American Journal of Physical Anthropology* 95: 1–26.

Jacobs, K., and T. D. Price, n.d. First radiocarbon dates for two Ukrainian Mesolithic and Neolithic cemeteries: implications for early Holocene human biogeography in eastern Europe. In preparation.

Jacobsen, T. W., 1976. 17,000 years of Greek prehistory. *Scientific American* 234(6): 76–87.

1981. Franchthi Cave and the beginning of settled village life in Greece. *Hesperia* 50: 303–19.

Janik, L., 1998. The appearance of food procuring societies in the southeastern Baltic region. In M. Zvelebil, L. Domanska, and R. Dennell (eds.), *Harvesting the Sea, Farming the Forest*, pp. 237–44. Sheffield: Sheffield Academic Press.

Jankowska, D., 1990. *Die Trichterbecherkultur: neue Forschungen und Hypothesen*. Material des Internationalen Symposiums Dymaczewo, 20–24 September 1988. Poznań.

Jarman, M., 1972. European deer economies and the advent of the Neolithic. In E. Higgs (ed.), *Papers in Economic Prehistory*, pp. 125–48. Cambridge: Cambridge University Press.

1996. Human influence in the development of the Cretan fauna. In D. Reese (ed.), *The Pleistocene and Holocene Fauna of Crete and Its First Settlers*, pp. 211–30. Madison, WI: Prehistory Press.

Jarman, M. R., G. N. Bailey, and H. N. Jarman, 1982. *Early European Agriculture: Its Foundations and Development*. Cambridge: Cambridge University Press.

Jazdzewski, K., 1938. Cmentarzyska kultury ceramiki wstegowej I swiazane z nimi slady osadnictwa w Brzesciu Kujawskim. *Wiadomosci Archeologiczne* 15: 1–105.

Jennbert, K., 1984. *Den produktiva gåvan: tradition och innovation i Sydskandinavien för omkring 5 300 år sedan*. Lund: Acta Archaeologica Lundensia 4.

1985. Neolithisation – a Scanian perspective. *Journal of Danish Archaeology* 4: 196–7.

1987. Neolithisation processes in the Nordic area. *Swedish Archaeology* 1981–5: 21–35.

Jensen, H. J., 1994. *Flint Tools and Plant Working*. Aarhus: Aarhus University Press.

Jeunesse, C., 1990. Habitats rubanés en grottes et abris sous roche. In D. Cahen and M. Otte (eds.), *Rubané et Cardial*, pp. 231–7. Etudes et Recherches Archéologiques de l'Université de Liège 39. Liège: Université de Liège.

1995. Les groupes régionaux occidentaux du Rubané (Rhin et bassin parisien) à travers les practiques funéraires. *Gallia Préhistoire* 37: 115–54.

Jeunesse, C., P. Y. Nicoud, P. L. van Berg, and J. L. Voruz, 1991. Nouveaux témoins d'âge néolithique ancien entre Rhône et Rhin. *Archives de la Société Suisse de Préhistoire et d'Archéologie* 74: 43–78.

Jochim, M., 1990. The Late Mesolithic in southwest Germany: culture change or population decline? In P. Vermeersch and P. Van Peer (eds.), *Contributions to the Mesolithic in Europe*, pp. 183–91. Leuven: Leuven University Press.

1992. Henauhof NW 2: ein neuer mittelsteinzeitlicher Fundplatz am Federsee. *Archäologische Ausgrabungen in Baden-Württemberg 1991*: 32–5.

1993. *Henauhof NW: ein mittelsteinzeitlicher Lagerplatz am Federsee*. Stuttgart: Konrad Theiss Verlag.

Johansen, Ø., 1989. Arkeologi, religion or kronologiske begrensninger. In M. Larsson and B. Wyszomirska (eds.), *Arkeologi och Religion*, pp. 7–19. Lund: Institute of Archaeology.

Johansen, O. S., 1979. Early farming north of the Arctic Circle. *Norwegian Archaeological Review* 12: 22–31.

Jones, G. D. B., 1987. *Apulia, I: Neolithic Settlement in the Tavoliere*. London: Society of Antiquaries.

Jones, J. S., 1991. Farming is in the blood. *Nature* 351: 97–8.

Jope, E. M., 1965. *An Archaeology Survey of County Down*. Belfast: HMSO.

Jorge, S. O., 1979. Contributo para o estudo de materiais provenientes de estações neolíticas dos arredores da Figueira da Foz. *Actas da 1ª MesaRedonda sobre o*

Neolítico e o Calcolítico em, pp. 53–82. Porto: Grupo de Estudos Arqueológicos do Porto.

Jovanovic, B., 1965. Starija Vincanska Grupa u juznom Banatu. *Rad Vojvodanskih Muzeja* 14:15–40.

1969. Chronological frames of the Iron Gates Group of the Early Neolithic period. *Archaeologica Iugoslavica* 10: 23–38.

1972. The autochthonous and the migrational components of the Early Neolithic of the Iron Gates. *Balcanica* 3:49–58.

1974. Relativno hronoloski odnos starijeg neolita Djerdapa i Vojvodine. *Godisnjak Zemaljskog Muzeja u Sarajevu* 10:31–50.

1975. The origin of the Early Neolithic in Djerdap. *Godisnjak Zemaljskog Muzeja u Sarajevu* 14 (12): 5–18.

1984. Naselje vinçanske kulture: stratigrafija. In M. Garasanin and D. Srejovi (eds.), *Vinça u praistoriji i srednjem veku*, pp. 23–33. Belgrade: Serbian Academy of Sciences and Arts.

1990. Die Vinca-Kultur und der Beginn der Metallnutzung auf dem Balkan. In D. Srejovic and N. Tasic (eds.), *Vinca and its World*, pp. 55–60. Belgrade: Serbian Academy of Sciences and Arts.

Juan-Cabaniles, J., 1990. Substrat épipaléolithique et néolithisation en Espagne: apport des industries lithiques à l'identification des traditions culturelles. In D. Cahen and M. Otte (eds.), *Rubané et Cardial*, pp. 417–36. Liège: Etudes et Recherches Archéologiques de l'Université de Liège 39.

1992. La neolitización de la vertiente mediterránea peninsular. Modelos y problemas. *Actas del Congreso Aragón/Litoral Mediterráneo. Intercambios culturales durante la Prehistoria*, pp. 255–68. Saragossa: Institución Fernando el Católico.

Kabacinski, J., 1992. Dabki site 9 and its relation to the Stone Age cultures of the southern Baltic coastal zone. *Dorzecze* 1: 6–41.

Kaiser, T., and B. Voytek, 1983. Sedentism and economic change in the Balkan Neolithic. *Journal of Anthropological Archaeology* 2:323–53.

Kalicz, N., 1993. The early phases of the Neolithic in western Hungary (Transdanubija). *Porocilo* 21: 85–136.

Kampffmeyer, U., 1983. Der neolitische Siedlungsplatz Hüde I am Dümmer. In G. Wagner (ed.), *Frühe Bauernkulturen in Niedersachsen*, pp. 119–35. Oldenburg: Staatliches Museum für Naturkunde und Vorgeschichte.

Kaplan, R., 1993. *Balkan Ghosts*. London: St Martin's Press.

Karlén, W., 1988. Scandinavian glacial and climatic fluctuations during the Holocene. *Quaternary Science Review* 7: 199–209.

Karsten, P., 1994. *Att kasta yxan i sjön: en studie över rituell tradition och förändring utfrån skånska neolitiska offerfynd*. Lund: Institute of Archaeology.

Keeley, L., 1992. The introduction of agriculture to the western North European Plain. In A. B. Gebauer and T. D. Price (eds.), *Transitions to Agriculture in Prehistory*, pp. 81–95. Madison, WI: Prehistory Press.

Keeley, L., and D. Cahen, 1989. Early Neolithic forts and villages in NE Belgium: a preliminary report. *Journal of Field Archaeology* 16: 157–76.

Kenyon, K., 1981. *Excavations at Jericho. 3: The Architecture and Stratigraphy of the Tell*. London: British School of Archaeology in Jerusalem.

Kervaso, B., and G. Mazière, 1989. Le gisement du Martinet à Sauveterre-la-Lémance

(Lot-et-Garonne). Nouvelles données et implications. *Bulletin de la Société Préhistorique Française* 86: 263–5.

Kihlstedt, B., 1996. Neolitiseringen i ostra Mellansverig – nagra reflektioner med utgangpunkt från nya ¹⁴C-dateringar. In B. Bratt (ed.), *Stenalder i Stokholms Lan: Tva Seminarier vid Stockholms Lans Museum*, pp. 72–9. Stockholm: Lans Museum.

Kind, C.-J., 1989. *Ulm-Eggingen: Bandkeramische Siedlung und mittelalterliche Wüstung.* Stuttgart: Konrad Theiss Verlag.

    1992. Der Freilandfundplatz Henauhof Nord II am Federsee und die Buchauer Gruppe des Endmesolithikums. *Archäologisches Korrespondenzblatt* 22: 341–53.

Kinnes, I., 1982. Les Fouaillages and megalithic origins. *Antiquity* 56: 24–30.

    1985. Circumstance not context, the Neolithic of Scotland as seen from outside. *Proceedings of the Society of Antiquaries of Scotland* 115: 15–57.

    1992. *Non-Megalithic Long Barrows and Allied Structures in the British Neolithic.* London: British Museum Occasional Paper 52.

Kinnes, I., and I. J. Thorpe, 1986. Radiocarbon dating: use and abuse. *Antiquity* 60: 221–3.

Kirch, P. V., 1984. *The Evolution of the Polynesian Chiefdoms.* Cambridge: Cambridge University Press.

Kirkowski, R., 1994. Neue Funde der Lengyel-Kultur in Chełmno Land. In P. Koötuøík (ed.), *Internationales Symposium über die Lengyel-Kultur 1888–1988*, pp. 156–66. Brno and Lódź: Masaryk University-Museum of Archaeology and Ethnography.

Knutsson, H., 1995. *Slutvandrat Aspekter på övergången från rörlig till bofast tillvaro.* Uppsala: Societas Archaeologica Upsaliensis.

Koch, E., 1994. Typeneinteilung und Datierung frühneolithischer Trichterbecher aufgrund ostdåanischer Opfergefässe. In J. Hoika and J. Meyers Balke (eds.), *Beiträge zur Frühneolithischen Trichterbecherkultur im westlichen Ostseegebiet*, pp. 165–93. Neumünster: Wachholz Verlag.

    1998. *Neolithic Bog-Pots from Zealand, Møn, and Lolland-Falster, Denmark.* Copenhagen: Nordiske Fortidsminder.

Kokelj, E. M., 1993. The transition from Mesolithic to Neolithic in the Trieste karst. *Porocilo* 21: 69–84.

Kolstrup, E., 1988. Late Atlantic and early Subboreal vegetational development at Trundholm, Denmark. *Journal of Archaeological Science* 15: 503–13.

Kosse (Krudy), K., 1968. Settlement types of the Early Neolithic Karanovo-Starçevo-Körös-Linear cultures in S.E. Europe. MA thesis, University of Edinburgh.

Kostrzewski, J., 1929. Osada starszej ceramiki wstêgowej w Chełmży w powiecie toruñskim na Pomorzu. *Roczniki Muzeum Wielkopolskiego* 4: 1–27.

Kot, M., M. A. Lewis, and P. Van den Driessche, 1996. Dispersal data and the spread of invading organisms. *Ecology* 77: 2027–42.

Kowalczyk, J., 1970. The Funnel Beaker culture. In T. Wislanski (ed.), *The Neolithic in Poland*, pp. 144–77. Wrocław.

Kozlowski, J., 1989. The Neolithization of south-east European: alternative approach. In S. Bökönyi (ed.), *Neolithic of Southeastern Europe and Its Near Eastern Connections*, pp. 131–48. Budapest: Varia Archaeologica Hungarica.

Kozlowski, J., and S. Kozlowski, 1986. Foragers of Central Europe and their accultu-ration. In M. Zvelebil (ed.), *Hunters in Transition*, pp. 95 –109. Cambridge: Cambridge University Press.

Kozlowski, S. K., 1973. Introduction to the history of Europe in early Holocene. In S. K. Kozlowski and J. K. Kozlowski (eds.), *The Mesolithic in Europe*, pp. 331–66. Warsaw: University of Warsaw Press.

1976. Les courants interculturels dans le Mésolithique de l'Europe occidentale. In S. K. Kozlowski (ed.), *Les civilisations du 8e au 5e millénaire avant notre ère en Europe*, pp. 135–60. Nice: Union Internationale des Sciences Préhistoriques et Protohistoriques.

1988. The pre-Neolithic base of the Early Neolithic stone industries in Europe. In J. K. Kozlowski and S. K. Kozlowski (eds.), *Chipped Stone Industries of the Early Farming Cultures in Europe*. Warsaw: University of Warsaw Press.

1990. Die ersten Bauern Mitteleuropas – eine archäobotanische Untersuchung zu Umwelt und Landwirtschaft der Ältesten Bandkeramik. *Analecta Praehistorica Leidensia* 23: 94–121.

Kozlowski, S. K., and J. K. Kozlowski, 1973. *The Mesolithic in Europe*. Warsaw: University of Warsaw Press.

Krantz, G., 1988. *Geographical Development of European Languages*. Bern: Peter Lang.

Krause, R., 1995. Ein bandkeramisches Dorf mit Dorfgraben und Friedhof bei Vaihingen an der Enz, Kreis Ludwigsburg. *Archäologische Ausgrabungen in Baden-Württemberg 1994*: 37–43.

1997. Grabenwerk – Siedlung – Gräberfeld: drei Jahre Ausgrabungen in der band-keramischen Siedlung bei Vaihingen an der Enz, Kreis Ludwigsburg. *Archäologische Ausgrabungen in Baden-Württemberg 1996*: 37–41.

Kreuz, A., 1990. Die ersten Bauern Mitteleuropas. Eine archäobotanische Untersuchung zu Umwelt und Landwirtschaft der ältesten Bandkeramik. *Analecta Prehistorica Leidensia* 13:40–61.

Kristensen, I. K., 1991. Storgård IV. An Early Neolithic long barrow near Fjelsø, North Jutland. *Journal of Danish Archaeology* 8: 72–87.

Kristiansen, K., 1987. From stone to bronze: the evolution of social complexity in northern Europe, 2300–1200 BC. In E. M. Brumfiel and T. K. Earle (eds.), *Specialization, Exchange and Complex Societies*, pp. 52–79. Cambridge: Cambridge University Press.

Kruk, J., 1973. *Studia Osadnicze nad Neolitem Wyżyn Lessowych*. Wrocław: Ossolineum.

1980. *The Neolithic Settlement of Southern Poland*. Oxford: British Archaeological Reports International Series 93.

Kuijt, I., 1994. Foeni, Romania, 1992. Preliminary report: analysis of the chipped stone tools. *Analele Banatului* 3: 86–93.

Kullman, L., 1988. Tree-limit history in the Scandes Mountains (central Sweden), Sweden, inferred from fossil wood. *Review of Palaeobotany and Palynology* 58: 163–71.

Kunkel, O., 1934. Die Bandkeramik in Pommern. *Germania* 18: 173–8.

Ladinsky, G., 1989. Origin and domestication of southwest Asian grain legumes. In D. Harris and G. C. Hillman (eds.), *Foraging and Farming: The Evolution of Plant Exploitation*, pp. 74–89. London: Unwin Hyman.

Lamb, H. H., 1995. *Climate, History, and the Modern World*. 2nd edn. London: Methuen.

Langenbrink, B., and J. Kneipp, 1990. Keramik vom Typ La Hoguette aus einer ältest-bandkeramischen Siedlung bei Steinfurth im Wetteraukreis. *Archäologisches Korrespondenzblatt* 20: 149–60.

Lanting, J. N., and J. van der Plicht, 1993–4. ^{14}C AMS; pros and cons for archaeology. *Palaeohistoria* 35–6: 1–12.

—— 1996. Wat Hebben Floris V, Skelet Swifterbant S2 en Visotters Gemeen? *Palaeohistoria*: 38: 1–39.

Larsson, L., 1984. The Skateholm Project. A Late Mesolithic settlement and cemetery complex at a southern Swedish bay. *Meddelanden från Lunds Universitets Historiska Museum* 1983–4: 5–38.

—— 1987. Some aspects of cultural relationship and ecological conditions during the Late Mesolithic and Early Neolithic. In G. Burenhult *et al.* (eds.), *Theoretical Approaches to Artefacts, Settlement and Society: Studies in Honour of Mats P. Malmer*, pp. 165–76. Oxford: British Archaeological Reports International Series 366.

—— 1988a. The use of the landscape during the Mesolithic and Neolithic in southern Sweden. In *Archeology en Landschap. Bijdragen aan het gelijknamige symposium gehouden op 19 en 20 oktober 1987, ter gelegenheid van het afscheid van H. T. Waterbolk*, pp. 31–48. Groningen: Biologisch-Archaeologisch Instituut.

—— 1988b. Aspects of exchange in Mesolithic societies. In B. Hårdh, L. Larsson, D. Olausson, and R. Petré (eds.), *Trade and Exchange in Prehistory: Studies in Honour of Berta Stjernquist*, pp. 25–32. Lund: Almquist and Wiksell International.

—— 1990. The Mesolithic of southern Scandinavia. *Journal of World Prehistory* 4: 257–310.

Larsson, L., J. Callmer, and B. Stjernquist (eds.), 1992. *The Archaeology of the Cultural Landscape*. Acta Archaeologica Lundensia 19. Stockholm: Almqvist and Wiksell International.

Larsson, L., and M. Larsson. 1991. The introduction and establishment of agriculture. In B. E. Bjerglund (ed.), *The Cultural Landscape during 6000 Years in Southern Sweden – the Ystad Project*, pp. 293–314. Ecological Bulletin 41.

Larsson, M., 1984. Tidigneolitikum i Sydvästskäne. Kronologi och bosättningsmön-ster. *Acta Archaeologica Lundensia* Ser. in 4, 17.

—— 1985. *The Early Neolithic Funnel-Beaker Culture in South-West Scania, Sweden: Social and Economic Change 3000–2500 BC*. Oxford: British Archaeological Reports International Series 264.

—— 1987. Neolithization in Scania – a Funnel Beaker perspective. *Journal of Danish Archaeology* 5: 244–7.

—— 1988. Exchange and society in the Early Neolithic in Scania, Sweden. In B. Hårdh, L. Larsson, D. Olausson, and R. Petré (eds.), *Trade and Exchange in Prehistory: Studies in Honour of Berta Stjernquist*, pp. 49–58. Lund: Almquist and Wiksell International.

—— 1992. The Early and Middle Neolithic Funnel Beaker culture in the Ystad area (southern Scania). Economic and social change 3100–2300 BC. In L. Larsson, J. Callmer, and B. Stjernquist (eds.), *The Archaeology of the Cultural Landscape*, pp. 17–90. Acta Archaeologica Lundensia 19. Lund: Almquist and Winksell International.

Larsson, M., and D. Olausson, 1992. Archaeological field survey-methods and prob-lems. In L. Larsson, J. Callmer, and B. Stjernquist (eds.), *The Archaeology of the*

Cultural Landscape, pp. 473–80. Acta Archaeologica Lundensia 19. Lund: Almquist and Winksell International.

Lazarovici, G., 1979. *Neoliticul Banatului.* Cluj: Bibliotheca Musei Napocensis.

Lazic, M., 1988. Fauna of mammals from the Neolithic settlements in Serbia. In D. Srejovic (ed.), *The Neolithic of Serbia,* pp. 24–38. Belgrade: University of Belgrade Center for Archaeological Research.

Leacock, E., and R. Lee, 1982. *Politics and History in Band Societies.* Cambridge: Cambridge University Press.

Lee, R., 1972. Population growth and the beginnings of sedentary life among the !Kung Bushmen. In B. Spooner (ed.), *Population Growth: Its Anthropological Implications,* pp. 329–50. Cambridge, MA: MIT Press.

Legge, A. J., and P. A. Rowley-Conwy, 1988. *Star Carr Revisited.* London: Centre for Extramural Studies, Birkbeck College.

Lekberg, P. (ed.), 1996. *Fågelbacken, eett fornlämningskomplex i östra Västmansland, 1: Lämningar från tidigneolitikum, mellanneolitikum och järnålder undersökta 1993.* Tryckta Rapporter från Arkeologikonsult 14. Uppsala.

Letica, Z., 1969. Vlasac – nouvel habitat de la culture de Lepenski Vir. *Archaeologica Iugoslavica* 10:7–11.

Lewthwaite, J., 1982. Cardial disorder: ethnographic and archaeological comparisons for problems in the early prehistory of the west Mediterranean. *Le Néolithique ancien méditerranéen,* Fédération Archéologique de l'Hérault, Sète: 311–18.

1985. The lacuna in the lagoon: an interdisciplinary research frontier in west Mediterranean Holocene palaeoecology and prehistory. *Cahiers Ligures de Préhistoire et de Protohistoire* 2: 253–64.

1986a. From Menton to the Mondego in three steps: application of the availability model to the transition to food production in Occitania, Mediterranean Spain and southern Portugal. *Arqueologia* 13: 95–112.

1986b. The transition to food production: a Mediterranean perspective. In M. Zvelebil (ed.), *Hunters in Transition,* pp. 53–66. Cambridge: Cambridge University Press.

Lichardus, J., 1976. *Rössen – Gatersleben – Baalberge: ein Beitrag zur Chronologie des Mitteldeutschen Neolitikums und zur Entstehung der Trichterbecher-Kulturen.* Bonn.

Lichardus, J., and M. Lichardus-Itten (eds.), 1985. *La protohistoire de l'Europe: le Néolithique et le Chalcolithique.* Paris: PUF.

Lichardus-Itten, M., 1993. La vallèe du Strymon: une route au Néolithique ancien? In V. Nikolov (ed.), *Praehistorische Funde und Forschungen: Festschrift zum Gedenken an Prof. Georgi I. Georgiev,* pp. 69–72. Sofia: Bulgarian Academy of Sciences.

Lidén, K. 1995a. *Prehistoric Diet Transitions.* Stockholm: Archaeological Research Laboratory.

1995b. Megaliths, agriculture, and social complexity: a diet study of two Swedish megalith populations. *Journal of Anthropological Archaeology* 14: 404–13.

Liese-Kleiber, H., 1990. Züge der Landschafts- und Vegetationsentwicklung im Federseegebiet. *Bericht der Römisch-Germanisch Kommission* 71: 58–83.

Lightfoot, R., 1994. *The Duckfoot Site, 2. Archaeology of the House and Household.* Cortez, CO: Crow Canyon Archaeological Center.

Lillie, M., 1996. Mesolithic and Neolithic populations of Ukraine: indications of diet from dental pathology. *Current Anthropology* 37: 135–42.

1998. The Mesolithic–Neolithic transition in Ukraine: new radiocarbon determinations for the cemeteries of the Dnieper Rapids region. *Antiquity* 72: 184–8.

Liversage, D., 1968. Excavations at Dalkey Island, Co. Dublin 1956–59. *Proceedings of the Royal Irish Academy* 66C: 53–233.

1981. Neolithic monuments at Lindebjerg, northwest Zealand. *Acta Archaeologica* 51: 85–152. Copenhagen.

1992. *Barkær: Long Barrows and Settlements*. Arkæologiske Studier 9. Copenhagen: Akademisk Forlag.

Louwe Kooijmans, L. P., 1993. The Mesolithic/Neolithic transformation in the lower Rhine Basin. In P. Bogucki (ed.), *Case Studies in European Prehistory*, pp. 95–145. Boca Raton, FL: CRC Press.

Lubell, D., and M. Jackes, 1985. Mesolithic–Neolithic continuity: evidence from chronology and human biology. *Actas da I Reunião do Quaternário Ibérico* 2: 113–33. Lisbon.

1988. *Portuguese Mesolithic–Neolithic Subsistence and Settlement*. Rivista di Antropologia, Supplement to vol. 66, pp. 231–48.

Lubell, D., M. Jackes, and C. Meiklejohn, 1989. Archaeology and human biology of the Mesolithic–Neolithic transition in southern Portugal: a preliminary report. In C. Bonsall (ed.), *The Mesolithic in Europe*, pp. 632–40. Edinburgh: John Donald.

Lubell, D., M. Jackes, H. Schwarcz, M. Knyf, and C. Meiklejohn, 1994. The Mesolithic–Neolithic transition in Portugal: isotopic and dental evidence of diet. *Journal of Archaeological Science* 21: 201–6.

Lüning, J., 1980. Getreideanbau ohne Dungung. *Archäologisches Korrespondenzblatt* 10: 117–22.

1986. Die Ausgrabungen zum Neolithikum in Schwanfeld, Landkreis Schweinfurt. *Mainfränkische Studien* 37: 916.

1988a. Frühe Bauern in Mitteleuropa im 6. und 5. Jahrausend v. Chr. *Jährbuch des Römisch-Germanischen Zentralmuseums* 35/1. Mainz.

1988b. Zur Verbreitung und Datierung bandkeramischer Erdwerke. *Archäologisches Korrespondenzblatt* 18: 155–8.

Lüning, J. (ed.), 1997. *Ein Siedlungsplatz der Altesten Bandkeramik in Bruchenbrucken, Stadt Freidberg/Hessen*. Universitätsforsch. Prähist. Arch. 39. Bonn.

Lüning, J., U. Kloos, and S. Albert, 1989. Westliche Nachbarn der bandkeramischen Kultur: La Hoguette und Limburg. *Germania* 67: 355–93.

Lüning, J., and P. Stehli, 1989. Die Bandkeramik in Mitteleuropa: von der Natur- zur Kulturlandschaft. *Spektrum der Wissenschaft*, April 1989, pp. 78–88.

Lynch, A., 1981. *Man and Environment in South West Ireland 4000 BC–AD 800: A Study of Man's Impact on the Development of Soil and Vegetation*. Oxford: British Archaeological Reports British Series 85.

1988. Poulnabrone. A stone in time. *Archaeology Ireland* 2(3): 105–7.

McCormick, F., 1985–6. Animal bones from prehistoric Irish burials. *Journal of Irish Archaeology* 3: 37–48.

McCorriston, J., and F. Hole, 1991. The ecology of seasonal stress and the origins of agriculture in the Near East. *American Anthropologist* 93:46–94.

MacLean, R., 1993. Eat your greens: an examination of the potential diet available in Ireland during the Mesolithic. *Ulster Journal of Archaeology* 56: 1–8.

MacNeish, R. M., 1992. *The Origins of Agriculture*. Norman: University of Oklahoma Press.

McPherron, A., and D. Srejovic (eds.), 1988. *Divostin and the Neolithic of Central Serbia*. Pittsburgh: University of Pittsburgh.

Madsen, B., 1993. Flint – extraction, manufacture, and distribution. In S. Hvass and B. Storgaard (eds.), *Digging into the Past*, pp. 126–30. Aarhus: Aarhus Universitetsforlag.

Madsen, T., 1979. Earthen long barrows and timber structures: aspects of the Early Neolithic mortuary practice in Denmark. *Proceedings of the Prehistoric Society* 45: 301–20.

   1982. Settlement systems of early agricultural societies in East Jutland: a regional study of change. *Journal of Anthropological Archaeology* 1: 197–236.

   1987. Where did all the hunters go? An assessment of an epoch-making episode in Danish prehistory. *Journal of Danish Prehistory* 5: 229–39.

   1990. Changing Patterns of land use in the TRB culture of south Scandinavia. In D. Jankowska, (ed.), *Die Trichterbecherkultur: Neue Forschungen und Hypothesen. Material des Internationalen Symposiums Dymaczewo*, I, pp. 27–41. Poznań.

   1991. The social structure of Early Neolithic society in south Scandinavia. In J. Lichardus (ed.), *Die Kupferzeit als historische Epoche*, pp. 489–96. Bonn: Saarbrücker Beiträge zur Altertumskunde.

Madsen, T., and H. J. Jensen, 1982. Settlement and land use in Early Neolithic Denmark. *Analecta Praehistorica Leidensia* 15: 63–86.

Madsen, T., and J. E. Petersen, 1984. Tidligneolitiske anlæg ved Mosegården. Regionale og kronologiske forskelle i tidligneolitikum. *Kuml* 1982–3: 61–120.

Malez, M., 1975. *Kvartarna fauna*. Niksis: Crvena Stijena.

Malinowski, B., 1922. *Argonauts of the Western Pacific* (1950 edn.). London: Routledge and Kegan Paul.

Mallory, J. P., 1989. *In Search of the Indo-Europeans*. London: Thames and Hudson.

Mallory, J. P., and B. Hartwell, 1984. Donegore Hill. *Current Archaeology* 8(9): 271–5.

Malmer, P., 1984. On the social function of pile dwellings and megaliths. In G. Burenhult (ed.), *The Archaeology of Carrowmore*, pp. 371–5. Theses and Papers in North European Archaeology 14. Stockholm: Institute of Archaeology.

Manby, T., 1988. The Neolithic in east Yorkshire. In T. Manby (ed.), *Archaeology in East Yorkshire*, pp. 35–88. Sheffield: University of Sheffield.

Manolakakis, L., 1987. L'industrie lithique de Sitagroi III: étude technologique du débitage. MA thesis, Department of Protohistory, University of Paris I.

   1994. L'industrie lithique taillée du chalcolithique des Balkans. Thèse du Doctorat, Department of Protohistory, University of Paris I.

Markevitch, V. I., 1974. *Bugo-Dnestrovksya kultura na territorii Moldavii*. Kishinev: Shiinsta.

Marks, A. E., N. Bicho, J. Zilhão, and C. R. Ferring, 1994. Upper Pleistocene prehistory in Portuguese Estremadura. Results of preliminary research. *Journal of Field Archaeology* 21: 53–68.

Marnival, P., 1988. Cueillette, agriculture et alimentation végétale de l'Epipaléolithique jusqu'au 2° Age du Fer en France méridionale. Apports palethnographiques de la carpologie. Thèse de doctorat. Paris: EHESS.

1992. Approche cartologie de la néolithisation du sud de la France. In P. Anderson (ed.), *Préhistoire de l'agriculture: nouvelles approches experimentales et ethnographiques*, pp. 255–63. Valbonne: Monographie du CRA no. 6.

Martí, B., J. Fortea, J. Bernabeu, M. Perez, J. D. Acuna, F. Robles, and M.-D. Gallart, 1987. El Neolitico antiguo en la zona oriental de la Peninsula Iberica. In J. Guilaine, J.-L. Roudil, and J.-L. Vernet (eds.), *Premières communautés paysannes en Méditerranée occidentale*, pp. 607–19. Paris: CNRS.

Martín, A., 1992. La economía de producción a lo largo del Neolítico en Cataluña. In A. Moure (ed.), *Elefantes, ciervos y ovicaprinos: economía y aprovechamiento del medio en la prehistoria de España y Portugal*, pp. 203–28. Santander: Universidad de Cantabria.

Masters, L. J., 1973. The Lochill long cairn. *Antiquity* 47: 96–100.

Masucci, M., 1994. Early Neolithic pottery production in the Rio Maior valley, Portuguese Estremadura. Paper presented in the World Ceramics Congress and Forum on New Materials, Florence, Italy.

Maury, J., 1997. Les niveaux post-glaciaires dans l'abri des Usclades (Nant, Aveyron). *Bulletin de la Société Préhistorique Française* 94: 509–26.

Meiklejohn, C., 1985. Review of Ammerman and Cavalli-Sforza. *American Anthropologist* 87: 974–5.

Meiklejohn, C., J. H. Baldwin, and Catherine T. Schentag, 1988. Caries as a probably dietary marker in the Western European Mesolithic. In B. V. Kennedy and G. M. LeMoine (eds.), *Diet and Subsistence: Current Archaeological Perspectives*, pp. 273–9. Calgary: The Archaeological Association of the University of Calgary.

Meiklejohn, C., C. Schentag, A. Venema, and P. Key, 1984. Socioeconomic change and patterns of pathology and variation in the Mesolithic and Neolithic of western Europe: some suggestions. In A. M. Cohen (ed.), *Paleopathology at the Origins of Agriculture*, pp. 75–100. New York: Academic Press.

Meiklejohn, C., and M. Zvelebil, 1991. Health status of European populations at the agricultural transition and the implications for the adoption of farming. In H. Bush and M. Zvelebil (eds.), *Health in Past Societies: Biocultural Interpretations of Human Skeletal Remains in Archaeological Contexts*, pp. 129–45. Oxford: British Archaeological Reports International Series 567.

Mellars, P. A., 1976. Fire ecology, animal populations and man: a study of some ecological relationships in prehistory. *Proceedings of the Prehistoric Society* 42: 15–45.

1987. *Excavations on Oronsay*. Edinburgh: Edinburgh University Press.

Mellars, P. A., and S. Rheinhardt, 1978. Mesolithic land use in southern England. In P. A. Mellars (ed.), *The Early Postglacial Settlement of Northern Europe*, pp. 243–95. London: Duckworth.

Menk, R., and J. Nemeskéri, 1989. The transition from Mesolithic to Early Neolithic in southeastern and eastern Europe: an anthropological outline. In I. Hershkovitz (ed.), *People and Culture in Change: Proceedings of the Second Symposium on Upper Palaeolithic, Mesolithic and Neolithic Populations of Europe and the Mediterranean Basin*, pp. 531–40. Oxford: British Archaeological Reports International Series 508.

Mercer, R., 1986. The Neolithic in Cornwall. *Cornish Archaeology* 25: 35–80.

Meurers-Balke, J., 1983. *Siggeneben-Süd. Ein Fundplatz der frühen Trichterbecherkultur an der holsteinischen Ostseeküste*. Offa-Bücher 50. Neumünster: Karl Wachholy Verlag.

Midgley, M., 1985. *The Origin and Function of the Earthen Long Barrows of Northern Europe*. Oxford: British Archaeological Reports International Series 259.

1993. *TRB culture*. Edinburgh: Edinburgh University Press.

Mikic, Z., 1980. Anthropologische Typen der Djerdap (Eisernen-tor) serie. In J. Kozlowski and J. Machnik (eds.), *Problèmes de la Neolithisation dans certaines régions de l'Europe*, pp. 151–61. Kraków.

1988. Anthropological remains from the Neolithic sites in Serbia. In D. Srejovic (ed.), *The Neolithic of Serbia*, pp. 20–3. Belgrade: Center for Archaeological Research, University of Belgrade.

1990. Lepenski Vir und das Neolithisations Problem in der Antropologie. In D. Srejovic and N. Tasic (eds.), *Vinca and its World*, pp. 1–5. Belgrade: Serbian Academy of Sciences and Arts.

Mikkelsen, E., 1982. Introduksjon av jordbruk i Øst-Norge. In T. Sjøvold (ed.), *Introduksjon av Jordbruk in Norden*, pp. 129–42. Olso: Universitetsforlaget.

1984. Neolitiseringen i Øst-Norge. *Universitetets Oldsaksamlingen Årbok* 1982/3: 86–128.

1989. *Fra jeger til bonde: Utviklingen av jordbrukssamfunn i Telemark i steinalder og bronsealder*. Universitetets Oldsaksamlings Skrifter, Ny rekke 11. Oslo: Universitets Oldsaksamlings.

Mikkelsen, E., and H. I. Høeg, 1979. A reconsideration of Neolithic agriculture in eastern Norway. *Norwegian Archaeological Review* 12(1): 33–47.

Milisauskas, S., 1978. *European Prehistory*. New York: Academic Press.

1986. *Early Neolithic Settlement and Society at Olszanica*. Ann Arbor: Museum of Anthropology, University of Michigan.

Milisauskas, S., and J. Kruk, 1989. Neolithic economy in Central Europe. *Journal of World Prehistory* 3(4): 403–46.

Miller, M. A., 1996. The manufacture of cockle shell beads at Early Neolithic Franchthi Cave, Greece: a case of craft specialization? *Journal of Mediterranean Archaeology* 9: 7–37.

Milles, A., D. Williams, and N. Gardner (eds.), 1989. *The Beginnings of Agriculture*. Oxford: British Archaeological Reports International Series 496.

Mills, N., 1983. The Neolithic of southern France. In C. Scarre (ed.), *Ancient France*, pp. 91–145. Edinburgh: Edinburgh University Press.

Milojcic, V., 1960. Prækeramisches Neolithikum auf der Balkanhalbinsel. *Germania* 38(3/4): 320–35.

Miroslavljevic, M., 1959. 'Jamina Sredi': prilog prethistorijskog kulturi na Otoku Cres. *Arheoloshki Radovi i Rasprave* 1: 131–69.

Misic, B., D. Colic, and A. Dinic, 1969. Ekolosko-Fitocenoloska Istrazivanja. In D. Srejovic (ed.), *Lepenski Vir*, pp. 207–23. Belgrade: Srpska Knizhevna Drushtva.

Mitchell, G. F., 1949. Further early kitchen middens in Co. Louth, *Co. Louth Archaeological Journal* 12: 14–20.

1956. An early kitchen midden at Sutton, Co. Dublin. *Journal of the Royal Society of Antiquaries of Ireland* 86: 1–16.

1971. The Larnian culture: a minimal view. *Proceedings of the Prehistoric Society* 37: 274–83.

1972a. A further excavation of the early kitchen-midden at Sutton, Co. Dublin. *Journal of the Royal Society of Antiquaries of Ireland* 102: 151–9.

1972b. Some ultimate Larnian sites in Lake Derravarragh, Co. Westmeath. *Journal of the Royal Society of Antiquaries of Ireland* 102: 160–73.

Mithen, S. J., 1990. *Thoughtful Foragers: A Study of Prehistoric Decision Making.* Cambridge: Cambridge University Press.

1991. 'A Cybernetic Wasteland'? Rationality, emotion and Mesolithic foraging. *Proceedings of the Prehistoric Society* 57(2): 9–14.

Modderman, P. J. R., 1970. *Linearbandkeramik aus Elsloo und Stein.* Leiden: Analecta Praehistorica Leidensia 3.

1971. Bandkeramiker und Wandernbauerntum. *Archäologisches Korrespondenzblatt* 1: 79.

1974. Die Limburger Keramik von Kesseley. *Archäologisches Korrespondenzblatt* 4: 511.

1977. Die neolithische Besiedlung bei Hienheim, Ldkr. Kelheim I: die Ausgrabungen am Weinberg. *Analecta Praehistorica Leidensia* 10.

1988. The Linear Pottery culture: diversity in uniformity. *Berichten van te Rijksdienst voor het Oudheidkundig Bodemonderzoek* 38: 63–139.

Mogosanu, F., 1978. Mezoliticul de la Ostrovul Corbului, o noua asezare de tip Schela Cladovei. *Studii si Cercetari de Istorie Veche si Arheologie* 29(3): 335–51.

Molloy, K., and M. O'Connell, 1988. Neolithic agriculture – fresh evidence from Cleggan, Connemara. *Archaeology Ireland* 2(2): 67–70.

Monk, M., 1993. People and environment: in search of the farmers. In E. Twohig and M. Ronayne (eds.), *Past Perceptions*, pp. 35–52. Cork: Cork University Press.

Moore, C., and A. K. Romney, 1992. Material culture, geographic propinquity, and linguistic affiliation on the north coast of New Guinea: a reanalysis of Welsch, Terrell, and Nadolski. *American Anthropologist* 94: 370–96.

Moore, J. A., 1985. Forager/farmer interactions: information, social organization, and the frontier. In S. Green and S. Perlman (eds.), *The Archaeology of Frontiers and Boundaries,* pp. 93–112. New York: Academic Press.

Moura, M. H., and T. Aubry, 1995. A pré-história recente da Serra do Sicó. *Trabalhos de Antropologia e Etnologia* 35 (3): 113–31.

Movius, H. L., 1935. Kilgreaney Cave, County Waterford. *Journal of the Royal Society of Antiquaries of Ireland* 65: 254–96.

Müller, J., 1988: Cultural definition of the Early Neolithic and its interaction in the eastern Adriatic. *Berytus* 36: 101–25.

1993. Modelle zur Neolithisierung aus mediterraner Sicht. *Archäologisches Informationen* 16(1): 32–8.

1994. *Das osadriatische Frühneolithikum: die Impresson-Kultur und die Neolithisierung des Adriaraumes.* Prähistorische Archäologie in Südosteuropa 9.

Nærøy, A. J., 1993. Chronological and technological changes in western Norway 6000–3800 BP. *Acta Archaeologica* 63: 77–95.

Nandris, J., 1970. Ground water as a factor in the first temperate Neolithic settlement in the Körös Region. *Zbornik Narodnog Muzeja* 6:59–69.

1972. Relations between the Mesolithic, the First Temperate Neolithic and the Bandkeramik: the nature of the problem. In J. Fitz (ed.), *Die aktuellen Fragen der Bandkeramik*, pp. 61–70. Szèkèsfehervar: Musée Roi St. Etienne.

Navarette, M.-S., 1976. *La cultura de las Cuevas con cerámica decorada en Andalucía orien-tal*. Granada: Universidad de Granada.

Navarette, M.-S., and F. Molina, 1987. Le processus de néolithisation et les débuts de la sédentarisation en Haute-Andalousie. In J. Guilaine., J.-L. Roudil, and J.-L. Vernet (eds.), *Premières communautés paysannes en Méditerranée occidentale*, pp. 645–51. Paris: CNRS.

Nemeskéri, J., 1969. Stanovisto Lepenskog Vira. In D. Srejovic (ed.), *Lepenski Vir*, pp. 239–57. Belgrade: Srpska Knizhevna Drushtva.

1978. Demographic structure of the Vlasac Epipalaeolithic population. In D. Srejovic and Z. Letica (eds.), *Vlasac*, pp. 97–134. Belgrade: Srpska Knizhevna Drushtva.

Neustupny, E., 1969. Absolute chronology of the Neolithic and Aeneolithic periods in central and south-east Europe II. *Archeologické Rozhledy* 21: 43–68.

1982. Prehistoric migrations by infiltration. *Archeologické Rozhledy* 34: 278–93.

1987. Comments on the establishment of agrarian communities on the North European Plain by P. Bogucki. *Current Anthropology* 28(1): 14–16.

Newell, R. R., D. Kielman, T. S. Constandse-Westerman, A. van Gijn, and W. A. B. van der Sanden, 1990. *An Inquiry into the Ethnic Resolution of Mesolithic Regional Groups: A Study of Their Decorative Ornaments in Time and Space*. Leiden: E. J. Brill.

Nielsen, E. K., 1987. Ertebølle and Funnel Beaker pots as tools. On traces of produc-tion techniques and use. *Acta Archaeologica* 57: 107–20. Copenhagen.

1992. Paläolithische und Mesolithische Fundstellen im zentralschweizerischen Wauwilermoos. *Archäologisches Korrespondenzblatt* 22: 27–40.

Nielsen, E. H., 1997. Fällanden ZH-Usserriet. Zum Übergangsbereich Spätmeso-lithikum-Frühneolithikum in der Schweiz. *Jahrbuch der Schweizerischen Gesellschaft für Ur- und Frühgeschichte* 80: 57–84.

Nielsen, P. O., 1979. Die Flintbeile der frühen Trichterbecherkultur in Dänemark. *Acta Archaeologica* 48: 61–138.

1985. De første bønder. Nye fund fra den tidligste Tragtbægerkultur ved Sigersted. *Aarbøger for Nordisk Oldkyndighed og Historie* 1984: 96–126.

1987. The beginning of the Neolithic – assimilation or complex change? *Journal of Danish Prehistory* 5: 240–3.

1993. The Neolithic. In S. Hvass and B. Storgaard (eds.), *Digging into the Past: 25 Years of Danish Archaeology*, pp. 84–7. Aarhus: Universitetsforlag.

Niesiolowska, E. 1994. Abriss der Probleme der frühen Trichterbecherkultur in Polen. Der Sarnowostufe und die Pikutkowo-Phase. In J. Hoika and J. Meyers Balke (eds.), *Beiträge zur frühneolithischen Trichterbecherkultur im westlichen Ostseegebiet*. Untersuchungen und Materialen zur Steinzeit in Schleswig-Holstein 1. Neumünster: Karl Wachholy Verlag.

Nieszery, N., and L. Breinl, 1993. Zur Trageweise des Spondylusschmucks in der Linearbandkeramik. *Archäologisches Korrespondenzblatt* 23: 427–38.

Nikolov, V., 1989a. Das Flusstal der Struma als Teil der Strasse von Anatolien nach Mitteleuropa. In S. Bökönyi (ed.), *Neolithic of Southeastern Europe and its Near Eastern Connections*, pp. 191–200. Budapest: Varia Archaeologica Hungarica.

1989b. Zu einigen Aspekten der Kultur Karanovo I. In S. Hiller (ed.), *Tell Karanovo und das Balkan-Neolithikum*, pp. 27–41. Salzburg: Institut für Klassische Archäologie der Universität Salzburg.

Noe-Nygaard, N., 1995. *Ecological, Sedimentary, and Geochemical Evolution of the Late-Glacial to Postglacial Åmose Lacustrine Basin, Denmark.* Oslo: Scandinavia University Press.

Nordqvist, B., 1991. Reduktionsprocesser av boplatsflinta från Halland. En spatial och kronologisk studie. In H. Browall, P. Persson, and K.-G. Sjögren (eds.), *Västsvenska stenålderstudier,* pp. 71–109. Göteborg: GOTARC.

Nygaard, S. E., 1988. Too many people, ritual porridge eating or was Hinsch right after all? In S. Indrelid, S. Kaland, and B. Solberg (eds.), *Festskrift til Anders Hagen,* pp. 147–55. Arkeologiske Skrifter 4. Bergen: Universitetet i Bergen, Historisk Museum.

    1989. The Stone Age of northern Scandinavia: a review. *Journal of World Prehistory* 3: 71–116.

O'Brien, S. R., P. A. Mayewski, L. D. Meeker, D. A. Meese, M. S. Twickler, and S. I. Whitlow, 1995. Complexity of Holocene climate as reconstructed from a Greenland ice core. *Science* 270: 1962–4.

O'Connell, M., 1987. Early cereal-type pollen cereals from Connemara, Western Ireland and their possible significance. *Pollen et Spores* 29(2–3): 207–24.

O Floinn, R., 1995. Recent research into Irish bog bodies. In R. C. Turner and R. G. Scaife (eds.), *Bog Bodies: New Discoveries and New Perspectives,* pp. 137–45. London: British Museum Press.

Odum, E. P., 1983. *Basic Ecology.* Philadelphia: Saunders College Publishing.

Olaria, C., 1988. *Cova Fosca: un asentamiento meso-neolitico de cazadores y pastores en la serrania dl Alto Maestrazgo.* Monografies de Prehistoria i Arqueologia Castellonenques 3. Castellon: Disputacion de Castellon.

Olsen, A. Bruen, 1992. *Kotedalen – en boplass gjennom 5000 år.* Bergen: University of Bergen Press.

    1995. Fagnstsedentisme og tidlig jordbrukspraksis. *Arkeologiske Skrifter* 8: 131–50.

Olsen, A. Bruen, and S. Alsaker, 1984. Greenstone and diabase utilization in the Stone Age of western Norway: technological and socio-cultural aspects of axe and adze production and distribution. *Norwegian Archaeological Review* 17: 71–103.

Olsen, B., 1988. Interaction between hunter-gatherers and farmers: ethnographical and archaeological perspectives. *Archaeologia Polski* 33: 425–34.

Oosterbeek, L., 1997. *Echoes from the East: Late Prehistory of the North Ribatejo.* Tomar: CEIPHAR.

Østmo, E., 1986. New observations on the Funnel Beaker culture in Norway. *Acta Archaeologica* 55: 190–8.

    1988. *Etableringen av jordbrukskultur i Østfold i steinalderen.* Universitets Oldsaksamlings Skrifter 10. Oslo: Universitets Oldsaksamlings.

    1990. The rise and fall of the TRB in southeastern Norway. In D. Jankowska (ed.), *Die Trichterbecherkultur: neue Forschungen und Hypothesen. Material des Internationalen Symposiums Dymaczewo, Poznan.*

    1993. Auve i Sandefjord – sanddynen, snorstemplekeramikken og c 14 dateringene. *Viking* 56: 37–64.

Østmo, E., B. Hulthèn, and S. Isaksson, 1996. The Middle Neolithic settlement at Auve. *Laborativ Arkeologi* 9: 31–40.

O'Sullivan, A., 1997. Last foragers or first farmers. *Archaeology Ireland* 11(2): 14–16.

Ottaway, B., 1973. Earliest copper ornaments in northern Europe. *Proceedings of the Prehistoric Society* 39: 294–333.

Otte, M., 1995. Diffusion des langues modernes in Eurasie préhistorique. *Comptes Rendues de l'Académie des Sciences de Paris* 321(2a): 1219–26.

Özdogan, M., 1983. Pendik: a Neolithic site of Fikirtepe culture in the Marmara region. In R. M. Boehmer and H. Hauptmann (eds.), *Beitrage zur Altertumskunde Kleinasiens: Festschrift fur Kurt Bittel*, pp. 401–11. Mainz: Karl Wachholy Verlag.

1989. Neolithic cultures of northwestern Turkey: a general appraisal of the evidence and some considerations. In S. Bökönyi (ed.), *Neolithic of Southeastern Europe and Its Near Eastern Connections*, pp. 201–15. Budapest: Varia Archaeologica Hungarica.

1993. Vinça and Anatolia: a new look at a very old problem. *Anatolica* 19 (Special Issue on Anatolia and the Balkans): 173–93.

1997. The beginning of the Neolithic economies in southeastern Europe: an Anatolian perspective. *Journal of European Archaeology* 5: 1–33.

Özdogan, M., and I. Gatsov, in press. The pre-pottery Neolithic sites of northwestern Turkey. *Anatolica*.

Paaver, K. C., 1965. *Formirovaniye Teriofauny i Izmenchivost Mlekopytayushchikh Pribaltiki v Goltsene*. Tartu: Akademiya Nauk Estonskoii SSR.

Palmer, S., 1968. A Mesolithic site at Portland Bill 1966. *Proceedings of the Dorset Natural History and Archaeological Society* 90: 183–206.

Paludan-Müller, C., 1978. High Atlantic food gathering in northwestern Zealand, ecological conditions and spatial representation. In K. Kristiansen and C. Paludan-Müller (eds.), *New Directions in Scandinavian Archaeology*, pp. 120–57. Odense: National Museum of Denmark.

Papathanassopoulos, G. A. (ed.), 1996. *Neolithic culture in Greece*. Athens: N.P. Goulandris Foundation.

Parry, W., and R. Kelly, 1987. Alternative models for exchange and spatial distribution. In J. K. Johnson and C. A. Morrow (eds.), *The Organization of Core Technology*, pp. 285–304. Boulder, CO: Westview Press.

Paul, I., 1981. Cultura Starcevo-Cris in sudul Transilvaiei. *Studii si Cercetari Istorie Veche si Archeologice* 32: 3–27.

1995. *Vorgeschichtliche Untersuchungen in Siebenbergen*. Alba Iulia: Universitatea 1 Decembrie 1918.

Paunescu, A., 1970. Epipalaeoliticul de la Cuina Turcului-Dubova. *Studii si Cercetari Istorie Veche si Archeologice* 21(1): 3–47.

1987. Tardenoisianul din Dobrogea. *Studii si Cercetari Istorie Veche si Archeologice* 38: 25–41.

Pearson, G. W., J. R. Pilcher, M. G. L. Baillie, D. M. Corbett, and F. Qua, 1986. High precision 14-C measurement of Irish oaks to show the natural 14-C variations from AD 1840 to 5210 BC. *Radiocarbon* 28: 911–34.

Pedersen, L., 1997. They put fences in the sea. In L. Pedersen, A. Fischer, and B. Aaby (eds.), *The Danish Storebælt since the Ice Age*, pp. 124–44. Copenhagen: A/S Storebælt Fixed Link.

Peglar, S. M., 1993. The mid-Holocene *Ulmus* decline at Diss Mere, Norfolk, UK: a year-by-year pollen stratigraphy from annual laminations. *The Holocene* 3: 1–13.

Peglar, S. M., and H. J. B. Birks, 1993. The mid-Holocene *Ulmus* fall at Diss Mere, south-east England – disease and human impact? *Vegetation History and Archaeobotany* 2: 61–8.

Pennington, W., 1975. The effect of Neolithic man on the environment of north west England: the use of absolute pollen diagrams. In J. G. Evans, S. Limbrey, and H. Cleere (eds.), *The Effects of Man on the Landscape: The Highland Zone*, pp. 74–85. London: Council for British Archaeology.

Perlès, C., 1989. La néolithisation de la Grèce. In O. Aurenche et J. Cauvin (eds.), *Néolithisations*, pp. 109–128. Oxford: British Archaeological Reports, International Series, 516.

1990a. L'outillage de pierre taillée néolithique en Grèce: approvisionnement et exploitation des matières premières. *Bulletin de Correspondance Hellénique* 114 (1): 1–42.

1992. Systems of exchange and organization of production in Neolithic Greece. *Journal of Mediterranean Archaeology* 5: 115–64.

1993. Les débuts du Néolithique en Grèce. *La Recherche* 266: 642–9.

1995. La transition Pléistocène/Holocène et le problème du Mésolithique en Grèce. In V. V. Bonilla (ed.), *Los Ultimos Cazadores: transforaciones culturales y económicas durante el Tardiglaciar y el inicio del Holoceno en el ámbito mediterráneo*, pp. 179–209. Alicante: Instituto de Cultura Juan Gil-Albert.

1996. Le Mésolithique de Grèce: données et problèmes. In V. Villaverde-Bonnilla and E. Auro-Tortosa (eds.), *Transformaciones culturales y economicas durante Tardiglaciar y el inicio de Holoceno en el ámbito mediterráneo*. Valencia: University of Valencia.

Perlès, C., and P. Vaughan, 1983. Pièces listrés, travail des plantes et moissons à Franchthi, Grèce (Xème–IVème mill. BC). In M.-C. Cauvin (ed.), *Traces d'utilisation sur les outils néolithiques du Proche-Orient*, pp. 209–24. Lyons: Maison de l'Orient.

Persson, O., and E. Persson, 1984. *Anthropological Report on the Mesolithic Graves from Skateholm, Southern Sweden, Excavation Seasons 1980–1982*. Lund: University of Lund, Institute of Archaeology.

Persson, P., 1987. *Etapper i Landbrukets Spridning: En Rekonstruktion utifrån de Tidigaste Spåren i Nordvåsteneuropa*. Series C. Arkeologiska Skrifter 4. Gothenburg: GOTARC.

Persson, P., and K.-G. Sjögren, 1996. Radiocarbon and the chronology of Scandinavian megalithic graves. *Journal of European Archaeology* 3(2): 59–88.

Petersen, K. S., 1992. Unitas Malacologica. *Eleventh International Malacological Congress*, pp. 129–32. Siena: Centro Offset.

Peterson, J. D., 1990. From foraging to food production in south east Ireland: some lithic evidence. *Proceedings of the Prehistoric Society* 56: 89–99.

Peterson, J. T., 1978. Hunter-gatherer/farmer exchange. *American Anthropologist* 80(2):335–51.

Piggott, S., 1954. *The Neolithic Cultures of the British Isles*. Cambridge: Cambridge University Press.

1965. *Ancient Europe*. Edinburgh: Edinburgh University Press.

1972. Excavations of the Dalladies long barrow, Fettercairn, Kincardineshire. *Proceedings of the Society of Antiquaries of Scotland* 106: 23–47.

Pilcher, J., 1993. Radiocarbon dating and the palynologist: a realistic approach to precision and accuracy. In F. M. Chambers (ed.), *Climate Change and Human Impact on the Landscape*, pp. 23–32. London: Chapman and Hall.

Pilcher, J. R., and A. G. Smith, 1979. Palaeoecological investigations at Ballynagilly, a Neolithic and Bronze Age settlement in Co. Tyrone, N. Ireland. *Philosophical Transactions of the Royal Society* (B) 286: 345–69.

Pitelka, Louis, and the Plant Migration Workshop Group, 1997. Plant migration and climate change. *American Scientist* 85: 464–73.

Pluciennik, M., 1996. Genetics, archaeology, and the wider world. *Antiquity* 70: 13–14.

1998a. Radiocarbon determinations and the Mesolithic–Neolithic transition in southern Italy. *Journal of Mediterranean Archaeology* 10: 115–50.

1998b. Deconstructung 'the Neolithic' in the Mesolithic–Neolithic transition. In M. Edmonds and C. Richards (eds.), *Understanding the Neolithic of North-Western Europe*, pp. 61–83. Glasgow: Cruithne Press.

Poplin, F., T. Poulain, P. Meniel, J. D. Vigne, D. Geddès, and D. Helmer, 1986. Les débuts de l'élevage en France. In J. P. Demoule and J. Guilaine, *Le Néolithique de la France*, pp. 37–51. Paris: Picard.

Porch, N., and J. Allen, 1995. Tasmania: archaeological and palaeo-ecological perspectives. *Antiquity* 69: 714–32.

Potekhina, I., and D. Telegin, 1995. On the dating of the Ukrainian Mesolithic–Neolithic transition. *Current Anthropology* 36: 823–36.

Prescott, C., 1995. The last frontier? Processes of Indo-Europeanization in northern Europe: the Norwegian case. *Journal of Indo-European Studies* 23: 257–78.

1996. Was there really a Neolithic in Norway? *Antiquity* 70: 77–87.

Price, R. P. S., 1993. The West Pontic 'Maritime Interaction Sphere': a long-term structure in Balkan prehistory? *Oxford Journal of Archaeology* 12: 176–96.

Price, T. D., 1981. Regional approaches to human adaptation in the Mesolithic of the North European Plain. In B. Gramsch (ed.), *Mesolithikum in Europa*, pp. 217–34. Potsdam: Museums für Ur- und Frühgeschicht.

1985. Complex foragers in southern Scandinavia. In T. D. Price and J. A. Brown (eds.), *Prehistoric Hunter-Gatherers*, pp. 341–63. Orlando: Academic Press.

1987. The Mesolithic of western Europe. *Journal of World Prehistory* 1: 225–305.

1989. The reconstruction of Mesolithic diets. In C. Bonsall (ed.), *The Mesolithic in Europe: Proceedings of the Third International Symposium*, pp. 48–59. Edinburgh: Edinburgh University Press.

1991. The Mesolithic of northern Europe. *Annual Review of Anthropology* 20: 211–33.

1995. Agricultural origins and social inequality. In T. D. Price and G. M. Feinman (eds.), *Foundations of Social Inequality*, pp. 129–51. New York: Plenum Press.

1996a. Agricultural origins and social inequality. In T. D. Price and G. M. Feinman (eds.), *Foundations of Social Inequality*, pp. 129–51. New York: Plenum.

1996b. The first farmers of southern Scandinavia. In D. R. Harris (ed.), *The Origins and Spread of Agriculture and Pastoralism in Eurasia*, pp. 346–62. London: University College Press.

Price, T. D., and J. A. Brown, 1985. Aspects of hunter-gatherer complexity. In T. D. Price and J. A. Brown (eds.), *Prehistoric Hunter-Gatherers: The Emergence of Cultural Complexity*, pp. 3–20. Orlando: Academic Press.

Price, T. D., and G. Feinman, 1993. *Images of the Past*. Mountain View, CA: Mayfield.

Price, T. D., and A. B. Gebauer, 1995a. New perspectives on the transition to agriculture. In T. D. Price and A. B. Gebauer (eds.) , *Last Hunters – First Farmers: New*

Perspectives on the Prehistoric Transition to Agriculture, pp. 3–19. Santa Fe, NM: School for American Research Press.

Price, T. D., and A. B. Gebauer (eds.), 1992. The final frontier: foragers to farmers in southern Scandinavia. In A. B. Gebauer and T. D. Price (eds.), *Transitions to Agriculture in Prehistory*, pp. 97–115. Madison, WI: Prehistory Press.

   1995b. *Last Hunters – First Farmers: New Perspectives on the Transition to Agriculture in Prehistory.* Santa Fe, NM: School for American Research Press.

Price, T. D., A. B. Gebauer, and L. H. Keeley, 1995. The spread of farming into Europe north of the Alps. In T. D. Price and A. B. Gebauer (eds.), *Last Hunters – First Farmers: New Perspectives on the Prehistoric Transition to Agriculture*, pp. 95–126. Santa Fe, NM: School for American Research Press.

Prinz, B., 1987. *Mesolithic Adaptations on the Lower Danube.* Oxford: British Archaeological Reports International Series 330.

Pucher, E., 1987. Viehwirtschaft und Jagd zur Zeit der ältesten Linearbandkeramik von Neckenmarkt (Burgenland) und Strögen (Niederösterreich). *Mitteilungen der Anthropologischen Gesellschaft in Wien* 117: 141–55.

Pumpelly, R. (ed.), 1908. *Explorations in Turkestan. Expedition of 1904. Prehistoric Civilizatons of Anau: Origins, Growth, and Influence of Environment.* Washington DC: Carnegie Institution.

Quitta, H., 1960. Zur Frage der ältesten Bandkeramik in Mitteleuropa. *Prähistorische Zeitschrift* 38: 153–89.

Radovanovic, I., 1992. Mezolit Djerdapa. PhD thesis, University of Belgrade.

   1996. *The Iron Gates Mesolithic.* Ann Arbor: International Monographs in Prehistory.

Radovanovic, I., M. Kaczanowska, J. Kozlowski, M. Pawlikowski, and B. Voytek, 1984. *The Chipped Stone Industry from Vinca.* Belgrade: University of Belgrade Press.

Rähle, W., 1978. Schmuckschnecken aus mesolithischen Kulturschichten Süddeutchlands und ihre Herkunft. In W. Taute (ed.), *Das Mesolithikum in Süddeutchland, 2: Naturwissenschaftliche Untersuchungen*, pp. 163–8. Tübingen: Verlag Archaeologica Venatoria.

Ralston, I. B. M., 1982. A timber hall at Balbridie Farm. *Aberdeen University Review* 168: 238–49.

Randsborg, K., 1975. Social dimensions of Early Neolithic Denmark. *Proceedings of the Prehistoric Society* 41: 105–18.

   1979. Resource distribution and the function of copper in Early Neolithic Denmark. In M. Ryan (ed.), *The Origins of Metallurgy in Atlantic Europe*, pp. 303–18. Proceedings of the Fifth Atlantic Colloquium. Dublin: Stationery Office.

Rasmussen, P., 1990. Leaf foddering in the earliest Neolithic agriculture: evidence from Switzerland and Denmark. *Acta Archaeologica* 60: 71–86.

Rausing, G., 1990. *Vitis* pips in Neolithic Sweden. *Antiquity* 64: 117–22.

Rech, M., 1979. *Studien zu Depotfunden der Trichterbecher- und Einzelgrabkultur des Nordens.* Offa-Bücher 39. Neumünster: Karl Wachholy Verlag.

Regnell, R., M.-J. Gaillard, T. S. Bartholin, and P. Karsten, 1995. Reconstruction of environment and history of plant use during the Late Mesolithic (Ertebølle Culture) at the inland settlement of Bökeberg III, southern Sweden. *Vegetation History and Archaeobotany* 4: 67–91.

Reim, H., 1995. Neue Baubefunde in der ältestbandkeramischen Siedlung von

Rottenburg, Kreis Tübingen. In J. Biel (ed.), *Archäologische Ausgrabungen in Baden-Württemberg 1994*, pp. 34–7. Stuttgart: Konrad Theiss.

Renfrew, A. C., 1977. Alternative models for exchange and spatial distribution. In T. Earle and J. Ericson (eds.), *Exchange Systems in Prehistory*, pp. 71–90. New York: Academic Press.

1987. *Archaeology and Language: The Puzzle of Indo-European Origins*. London: Cape.

1989. The origins of Indo-European languages. *Scientific American* 261(4): 106–14.

1992. Archaeology, genetics and linguistic diversity. *Man* 27: 445–78.

1994. World linguistic diversity. *Scientific American* 270(1): 104–10.

1996. Language families and the spread of farming. In D. H. Harris (ed.), *The Origins and Spread of Agriculture and Pastoralism in Eurasia*, pp. 70–92. London: University of London Press.

Renfrew, J. M., 1979. The first farmers in south-east Europe. *Archaeo-Physika* 8:243–65.

Richards, M., H. Corte-Real, P. Forster, V. Macaulay, H. Wilkinson-Herbots, A. Demaine, S. Papiha, R. Hedges, H.-J. Bandelt, and B. Sykes, 1996. Palaeolithic and Neolithic lineages in the European mitochondrial gene pool. *American Journal of Human Genetics* 59: 185–203.

Richards, M., V. Macaulay, B. Sykes, P. Pettitt, R. Hedges, P. Forster, and H.-J. Bandelt, 1997. Reply to Cavalli-Sforza and Minch. *American Journal of Human Genetics* 61: 251–4.

Ricq-de Bouard, M., 1987. L'outillage de pierre polie des Alpes aux Pyrénées au Néolithique ancien: la naissance d'une industrie. In J. Guilaine, J. Courtin, J.-L. Roudil, and J.-L. Vernet (eds.), *Premières communautés paysannes en Méditerranée occidentale*, pp. 305–15. Paris: CNRS.

Ricq-de Bouard, M., R. Compagnoni, J. Desmons, and F. Fedele, 1990. Les roches alpines dans l'outillage poli néolithique de la France méditerranéenne. *Gallia Préhistoire* 32: 125–49.

Ricq-de Bouard, M., and F. G. Fedele, 1993. Neolithic rock resources across the western Alps: circulation data and models. *Geoarchaeology* 8(1): 1–22.

Rimantienè, R., 1992. Neolithic hunter-gatherers at Šventoji in Lithuania. *Antiquity* 66: 367–76.

Rindos, D., 1984. *The Origins of Agriculture: An Evolutional Approach*. Orlando: Academic Press.

Roberts, L., 1992. Using genes to track down Indo-European migrations. *Science* 257: 1346.

Roche, J. 1977. Les amas coquilliers mésolithiques de Muge (Portugal). Chronologie, milieu naturel et leurs incidences sur le peuplement humain. *Approche écologique de l'homme fossile*, supplément au *Bulletin de l'Association Française pour l'Etude du Quaternaire* 47: 353–9. Paris.

Roksandic, M. 1999. Transition from Mesolithic to Neolithic in the Iron Gates Gorge: physical anthropology perspective. PhD thesis, Simon Fraser University, Burnaby.

Rodden, R. J., 1962. Excavations at the Early Neolithic site at Nea Nikomedeia, Greek Macedonia. *Proceedings of the Prehistoric Society* 28: 267–88.

Ronayne, M., 1994. Located practices: deposition, architecture and landscape in Irish court tombs. MA thesis, University College Cork.

Ronen, A., 1995. Core, periphery, and ideology in Aceramic Cyprus. *Quartär* 45/46: 177–206.

Roth, H. L., 1887. On the origin of agriculture. *Journal of the Royal Anthropological Institute of Great Britain and Ireland* 16: 102–36.

Roudil, Jean-Louis, and M. Soulier, 1983. Le gisement néolithique ancien de Peiro Signado (Portiragnes, Hérault): étude préliminaire. *Congrès Préhistorique de France*, pp. 258–79. Paris: Société préhistorique.

Rouse, I., 1958. The inference of migrations from anthropological evidence. In R. H. Thompson (ed.), *Migration in New World Culture History*, pp. 63–8. Social Science Bulletin 27. Tucson: University of Arizona.

Roussot-Larroque, J., 1977. Néolithisation et Néolithique ancien d'Aquitaine. *Bulletin de la Société Préhistorique Française* 74: 559–82.

  1989. Imported problems and home-made solutions: late foragers and pioneer farmers seen from the west. In S. Bökönyu (ed.), *Neolithic of Southeastern Europe and its Near Eastern Connections*, pp. 253–76. Budapest: Varia Archaeologica Hungarica.

Rowley-Conwy, P., 1980. Continuity and change in the prehistoric economies of Denmark, 3700–2300 BC. PhD thesis, Cambridge University.

  1981. Slash and burn in the temperate European Neolithic. In R. Mercer, (ed.), *Farming Practice in British Prehistory*, pp. 85–96. Edinburgh: Edinburgh University Press.

  1983. Sedentary hunters: the Ertebølle example. In G. Bailey (ed.), *Hunter-Gatherer Economy*, pp. 111–26. Cambridge: Cambridge University Press.

  1984. The laziness of the short-distance hunter: the origin of agriculture in western Denmark. *Journal of Anthropological Archaeology* 3: 300–24.

  1985. The origin of agriculture in Denmark: a review of some theories. *Journal of Danish Archaeology* 4:188–95.

  1986. Between cave painters and crop planters: aspects of the Temperate European Mesolithic. In M. Zvelebil (ed.), *Hunters in Transition*, pp. 17–32. Cambridge: Cambridge University Press.

  1987. Animal bones in Mesolithic studies: recent progress and hopes for the future. In P. Rowley-Conwy, M. Zvelebil, and H. P. Blankholm (eds.), *Mesolithic Northwest Europe: Recent Trends*, pp. 74–81. Sheffield: University of Sheffield.

  1991. Arene Candide: a small part of a larger pastoral system? In B. Bordighera (ed.), *Archeologia della pastorizia nell'Europa meridionale*, pp. 95–116. Istituto internazionale di Studi Liguri.

  1992. The Early Neolithic animal bones from Gruta do Caldeirão. In J. Zilhão (ed.), *Gruta do Caldeirão: O Neolítico Antigo*, pp. 231–57. Trabalhos de Arqueologia 6. Lisbon: Instituto Português do Património Arquitectónico e Arqueológico.

  1995. Making the first European farmers younger. *Current Anthropology* 36: 346–53.

Rowley-Conwy, P., and M. Zvelebil, 1989. Saving it for later: storage by prehistoric hunter-gatherers in Europe. In P. Halstead, and J. O'Shea (eds.), *Bad Year Economics*, pp. 40–56. Cambridge: Cambridge University Press.

Rowley-Conwy, P., M. Zvelebil, and P. Blankholm (eds.), 1987. *Mesolithic Northwest Europe: Recent Trends* 2. Sheffield: University of Sheffield.

Rozoy, J. G., 1978. *Les derniers chasseurs: l'Epipaléolithique en France et en Belgique, essai de synthèse*. Charleville: Chez l'auteur. Supplément au Bulletin de la Société Archéologique Champenoise.

Rubel, P. G., and A. Rosman, 1983. The evolution of exchange structures and ranking:

some Northwest Coast and Athapaskan examples. *Journal of Anthropological Research* 39: 1–25.

Rudebeck, E., 1987. Flint mining in Sweden during the Neolithic period: new evidence from the Kvarnby-S. Sallerup area. In G. de G. Sieveking and M. H. Newcomer (eds.), *The Human Uses of Flint and Chert*, pp. 151–7. Cambridge: Cambridge University Press.

Runeson, H. 1994. Arkeologisk undersokning Soderbytorp, Sodermanland, Osterhaninge socken. *RAA 387 UV Stockholm*, Rapport 1994: 76.

Runnels, C., 1988. A prehistoric survey of Thessaly: new light on the Greek Middle Paleolithic. *Journal of Field Archaeology* 15: 277–90.

1995. Review of Aegean prehistory IV: the Stone Age of Greece from the Palaeolithic to the advent of the Neolithic. *American Journal of Archaeology* 99: 699–728.

Runnels, C., and T. H. van Andel, 1988. Trade and the origins of agriculture in the eastern Mediterranean. *Journal of Mediterranean Archaeology* 1: 83–109.

Ryan, W. B. F., W. C. Pitman III, C. O. Major, K. Shimkus, V. Moskalenko, G. A. Jones, P. Dimitrov, G. Naci, M. Sakinç, and H. Yuce, 1997. An abrupt drowning of the Black Sea Shelf. *Marine Geology* 138: 119–26.

Sahlins, M., 1974. *Stone Age Economics*. London: Tavistock.

Sakellardis, M., 1979. *The Mesolithic and Neolithic of the Swiss Area*. Oxford: British Archaeological Reports International Series.

Sanchez, M. J., 1996. *Ocupação prehistórica do nordeste de Portugal*. Zamora: Fundación Rei Afonso Henriques.

Sanchez, M. J., A. M. Soares, and F. M. Alonso, 1993. Buraco da Pala (Mirandela): datas de carbono 14 calibradas e seu poder de resolução. Algumas reflexões. *Trabalhos de Antropologia e Etnologia* 33(12): 223–43.

Sanger, D., 1975. Culture change as an adaptive process in the Maine-Maritimes region. *Arctic Anthropology* 12(2): 60–75.

Schietzel, K., 1965. *Müddersheim, eine Ansiedlung der jüngeren Bandkeramik in Rheinland*. Cologne: Böhlau.

Schrire, C. (ed.), 1984. *Past and Present in Hunter Gatherer Studies*. Orlando, FL: Academic Press.

Schütrumpf, R. 1972, Stratigrahie und pollenanalytische Ergebnisse der Ausgrabung des Ellerbek-zeitlische Wohnplatzes Rosenhof (Ostholstein). *Arkäologisches Korrespondenzblatt* 2: 9–16.

Schütz, C., H. C. Strien, and W. Taute, 1992. Ausgrabungen in der Wilhelmina von Stuttgart-Bad Cannstatt: die erste Siedlung der altneolitischen La-Hoguette-Kultur. *Archäologische Auggrabungen in Baden-Württemberg* 1991: 45–9.

Schvorer, M., C. Bordier, J. Evin, and G. Delibrias, 1979. Chronologie absolue de la fin des temps glaciaires en Europe. Recensement et présentation des datations se rapportant à des siets Françasi. In D. de Sonneville-Bordes (ed.), *La fin des temps glaciaires en Europe*, pp. 21–41. Paris: CNRS.

Schwabedissen, H., 1966. Ein horizontierer Breitkeil aus Satrup und die Manninfachen Kulturverbindungen des Beginn den Neolitikums im Norden und Nordwesten. *Palaeohistoria* 12: 409–68.

1979. Der Begin des Neolithikums in nordwestlichen Deutschland. In H. Schirnig (ed.), *Grosssteingräber in Niedersachsen*, pp. 203–22.

1981. Ertebølle/Ellerbek-Mesolithilum oder Neolithikum? In B. Gramsch (ed.),

Mesolithikum in Europa, pp. 129–43. Berlin: VEB Deutcher Verlag der Wissenschaften.

1994. Die Ellerbek-Kultur in Schleswig-Holstein und das Vordringen des Neolithikums über die Elbe nach Norden. In J. Hoika and J. Meyers Balke (eds.), *Beiträge zur frühneolithischen Trichterbecherkultur im westlichen Ostseegebiet*, pp. 361–81. Untersuchungen und Materialen zur Steinzeit in Schleswig-Holstein 1. Neumünster: Karl Wachholy Verlag.

Schwarz-Mackensen, G., 1983. Sie Siedlung der ältesten Linienbandkeramik von Eitzum, Ldkr. Wolfenbüttel. In G. Wegner (ed.), *Frühe Bauernkulturen in Niedersachsen*, pp. 23–36. Oldenburg: Museum für Naturkunde und Vorgeschichte.

Schwarz-Mackensen, G., and W. Schneider, 1983. Fernbeziehungen im Frühneolithikum – Rohstoffversorgung am Beispiel des Aktinolith-Hornblendschiefers. In G. Wegner (ed.), *Frühe Bauernkulturen in Niedersachsen*, pp. 165–76. Oldenburg: Museum für Naturkunde und Vorgeschichte.

Schwidetsky, I. (ed.), 1973. *Anfänge des Neolithikums vom Orient bis Europa, VIII, Anthropologie*. Cologne: Bohlau.

Séfériadès, M. L., 1993. The European Neolithisation process. *Porocilo* 21: 137–62.

Segerberg, A., 1985. Bälinge Mossar. Hunters and farmers during the Early and Middle Neolithic in Central Sweden. *Iskos* 5: 157–63.

1986. En felande länk från tidigneolitikum? *Populär Arkeologi* 4: 15–22.

Shea, S., 1931. Report on the human skeleton found in Staney Island bog, Portumna. *Journal of the Galway Archaeological and Historical Society* 15: 73–9.

Sherratt, A., 1980. The beginnings of agriculture in the Near East and Europe. In A. Sherrat (ed.), *The Cambridge Encyclopedia of Archaeology*, pp. 102–11. Cambridge: Cambridge University Press.

1981. Plough and pastoralism: aspects of the secondary products revolution. In I. Hodder, F. Isaac, and N. Hammond (eds.), *Pattern of the Past: Studies in Honour of David Clarke*, pp. 261–306. Cambridge: Cambridge University Press.

1982. Mobile resources: settlement and and exchange in early agricultural Europe. In C. Renfrew and S. Shennan (eds.), *Ranking, Resource, and Exchange: Aspects of the Archaeology of Early European Society*, pp. 13–26. Cambridge: Cambridge University Press.

1984. Social evolution: Europe in the later Neolithic and Copper Ages. In J. Bintliff (ed.), *European Social Evolution*, pp. 123–34. Bradford: University of Bradford Press.

1987. Neolithic exchange systems in central Europe. In G. de G. Sieveking and M. Newcomer (eds.), *The Human Uses of Flint and Chert*, pp. 193–204. Cambridge: Cambridge University Press.

1990. The genesis of megaliths: monumentality, ethnicity, and social complexity in Neolithic northwest Europe. *World Archaeology* 22: 147–67.

Sherratt, A., and S. Sherratt, 1988. The archaeology of Indo-European: an alternative view. *Antiquity* 62: 584–95.

Shnirelman, V., 1992a. Crises and economic dynamics in traditional societies. *Journal of Anthropological Archaeology* 11: 25–46.

1992b. The emergence of a food-producing economy in the steppe and forest-steppe zones of eastern Europe. *The Journal of Indo-European Studies* 20: 123–43.

Sielmann, B., 1971. Die frühneolithische Besiedlung Mitteleuropas. *Fundamenta* 3(Va): 1–65.

Sieveking, G. de G., *et al.*, 1972. Prehistoric flint mines and their identification as sources of raw material. *Archaeometry* 14:151–76.

Silva, C. T., and J. Soares, 1981. *Préhistória da área de Sines*. Lisbon: Gabinete da Área de Sines.

Silva, R. J., and L. H. Keeley, 1994. 'Frits' and specialized hide preparation in the Belgian Early Neolithic. *Journal of Archaeological Science* 21: 91–9.

Simmons, I. G., 1979. Late Mesolithic societies and the environment of the uplands of England and Wales. *Bulletin of the Institute of Archaeology London* 16: 11–129.

   1996. *The Environmental Impact of Later Mesolithic Cultures*. Edinburgh: Edinburgh University Press.

Simões, T., 1996. O sítio neolítico de São Pedro de Canaferrim (Sintra). *Actes. I Congrés del Neolític a la Península Ibérica* 1, pp. 329–6. Gavà: Museu de Gavà.

Simonsen, P., 1975. When and why did occupational specialization begin at the Scandinavian north coast? *Papers of the IX International Anthropological Congress. Prehistoric Maritime Adaptations*, pp. 75–85. Chicago.

   1988. Exchange of raw materials between coast and inland in northernmost Scandinavia in the Late Stone Age. *Acta Archaeologica Ludensia* 8(14): 99–106.

   1996. Trade in north Scandinavia in Neolithicum. Paper presented at the Xth UISPP Congress. Forli, Italy.

Simpson, D. D. A., 1995. The Neolithic settlement site at Ballygalley, Co. Antrim. In E. Grogan and C. Mount (eds.), *Annus Archaeologiae: Archaeological Research 1992*, pp. 37–44. Dublin: Organisation of Irish Archaeologists.

Sjögren, K.-G., 1986. Kinship, labor, and land in Neolithic southwest Sweden: social aspects of megalithic graves. *Journal of Anthropological Archaeology* 5: 229–65.

   1994. Det tidliga jordbruket i Västsverige. In *Mylla Mule Människa: Västergötlands Fornminnesförenings Tidsskrift* 1993–4: 147–57.

Sjøvold, T. (ed.), 1982. *Introduksjonen av Jordbruk i Norden*. Oslo: Universitetsforlaget.

Skaarup, J., 1973, *Hesselø-Sølager: Jagdstationen der südskandinavischen Trichterbecherkultur*. Copenhagen: Akademisk Forlag.

   1975. *Stengade: ein langeländischer Wohnplatz mit Hausresten aus der frühneolithischen Zeit*. Rudkøping: Meddelelser fra Langelands Museum.

   1983. Submarine stenalderbopladser i det fynske øhav. *Antikvariske Studier* 6: 137–61.

   1988. Burials, votive offerings and social structure in Early Neolithic farmer society of Denmark. *Rivista di Antropologia* (Rome) 66: 435–54.

Skeates, R., and R. Whitehouse, 1997. New radiocarbon dates for prehistoric Italy 2. *The Accordia Research Papers* 6: 179–91.

Sleeman, D. P., R. J. Devoy, and P. C. Woodman, 1984. *The Proceedings of the Postglacial Colonization Conference*. Occasional Publication of the Irish Biogeographical Society 1. Cork.

Smith, B. D., 1994. *The Emergence of Agriculture*. San Francisco: W. H. Freeman.

Smith, C., 1992. *Late Stone Age Hunters of the British Isles*. London: Routledge.

Smith, P. E. L., 1995. Transhumance among European settlers in Atlantic Canada. *The Geographical Journal* 161: 79–86.

Snow, D., 1995. Migration in prehistory: the Northern Iroquoian case. *American Antiquity* 60: 59–79.

Soares, A. M., 1989. *O efeito de reservatório oceânico nas águas costeiras de Portugal continental*. Lisbon: ICEN-LNETI.

1993. The ¹⁴C content of marine shells: evidence for variability in coastal upwelling off Portugal during the Holocene. *Isotope Techniques in the Study of Past and Current Environmental Changes in the Hydrosphere and the Atmosphere*, pp. 471–85. Vienna: International Atomic Energy Agency,

Soares, J., 1992. Les territorialités produites sur le littoral centre-sud du Portugal au cours du processus de néolithisation. *Setúbal Arqueológica* 9–10: 1735.

1995. Mesolítico-Neolítico na costa sudoeste: transformações e permanências. *Trabalhos de Antropologia e Etnologia* 35(2): 27–54.

1997. A transição para as formações sociais neolíticas na costa sudoeste portuguesa. In A. A. Rodríguez Casal (ed.), *O Neolítico atlántico e as orixes do megalitismo*, pp. 587–608. Santiago de Compostela: Universidade de Santiago de Compostela.

Sokal, R. R., G. Jacquez, N. Oden, D. Digiovanni, A. Falsettin, E. McGee, and B. Thomson, 1993. Genetic relationships of European populations reflect their ethnohistorical affinities. *American Journal of Physical Anthropology* 91: 55–70.

Sokal, R. R., R. L. Jantz, and B. A. Thomson, 1996. Dermatoglyphic variation in Europe. *American Journal of Physical Anthropology* 100: 35–47.

Sokal, R. R., and G. Livshits, 1993. Demographic variation of six dermatoglyphic traits in Eurasia. *American Journal of Physical Anthropology* 90: 393–407.

Sokal, R. R., N. L. Oden, P. Legendre, M.-J. Fortin, J. Kim, B. A. Thomson, A. Vaudor, R. M. Harding, and G. Barbujani, 1990. Genetics and language in European populations. *American Naturalist* 135(2): 157–75.

Sokal, R. R., N. L. Oden, P. Legendre, M.-J. Fortin, J. Kim, and A. Vaudor, 1989. Genetic differences among language families in Europe. *American Journal of Physical Anthropology* 79: 489–502.

Sokal, R. R., N. L. Oden, and B. A. Thompson, 1992. Origins of the Indo-Europeans: genetic evidence. *Proceedings of the National Academy of Sciences U.S.A.* 89: 7669–73.

Sokal, R. R., N. L. Oden, J. Walker, D. Di Giovanni, and B. A. Thomson, 1996. Historical population movements in Europe influence genetic relationships in modern samples. *Human Biology* 68:873–98.

Sokal, R. R., N. L. Oden, and A. C. Wilson, 1991. New genetic evidence supports the origin of agriculture in Europe by demic diffusion. *Nature* 351:143–4.

1992. Patterns of population spread. *Nature* 355: 214.

Solberg, B., 1989. The Neolithic transition in southern Scandinavia: internal development or migration. *Oxford Journal of Archaeology* 8: 261–96.

Sondaar, P. Y., 1971. Paleozoogeography of the Pleistocene mammals from the Aegean. *Opera Botanica* 30: 65–70.

Sordinas, A., 1969. Investigations on the prehistory of Corfu. *Balkan Studies* 10(2): 393–420.

Sørensen, S. A., 1995. Lollikhuse – a dwelling site under a kitchen midden. *Journal of Danish Archaeology* 11: 19–29.

Soudsky, B., 1969. Etude de la maison néolithique. *Slovenská Archeologia* 17: 5–96.

Spång, K., S. Welinder, and B. Wyszomirski, 1976. The introduction of the Neolithic stone age into the Baltic area. In S. J. de Laet (ed.), *Acculturation and Continuity in Atlantic Europe*, pp. 235–49. Bruges: De Tempel.

Spencer, C., 1993a. Factional ascendance, dimensions of leadership, and the development of centralized authority. In E. Brumfiel and J. Fox (eds.), *Factional Competition and Political Development in the New World*, pp. 31–73. Cambridge: Cambridge University Press.

1993b. Human agency, biased transmission, and the cultural evolution of chiefly authority. *Journal of Anthropological Archaeology* 12: 41–74.

Speth, J., 1991. Some unexplored aspects of mutualistic Plains–Pueblo food exchange. In K. Spielman (ed.), *Farmers, Hunters and Colonists: Interaction between the Southwest and the Southern Plains*, pp. 18–36. Tucson: University of Arizona Press.

Spielman, K. A. (ed.), 1991. *Farmers, Hunters and Colonists: Interaction Between the Southwest and the Southern Plains*. Tucson: University of Arizona Press.

Srejovic, D., 1966. Lepenski Vir: a new prehistoric culture in the Danubian region. *Archaeologica Jugoslavica* 7:13–18.

1969a. *Lepenski Vir*. Belgrade: Srpska Knizhevna Zadruga.

1969b. The roots of the Lepenski Vir culture. *Archaeologica Jugoslavica* 10:13–22.

1971. Die Lepenski Vir Kultur und der Beginn der Jungsteinzeit an der mittleren Donau. In H. Schwabedissen (ed.), *Die Anfang des Neolithikums vom Orient bis Nordeuropa*, pp. 1–19. Cologne: Böhlau Verlag.

1972. *Europe's First Monumental Sculpture: New Discoveries at Lepenski Vir*. New York: Stein and Day.

1974. Mezolitske osnove Neolitskih kultura u juznom Podunavlju. *Materijali* 10:21–30.

1975. The Odmut Cave – a new facet of the Mesolithic culture of the Balkan peninsula. *Archaeologica Jugoslavica* 15:3–12.

1979. Protoneolit – kultura lepenskogo vira. *Praistoria Jugoslavenskih zemalja*,2: *Neolitsko doba*. Sarajevo.

1984. Umetnost i Religija. In M. Garasanin and D. Srejovic (eds.), *Vinça u praistoriji i srednjem veku*, pp. 42–57. Belgrade: Srpska Akademija Nauka i Umetnosti.

1988. The Neolithic of Serbia: a review of research. In D. Srejovic (ed.), *The Neolithic of Serbia: Archaeological Research 1948–1988*, pp. 5–19. Belgrade: Center for Archaelogical Research, University of Belgrade.

Srejovic, D., and L. Babovic, 1981. *Lepenski Vir: Menschenbilder einer frühen europäischen Kultur*. Cologne: Römisch-Germanisch Museum.

Srejovic, D., and Z. Letica, 1978. *Vlasac: A Mesolithic Settlement in the Iron Gates*. Belgrade: Serbian Academy of Sciences and Art.

Stafford, M., 1998. *From Forager to Farmer in Flint: Stone Tools and the Transition to Agriculture in Southern Scandinavia*. Aarhus: Aarhus University Press.

Starkel, L., 1995. Reconstruction of hydrological changes between 7000 and 3000 BP in the upper and middle Vistula river basin, Poland. *The Holocene* 5(1): 34–42.

Startin, W., 1978. Linear Pottery culture houses: reconstruction and manpower. *Proceedings of the Prehistoric Society* 44: 143–59.

Stäuble, H., 1995. Radiocarbon dates of the earliest Neolithic in central Europe. *Radiocarbon* 37/2: 227–37.

Stephens, N., and A. E. P. Collins, 1961. The Quaternary deposits at Ringneil Quay and Ardmillan. *Proceedings of the Royal Irish Academy* 61C: 41–77.

Stordeur, D., 1993. Sédentaires et nomades du PPNB final dans le désert de Palmyre (Syrie). *Paléorient* 19: 187–204.

Strand Petersen, K., 1992. Environmental changes recorded in the Holocene molluscan fauna, Djursland, Denmark. *Unitas Malacologica*, pp. 129.

Straus, L. G., 1988. Archaeological Surveys and Excavations in Southern Portugal. *Old World Archaeology Newsletter* 12(3): 13–17.

Straus, L. G., and B. J. Vierra, 1989. Preliminary investigation of the concheiro at Vidigal (Tagus, Portugal). *Mesolithic Miscellany* 10(1): 2–11.

Tarrus, J., J. Chinchilla, and A. Bosch, 1994. La Draga (Banyoles): un site lacustre du Néolithique ancien Cardial en Catalogne. *Bulletin de la Société Préhistorique Française* 91: 449–56.

Tasic, N., B. Jovanovic, and S. Dimitrijevic, 1979. *Praistorija Jugoslovenskih Zemalja, 3 Eneolitska Doba*, Sarajevo.

Tasic, N., D. Srejovic, and B. Stojanovic, 1990. *Vinca: Centre of the Neolithic Culture of the Danubian Region*. Belgrade: Kultura.

Tauber, H., 1972. Radiocarbon chronology of the Danish Mesolithic and Neolithic. *Antiquity* 46:106–10.

  1981. δ^{13}C evidence for dietary habits of prehistoric man in Denmark. *Nature* 292: 332–3.

Taute, W., 1967. Das Felsdach Lautereck, eine mesolithisch-neolithisch-bronzezeitliche Stratigraphie an der oberen Donau. *Palaeohistoria* 12: 483–504.

  1973. Neue Forschungen zur Chronologie von Spätpaläolithikum und Frühmesolithikum in Süddeutschland. *Archäologische Informationen* 2/3: 59–66.

  1978. *Das Mesolithikum in Süddeutschland, 2: Naturwissenschaftliche Untersuchungen.* Tübinger Monographien zur Urgeschichte 5/2. Tübingen: Archaeologica Venatoria.

Telegin, D. Y., 1987. Neolithic cultures of the Ukraine and adjacent areas and their chronology. *Journal of World Prehistory* 1: 307–31.

Telegin, D. Y. and Pothekina, I. D. 1987. *Neolithic cemeteries and populations in the Dnieper basin*. Oxford: British Archaeological Reports, International Series S383.

Telegin, D. Y., and E. N. Titov, 1993. La Zone des Steppes. In *Atlas du Néolithique européen: l'Europe orientale*, pp. 463–94. Etudes et Recherches Archéologiques de l'Université de Liège. Liège: Université de Liège.

Testart, A., 1982. The significance of food storage among hunter-gatherers: residence patterns, population densities and social inequalities. *Current Anthropology* 23: 523–37.

Theocharis, D., 1973. *Neolithic Greece*. Athens: National Bank of Greece.

Thomas, J. 1987. Relations of production and social change in the Neolithic of north-west Europe. *Man* 22: 405–30.

  1988. Neolithic explanations revisited: the Mesolithic–Neolithic transition in Britain and south Scandinavia. *Proceedings of the Prehistoric Society* 54: 59–66.

  1991a. The hollow men? A reply to Steven Mithen. *Proceedings of the Prehistoric Society* 57(2): 15–20.

  1991b. *Rethinking the Neolithic*. Cambridge: Cambridge University Press.

1996a. The cultural context of the first use of domesticates in continental central and northwest Europe. In D. R. Harris (ed.), *The Origins and Spread of Agriculture and Pastoralism in Eurasia*, pp. 310–22. London: University College London Press.

1996b. *Time, Culture, and Identity*. London: Routledge.

Thorpe, I. J., 1996. *The Origins of Agriculture in Europe*. London: Routledge.

Thorpe, O. W., S. E. Warren, and L. H. Barfield, 1979. The sources and distribution of archaeological obsidian in northern Italy. *Preistoria alpina* 15: 73–92.

Thrane, H., 1991. Danish plough-marks from the Neolithic and Bronze Age. *Journal of Danish Archaeology* 9: 111–25.

Tilley, C., 1996. *An Ethnography of the Neolithic*. Cambridge: Cambridge University Press.

Tillmann, A., 1994. Kontinuität oder Diskontinuität? Zur Frage einer bandkeramischen Landnahme im südlichen Mitteleuropa. *Arch. Informationen* 17: 157–87.

Timofeev, V. I., 1987. On the problem of the Early Neolithic of the east Baltic area. *Acta Archaeologica* 58: 207–12.

1990. On the links of the east Baltic Neolithic and the Funnel Beaker Culture. In D. Jankovska (ed.), *Die Trichterbeckerkultur*, pp. 135–49. Poznań.

Tinè, S., 1986. Nuovi scavi nella caverna delle Arene Candide. In J. P. Demoule and J. Guilaine (eds.), *Le Néolithique de la France: hommage à Gérard Bailloud*, pp. 95–111. Paris: Picard.

Tinè, S., and M. Bernabo Bréa, 1980. Il villagio del Guadone di S. Severo (Foggia). *Rivista di Scienze Preistoriche* 35: 45–74.

Tinè, V. (ed.), 1996. *Forme e tempi della Neolitizzazione in Ialia meridionale e in Sicilia*. Genoa: Istituto Regionale per le Antichità Calabresi e Bizantine.

Todorova, H., and I. Vajsov, 1993. *Novo-Kamennata Epokha v Balgaria*. Sofia: Izdatelstvo Nauka i Izkustvo.

Tomaszewski, A. J., 1988. Foragers, farmers and archaeologists. *Archaeologia Polski* 33: 434–40.

Tringham, R., 1968. A preliminary study of the Early Neolithic and latest Mesolithic blade industries in southeast and central Europe. In J. Coles and D. Simpson (eds.), *Studies in Ancient Europe: Essays Presented to Stuart Piggott*, pp. 45–70. Leicester: Leicester University Press.

1969. Animal domestication in the Neolithic cultures of the south-west part of European USSR. In P. J. Ucko and G. Dimbelby (eds.), *The Domestication and Exploitation of Plants and Animals*, pp. 381–92. London: Duckworth.

1971. *Hunters, Fishers and Farmers of Eastern Europe*. London: Hutchinson.

1973. The Mesolithic of southeastern Europe. In S. K. Kozlowski (ed.), *The Mesolithic in Europe*, pp. 551–72. Warsaw: Warsaw University Press.

1974. The concept of 'civilization' in European archaeology. In J. Sabloff and C. C. Lamberg-Karlovsky (eds.), *The Rise and Fall of Civilization*, pp. 470–85. San Francisco: Cummings.

1978. Experimentation, ethnoarchaeology and the leapfrogs in archaeological methodology. In R. Gould (ed.), *Explorations in Ethnoarchaeology*, pp. 169–99. Albuquerque: University of New Mexico Press.

1988. Microwear analysis of the chipped stone assemblage from Divostin. In A. McPherron and D. Srejovic (eds.), *Divostin and the Neolithic of central Serbia*, pp. 203–24. Pittsburgh, PA: University of Pittsburgh Press.

In press. Analysis of the chipped stone assemblage at Sitagroi. In E. Elster and

C. Renfrew (eds.), *Excavations at Sitagroi* 2. Los Angeles: UCLA Institute of Archaeology Press.

Tringham, R., B. Brukner, T. Kaiser, K. Borojevic, N. Russell, R. Steli, M. Stevanovic, and B. Voytek, 1992. The Opovo Project: a study of socio-economic change in the Balkan Neolithic. 2nd preliminary report. *Journal of Field Archaeology* 19(3):351–86.

Tringham, R., and D. Krstić, 1990. Conclusion. In R. Tringham and D. Krstic (eds.), *Selevac, a Neolithic Village in Yugoslavia*, pp. 567–616. Los Angeles: UCLA Institute of Archaeology Press.

Troels-Smith, J., 1953. Ertebøllekultur – Bondekultur. Resultater af de sidste 10 aars undersøgelser i Aamosen. *Aarbøger for Nordisk Oldkyndighed og Historie* 1953: 5–62.

 1960. Ivy, mistletoe, and elm. Climate indicators – fodder plants. *Danmarks Geologiske Undersøgelse* 4(4): 4–32.

 1967. The Ertebølle culture and its background. *Palaeohistoria* 12: 505–28.

 1982. Vegetationshistoriske vidnesbyrd om skovrydning, planteavl og husdyrhold i Europa, specielt Skandinavien. In T. Sjövold (ed.), *Introduksjonen av jordbruk i Norden*, pp. 39–62. Tromsø: Universitetsforlaget.

Turk, I., 1993. Podmol pri Kastelcu – novo vecplastno arheolosko najdisce na Krasu. *Slovenija Arheol. Vestnik* 44: 130–52. Ljubljana.

Twohig, E., 1990. *Irish Megalithic Tombs*. London: Shire.

Tykot, R., 1992. Regional interaction in the prehistoric central Mediterranean: chronological variation as evidenced by obsidian exchange. Paper presented at the 57th annual meeting of the SAA, Pittsburgh.

 1996. Obsidian procurement and distribution in the central and western Mediterranean. *Journal of Mediterranean Archaeology* 9(1): 39–82.

 n.d. Mediterranean islands and multiple flows: the sources and exploitation of Sardinian obsidian. In M. S. Shackley (ed.), *Method and Theory in Archaeological Obsidian Studies*. New York: Plenum.

Uerpmann, H. P., 1977. Betrachtungen zur Wirtschaftsform neolithischer Gruppen in Südwestdeutschland. *Fundberichte aus Baden-Württemburg* 3: 144–61.

van Andel, T. H., and C. N. Runnels, 1995. The earliest farmers in Europe. *Antiquity* 69: 481–500.

van de Velde, P. 1993. Soziale Struktur, Gräberanalyse, und Repräsentivität. Der Fall der nordwestlichen Bandkeramik. *Helinium* 33: 157–67.

van der Waals, J. D., and H. T. Waterbolk, 1976. Excavations at Swifterbant – discovery, progress, aims, and methods. *Helinium* 16: 3–14.

van Diest, H., 1981. Zur Frage der Lampen nach den Ausgrabungsfunden von Rosenhof (OstHolstein). *Archäologisches Korrespondenzblatt* 11: 301–14.

Vang Petersen, P., 1984. Chronological and regional variation in the Late Mesolithic of eastern Denmark. *Journal of Danish Archaeology* 3: 7–18.

Vankina, L. V., 1970. *Torfyanikovaya Stoyanka Sarnate*. Riga: Zinatne.

Vaquer, J., 1989. Innovation et inertie dans le processus de néolithisation en Languedoc occidental. In O. Aurenche and J. Cauvin (eds.), *Néolithisations*, pp. 187–98. Oxford: British Archaeological Reports International Series 516.

Vaquer, J., D. Geddes, M. Barbaza, and J. Erroux, 1986. Mesolithic plant exploitation at the Balma Abeurador (France). *Oxford Journal of Archaeology* 5: 1–18.

Vásquez Varela, J. M., 1994. El Mesolítico costero de Galicia: una panorámica actual.

Paper presented to the Old People and the Sea. International Conference on the Mesolithic of the Atlantic Façade, Santander (Spain).

Vavilov, N. I., 1926. *Studies on the Origin of Cultivated Plants*. Leningrad: Institut Botanique Appliqué et d'Amélioration des Plantes.

Vencl, S., 1986. The role of hunting-gathering populations in the transition to farming: a central-European perspective. In M. Zvelebil (ed.), *Hunters in Transition*, pp. 43–51. Cambridge: Cambridge University Press.

Verhart, L. B. M., and M. Wansleeben, 1997. Waste and prestige; the Mesolithic–Neolithic transition in the Netherlands from a social perspective. *Analecta Praehistorica Leidensia* 29: 65–73.

Vermeersch, P. M., and P. Van Peer, 1990. *Contributions to the Mesolithic in Europe*. Studia Praehistoric Belgica 5. Leuven: Leuven University Press.

Vigne, J.-D., 1989. Origine des principaux mammifères domestiques de l'Ancien Monde. *Ethnozootechnie* 42: 1–5.

Vigne, J.-D., and D. Helmer, 1994. Origine et évolution de l'élevage au Néolithique sur la bordure nord-occidentale de la Méditerranée. Les civilisations méditerranéennes (résumé des communications). *Société préhistorique française, Carcassonne* 31.

Vilaça, R., 1988. *Subsídios para o estudo da Pré-História recente do Baixo Mondego*. Trabalhos de Arqueologia 5. Lisbon: Instituto Português do Património Cultural.

Villa, P., J. Courtin, and D. Helmer, 1985. Restes osseux et structures d'habitat en grotte: l'apport des remontages dans la Baume de Fontbrégoua. *Bulletin de la Société Préhistorique Française* 82: 389–421.

Vitelli, K. D., 1993. *Franchthi Neolithic Pottery: Classification and Ceramic Phases 1 and 2. Excavations at Franchthi Cave 8*. Bloomington: Indiana University Press.

1995. Pots, potters, and the shaping of Greek Neolithic society. In W. K. Barnett and J. W. Hoopes (eds.), *The Emergence of Pottery: Technology and Innovation in Ancient Societies*, pp. 55–63. Washington DC: Smithsonian Institution Press.

Vlassa, N., 1972. Cea mai veche faza a complexului cultural Starcevo-Cris in Romania. *Acta Musei Napocensis* 9:7–28.

1976. *Neoliticul Transilvanei*. Cluj: Bibliotheca Musei Napocensis

Voytek, B., 1990. The use of stone resources at Selevac. In R. Tringham and D. Krstic (eds.), *Selevac: A Neolithic Village in Yugoslavia*, pp. 437–94. Los Angeles: UCLA Institute of Archaeology.

Voytek, B., and R. Tringham, 1989. Rethinking the Mesolithic: the case of south-east Europe. In C. Bonsall (ed.), *The Mesolithic in Europe*, pp. 492–500. Edinburgh: John Donald.

Vuorela, I., and T. Lempiainen, 1988. Archaeobotany of the oldest cereal grain find in Finland. *Annales Botanici Fennici* 25: 33–45.

Waddell, J., 1978. The invasion hypothesis in Irish prehistory. *Antiquity* 52: 121–8.

Wahl, J., and H. G. König, 1987. Anthropologischchtraumatologische Untersuchung der menschlichen Skelettreste aus dem bandkeramischen Massengrab bei Talheim, Kreis Heilbronn. *Fundberichte aus BadenWürttemberg* 12: 65–193.

Waldrop, M. M., 1992. *Complexity: The Emerging Science at the Edge of Order and Chaos*. New York: Touchstone/Simon and Schuster.

Walker, A. J., and R. L. Otlet, 1985. Briar Hill: the carbon 14 measurements. In H. Bamford (ed.), *Briar Hill: Excavations 1974–78*, pp. 126–8. Northampton Development Corporation Archaeological Monograph 3. Northampton.

Warner, R. B., 1990. A proposed adjustment for the old wood effect. *PACT* 29: 159–72.

Waterbolk, H. T., 1982. The spread of food production over the European continent. In T. Sjøvold (ed.), *Introduksjonen av jordbruk i Norden*, pp. 19–37. Oslo: Universitetsforlaget.

Watson, P. J., 1995. Explaining the transition to agriculture. In T. D. Price and A. B. Gebauer (eds.), *Last Hunters–First Farmers: New Perspectives on the Origins of Agriculture*, pp. 21–38. Santa Fe, NM: School for American Research Press.

Wattez, J., 1992. Dynamique de formation des structures de combustion de la fin du Paléolithique au Néolithique moyen. Approches méthodologiques et implications culturelles. Thése de doctorat, Université de Paris I.

Weber, A., and J. Piontek, 1985. Social context of the unchambered megalithic long barrows in Middle Pomerania, Poland. *Journal of Anthropological Anthropology* 4: 116–32.

Weber, T., 1981. Flintinventare der Ertebölle- und der Trichterbecherkultur im südwestlichen Ostseeraum. *Veröffentlichungen des Museums für Ur- und Frühgeschichte Potsdam* 14/15: 143–50.

Wechler, K.-P., 1993. Mesolithikum – Bandkeramik – Trichterbecherkultur. Zur Neolithisierung Mittel- und Ostdeutschlands aufgrund vergleichender Untersuchungen zum Silexinventar. *Beiträge zur Ur- und Frühgeschichte Mecklenburg-Vorpommern* 27.

Weissner, P., 1984. Reconsidering the behavioral basis for style: a case study among the Kalahari San. *Journal of Anthropological Archaeology* 3: 190–234.

Welinder, S., 1978. Acculturation of the Pitted Ware culture in Eastern Sweden. *Meddelanden fran Lunds Universitets Historiska Museum* 1977/8.

    1987. Keramikstilar på Fagelbacken för 5000 ar sedan. *Vastmanlands lans fornminnesforenings Arskrift* 1987.

    1988. Exchange of axes in the Early Neolithic farming society of middle Sweden. In B. Hårdh, L. Larsson, D. Olausson, and R. Petré (eds.), *Trade and Exchange in Prehistory: Studies in Honour of Berta Stjernquist*, pp. 41–8. Lund: Almquist and Wiksell International.

Welsch, R. L., and J. Terrell, 1994. Reply to Moore and Romney. *American Anthropologist* 96: 392–6.

Welsch, R. L., J. Terrell, and J. A. Nadolski, 1992. Language and Culture on the north coast of New Guinea. *American Anthropologist* 94: 565–600.

Whitehouse, R. D., 1992. *Underground Religion: Cult and Culture in Prehistoric Italy.* London: Accordia Research Centre.

    1994. The British Museum 14C programme for Italian prehistory. In R. Skeates and R. Whitehouse (eds.), *Radiocarbon Dating and Italian Prehistory*, pp. 85–98. London: Accordia Research Centre.

Whittle, A., 1985. *Neolithic Europe: A Survey.* Cambridge: Cambridge University Press.

    1987. Neolithic settlement patterns in temperate Europe: progress and problems. *Journal of World Prehistory* 1(1): 5–52.

    1990a. Radiocarbon dating of the Linear Pottery culture: the contribution of cereals and bone samples. *Antiquity* 64: 297–302.

    1990b. Prolegomena to the study of the Mesolithic–Neolithic transition in Britain and Ireland. In D. Cahen and M. Otte (eds.), *Rubané et Cardial*. Liège: Université de Liège.

    1991. Wayland's Smithy, Oxfordshire: excavations at the Neolithic tomb in

1962–63 by R. J. C. Atkinson and S. Piggott. *Proceedings of the Prehistoric Society* 57(2): 61–102.

1996. *Europe in the Neolithic.* Cambridge: Cambridge University Press.

Wickham-Jones, C. R., 1994. *Scotland's First Settlers.* London: Batsford/Historic Scotland.

Wijngaarden Bakker, L. van, 1989. Faunal remains and the Irish Mesolithic. In C. Bonsall (ed.), *The Mesolithic in Europe: Papers Presented at the 3rd International Symposium.* Edinburgh: John Donald.

Wilkens, B., 1992. Il ruolo della pastorizia nelle economie preistoriche dell'Italia centro-meridionale. In B. Bordighera (ed.), *Archeologia della pastorizia nell'Europa meridionale*, pp. 81–94. Istituto internazionale di Studi Liguri.

Wilkinson-Herbots, H. M., M. B. Richards, P. Forster, and B. C. Sykes, 1996. Site 73 in hypervariable region II of the human mitochrondrial genome and the origin of European populations. *Annals of Human Genetics* 60: 499–508

Williams, B., 1986. Excavations at Altanagh, County Tyrone. *Ulster Journal of Archaeology* 49: 33–88.

Williams, E., 1989. Dating the introduction of food production into Britain and Ireland. *Antiquity* 63: 510–21.

Willis, K. J., and K. D. Bennett, 1994. The Neolithic transition – fact or fiction? Palaeoecological evidence from the Balkans. *The Holocene* 4: 326–30.

Wislanski, T., 1973. Studies on the origin of Funnel Beaker culture. *Archeologia Polski* 18: 123–6.

Woodburn, J., 1982. Egalitarian societies. *Man* (N.S.) 17: 431–51.

1988. African hunter-gatherer social organization: is it best understood as a product of encapsulation? In T. Ingold, D. Riches, and J. Woodburn (eds.), *Hunters and Gatherers*, pp. 131–64. Oxford: Berg.

Woodman, P. C., 1976. The Irish Mesolithic/Neolithic transition. In S. J. de Laet (ed.), *Acculturation and Continuity in Atlantic Europe*, Proceedings of the IVth Atlantic Colloquium, pp. 196–309. Bruges: De Tempel.

1977. Recent excavations at Newferry, Co. Antrim. *Proceedings of the Prehistoric Society* 43: 155–200.

1978. *The Mesolithic in Ireland.* Oxford: British Archaeological Reports British Series 58.

1985a. Prehistoric settlement and environment. In K. J. Edwards and W. P. Warren (eds.), *The Quaternary History of Ireland*, pp. 251–78. London: Academic Press.

1985b. *Excavations at Mt Sandel 1973–77, Northern Ireland.* Archaeological Research Monographs 2. Belfast: HMSO.

1992a. Excavations at Mad Mans Window, Glenarm, Co. Antrim: problems of flint exploitation in East Antrim. *Proceedings of the Prehistoric Society* 58: 77–106.

1992b. Filling in the spaces in Irish prehistory. *Antiquity* 66: 295–314.

1992c. The Komsa culture: a re-examination of its position in the Stone Age of Finnmark. *Acta Archaeologica* 63: 57–76.

1994. Towards a definition of the Irish Early Neolithic lithic assemblages. In N. Ashton and A. David (eds.), *Stories in Stone*, pp. 221–8. Lithic Studies Society Occasional Paper 4. London: Lithic Studies Society.

In press. The exploitation of Ireland's coastal resources: a marginal resource through time? In M. R. Gonzalez-Morales and G. A. Clarke (eds.), *The Mesolithic of the Atlantic Façade.*

Woodman, P. C., and E. Anderson, 1990. The Irish Later Mesolithic, a partial picture. In P. M. Vermeersch and P. Van Geer (eds.), *Contributions to the Mesolithic in Europe 4th International Symposium*. Leuven: Leuven University Press.

Woodman, P. C., E. Anderson, and N. Finlay, 1999. *Excavations at Ferriter's Cove 1983–1995: last foragers and first farmers on the Dingle Peninsula*. Bray: Wordwell.

Woodman, P. C., and G. Johnson, 1996. Excavations at Bay Farm, Carnlough, Co. Antrim. *Proceedings of the Royal Irish Academy* 96(6): 136–235.

Woodman, P. C., M. McCarthy, and N. Monahan, 1997. The Irish Quaternary Faunas Project, a survey of the ^{14}C evidence. *Quaternary Science Review* 16: 129–59.

Wright, H. E., 1977. Environmental change and the origin of agriculture in the Old and New Worlds. In C. A. Reed (ed.), *Origins of Agriculture*, pp. 281–318. The Hague: Mouton.

y'Edynak, G., 1978. Culture, diet and dental reduction in Mesolithic forager-fishers of Yugoslavia. *Current Anthropology* 19: 616–17.

　　1989. Yugoslav Mesolithic dental reduction. *American Journal of Physical Anthropology* 78: 17–36.

y'Edynak, G., and S. Fleisch, 1983. Microevolution and biological adaptability in the transition from food-collecting to food-producing in the Iron Gates of Yugoslavia. *Journal of Human Evolution* 12:279–96.

Zapata, L., 1994. The shell-midden of Pico Ramos Cave (Muzkiz, Biscay). Paper presented to the Old People and the Sea. International Conference on the Mesolithic of the Atlantic Façade, Santander (Spain).

Zilhão, J., 1992. *Gruta do Caldeirão: O Neolítico Antigo*. Lisbon: Instituto Português do Património Arquitectónico e Arqueológico.

　　1993. The spread of agro-pastoral economies across Mediterranean Europe: a view from the far west. *Journal of Mediterranean Archaeology* 6: 5–63.

　　1995. *O Paleolítico Superior da Estremadura portuguesa*. Lisbon: Colibri.

　　1998. Maritime pioneer colonisation in the Early Neolithic of the west Mediterranean. Testing the model against the evidence. *Porocilo o rziskovanju paleolitika, neolitika in eneolitika v Slovejini* 34 (in press).

Zilhão, J., T. Aubry, A. F. Carvalho, A. M. Baptista, M. V. Gomes, and J. Meireles, 1997. The rock art of the Côa Valley (Portugal) and its archaeological context. *Journal of European Archaeology* 5: 7–49.

Zilhão, J., and A. M. Faustino de Carvalho, 1996. O Neolítico do Maciço Calcário Estremenho. Crono-estratigrafia e povoamento. *Actes. I Congrés del Neolític a la Península Ibérica* 2, pp. 659–671. Gavà, Museu de Gavà.

Zilhão, J., E. Carvalho, and A. C. Araújo, 1987. A estação epipaleolítica da Ponta da Vigia (Torres Vedras). *Arqueologia* 16: 818.

Zilhão, J., J. Maurício, and P. Souto, 1991. A arqueologia da Gruta do Almonda. Resultados das escavações de 1988–89. *Actas das IV Jornadas Arqueológicas*, pp. 161–71. Lisbon: Associação dos Arqueólogos Portugueses.

Zohary, D., and J. Hopf, 1993. *Domestication of Plants in the Old World: The Origin and Spread of Cultivated Plants in West Asia, Europe, and the Nile Valley*. Oxford: Oxford University Press.

Zubrow, E., 1989. The demographic modelling of Neanderthal extinction. In P. A. Mellars and C. Stringer (eds.), *The Human Revolution*, pp. 212–31. Edinburgh: Edinburgh University Press.

Zvelebil, M., 1981. *From Forager to Farmer in the Boreal Zone*. Oxford: British Archaeological Reports International Series 115.

    1985. Iron Age transformations in northern Russia and the northeast Baltic. In G. Barker and C. Gamble (eds.), *Beyond Domestication in Prehistoric Europe*, pp. 147–80. Cambridge: Cambridge University Press.

    1986a. Mesolithic prelude and Neolithic revolution. In M. Zvelebil (ed.), *Hunters in Transition: Mesolithic Societies of Temperate Eurasia and Their Transition to Farming*, pp. 5–15. Cambridge: Cambridge University Press.

    1986b. Mesolithic societies and the transition to farming: problems of time, scale and organisation. In M. Zvelebil (ed.), *Hunters in Transition: Mesolithic Societies of Temperate Eurasia and Their Transition to Farming*, pp. 167–88. Cambridge: Cambridge University Press.

    1989. On the transition to farming in Europe, or what was spreading with the Neolithic: a reply to Ammerman. *Antiquity* 63: 379–83.

    1992a. Hunting in farming societies: the prehistoric perspective. *Anthropozoologica* 16: 7–18.

    1992b. Les chasseurs pêcheurs de la Scandinavie préhistorique. *La Recherche* 246:982–90.

    1993. Hunters or farmers? The Neolithic and Bronze Age societies of north-east Europe. In J. Chapman and P. Dolukhanov (eds.), *Cultural Transformation and Interactions in Eastern Europe*, pp. 146–62. Aldershot: Avebury.

    1994a. Plant use in the Mesolithic and its role in the transition to farming. *Proceedings of the Prehistoric Society* 60: 35–74.

    1994b. Social structure and ideology of the Late Mesolithic communities in north temperate Europe. Paper presented at the Old People and the Sea. International Conference on the Mesolithic of the Atlantic Façade, Santander (Spain).

    1995a. Neolithization in eastern Europe: A view from the frontier. *Porocilo* 22: 107–50

    1995b. At the interface of archaeology, linguistics and genetics: Indo-European dispersals and the agricultural transition in Europe. *Journal of European Archaeology* 3: 33–70.

    1995c. Hunting, gathering or husbandry? Management of food resources by the Late Mesolithic communities in temperate Europe. In D. Campana (ed.), *Before Farming*, pp. 79–105. Masca Research Papers in Science and Archaeology. Philadelphia: University of Pennsylvania Press,

    1996. The agricultural frontier and the transition to agriculture in the circum-Baltic region. In D. R Harris (ed.), *The Origins and Spread of Agriculture and Pastoralism in Eurasia*, pp. 323–35. London: University of London Press.

    1998. What's in a name: the Mesolithic, the Neolithic, and social change at the Mesolithic–Neolithic transition. In M. Edmonds and C. Richards (eds.), *Understanding the Neolithic of North-West Europe*, pp. 1–35. Glasgow: Cruithne Press.

Zvelebil, M. (ed.), 1986c. *Hunters in Transition: Mesolithic Societies of Temperate Eurasia and Their Transition to Farming*. Cambridge: Cambridge University Press.

Zvelebil, M., and P. Dolukhanov, 1991. Transition to farming in eastern and northern Europe. *Journal of World Prehistory* 5: 233–78.

Zvelebil, M., L. D. Domaynska, and R. Dennell (eds.), 1998. *Harvesting the Sea, Farming the Forest*. Sheffield: Sheffield University Press.

Zvelebil, M., J. Moore, S. Green, and D. Henson, 1987. Regional survey and analysis of lithic scatters: a case study from southeast Ireland. In P. Rowley-Conwy, M. Zvelebil, and H. P. Blankholm (eds.), *Mesolithic North-West Europe: Recent Trends*, pp. 9–32. Sheffield: Sheffield University Press

Zvelebil, M., and P. Rowley-Conwy. 1984. Transition to farming in northern Europe: a hunter-gatherer perspective. *Norwegian Archaeological Review* 17: 104–28.

    1986. Foragers and farmers in Atlantic Europe. In M. Zvelebil (ed.), *Hunters in Transition: Mesolithic Societies of Temperate Eurasia and Their Transition to Farming*, pp. 67–93. Cambridge: Cambridge University Press.

Zvelebil, M., and K. V. Zvelebil, 1988. Agricultural transition and Indo-European dispersals. *Antiquity* 62: 574–83.

Index

Page numbers in bold denote illustrations.